1596955-1

7/28/04

Fuzzy Grammar

Fuzzy Grammar

A Reader

Edited by

BAS AARTS
DAVID DENISON
EVELIEN KEIZER
GERGANA POPOVA

OXFORD
UNIVERSITY PRESS

OXFORD

UNIVERSITY PRESS

Great Clarendon Street, Oxford OX2 6DP

Oxford University Press is a department of the University of Oxford.
It furthers the University's objective of excellence in research, scholarship,
and education by publishing worldwide in

Oxford New York

Auckland Bangkok Buenos Aires Cape Town Chennai
Dar es Salaam Delhi Hong Kong Istanbul Karachi Kolkata
Kuala Lumpur Madrid Melbourne Mexico City Mumbai Nairobi
São Paulo Shanghai Taipei Tokyo Toronto

Oxford is a registered trade mark of Oxford University Press
in the UK and in certain other countries

Published in the United States
by Oxford University Press Inc., New York

© Oxford University Press, 2004

The moral rights of the author have been asserted
Database right Oxford University Press (maker)

First published 2004

A catalogue record for this title is available from the British Library

Library of Congress Cataloging in Publication Data
(Data available)
ISBN 0 19 926256 X (hbk)
      0 19 926257 8 (pbk)

10 9 8 7 6 5 4 3 2 1

Typeset by Newgen Imaging Systems (P) Ltd., Chennai, India
Printed in Great Britain
on acid-free paper by
Antony Rowe Ltd, Chippenham, Wiltshire

P
158
.6
eF899x
2004

Contents

Preface

The aim of this book is to bring together a number of classical and recent writings from philosophy and linguistics in the areas of vagueness and fuzziness. We present a collection of carefully selected key texts which have influenced thinking in these domains. The introductory chapter contextualizes the passages within the field of linguistics, and assesses the impact they have made. It also discusses recent developments and future prospects.

Why did we compile this Reader? The most important reason is that we feel that the study of indeterminacy has been an important thread of thinking in the history of philosophy, psychology, and linguistics. Bringing together papers from these domains gives an idea of the richness of thought in this area and will, we hope, stimulate further cross-disciplinary work. Secondly, we feel that linguistics has been unfavourably dominated by approaches that advocate strictly Aristotelian categories, and that some counterbalancing is required. Modern descriptive linguistics has always been conscious of the fact that grammatical systems are subject to fuzziness, but there are now signs in present-day linguistics that increasing numbers of linguists are reluctant to be bullied by the categories, especially in formal linguistic theory. We regard this as a welcome development. As we will see in the Introduction, mechanisms are being proposed in Head-Driven Phrase Structure Grammar, Lexical Functional Grammar, Optimality Theory, Probability Theory, and even in Generative Grammar to deal with gradient linguistic phenomena.

The criterion for inclusion of a paper in this reader was principally the contribution it has made, and continues to make, to the study of fuzziness in grammar. In this sense almost all the papers are 'classics'. However, given the recent renewed interest in fuzziness signalled above we have not neglected more recent work. We also bore in mind the fact that this book will be used on taught courses, and for this reason we selected papers that would offer useful starting points for discussions of a whole array of topics in grammatical indeterminacy.

We expect that this book will appeal to a wide range of readers. It will provide specialists and students in the fields of language, philosophy, and cognitive science with a focused and balanced introduction to the work of key thinkers. The value of the reader lies in bringing together works from various subdisciplines and points of view, which will enable linguists to become acquainted with the thinking of philosophers and cognitivists, and, conversely, will allow philosophers to get a feel for the kinds of issue and problem that language confronts us with. We believe that this publication will give fresh impetus to ongoing research in this area.

Our thanks are due first and foremost to all the authors, the quick and the dead, whose work is collected here. We also thank John Davey of OUP and a number of anonymous referees who gave us useful feedback on our initial proposal and on the final product. Finally, thanks are due to Marie Gibney, Gabriel Ozón, Yordanka Kostadinova-Kavalova, and Shaw Hubbard for help with the gargantuan task of scanning and proofreading the papers.

London, Manchester, and Amsterdam
May 2003

Bas Aarts
David Denison
Evelien Keizer
Gergana Popova

Introduction: The Nature of Grammatical Categories and their Representation

PRELIMINARIES

Categorization is a notion that lies at the heart of virtually all approaches to grammar, be they descriptive, theoretical, or cognitive. All linguists would agree that you cannot do linguistics without assuming that grammatical categories exist in some shape or other. What linguists disagree about is the nature of those categories. Are they discrete, as the classical Aristotelian tradition has it, or are they blurred at the edges, as has been argued more recently, especially by cognitive linguists? In this Introduction we will provide an overview of work on categorization in the domains of philosophy, psychology, and linguistics, and we will discuss the significance of each of the papers contained in this book within the general framework of fuzzy grammar. We have grouped the papers into the following five parts:

Part I: Philosophical background
Part II: Categories in cognition
Part III: Categories in grammar
Part IV: Gradience in grammar
Part V: Criticisms and responses

The sections below will use the same headings as those shown above. The final section of this chapter looks at current developments and future prospects.[1]

PHILOSOPHICAL BACKGROUND

There is no doubt that the most influential thinker in the domain of categorization was Aristotle. The Aristotelian ('scholastic' or 'classical') tradition holds that the categories we use in everyday life are 'hard', i.e. have clear boundaries, and that the elements that populate those categories have unambiguously been assigned to those categories, and to no other. There is no room for compromise: an element cannot be more or less a member of a category, nor can it belong to more than one category. Aristotle stresses the importance of distinguishing between defining properties and accidental properties in assigning elements to categories: in defining the notion of 'man', his being two-footed and an animal are essential attributes; his being white is not. Aristotle's views become clear in the passages we included in this book. When speaking of language he says: 'language also is one of the discrete quantities: . . . For its parts do not join together at any common boundary. For there is no common boundary at which the syllables join together, but each is separate in itself'

---

[1] In this chapter, references to the papers included in this Reader will be to the page numbers of the articles as they appear in this book.

(*The Categories*, 31). A number of factors have been identified to explain the popularity of Aristotelian thinking. Taylor (1995: 75) suggests that the influence of the Bible was important, as well as formal education. Michael (1970: 490) attributes the 'hardening of categories' in the thinking of grammarians over time to the fact that there was no science of language, and argues that this resulted in an obsession with classification. A further factor may have been the argument that science is all about the pursuit of precision. Under this view there is no role for notions like fuzziness. Finally, part of the attraction of the Aristotelian model may be the fact that it is the simplest way of approaching the bewildering reality that confronts us every day.

Aristotle's thinking influenced Gottlob Frege's writings on logic, as the passage from his *Grundgesetze der Arithmetik* show. For Frege the Law of the Excluded Middle must hold when defining concepts: 'Any object Δ that you choose to take either falls under the concept Φ or does not fall under it; *tertium non datur*' (Frege 1903/97: 33).

Philosophers have studied fuzziness under the heading 'vagueness', and this concept has troubled them ever since Eubulides of Megara formulated his famous Sorites Paradox (or Paradox of the Heap): when we start forming a heap out of grains of sand, is it possible to say which grain n makes the difference between the collection of grains being called a heap and not being called a heap? In other words, is there a sharp boundary between [Heap] and [~Heap], or is this boundary blurred? In the paper reproduced in this volume Bertrand Russell presents his own version of the Sorites paradox: the Paradox of the Bald Man: 'It is supposed that at first he was not bald, that he lost his hairs one by one, and that in the end he was bald; therefore, it is argued, there must have been one hair the loss of which converted him into a bald man' (p. 36). However, Russell argues, vagueness is not a property of entities— 'things are what they are, and there is an end of it' (pp. 35–6)—but of representations. Language is a representation, and as such it is vague. From this we can conclude that vagueness rears its head when we start using language to talk about concepts like heaps and baldness. But what is a vague representation? According to Russell, a representation is vague if there is no one-to-one relationship between a representation and the entity that is being represented. It follows that '[v]agueness, clearly, is a matter of degree, depending upon the extent of the possible differences between different systems represented by the same representation' (p. 38). Thus, for example, a quick sketch of a person drawn in pencil is a vaguer representation of that person than a photograph. Keefe and Smith (1996: 9) find Russell's position perhaps too radical:

> Russell takes it that logic assumes precision, and since natural language is not precise it cannot be in the province of logic at all. If Russell's 'no logic' thesis requires wholesale rejection of reasoning with vague predicates—and hence of most reasoning in natural language—it would certainly seem extreme. Are there no distinctions to be drawn between good and bad arguments couched in a vague language? If not, it would seem e.g. that we would have no reason to trust the very arguments, themselves expressed in vague terms, that Russell and others present to support their 'no logic' thesis.

Ludwig Wittgenstein was another philosopher who concerned himself with vagueness in the guise of indeterminacy. In his study of the notion of 'game' in his *Philosophical Investigations*—the key passages of which are reproduced here—he noticed that there are many human pastimes that we might call games, but it is very hard to come up with a tight definition of the notion, given that some characteristics of games are shared by one group of games, others by different groups, but there is no one set of properties that will exhaustively define all games. All games show similarities.

> I can think of no better expression to characterize these similarities than 'family resemblances'; for the various resemblances between members of a family: build, features, colour of eyes, gait, temperament,

etc. etc. overlap and criss-cross in the same way.—And I shall say: 'games' form a family. (Wittgenstein 1953/58: 41)

Wittgenstein's thinking prefigured the ideas on *prototypes* presented by psychologists like Eleanor Rosch (see the next section below).

Vagueness has continued to be a focus of interest in modern philosophy: see e.g. Sainsbury (1988), Burns (1991), Chatterjee (1994), Williamson (1994), Sainsbury and Williamson (1997), as well as the collections of papers in Ballmer and Pinkel (1983) and Keefe and Smith (1996). The last paper in this part of this reader, by Rosanna Keefe, is a recent contribution to the vagueness debate. It offers a useful summary of theories of vagueness, and contains a discussion of linguistic vagueness.

CATEGORIES IN COGNITION

Despite numerous voices of dissent, the traditional view of categories as definable solely in terms of the common properties of their members remained the predominant view in philosophy, psychology, and linguistics until well into the twentieth century. The assumption that categorization is an unambiguous, clear-cut process turned out to be too attractive and convenient for most scholars to question its premises—as, indeed, it still proves to be for a new generation of computer scientists. This is presumably the main reason why the traditional view remained relatively unchallenged for so long: what was originally the result of a priori speculation came to be taken for granted; it was a position that was assumed rather than investigated (Labov 1973: 72; Lakoff 1987: 140, 142). Moreover, although vagueness in categorization had been recognized by scholars from different scientific disciplines, e.g. philosophy, evidence for an alternative view remained fragmented, while those advocating such a view found themselves desperately seeking for a scientific way to deal with the elusive phenomenon of non-discreteness. What was needed was the realization that the evidence from the various disciplines taken together could lead to an entirely different, scientifically based view of categorization.

The answer came in the late 1960s and early 1970s, with the emergence of cognitive science, a new discipline concentrating on the workings of the mind which at last offered a coherent framework into which the scattered evidence from philosophy, linguistics, anthropology, and psychology could be brought together to build a unified picture of the way in which people perceive and categorize the world around them. Chapter 1 from Lakoff (1987), reproduced here, discusses these developments. Gradually, it came to be recognized that categorization was not only a process of extreme importance in every aspect of human existence, but also a process of almost incredible complexity—a complexity which the traditional view of categorization could not account for.

Thus it turned out that while some categories are based simply on the presence of a set of invariable common properties, most categories include members which do not share properties with all other members; or, if they do, these properties may vary from context to context, or from person to person. In other words, whereas some categories may have strict and fixed boundaries, in other cases boundaries between categories may be fuzzy or variable. Moreover, experiments of various kinds provided evidence that, even within clearly bounded categories, not all members necessarily possess the same degree of category membership, with some members consistently being regarded as better examples of the category than others. In addition, research on categorization was no longer restricted to concrete objects, as it came to be recognized that abstract entities (such as actions and events, relationships, emotions or illnesses), too, form categories in the mind. Nor did there appear to be any reason to assume that categories were fixed or conventional, as people were found to make up ad hoc categories (e.g. 'things to take from one's house during a fire' or 'what to get for a birthday present') for immediate purposes (Barsalou 1983). With the steady accumulation of evidence concerning the formation and function of categories, their internal structure, and the interaction between contrasting categories, the traditional view became less and less tenable.

One of the first studies to play an important role in the development of an alternative view of categorization is Labov's (1973) report on a number of experiments carried out to measure vagueness in the categorization (or naming) of concrete objects, which we have included in this book. Labov starts by explaining why the study of word meaning has been neglected in linguistics for so long:

Words have often been called slippery customers, and many scholars have been distressed by their tendency to shift their meaning and slide out from formal definition . . . It is not only words that are shifters; the objects to which they must be applied shift with even greater rapidity . . . Words as well as the world itself display the 'orderly heterogeneity' which characterizes language as a whole. (Labov 1973: 67)

The recognition of an 'orderly heterogeneity' (reminiscent of Shakespeare's 'Though this be madness, yet there is method in 't', *Hamlet* II. ii) did, however, pose a problem for the prevalent view that language translates meaning into sound through the categorization of reality into discrete units and sets of units. On this 'categorical' view (the term used by Labov), linguistic categories are implicitly assumed to be:

    (i) discrete: categories are separated from each other by clear-cut discontinuities of form and function;
    (ii) invariant: the category as a type recurs as precisely the same in each occurrence;
    (iii) qualitatively distinct: categories are completely different from each other, i.e. not elements in a linear or ordered sequence;
    (iv) conjunctively defined: each category is defined by a set of criterial or necessary (as opposed to unnecessary or redundant) properties, each of which must be present for the category to be recognised;
    (v) composed of atomic primes: all categories are ultimately composed of a set of integral categories which cannot be further subdivided. (Labov 1973: 68)

An alternative approach to categorization was therefore called for—one which could account for the fact that categories, like the continuous substratum of reality they represent, are not always separated by distinct boundaries. Labov's proposal can be seen as offering such an alternative, albeit a relatively modest one. Thus, he realizes that, given the aims and the nature of linguistic analysis, total abandonment of the assumptions underlying the categorical view may have unfortunate effects. What he urges, therefore, is some modification which can bring the categorical view more in line with the non-discrete nature of the boundaries between categories suggested by experiments reported both in Labov (1973) and earlier work (e.g. Weinreich et al. 1968). As pointed out by Labov, this requires a new approach to the study of linguistic categorization: instead of taking the categorical view for granted and concentrating on problematic cases, linguists must go beyond that view, must focus on the process of categorization itself and turn their attention to the nature of the boundaries between categories.

This is precisely the approach taken by Labov in a series of experiments which required groups of subjects to name a variety of cup-like objects. The results show that there is no clear cut-off point between, for instance, a cup and a bowl. Instead, there are clear cases of cups and clear cases of bowls, but in between the two is a 'fringe area', where the object in question can with equal truth be called a cup or a bowl. Moreover, it turns out that the position of this fringe area shifts with a change of context. Thus, in a food context, objects at or near the fringe areas which might be named cups in a neutral context were referred to as bowls, while the reverse was true in a context mentioning coffee. Similarly, in a flower context, objects which might otherwise be named cups were more likely to be called vases.

Labov (1973: 81–2) concludes that, potentially, there are three types of category. The first type conforms to the categorical view: categories of this type are bounded and non-graded, with distinct and invariable outer limits, characterized by a fixed set of necessary attributes and simple yes-or-no membership. The second type of category is bounded, but at the same time graded. These categories have strict boundaries, but allow for within-category gradience, with some members being better examples of the category than others. The third type of category is both unbounded and graded. Categories of this type do not have boundaries; rather, they fade off into each other, with the more peripheral members having more in common with members of other (contrasting) categories.

For Labov, the cup-like objects used in his experiments constitute categories of the second type. Thus, they have an invariable core (some objects will always be named cups) as well as boundaries (some objects will never be named cups). However, the location of the boundary between categories may vary from context to context. Labov's conclusion, therefore, is that

> It is not true that everything varies, anymore than it is true that everything remains distinct and discrete. We must locate the boundary between the invariable and the variable areas of language with the same precision that we have learned to use in studying the variable elements themselves. (Labov 1973: 87)

Labov's study was by no means the only one to provide evidence against the categorical view of categorization. His findings were consistent with the results of various contemporary studies from different disciplines. See chapter 2 from Lakoff (1987), included in this reader, for an overview. Many of these came from language philosophy (see Part I) and linguistics, e.g. Ross's (1973a; 1973b) recognition of fuzziness in syntactic categorization and Lakoff's (1972) description of 'hedges'. In logic, too, the need was acknowledged to rethink classical set theory, as reflected in Zadeh's (1965) proposal for a 'fuzzy set theory'. Further evidence for fuzzy boundaries, as well as for the existence of central or focal members within categories, came from various anthropological studies, such as Lounsbury's study (1964) of American Indian kinship names and the work of Berlin and Kay (1969) and Kay and McDaniel (1978) on the categorization of colours. Other important contributions to the development of an alternative view of categorization could be found in the ethnobiological research of Berlin and his associates on the naming of plants and animals (e.g. Berlin et al. 1974; Berlin 1976; 1978), in psychology (e.g. Brown's 1965 first indication of the existence of basic-level categories), and in physiology (e.g. Ekman's research on basic emotions and facial gestures; see Ekman 1971; Ekman et al. 1972).

The first scholar to recognize and describe the general cognitive principles which could accommodate the findings of these diverse studies was Eleanor Rosch. From the late 1960s, Rosch and her associates had been conducting experiments on colour and form which suggested the existence of nonarbitrary categories centred on 'natural prototypes' (Rosch 1973). In later publications, the idea of prototypes as an organizing principle in human categorization was extended to other domains, eventually resulting in a coherent perspective on human thinking in general which could serve as an alternative to the traditional view of categorization.

This perspective on categorization, which came to be known as 'prototype theory', depended on the acceptance of two basic general principles for the formation of categories (Rosch 1978: 92–3). The first of these, Cognitive Economy, asserts that 'the task of category systems is to provide maximum information with the least cognitive effort' (Rosch 1978: 92). More specifically this means that (a) in categorizing an object, we not only consider the ways in which it resembles objects in the same category, but also the ways in which it differs from objects not in the same category; and (b) categorization is not invariant but depends on the purpose it serves: we only differentiate objects from other objects when it is relevant to do so given the purposes at hand. According to the second general principle, that of Perceived World Structure, the perceived world is not an unstructured set of arbitrary and unpredictable attributes; instead, objects in this world possess high correlational structure. Thus, certain attributes are perceived by humans as coming in clusters (wings tend to co-occur with feathers), while in other cases the co-occurrence is of a functional nature (chairs and the function of sitting) (Rosch 1978: 92).

Together, these principles make it possible to account for two types of effect in categorization: basic-level effects and prototype effects. The former can be seen as the vertical dimension of a category system and concerns the level of inclusiveness of the category—that is, the variation between superordinate categories (e.g. animals, vehicles) and lower-level categories (e.g. dog and cat; car and bus) (Rosch et al. 1976; see also Rosch 1978). The latter, which can be seen as the horizontal dimension, concerns categorization at the same level of inclusiveness—that is, the variation between dog and cat, and between car and bus (e.g. Rosch 1973; 1978).

Basic-level objects are situated at the most inclusive (highest) level of categorization at which there are attributes common to all or most members of the category (Rosch et al. 1976: 385ff.; 1978: 93). In addition, this basic level was found to be the most inclusive level at which highly similar sequences of motor movements (e.g. 'sitting on') apply to all objects of a class, as well as the highest level at which the shapes of objects of a category are perceived as similar, allowing for a mental image of some 'average' member which possesses a relatively concrete shape (or 'gestalt'). For example, in the hierarchy 'furniture-chair-kitchen chair', the basic-level category is that of chair, as this category forms the highest level at which a consistent mental image can be formed of the average member, while members of this category also share highly similar motor programmes. This is not the case for the superordinate category of furniture, which includes objects (chairs, tables, and beds) which, taken together, cannot be readily identified by shape, cannot be represented by one more or less concrete mental image, and which are not used in the same way ('sitting on', 'eating from', 'sleeping in', etc.). Lower-level categories (e.g. kitchen chair, director's chair), on the other hand, share these perceptual and functional properties with the basic level category, differing from them, and each other, only in terms of more specific attributes.

Because of these characteristics, basic-level object categories are believed to have a special cognitive status: it is at this level that the differentiability of categories is maximized, making it universally the most useful and necessary level of classification. Experimental evidence supporting this special cognitive status can be found in the fact that these categories have been shown to be the first to be learned and named by children, the first to be coded in any language, and the easiest categories to identify and remember (Rosch et al. 1976; see also Lakoff 1987: 168).

The second major contribution made by Rosch and her associates to the study of human categorization concerned the internal structure of categories. Thus, like Labov, Rosch argues that since most categories do not have clear-cut boundaries, categorization cannot take place on the basis of necessary and sufficient criteria. However, where Labov shifted the focus of attention to the boundaries between the categories, Rosch chooses 'to achieve separateness and clarity of actually continuous categories . . . by conceiving of each category in terms of its clear cases rather than its boundaries' (Rosch 1978: 98). The clearest cases of category membership constitute 'prototypes'. Operationally, they are defined by people's judgements of goodness of membership in the category: as it turned out, people overwhelmingly agree on how good an example members are of a category, even if they disagree about the boundary of that category (e.g. McCloskey and Glucksburg 1978; Barsalou 1983). Thus, the more prototypical of a category a member is rated, the more attributes it has in common with other members of the category, and the fewer it has in common with members of contrasting categories (Rosch and Mervis 1975).

Further evidence for the existence of prototypes includes the fact that in experiments asking subjects to judge, as true or false, statements of category membership, responses of true were invariably faster for more prototypical items. Moreover, children were found to learn category membership of good examples of categories before that of poor examples (Rosch 1973). Evidence can also be found in linguistics, as demonstrated by the use of 'hedges' (Lakoff 1972), such as 'almost' and 'virtually'. Thus, it is acceptable to say that a penguin is technically a bird, but not that a robin is technically a bird, because robins (but not penguins) are rated as prototypes of the category bird.

It is, however, important to realize that, as pointed out by Rosch in her later work (1978; 1981), prototype and basic-level effects are, indeed, effects and do not themselves constitute a theory of the way categories are processed or learned:

The principles of categorization proposed are not as such intended to constitute a theory of the development of categories in children born into a culture nor to constitute a model of how categories are processed (how categorizations are made) in the minds of adult speakers of a language. (Rosch 1978: 92–3)

Nor does prototype theory make any claims about how prototypes are represented in the mind. Thus, Rosch (1978: 102) observes that 'prototypes can be represented either by propositional or image systems . . . the facts about prototypes can only constrain, but do not determine, models of representation'. (For later developments in the acquisition and processing of categories, see e.g. Keil and Kelly 1987; Medin and Barsalou 1987. On category representation, see also Scholnick 1983; Harnad 1987: 551ff.)

It will be clear that, due to the role of naming and the importance of words and their meaning in the experiments conducted, linguistics has been one of the major areas to contribute to, and be influenced by, the new developments in cognitive psychology. Among the first to recognize the implications of Rosch's work for linguistic theory were linguists who were unhappy with the way in which generative grammar was developing, with its assumption of a strict division between syntax, semantics, and lexicon, and its insistence on the autonomy and primacy of syntax within the language faculty (e.g. Lakoff 1971; Jackendoff 1972; Langacker 1973). After a largely unsuccessful experiment with generative semantics, these linguists all proceeded to develop cognitively grounded models of grammar which were not merely consistent with, but actually started from, recent views concerning the nature of human categorization. (For a brief comparison between generative semantics and cognitive linguistics, see Lakoff 1987: 582–5.)

Throughout his career, one of the main concerns of Ray Jackendoff has been with semantic structure and with finding a formalism to represent this structure which is consistent with psychological evidence. The overall aim of his book *Semantics and Cognition* (1983), parts of which are reprinted here, is to show that, although linguistics and psychology approach the study of meaning from different points of view, the questions they ask ('What is the nature of the meaning in language?' and 'What does grammatical structure reveal about the nature of cognition?') are inseparable: 'to study semantics of natural language *is* to study cognitive psychology' (Jackendoff 1983: 3; emphasis in original). He then sets out to develop a theory of 'conceptual semantics', which he believes to be 'considerably richer in both formal and substantive respects than standard logical approaches' (for further development and refinement of the theory, see also Jackendoff 1990; 1992).

One of the advantages of Jackendoff's theory over traditional logical approaches is that the representation of categorization it offers is consistent with the main tenets of prototype theory. Thus, Jackendoff (1983: 110) takes 'the theory of categorization to concern not whether a particular categorization is true, but what information and processing must be ascribed to an organism to account for its categorization judgements'. These categorization judgements, Jackendoff continues, should not be seen as resulting from a simple comparison of some real-world entity *a* to some pre-existing category. Instead, 'the mechanism of categorization must be assigned to the level of conceptual structure'. With regard to the formalism Jackendoff proposes for representing categories (1983: ch. 5), this means that he rejects the idea that in a sentence such as '*a* is a dog', the token *a* and the type *dog* provide different kinds of information, and should be seen as having different internal structures. Instead, he claims that the internal organization of tokens and types is the same, the difference between them corresponding to a difference not in conceptual structure but in referentiality: whereas token constituents are referential, type constituents are non-referential. Moreover, Jackendoff rejects the view that word meaning can be decomposed exhaustively in semantic primitives (Jackendoff 1983: 112–15), and accepts fuzziness as 'an inescapable characteristic of the concepts that language expresses' (p. 125). As far as the internal organization of categories is concerned, Jackendoff agrees with Wittgenstein's characterization in terms of family resemblances and with Rosch's notion of centrality (1983: 125–8).

A second major influence of cognitive science on linguistics can be found in the work of Ronald Langacker, in particular in his highly innovative *Foundations of Cognitive Grammar* (1987; 1991), parts of which we have reprinted in this volume. In this work, Langacker presents a model of Cognitive Grammar (CG), a linguistic framework using image-schematic representation which emerges 'from a comprehensive and unified view of linguistic organization characterized in terms of cognitive processing' (1987: 1; see also Langacker 1999; 2002). Although at the time of its conception Langacker's model seemed to row against the tide, over the years CG has, in fact, proved to offer an extremely viable conception of grammatical structure. One important difference between CG and most of the prevailing linguistic theories is that it assumes that semantic structure is based on conventional imagery and is characterized relative to knowledge structures. Like Jackendoff, Langacker thus equates semantic structure with conceptual structure (Langacker 1987: 2). A second difference concerns the fact that in CG syntax is not perceived as constituting an autonomous formal level of representation. Rather, syntax, morphology and the lexicon are seen as forming a continuum: all three are symbolic in nature, and serve to symbolize semantic structure. For a recent textbook overview of the theory of Cognitive Grammar, see Taylor (2002).

In accordance with prototype theory, Cognitive Grammar thus accepts that much in language is a matter of degree and is geared to deal with non-discreteness in the categorization of word meaning, as well as of morphological and syntactic patterns. In addition, the idea of a continuum is extended to many other distinctions commonly treated by linguists as rigid dichotomies, such as competence vs. performance, grammar vs. lexicon, morphology vs. syntax, semantics vs. pragmatics, rule vs. analogy, grammatical vs. ungrammatical, and literal vs. figurative. In other words, instead of regarding non-discreteness as a problem, CG starts from the idea that 'non-discrete aspects of language must be accommodated in the basic design of an adequate linguistic theory' (Langacker 1987: 14). This recognition of gradation does not, in Langacker's view, weaken the theory:

... to posit a continuum is not to abandon the goal of rigorous description: we must still describe the individual constructions in explicit detail, even as we articulate their parameters of gradation. Nor does recognizing a continuum render us impotent to make valid distinctions or interesting claims ... Rules and generalizations can perfectly well refer to [non-discrete] categories; we need only realize that predictions inspired by representative instances of a category, found near one pole of a continuum, hold with progressively less force as one moves away from that pole to the opposite extreme. (Langacker 1987: 135)

Published in the same year as the first volume of Langacker's *Foundations of Cognitive Grammar*, Lakoff's study *Women, Fire and Dangerous Things* (1987) also embraces the new views on human categorization. However, where these inspired Langacker to develop a new grammar model, Lakoff's main concern is with the more general question of how human beings think; more specifically, with the question of what categorization tells us about the mind. Building on evidence from cognitive science concerning category structure (summarized in his chapter 2, reprinted here), and combining ideas on the representation and organization of knowledge from Fillmore's (1982) frame semantics, Lakoff and Johnson's (1980) theory of metaphor and metonymy, Langacker's (1987) cognitive grammar, and Fauconnier's (1985) theory of mental spaces, Lakoff presents the view that human thought is organized in terms of 'idealized cognitive models':

The main thesis of this book is that we organize our knowledge by means of structures called *idealized cognitive models*, or ICMs, and that category structures and prototype effects are by-products of that organization. (Lakoff 1987: 68; emphasis in original)

The basic assumptions of Lakoff's proposal are (i) that reason has a bodily basis and (ii) that imaginative aspects of reason—metaphor, metonymy, mental imagery—are central to reason, rather than a peripheral and inconsequential adjunct to the literal (Lakoff 1987: xi). More specifically, the cognitive models he proposes to describe conceptual structure are developed to accommodate the following ideas:

(i) thought is embodied, i.e. the structures used to put together our conceptual systems grow out of bodily experience and make sense in terms of it;
(ii) thought is imaginative, in that those concepts which are not directly grounded in experience employ metaphor, metonymy and mental imagery;
(iii) thought has gestalt properties and is thus not atomic;
(iv) thought has an ecological structure; i.e. the efficiency of cognitive processing, as in learning and memory, depends on the overall structure of the conceptual system and on what the concepts mean. (Lakoff 1987: xiv–xv)

The second part of Lakoff's book presents a number of case studies illustrating and supporting this proposal.

It would be wrong, however, to assume that only models developed within cognitive linguistics can be consistent with prototype theory. Both new and existing linguistic frameworks can attain at least a certain degree of cognitive adequacy provided they accept the central role of semantic structure in linguistics, the conceptual nature of meaning, and the fact that concepts are organized in terms of potentially, or perhaps typically, non-discrete categories. Obviously, such aspects as non-discrete boundaries and graded category membership can more easily be incorporated in approaches which either make no use of formalisms, or whose formalisms are of a purely practical nature, used as a notational convenience to allow appropriate precision in representation, but without any suggestion of psychological reality. On the other hand, any theory using a formalism derived from predicate logic, or any other type of underlying representation requiring clear-cut syntactic categories (word classes, syntactic functions, construction types, etc.) defined in terms of features or unambiguous structural relations, will have difficulty in representing prototype effects in language.

Consequently, non-formalistic, semantically based approaches to language, such as the 'Columbia school' of linguistics (e.g. García 1977), or functionally oriented approaches such as that of Givón (e.g. 1983; 1984; 1986; 1995) and Hopper and Thompson (1980), have proved capable of accommodating prototypicality effects. The same seems to be true for a large number of (more or less) formal theories taking what Van Valin and LaPolla (1997: 11) refer to as the 'communication-and-cognition perspective' to language. Examples are Functional Grammar (Dik 1997), Role and Reference Grammar (Van Valin 1993), Functional-Systemic Grammar (Halliday 1994), Lexical-Functional Grammar (Bresnan 1982; 2000), Construction Grammar (Fillmore 1988; Kay and Fillmore 1999), and Radical Construction Grammar (Croft 2001). What these theories have in common is the basic assumption that language is principally a means of communication, and that the form of linguistic utterances is determined first and foremost by their use. In addition, it is recognized that the study of language use must take place within the perspective of broader cognitive processes such as reasoning and conceptualization. Apart from these basic assumptions, however, these theories differ widely, not only with regard to the grammar models developed (taxonomies, rules, and representations), but also in their definitions of psychological or cognitive adequacy and in their concern with the cognitive status of the grammar itself. It will not, therefore, come as a surprise that these theories succeed in varying ways and to different degrees in accounting for prototype effects in language.

CATEGORIES IN GRAMMAR

Grammatical systems cannot do without categories, as grammarians have recognized ever since ancient times. This is not to say that there has always been agreement as to exactly which categories should be used in describing languages. Ian Michael's 1970 book gives us interesting insights into the history of categorization in the grammar of English. He notes that by 1800 some fifty-six systems of word classes had been proposed by English grammarians. Some of these grammarians were aware of the fact that the word classes cannot be rigidly kept apart, as the passage below from Bullen makes clear:

In parsing English it is not to be expected that every word should upon all occasions preserve its proper title; there is a certain blending of the parts of speech by which each sort of words is connected with the rest. (Bullen 1797: 133; quoted in Michael 1970: 224)

Most modern grammar books recognize eight parts of speech. Among them, nouns and verbs are regarded as primary. The oldest way of defining the parts of speech is by using notional criteria. Dionysius Thrax must have been the first grammarian to note that nouns are words that are 'inflected for case, signifying a concrete or abstract entity' (Robins 1990: 39). The notional part of this definition has been progressively downplayed by grammarians in recent times.

John Lyons and John Anderson have revalued the notional aspects of the definitions of the parts of speech, as the passages from their work included here make clear. Lyons points out that verbs and adjectives are similar, as Plato and Aristotle had observed, and that modern linguists, in keeping verbs and adjectives apart, have stressed the inflectional properties of verbs, neglecting or ignoring their notional properties. Lyons notes, however, that notional properties cannot be disregarded. Thus, while verbs take inflectional endings and usually denote actions, adjectives do not have inflections, and are usually stative. But how then do we explain expressions like *Mary is being silly*, where *silly* combines in its immediate environment with an *-ing* ending which denotes progressive (i.e. actional) aspect? The solution is to speak of 'non-stative adjectives', but in doing so, we are crucially referring to notional properties.

John Anderson in the excerpt included in this reader sets up a 'minimal categorial system' of word classes as follows:

{P} {N} {N,P} { }
verb name noun   functor

This classification is based not only on the fact that verbs are 'event-specific', while nouns are 'entity-specific', but also on the 'predicativity/predicability' of verbs (indicated by the feature P) and the 'referentiality/referentiability' of nouns (indicated by the feature N). This system is modified in Anderson (1997: 59–60) for English and other languages as follows:

{P} {P;N} {P:N}   {N;P} {N}   { }
aux verb   adjective noun   name functor

Names are typical arguments which refer, but are never predicative. Nouns are considered intermediate between verbs and names: they are also typical arguments, but, unlike names, they can be predicative, hence the conjunction of the features N and P. Nouns and verbs are universal categories which can have central and peripheral members. Anderson notes that 'the notional characterization of further categories involves the interaction of just these two features'. The notation {A;B} signifies that a category is characterized by the features A and B, with A being the more dominant. In the case of {A:B} the features simply combine. As for gradience, elsewhere in his book Anderson distinguishes what he calls 'strong gradience' from 'relative gradience'. The former involves an indefinite number of intermediate points between two points on a gradient. The latter is exemplified below (1997: 72):

4P::0N 3P::1N 2P::2N   1P::3N 0P::4N 0P,0N
aux   verb   adjective noun   name   functor

As we have seen, P and N stand for the features 'Predicativity' and 'Nominal/referential'. In the representation above each word class is defined in terms of the 'preponderance' (Anderson 1997) of the features 'Predicativity' and 'Nominal/referential', expressed by the integers, determined as follows:

X alone = 4 X; = 3 X: = 2 ;X = 1 absence of X = 0

Another approach to defining word classes is exemplified in a chapter from Otto Jespersen's *Philosophy of Grammar* and in an article by David Crystal, both reprinted here. Under this approach elements are assigned to classes primarily on the basis of their morphosyntactic behaviour. Both authors make clear that devising definitions for the word classes is not always straightforward, and they attempt to be more precise in defining particular word classes. They agree that meaning is not a reliable criterion. Crystal argues that the best way to set up word classes is to enumerate a number of morphological and distributional criteria. If you then apply these to elements that you want to classify, some end up in the core of a particular class, while others belong to the periphery, depending on how many criteria each element satisfies. In addition to discussing the difficulties of defining word classes, Jespersen also makes an interesting case for recognizing a gradient between proper names and common names.

A third method of defining word classes is employed by cognitive linguists and linguists who are interested in discourse phenomena. They argue that definitions of word classes should be based on semantic and/or pragmatic considerations. For them the syntax of languages is driven by meaning. As an example of this approach we have included in this Reader a passage from Langacker's *Foundations of Cognitive Linguistics* where he stresses the importance of meaning in defining the parts of speech:

Counter to received wisdom, I claim that basic grammatical categories such as **noun, verb, adjective**, and **adverb** are semantically definable. The entities referred to as nouns, verbs, etc. are symbolic units, each with a semantic and a phonological pole, but it is the former that determines the categorization. All members of a given class share fundamental semantic properties, and their semantic poles thus instantiate a single abstract schema subject to reasonably explicit characterization. (Langacker 1987: 239)

Under this view a noun is a symbolic element whose semantic characteristic is that it instantiates a schema, which is referred to as [THING]. Things are then said to be 'regions in a domain'. Verbs, by contrast, designate processes, whereas adjectives and adverbs designate atemporal relations. As we have seen in the section 'Categories in cognition' above, cognitive linguists recognize the importance of prototypes, and have argued that the boundaries between classes cannot be sharply delimited:

[Another] dimension of the discreteness issue concerns the propriety of positing sharp distinctions between certain broad classes of linguistic phenomena, thereby implying that the classes are fundamentally different in character and in large measure separately describable. The nondiscrete alternative regards these classes as grading into one another along various parameters. They form a continuous spectrum (or field) of possibilities, whose segregation into distinct blocks is necessarily artifactual. (Langacker 1987: 134)

For further discussion, see also Taylor (2002).

Hopper and Thompson, in their paper in this volume, set out to show that in addition to looking at the semantics of words, we must also take pragmatic considerations into account. They claim that

the lexical semantic facts about Ns and Vs are secondary to their *discourse roles*; and that the semantic facts (perceptibility etc.) which are characteristic features of prototypical Ns and Vs are in fact derivative of (and perhaps even secondary to) their discourse roles. (Hopper and Thompson 1984: 251)

For these authors nouns typically introduce participants into the discourse, while typical verbs report on events in the discourse. They also claim that there is a correlation between the degree to which word classes display the morphosyntactic features typical of their class and the degree to which they perform the discourse functions that are typical of them, as mentioned above. Thus, for example, nouns that do not refer show fewer nominal morphosyntactic features, and verbs that are stative display fewer typically verbal morphosyntactic properties. At the end of their paper Hopper and Thompson make the perhaps rather startling suggestion that linguistic entities set out as acategorial elements which only acquire categorical properties when they are actually used in discourse:

[F]ar from being 'given' aprioristically for us to build sentences out of, the categories of N and V actually manifest themselves only when the discourse requires it. Such a perspective may help remind us that questions of the relationship between language and the mind can be approached only by considering language in its natural functional context. (Hopper and Thompson 1984: 287)

Part III of the book ends with a chapter by John Taylor which offers a useful overview of work on categorization in linguistics.

GRADIENCE IN GRAMMAR

The 1960s saw sporadic reactions against the dominant syntactic approach of American structuralism, one of the earliest being Dwight Bolinger's slim 1961 book, half of which is excerpted here. Bolinger, always a subtle observer of language in use, draws a distinction between *ambiguity*—where a choice must be made between possible readings—and what he calls *generality*, which seems to be a kind of underspecification, later apparently taken to be also a type of *blend*. He concedes Joos's example *They put their glasses on their noses* to be ambiguous: you have to choose either a present- or past-tense reading of *put*. But Bolinger's counter-example, the elliptical question *Put them away yet?*, is not ambiguous: the normal choice between infinitive after *did* (past tense) and past participle after *have* (present perfect) is neutralized in this particular context, since infinitive and past participle happen to be identical in *put*, and furthermore the past tense and present perfect are semantically compatible here. Bolinger suggests that blends occur not just in lexical semantics and nonce word formation but in everyday syntax and phonology too, and that therefore it just will not do to assume that all core linguistic phenomena are strictly all-or-none in their behaviour. The argument is essentially critical: current linguistics is shutting its eyes to real phenomena of gradience.

Randolph Quirk draws on Bolinger for his 1965 piece, given in full here, as well as on fellow British linguists, American structuralists, and the then emerging paradigm of generative grammar. He starts from that structuralist staple, the binary feature, and shows that careful analysis of corpus data can reveal degrees of similarity between structures according to how far their sets of features overlap. ('Feature' covers a much wider range of phenomena than in generative grammar: broadly, any distributional property.) A convenient notation is a two-dimensional matrix whose columns represent features and whose rows represent constructions or lexical items or classes of lexical item (rather like the verb classes identified by Levin 1993). Cells are marked with pluses or minuses, or question marks where there is divided or uncertain usage. Rearrangement of the matrix puts similar structures or items together—with the acknowledgement that more complex distributions would require polydimensional matrices. Further rearrangement of rows or columns can sometimes demonstrate gradience, where a sequence of neighbouring constructions or items offers a progressive change in the distribution of features, showing up visually as a break in the pattern of pluses and minuses along a roughly diagonal line. Quirk claims several explanatory benefits for this mode of presentation. It predicts where usage is likely to be divided, and it explains certain constructions which transformational grammar would find baffling, since they are not 'generated' by a horizontal relationship in the matrix (constructions in different columns thought to be related by transformation), as, say, passive from active, but by a vertical relationship dependent on the availability of otherwise similar structures or items. Hence the passive *He is said to be careful*, despite the lack of a corresponding active.

Quirk's ground-breaking proposal was intended to supplement the insights gained by structuralist and transformational grammar. Perhaps because of the difficulty of integrating it into a formal theory, it does not appear to have had much explicit influence, except via the work of Ross (see below). Denison (1990: 130–4) used it to map the subcategorizations of certain Old English impersonal verbs, and the concept turns up repeatedly in the Quirk-led descriptive grammars of present-day English. See also Svartvik (1966) on the English passive and Coates (1971) on denominal adjectives.

Problems in the taxonomy of morphosyntactic categories are widely recognized, for instance by Quirk et al. (1985: 73), who also allow for membership of their categories to range from prototypical to marginal cases, as for example with adjectives (1985: 403–4). This does not amount to admitting gradience between categories. To take a case in point, although Quirk et al. show there to be a gradient in terms of syntactic features from coordinators (*and*, *or*) through conjuncts (*yet*, *nor*) to subordinators (*for*, *because*), the tripartite division is maintained (1985: 921–8; sections 13.6–19, reproduced here). The basis of the tripartite division remains, however, unclear. Is it functional or structural? All such items have the function of linking clauses. There is no morphological distinction: all are uninflected, and all three classes contain morphologically simplex items. Each of the three classes is divided into two subclasses, and a number of purely syntactic tests are offered to help distinguish them. The resulting 6×6 table is arranged to show a gradient, though it is unclear from the table why *for* and *so that* are subordinators placed below the conjuncts *however* and *therefore*, since the gradient would be much neater if they were reclassified and the rows swapped.

Jiří V. Neustupný's article (1966), reproduced here in full,[2] is almost entirely data-free, drawing instead on a wide range of recent publications. The main concern of his programmatic paper is to show that linguistic vagueness is a necessary property of any successful linguistic description, and that linguists can and should distinguish between core membership of a linguistic class (the *centre*), and two kinds of non-core membership (the *margin*). The margin covers both the *periphery*, whose members are clearly members of one class rather than another, but without all the features which characterize that class, and the *boundary*, whose members are no closer to one class than to another, neighbouring class.

John Robert Ross's (1973b) paper, also given here in full, comes from a book that grew out of a series of invited lectures given in Japan by Ross, James D. McCawley, and Paul Kiparsky. It is the most specific to be discussed in this section and is also by far the most detailed. Ross's work on 'nouniness' has stimulated a considerable amount of discussion in theoretical syntax, probably in the end more hostile than supportive, but nevertheless testifying to its importance. Two other, shorter papers of his, published around the same time (1972; 1973a), have been more easily available and are better known. The present paper is his fullest exposition of this material. To use more recent terminology, its essence is an attempt to demonstrate that the phrasal category NP exhibits prototype effects, with the following hierarchy of noun phrase heads moving from least to most prototypical (or in Ross's terms, from most 'sentency' to most 'nouny'):

(1)   *that > for to > Q > Acc Ing > Poss Ing >* Action Nominal > Derived Nominal > Noun.

The abbreviations in (1) are explained on his opening page. As is conventional with typological hierarchies, the relation > does not mean 'greater than': rather, if a given item displays a particular property, then the hierarchy predicts that all the items to its left will do so too—and conversely, that properties which belong to the 'nouny' end of the spectrum will only be exhibited by a contiguous set of items starting from the right-hand end of the hierarchy. Ross invented the term 'squish' for such a gradient. To illustrate with one of Ross's early sets of data, consider the operation which disallows prepositions before clauses even when required before conventional NPs:

(2) a. I was surprised that you were ill.
    b. I was surprised at your illness.

Ross works with a transformational model in which *at* is assumed to be underlyingly present, as in (2b), and (2a) is derived by an operation of preposition deletion. He shows that this deletion transformation is obligatory before *that-* and *(for) to*-clauses, often optional before embedded questions, and impossible before the remaining items on the hierarchy:

(3)   I was surprised
$$\left\{\begin{array}{l} \text{(*at) that you had hives} \\ \text{(*at) to find myself underwater} \\ \text{(at) how far I could throw the ball} \\ \text{*(at) Jim('s) retching} \end{array}\right\}$$

[2] We have silently corrected some obvious, mainly typographical, slips.

In similar fashion, a whole series of syntactic and morphological properties is invoked to demonstrate the reality and constancy of the hierarchy in (1), first external to the putative NP, then internal to it, then involving the 'accessibility' of its constituents.

Ross's squishes are demonstrated in matrices closely similar to those used by Quirk, though using finer distinctions: thus rather than Quirk's $< + ? ->$, Ross has $< OK ? ?? ? * * **>$. The overall summary of the evidence is shown in his (2–111). A well-behaved squish is one which shows a monotonic progression of grammaticality in every row and column, so that a cell has either the same grammaticality value as its predecessor or a worse one. A cell which 'misbehaves' by showing higher grammaticality than its left or upper neighbour is a problem which needs explanation, and if no explanation can be found, such misbehaviour is counter-evidence to the squish. (After the first matrix, Ross starts marking such rogue cells with bars which indicate whether the disruption affects the horizontal and/or vertical axes.) Ross believes that the squishiness he claims to have demonstrated here in NPs, and elsewhere in other categories, cannot be satisfactorily handled in a discrete theory.

He concedes that dialectal variation is great—certainly the present authors get hardly any of the progression he finds in (2.78, p. 378), for instance—and his assessments are explicitly based on his own idiolect. He also notes that in some tests, results may be distorted by memories of prescriptive teaching ('Miss Fidditchism', Miss Fidditch being the archetypal pedantic American schoolmarm).

Ross goes further than Quirk in several respects, one of which is to sketch a model of squishes with a metric for degree of category membership, a variable α whose values range from 0 to 1. He then advocates measuring the change in grammaticality between vertically adjacent cells to show whether rows are evenly distributed or bunched in their degree of nouniness; to give some precision to these notions; and to provide an estimate of α. Squishiness, or fuzzy applicability, is then to be extended from category membership to syntactic relationships like 'command' (not the same as 'c-command') and transformational rules. The idea of variable rules was of course taken up in some branches of sociolinguistics in the 1970s and 1980s, though perhaps independently of Ross.[3] However, this part of Ross's paper is largely programmatic. We have reprinted the whole paper despite some digressions irrelevant to the theme of this book, such as an attack on Chomsky's lexicalist hypothesis, partly in order to make an important paper more easily available, partly because the notion of squish recurs throughout.

Now we follow a parallel strand in discussions of gradience since the 1960s. Noam Chomsky (1961) opens a debate on a different kind of gradedness: whether or not grammaticality (Chomsky prefers 'grammaticalness') is a graded property rather than dichotomous. Ever since his inauguration of generative grammar, Chomsky has argued that grammar itself does not, and grammars as produced by linguists should not, involve gradience. In the construction of generative grammars, introspection plays a central role by providing the grammaticality judgements linguists rely on. In this early paper, whose fifth and last section is reproduced here, Chomsky concedes that the grammarian and the native speaker can do more than simply judge a sentence to be grammatical or not: they can often sense *degrees* of grammaticality—or rather, degrees of deviance from grammaticality. His paper is an attempt to reconcile this particular kind of gradedness with the firm either/or properties encoded in a grammar. In effect, degree of deviance is an integer measure based on the level of generality at which a given example violates some rule of the grammar (at least

---

[3] Charles-James N. Bailey, for example, cites Ross's work on squishes with approval (1973: xii), and in a recent essay he includes Ross among those having provided independent confirmation at that time of his own ideas on gradience (1996: 49).

three levels, in Chomsky 1965: 148–53). At the end of our extract Chomsky shifts the focus from deviant sentences to the grammar of a (presumably non-deviant) corpus. Such a grammar is optimal if it successfully accounts for the sentences of the corpus with the least possible over-generation. The metric, again an integer, now represents the number of categories needed in the grammar.

Carson T. Schütze's book (1996) is a study of the theory and methodology of grammaticality judgements. In the sections excerpted here he considers whether grammaticality is inherently dichotomous, and then reports on some indirect experimental testing of levels of (un)grammaticality. Section 3.3.1 examines the nature of graded judgements, taking it for granted that they do occur in practice. Is this because grammaticality itself is graded, or is it an artefact of the judgement process (with grammaticality a pure dichotomy)? Schütze seems to be sympathetic to the former idea, as espoused by Lakoff and Ross, although he concedes that arguments from learnability might point the other way. Then he explicates Chomsky's view of degrees of ungrammaticality as involving an overarching dichotomy—fully grammatical vs. ungrammatical—with the gradedness applying only to the second term; that is, grammaticality is undifferentiated, whereas ungrammaticality can be differentiated into levels. However, he is sceptical both as to whether undifferentiated grammaticality has actually been demonstrated and as to the significance of graded judgements of deviance. On the latter point he leans towards the view that acceptability judgements probably exhibit prototype phenomena even though the underlying (mental) representation may involve classical, Aristotelian category choices.

Schütze's section 3.3.2 considers some experimental evidence for degrees of grammaticality which comes from subjects' acceptability judgements and their processing times for different kinds of deviant sentence. Note his warning that degrees of acceptability are not the same thing as degrees of grammaticality. Most of the studies he reports seem to give broad support to Chomsky's (1965) claim—already prefigured in our extract from Chomsky (1961)—that there is a hierarchy of deviance based on the kind of rule which is violated:

(4) a. *Gandhi hated destroy.
    b. *Gandhi frowned destruction.
    c. *Destruction hated Gandhi.

A lexical category violation like (4a) (the verb *destroy* occurs where an object NP is required) is claimed to be worse—a higher-level violation—than a subcategorization violation like (4b) (a direct object with the intransitive verb *frown*), which is in turn worse than a selectional violation like (4c) (an inanimate subject for the verb *hate*).

CRITICISMS AND RESPONSES

Part V of this Reader presents the views of linguists who explicitly deny gradience and/or fuzziness a place in grammatical analysis. In an article dating from the 1950s Martin Joos puts forward a case for linguistics as a kind of discrete mathematics by definition. It is the task of linguists, so Joos argues, to describe how language is designed (not why it is designed this way), and in doing so they must speak about language precisely. This precision can be achieved under two conditions: one is to limit the field of study, and thus '[a]ll continuity, all possibilities of infinitesimal gradation, are shoved outside of linguistics in one direction or another. There are in fact two such directions, in which we can and resolutely do expel continuity: semantics and phonetics' (Joos 1950/57: 451). The second condition is to adopt a precise approach to linguistic description which is by definition mathematical. This would make conflicting statements possible only when they are derived from a different set of axioms. Linguistic statements must be true or false, and there can be no in-between truth value. It is perhaps possible to represent language with continuous mathematical techniques, but practice has shown that an account in discrete terms is more elegant and therefore preferable, since language is a symbolic system, a code with a high degree of complexity, consisting of signals built out of invariant atoms.

In such an approach to linguistic study linguistic categories are absolutes. Not all languages have the same categorizations: e.g. English and German have the singular/plural distinction, but Chinese does not. But where a category exists, it can be distinguished in all relevant cases without indeterminacy, without partiality or ambiguity. Thus, argues Joos, every noun in English or German has to be singular or plural, regardless of its meaning (a singular noun may denote a plurality of entities) or form (a noun may have the same form for the singular and for the plural). Whereas continuity is to be found in the real world, linguistic categories must be discrete. This is an empirical observation for Joos, since '[no] ... gradation or continuity *in either form or meaning*, has ever been found *in any language* on this planet' (p. 452, emphasis in original). Gradience, then, is outside grammar for Joos, where grammar is a set of statements of possibility or impossibility of occurrence of combinations of units on the various different levels of analysis (phonemic, morphological, syntactic). This is so because of the way language is, and because of the tasks and nature of the linguistic enterprise.

But does this denial of gradience mean that things linguistic cannot be partially the same or partially different? Joos admits such a possibility, but this partiality is not the same as gradience. Similarity cannot be gradual; it is instead quantized. To use his example, let's say phoneme /A/ can be assigned to the categories x, y and z, whereas phoneme /B/ can be assigned to the categories v, w, and z. /A/ and /B/ are identical to the extent that they share z, but different in all other respects.

Joos does not argue against specific linguistic analyses which allow for gradience. He takes a principled stance. The other linguists whose work appears in this part of the book, however, set out to demonstrate that where claims have been made for gradience in grammar, an alternative account is possible and even preferable.

From the point of view of Joos's position the task Wierzbicka sets herself in the article we reproduce here is perhaps the most challenging. Whereas Joos pushed meaning (at least meaning in the sense of the relation between language and the real world) outside the linguistic enterprise, leaving it to sociologists, it is precisely meaning that concerns Wierzbicka, and more specifically the meaning of words. Although for Wierzbicka meaning is very much within the realm of linguistics, her agenda is not very different from that of Joos: she sets out to prove with concrete argumentation and counteranalyses that we not only can, but also must, talk about the meaning of words in precise terms, using discrete semantic features. In the first half of her paper Wierzbicka recounts analyses of words like *bird, lie, furniture,* and *game,* and seeks to disprove claims that capturing their meaning with precise definitions in terms of necessary and sufficient conditions is impossible. She strives to convince us that appeals to vagueness, fuzziness, and prototypicality effects are precipitate. Linguists have abused the concept of prototype and have employed it to excuse themselves from the duty of finding a precise definition of word meanings, so claims Wierzbicka. In the second half of her paper she demonstrates that the notion of prototype can in fact be harnessed and used profitably to help us find the right definitions, because 'there is no conflict between prototypes and definitions' (1990: 360). She exemplifies her claim with semantic accounts of colour terms, words for emotions, and the words *cup, uncle, bird, tomato, cabbage, apple,* and *climb.* The problem with the concept of prototype, according to Wierzbicka, is that all too often it has been used 'as an excuse for intellectual theorizing and sloppiness' (p. 474). It has to 'prove its usefulness through semantic description, not through semantic theorizing'. Wierzbicka acknowledges that vagueness exists. But, like Joos, she is eager to ban it from linguistics: 'Concepts encoded in natural language are, in a sense, vague . . . but this does not mean that their semantic description should be vague, too. The challenge consists in portraying the vagueness inherent in natural language with precision' (p. 474).

The desire to place fuzziness, indeterminacy, and vagueness outside linguistic concerns is echoed in the excerpt from Bouchard we present here. He discusses claims similar to those reviewed in Wierzbicka—that the meaning of words such as *colour, bird, cup, game,* and others is inherently vague and fuzzy. However, the focus of Bouchard's counter-arguments differs somewhat from that of Wierzbicka's. Perhaps fuzziness permeates the concepts words denote, but it has no effect on the grammatical behaviour of words—therefore it is of no concern to the linguist. Even though the crucial consideration is their grammatical behaviour, for Bouchard, as for Wierzbicka, words have 'definite and precise meanings that can be exhaustively decomposed into necessary and sufficient conditions, once the effects of the background have been removed' (1995: 483).

However, as we have seen, researchers have argued explicitly that prototypicality effects *can* be observed in grammar. If so, linguists cannot so easily wash their hands of fuzziness and prototypicality. In response, Bouchard first takes on Ross's argument that nouns fall into a hierarchy of nouniness and that syntactic processes reflect this in their (non)applicability. According to Bouchard, Ross's claim that some nouns are 'nounier' than others can be explained not as differences in behaviour between members of the same syntactic category, but as differences in the referentiality of the different NPs. Fuzziness, in this case, 'is in the web, the background knowledge on which language is woven, and therefore it has no effect on the form and function of language' (Bouchard 1995: 482). Bouchard also hints at alternative, fuzzy-less, accounts for phenomena like modal verbs, serial verb constructions in West African languages, extraction facts, and for the category of the word *faim* 'hunger' in French. His general conclusion is that grammar only employs classical categorization (a fact to be established empirically). Fuzzy categorization is related to the way we perceive the real world, and is external to language.

In the last study in Part V the investigation is narrower—Frederick Newmeyer limits himself to a discussion of syntactic categories. Like Bouchard, one of his aims is to show that prototypicality effects exhibited by categories are invisible to the rules and processes of grammar. This places doubt on the very existence of such prototypicality effects. Newmeyer also reviews the hierarchies proposed by Ross which substantiate the claims for both proto-typicality and fuzziness, as well as the reasons why the particulars of Ross's theories (if not his basic ideas) were eventually abandoned by his followers.

According to Newmeyer, prototypicality effects have recently been seen most often in the degree of 'paradigmatic complexity' of forms, i.e. more prototypical forms are claimed to have a richer set of inflectional endings and/or are able to participate in more construction types. Newmeyer discusses four versions of this idea: Direct Mapping Prototypicality, Strong Cut-off Point Prototypicality, Weak Cut-off Point Prototypicality, and Correlation-only Prototypicality. Direct Mapping Prototypicality makes the strongest claim: as the name suggests, there is a direct interdependence between the degree of prototypicality of a linguistic unit and the grammatical processes it is involved in. Ross's notion of a squish is an example. Strong Cut-off Point Prototypicality says something about which kinds of grammar are possible: if a morphosyntactic process applies to less prototypical members, then it should apply to all the prototypical members too. Weak Cut-off Point

Prototypicality differs from Strong Cut-off Point Prototypicality in that it allows some, albeit rare, exceptions to the foregoing, i.e. some processes are allowed to apply to non-prototypical members even though they do not apply to prototypical ones. The exceptions are arbitrary, and there is a non-random, but unpredictable relationship between them and the central cases. Finally, Correlation-only Prototypicality is also well explained by its name—all it claims is that there is some interdependence between the morphosyntax of a linguistic unit and the degree of prototypicality it displays.

Newmeyer discusses three phenomena to justify his assertion that all of the above (with the possible exception of the weakest claim) are disproved: the English progressive, adjectives, and English verbal alternations. First, the English progressive seems to be possible with less prototypical verbs (e.g. temporary state and psychological predicate verbs) and impossible with more prototypical verbs (e.g. achievement verbs). What is more, when used to denote planned events, the use of the progressive is clearly not related to the prototypicality of the verb. It is likely that the (im)possibility of the progressive should be explained with reference to semantic and pragmatic factors, as indeed linguists have done. Second, with regard to adjectives, data from languages like Rotuman and Acooli show that some prototypical adjectives will manifest the available inflectional distinctions, while a large number fail to do so. And third, as regards English verbal alternations, a considerable number of these are restricted to not very prototypical stative and psychological predicates. All of the above phenomena falsify the two kinds of Cut-off Point Prototypicality.

And yet, there are cases where a correlation between prototypicality and morphosyntax has been claimed, and seemingly with sound justification. Newmeyer proposes or calls upon alternative analyses which provide an explanation for this apparent correlation, with recourse only to discrete categories and certain independently needed principles of grammar. He reviews phenomena like English measure verbs and passives, the case of *there* as a non-prototypical NP, English Idiom Chunks, event structure, and inflectional possibilities. Rather than appeal to prototypicality or defectiveness, as in Ross (1995), the failure of English measure verbs to passivize can be explained by the fact that direct objects passivize, whereas predicate nominatives do not (an observation which, according to Newmeyer, goes back to the work of Bresnan (1978)). The inability of the expletive *there* to undergo a number of syntactic processes (as argued in Ross's 'Fake NP squish' paper, 1973a) can be explained through the lexical semantics of *there* and the pragmatics of its use. In all but one of the cases, the varied and often defective syntactic behaviour of English Idiom Chunks can be explained in a number of alternative ways, without reference to prototypicality, claims Newmeyer, in contradistinction to Ross (1973b; 1981) and Lakoff (1987). To prove this, Newmeyer brings to our attention independent properties of the linguistic units involved, interaction with information structure, semantic factors, and in some cases new data. Inflectional complexity seems to correlate with the degree of prototypicality of verbs (agentive verbs being more prototypical than stative ones). However, following Pustejovky (1991), Newmeyer asserts that achievements and accomplishments have a more complex event structure than do processes, whose structure is in turn more complex than that of states. A more complex event structure will mean more scope for aspectual distinctions, which will lead to a more complex functional structure (in terms of number of projections), which would account for the greater inflectional complexity, without invoking prototypicality effects. A similar claim can be made for nouns, since concrete nouns allow for individuation, whereas abstract nouns do not.

There are cases where semantic accounts of inflectional complexity seem problematic, e.g. when an inflectional distinction is possible for one lexical class but not for another without there being a semantic motivation for it, and when a semantically empty inflection like agreement also exhibits prototypicality effects. Newmeyer makes a (tentative) claim that in cases like these pragmatic factors override semantic factors.

Another task Newmeyer sets himself is the refutation of fuzzy categories. Fuzzy categories have been defended by Ross, as we have seen. Newmeyer takes two phenomena that Ross used to support his position, and shows that the facts can be accounted for without assuming fuzzy boundaries between categories. In response to Ross's claim that the English word *near* is somewhere on a cline between a preposition and an adjective, Newmeyer asserts that it is in fact both, as it passes both the adjective tests and the preposition tests. He also claims that in Ross's nouniness squish one cannot in fact find evidence for the lack of discreteness between the category of sentence and that of noun. He disputes some of the grammaticality judgements in Ross's work, and argues that the data can be accounted for with the available syntactic tools and without assuming fuzzy categories.

RECENT APPROACHES AND FUTURE PROSPECTS

Recently there has been a revaluation of ideas on gradience and other types of variability in many current approaches to linguistics. A convergence of ideas is emerging, as signalled also in a recent book on sociolinguistics:

> Among the most promising recent developments in theoretical syntax and phonology are attempts at relaxing the axiom of categoricity along the lines promulgated by Cedergen and Sankoff (1974) in order to encompass linguistic variation (for example, Hayes 2000, Henry 2002, Anttila 2002). The motivation for these initiatives, which should ultimately redefine the venerable *langue/parole* distinction as poles on a continuum, comes directly from sociolinguistic breakthroughs in dealing with variable data. In a larger sense, it represents a general re-alignment of goals that has taken place in numerous disciplines in recent times. (Chambers 2003: 36)

We review some recent work on gradience and variability in this section.

Work has been done on mixed categories, witness studies like Bresnan (1997) and Malouf (2000a; 2000b). Working in Lexical Functional Grammar, Joan Bresnan claims that mixed categories are 'very common crosslinguistically' (1997: 3). Words in various languages are shown to exhibit characteristic properties of two different lexical categories simultaneously, as if the item were dominated by both categories (which are conveniently adjacent in the linear string in the analyses offered of the initial examples). Bresnan's preferred solution exploits this idea. Her theoretical apparatus uses—and indeed extends—Extended Head Theory, crucially involving the distinction in LFG between c-structure (a level which encodes constituent structure) and f-structure (which encodes grammatical relations, or functions). Suppose, for example, the mixed item is a nominalized verb which is morphologically a noun. It will be analysed as a lexical head N with a VP sister within its NP (1997: 14). The f-structure of the head corresponds both to the head itself (here a N) and to the sister (here a VP), so that in effect it is from f-structure that the item gets both nominal and verbal properties, while in c-structure the tree looks conventional and does not involve dual heads. Now, however common mixed categories may be, they are surely in the minority. Bresnan suggests that composition of argument structures in lexical word formation will determine which categories are mixed and which are not, following a proposal of Spencer.

On the way to presenting the Extended Head Theory analysis, Bresnan explores some other approaches. She rejects solutions which rely on a lexically indeterminate head, on the grounds that in many examples the head is—at least morphologically—unambiguous in category.

Furthermore, given that there are no mixed constructions which allow interleaving of constituents, except as complete phrases, there is allegedly no explanation available if headship is allowed to be indeterminate. The transformational approach of morphological derivation in syntax fails because it cannot explain why syntactically derived words behave just like lexical derivations. There are lexicalist theories which allow dual categories like N/V (projecting up to a VP and then further to an NP, for instance). These fail with mixed categories where the two head categories are not adjacent, making wrong predictions about constituency or the location of the head.

Malouf (2000a: 153) treats the English gerund as a mixed category construction, and implements the insight that gerunds are nominal in their external syntax and verbal in their internal syntax through a cross-classification of head values:

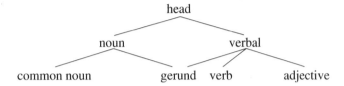

In this representation gerunds are a subtype of the category 'noun', as well as a subtype of the category 'verbal'. Hudson accepts and extends much of this analysis of gerunds, recasting it in his own dependency framework (Hudson 2003).

Even in the Chomskyan paradigm there is recent work which recognizes gradience and categorial indeterminacy. Working in the Minimalist framework Bernstein (2001: 547) claims that there exists 'a continuum between relatively robust and relatively weak noun movement'. And in Corver and van Riemsdijk (2001: 3) we read:

[A]s with all types of categorization, there are elements, which cannot be put straightforwardly under one of the two classes [lexical and functional]. Certain lexical items display ambiguous behavior: they share properties with lexical categories and at the same time they display functional characteristics.

The word class of preposition is given as an example: 'Although they seem less functional in a sense than determiners, they are more "grammatical" than N, V and A' (2001: 3).

In Optimality Theory (OT; see Barbosa et al. 1998; Dekkers et al. 2000; Legendre et al. 2001; McCarthy 2002) the output representations of a given candidate set are ranked against a set of violable criteria, and the candidate which violates the fewest criteria is 'optimal' and wins out. Keller (1997; 1998; 2000) proposes an extended OT framework in which a ranking of candidates is envisaged in terms of their degree of grammaticality, while Hayes's (2000) attempts to model gradient well-formedness in the OT framework.

In an important paper which provides useful coverage of many related fields, Manning (2003) takes up the question of gradient grammaticality. He cites such material as low-frequency patterns in recent corpus material and the arbitrariness of the complement~adjunct distinction to advocate a probabilistic approach to syntax. Large corpora can be used to estimate probability mass functions over certain discrete random variables—that is, say, for each subcategorization possibility occurring with a given verb in the corpus, its probability of occurrence. By this means one builds gradience into the grammatical model and relegates rather less to 'performance' than formal grammar used to do—only entirely non-linguistic facts about the speaker or the world. But the grammar remains formal and structural. He illustrates the concept of continuous categories by looking at the progress of English *following* from V to P, and takes up an extended example involving the interaction of voice, topicality, and person to show that, say, a mere dispreference for indefinite subjects in English and an outright ban on them in Krio can be modelled in the same way, giving an overall economy in linguistic theory. As for English, a discrete formal grammar will miss the genuine and important linguistic fact that certain forms, however grammatical, are particularly rare in practice. The model involves competing constraints, which obviously brings us into the territory of Optimality Theory. Manning sketches a probabilistic version of OT called Stochastic Optimality Theory, in which the constraints are not merely ranked in linear order, but are given a numerical value which reflects their relative distance from each other. Furthermore, an arbitrary level of 'noise' is added to the model to produce occasional re-rankings and thus allow for the variation seen in natural language. The paper concludes with an introduction to generalized linear models as a statistical tool for grammar-building, already widely used in natural language processing software.

At this point it is appropriate to mention some other work which has invoked fuzzy grammar in diachronic studies. Romaine (1983: 13–15) briefly invokes squishy category membership in her discussion of category change. It is left unclear whether the category of a particular item is squishy for a particular speaker at a particular time, since Romaine also believes in multiple grammars in a population during the lexical and social diffusion of a change. Haspelmath simply takes it for granted 'that linguistic expressions cannot always be categorized clearly into categories such as N, P, V, Aux, C, D, and that instead what we have are continua (N ↔ P, V ↔ Aux, etc.)' (1999: 1045), regarding this as an essential assumption if grammaticalization is to be modelled as a gradual process. Kemmer too commends the prototype model in the description of diachrony (1992).[4] Denison (2001) explores recent diachronic change from Noun to Adjective in English, showing that there is non-abrupt change and speculating that intermediate states are usually marked and unstable. (Compare Bailey's contention that 'few of the rules of a language will be variable at any given time. Variable rules usually have sociolinguistic significance' (1973: 33).) Givón (1975: 80–7) makes a case for various gradual changes from V to P in so-called serial verbs:

It is highly unlikely that a verb would change suddenly into a preposition by all semantic, morphological and syntactic criteria at once. One thus expects to find, for a long time, many different types of intermediate cases in the language.... (Givón 1975: 86)

Syntactic blending has also been advanced frequently, for example by Jespersen (1909–49: VII 385–7, 393). Tabor (1993) posits transient hybrid constructions as stepping stones in the history of *sort of* and *kind of* constructions, sketching a connectionist model of change. Although Keizer and Denison (2002) advocate constructional gradience in *sort of* constructions, they take issue with some of the details in Tabor's account.

Charles-James N. Bailey has been writing for over thirty years on ideas to do with wave theory and developmentalism, in which synchrony and diachrony are integrated in the spread of features in time and place. A convenient gathering and updating of papers is Bailey (1996). His principal concerns are language contact, polylectal grammars, and phonology, but grammar and syntax also receive some discussion. Bailey favours an adaptation of formal, Chomskian analyses to allow for both gradient categorizations and for the variable application of rules:

Binary models have got no special place in developmentalism, being viewed as special (infrequent) instances of ternary features (whose mid values are often gradient). (Bailey 1996: 29)

Gradient models are needed not just for intonation. The developmental approach quite generally requires non-discrete models.... (1996: 87)

---

[4] Winters uses it in her account of the evolution of the French subjunctive (1989), though her prototype is essentially a semantic rather than a morphosyntactic one.

However, the term 'gradience' appears to be used more for differences between lects than for the grammatical analysis of a single variety.

Neural support for the scalar nature of human language processing can be found in research carried out within the Berkeley Neural Theory of Language project, which aims (among other things) at supplying the kind of graded (probabilistic) computational models of language processing needed to capture and extend the insights from cognitive linguistics and construction grammar (e.g. Narayanan and Jurafsky 1998; Chang et al. 2002; Bergen 2002a, b). The basic assumptions are (a) that human language processing relies on various interactive sources of linguistic knowledge (e.g. lexical, phonological, semantic, syntactic, pragmatic), and is sensitive to their relative frequency; and (b) that during on-line processing multiple interpretations are maintained in parallel. The question to be answered is how the various knowledge sources, which are all probabilistic, are combined to favour a particular interpretation. By using a 'belief net' (or 'probabilistic independence net', a connectionist model for representing uncertain propositional knowledge), probabilistic models are being developed which can compute the likelihood of parallel interpretations at any stage of the process on the basis of linguistic input from the various sources, whether top-down (e.g. semantic, syntactic, and pragmatic knowledge sources) or bottom-up (phonological or graphological evidence). Although research in this area is only just beginning, it is believed that these models can succeed where deterministic models of language processing have failed, in that they can deal both with the graded nature of linguistic knowledge and with the interaction between various types of probabilistic information.

Finally, Aarts (2004) attempts to reconcile an Aristotelian conception of word classes in English with a recognition of the fact that categories resemble each other in their distributional behaviour. Category boundaries must be drawn sharply, but are subject to two kinds of gradience: Subsective Gradience is an intra-categorial phenomenon that allows members of form classes to display the properties of that class to varying degrees, while Intersective Gradience is an inter-categorial phenomenon which obtains when two form classes 'converge' on each other.

REFERENCES

Aarts, B. (2004). 'Modelling linguistic gradience'. *Studies in Language* 28(1): 1–50.

Anderson, J. M. (1997). *A Notional Theory of Syntactic Categories*. Cambridge: Cambridge University Press.

Anttila, A. (2002). 'Variation and phonological theory'. In J. K. Chambers, P. Trudgill, and N. Schilling-Estes (eds.), *The Handbook of Language Variation and Change*. Oxford: Blackwell, 206–43.

Aristotle (1984). *The Categories*. In *The Complete Works of Aristotle*, the revised Oxford translation, ed. J. Barnes, trans. J. L. Ackrill. Princeton, NJ: Princeton University Press, 3–24.

Bailey, C.-J. N. (1973). 'Introduction'. In C.-J. N. Bailey and R. W. Shuy (eds.), *New Ways of Analyzing Variation in English*. Washington, DC: Georgetown University Press, xi–xv.

——(1996). *Essays on Time-Based Linguistic Analysis*. Oxford: Clarendon Press.

Ballmer, T. T., and M. Pinkel (eds.) (1983). *Approaching Vagueness*. Amsterdam: North Holland.

Baltin, M., and C. Collins (2001). *The Handbook of Contemporary Syntactic Theory*. Oxford: Blackwell.

Barbosa, P., D. Fox, P. Hagstrom, M. McGinnis and D. Pesetsky (eds.) (1998). *Is the Best Good Enough?* Cambridge, Mass.: MIT Press and MIT Working Papers in Linguistics.

Barsalou, L. W. (1983). 'Ad-hoc categories'. *Memory and Cognition* 11: 211–27.

Bergen, B. K. (2000a). 'Probability in phonological generalizations: modeling optional French final consonants'. In A. Yu et al. (eds.), *Proceedings of the 26th Annual Meeting of the Berkeley Linguistics Society*.

Bergen, B. K. (2000b). 'Ramifications of phonology–syntax interactions for phonological models'. In *Proceedings of the 24th Annual Penn Linguistics Colloquium*.

Berlin, B. (1976). 'The concept of rank in ethnobotanical classification'. *American Ethnologist* 3: 381–99.

——(1978). 'Ethnobotanical classification'. In E. Rosch and B. B. Lloyd (eds.), *Cognition and Categorization*. Hillsdale, NJ: Erlbaum, 1–26.

——and P. Kay (1969). *Basic Color Terms: Their Universality and Evolution*. Berkeley, Calif.: University of California Press.

——D. E. Breedlove, and P. H. Raven (1974). *Principles of Tzeltal Plant Classification*. New York: Academic Press.

Bernstein, J. B. (2001). 'The DP hypothesis'. In Baltin and Collins (2001: 536–61).

Bolinger, D. L. (1961). *Generality, Gradience, and the All-or-None*. 's-Gravenhage: Mouton.

Bouchard, D. (1995). *The Semantics of Syntax: A Minimalist Approach to Grammar*. Chicago: University of Chicago Press.

Bresnan, J. W. (1978). 'A realistic transformational grammar'. In M. Halle, J. Bresnan, and G. Miller (eds.), *Linguistic Theory and Psychological Reality*. Cambridge, Mass.: MIT Press, 1–59.

——(1982). *The Mental Representation of Grammatical Relations*. Cambridge, Mass.: MIT Press.

——(1997). 'Mixed categories as head sharing constructions'. http://www-lfg.stanford.edu/lfg/ms/ms.html.

——(2000). *Lexical-Functional Syntax*. Oxford: Blackwell.

Brown, R. (1965). *Social Psychology*. New York: Free Press.

Burns, L. C. (1991). *Vagueness: An Investigation into Natural Languages and the Sorites Paradox*. Dordrecht: Kluwer.

Cedergren, H., and D. Sankoff (1974). 'Variable rules: performance as a statistical reflection of competence'. *Language* 50: 333–55.

Chambers, J. K. (2003). *Sociolinguistic Theory*, 2nd edn. Oxford: Blackwell.

Chang, N., J. Feldman, R. Porzel, and K. Sanders (2002). 'Scaling cognitive linguistics: formalisms for language understanding'. In *Proceedings of the 1st International Workshop on Scalable Natural Language Understanding*. Heidelberg.

Chatterjee, A. (1994). *Understanding Vagueness*. Delhi: Pragata.

Chomsky, N. (1961). 'Some methodological remarks on generative grammar'. *Word* 17: 219–39.

——(1965). *Aspects of the Theory of Syntax*. Cambridge, Mass.: MIT Press.

Coates, J. (1971). 'Denominal adjectives: a study in syntactic relationships between modifier and head'. *Lingua* 27: 160–69.

Corver, N., and H. van Riemsdijk (2001). 'Semi-lexical categories'. In Corver and van Riemsdijk (eds.), *Semi-lexical Categories: The Function of Content Words and the Content of Function Words*. Berlin: Mouton de Gruyter, 1–19.

Craig, C. (ed.) (1986). *Noun Classes and Categorization: Proceedings of a Symposium on Categorization and Noun Classification, Eugene, Oregon, October 1983*. Amsterdam: Benjamins.

Croft, W. (2001). *Radical Construction Grammar: Syntactic Theory in Typological Perspective*. Oxford: Oxford University Press.

Crystal, D. (1967). 'English'. *Lingua* 17: 24–56.

Dekkers, J., F. van der Leeuw, and J. van de Weijer (eds.) (2000). *Optimality Theory: Phonology, Syntax and Acquisition*. Oxford: Oxford University Press.

Denison, D. (1990). 'The Old English impersonals revived'. In S. Adamson, V. A. Law, N. Vincent, and S. Wright (eds.), *Papers from the 5th International Conference on English Historical Linguistics: Cambridge, 6–9 April 1987*. Amsterdam: Benjamins, 111–40.

——(2001). 'Gradience and linguistic change'. In L. Brinton (ed.) *Historical Linguistics 1999: Selected Papers from the 14th International Conference on Historical Linguistics*. Amsterdam: Benjamins, 119–44.

Dik, S. C. (1997). *The Theory of Functional Grammar*. Berlin: Mouton de Gruyter.

Ekman, P. (1971). *Universals and Cultural Differences in Facial Expressions of Emotions*. Lincoln: University of Nebraska Press.

——R. W. Levenson, and P. Ellsworth (1972). *Emotion in the Human Face*. Elmsford, NY: Pergamon Press.

Fauconnier, G. (1985). *Mental Spaces*. Cambridge, Mass.: MIT Press.

Fillmore, C. J. (1982). 'Frame semantics'. In Linguistic Society of Korea (ed.), *Linguistics in the Morning Calm*. Seoul: Hanshin, 111–38.

——(1988). 'The mechanism of "Construction Grammar"'. In *Proceedings of the 14th Annual Meeting of the Berkeley Linguistics Society*, 95–107.

Frege, G. (1903/70). *Grundgesetze der Arithmetik*, vol. ii, taken from *The Frege Reader*, ed. Michael Beaney. Oxford: Blackwell.

García, E. (1977). 'On the practical consequences of theoretical principles'. *Lingua* 43: 129–70.

Givón, T. (1975). 'Serial verbs and syntactic change: Niger-Congo'. In C. N. Li (ed.), *Word Order and Word Order Change*. Austin: University of Texas Press, 47–112.

——(1983). *Topic Continuity in Discourse: A Quantitative Cross-Language Study*. Amsterdam: Benjamins.

——(1984). *Syntax: A Functional-Typological Introduction*, vol. i. Amsterdam: Benjamins.

——(1986). 'Prototypes: between Plato and Wittgenstein'. In Craig (1986: 77–102).

——(1995). *Functionalism and Grammar*. Amsterdam: Benjamins.

Halliday, M. A. K. (1994). *An Introduction to Functional Grammar*. London: Arnold.

Harnad, S. (1987). 'Category induction and representation'. In S. Harnad (ed.), *Categorial Perception: The Groundwork of Cognition*. Cambridge: Cambridge University Press, 535–65.

Haspelmath, M. (1998). 'Does grammaticalization need reanalysis?' *Studies in Language* 22: 49–85.

——(1999). 'Why is grammaticalization irreversible?' *Linguistics* 37: 1043–68.

Hayes, B. P. (2000). 'Gradient well-formedness in optimality theory'. In Dekkers et al. (2000: 88–120).

Henry, A. (2002). 'Variation and syntactic theory'. In: J. K. Chambers, P. Trudgill, and N. Schilling-Estes (eds.), *The Handbook of Language Variation and Change*. Oxford: Blackwell, 267–82.

Hopper, P. J., and S. A. Thompson (1980). 'Transitivity in grammar and discourse'. *Language* 56: 251–99.

——(1984). 'The discourse basis for lexical categories in Universal Grammar'. *Language* 60: 703–52.

Hudson, Richard (2003). 'Gerunds without phrase structure'. *Natural Language and Linguistic Theory*: 579–615.

Jackendoff, R. J. (1972). *Semantic Interpretation in Generative Grammar*. Cambridge Mass.: MIT Press.

——(1983). *Semantics and Cognition*. Cambridge, Mass.: MIT Press.

——(1990). *Semantic Structures*. Cambridge, Mass.: MIT Press.

——(1992). *Languages of the Mind*. Cambridge, Mass.: MIT Press.

Jespersen, O. (1924). *The Philosophy of Grammar*. London: Allen & Unwin.

——(1909–49). *A Modern English Grammar on Historical Principles*. 7 vols. London: Allen & Unwin; Copenhagen: Munksgaard.

Joos, M. (1950/57). 'Description of language design'. *Journal of the Acoustical Society of America* 22: 701–8; also in Joos (1957).

——(ed.) (1957). *Readings in Linguistics: The Development of Descriptive Linguistics in America 1925–56*, 4th edn. Chicago: University of Chicago Press, 349–56.

Kay, P., and C. McDaniel (1978). 'The linguistic significance of the meanings of basic color terms'. *Language* 54: 610–46.

—— and C. J. Fillmore (1999). 'Grammatical constructions and linguistic generalizations: the *What's X doing Y?* construction'. *Language* 75: 1–33.

Keefe, R., and P. Smith (eds.) (1996). *Vagueness: A Reader*. Cambridge, Mass.: MIT Press.

Keil, F. C., and M. H. Kelly (1987). 'Development changes in category structure'. In S. Harnad (ed.), *Categorial Perception: The Groundwork of Cognition*. Cambridge: Cambridge University Press, 491–510.

Keizer, E., and D. Denison (2002). '*Sort of* constructions: grammar and change'. MS, University College London and University of Manchester.

Keller, F. (1997). 'Extraction, gradedness and optimality'. In A. Dimitriadis, L. Siegel, C. Surek-Clark, and A. Williams (eds.), *Proceedings of the 21st Annual Penn Linguistics Colloquium*. Penn Working Papers in Linguistics 4.2: 169–86.

Keller, F. (1998). 'Gradient grammaticality as an effect of selective constraint re-ranking'. In M. Gruber, D. Higgins, K. S. Olson, and T. Wysocki (eds.), *Papers from the Thirty-Fourth Regional Meeting of the Chicago Linguistic Society*, vol. ii: *The Panels*, 95–109.

——(2000). 'Gradience in Grammar: Experimental and Computational Aspects of Degrees of Grammaticality'. Ph.D. thesis, University of Edinburgh.

Kemmer, S. (1992). 'Grammatical prototypes and competing motivations in a theory of linguistic change'. In G. W. Davis and G. K. Iverson (eds.), *Explanation in Historical Linguistics*. Amsterdam: Benjamins, 145–66.

Labov, W. (1973). 'The boundaries of words and their meanings'. In C.-J. Bailey and R. W. Shuy (eds.), *New Ways of Analyzing Variation in English*. Washington, DC: Georgetown University Press, 340–73.

Lakoff, G. (1971). 'On generative semantics'. In D. Steinberg and L. Jakobovits (eds.), *Semantics: An Interdisciplinary Reader*. New York: Cambridge University Press, 232–96.

——(1972). 'Hedges: a study in meaning criteria and the logic of fuzzy concepts'. In *Papers from the Eighth Regional Meeting of the Chicago Linguistics Society*, 183–228.

——(1987). *Women, Fire and Dangerous Things: What Categories Reveal about the Mind*. Chicago: University of Chicago Press.

——and M. Johnson (1980). *Metaphors We Live By*. Chicago: University of Chicago Press.

Langacker, R. W. (1973). 'Predicate raising: some Uto-Aztecan evidence'. In B. B. Kachru et al. (eds.), *Issues in Linguistics: Papers in Honor of Henry and Renée Kahane*. Urbana: University of Illinois Press, 468–91.

——(1987). *Foundations of Cognitive Grammar*, vol. i: *Theoretical Prerequisites*. Stanford, Calif.: Stanford University Press.

——(1991). *Foundations of Cognitive Grammar*, vol. ii: *Descriptive Application*. Stanford, Calif.: Stanford University Press.

——(1999). *Grammar and Conceptualization*. Berlin: Mouton de Gruyter.

——(2002). *Concept, Image, and Symbol: The Cognitive Basis of Grammar*, 2nd edn. Berlin: Mouton de Gruyter.

Legendre, G., J. Grimshaw, and S. Vikner (eds.) (2001). *Optimality-Theoretic Syntax*. Cambridge, Mass.: MIT Press.

Levin, B. (1993). *English Verb Classes and Alternations: A Preliminary Investigation*. Chicago: University of Chicago Press.

Lounsbury, F. (1964). 'A formal account of the Crow- and Omaha-type kinship terminologies'. In W. H. Goodenough (ed.), *Explorations in Cultural Anthropology*. New York: McGraw-Hill, 351–94. Repr. in S. A. Tyler (ed.) (1969), *Cognitive Anthropology*. New York: Holt, Rinehart Winston, 212–54.

Malouf, R. P. (2000a). 'Verbal gerunds as mixed categories in Head-Driven Phrase Structure grammar'. In R. D. Borsley (ed.), *The Nature and Function of Syntactic Categories*. New York: Academic Press, 133–66.

——(2000b). *Mixed Categories in the Hierarchical Lexicon*. Stanford, Calif.: CSLI.

Manning, C. D. (2003). 'Probabilistic syntax'. In R. Bod, J. Hay, and S. Jannedy (eds.), *Probabilistic Linguistics*. Cambridge, Mass.: MIT Press, 289–341.

McCarthy, J. J. (2002). *A Thematic Guide to Optimality Theory*. Cambridge: Cambridge University Press.

McCloskey, M., and S. Glucksburg (1978). 'Natural categories: well-defined or fuzzy sets?' *Memory and Cognition* 6: 462–72.

Medin, D. L., and L. W. Barsalou (1987). 'Categorization processes and categorical perception'. In S. Harnad (ed.), *Categorial Perception: The Groundwork of Cognition*. Cambridge: Cambridge University Press, 455–90.

Michael, I. (1970). *English Grammatical Categories and the Tradition to 1800*. Cambridge: Cambridge University Press.

Narayanan, S., and D. Jurafsky (1998). 'Bayesian models of human sentence processing'. In *Proceedings of the 20th Cognitive Science Society Conference*. Hillsdale, NJ: Erlbaum, 84–90.

Neustupný, J. V. (1966). 'On the analysis of linguistic vagueness'. *Travaux linguistiques de Prague* 2: 39–51.

Pustejovsky, J. (1991). 'The syntax of event structure'. *Cognition* 41: 47–81.

Quirk, R. (1965). 'Descriptive statement and serial relationship'. *Language* 41: 205–17.

——S. Greenbaum, G. Leech, and J. Svartvik (1985). *A Comprehensive Grammar of the English Language*. London: Longman.

Robins, R. H. (1990). *A Short History of Linguistics*, 3rd edn. London: Longman.

Romaine, S. (1983). 'Syntactic change as category change by re-analysis and diffusion: some evidence from the history of English'. In M. Davenport, E. Hansen, and H. F. Nielsen (eds.), *Current Topics in English Historical Linguistics*. Odense: Odense University Press, 9–27.

Rosch, E. (1973). 'Natural categories'. *Cognitive Psychology* 4: 328–50.

——(1978). 'Principles of categorization'. In E. Rosch and B. B. Lloyd (eds.), *Cognition and Categorization*. Hillsdale, NJ: Erlbaum, 27–48.

——(1981). 'Prototype classification and logical classification: the two systems'. In E. Scholnick (ed.), *New Trends in Conceptual Representation: Challenges to Piaget's Theory*. Hillsdale, NJ: Erlbaum, 73–86.

——and C. B. Mervis (1975). 'Family resemblances: studies in the internal structure of categories'. *Cognitive Psychology* 7: 573–605.

——W. D. Gray, and D. M. Johnson (1976). 'Basic objects in natural categories'. *Cognitive Psychology* 8: 382–439.

Ross, J. R. (1972). 'The category squish: Endstation Hauptwort'. *Papers from the Eighth Regional Meeting of the Chicago Linguistic Society*, 316–28.

——(1973a). 'A fake NP squish'. In C.-J. Bailey and R. W. Shuy (eds.) *New Ways of Analyzing Variation in English*. Washington DC: Georgetown University Press, 96–140.

——(1973b). 'Nouniness'. In O. Fujimura (ed.), *Three Dimensions of Linguistic Theory*. Tokyo: TEC, 137–257.

——(1981). 'Nominal decay'. Unpublished MS, Massachusetts Institute of Technology.

——(1995). 'Defective noun phrases'. In *Papers from the Thirty-First Regional Meeting of the Chicago Linguistic Society*, 309–20.

Russell, B. (1923). 'Vagueness'. *Australian Journal of Philosophy and Psychology* 1: 84–92.

Sainsbury, R. M. (1988). *Paradoxes*. Cambridge: Cambridge University Press.

——and T. Williamson (1997). 'Sorites'. In C. Wright and B. Hale (eds.), *Companion to Philosophy of Language*. Oxford: Blackwell, 458–84.

Scholnick, E. (ed.) (1983). *New Trends in Conceptual Representation: Challenges to Piaget's Theory*. Hillsdale, NJ: Erlbaum.

Schütze, C. T. (1996). *The Empirical Base of Linguistics: Grammaticality Judgments and Linguistic Methodology*. Chicago: Chicago University Press.

Svartvik, J. (1966). *On Voice in the English Verb*. The Hague: Mouton.

Tabor, W. (1993). 'The gradual development of degree modifier *sort of* and *kind of*: a corpus proximity model'. In *Papers from the Twenty-Ninth Regional Meeting of the Chicago Linguistic Society*, 451–65.

Taylor, J. (1995). *Linguistic Categorization: Prototypes in Linguistic Theory*, 2nd edn. Oxford: Oxford University Press.

——(2002). *Cognitive Grammar*. Oxford: Oxford University Press.

Tsohatzidis, S. L. (ed.) (1990). *Meanings and Prototypes: Studies in Linguistic Categorization*. London: Routledge.

Van Valin, R. D. (ed.) (1993). *Advances in Role and Reference Grammar*. Amsterdam: Benjamins.

——and R. J. LaPolla (1997). *Syntax: Structure, Meaning and Function*. Cambridge: Cambridge University Press.

Weinreich, U., W. Labov, and M. Herzog (1968). 'Empirical foundations for a theory of language change'. In W. Lehmann and Y. Malkiel (eds.), *Directions for Historical Linguistics*. Austin: University of Texas Press, 97–195.

Wierzbicka, A. (1990). ' "Prototypes save": on the uses and abuses of of the notion of "prototype" in linguistics and related fields'. In Tsohatzides (1990: 347–67). Also in Wierzbicka (1996).

——(1996). *Semantics: Primes and Universals*. Oxford: Oxford University Press.

Williamson, T. (1994). *Vagueness*. London: Routledge.

Winters, M. E. (1989). 'Diachronic prototype theory: on the evolution of the French subjunctive'. *Linguistics* 27: 703–30.

Wittgenstein, L. (1953/58). *Philosophical Investigations*, 3rd edn. 1968, trans. G. E. M. Anscombe. Oxford: Blackwell.

Zadeh, L. (1965). 'Fuzzy sets'. *Information and Control* 8: 338–53.

PART I
Philosophical Background

1

Categories

ARISTOTLE

Categories

4^b20. Of quantities some are discrete, others continuous; and some are composed of parts which have position in relation to one another, others are not composed of parts which have position.

4^b22. Discrete are number and language; continuous are lines, surfaces, bodies, and also, besides these, time and place. For the parts of a number have no common boundary at which they join together. For example, if five is a part of ten the two fives do not join together at any common boundary but are separate; nor do the three and the seven join together at any common boundary. Nor could you ever in the case of a number find a common boundary of its parts, but they are always separate. Hence number is one of the discrete quantities. Similarly, language also is one of the discrete quantities (that language is a quantity is evident, since it is measured by long and short syllables; I mean here language that is *spoken*). For its parts do not join together at any common boundary. For there is no common boundary at which the syllables join together, but each is separate in itself. A line, on the other hand, is a continuous quantity. For it is possible to find a common boundary at which its parts join together, a point. And for a surface, a line; for the parts of a plane join together at some common boundary. Similarly in the case of a body one could find a common boundary—a line or a surface—at which the parts of the body join together. Time also and place are of this kind. For present time joins on to both past time and future time. Place, again, is one of the continuous quantities. For the parts of a body occupy some place, and they join together at a common boundary. So the parts of the place occupied by the various parts of the body, themselves join together at the same boundary at which the parts of the body do. Thus place also is a continuous quantity, since its parts join together at one common boundary.

* Aristotle, *Categories and De Interpretatione*, ch. 6, sections 4^b20 and 4^b22, pp. 12–13. Translated by J. L. Ackrill. Clarendon Aristotle Series. © 1963 Oxford: Clarendon Press. Reprinted by permission.

Metaphysics

1006^{b}28. It is accordingly necessary, if it is true of anything to say that it is a man, that it be a two-footed animal (for that was what 'man' signified); and if that is necessary, it is not possible that the same thing should not be, at that time, a two-footed animal (for 'to be necessary' signifies this: to be incapable of not being). Consequently it is not possible that it should be simultaneously true to say that the same thing is a man and is not a man.

1008^{b}31. Again, however much everything is so-and-so and not so-and-so, at least the more and the less are present in the nature of things-that-are. For we would not assert that two and three are *equally* even, or that one who considered that four things were five and one who considered that they were a thousand were *equally* in error. So if they are not equally, it is plain that one of them is less, so that he has more truth. So if what is more is nearer, there must be something true which the more true view is nearer. And even if that is not so, at least there is already something more firm and more truthlike, and we should be rid of the unadulterated thesis which would prevent us from having anything definite in our thinking.

---

* From: Aristotle, *Metaphysics*, Books Γ, Δ, and Σ. Book Γ, ch. 4, section 1006^{b}28, p. 10, and Book Γ, chapter 4, section 1008^{b}31, pp. 15–16. Translated by Christopher Kirwan. Clarendon Aristotle Series. © 1971 Oxford: Clarendon Press. Reprinted by permission.

2

Concepts

GOTTLOB FREGE

§56

A definition of a concept (of a possible predicate) must be complete; it must unambiguously determine, as regards any object, whether or not it falls under the concept (whether or not the predicate is truly assertible of it). Thus there must not be any object as regards which the definition leaves in doubt whether it falls under the concept; though for us men, with our defective knowledge, the question may not always be decidable. We may express this meta-phorically as follows: the concept must have a sharp boundary. If we represent concepts in extension by areas on a plane, this is admittedly a picture that may be used only with caution, but here it can do us good service. To a concept without sharp boundary there would cor-respond an area that had not a sharp boundary-line all round, but in places just vaguely faded away into the background. This would not really be an area at all; and likewise a concept that is not sharply defined is wrongly termed a concept. Such quasi-conceptual constructions cannot be recognized as concepts by logic; it is impossible to lay down precise laws for them. The law of excluded middle is really just another form of the requirement that the concept should have a sharp boundary. Any object Δ that you choose to take either falls under the concept Φ or does not fall under it; *tertium non datur*. E.g. would the sentence 'any square root of 9 is odd' have a comprehensible sense at all if *square root of* 9 were not a concept with a sharp boundary? Has the question 'Are we still Christians?' really got a sense, if it is inde-terminate whom the predicate 'Christian' can truly be asserted of, and who must be refused it?

* From: Gottlob Frege, *Grundgesetze der Arithmetik*, vol. ii (1903/70). In Peter Geach and Max Black (eds.), *Translations from the Philosophical Writings of Gottlob Frege* (Oxford: Basil Blackwell, 1970), section 56, p. 159. © 1970 Blackwell Publishers. Reprinted by permission.

3

Vagueness

BERTRAND RUSSELL

Reflection on philosophical problems has convinced me that a much larger number than I used to think, or than is generally thought, are connected with the principles of symbolism, that is to say, with the relation between what means and what is meant. In dealing with highly abstract matters it is much easier to grasp the symbols (usually words) than it is to grasp what they stand for. The result of this is that almost all thinking that purports to be philosophical or logical consists in attributing to the world the properties of language. Since language really occurs, it obviously has all the properties common to all occurrences, and to that extent the metaphysic based upon linguistic considerations may not be erroneous. But language has many properties which are not shared by things in general, and when these properties intrude into our metaphysic it becomes altogether misleading. I do not think that the study of the principles of symbolism will yield any *positive* results in metaphysics, but I do think it will yield a great many negative results by enabling us to avoid fallacious inferences from symbols to things. The influence of symbolism on philosophy is mainly unconscious; if it were conscious it would do less harm. By studying the principles of symbolism we can learn not to be unconsciously influenced by language, and in this way can escape a host of erroneous notions.

Vagueness, which is my topic tonight,[1] illustrates these remarks. You will no doubt think that, in the words of the poet: 'Who speaks of vagueness should himself be vague.' I propose to prove that all language is vague and that therefore my language is vague, but I do not wish this conclusion to be one that you could derive without the help of the syllogism. I shall be as little vague as I know how to be if I am to employ the English language. You all know that I invented a special language with a view to avoiding vagueness, but unfortunately it is unsuited for public occasions. I shall therefore, though regretfully, address you in English, and whatever vagueness is to be found in my words must be attributed to our ancestors for not having been predominantly interested in logic.

There is a certain tendency in those who have realized that words are vague to infer that things also are vague. We hear a great deal about the flux and the continuum and the unanalysability of the Universe, and it is often suggested that as our language becomes more precise, it becomes less adapted to represent the primitive chaos out of which man is supposed to have evolved the cosmos. This seems to me precisely a case of the fallacy of verbalism—the fallacy that consists in mistaking the properties of words for the properties of things. Vagueness and precision alike are characteristics which can only belong to a representation, of which language is an example. They have to do with the relation between a representation and that which it represents. Apart from representation, whether cognitive or mechanical, there can be no such thing as vagueness or precision; things are what they are, and there is an end of

* Bertrand Russell, 'Vagueness', *Australasian Journal of Philosophy and Psychology* 1 (1923): 84–92. © Oxford University Press. Reprinted by permission.
[1] Read before the Jowett Society, Oxford, 22 Nov. 1922.

it. Nothing is more or less what it is, or to a certain extent possessed of the properties which it possesses. Idealism has produced habits of confusion even in the minds of those who think that they have rejected it. Ever since Kant there has been a tendency in philosophy to confuse knowledge with what is known. It is thought that there must be some kind of identity between the knower and the known, and hence the knower infers that the known also is muddle-headed. All this identity of knower and known, and all this supposed intimacy of the relation of knowing, seems to me a delusion. Knowing is an occurrence having a certain relation to some other occurrence, or groups of occurrences, or characteristic of a group of occurrences, which constitutes what is said to be known. When knowledge is vague, this does not apply to the knowing as an occurrence; as an occurrence it is incapable of being either vague or precise, just as all other occurrences are. Vagueness in a cognitive occurrence is a characteristic of its relation to that which is known, not a characteristic of the occurrence in itself.

Let us consider the various ways in which common words are vague, and let us begin with such a word as 'red'. It is perfectly obvious, since colours form a continuum, that there are shades of colour concerning which we shall be in doubt whether to call them red or not, not because we are ignorant of the meaning of the word 'red', but because it is a word the extent of whose application is essentially doubtful. This, of course, is the answer to the old puzzle about the man who went bald. It is supposed that at first he was not bald, that he lost his hairs one by one, and that in the end he was bald; therefore, it is argued, there must have been one hair the loss of which converted him into a bald man. This, of course, is absurd. Baldness is a vague conception; some men are certainly bald, some are certainly not bald, while between them there are men of whom it is not true to say they must either be bald or not bald. The law of excluded middle is true when precise symbols are employed, but it is not true when symbols are vague, as, in fact, all symbols are. All words describing sensible qualities have the same kind of vagueness which belongs to the word 'red'. This vagueness exists also, though in a lesser degree, in the quantitative words which science has tried hardest to make precise, such as a metre or a second. I am not going to invoke Einstein for the purpose of making these words vague. The metre, for example, is defined as the distance between two marks on a certain rod in Paris, when that rod is at a certain temperature. Now the marks are not points, but patches of a finite size, so that the distance between them is not a precise conception. Moreover, temperature cannot be measured with more than a certain degree of accuracy, and the temperature of a rod is never quite uniform. For all these reasons the conception of a metre is lacking in precision. The same applies to a second. The second is defined by relation to the rotation of the earth, but the earth is not a rigid body, and two parts of the earth's surface do not take exactly the same time to rotate; moreover all observations have a margin of error. There are some occurrences of which we can say that they take less than a second to happen, and others of which we can say that they take more, but between the two there will be a number of occurrences of which we believe that they do not all last equally long, but of none of which we can say whether they last more or less than a second. Therefore, when we say an occurrence lasts a second, all that it is worth while to mean is that no possible accuracy of observation will show whether it lasts more or less than a second.

Now let us take proper names. I pass by the irrelevant fact that the same proper name often belongs to many people. I once knew a man called Ebenezer Wilkes Smith, and I decline to believe that anybody else ever had this name. You might say, therefore, that here at last we have discovered an unambiguous symbol. This, however, would be a mistake. Mr Ebenezer Wilkes Smith was born, and being born is a gradual process. It would seem natural to suppose that the name was not attributable before birth; if so, there was doubt, while birth was taking place, whether the name was attributable or not. If it be said that the name was attributable before birth, the ambiguity is even more obvious, since no one can decide how long before birth the name became attributable. Death also is a process: even when it is what is called instantaneous, death must occupy a finite time. If you continue to apply the name to the corpse, there must gradually come a stage in decomposition when the name ceases to be attributable, but no one can say precisely when this stage has been reached. The fact is that all words are attributable without doubt over a certain area, but become questionable within a penumbra, outside which they are again certainly not attributable. Someone might seek to obtain precision in the use of words by saying that no word is to be applied in the penumbra, but unfortunately the penumbra itself is not accurately definable, and all the vaguenesses which apply to the primary use of words apply also when we try to fix a limit to their indubitable applicability. This has a reason in our physiological constitution. Stimuli which for various reasons we believe to be different produce in us indistinguishable sensations. It is not clear whether the sensations are really different like their stimuli and only our power to discriminate between sensations is deficient, or whether the sensations themselves are sometimes identical in relevant respects even when the stimuli differ in relevant respects. This is a kind of question which the theory of quanta at some much later stage in its development may be able to answer, but for the present it may be left in doubt. For our purpose it is not the vital question. What is clear is that the knowledge that we can obtain through our sensations is not as fine-grained as the stimuli to those sensations. We cannot see with the naked eye the difference between two glasses of water of which one is wholesome while the other is full of typhoid bacilli. In this case a microscope enables us to see the difference, but in the absence of a microscope the difference is only inferred from the differing effects of things which are sensibly indistinguishable. It is this fact that things which our senses do not distinguish produce different effects—as, for example, one glass of water gives you typhoid while the other does not—that has led us to regard the knowledge derived from the senses as vague. And the vagueness of the knowledge derived from the senses infects all words in the definition of which there is a sensible element. This includes all words which contain geographical or chronological constituents, such as 'Julius Caesar', 'the twentieth century', or 'the solar system'.

There remains a more abstract class of words: first, words which apply to all parts of time and space, such as 'matter' or 'causality'; secondly, the words of pure logic. I shall leave out of discussion the first class of words, since all of them raise great difficulties, and I can scarcely imagine a human being who would deny that they are all more or less vague. I come therefore to the words of pure logic, words such as 'or' and 'not'. Are these words also vague or have they a precise meaning?

Words such as 'or' and 'not' might seem, at first sight, to have a perfectly precise meaning: 'p or q' is true when p is true, true when q is true, and false when both are false. But the trouble is that this involves the notions of 'true' and 'false'; and it will be found, I think, that all the concepts of logic involve these notions, directly or indirectly. Now 'true' and 'false' can only have a *precise* meaning when the symbols employed—words, perceptions, images, or what not—are themselves precise. We have seen that, in practice, this is not the case. It follows that every proposition that can be framed in practice has a certain degree of vagueness; that is to say, there is not one definite fact necessary and sufficient for its truth, but a certain region of possible facts, any one of which would make it true. And this region is itself ill-defined: we cannot assign to it a definite boundary. This is the difference between vagueness and generality. A proposition involving a general concept—e.g. 'This is a man'—will be verified by a number of facts, such as 'This' being Brown or Jones or Robinson. But if 'man' were a precise idea, the set of possible facts that would verify 'this is a man' would be quite definite. Since, however, the conception 'man' is more or less vague, it is possible to discover prehistoric specimens concerning which there is not, even in theory, a definite answer to the question, 'Is this a man?' As applied to such specimens, the proposition 'this is a man' is neither definitely true nor definitely false. Since all non-logical words have this kind of vagueness, it follows that the conceptions of truth and falsehood, as applied to propositions composed of or containing non-logical words, are themselves more or less vague. Since propositions containing non-logical words are the substructure on which logical propositions are built, it follows that logical propositions also, so far as we can know them, become vague through the vagueness of 'truth' and 'falsehood'. We can see an ideal of precision, to which we can approximate indefinitely; but we cannot attain this ideal. Logical words, like the rest, when used by human beings, share the vagueness of all other words. There is, however, less vagueness about logical words than about the words of daily life, because logical words apply essentially to symbols, and may be conceived as applying rather to possible than to actual symbols. We are capable of imagining what a precise symbolism would be, though we cannot actually construct such a symbolism. Hence we are able to *imagine* a precise meaning for such words as 'or' and 'not'. We can, in fact, see precisely what they would mean if our symbolism were precise. All traditional logic habitually assumes that precise symbols are being employed. It is therefore not applicable to this terrestrial life, but only to an imagined celestial existence. Where, however, this celestial existence would differ from ours, so far as logic is concerned, would be not in the nature of what is known, but only in the accuracy of our knowledge. Therefore, if the hypothesis of a precise symbolism enables us to draw any inferences as to what is symbolized, there is no reason to distrust such inferences merely on the ground that our actual symbolism is not precise. We are able to conceive precision; indeed, if we could not do so, we could not conceive vagueness, which is merely the contrary of precision. This is one reason why logic takes us nearer to heaven than most other studies. On this point I agree with Plato. But those who dislike logic will, I fear, find my heaven disappointing.

It is now time to tackle the definition of vagueness. Vagueness, though it applies primarily to what is cognitive, is a conception applicable to every kind of representation—for example, a photograph, or a barograph. But before defining vagueness it is necessary to define accuracy. One of the most easily intelligible definitions of accuracy is as follows: one structure is an accurate representation of another when the words describing the one will also describe the other by being given new meanings. For example, 'Brutus killed Caesar' has the same structure as 'Plato loved Socrates', because both can be represented by the symbol 'xRy', by giving suitable meanings to x and R and y. But this definition, though easy to understand, does not give the essence of the matter, since the introduction of words describing the two systems is irrelevant. The exact definition is as follows: one system of terms related in various ways is an accurate representation of another system of terms related in various other ways if there is a one–one relation of the terms of the one to the terms of the other, and likewise a one–one relation of the relations of the one to the relations of the other, such that, when two or more terms in the one system have a relation belonging to that system, the corresponding terms of the other system have the corresponding relation belonging to the other system. Maps, charts, photographs, catalogues, etc. all come within this definition in so far as they are accurate.

Per contra, a representation is *vague* when the relation of the representing system to the represented system is not one–one, but one–many. For example, a photograph which is so smudged that it might equally represent Brown or Jones or Robinson is vague. A small-scale map is usually vaguer than a large-scale map, because it does not show all the turns and twists of the roads, rivers, etc. so that various slightly different courses are compatible with the representation that it gives. Vagueness, clearly, is a matter of degree, depending upon the extent of the possible differences between different systems represented by the same representation. Accuracy, on the contrary, is an ideal limit.

Passing from representation in general to the kinds of representation that are specially interesting to the logician, the representing system will consist of words, perceptions, thoughts, or something of the kind, and the would-be one–one relation between the representing system and the represented system will be *meaning*. In an accurate language, meaning would be a one–one relation; no word would have two meanings, and no two words would have the same meaning. In actual languages, as we have seen, meaning is one–many. (It happens often that two words have the same meaning, but this is easily avoided, and can be assumed not to happen without injuring the argument.) That is to say, there is not only one object that a word means, and not only one possible fact that will verify a proposition. The fact that meaning is a one–many relation is the precise statement of the fact that all language is more or less vague. There is, however, a complication about language as a method of representing a system, namely that words which mean relations are not themselves relations, but just as substantial or unsubstantial as other words.[2] In this respect a map, for instance, is superior to language, since the fact that one place is to the west of another is represented by the fact that the corresponding place on the map is to the left of the other; that is to say, a relation is represented by a relation. But in language this is not the case. Certain relations of higher order are represented by relations, in accordance with the rules of syntax. For example, '*A* precedes *B*' and '*B* precedes *A*' have different meanings, because the order of the words is an essential part of the meaning of the sentence. But this does not hold of elementary relations; the word 'precedes', though it means a relation, is not a relation. I believe that this simple fact is at the bottom of the hopeless muddle which has prevailed in all schools of philosophy as to the nature of relations. It would, however, take me too far from my present theme to pursue this line of thought.

It may be said: How do you know that all knowledge is vague, and what does it matter if it is? The case which I took before, of two glasses of water, one of which is wholesome while the other gives you typhoid, will illustrate both points. Without calling in the microscope, it is obvious that you cannot distinguish the wholesome glass of water from the one that will give you typhoid, just as, without calling in the telescope, it is obvious that what you see of a man who is 200 yards away is vague compared to what you see of a man who is 2 feet away; that is to say, many men who look quite different when seen close at hand look indistinguishable at a distance, while men who look different at a distance never look indistinguishable when seen close at hand. Therefore, according to the definition, there is less vagueness in the near appearance than in the distant one. There is still less vagueness about the appearance under the microscope. It is perfectly ordinary facts of this kind that prove the vagueness of most of our knowledge, and lead us to infer the vagueness of all of it.

It would be a great mistake to suppose that vague knowledge must be false. On the contrary, a vague belief has a much better chance of being true than a precise one, because there are more possible facts that would verify it. If I believe that so-and-so is tall, I am more likely to be right than if I believe that his height is between 6 ft. 2 in. and 6 ft. 3 in. In regard to beliefs and propositions, though not in regard to single words, we can distinguish between accuracy and precision. A belief is *precise* when only one fact would verify it; it is *accurate* when it is both precise and true. Precision diminishes the likelihood of truth, but often increases the pragmatic value of a belief if it is true—for example, in the case of the water that contained the typhoid bacilli. Science is perpetually trying to substitute more precise beliefs for vague ones; this makes it harder for a scientific proposition to be true than for the vague beliefs of uneducated persons to be true, but makes scientific truth better worth having if it can be obtained.

Vagueness in our knowledge is, I believe, merely a particular case of a general law of physics, namely the law that what may be called the appearances of a thing at different places

---

[2] A word is a class of series, and both classes and series are logical fictions. See Russell (1920: ch. 10); Russell (1919: ch. 17).

are less and less differentiated as we get further away from the thing. When I speak of 'appearances' I am speaking of something purely physical—the sort of thing, in fact, that, if it is visual, can be photographed. From a close-up photograph it is possible to infer a photograph of the same object at a distance, while the contrary inference is much more precarious. That is to say, there is a one–many relation between distant and close-up appearances. Therefore the distant appearance, regarded as a representation of the close-up appearance, is vague according to our definition. I think all vagueness in language and thought is essentially analogous to this vagueness which may exist in a photograph. My own belief is that most of the problems of epistemology, in so far as they are genuine, are really problems of physics and physiology; moreover, I believe that physiology is only a complicated branch of physics. The habit of treating knowledge as something mysterious and wonderful seems to me unfortunate. People do not say that a barometer 'knows' when it is going to rain; but I doubt if there is any essential difference in this respect between the barometer and the meteorologist who observes it. There is only one philosophical theory which seems to me in a position to ignore physics, and that is solipsism. If you are willing to believe that nothing exists except what you directly experience, no other person can prove that you are wrong, and probably no valid arguments exist against your view. But if you are going to allow any inferences from what you directly experience to other entities, then physics supplies the safest form of such inferences. And I believe that (apart from illegitimate problems derived from misunderstood symbolism) physics, in its modern forms, supplies materials for answers to all philosophical problems that are capable of being answered, except the one problem raised by solipsism, namely: Is there any valid inference ever from an entity experienced to one inferred? On this problem, I see no refutation of the sceptical position. But the sceptical philosophy is so short as to be uninteresting; therefore it is natural for a person who has learnt to philosophize to work out other alternatives, even if there is no very good ground for regarding them as preferable.

REFERENCES

Russell, B. (1919). *Introduction to Mathematical Philosophy*. London: Allen & Unwin.
——(1920). *The Analysis of Mind*. London: Allen & Unwin.

4

Family Resemblances

LUDWIG WITTGENSTEIN

66. Consider for example the proceedings that we call "games". I mean board-games, card-games, ball-games, Olympic games, and so on. What is common to them all?—Don't say: 'There *must* be something common, or they would not be called "games"'—but *look and see* whether there is anything common to all.—For if you look at them you will not see something that is common to *all*, but similarities, relationships, and a whole series of them at that. To repeat: don't think, but look!—Look for example at board-games, with their multifarious relationships. Now pass to card-games; here you find many correspondences with the first group, but many common features drop out, and others appear. When we pass next to ball-games, much that is common is retained, but much is lost.—Are they all 'amusing'? Compare chess with noughts and crosses. Or is there always winning and losing, or competition between players? Think of patience. In ball games there is winning and losing; but when a child throws his ball at the wall and catches it again, this feature has disappeared. Look at the parts played by skill and luck; and at the difference between skill in chess and skill in tennis. Think now of games like ring-a-ring-a-roses; here is the element of amusement, but how many other characteristic features have disappeared! And we can go through the many, many other groups of games in the same way; can see how similarities crop up and disappear.

And the result of this examination is: we see a complicated network of similarities overlapping and criss-crossing: sometimes overall similarities, sometimes similarities of detail.

67. I can think of no better expression to characterize these similarities than "family resemblances"; for the various resemblances between members of a family: build, features, colour of eyes, gait, temperament, etc. etc. overlap and criss-cross in the same way.—And I shall say: 'games' form a family.

And for instance the kinds of number form a family in the same way. Why do we call something a "number"? Well, perhaps because it has a—direct—relationship with several things that have hitherto been called number; and this can be said to give it an indirect relationship to other things we call the same name. And we extend our concept of number as in spinning a thread we twist fibre on fibre. And the strength of the thread does not reside in the fact that some one fibre runs through its whole length, but in the overlapping of many fibres.

But if someone wished to say: "There is something common to all these constructions—namely the disjunction of all their common properties"—I should reply: Now you are only playing with words. One might as well say: "Something runs through the whole thread—namely the continuous overlapping of those fibres".

68. "All right: the concept of number is defined for you as the logical sum of these individual interrelated concepts: cardinal numbers, rational numbers, real numbers, etc.; and in the same

* From: Ludwig Wittgenstein, *Philosophical Investigations* (1953). Translated by G. E. M. Anscombe. (Oxford: Blackwell, 3rd edn., 1968), sections 66–78. © 1987 Blackwell Publishers. Reprinted by permission.

way the concept of a game as the logical sum of a corresponding set of sub-concepts."—It need not be so. For I *can* give the concept 'number' rigid limits in this way, that is, use the word "number" for a rigidly limited concept, but I can also use it so that the extension of the concept is *not* closed by a frontier. And this is how we do use the word "game". For how is the concept of a game bounded? What still counts as a game and what no longer does? Can you give the boundary? No. You can *draw* one; for none has so far been drawn. (But that never troubled you before when you used the word "game".)

"But then the use of the word is unregulated, the "game" we play with it is unregulated."—It is not everywhere circumscribed by rules; but no more are there any rules for how high one throws the ball in tennis, or how hard; yet tennis is a game for all that and has rules too.

69. How should we explain to someone what a game is? I imagine that we should describe *games* to him, and we might add: 'This *and similar things* are called "games"'. And do we know any more about it ourselves? Is it only other people whom we cannot tell exactly what a game is?—But this is not ignorance. We do not know the boundaries because none have been drawn. To repeat, we can draw a boundary—for a special purpose. Does it take that to make the concept usable? Not at all! (Except for that special purpose.) No more than it took the definition: 1 pace = 75 cm to make the measure of length 'one pace' usable. And if you want to say "But still, before that it wasn't an exact measure", then I reply: very well, it was an inexact one.—Though you still owe me a definition of exactness.

70. 'But if the concept "game" is uncircumscribed like that, you don't really know what you mean by a "game".'—When I give the description: "The ground was quite covered with plants"—do you want to say I don't know what I am talking about until I can give a definition of a plant?

My meaning would be explained by, say, a drawing and the words "The ground looked roughly like this". Perhaps I even say "it looked *exactly* like this."—Then were just *this* grass and *these* leaves there, arranged just like this? No, that is not what it means. And I should not accept any picture as exact in *this* sense.

Someone says to me: "Shew the children a game." I teach them gaming with dice, and the other says "I didn't mean that sort of game." Must the exclusion of the game with dice have come before his mind when he gave me the order?

71. One might say that the concept 'game' is a concept with blurred edges.—"But is a blurred concept a concept at all?"—Is an indistinct photograph a picture of a person at all? Is it even always an advantage to replace an indistinct picture by a sharp one? Isn't the indistinct one often exactly what we need?

Frege compares a concept to an area and says that an area with vague boundaries cannot be called an area at all. This presumably means that we cannot do anything with it.—But is it senseless to say: "Stand roughly there"? Suppose that I were standing with someone in a city square and said that. As I say it I do not draw any kind of boundary, but perhaps point with my hand—as if I were indicating a particular *spot*. And this is just how one might explain to someone what a game is. One gives examples and intends them to be taken in a particular way.—I do not, however, mean by this that he is supposed to see in those examples that common thing which I—for some reason—was unable to express; but that he is now to *employ* those examples in a particular way. Here giving examples is not an *indirect* means of explaining—in default of a better. For any general definition can be misunderstood too. The point is that *this* is how we play the game. (I mean the language-game with the word "game".)

72. *Seeing what is common.* Suppose I shew someone various multi-coloured pictures, and say: 'The colour you see in all these is called "yellow ochre"'.—This is a definition, and the

other will get to understand it by looking for and seeing what is common to the pictures. Then he can look *at*, can point *to*, the common thing.

Compare with this a case in which I shew him figures of different shapes all painted the same colour, and say: 'What these have in common is called "yellow ochre"'.

And compare this case: I shew him samples of different shades of blue and say: 'The colour that is common to all these is what I call "blue"'.

73. When someone defines the names of colours for me by pointing to samples and saying 'This colour is called "blue", this "green"......' this case can be compared in many respects to putting a table in my hands, with the words written under the colour-samples.—Though this comparison may mislead in many ways.—One is now inclined to extend the comparison: to have understood the definition means to have in one's mind an idea of the thing defined, and that is a sample or picture. So if I am shewn various different leaves and told "This is called a "leaf"', I get an idea of the shape of a leaf, a picture of it in my mind.—But what does the picture of a leaf look like when it does not shew us any particular shape, but 'what is common to all shapes of leaf'? Which shade is the 'sample in my mind' of the colour green—the sample of what is common to all shades of green?

"But might there not be such "general" samples? Say a schematic leaf, or a sample of *pure* green?"—Certainly there might. But for such a schema to be understood as a *schema*, and not as the shape of a particular leaf, and for a slip of pure green to be understood as a sample of all that is greenish and not as a sample of pure green—this in turn resides in the way the samples are used.

Ask yourself: what *shape* must the sample of the colour green be? Should it be rectangular? Or would it then be the sample of a green rectangle?—So should it be 'irregular' in shape? And what is to prevent us then from regarding it—that is, from using it—only as a sample of irregularity of shape?

74. Here also belongs the idea that if you see this leaf as a sample of 'leaf shape in general' you *see* it differently from someone who regards it as, say, a sample of this particular shape. Now this might well be so—though it is not so—for it would only be to say that, as a matter of experience, if you *see* the leaf in a particular way, you use it in such-and-such a way or according to such-and-such rules. Of course, there is such a thing as seeing in *this* way or *that*; and there are also cases where whoever sees a sample like *this* will in general use it in *this* way, and whoever sees it otherwise in another way. For example, if you see the schematic drawing of a cube as a plane figure consisting of a square and two rhombi you will, perhaps, carry out the order "Bring me something like this" differently from someone who sees the picture three-dimensionally.

75. What does it mean to know what a game is? What does it mean, to know it and not be able to say it? Is this knowledge somehow equivalent to an unformulated definition? So that if it were formulated I should be able to recognize it as the expression of my knowledge? Isn't my knowledge, my concept of a game, completely expressed in the explanations that I could give? That is, in my describing examples of various kinds of game; shewing how all sorts of other games can be constructed on the analogy of these; saying that I should scarcely include this or this among games; and so on.

76. If someone were to draw a sharp boundary I could not acknowledge it as the one that I too always wanted to draw, or had drawn in my mind. For I did not want to draw one at all. His concept can then be said to be not the same as mine, but akin to it. The kinship is that of two pictures, one of which consists of colour patches with vague contours, and the other of patches similarly shaped and distributed, but with clear contours. The kinship is just as undeniable as the difference.

77. And if we carry this comparison still further it is clear that the degree to which the sharp picture *can* resemble the blurred one depends on the latter's degree of vagueness. For imagine having to sketch a sharply defined picture 'corresponding' to a blurred one. In the latter there is a blurred red rectangle: for it you put down a sharply defined one. Of course—several such sharply defined rectangles can be drawn to correspond to the indefinite one.—But if the colours in the original merge without a hint of any outline won't it become a hopeless task to draw a sharp picture corresponding to the blurred one? Won't you then have to say: "Here I might just as well draw a circle or heart as a rectangle, for all the colours merge. Anything— and nothing—is right."—And this is the position you are in if you look for definitions corresponding to our concepts in aesthetics or ethics.

In such a difficulty always ask yourself: How did we *learn* the meaning of this word ("good" for instance)? From what sort of examples? In what language-games? Then it will be easier for you to see that the word must have a family of meanings.

78. Compare *knowing* and *saying*:

> how many feet high Mont Blanc is—
> how the word "game" is used—
> how a clarinet sounds.

If you are surprised that one can know something and not be able to say it, you are perhaps thinking of a case like the first. Certainly not of one like the third.

5

The Phenomena of Vagueness

ROSANNA KEEFE

I. CENTRAL FEATURES OF VAGUE EXPRESSIONS

The parties to the vigorous debates about vagueness largely agree about which predicates are vague: paradigm cases include 'tall,' 'red,' 'bald,' 'heap,' 'tadpole', and 'child'. Such predicates share three interrelated features that intuitively are closely bound up with their vagueness: they admit borderline cases, they lack (or at least apparently lack) sharp boundaries and they are susceptible to sorites paradoxes. I begin by describing these characteristics.

Borderline cases are cases where it is unclear whether or not the predicate applies. Some people are borderline tall: not clearly tall and not clearly not tall. Certain reddish-orange patches are borderline red. And during a creature's transition from tadpole to frog, there will be stages at which it is a borderline case of a tadpole. To offer at this stage a more informative characterisation of borderline cases and the unclarity involved would sacrifice neutrality between various competing theories of vagueness. Nonetheless, when Tek is borderline tall, it does seem that the unclarity about whether he is tall is not merely epistemic (i.e. such that there is a fact of the matter, we just do not know it). For a start, no amount of further information about his exact height (and the heights of others) could help us decide whether he *is* tall. More controversially, it seems that there is no fact of the matter here about which we are ignorant: rather, it is *indeterminate* whether Tek is tall. And this indeterminacy is often thought to amount to the sentence 'Tek is tall' being neither true nor false, which violates the classical principle of bivalence. The law of excluded middle may also come into question when we consider instances such as 'either Tek is tall or he is not tall'.

Second, vague predicates apparently lack well-defined extensions. On a scale of heights there appears to be no sharp boundary between the tall people and the rest, nor is there an exact point at which our growing creature ceases to be a tadpole. More generally, if we imagine possible candidates for satisfying some vague *F* to be arranged with spatial closeness reflecting similarity, no sharp line can be drawn round the cases to which *F* applies. Instead, vague predicates are naturally described as having fuzzy, or blurred, boundaries. But according to classical logic and semantics all predicates have well-defined extensions: they cannot have fuzzy boundaries. So again this suggests that a departure from the classical conception is needed to accommodate vagueness.

Clearly, having fuzzy boundaries is closely related to having borderline cases. More specifically, it is the *possibility* of borderline cases that counts for vagueness and fuzzy boundaries, for if all actually borderline tall people were destroyed, 'tall' would still lack sharp boundaries. It might be argued that for there to be no sharp boundary between the *F*s and the

---

* Rosanna Keefe, 'The phenomena of vagueness', ch. 1 of *Theories of Vagueness* (Cambridge: Cambridge University Press, 2000), 6–36. © Cambridge University Press. Reprinted by permission. With thanks to the author for supplying an electronic version of this chapter incorporating minor amendments and corrections.

not-*F*s just *is* for there to be a region of possible borderline cases of *F* (sometimes known as the penumbra). On the other hand, if the range of possible borderline cases between the *F*s and the not-*F*s was itself sharply bounded, then *F* would have a sharp boundary too, albeit one which was shared with the borderline *F*s, not with the things that were definitely not *F*. The thought that our vague predicates are not in fact like this—their borderline cases are not sharply bounded—is closely bound up with the key issue of higher-order vagueness.

Third, typically vague predicates are susceptible to sorites paradoxes. Intuitively, a hundredth of an inch cannot make a difference to whether or not a man counts as tall—such tiny variations, undetectable using the naked eye and everyday measuring instruments, are just too small to matter. This seems part of what it is for 'tall' to be a *vague* height term lacking sharp boundaries. So we have the principle [S$_1$] if *x* is tall, and *y* is only a hundredth of an inch shorter than *x*, then *y* is also tall. But imagine a line of men, starting with someone seven foot tall, and each of the rest a hundredth of an inch shorter than the man in front of him. Repeated applications of [S$_1$] as we move down the line imply that each man we encounter is tall, however far we continue. And this yields a conclusion which is clearly false, namely that a man less than five foot tall, reached after three thousand steps along the line, is also tall.

Similarly there is the ancient example of the heap (Greek *soros*, from which the paradox derives its name). Plausibly, [S$_2$] if *x* is a heap of sand, then the result *y* of removing one grain will still be a heap—recognising the vagueness of 'heap' seems to commit us to this principle. So take a heap and remove grains one by one; repeated applications of [S$_2$] imply absurdly that the solitary last grain is a heap. The paradox is supposedly owed to Eubulides, to whom the liar paradox is also attributed. (See Barnes 1982 and Burnyeat 1982 for detailed discussion of the role of the paradox in the ancient world.)

Arguments with a sorites structure are not mere curiosities: they feature, for example, in some familiar ethical 'slippery slope' arguments (see e.g. Walton 1992 and Williams 1995). Consider the principle [S$_3$] if it is wrong to kill something at time *t* after conception, then it would be wrong to kill it at time *t* minus one second. And suppose we agree that it is wrong to kill a baby nine months after conception. Repeated applications of [S$_3$] would lead to the conclusion that abortion even immediately after conception would be wrong. The need to assess this kind of practical argumentation increases the urgency of examining reasoning with vague predicates.

Wright (1975, p. 333) coined the phrase *tolerant* to describe predicates for which there is 'a notion of degree of change too small to make any difference' to their applicability. Take '[is] tall' (for simplicity, in mentioning predicates I shall continue, in general, to omit the copula). This predicate will count as tolerant if, as [S$_1$] claims, a change of one-hundredth of an inch never affects its applicability. A tolerant predicate must lack sharp boundaries; for if *F* has sharp boundaries, then a boundary-crossing change, however small, will always make a difference to whether *F* applies.[1] Moreover, a statement of the tolerance of *F* can characteristically serve as the inductive premise of a sorites paradox for *F* (as in the example of 'tall' again).

Russell provides one kind of argument that predicates of a given class are tolerant: if the application of a word (a colour predicate, for example) is paradigmatically based on unaided sense perception, it surely cannot be applicable to only one of an indiscriminable pair (1923, p. 87 [included in this volume]). So such 'observational' predicates will be tolerant with respect to changes too small for us to detect. And Wright develops, in detail, arguments supporting

---

[1] Note that throughout this book, when there is no potential for confusion I am casual about omitting quotation marks when natural language expressions are not involved, e.g. when talking about the predicate *F* or the sentence *p* & ¬*p*.

the thesis that many of our predicates are tolerant (1975 and 1976). In particular, consideration of the role of ostension and memory in mastering the use of such predicates appears to undermine the idea that they have sharp boundaries which could not be shown by the teacher or remembered by the learner. Arguments of this kind are widely regarded as persuasive: I shall refer to them as 'typical arguments for tolerance'. A theory of vagueness must address these arguments and establish what, if anything, they succeed in showing, and in particular whether they show that the inductive premise of the sorites paradox holds.

Considerations like Russell's and Wright's help explain why vague predicates are so common (whatever we say about the sorites premise). And they also seem to suggest that we *could* not operate with a language free of vagueness. They make it difficult to see vagueness as a merely optional or eliminable feature of language. This contrasts with the view of vagueness as a defect of natural languages found in Frege (1903, §56) and perhaps in Russell's uncharitable suggestion (1923, p. 84) that language is vague because our ancestors were lazy. A belief that vagueness is inessential and therefore unimportant may comfort those who ignore the phenomenon. But their complacency is unjustified. Even if we could reduce the vagueness in our language (as science is often described as striving to do by producing sharper definitions, and as legal processes can accomplish via appeal to precedents), our efforts could not in practice eliminate it entirely. (Russell himself stresses the persistent vagueness in scientific terms, p. 86; and it is clear that the legal process could never reach absolute precision either.) Moreover, in natural language vague predicates are ubiquitous, and this alone motivates study of the phenomenon irrespective of whether there could be usable languages entirely free of vagueness. Even if 'heap' could be replaced by some term 'heap*' with perfectly sharp boundaries and for which no sorites paradox would arise, the paradox facing our actual vague term would remain.[2] And everyday reasoning takes place in vague language, so no account of good ordinary reasoning can ignore vagueness.

In the next section I shall discuss the variety of vague expressions—a variety which is not brought out by the general form of arguments for tolerance. First, I clarify the phenomenon by mentioning three things that vagueness in our sense (probably) is not.

(a) The remark 'Someone said something' is naturally described as vague (who said what?). Similarly, 'X is an integer greater than thirty' is an unhelpfully vague hint about the value of X. Vagueness in this sense is underspecificity, a matter of being less than adequately informative for the purposes in hand. This seems to have nothing to do with borderline cases or with the lack of sharp boundaries: 'is an integer greater than thirty' has sharp boundaries, has no borderline cases, and is not susceptible to sorites paradoxes. And it is not because of any possibility of borderline people or borderline cases of saying something that 'someone said something' counts as vague in the alternative sense. I shall ignore the idea of vagueness as underspecificity: in philosophical contexts, 'vague' has come to be reserved for the phenomenon I have described.

(b) Vagueness must not be straightforwardly identified with paradigm context-dependence (i.e. having a different extension in different contexts), even though many terms have both features (e.g. 'tall'). Fix on a context which can be made as definite as you like (in particular, choose a specific comparison class, e.g. current professional American basketball players): 'tall' will remain vague, with borderline cases and fuzzy boundaries, and the sorites paradox

---

[2] See Carnap (1950: ch. 1), Haack (1974: ch. 6), and Quine (1981) on the replacement of vague expressions by precise ones, and see Grim (1982) for some difficulties facing the idea. Certain predicates frequently prompt the response that there *is* in fact a sharp boundary for their strict application, though we use them more loosely—in particular, strictly no one is bald unless they have absolutely no hair (see e.g. Sperber and Wilson 1986). But even if this line is viable in some cases, it is hopeless for the majority of vague predicates. E.g. should someone count as 'tall' only if they are as tall as possible? How about 'quite tall'? Or 'very hairy'? And where is the strict boundary of 'chair'?

will retain its force. This indicates that we are unlikely to understand vagueness or solve the paradox by concentrating on context-dependence.[3]

(c) We can also distinguish vagueness from ambiguity. Certainly, terms can be ambiguous *and* vague: 'bank' for example has two quite different main senses (concerning financial institutions or river edges), both of which are vague. But it is natural to suppose that 'tadpole' has a univocal sense, though that sense does not determine a sharp, well-defined extension. Certain theories, however, do attempt to close the gap between vagueness and a form of ambiguity.

2. TYPE OF VAGUE EXPRESSIONS

So far, I have focused on a single dimension of variation associated with each vague predicate, such as height for 'tall' and number of grains for 'heap'. But many vague predicates are *multi-dimensional*: several different dimensions of variation are involved in determining their applicability. The applicability of 'big', used to describe people, depends on both height and volume; and even whether something counts as a 'heap' depends not only on the number of grains but also on their arrangement. And with 'nice', for example, there is not even a clear-cut set of dimensions determining the applicability of the predicate: it is a vague matter which factors are relevant and the dimensions blend into one another.

The three central features of vague predicates are shared by multi-dimensional ones. There are, for example, borderline nice people: indeed, some are borderline *because* of the multi-dimensionality of 'nice', by scoring well in some relevant respects but not in others. Next consider whether multi-dimensional predicates may lack sharp boundaries. In the one-dimensional case, F has a sharp boundary (or sharp boundaries) if possible candidates for it can be ordered with a point (or points) marking the boundary of F's extension, so that everything that falls on one side of the point (or between the points) is F and nothing else is F. For a multi-dimensional predicate, there may be no uniquely appropriate ordering of possible candidates on which to place putative boundary-marking points. (For instance, there is no definite ordering of people where each is bigger than the previous one; in particular, if ordered by height, volume is ignored, and vice versa.) Rather, for a sharply bounded, two-dimensional predicate the candidates would be more perspicuously set out in a two-dimensional space in which a boundary could be drawn, where the two-dimensional region enclosed by the boundary contains all and only instances of the predicate. With a *vague* two-dimensional predicate no such sharp boundary can be drawn. Similarly, for a sharply bounded predicate with a clear-cut set of n dimensions, the boundary would enclose an n-dimensional region containing all of its instances; and vague predicates will lack such a sharp boundary.[4] When there is no clear-cut set of dimensions—for 'nice', for example—this model of boundary-drawing is not so easily applied: it is then not possible to construct a suitable arrangement of candidates on which to try to draw a boundary of the required sort. But this, I claim, is distinctive of the vagueness of such predicates: they have no sharp boundary, but nor do they have a fuzzy boundary in the sense of a rough boundary-area of a representative space. 'Nice'

---

[3] There have, however, been some attempts at this type of solution to the sorites paradox using, for example, more elaborate notions of the context of a subject's judgement (see e.g. Raffman 1994).

[4] Could there be a single, determinate way of balancing the various dimensions of a multi-dimensional predicate that *does* yield a unique ordering? Perhaps, but this will usually not be the case, and when it is, it may then be appropriate to treat the predicate as one-dimensional, even if the 'dimension' is not a natural one. Further discussion of this point would need a clearer definition of 'dimension', but this is not important for our purposes.

is so vague that it cannot even be associated with a neat array of candidate dimensions, let alone pick out a precise area of such an array.

Finally, multi-dimensional vague predicates are susceptible to sorites paradoxes. We can construct a sorites series for 'heap' by focusing on the number of grains and minimising the difference in the arrangement of grains between consecutive members. And for 'nice' we could take generosity and consider a series of people differing gradually in this respect, starting with a very mean person and ending with a very generous one, where, for example, other features relevant to being nice are kept as constant as possible through the series.

Next, I shall argue that comparatives as well as monadic predicates can be vague. This has been insufficiently recognised and is sometimes denied. Cooper (1995), for example, seeks to give an account of vagueness by explaining how vague monadic predicates depend on comparatives, taking as a starting point the claim that 'classifiers in their grammatically positive form [e.g. "large"] are vague, while comparatives are not' (p. 246). With a precise comparative, 'F-er than', for any pair of things x and y, either x is F-er than y, y is F-er than x, or they are equally F. This will be the case if there is a determinate ordering of candidates for F-ness (allowing ties). For example, there is a one-dimensional ordering of the natural numbers relating to the comparative 'is a smaller number than', and there are no borderline cases of this comparative, which is paradigmatically precise. Since 'is a small number' is a vague predicate, this shows how vague positive forms can have precise comparatives. It may seem that 'older than' also gives rise to an ordering according to the single dimension of age, and hence that 'older than' must be precise. But, in fact, there could be borderline instances of the comparative due to indeterminacy over exactly what should count as the instant of someone's birth and so whether it is before or after the birth of someone else. And such instances illustrate that there is *not*, in fact, an unproblematic ordering of *people* for 'older than', even though there is a total ordering of *ages*, on which some people cannot be exactly placed. Similarly, though there is a single dimension of height, people cannot always be exactly placed on it and assigned an exact height. For what exactly should count as the top of one's head? Consequently there may also be borderline instances of 'taller than'.

Comparatives associated with multi-dimensional predicates—for example 'nicer than' and 'more intelligent than'—are typically vague. They have borderline cases: pairs of people about whom there is no fact of the matter about who is nicer/more intelligent, or whether they are equally nice/intelligent. This is particularly common when comparing people who are nice/intelligent in different ways. There are, however, still clear cases of the comparative in addition to borderline cases—it is not that people are *never* comparable in respect to niceness—thus the vague 'nicer than', like 'nice' itself, has clear positive, clear negative, and borderline cases.

Can comparatives also lack sharp boundaries? Talk of boundaries, whether sharp or fuzzy, is much less natural for comparatives than for monadic predicates. But we might envisage precise comparatives for which we could systematically set out ordered pairs of things, $\langle x, y \rangle$ and draw a sharp boundary around those for which it is true that x is F-er than y. For example, if F has a single dimension then we could set out pairs in a two-dimensional array, where the x coordinate of a pair is determined by the location along the dimension of the first of the pair, and the y coordinate by that of the second. The boundary line could then be drawn along the diagonal at $x = y$, where pairs falling beneath the diagonal are definitely true instances of the comparative 'x is F-er than y', and those on or above are definitely false. But for many comparatives, including 'nicer than', there could not be such an arrangement and this gives a sense in which those comparatives lack sharp boundaries.

Another possible sense in which comparatives may lack sharp boundaries is the following. Take the comparative 'redder than' and choose a purplish-red patch of colour, *a*. Then consider a series of orangeish-red patches, x_i, where x_{i+1} is redder than x_i. It could be definitely true that a is redder than x_0 (which is nearly orange), definitely not true that a is redder than x_{100}, where not only are there borderline cases of 'a is redder than x_i' between them, but there is no point along the series of x_i at which it suddenly stops being the case that a is redder than x_i. So, certain comparatives have borderline cases and exhibit several features akin to the lack of sharp boundaries: they should certainly be classified as vague.

Having discussed vague monadic predicates and vague comparatives, I shall briefly mention some other kinds of vague expressions. First, there can be other vague dyadic relational expressions. For example, 'is a friend of' has pairs that are borderline cases. Adverbs like 'quickly', quantifiers like 'many', and modifiers like 'very' are also vague. And, just as comparatives can be vague, particularly when related to a multi-dimensional positive, so can superlatives. 'Nicest' and 'most intelligent' have vague conditions of application: among a group of people it may be a vague matter, or indeterminate, who is the nicest or the most intelligent. And vague superlatives provide one way in which to construct vague singular terms such as 'the nicest man' or 'the grandest mountain in Scotland', where there is no fact of the matter as to which man or mountain the terms pick out. Terms with plural reference like 'the high mountains of Scotland' can equally be vague.

A theory of vagueness should have the resources to accommodate all the different types of vague expression. And, for example, we should reject an account of vagueness that was obliged to deny the above illustrated features of certain comparatives in order to construct its own account of vague monadic predicates. The typical focus on monadic predicates need not be mistaken, however. Perhaps, as Fine suggests, all vagueness is reducible to predicate vagueness (1975, p. 267), though such a claim needs supporting arguments. Alternatively, vagueness might manifest itself in different ways in different kinds of expression, and this could require taking those different expression-types in turn and having different criteria of vagueness for comparatives and monadic predicates. Another possibility is to treat complete sentences as the primary bearers of vagueness, perhaps in their possession of a non-classical truth-value. This approach would avoid certain tricky questions about whether the vagueness of a particular sentence is 'due to' a given expression. For example, in a case where it is indeterminate exactly what moment a was born and whether it was before the birth of b, we would avoid the question whether this shows 'older than' to be vague, or whether the indeterminacy should be put down to vagueness in a itself. Provided one can still make sense of a typical attribution of vagueness to some element of a sentence in the uncontroversial cases, I suggest that this strategy is an appealing one.

3. VAGUENESS IN THE WORLD?

Is it only linguistic items—words or phrases—that can be vague? Surely not: thoughts and beliefs are among the mental items which share the central characteristics of vagueness; other controversial cases include perceptions. What about the world itself: could the world be vague as well as our descriptions of it? Can there be vague objects? Or vague properties (the ontic correlates of predicates)? Consider Ben Nevis: any sharp spatio-temporal boundaries drawn around the mountain would be arbitrarily placed, and would not reflect a natural boundary. So it may seem that Ben Nevis has fuzzy boundaries, and so, given the common view that a vague object is an object with fuzzy, spatio-temporal boundaries, that it is a vague object. (See e.g. Parsons 1987, Tye 1990, and Zemach 1991 for arguments that there are vague objects.) But there are, of course, other contending descriptions of the situation here. For example, perhaps the only objects we should admit into our ontology are precise/sharp although we fail to pick out a single one of them with our (vague) name 'Ben Nevis'. It would then be at the level of our representations of the world that vagueness came in.[5]

My concern is with linguistic vagueness and I shall generally ignore ontic vagueness. This would be a mistake if a theory of linguistic vagueness had to rely on ontic vagueness. But that would be surprising since it seems at least possible to have vague language in a non-vague world. In particular, even if all objects, properties and facts were precise, we would still have reason, for everyday purposes, to use a vague expression such as 'tall', which would still have borderline cases (even if those cases could also be described in non-vague terms involving precise heights etc.). Similarly, in a precise world we would still use vague singular terms, perhaps to pick out various large collections of precise fundamental particulars (e.g. as clouds or mountains) where the boundaries of those collections are left fuzzy. So it seems that language could still be vague if the concrete world were precise.[6]

The theories of vagueness of this book are theories of linguistic vagueness and in the next section I briefly introduce them.

4. THEORIES OF VAGUENESS

The candidate theories of vagueness can be systematically surveyed by considering how they address two central tasks. The first is to identify the logic and semantics for a vague language—a task bound up with providing an account of borderline cases and of fuzzy boundaries. The second task is that of addressing the sorites paradox.

The logic and semantics of vagueness

The simplest approach is to retain classical logic and semantics. Borderline case predications *are* either true or false after all, though we do not and cannot know which. Similarly, despite appearances, vague predicates have well-defined extensions: there is a sharp boundary between the tall people and the rest, and between the red shades of the spectrum and the other colours. The *epistemic view* takes this line and accounts for vagueness in terms of our ignorance—for example, ignorance of where the sharp boundaries to our vague predicates lie. And a *pragmatic account* of vagueness also seeks to avoid challenging classical logic and semantics, but this time by accounting for vagueness in terms of pragmatic relations between speakers and their language.

If we do not retain classical logic and semantics, we can say instead that when *a* is a borderline case of *F*, the truth-value of '*a* is *F*' is, as Machina puts it, 'in some way peculiar, or indeterminate or lacking entirely' (1976, p. 48). This generates a number of non-classical options.

Note that a borderline case of the predicate *F* is equally a borderline case of not-*F*: it is unclear *whether or not* the candidate is *F*. This symmetry prevents us from simply counting a borderline *F* as not-*F*. But there are several ways of respecting this symmetry. Some take the

---

[5] The most discussed strand of the ontic vagueness debate focuses on Evans's formal argument which aims to establish a negative answer to his question 'Can there be vague objects?' (1978; see Keefe and Smith 1997b: §5 for an overview of the debate).

[6] These are only *prima facie* reasons for not approaching linguistic vagueness via ontic vagueness: a tighter case would require clarification of what vagueness in the world would be. They also do not seem to bear on the question whether there can be vague *sets*, which might also be counted as a form of ontic vagueness. Tye, for example, believes that there are vague sets and maintains that they are crucial to his own theory of the linguistic phenomena (see Tye 1990).

line that a predication in a borderline case is both true *and* false: there is a truth-value glut. This can be formalised within the context of a paraconsistent logic—a logic that admits true contradictions (see Hyde 1997 for discussion of that view).

A more popular position is to admit truth-value *gaps*: borderline predications are neither true nor false. One elegant development is *supervaluationism*. The basic idea is that a pro-position involving the vague predicate 'tall', for example, is true (false) if it comes out true (false) on all the ways in which we can make 'tall' precise (ways, that is, which preserve the truth-values of uncontentiously true or false cases of '*a* is tall'). A borderline case, 'Tek is tall', will be neither true nor false, for it is true on some ways of making 'tall' precise and false on others. But a classical tautology like 'either Tek is tall or he is not tall' *will* still come out true because wherever a sharp boundary for 'tall' is drawn, that compound sentence will come out true. In this way, the supervaluationist adopts a non-classical *semantics* while aiming to minimise divergence from classical *logic*.

Rather than holding that predications in borderline cases lack a truth-value, another option is to hold that they have a third value—'neutral', 'indeterminate', or 'indefinite'—leading to a three-valued logic. Alternatively, *degree theories* countenance degrees of truth, introducing a whole spectrum of truth-values from 0 to 1, with complete falsity as degree 0 and complete truth as degree 1. Borderline cases each take some value between 0 and 1, with '*x* is red' gradually increasing in truth-value as we move along the colour spectrum from orange to red. This calls for an infinite-valued logic or a so-called 'fuzzy logic', and there have been a variety of different versions.

So far the sketched positions at least agree that there is *some* positive account to be given of the logic and semantics of vagueness. Other writers have taken a more pessimistic line. In particular, Russell claims that logic assumes precision, and since natural language is not precise it cannot be in the province of logic at all (1923, pp. 88–9). If such a 'no logic' thesis requires wholesale rejection of reasoning with vague predicates—and hence of most reasoning in natural language—it is absurdly extreme. And arguments involving vague predicates are clearly not all on a par. For example, 'anyone with less than 500 hairs on his head is bald; Fred has less than 500 hairs on his head; therefore Fred is bald' is an unproblematically good argument (from Cargile 1969, pp. 196–7). And, similarly, there are other ways of arguing with vague predicates that should certainly be rejected. Some account is needed of inferences that are acceptable and others that fail, and to search for systematic principles capturing this is to seek elements of a logic of vague language. So, I take the pessimism of the no-logic approach to be a very last resort, and in this book I concentrate on more positive approaches.

Focusing on the question how borderline case predication should be classified, we seem to have exhausted the possibilities. They may be true or false, or have no truth value at all (in particular, being neither true nor false), or be both true and false, or have a non-classical value from some range of values. When it comes to surveying solutions to the sorites paradox, however, there may additionally be alternatives that do not provide a theory of vagueness and perhaps do not answer the question how borderline cases are to be classified. I concentrate on those which do fit into a theory of vagueness.

The sorites paradox

A paradigm sorites set-up for the predicate F is a sequence of objects x_i, such that the two premises

(1) Fx_1
(2) For all i, if Fx_i then Fx_{i+1}

both appear true, but, for some suitably large n, the putative conclusion

(3) Fx_n

seems false. For example, in the case of 'tall', the x_i might be the series of men described earlier, each a hundredth of an inch shorter than the previous one and where x_1 is seven foot tall. (1) 'x_1 is tall' is then true; and so, it seems, is the inductive premise, (2) 'for all i, if x_i is tall, so is x_{i+1}'. But it is surely false that (3) x_{3000}—who is only 4 feet 6 inches—is tall.

A second form of sorites paradox can be constructed when, instead of the quantified inductive premise (2), we start with a collection of particular conditional premises, (2C_i), each of the form 'if Fx_i then Fx_{+1}'. For example,

(2C_1) if x_1 is tall, so is x_2
(2C_2) if x_2 is tall, so is x_3

and so on. And the use of conditionals is not essential: we can take a sequence of premises of the form $\neg(Fx_i \ \& \ \neg Fx_{+1})$—a formulation that goes back at least to Diogenes Laertius (see Long and Sedley 1987, p. 222). Alternatively, (2) could be replaced by a quantification over the negated conjunctions of that form.

As well as needing to solve the paradox, we must assess that general form of argument because it is used both in philosophical arguments outside the discussion of vagueness (e.g. with the story of the ship of Theseus) and in various more everyday debates (the slippery slope arguments mentioned in §1).[7]

Responses to a sorites paradox can be divided into four types. We can:

(a) deny the validity of the argument, refusing to grant that the conclusion follows from the given premises; or
(b) question the strict truth of the general inductive premise (2) or of at least one of the conditionals (2C_i); or
(c) accept the validity of the argument and the truth of its inductive premise (or of all the conditional premises) but contest the supposed truth of premise (1) or the supposed falsity of the conclusion (3); or
(d) grant that there are compelling reasons both to take the argument form as valid, and to accept the premises and deny the conclusion, concluding that this demonstrates the incoherence of the predicate in question.

I shall briefly survey these in turn, ignoring here the question whether we should expect a uniform solution to all sorites paradoxes whatever their form and whatever predicate is involved. (Wright 1987 argues that different responses could be required depending on the reasons that support the inductive premise.) Any response must explain away apparent difficulties with accepting the selected solution; for example, if the main premise is denied, it must be explained why that premise is so plausible. More generally, a theory should account for the persuasiveness of the paradox as a paradox and should explain how this is compatible with the fact that we are never, or very rarely, actually led into contradiction.

(a) Denying the validity of the sorites argument seems to require giving up absolutely fundamental rules of inference. This can be seen most clearly when the argument takes the

---

[7] As a further example of the former, consider Kirk (1986: 217 ff.). Regarding Quine's thesis about the indeterminacy of translation, Kirk uses an argument with the form of the quantificational version of the paradox to argue that there can be no indeterminacy of translation because, first, there would be no indeterminacy in translating between the languages of infants each of whom is at an early stage of language-acquisition and, second, if there is no indeterminacy at one step of acquisition then there is none at the next. He presents his argument as using mathematical induction but does not ask whether its employment of vague predicates casts doubt on that mode of argument.

second form involving a series of conditionals, the $(2C_i)$. The only rule of inference needed for this argument is modus ponens. Dummett argues that this rule cannot be given up, as it is constitutive of the meaning of 'if' that modus ponens is valid (1975, p. 306). To derive the conclusion in the first form of sorites, we only need universal instantiation in addition to modus ponens; but, as Dummett again argues, universal instantiation seems too central to the meaning of 'all' to be reasonably challenged (1975, p. 306). I agree on both points and shall not pursue the matter further here.

There is, however, a different way of rejecting the validity of the many-conditionals form of the sorites. It might be suggested that even though each step is acceptable on its own, chaining too many steps does not guarantee the preservation of truth if what counts as preserving truth is itself a vague matter. (And then the first form of sorites could perhaps be rejected on the grounds that it is in effect short hand for a multi-conditional argument.) As Dummett again notes, this is to deny the transitivity of validity which would be another drastic move, given that chaining inferences is normally taken to be essential to the very enterprise of proof.[8]

Rather than questioning particular inference rules or the ways they can be combined, Russell's global rejection of logic for vague natural language leads him to dismiss 'the old puzzle about the man who went bald', simply on the grounds that 'bald' is vague (1923, p. 85). The sorites arguments, on his view, cannot be valid because, containing vague expressions, they are just not the kind of thing that can be valid or invalid.

(b) If we take a formulation of the paradox that uses negated conjunctions (or assume that 'if' is captured by the material conditional), then within a classical framework denying the quantified inductive premise or one of its instances commits us to there being an i such that 'Fx_i and not-Fx_{i+1}' is true. This implies the existence of sharp boundaries and the epistemic theorist, who takes this line, will explain why vague predicates appear not to draw sharp boundaries by reference to our ignorance (see chapter 3).

In a non-classical framework there is a wide variety of ways of developing option (b), and it is not clear or uncontroversial which of these entail a commitment to sharp boundaries. For example, the supervaluationist holds that the generalised premise (2) 'for all i, if Fx_i then Fx_{i+1}' is false: for each F^* which constitutes a way of making F precise, there will be *some x_i* or other which is the last F^* and is followed by an x_{i+1} which is not-F^*. But since there is no particular i for which 'Fx_i and not-Fx_{i+1}' is true—i.e. true however F is made precise—supervaluationists claim that their denial of (2) does not mean accepting that F is sharply bounded. And other non-classical frameworks may allow that (2) is not true, while not accepting that it is *false*. Tye 1994, for example, maintains that the inductive premise and its negation both take his intermediate truth-value, 'indefinite'.

Degree theorists offer another non-classical version of option (b): they can deny that the premises are strictly true while maintaining that they are *nearly* true. The essence of their account is to hold that the predications Fx_i take degrees of truth that encompass a gradually decreasing series from complete truth (degree 1) to complete falsity (degree 0). There is never a substantial drop in degree of truth between consecutive Fx_i, so, given a natural interpretation of the conditional, the particular premises 'if Fx_i then Fx_{i+1}' can each come out at least very nearly true, though some are not completely true. If the sorites argument based on many conditionals is to count as strictly valid, then an account of validity is needed that allows a valid argument to have nearly true premises but a false conclusion. But with some degree theoretic accounts of validity, the sorites fails to be valid—thus a degree theorist can combine responses (a) and (b).

Intuitionistic logic opens up the possibility of another non-classical position that can respond to the sorites by denying the inductive premise (2), while not accepting the classical

---

[8] But see Parikh (1983).

equivalent of this denial, $(\exists x_i)(Fx_i \& \neg Fx_{i+1})$, which is the unwanted assertion of sharp boundaries. Putnam (1983) suggests this strategy. But critics have shown that with various reasonable additional assumptions, other versions of sorites arguments still lead to paradox. In particular, if, as might be expected, you adopt intuitionistic semantics as well as intuitionistic logic, paradoxes recur (see Read and Wright 1985). And Williamson 1996 shows that combining Putnam's approach to vagueness with his epistemological conception of truth still faces paradox. (See also Chambers 1998, who argues that, given Putnam's own view on what would make for vagueness, paradox again emerges.) The bulk of the criticisms point to the conclusion that there is no sustainable account of vagueness that emerges from rejecting classical logic in favour of intuitionistic logic.

(c) Take the sorites (H+) with the premises 'one grain of sand is not a heap' and 'adding a single grain to a non-heap will not turn it into a heap'. If we accept these premises and the validity of the argument, it follows that we will never get a heap, no matter how many grains are piled up: so there are no heaps. Similarly, sorites paradoxes for 'bald', 'tall', and 'person' could be taken to show that there are no bald people, no tall people and indeed no people at all. Unger bites the bullet and takes this nihilistic line, summarised in the title of one of his papers: 'There are no ordinary things' (Unger 1979; see also Wheeler 1975, 1979, and Heller 1988).

The thesis, put in linguistic terms, is that all vague predicates lack serious application, i.e. they apply either to nothing ('is a heap') or to everything ('is not a heap'). Classical logic can be retained in its entirety, but sharp boundaries are avoided by denying that vague predicates succeed in drawing *any* boundaries, fuzzy or otherwise. There will be no borderline cases: for any vague *F*, everything is *F* or everything is not-*F*, and thus nothing is borderline *F*.[9]

The response of accepting the conclusion of every sorites paradox cannot be consistently sustained. For in addition to (H+), there is the argument (H−) with the premises 'ten thousand grains make a heap' and 'removing one grain from a heap still leaves a heap', leading to the conclusion that a single grain of sand is a heap, which is incompatible with the conclusion of (H+). Such reversibility is typical; given a sorites series of items, the argument can be run either way through them. Unger's response to (H−) would be to deny the initial premise: there are no heaps—as (H+) supposedly shows us—so it is not true that ten thousand grains make a heap. Systematic grounds would then be needed to enable us to decide which of a pair of sorites paradoxes is sound (e.g. why there are no heaps rather than everything being a heap).

Unger is driven to such an extreme position by the strength of the arguments in support of the inductive premises of sorites paradoxes. If our words determined sharp boundaries, Unger claims, our understanding of them would be a miracle of conceptual comprehension (1979, p. 126). The inductive premise, guaranteeing this lack of sharp boundaries, reflects a semantic rule central to the meaning of the vague *F*. But, we should ask Unger, can the tolerance principle expressed in the inductive premise for 'tall' really be more certain than the truth of the simple predication of 'tall' to a seven-foot man? Is it plausible to suppose that the expression 'tall' is meaningful and consistent but that there could not be anything tall, when learning the term typically involves ostension and hence confrontation with alleged examples? A different miracle of conceptual comprehension would be needed then to explain how we can understand that meaning and, in general, how we can use such empty predicates successfully to communicate anything at all. It may be more plausible to suppose that if there are any rules governing the application of 'tall', then, in addition to tolerance rules, there are ones dictating

---

[9] See Williamson (1994: ch. 6) for a sustained attack on various forms of nihilism. For example, he shows how the nihilist cannot state or argue for his own position on his own terms (e.g. the expressions he tries to use must count as incoherent).

that 'tall' applies to various paradigmatic cases and does not apply to various para-digmatically short people. Sorites paradoxes could then demonstrate the inconsistency of such a set of rules, and this is option (d).

Responses (c) and (d) are not always clearly distinguished. Writers like Unger are primarily concerned with drawing ontological conclusions. It is enough for them to emphasise the tolerance of a predicate like 'tall' which already guarantees, they claim, that the world con-tains nothing that strictly answers to that description: they are not so concerned to examine what further rules might govern the predicate and perhaps render it incoherent. But other writers, for example Dummett, explore these conceptual questions.

(d) Having argued in detail against alternative responses to the paradox, Dummett (1975) maintains that there is no choice but to accept that a sorites paradox for F exemplifies an undeniably valid form of argument from what the semantic rules for F dictate to be true premises to what they dictate to be a false conclusion. The paradoxes thus reveal the in-coherence of the rules governing vague terms: by simply following those rules, speakers could be led to contradict themselves. This inconsistency means that there can be no coherent logic governing vague language.[10]

Once (d)-theorists have concluded that vague predicates are incoherent, they may agree with Russell that such predicates cannot appear in valid arguments. So option (d) can be developed in such a way that makes it compatible with option (a), though this route to the denial of validity is very different from Russell's. (Being outside the scope of logic need not make for incoherence.)

The acceptance of such pervasive inconsistency is highly undesirable and such pessimism is premature; and it is even by Dummett's own lights a pessimistic response to the paradox, adopted as a last resort rather than as a positive treatment of the paradox that stands as competitor to any other promising alternatives. Communication using vague language is overwhelmingly successful and we are never in practice driven to incoherence (a point stressed by Wright, e.g. 1987, p. 236). And even when shown the sorites paradox, we are rarely inclined to revise our initial judgement of the last member of the series. It looks unlikely that the success and coherence in our practice is owed to our grasp of inconsistent rules. A defence of some version of option (a) or (b) would provide an attractive way of escaping the charge of inconsistency and avoiding the extreme, pessimistic strategies of options (c) and (d).

Rather like the liar paradox ('this sentence is false'), where supposed solutions are often undermined by the more resilient 'strengthened liar paradox' (e.g. 'this sentence is false or X' when the response to the original liar is to call it X), a solution to the original sorites paradox can leave untackled other persistent forms of the sorites, or other arguments of a very similar nature. First, consider the phenomenon of higher-order vagueness noted in §1: not only are there no sharp boundaries between the tall and the not-tall, there are no sharp boundaries between the tall and the borderline tall either (see §6). Like the former lack of sharp boundaries, the latter can also be reflected in a sorites premise, e.g. 'growing one-thousandth of an inch cannot turn a borderline tall person into a tall one'. Such higher-order paradoxes must also be addressed.

There are also related metalinguistic paradoxes which threaten any theory of vagueness that introduces extra categories for borderline cases assuming they can thereby classify every predication of a given vague predicate in some way or other. In particular, Sainsbury's

---

[10] See also Rolf (1981; 1984). Horgan (1994; 1998) advocates a different type of the inconsistency view. He agrees that the sorites paradox (and other related arguments) demonstrate logical incoherence, but considers that in-coherence to be *tempered* or *insulated*, so that it does not infect the whole language and allows us to use the language successfully despite the incoherence (see chapter 8, §2).

'transition question' (1992) and Horgan's 'forced march sorites paradox' (1994) raise similar issues, both emphasising the need to avoid commitment to a sharp boundary between any two types of semantic classification. Horgan instructs us to take, in turn, successive pairs of a sorites series (x_1 and x_2, x_2, and x_3, etc.) and report whether they have the same semantic status. If the answer is 'no' for some particular pair then a sharp boundary is drawn between them, contrary to the vague nature of the predicate, but if the answer is always 'yes', all cases will be absurdly classified the same (e.g. the four-foot man will count as tall). And, as Horgan stresses, if a theory commits us to assigning some semantic category to every predication in turn then, assuming they are not all classified the same way, the theory will be stuck on the first horn of his dilemma and committed to sharp boundaries. This emphasises how theorists need to avoid solutions to the original sorites which are still committed to sharp boundaries between semantic categories.

To finish this section I shall briefly mention that there are approaches to the sorites paradox that, I claim, fail to tackle the primary issues those paradoxes raise. These discussions of the paradox do not slot conveniently into my classification of possible responses, or at least they are not presented as so doing. Unlike most the solutions I have been outlining in (a) to (d), these treatments are not situated in the context of a theory of vagueness more generally. Some, I suggest, may be better seen as tackling a somewhat different issue. For example, sometimes the approach seems to be more of a psychological study of how we respond to successive members of a sorites series and of how our classificatory mechanisms might work such as to prevent us from applying the predicate right through the series. Stories of these kinds do not settle the normative issues of how we *should* classify using vague predicates, what truth-values the problem ascriptions take and what logic governs the language, the very issues I have identified as central to the project in question.[11]

5. THE 'DEFINITELY' OPERATOR

When we construct an account of vagueness, in addition to considering the truth-values of borderline predications, we may seek to *express* the fact that a given predication is or is not of borderline status. Informally, our statement of the fact has relied on semantic ascent—e.g. talking about truth-values of predications. But we may hope to express it without that device. To do so we can introduce into the object language the sentence operators D and I such that Dp holds when p is determinately or definitely true, and Ip (equivalent to $\neg Dp \mathbin{\&} \neg D\neg p$) holds when p is indeterminate or borderline. (The terms 'determinately' and 'definitely' are both used in the literature, but marking no agreed distinction.[12]) This is comparable to the introduction of the sentence operators $\square$ and $\lozenge$ modal logics: these operators allow an

---

[11] Though I will not argue it here, I consider the treatment in, e.g. Raffman (1994) to be of the described type. Among other non-solutions are discussions which give some remedy through which we can avoid actually being driven to paradox (as if it wasn't already clear how this could be done). For example, Shapiro (1998) distinguishes serial processes from parallel ones and attributes the paradox to the use of a serial process that assigns values to predications on the basis of the assignment to the previous member of the ordered sorites series. Such a procedure is wrong because it yields absurd results, Shapiro argues, but he gives no indication of why it is plausible nonetheless (and reliable in other contexts), or what the consequences are regarding sharp boundaries. Moreover, in treating something like the inductive premise of the sorites as an instruction for applying the predicate given certain other members of its extension, Shapiro appears to ignore the fact that it can be treated as a plausible generalisation about the members of the series. On this typical interpretation the paradox persists in abstraction from contexts of running through the sorites sequence via some chosen procedure.

[12] Some authors use Δ and ∇ in place of D and I, others use *Def* or *Det* for D; and some chose an operator for 'definite *whether*' (i.e. $Dp \vee D\neg p$ in my terms).

object-language reflection of the meta-linguistic device employed when we report on whether a sentence is possibly or necessarily true. And just as $\square$ and $\diamond$ can be straightforwardly iterated to express, for example, that necessarily possibly p, the D and I operators can be iterated, where this iteration could perhaps be employed to express higher-order vagueness. For, just as we want to admit borderline cases of F, where $\neg DFx$ & $\neg D \neg Fx$, we may want to allow borderline cases of 'definitely F', where we will have $\neg DDFx$ & $\neg D \neg DFx$. So one motivation for introducing the D operator is for the treatment of higher-order vagueness, the issue to which I turn in §6.

We may hold that no sentence can be true without being determinately true. For how can *a* be F without being determinately F? Dp and p will then be true in exactly the same situations. But the operator is not thereby redundant: for example, $\neg Dp$ will be true in a borderline case, when $\neg p$ is indeterminate. When there is some deviation from classical logic and semantics, the fact that p and Dp coincide in the way described does not guarantee that they are equivalent in the embedded contexts generated by negating them. (According to the epistemic view, which allows no deviation from classical logic, p *can* be true without Dp being true, namely when p is borderline and not known to be true. For the D operator must, on that account, be an epistemic operator.)

The degree theorist can say that Dp is true if p is true to degree 1 and is false if p is true to any lesser degree. A supervaluationist, on the other hand, will say that Dp is true just in case p is true on all ways of making it precise and is false otherwise (so if p is borderline, p itself will be neither true nor false, but Dp will be false). Ways of making the whole language precise each yield a model of the language, and definite truth, as truth on all models, may be expected to share structural and logical features with *necessary* truth construed as truth in all worlds.[13] Alternatively the D operator could perhaps be taken as primitive, in the sense that there is no account of it that is derivative from other resources used in a theory of vagueness.

Wright claims that 'when dealing with vague expressions, it is essential to have the expressive resources afforded by an operator expressing *definiteness* or *determinacy*' (1987, p. 262). I take this to imply that we will fail to fulfil the central tasks of a theory of vagueness unless we introduce the D operator. It is only when we have that operator that we can state that borderline cases occupy a gap between definite truth and definite falsity without committing ourselves to a gap between truth and falsity (Wright 1995, p. 142). And, Wright also maintains, we need to use the D operator to say what it is for a predicate to lack sharp boundaries. Consider a series of objects x_i forming a suitable sorites series for F (e.g. our line of men of decreasing heights for 'tall'). Wright proposes (1987, p. 262)

(W) F is not sharply bounded when there is no i for which DFx_i & $D \neg Fx_{i+1}$.

This can be contrasted with the suggestion that a predicate lacks sharp boundaries when there is no i such that Fx_i & $\neg Fx_{i+1}$. This latter condition gives rise to paradox; but lacking sharp boundaries in the sense of (W) does *not* lead straight to paradox. In particular, suppose that there are some indefinitely F cases between the definitely F cases and the definitely not-F cases. Then, as (W) requires, there will be no immediate leap from DFx_i to $D \neg Fx_{i+1}$ (see also Campbell 1974).

Suppose someone were to take Wright's claim about the importance of D to show that a theory of vagueness should proceed by introducing a primitive D operator and focusing on its logic and semantics. They would, I argue, be pursuing the wrong approach. Having a primitive D operator will not enable us to fulfil the tasks facing a theory of vagueness. In particular,

---

[13] Note that it is not only on the supervaluationist scheme that the comparison with modal logics is appropriate. Williamson, for example, explains its applicability within an epistemic view of vagueness (see esp. his 1999).

replacing statements naturally used to express our intuitions about borderline cases and the lack of sharp boundaries with *different* (but similar) statements involving the *D* operator does not provide an excuse to ignore the very questions that are, and should be, at the centre of the debate, namely ones about the original intuitions.

For example, suppose the claim is that we are confusing the standard premise with something else which does not lead to paradox, namely the claim that there is no successive pair in the series of which the first is definitely *F* and the second is definitely not-*F*. We need still to ask how we should classify the original premise itself. If we say that premise is true, as it seems to be, the paradox remains untouched. But can we be content to call it false and hence accept that there is a last patch of a sorites series that is red and an adjacent pair in the series of which one is *F* and the other is not-*F*? Wright suggests that the inductive premises of some (but not all) sorites paradoxes may be of indeterminate status (1987, p. 267). But how are we to understand this claim? At the least it seems to imply that attaching a 'definitely' operator to the front of the premise-statement would result in a statement that was not true. But what should we say when we do *not* attach that operator? If regarding that premise as having indeterminate status is to be taken as ascribing it a non-classical truth-value (or just not ascribing a classical value), then a non-classical logic and semantics of vagueness needs to be provided to fill out the picture. But then surely providing such a system should be the central task, rather than concentrating on the logic and semantics of the *D* operator, which would then be an optional extra. Similarly for the claim that our intuition that a borderline pre-dication is neither true nor false should be accounted for by the fact that it is actually neither *definitely* true nor *definitely* false. For are we then to say that it *is* either true or false, and if so, how are we to avoid the unwanted consequences of bivalence? And if, instead, it is said to be of indeterminate status, again we will need a logic that can accommodate such a non-classical truth-value status.[14]

In summary, how can it help to add a *D* operator to the language—creating new sentences that may be shown to be unproblematically true or false—when the task is to illuminate the semantics of the old statements which do not contain this operator? Using a *D* operator may allow us to say that it is not definitely the case that *a* is red, but how can this illuminate the semantics of the vague '*a* is red' itself?

It might be suggested that even if introducing the *D* operator does not provide the *key* to a theory of vagueness, such a theory must at least accommodate and give a plausible semantics for the operator. For, in describing the semantics of our language we should acknowledge that expressions such as 'borderline' and 'definitely' are part of it. Moreover, the *D* operator enables us to make assertions about candidates for *F*-ness (e.g. borderline cases) as assertions about the things themselves, whereas without the operator we are strangely limited to judge-ments about the *language* if we are to say anything like what we want to say. But though I agree that there is a pre-theoretic notion of 'definitely', we should be wary of constructing an account of *D* via one's theory and assuming that it corresponds exactly to a pre-theoretic notion (even if the theory appropriately captures vague language without that operator). The ordinary use and apprehension of 'definitely' may well not straightforwardly conform to the kind of formal theory of the *D* operator that theorists seek. Intuitions about the operator may be inconsistent (just like those leading to sorites paradoxes). And, anyway, the consequences of the theory of *D* will outstrip the consequences we would expect given only our intuitions

---

[14] Could there be a coherent theory that retains bivalence but still maintains that some sentences are of inde-terminate status? This would imply that there could be sentences that were both true and indeterminate, which goes against the earlier assumption that no sentence can be true without being determinately true. Williamson (1995) argues that such a theory is not possible unless the indeterminacy is taken to be epistemic.

about 'definitely'. We should beware unargued theoretical assumptions that, for example, D can be used to capture the vagueness of *any* expression, including 'D' itself.[15]

It is thus reasonable, and perhaps necessary, to give 'definitely' a technical sense that depends on and is dictated by the theory of vagueness offered for the D-free part of language. And the theory may dictate that there is some departure from uniformity between the treatment of sentences with the operator and that of those without. For example, according to supervaluationism, though the logic of the D-free language is classical, the logical behaviour of the D operator has to be non-classical. So, although an account of the D operator may provide further details of a theory of vagueness, it forms the second and less central stage of such a theory. My prime concern is with the first stage: discussion of the second stage needs to be built on my account of the logic and semantics of D-free language.

I now turn to higher-order vagueness, in relation to which the D operator remains highly relevant.

6. HIGHER-ORDER VAGUENESS

Imagine—if we can—a predicate G that has a sharply bounded set of clear positive cases, a sharply bounded set of clear negative cases, and a sharply bounded set of cases falling in between. Although G is stipulated to have borderline cases in the sense of instances which are neither clearly G nor clearly not-G, it still has sharp boundaries—one between the Gs and the borderline cases and another between the borderline cases and the not-Gs. Our ordinary vague predicates such as 'tall', 'red', and 'chair' surely do not yield a threefold sharp classification of this sort, with two sharp boundaries around the borderline cases. The familiar arguments that there is no sharp boundary between the positive and negative extensions of 'tall' would equally count against any suggestion that there is a sharp boundary between the positive extension and the borderline cases (consider the typical arguments for tolerance discussed in Wright 1976). For example, one-hundredth of an inch should not make the difference as to whether someone counts as borderline tall. And a sharp boundary to the borderline cases of F would mean that there could be two things that are indiscriminable by those who use that word but yet that differ over whether F applies. More generally, just as the meaning of a vague predicate does not determine a sharp boundary between the positive and negative extensions, nor does it determine sharp boundaries to the borderline cases or other sharp boundaries. (On the epistemic view the requirement would need to be formulated differently, but parallel issues arise.) With the D operator, the lack of sharp boundaries to the borderline cases of F can be expressed as the lack of abrupt transition between the DFx cases and the $\neg DFx$ cases (and between the $D\neg Fx$ cases and the $\neg D\neg Fx$ cases), or the lack of a last x in a sorites series for which DFx is true (and the lack of a first x in a sorites series for which $D\neg Fx$ is true).

It is widely recognised in the literature from Russell onwards (1923, p. 87) that the borderline cases of a vague predicate are not sharply bounded. There is disagreement over whether or not a predicate with sharply bounded borderline cases should count as vague (for example, Sainsbury suggests not, 1991, p. 173, in contrast with Fine, 1975, p. 266). But however that question is settled, our ordinary vague predicates typically have borderline cases that are not sharply bounded, so that phenomenon needs to be examined.

---

[15] Wright offers principles governing the D operator, but these are insufficiently defended and are disputed in Sainsbury (1991), Edgington (1993), and Heck (1993). Evans's celebrated argument concerning indeterminate identity uses a determinately operator (frequently taken to be 'determinate whether') and again employs unjustified assumptions about its logic (1978).

Closely related to the lack of sharp boundaries to the borderline cases is the phenomenon of having possible borderline borderline cases (also known as second-order borderline cases), where borderline borderline cases of F are values of x for which 'Fx is borderline' is itself borderline. Suppose we accept that the borderline cases of H are not sharply bounded. We can infer that H has possible second-order borderline cases given a widely held assumption:

(A_1) The lack of sharp boundaries between the Fs and the Gs shows that there are possible values of x for which 'x is borderline F' and 'x is borderline G' both hold.

For the lack of a sharp boundary between the definite Hs and the borderline Hs will then imply that there are possible cases between them which are borderline borderline cases of H as well as borderline cases of 'defintely H'. (And there will be a second variety of possible borderline borderline cases arising from the lack of a sharp boundary between the borderline cases and the definitely false predications.)

This argument for second-order borderline cases looks as though it should now iterate: if H is to be genuinely vague there should be no sharp boundaries to the borderline borderline Hs either, and this, in turn, will yield possible borderline borderline borderline Hs; and so on. If there is no order of borderline case which we are willing to acknowledge as having sharp boundaries, the iteration will continue indefinitely, resulting in an unlimited hierarchy of possible borderline cases of different orders; we can call this unlimited higher-order vagueness.

The term 'higher-order vagueness' has been used for several phenomena which we may wish to keep apart. In particular, sometimes it amounts to having borderline cases of any order above the first; sometimes the term is used to refer to the lack of sharp boundaries to the borderline cases; and occasionally it is used to mean the same as my 'unlimited higher-order vagueness'. When it is not important to make these distinctions, I shall use 'higher-order vagueness' for this cluster of phenomena, though elsewhere it will be preferable to use descriptions without this potential ambiguity (such as 'the lack of sharp boundaries to the borderline cases').[16]

Another argument for unlimited higher-order vagueness can be constructed as follows. When F is vague, typically the predicate 'is a borderline case of F' is also vague. Given the assumption that if a predicate is vague, then it has possible borderline cases—call it (A_2)—it follows from the vagueness of H that there are possible borderline borderline cases of H, since the borderline cases of 'is borderline H' are themselves borderline borderline cases of H. And accepting 'if F is vague then "is a borderline F" is also vague' would guarantee that if a predicate is vague at all, it has possible borderline cases of all orders. Moreover, since the first-order borderline cases of one predicate coincide exactly with the second-order borderline cases of another, this suggests another (plausible) requirement, namely that higher-order borderline cases be given the same treatment as first-order ones: there should be consistency and uniformity in the treatment of different orders of vagueness.

Should we accept the commitment to an unlimited hierarchy of orders of borderline case associated with each of our typical everyday predicates?[17] It might be thought an extravagant

---

[16] Williamson (1999) defends a different characterisation of the hierarchy of orders of vagueness such that there can be third-order vagueness in his sense without third-order borderline cases in the above sense. The dispute does not matter for our current purposes. Also relevant to a detailed discussion of the various related phenomena would be Williamson's argument that if F is second order vague, it must be vague at all orders.

[17] Burgess argues against unlimited higher-order vagueness, maintaining that higher-order vagueness terminates at a 'rather low finite level' (1990: 431), at least for secondary-quality predicates. He does this via a proposed analysis of one of the relevant notions, each of the elements of which, he argues, is only vague to a finite level. The strength of his arguments must rest in their detail—for instance they must avoid the objection that precision is simply assumed at some key stage of the account (see Williamson 1994: 296).

and unrealistic commitment. Moreover, the hierarchy of borderline cases may still fail to capture the complete lack of sharp boundaries for F if there is a sharp boundary between those cases which are borderline cases of some order and those that are, as we might say, absolutely definitely F. (See e.g. Sainsbury 1990, p. 11.) And, relatedly, the hierarchy will be of limited benefit if it is such as to pin every candidate for being F into exactly one of the orders of borderline case, since again this seems to impose a determinacy where there is none.

(A_1) and (A_2), the principles used above in generating the hierarchy, both reflect the common emphasis on borderline cases, which seems reasonable at the first level, but may be less compelling once they are seen to draw us into the hierarchy. (A_2) amounts to the standard criterion of vagueness in terms of borderline cases (a criterion that can be found in Peirce 1902). It is particularly amenable to an iterative structure. To test whether a predicate F is vague, ask whether it has borderline cases. If so, this yields a set of cases (those borderline cases) and with regard to them we can apply the same test and ask whether they too have borderline cases (which, if so, will give second-order borderline cases of F). And so on through the progressive sets of higher-order borderline cases. An alternative criterion that takes vague predicates to be those lacking sharp boundaries would not have the same scope for the generation of a hierarchy of levels. (Testing whether the borderline cases themselves have borderline cases is no longer iterating the test for vagueness at the first level with this new criterion.) For the fact that there are no sharp boundaries to the positive extension is not a feature susceptible to iteration, just as precision, interpreted as the existence of a sharp boundary, leaves no scope for a notion of higher-order precision. Sainsbury (1990), claiming that there is no such thing as an unsharp boundary, identifies the defining feature of vagueness as 'boundarylessness'. He argues that recognising the feature of boundarylessness is essential for a genuine understanding of vagueness and an account of its semantics. At the very least, we should say that it is more important to capture the lack of sharp boundaries to the borderline cases than to focus on the hierarchy of borderline cases, and this may mean not taking borderline cases as the centre of the debate.

A key issue here concerns vagueness in the metalanguage—the language in which we frame our theory and report the borderline status of some predications. If the metalanguage contains the object-language, so that sentences of the object-language are also sentences of the metalanguage, then the metalanguage will be vague given that the object-language is vague. The interesting issues concern whether the proper part of the metalanguage which is not also part of the object-language is also vague. This part will contain all truth-value predicates, plus expressions for the consequence relation etc. Or if the metalanguage is the same language as the object-language, then we can still ask about the cited elements of the language (they are still called upon to talk *about* the language). If these elements were all precise, then the (precise) metalinguistic predicate applicable to all and only those sentences of borderline case status would pick out a sharply bounded set of cases. But this would guarantee that, for all F, the borderline cases of F themselves had sharp boundaries. So accommodating the lack of such sharp boundaries requires a vague metalanguage. And the existence of higher-order borderline cases would impose the same requirement. For if x is a borderline borderline case of F, the metalinguistic report that Fx is borderline will itself be of borderline status, so the metalinguistic predicate it uses must have borderline cases. Whether and how to accommodate vague metalanguages is a question for any theory of vagueness, and the need for a vague metalanguage is emphasised in Sainsbury (1990), Tye (1990), and Williamson (1994). And Horgan's forced march paradox described in §4 bears on this issue, for with a non-vague metalanguage we can assume that some semantic status or other will be assigned to each object-language sentence, and, as Horgan argues, this will mean sharp boundaries along the relevant series.

There are difficulties, however, facing the idea of vague metalanguages. [I shall argue later that] certain theories cannot be consistently defended on the supposition that their meta-languages are vague. But even if the metalanguage for some theory could be vague, the following question arises: can we succeed in illuminating the vagueness of our language if we need to draw on a metalanguage that itself exhibits vagueness? There is at least a suspicion of circularity or triviality here, which has been alluded to in the literature. And Fine suggests that in constructing and assessing theories of vagueness, we might 'require that the meta-language not be vague, or, at least, not so vague in its proper part as the object-language' (1975, p. 297). This tension between needing and resisting vague metalanguages will be explored in later chapters in the context of specific theories.

If we approach higher-order vagueness by using the D operator within the object language, can we ignore the vagueness or otherwise of the metalanguage? I think not. With the statement (BB) $\neg DDp$ & $\neg DIp$, we may be able to express the fact that p is a second-order borderline case that is not definitely definitely true and not definitely borderline. And (BB) can be unproblematically assigned the value 'true' in a non-vague metalanguage. But when we come to assign truth-values to *all* statements of the object language, we will *still* be required to assess the truth-value of p itself. Being a second-order borderline case, p is appropriately called neither 'true' nor 'borderline', so even if the metalanguage has an expression for borderline status, that will not be enough unless that expression is itself vague. So a precise metalanguage cannot capture the truth-value status of a second-order borderline case, and it is not to the point to note that by using D and I we can still express the fact that p is a second-order borderline case.

In summary, I maintain that any putative theory of vagueness must accommodate the apparent lack of sharp boundaries to the borderline cases, and address the issue of higher-order vagueness. And, relatedly, it must answer the question whether the metalanguage for the theory is vague, while tackling the difficulties facing the chosen answer.

REFERENCES

Barnes, J. (1982). 'Medicine, experience and logic'. In J. Barnes, J. Brunschwig, M. Burnyeat, and M. Schofield (eds.), *Science and Speculation*. Cambridge: Cambridge University Press.

Burgess, J. A. (1990). 'The sorites paradox and higher-order vagueness'. *Synthese* 85: 417–74.

Burnyeat, M. F. (1982). 'Gods and heaps'. In M. Schofield and M. C. Nussbaum (eds.), *Language and Logos*. Cambridge: Cambridge University Press.

Campbell, R. (1974). 'The sorites paradox'. *Philosophical Studies* 26: 175–91.

Cargile, J. (1969). 'The sorites paradox'. *British Journal for the Philosophy of Science* 20: 193–202. Repr. in Keefe and Smith (1997a).

Carnap, R. (1950). *The Logical Foundations of Probability*. Chicago: University of Chicago Press.

Chambers, T. (1998). 'On vagueness, sorites, and Putnam's "Intuitionistic Strategy"'. *Monist* 81: 343–8.

Cooper, N. (1995). 'Paradox lost: understanding vague predicates'. *International Journal of Philosophical Studies* 3: 244–69.

Dummett, M. (1975). 'Wang's paradox'. *Synthese* 30: 301–24. Repr. in Keefe and Smith (1997a).

Edgington, D. (1993). 'Wright and Sainsbury on higher-order vagueness'. *Analysis* 53: 193–200.

Evans, G. (1978). 'Can there be vague objects?' *Analysis* 38: 208. Repr. in Keefe and Smith (1997a).

Fine, K. (1975). 'Vagueness, truth and logic'. *Synthese* 30: 265–300. Repr. in Keefe and Smith (1997a).

Frege, G. (1903). *Grundgesetze der Arithmetik, begriffsschriftlich abgeleitet*, vol. ii. Jena: Hermann Pohle.

Grim, P. (1982). 'What won't escape sorites arguments'. *Analysis* 42: 38–43.

Haack, S. (1974). *Deviant Logic*. Cambridge: Cambridge University Press.

Heck, R. G., Jr. (1993). 'A note on the logic of (higher-order) vagueness'. *Analysis* 53: 201–8.

Heller, M. (1988). 'Vagueness and the standard ontology'. *Noûs* 22: 109–31.

Horgan, T. (1994). 'Robust vagueness and the forced-march sorites paradox'. In J. E. Tomberlin (ed.), *Philosophical Perspectives* 8: *Logic and Language*. Atascadero, Calif.: Ridgeview.

Hyde, D. (1997). 'From heaps and gaps to heaps of gluts'. *Mind* 106: 641–60.

Keefe, R., and P. Smith (eds.) (1997a). *Vagueness: A Reader*. Cambridge, Mass.: MIT Press.

—— —— (1997b). 'Theories of vagueness'. In Keefe and Smith (1997a).

Kirk, R. (1986). *Translation Determined*. Oxford: Oxford University Press.

Long, A. A., and D. N. Sedley (eds.) (1987). *The Hellenistic Philosophers*. Cambridge: Cambridge University Press. Excerpted in Keefe and Smith (1997a).

Machina, K. F. (1976). 'Truth, belief, and vagueness'. *Journal of Philosophical Logic* 5: 47–78. Repr. in Keefe and Smith (1997a).

Parikh, R. (1983). 'The problem of vague predicates'. In R. S. Cohen and M. W. Wartofsky (eds.), *Language, Logic, and Method*. Dordrecht: Reidel.

Parsons, T. (1987). 'Entities without identity'. In J. E. Tomberlin (ed.), *Philosophical Perspectives* 1: *Metaphysics*. Atascadero, Calif.: Ridgeview.

Peirce, C. S. (1902). 'Vague'. In J. M. Baldwin (ed.), *Dictionary of Philosophy and Psychology*. New York: Macmillan, 748.

Putnam, H. (1983). 'Vagueness and alternative logic'. *Erkenntnis* 19: 297–314.

Quine, W.V. (1981). 'What price bivalence?' *Journal of Philosophy* 78: 90–5.

Raffman, D. (1994). 'Vagueness without paradox'. *Philosophical Review* 103: 41–74.

Read, S., and C. Wright (1985). 'Hairier than Putnam thought'. *Analysis* 45: 56–8.

Rolf, B. (1981). *Topics on Vagueness*. Lund: Studentlitteratur.

——(1984). 'Sorites'. *Synthese* 58: 219–50.

Russell, B. (1923). 'Vagueness'. *Australasian Journal of Philosophy and Psychology* 1: 84–92. Repr. in Keefe and Smith (1997a) and in this volume.

Sainsbury, R. M. (1990). 'Concepts without boundaries'. Inaugural lecture published by the King's College London Department of Philosophy. Repr. in Keefe and Smith (1997a).

——(1991). 'Is there higher-order vagueness?' *Philosophical Quarterly* 41: 167–82.

——(1992). 'Sorites paradoxes and the transition question'. *Philosophical Papers* 21: 177–90.

Shapiro, S. C. (1998). 'A procedural solution to the unexpected hanging and sorites paradoxes'. *Mind* 107: 751–61.

Sperber, D., and D. Wilson (1985–6). 'Loose talk'. *Proceedings of the Aristotelian Society* 86: 153–71.

Tye, M. (1990). 'Vague objects'. *Mind* 99: 535–57.

Unger, P. (1979). 'There are no ordinary things'. *Synthese* 41: 117–54.

Walton, D. N. (1992). *Slippery Slope Arguments*. Oxford: Clarendon Press.

Wheeler, S. C. (1975). 'Reference and vagueness'. *Synthese* 30: 367–79.

——(1979). 'On that which is not'. *Synthese* 41: 155–73.

Williams, B. (1995). 'Which slopes are slippery?' In *Making Sense of Humanity*. Cambridge: Cambridge University Press.

Williamson, T. (1994). *Vagueness*. London: Routledge.

——(1995). 'Definiteness and knowability'. *Southern Journal of Philosophy* 33 (supplement): 171–91.

——(1996). 'Putnam on the sorites paradox'. *Philosophical Papers* 25: 47–56.

——(1999). 'On the structure of higher-order vagueness'. *Mind* 108: 127–43.

Wright, C. (1975). 'On the coherence of vague predicates'. *Synthese* 30: 325–65.

——(1976). 'Language-mastery and the sorites paradox'. In G. Evans and J. McDowell (eds.), *Truth and Meaning: Essays in Semantics*. Oxford: Clarendon Press. Repr. in Keefe and Smith (1997a).

——(1987). 'Further reflections on the sorites paradox'. *Philosophical Topics* 15: 227–90. Excerpted in Keefe and Smith (1997a).

——(1995). 'The epistemic conception of vagueness'. *Southern Journal of Philosophy* 33 (supplement): 133–59.

Zemach, E. M. (1991). 'Vague objects'. *Noûs* 25: 323–40.

PART II
Categories in Cognition

6

The Boundaries of Words and their Meanings

WILLIAM LABOV

If we take seriously the traditional notion that linguistic signs represent the union of a form and a meaning, there can be no limit to our interest in the meanings of words. But for a number of reasons, linguists have concentrated their attention on the forms of words and their combinations, and the meanings of only a small number of grammatical particles. The description of the meanings of words has been left to the lexicographers, for better or for worse; and linguists have long contented themselves with glosses which are labels but not descriptions. Recent activity in combinatorial semantics has not extended as yet to the meanings of words.

The reason for this neglect is certainly not a lack of interest, since linguists like any other speakers of a language cannot help focusing their attention on the word, which is the most central element in the social system of communication.[1] It is the difficulty of the problem, and its inaccessibility to the most popular methods of inquiry, which is responsible for this neglect.

We encounter many ordinary objects that are clearly and easily named, but many more where it is difficult to say exactly what they are if we confront them directly. In any kitchen, there are many containers that are obviously bowls, cups, mugs, and dishes. But there are others that might be called cups, or might not; or might be a kind of a cup, according to some, but a kind of a dish according to others. This is a problem of formal description more than a problem of the language; for the puzzled expressions that we get when we hold up such an object for naming rarely appear in the everyday use of the language. The most casual observation suggests that the language has many adroit ways of dealing with the problem, but that has not helped lexicographers when they attempted formal definitions of words.

Words have often been called slippery customers, and many scholars have been distressed by their tendency to shift their meanings and slide out from under any simple definition. A goal of some clear thinkers has been to use words in more precise ways. But though this is an excellent and necessary step for a technical jargon, it is a self-defeating program when applied to ordinary words. It is not only that words are shifters; the objects to which they must be applied shift with even greater rapidity. Words that are bound to simple conjunctive definitions will have little value for application in a world which presents us with an unlimited range

---

* William Labov, 'The boundaries of words and their meanings', in C.-J. Bailey and R. W. Shuy (eds.), *New Ways of Analyzing Variation in English* (Washington, DC: Georgetown University Press, 1973), 340–73. © 1973 Georgetown University Press. Reprinted by permission.

[1] One of the classic problems of defining the boundaries of a category is that of defining the word in English (Hockett 1958: 166). The difficulties of providing a categorical definition are so great that many linguists have abandoned *word* as a technical term and substituted *lexeme, formative*, etc. But the word seems to be the linguistic unit of greatest social significance in our own and many other cultures. The problem of defining the category *word* can be taken as one of the important issues to be attacked as linguistics shifts from being a theory of category to a theory of limits and boundaries (see section 1).

of new and variable objects for description. Words as well as the world itself display the 'orderly heterogeneity' which characterizes language as a whole (Weinreich, Labov, and Herzog 1968). Again we would argue that this orderly heterogeneity is functional. Rather than complain about the variable character of the meanings of words, we should recognize the existence of an extraordinary ability of human beings to apply words to the world in a creative way. The problem is no less central than the one which Chomsky has identified in relation to syntax. Just as we employ a finite set of rules to produce an unlimited number of sentences, so we employ a finite set of words to describe an unlimited number of objects in the real world around us.

The ordinary methods of investigation which have been used to define words represent only a part of the methods which might be used to attack this problem. Language can be studied through introspection, formal elicitation, the study of texts, experiment, and/or observation (Labov 1971). But only the first three approaches have been taken to the study of words and their meanings. This paper will report for the first time a series of experimental studies of the use of words which have been carried out over the past ten years.[2] The main focus has been on the denotation of cups and cuplike containers, and the use of words such as *cup, bowl, dish, mug, glass, pitcher*, etc., and their corresponding terms in other languages. New techniques have been developed for the study of the variable conditions which govern denotation. But there are also invariant components among these conditions, and the entire study must be firmly located as an aspect of the basic categorizing activity of human beings. Before we consider the experiments themselves, it will be necessary to outline the traditional categorical view which attempts to capture this aspect of linguistic behavior and the problem of defining boundary conditions within that view.

I. THE CATEGORICAL VIEW AND ITS LIMITATIONS

If linguistics can be said to be any one thing it is the study of categories: that is, the study of how language translates meaning into sound through the categorization of reality into discrete units and sets of units. This categorization is such a fundamental and obvious part of linguistic activity that the properties of categories are normally assumed rather than studied. Behind all of the theories of linguistic structure that have been presented in the twentieth century there is a common set of assumptions about the nature of structural units. This set of assumptions can be called the 'categorical view'. It includes the implicit assertions that all linguistic units are categories which are:

(1) discrete
(2) invariant
(3) qualitatively distinct
(4) conjunctively defined
(5) composed of atomic primes

By 'discrete', it is meant that the categories are separated from each other by clear-cut discontinuities of form or function; by 'invariant', that the category as a type recurs as precisely the same in each occurrence, despite the fact that tokens may vary; by 'qualitatively different', that the units are completely different from each other, and not distinguished as homogeneous elements in a linear or ordered sequence; by 'conjunctively defined', that there is a set of

---

[2] The first report of this work was to the Linguistic Society of America at the Annual Meeting in New York City on December 28, 1964, entitled 'Interdependent conditions for denotation'. The present report incorporates results from a number of further studies carried out at Columbia University, and recent work at the University of Pennsylvania in 1972 with the help of Franklin Jones.

properties associated with the unit which are in some way criterial or necessary, essential as opposed to other properties which are unnecessary, accidental, or redundant, and that all of these essential properties must be present for the category to be recognized.

The fifth property may be considered an extension of discreteness: although some categories are compounded of others, there is a limit to any such subdivision and all categories are ultimately composed of a set of integral categories which cannot be subdivided.

Membership in these categories, and relations of inclusion and exclusion among categories, are established by rules which are obligatory or optional, but optionality cannot be further characterized. No statements can be made as to whether one such rule applies more often than another.[3]

These properties of linguistic categories are far from arbitrary. They appear to correspond well to the basic structure of language as we deal with it everyday. It is sometimes said that man is a categorizing animal; it is equally appropriate to say that language is a categorizing activity. The total abandonment of any one of these properties might be shown to have unfortunate consequences for linguistic analysis. But some modification appears to be necessary, as the present report and other recent work demonstrates.

Scholars have assumed the properties of the categorical view for a wide range of categories: features, phonemes, morphemes, intonation contours, verbs, modals, nouns, nodes, cycles, derivations, styles, languages, manner adverbs, dialects, etc. Because this characterization of language seems to be firmly based on the nature of linguistic activity, it has provided a useful base for a first approximation to grammars and the principles of writing grammars.

But this view of man as a categorizing animal fails if it takes categorizing activity for granted, since it cannot deal with the facts of linguistic change which have been studied over several centuries, nor with the orderly variation within linguistic structure which we have charted in some detail in recent years (Weinreich, Labov, and Herzog 1968).

In the categorical view, the properties of categories are assumed. Scholars then typically argue how many categories exist, and what items are assigned to what categories.[4] This is an important and essential activity: many fields which study human behavior deal with categories which are not firmly enough established to allow the question, one category or two?[5] But in many areas of linguistics, we have extracted as much profit as we can from these debates, and we can turn to the resolution of long-standing questions by examining the correspondence of the categorizing process to linguistic activity. Instead of taking as problematical the existence of categories, we can turn to the nature of the boundaries between them. As linguistics then becomes a form of boundary theory rather than a category theory, we discover that not all linguistic material fits the categorical view: there is greater or lesser success in imposing categories upon the continuous substratum of reality.

There are cases where the categorical nature of a boundary is immediate and obvious, as suggested in a property-item matrix such as Figure 1. Here there are a series of eight items (a–h) which may be thought of variously as languages, dialects, villages, parts of speech, words, phonemes, etc., and seven properties (1–7) detectable in them. The presence of these properties is associated with category X, their absence with category Y. In Figure 1 it is plain that items a–d are Xs, and e–h are Ys. Though it is possible to select a single property as the

---

[3] The analysis of the categorical view presented here is based upon Labov (1965); for the additional consideration of the prohibition on constraining free variation, see Labov (1971).

[4] See for example Martinet 'Un ou deux phonèmes' (1939) and countless other discussions of category assignment in the literature.

[5] Several other fields concerned with human behavior have not yet been able to formulate questions precisely enough to answer such questions. For example, it is very difficult to argue in role theory whether certain small differences in rights, duties, and obligations represent one role or two; there seems to be no principled way of deciding whether being the father of a five-year-old child is a different role from being the father of an eight-year-old child.

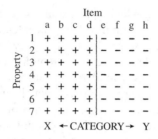

FIG. 1   Property-item matrix for a clearly categorical boundary.

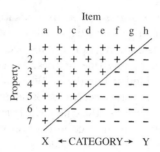

FIG. 2   Property-item matrix for the absence of a boundary between two categories.

distinctive, or criterial, or essential one, we feel much more confident about categories which are defined by the co-occurrence of a large number of items. Thus it is clear that French and English are different systems, and we use these terms without misgivings. But we are not so happy with such categories as dialects established by the evidence that two speakers disagree with each other on the acceptability of a single sentence type[6] and we are particularly critical of sub-categorizations of parts of speech which are justified by only one property.[7]

However, a certain degree of vagueness is often characteristic of boundaries. In the most extreme case, categories can be justified even when no boundaries can be set up between them.

Thus, in Figure 2, any decision to locate the boundary between categories X and Y would obviously be an arbitrary one. Yet the fact that the data on properties (1–7) can be organized in the implicational series shows that there is a structure here, which effectively constrains the data to eliminate at least half of the possible permutations of items and properties. Given empirical data which resembled Figure 2, we could not say with any certainty whether any given item b–g was to be classed as a sonorant or an obstruent, a verb or a modal, a speaker of the white vernacular or of the black vernacular, a Romance or a Germanic language, a pidgin or a creole, as the categories X and Y may variously assign membership. The transition between X and Y occupies the entire property-item space. Such matrices have been discussed as theoretical possibilities by a number of recent writers, beginning with Quirk (1965) in regard to grammatical categories, and DeCamp (1971) in regard to sociolinguistic systems and the Creole continuum. But in regard to geographical dialects, it has long been argued that such gradient models are characteristic of the diffusion of linguistic features across a territory

---

[6] On the questionable status of such idiosyncratic dialects, see Labov (1972a).

[7] Such ad hoc categories are regularly criticized in syntax as having no explanatory adequacy. But when a category can be shown to have two relatively independent properties, one property at least is said to be 'explained'; that is, the overall rule statements can then be simplified by the use of the category in question. The distinction of count-nouns vs. mass nouns, for example, is associated with differences in co-occurrence with the plural, with the indefinite article, and partitive quantifiers like *some*.

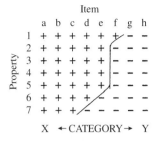

FIG. 3   Discontinuity reflecting co-occurrence restrictions on properties in a variable matrix.

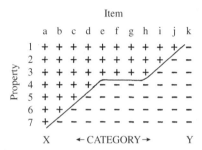

FIG. 4   Discontinuity reflecting a concentration of homogeneous items in a variable matrix.

and the challenge has been to establish that boundaries between dialects are anything but arbitrary (Weinreich 1954, Stankiewicz 1957).

The most vigorous development of the modal of Figure 2, on both the theoretical and empirical side, is to be found in the work of Bickerton, who proposes that linguistic structures contain no homogeneous categories at all, but only continuous transitions bound by implicational series, with no properties showing co-occurrence restrictions at all (1971, 1972). Nevertheless, even in dialect geography, most investigators agree that properties do bundle, and that it is possible to show boundaries of varying degrees of clarity even when all variable features are superimposed upon a single map. This type of bundling or co-occurrence of properties in a variable matrix is illustrated in Figure 3, where the division between categories X and Y appears to be less arbitrary than in Figure 2. Items a, b, c are clearly X, and d and e appear to be X's as well, though a bit defective in relation to properties 6 and 7. Items g and h are clearly Y, and f is again a Y, though imperfect. The important feature of Figure 3 which makes this division possible is the simultaneous shift or co-occurrence restrictions exhibited by properties 2–5. These provide us with evidence of systematicity within the rules which govern property 2 and tie them to those which govern properties 3, 4, and 5. In dialect geography, the discontinuity of Figure 3 would represent a bundle of isoglosses; in an urban speech community, it would represent a subsystem characteristic of a class or ethnic dialect. If Figure 3 represents the distinction between modals and other verbs, the bundling properties might be subject to inversion, reproduction in tag questions, and *not* contraction. In phonology, we find that initial stops show co-occurrence of initial aspiration, voicing lag, and stronger release of air pressure. Whether or not we choose one of these properties as distinctive, the co-occurrence reinforces our confidence in the existence of the categories.

Another sort of discontinuity in a variable matrix appears in Figure 4. Here there is no co-occurrence of any two properties, but there are items that clump together. Items e–h are all characterized by properties 1–3 but not properties 4–7. This situation tempts us to redefine our category system, possibly setting up a third category X′ which is defined by properties 1–3 only. In dialect geography, this would mean that relatively homogeneous speech communities exist; in phonology, it would mean that some combinations of features were more heavily exploited than others for some functional reason. It is clear that this second type of discontinuity appears in Bickerton's data, and is one of the main focuses of Bailey's approach in building rate into models of phonological linguistic description (1971).

In large-scale studies which are accountable to a given population or body of data, we may find no examples of perfect co-occurrence or perfectly homogeneous groups. But given an empirical approach to the problems of linguistic analysis we can report the actual discontinuities in transition which exist. Thus if we are to take seriously the categorical property of language, we must pass beyond the categorical view which takes it as given, and study the process of categorization itself by focusing on such discontinuities directly. By avoiding the categorical view, or some equally rigid principle of distribution, we are free to study the real properties of such boundaries, and deduce the higher level properties which govern the use of language.

This paper will introduce the study of variability in denotation, systematically displacing the categorical view which has dominated previous studies in order to discover the regularities which relate the properties of shape, function, material, etc. as they govern the conditions for the act of denotation. To do so, we will have to reject in particular property (d)—the notion that categories are to be defined conjunctively through their distinctive features. These distinctive features or essential attributes are the working apparatus of the scholastic tradition which has dominated almost every school of linguistic thought until recently, and our pursuit of a secular mode of inquiry will inevitably bring us into conflict with that tradition.

2. CONDITIONS FOR DENOTATION

In this study, we will be dealing with the conditions which govern denotation, that is, the act of naming or reference which associates a linguistic sign with an element of the extra-linguistic world. Denotation or reference has been especially excluded from some recent studies of combinatorial semantics, as if this topic were outside of the proper domain of linguistics (Katz and Fodor 1963). Yet the fundamental relation of form to meaning in designation is to be seen only in the conditions which govern the act of reference: that is, the significatum of the sign.

Though this investigation deals with the application of signs to concrete objects, it is not a study of the act of reference, and should not be confused with the point of view that identifies meaning with use. We are dealing rather with the knowledge of ability to apply a term to a range of objects in a way that reflects the communicative system utilized by others. Following Weinreich (1962), we define the significatum or meaning of a sign, as the conditions which govern denotation. Given a situation in which such conditions are actually fulfilled, so that the sign can be used in reference to the situation, the token of the sign is said to denote. Thus

(1) L(x) if C_1 and C_2 and C_3.

That is, the sign L denotes the object x if all of the conditions C_1, C_2... are fulfilled. These conditions C_1, C_2... are sometimes called criteria, or conditions of criteriality. The relationship here is one of intersection: each of them must be fulfilled, or the sign does not denote. In other words, these are essential conditions, or distinctive features of the designatum. They are quite parallel in this respect to the distinctive features of the Jakobson–Halle framework (1952): essential properties that are always present (except when they are replaced), and the only properties which need to be included in a specification of the phoneme or the sign. All other—redundant—properties can be discarded from the specification of meaning.

In the present state of semantic investigations, most articles draw upon the intuitions of the theorist in order to isolate these distinctive features and their internal structure. A great deal can be learned through such introspection, especially if intuitions are sharpened, by the use of the right linguistic frames. Let us see how much can be achieved within the categorical view by the use of our linguistic intuitions, beginning with a definition of a cup cast in the model of (1):

(2) The term cup is used for an object which is (a) concrete and (b) inanimate and (c) upwardly concave and (d) a container (e) with a handle (f) made of earthenware or other vitreous material and (g) set on a saucer and (h) used for the consumption of food (i) which is liquid [(j) and hot] . . .

In order to find out which of these ten conditions are criterial, we can apply the test frame proposed by Weinreich, *It's an L but C*. If the property is essential and expected to be present, the result is absurd since *but* implies something contrary to expectation. Thus the absurdity of *It's a chair but you can sit in it* establishes that there is something about the property of seating someone that is essential to chairs. In the test sentences given below, we insert first the property listed as an essential condition in definition (2); on the right, a contrary or opposing property. If the original property cited is essential, criterial, or distinctive, we should have unacceptable or absurd sentences on the left, and acceptable or sensible sentences on the right.

(3)   It's a cup but . . .
a. *it's concrete.   it's abstract.
b. *it's inanimate.   it's alive.
c. *it's concave.   it's convex.
d. *it holds things.   it doesn't hold anything.
e. *it has a handle.   it doesn't have a handle.
f. *it's pottery.   it's made of wax.
g. *it's on a saucer.   it has no saucer.
h. *it's used at meal times.   they use it to store things.
i. *you can drink out of it.   you can eat out of it.
j. ?you can drink hot milk out of it. ?you can drink cold milk out of it.
k. ?it has a stripe on it.   ?it doesn't have a stripe on it.

My own reactions to these sentences are indicated by asterisks or question marks; they suggest that properties (a–i) satisfy this approach to essentiality or criteriality. For item (j) we get two sentences that are equally irrelevant or questionable. There is no reason to think it surprising that we can drink hot milk out of a cup; but equally so, it is not surprising that we can drink cold milk out of it. Similarly, if we add a feature which is obviously accidental and not essential, like a stripe (k), we get questionable results on both sides.[8] It is of course the lack of symmetry between the two opposing sentences rather than the absolute judgment which makes the test reasonably precise.

If the study of linguistic intuitions were a satisfactory approach to the defining of terms, it would seem that linguists have a great deal to contribute to the writing of dictionaries. But lexicography as it has been practised is an art of a different kind, where the intuitions of the

---

[8] Of course one can construct contexts in which it is reasonable to say either form of (k). For example, 'All of the cups in this store have stripes on them. This is a cup but it doesn't have a stripe on it.' But such contexts can be constructed with equal facility for both the positive and negative forms.

lexicographer combine with traditional lore (the definitions found in other dictionaries) and a large body of citations from published sources. The dictionary maker does not rely upon his intuitions to cover the full range of applications and meanings which the term *cup* might have, but tries instead to frame a definition that circumscribes as narrowly as possible the whole range of uses that he can collect. The result is a kind of definition which linguists usually find quite unsatisfactory.

(4) *cup*, n. I. A small open bowl-shaped vessel used chiefly to drink from, with or without a handle or handles, a stem and foot, or a lid; as a wine cup, a Communion cup; specif., a handled vessel of china, earthenware, or the like commonly set on a saucer and used for hot liquid foods such as tea, coffee, or soup.—Webster's New International Dictionary, Second edition.

There are quite a few features of this definition which linguists might find peculiar, but the most objectionable is the use of qualifying words like *chiefly, commonly, or the like,* etc. These are the kinds of indefinite quantifiers that linguistics has been trying to escape from since the early days of comparative method. In the current linguistic framework, a property can be optional or obligatory. If it is optional, then it is in 'free variation' and nothing more can be said about its frequency.[9] Even more objectionable is *with or without a handle, or handles.* Such a phrase is hardly specific to cups; it can be applied to any object in the universe. I myself, for example, come with or without a handle or handles.

Let us ask how a reader is expected to use this definition. Suppose an object is not used to drink from. How does the reader utilize the expression *used chiefly to drink from*? Is the object he is examining less of a cup? Should he then call it *cuppish*, or *a thing like a cup*, or can he go ahead and call it *a cup* just the same? The definition does not help to make the kind of decision which was discussed in section I, where the categorizing spirit of language is invoked to decide if in fact, an object is, or is not, a cup.

Webster's definition goes far beyond this categorizing activity; it has an encyclopedic quality, which could seemingly expand indefinitely to tell us anything or everything ever known about cups. There are of course many other entries besides the principal one that I have quoted. The sixth is the principle generalizing entry which covers the extended and metaphorical uses of cup most freely.

(5)   6. A thing resembling a cup (sense I) in shape or use, or likened to such a utensil; as (*a*) a socket or recess in which something turns, as the hip bone, the recess which a capstan spindle turns, etc. (*b*) any small cavity in the surface of the ground. (*c*) an annular trough, filled with water, at the face of each section of a telescopic gas holder, into which fits the grip of the section next outside. (*d*) in turpentine orcharding, a receptacle shaped like a flowerpot, metal or earthenware, attached to the tree to collect resin.

We wonder whether the first part of this definition could not be added to every noun in the dictionary. Is there any term which cannot be applied to a thing resembling its main referent in shape or use, or likened to it? Beyond this, we have four uses of dazzling specificity, which are obviously inserted only to cover some particular three-by-five slips which the dictionary staff happened to have collected. If the reader is not capable of understanding uses (a–d) without help from the dictionary, it seems unlikely that he will be able to survive in everyday life where terms are freely extended in such a way to even more specific objects.

---

[9] This is a property associated with the categorical view, as discussed in section I above; for further discussion, see Labov (1971).

Thus the Webster definition seems to be overly specific in some areas, but terribly vague in others. No current linguistic text would hold it up as a proper model or guide for semantic description. It is true that it will be contradicted far less often by experience than definition (2). But definition (2) can be defended by saying that it covers only the essential or distinctive properties of a cup; the Webster definition seems to be governed only by the need to cover all of the uses of *cup* that have been accumulated in its files.

The balance of this paper will report experimental studies of the use of the term *cup*. Surprisingly enough, these studies will show that the Webster definition is superior to the criterial definition (2) in every respect. A first indication of this situation appears when we consider some properties of such criterial statements which raise great difficulties for empirical investigations.

The conditions specified in formula (1) are usually taken to indicate the presence or absence of a given feature: that is, they govern the denotation of L by binary decisions. Thus a cup may or may not be concave, may or may not be used as a container. Similarly, in componential analysis we define a relative as either male or female, either colineal or ablineal. But the generation condition is a linear scale; we must establish some criterial value along that scale, such as first ascending generation, to locate *father* (Wallace and Atkins 1960). We do find many such cases of simply yes–no conditions, such as whether a tree has cones or not. But we more commonly encounter dimensions which require us to establish criterial values to complete our definition. For L to denote, C_1 must achieve a critical value. Thus we need a formulation such as

(6) $L(x)$ if C_p and D_r and E_t

where C, D, and E each vary along separate dimensions, and L does not denote if the value of C is less than p, etc. Thus a tree is not a white pine unless it has five needles in each fascicle. But again, it is unusual to find such discrete criterial values in empirical work: normally, the criterial condition is a range of values within which L will denote. Thus we must formulate

(7) $L(x)$ if C_p^q and D_r^s and E_t^u ...

where L does not denote if the value of C is less than p or greater than q, etc. Thus a tree is not a yellow pine if its needles are in bundles of less than two or more than three.

We may note here one further limitation of the traditional, categorical approach to denotative conditions which may cause difficulties: the various conditions C, D, E are normally considered to be independent of each other. It is possible that one condition is dependent on the other in the sense that it is a precondition for the other. Thus the leaves of a pine tree must be needles, implying some maximum of cross-section relative to length. And the needles must be in bundles of a certain number, entailing the existence of needles as a feature superordinate in the taxonomy. But the criterial values for a needle, and the criterial values for numbers of needles in a fascicle, are independent of each other. The number of needles in a bundle required if white pine is to denote are usually independent of the specification of maximum cross-section of the leaves. We do not, for example, say that a white pine is a tree with bundles of five needles if they are thick or three to four when they are thin.[10]

---

[10] There are a few disjunctive statements of this sort in plant taxonomy, but they are rare. As a plant grows, its leaves may become thicker, develop more lobes, and its bark may develop an entirely different form. The difficulties of recognizing immature specimens may require such interdependence of the criterial properties. The fact that the formal taxonomy usually does not reflect such interdependence does not mean that people do not utilize more sophisticated models when they actually recognize trees.

This property of independence of criterial conditions is firmly entrenched in the componential analysis of kinship terms, plant taxonomy, etc., which is the area where the most progress has been made in descriptive semantics. Nevertheless, our empirical investigations will show us that the independence of criterial values is not a fundamental property which governs native competence in the use of words. The formal modifications of (7) necessary to cope with this situation will be developed at the conclusion of our report.

The remaining limitation of the modified categorical formula (7) which we must amend is its discreteness. The criterial conditions C_p^q imply discrete cutting points p and q. Yet in the world of experience boundaries show some degree of *vagueness*, and any formal system which is useful for semantic description must allow us to record, or even measure, this property.

3. THE MEASUREMENT OF VAGUENESS

When we approach the empirical problems of naming things, we find that vagueness is almost a universal property of the criterial ranges C_p to C^q. In kinship terminology, we have ready-made discreteness: there is no intermediate step in the nuclear family between first and second generation, and no vague borderland or fringe area between them. But the borderline between a tree and a shrub is not discrete. Leaves may be deeply lobed or shallowly lobed, but there is a vague area in between where we are in doubt. This vagueness is not a property of our perception or the weakness of our instruments, nor the abstractness of our objects. Some of the most concrete data are by nature vague, and some concrete objects are in themselves vague, as for example, fog.

Can we measure vagueness? At first glance, this may seem to be a self-defeating idea. Yet if we follow the reasoning of Max Black (1949), it seems quite feasible to measure the vagueness of terms within a given context. A term's vagueness, following Black, consists of the existence of objects concerning which it is impossible to say either that the term does or does not denote. He constructs a consistency profile upon three fundamental notions: (1) users of a language; (2) a situation in which a user of a language is trying to apply a term L to an object x; and (3) the consistency of application of L to x. The subjective aspect of vagueness may be thought of as the lack of certainty as to whether the term does or does not denote; and this may be transformed into the consistency with which a given sample of speakers does in fact apply the term. The problem of vagueness is seen most clearly when we have a large number of objects which differ by only small degrees from each other, as in Black's example of a series of chairs which gradually become indistinguishable from a series of blocks of wood. At one end of the series, a single term L clearly denotes; at the other end, it does not; and in the middle we are left in doubt. If the consistency of application of L to x for each of these objects is measured, we obtain a consistency profile. Measurements are not of course comparable except in a given situation, but we can distinguish various types of gradients and opposing relations within that situation and regular transformations of it. A precise symbol will show a sharp gradient, while a vague term will show a very slight one. But more importantly, we will be able to use this mechanism to demonstrate the effect of changes in various properties upon the application of the term, and their mutual interaction.

The present series of studies is based upon the series of cup-like objects shown in Figure 5. The first four cups across the top show increasing ratios of width to depth. If the proportional width of the cup at upper left is taken as 1, then the widths of the cups 1, 2, 3, 4 increase in the

FIG. 5   Series of cup-like objects.

ratios of 1.2, 1.5, and 1.9 to 1, all with constant depth.[11] A fifth decrease in width (No. 20, not shown here) gives us a ratio of 2.5 to 1. Proceeding downward along the left margin, we have five increments of depth with constant width; the depth is increased in the ratios of 1.2, 1.5, 1.9, 2.4, and 3.0 to 1. In the center of the diagram are cups which depart from the concave shape of 1–4 and 5–9. Cups 10, 11, 12 are cylindrical, with increasing depth; and cups 13, 14, 15

[11] The actual ratio of width to depth in the drawings is not immediately obvious, since they are slightly fore-shortened in depth. The figures used throughout this discussion are the relation of the width or depth of a given cup to the width and depth of cup No. 1. I am indebted to Felix Cooper, the well-known illustrator of scientific texts, for the precise execution of this series of drawings.

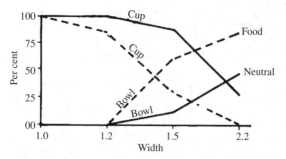

FIG. 6   Consistency profiles for *cup* and *bowl* in Neutral and Food contexts, Group A, N = 11.

show the same increments for the tapering pattern of a truncated cone. In the lower right we have forms that depart maximally from the modal cup at upper left. The short- and long-stemmed cups show variation in the form of the base, and the square and triangular objects show variation in the contour of the perimeter. The drawings of cups are presented to subjects one at a time, in two different randomized orders; the subjects are simply asked to name them. They are then shown the same series of drawings again, and this time asked to imagine in each case that they saw someone with the object in his hand, stirring in sugar with a spoon, and drinking coffee from it (or in some languages, tea), and to name them in this context. In a third series, they are asked to imagine that they came to dinner at someone's house and saw this object sitting on the dinner table, filled with mashed potatoes (rice for some languages). In a fourth series, they are asked to conceive of each of these objects standing on a shelf, each with cut flowers in it. We will refer to these four contexts as the 'Neutral', 'Coffee', 'Food', and 'Flower' contexts.

There is another set of diagrams with no handles, and a third with two handles, which are used in a more limited series of namings. In other series, we specify the material of these cups as china, glass, paper, and metal.

The responses to these tests are in the form of noun phrases, often with a wide range of modifiers. In our present analyses, we consider only the head noun. That is, we do not care whether the object is called *a long cup*, *a funny cup with a stem*, or *a kind of a cup*; as long as the head noun is *cup*, it will be classed here as 'cup'. We have carried out these tests in a fair range of languages, and recently extended this study to contrast bilingual and monolingual speakers of Spanish and English, in various degrees of proficiency. But the material reported here will be drawn from a series of eight investigations of speakers of English, with sample sizes ranging from eleven to twenty-four subjects. The fundamental relations to be discussed here are confirmed with great consistency in each of these tests. The first series was drawn from exploratory interviews in the speech community, but most of the others from classes or series of individual students at Columbia University and at the University of Pennsylvania.[12]

Figures 6 and 7 show a series of consistency profiles for the application of *cup* to a series of objects of increasing width. Figure 6 is for Group A of eleven subjects from the first series in 1964 (without cup No. 20), and Figure 7 is an immediately following series with Group B, also with eleven subjects. The solid lines show the consistency profiles for *cup* and *bowl* in the first, Neutral context. For Group A, the applicability of *cup* is 100 per cent for the first two cups, drops slightly for a ratio of 1.5 to 1, and then plunges sharply to less that 25 per cent for the

[12] I am indebted to Franklin Jones of the University of Pennsylvania, who carried out an extensive series of studies of the denotation of cups and other objects in connection with a study of differences in Spanish and English bilingualism, and to Beatriz Lavandera who completed a comparable series in Buenos Aires.

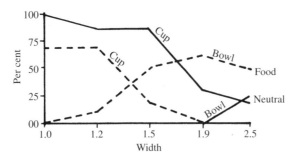

FIG. 7   Consistency profiles denoted as *cup* and *bowl* in Neutral and Food contexts, Group B, N = 11.

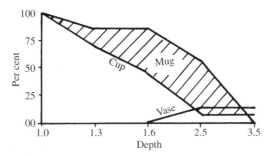

FIG. 8   Consistency profiles denoted as *cup*, *mug*, and *bowl* in Neutral context, by depth for Group A, N = 11.

wider objects. The line crossing from lower left shows the percentage of applications of *bowl* to the same objects. At about the width of 2.2 to 1, the likelihood of the object being called a bowl is roughly equal to the likelihood of its being called a cup. This is the fringe area, in which it is possible to assert with equal truth that the object is a cup and that it is not a cup.

The same relations for the Neutral context appear again in Figure 7, this time with five degrees of width. Again the fringe area cross-over point is at a width ratio of 2.2 to 1.

The dotted lines show the effect of switching the context of denotation to Food—that is, containing mashed potatoes. The pattern is the same as for Neutral, but it is shifted to the left. Now the abrupt drop in the *cup* pattern is after cup No. 2, and the cross-over point is between 2 and 3, that is between the width ratios of 1.2 and 1.5. The same phenomenon appears in both Figures 6 and 7. The term *bowl* is applied more frequently in the transitional area than *cup*, although the modal values are immune from the shift.

Figure 8 shows consistency profiles for objects of increasing depth. Only Group A is shown here; Group B gives similar results. The term *mug* is shown superimposed on instances of *cup*, since as all informants agree that *cup* is a superordinate term for *mug*: that is, *mug* is a kind of *cup*.[13] On the other hand, vases are not kinds of cups. The number of items named as *vase* in the Neutral context is shown by the solid line at the lower right of Figure 8. In Figure 9, the same series of objects are shown in the Flower context; more favorable to *vase* and less favorable to *cup* and *mug*. In fact, *mug* does not appear in the Flower context at all. Here again we see a regular shift of consistency profiles, so that now the cross-over area lies between depths of 1.3 and 1.6, rather than at 3.5.

[13] For more objective evidence on this point, see below.

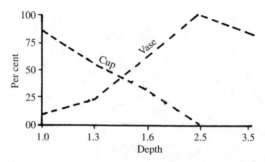

FIG. 9   Consistency profiles denoted as *cup* and *vase* in Flower context, by depth, for Group A, N=11.

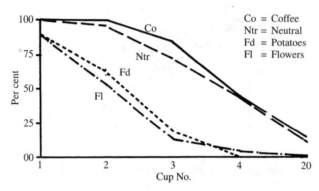

FIG. 10   Consistency profiles for *cup* by width in four contexts, Group C, N=24.

4. THE INTERDEPENDENCE OF CONDITIONS FOR DENOTATION

Many different dimensions and sub-tests within these series confirm the general pattern of Figures 5 and 6: the consistency profiles for any given term are radically shifted as the subjects conceive of the objects in different functional settings.[14] The consistency profiles are regularly elevated for *cup* by the Coffee context, depressed by Food, and even further depressed by the Flower context. The clarity and strength of the effect is illustrated by the fact that it emerges consistently with groups of less than ten subjects. Figure 10 shows the effect of all four contexts on the application of *cup* to containers of increasing width, and Figure 11 the effect on containers of increasing depth. This was a series carried out in 1968 on Group C, with twenty-four subjects. The increment of Coffee over the Neutral context is a slight one in Figure 10, and for these shallow containers the Flower context decreases the use of the term only a little more than Food. In Figure 11 this effect is much greater, as *bowl* competes with *cup* less in the Food context and *vase* competes more with *cup*. The effect contributed by *mug* to *cup* is shown here for the Neutral context only; in the others, *mug* is added to cup, but not shown separately.

---

[14] The subjects show an extraordinary ability to register the effect of different contexts through verbal instructions. Some preliminary tests with more concrete instances of contextual shifting did not show any clearer results, although this is an area to be explored further.

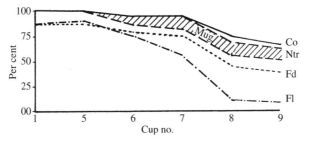

FIG. 11   Consistency profiles for *cup* and *mug* (Neutral) by depth in Group C, N = 24.

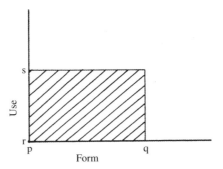

FIG. 12   Orthogonal model for independent conditions for denotation.

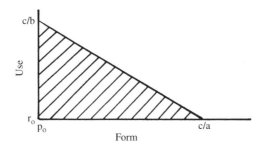

FIG. 13   Linear model for relations between conditions for denotation.

Formal representations

It is normally assumed, as we noted above, that the criteria for denotation are established and selected independently of each other. The relations of form and function would therefore appear on a two-dimensional graph as a rectangular block bounded by the straight lines $C = p$ and $C = q$, as in Figure 12. This is the pattern which we normally find in the schematic representations of componential analysis (Wallace and Atkins 1960, Figure 1). If we take condition C as referring to form (e.g. ratio of width to depth), and condition D as referring to use (e.g. function as a container), then the term always denotes if C lies between p and q, and D lies between r and s. This is the categorical view of denotation, corresponding to formula (1).

The data we derive from our studies of *cup*, *bowl*, *vase*, etc., corresponds to a very different model. Figure 13 shows a linear model which approximates the data. Instead of locating the

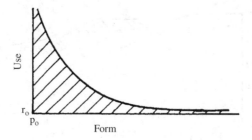

FIG. 14   Hyperbolic model for relations between two conditions for denotation.

outer and inner limits of the conditions C and D, we locate at the origin the modal values of C and D, p_o and r_o. The values of p and r which depart in various ways from this modal value will be located along the ordinate and abscissa respectively. The diagonal line shown in Figure 13 is merely one of many that connect points of equal probability of the term L denoting. To express a quantitative relationship between the values of form and function presupposes that function has been quantified, and in our present state of knowledge this does not seem likely. If that could be done, however, the relationship between form and function might appear as

(8) $a \cdot (p - p_o) + b \cdot (r - r_o) = c$

If the diagonal line of Figure 13 is taken to represent the outer limits of all cases where the probability of L denoting is more than zero, then it will show two specific limits of form and function for cup. When p is equal to the modal value for form p_o, then $(r_o - r) = c/b$, and similarly, when r is equal to the modal value for form r_o, then the outer limits of $(p_o - p)$ will be equal to a quantity c/a. This means that under no circumstances will any object with a form beyond c/a be called a cup.

If this is not the case, and if there is no outer limit of shape or function which limits the use of *cup*, then we would have a hyperbolic model such as Figure 14. Here there are no outer limits. When $p = p_o$, then almost any value of r will permit the application of the term cup, and when $r = r_o$, then any value of the shape p will permit the term to denote. In this case, the relations of use and form would appear as

(9) $(p - p_o) \times (r - r_o) = c$

Thus as $(p - p_o)$ approaches zero, $(r - r_o)$ becomes indefinitely large.

We do not yet have a wide enough range of data to test these models, although the evidence of Figures 6, 8, 9, 10, and 11 argues for an approximation to the linear model of Figure 13. The linearity is most evident in the slopes for *cup*, especially in Neutral and Coffee contexts. In some arrays, we note sudden discontinuities when *vase*, for example, begins to compete actively with *cup* and *mug* in the deepest containers. There are further interrelationships between the invariant core or modal values of one term and the variable skirt of another which must be explored if the model is to be refined.

The location of a subordinate term

Figure 10 showed combined figures for *cup* and *mug*, based on the notion that *mug* is included within the superordinate *cup*. This claim can be supported by examining responses to the cylindrical series of cups 10, 11, and 12, where *mug* is most strongly favored. Figure 15 shows that in the Coffee and Neutral contexts, *mug* expands to its maximum extent with No. 11; in

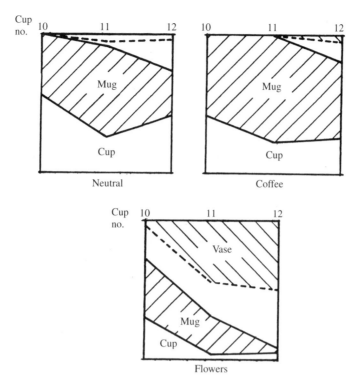

FIG. 15   Consistency profiles for *cup*, *mug*, and *vase* for cylindrical cups of increasing depth in three contexts, Group C, N = 24.

the Coffee context it denotes in over three-quarters of the total responses. Note that the most sensitive index of the predominance of *mug* is its relation to *cup*, for No. 11, the ratio of *mug* to *cup* is quite high, but in No. 10, it represents only about half of the combined category, and in the longer cylinder of No. 12, the proportion of *mug* to *cup* again recedes. The fact that *mug* reaches a maximum at a certain depth, and then recedes, flanked by greater proportions of *cup* on both sides, indicates that *cup* is the residual or unmarked category out of which *mug* is specified. Thus in the most favored Coffee and Neutral contexts, we observe the following pattern in the ratios of mug to cup:

	Mug/Cup		
	No. 10	No. 11	No. 12
Coffee context	1.4	2.4	1.5
Neutral context	.8	1.8	.8

It appears that the empirical study of denotation can offer us further insight into the superordinate/subordinate relationship through the study of such regular patterns.

Further articulation of function and form

In recent tests we have explored the possibility of further subdividing the functional scale, in order to show more delicate shifting, and looking forward to ordering the functional contexts by more exact criteria. Figure 16 shows the consistency profile for *cup* in a recent test with the

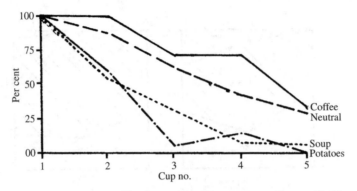

FIG. 16   Consistency profiles for *cup* in four contexts, Group D, N = 15.

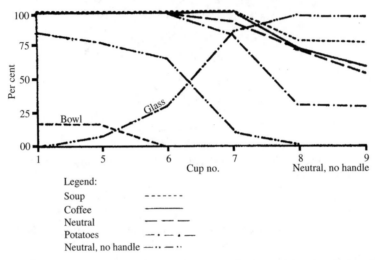

FIG. 17   Consistency profiles for *cup* in five contexts by depth, and *bowl* and *glass* in one context (Neutral, no handle). Group D, N = 15.

fifteen subjects of Group D, where the Food context was subdivided into Soup and Potatoes. Soup is normally a hot liquid, like coffee, but it is eaten rather than drunk, and is often served in a bowl. Potatoes, as a solid food, are regularly served in a bowl and never in a cup, and we would thus expect that Potatoes favors *cup* even less than Soup. Figure 16 does not bear out this expectation, however. Again, the largest break is between Coffee and Neutral contexts, on the one hand, and the food contexts on the other. But Soup and Potatoes are evidently not distinguished. This may be due to the fact that both of these contexts favor *bowl* strongly at the expense of *cup*, except in the modal values of *cup*.

Figure 17 shows the same contexts in a range of cups of increasing depth, with some additional details. Here the role of Soup is suddenly reversed. Instead of being confounded with the Potato context, it now appears to be the context which favors *cup* more strongly than any other, even Coffee. This must be because *cup* is not now competing with *bowl* in the Soup context, since the deeper containers are less like bowls than the modal cup container No. 1. Again, we note that the largest difference between contexts is that which separates Food (potatoes) from the others.

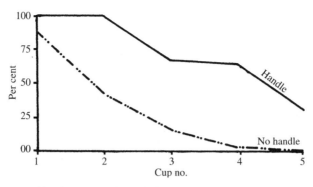

FIG. 18   Consistency profiles for *cup* with and without a handle in Neutral context, for Group D, N = 15.

Below the Potatoes profile, there is one in which *cup* is even more disfavored. This is the series of diagrams of cup without handles (see Figure 17). Even in the neutral context, the effect of removing the handle appears to be greater than the shifting context with the handle. Here we can see how strongly *glass* competes with *cup* in this handle-less condition, with a cross-over point between Nos. 6 and 7. The effect of removing the handle from the containers is seen even more clearly in Figure 18, which shows the application of *cup* to objects of increasing width, with and without a handle.

5. REDEFINING CUP

We may now attempt to utilize our new information about the conditions for denotation of cup in reconstructing the definition of this term. Returning to the two definitions presented in section 2, we find that (2) is even less attractive than ever, but Webster's second edition definition (4) does not look quite as bad as it did at first. The expression *with or without a handle* can now be read as *usually with a handle, sometimes without*, in line with the findings presented in Figure 18. Expressions such as *used chiefly to drink from, commonly set on a saucer, used for hot liquid foods*, etc., express the regularities which were brought out in Figures 6–11. The writers of the definition seemed to anticipate by one means or another many of the findings of our more objective procedures, and they have resolutely adhered to terms which may appear uselessly vague to less experienced lexicographers. This should not be surprising, as we have found similar tendencies in the treatment of variability by practising phonologists, who have undertaken the task of describing new languages (Labov 1971). Though the theory they are operating under strongly forbids them to characterize the frequency of free variants, they regularly insist on inserting such informal qualifiers after they have stated the principal allophonic distributions. Thus we find Bucca and Lesser writing about Kitsai voiceless *I*:

It is in free variation with i. The free variation is less frequent in final position where i is more used; and in medial position before the consonantal groups ts, st, sk, sn, tjk, where I is predominant (1969: 11).

Such statements about relations more or less express informally the variable constraints which are formalized in recent direct studies of variability (Labov 1969, Cedergren and Sankoff 1974). In the same way, good lexicographers make an informal attempt to capture the variable properties which reflect the deep and subtle competence of the native speaker, a competence he must have to name the wide variety of new and intermediate objects in the world.

But the Webster definition still fails to capture the most systematic and intricate aspect of variability in the use of *cup*. On the one hand, there seems to be a wide range of objects that we call cup without hesitation. But the size of that invariant range fluctuates systematically according to function, material, and other properties. As we examine the figures given above, there appears beyond the invariant range a systematic decline, almost linear, in the probability of an object being called a cup. Though a hyperbolic, asymptotic model like Figure 14 may be possible, most of our data is linear, and whenever we actually observe a terminal point, it is quite sharp. We can therefore construct a definition which reflects this double variability: the invariant core is itself variable in extent, controlled by the interrelation of a number of factors, while the variable skirt follows a relatively simple downward slope.[15]

> The term *cup* is regularly used to denote round containers with a ratio of width to depth of $1 \pm r$ where $r \leq r_b$, and $r_b = \alpha_1 + \alpha_2 + \dots \alpha_v$ and α_i is a positive quantity when the feature i is present and 0 otherwise.
> feature 1 = with one handle
> 2 = made of opaque vitreous material
> 3 = used for consumption of food
> 4 = used for consumption of liquid food
> 5 = used for consumption of hot liquid food
> 6 = with a saucer
> 7 = tapering
> 8 = circular in cross-section

> *Cup* is used variably to denote such containers with ratios of width to depth of $1 \pm r$ where $r_b \leq r \leq r_t$ with a probability of $r_t - r/r_t - r_b$. The quantity $1 \pm r_b$ expresses the distance from the modal value of width to height.[16]

The various factors controlling the invariant core are ordered in accordance with the data presented here, rather than the dictionary definition itself, but there is no contradiction between them. The expression *regularly used* is intended to capture the fact that there are objects which in the range of contexts indicated will be called *cups* by practically all speakers.

The second half of the definition reflects the general fact that the vagueness profile of *cup* is approximately linear, so that the probability of applying *cup* to an object is proportional to the distance one has moved from the outer limit of the invariant core and the cut-off point r_t. The quantity $(r_t - r_b)$ may vary considerably, and so alter the slope of the variable skirt or fringe of cup-like objects.[17]

This definition is thus designed to register the categorical character of our lexicon along with its flexibility and adaptability for application to a wide range of objects. We can schematize this relation by Figure 19, which shows the two aspects of variability superimposed upon an item-speaker matrix similar to the item-property matrices of section 1.

---

[15] The basic form of the rule presented here is due to David Sankoff of the Centre des Recherches Mathématiques in Montreal.

[16] The slope of the variable area is itself quite variable, but it cannot be specified as long as function is not a quantified linear scale.

[17] In actual fact, the ratio of width to height which is most typical of coffee cups in American households is considerably less than 1, reflected in the way we have located cup No. 1. Cup No. 5 exhibits in perspective this 1:1 ratio, and a glance at the various representations of increasing depth shows that it is in fact favored as strongly as No. 1.

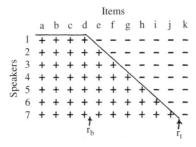

Fig. 19　Invariant core and variable range for denotation of items by speakers.

The model of Figure 19 is an elaboration of Figure 3: it reflects the categorical nature of the phenomenon by delineating an invariant core; but it also specifies the variable location of the boundary which marks the limits of categories and the limitations of the categorizing process.

The study of variability is the obverse of the study of invariance; one without the other has little significance, and a linguistic study devoted to only one or the other misses the richness of the phenomenon. It is not true that everything varies, anymore than it is true that everything remains distinct and discrete. We must locate the boundary between the invariant and variable areas of language with the same precision that we have learned to use in studying the variable elements themselves (Labov 1972b). We cannot escape the overall implications of section 1: that language is essentially a categorical device. If we want to understand it, we have to do more than count the categories; we have to measure them, weigh them, and eventually record them at work.

6. HOW AN OBJECT IS NOT KNOWN PER SE

A review of the linguistic literature on distinctive features reinforces our conviction that there is no significant difference between the distinctive/redundant opposition and the Aristotelian notion of essence and accident. A search for distinctive features is fundamentally a search for the Aristotelian essence, through which the thing itself is to be known.

The essence (τὸ τί ἦν) of each thing is that which it is said to be *per se* (καδ αὐτο). (*Metaphysics* VII.IV.4)

Essence is opposed to accident, and reflects the way things really are, intrinsically, and cannot help being. One's essence is identical with one's own nature, as Aristotle points out, continuing the above passage:

'To be you' is not 'to be cultured', because you are not of your own nature cultured. Your essence, then, is that which you are said to be of your own nature.

Furthermore, it is clear that for Aristotle, the essence of a substance is identical with and inseparable from the thing itself. But essence is somehow the verbalizable aspect of substance:

It is obvious, then, that the definition is the formula (λόγος) of the essence. (VII.V.7)

The definition we have presented in section 4 is obviously not the essence of a cup, nor limited to essential attributes. There is no question of a handle or a saucer being an essential attribute of a cup, anymore than 'white' is an essential part of the essence of 'man' (to use Aristotle's favorite example). One cannot separate an essential attribute from the object, and cups without handles are common enough. In our definition, properties such as these play an important role in circumscribing the outer range of regular usage, which varies with their presence or absence. Our ability to recognize a cup depends upon our ability to recognize such accidents, contrary to the opinion of Aristotle:

That each individual thing is one and the same thing with its essence, and not merely accidentally so, is apparent, not only from the foregoing considerations, but because to have knowledge of the individual is to have knowledge of its essence. (VII.VI.9)

These quotations from the philosopher should make it quite evident that scholastic linguistic theory is quite in harmony with Aristotle's categorical viewpoint, which is in almost every detail the categorical view sketched in section 1. It is not uncommon for linguists to insist that one or the other aspect or property of an object is the essential property for the naming of it; as for example, the claim that function is the essential thing in naming objects while form is accidental.[18] The empirical evidence presented here will serve to underline the interrelation of form and function, and their symmetry in the process of denotation. A secular approach to further research in semantic description will necessarily carry us outside of the schools, beyond the limitations of scholastic intuitions, and beyond the categorical view which survives intact in the doctrines of the schoolmen.

The experimental studies reported here represent only one step outward from this scholastic setting. Further research will carry us towards experimentation in a more natural setting (Labov 1971). But the results so far are encouraging enough to suggest that semantic theory, like phonological theory, can find firm ground if we take even one step away from the intuition of the theorist and towards the observation of language in use.

REFERENCES

Aristotle (1933). *The Metaphysics*. With translation by H. Tredennick. Cambridge, Mass.: Harvard University Press.

Bailey, C.-J. N. (1971). 'Building rate into a dynamic theory of linguistic description'. *Working Papers in Linguistics*. Honolulu: University of Hawaii.

Bickerton, D. (1971). 'Inherent variability and variable rules'. *Foundations of Language* 7: 457–92.

——(1972). 'The structure of polylectal grammars'. In Georgetown University Monograph Series on Languages and Linguistics, Monograph 25, *Report of the 23rd Annual Round Table*. Washington, DC: Georgetown University Press.

Black, M. (1949). *Language and Philosophy*. Ithaca, NY: Cornell University Press.

Bucca, S., and A. Lesser (1969). 'Kitsai phonology and morphophonemics'. *IJAL* 35: 7–19.

Cedergren, H., and D. Sankoff (1974). 'Variable rules: performance as a statistical reflection of competence'. *Language* 50: 333–55.

DeCamp, D. (1971). 'Toward a generative analysis of a post-creole speech continuum'. In D. Hymes (ed.), *Pidginization and Creolization of Languages*. Cambridge: Cambridge University Press.

Hockett, C. F. (1958). *A Course in Modern Linguistics*. New York: Macmillan.

Jakobson, R., G. Fant, and M. Halle (1952). *Preliminaries to Speech Analysis*. Cambridge, Mass.: MIT Press.

Katz, J. J., and J. A. Fodor (1963). 'The structure of a semantic theory'. *Language* 39: 170–210.

Labov, W. (1966). 'The linguistic variable as a structural unit'. *Washington Linguistics Review* 3: 4–22.

——(1969). 'Contraction, deletion, and inherent variability of the English copula'. *Language* 45: 715–62.

---

[18] From an oral presentation of Noam Chomsky in Los Angeles, 1966, developing a point of view based upon thought experiments performed by Philippa Foot.

——(1971). 'Methodology'. In W. Dingwall (ed.), *A Survey of Linguistic Science*. College Park, Md.: Linguistics Program, University of Maryland, 412–97.

——(1972a). 'For an end to the uncontrolled use of linguistic intuitions'. Paper presented to the Linguistic Society of America, Atlanta, Dec.

——(1972b). 'Negative attraction and negative concord in English grammar'. *Language* 48: 773–818.

Martinet, A. (1939). 'Un ou deux phonèmes?' *Acta Linguistica* 1: 94–103.

Quirk, R. (1965). 'Descriptive statement and serial relationship'. *Language* 41: 205–17.

Stankiewicz, E. (1957). 'On discreteness and continuity in structural dialectology'. *Word* 13: 44–59.

Wallace, A. F., and J. Atkins (1960). 'The meaning of kinship terms'. *American Anthropologist* 62: 58–80.

Weinreich, U. (1954). 'Is a structural dialectology possible?' *Word* 10: 388–400.

——(1962). 'Lexicographic definition in descriptive semantics'. *Problems in Lexicography* 28(4) April.

—— W. Labov, and M. Herzog (1968). 'Empirical foundations for a theory of language change'. In W. Lehmann and Y. Malkiel (eds.), *Directions for Historical Linguistics*. Austin: University of Texas Press, 97–195.

Principles of Categorization

ELEANOR ROSCH

The following is a taxonomy of the animal kingdom. It has been attributed to an ancient Chinese encyclopedia entitled the *Celestial Emporium of Benevolent Knowledge*:

On those remote pages it is written that animals are divided into (a) those that belong to the Emperor, (b) embalmed ones, (c) those that are trained, (d) suckling pigs, (e) mermaids, (f) fabulous ones, (g) stray dogs, (h) those that are included in this classification, (i) those that tremble as if they were mad, (j) innumerable ones, (k) those drawn with a very fine camel's hair brush, (l) others, (m) those that have just broken a flower vase, (n) those that resemble flies from a distance. (Borges, 1966, p. 108)

Conceptually, the most interesting aspect of this classification system is that it does not exist. Certain types of categorizations may appear in the imagination of poets, but they are never found in the practical or linguistic classes of organisms or of man-made objects used by any of the cultures of the world. For some years, I have argued that human categorization should not be considered the arbitrary product of historical accident or of whimsy but rather the result of psychological principles of categorization, which are subject to investigation. This chapter is a summary and discussion of those principles.

The chapter is divided into five parts. The first part presents the two general principles that are proposed to underlie categorization systems. The second part shows the way in which these principles appear to result in a basic and primary level of categorization in the levels of abstraction in a taxonomy. It is essentially a summary of the research already reported on basic level objects (Rosch et al., 1976). Thus the second section may be omitted by the reader already sufficiently familiar with that material. The third part relates the principles of categorization to the formation of prototypes in those categories that are at the same level of abstraction in a taxonomy. In particular, this section attempts to clarify the operational concept of prototypicality and to separate that concept from claims concerning the role of prototypes in cognitive processing, representation, and learning for which there is little evidence. The fourth part presents two issues that are problematical for the abstract principles of categorization stated in Part I [not included in this volume]: (1) the relation of context to basic level objects and prototypes; and (2) assumptions about the nature of the attributes of real-world objects that underlie the claim that there is structure in the world. The fifth part is a report of initial attempts to base an analysis of the attributes, functions, and contexts of objects on a consideration of objects as props in culturally defined events.

It should be noted that the issues in categorization with which we are primarily concerned have to do with explaining the categories found in a culture and coded by the language of that culture at a particular point in time. When we speak of the formation of categories, we mean their formation in the culture. This point is often misunderstood. The principles of

* Eleanor Rosch, 'Principles of categorization', in Eleanor Rosch and Barbara B. Lloyd (eds.), *Cognition and Categorization* (Hillsdale, NJ: Lawrence Erlbaum Associates, 1978), 27–48. © 1978 Lawrence Erlbaum Associates. Reprinted by permission.

categorization proposed are not as such intended to constitute a theory of the development of categories in children born into a culture nor to constitute a model of how categories are processed (how categorizations are made) in the minds of adult speakers of a language.

THE PRINCIPLES

Two general and basic principles are proposed for the formation of categories: the first has to do with the function of category systems and asserts that the task of category systems is to provide maximum information with the least cognitive effort; the second has to do with the structure of the information so provided and asserts that the perceived world comes as structured information rather than as arbitrary or unpredictable attributes. Thus maximum information with least cognitive effort is achieved if categories map the perceived world structure as closely as possible. This condition can be achieved either by the mapping of categories to given attribute structures or by the definition or redefinition of attributes to render a given set of categories appropriately structured. These principles are elaborated in the following.

Cognitive economy

The first principle contains the almost common-sense notion that, as an organism, what one wishes to gain from one's categories is a great deal of information about the environment while conserving finite resources as much as possible. To categorize a stimulus means to consider it, for purposes of that categorization, not only equivalent to other stimuli in the same category but also different from stimuli not in that category. On the one hand, it would appear to the organism's advantage to have as many properties as possible predictable from knowing any one property, a principle that would lead to formation of large numbers of categories with as fine discriminations between categories as possible. On the other hand, one purpose of categorization is to reduce the infinite differences among stimuli to behaviorally and cognitively usable proportions. It is to the organism's advantage not to differentiate one stimulus from others when that differentiation is irrelevant to the purposes at hand.

Perceived world structure

The second principle of categorization asserts that unlike the sets of stimuli used in traditional laboratory-concept attainment tasks, the perceived world is not an unstructured total set of equiprobable co-occurring attributes. Rather, the material objects of the world are perceived to possess (in Garner's, 1974, sense) high correlational structure. That is, given a knower who perceives the complex attributes of feathers, fur, and wings, it is an empirical fact provided by the perceived world that wings co-occur with feathers more than with fur. And given an actor with the motor programs for sitting, it is a fact of the perceived world that objects with the perceptual attributes of chairs are more likely to have functional sit-on-able-ness than objects with the appearance of cats. In short, combinations of what we perceive as the attributes of real objects do not occur uniformly. Some pairs, triples, etc., are quite probable, appearing in combination sometimes with one, sometimes another attribute; others are rare; others logically cannot or empirically do not occur.

It should be emphasized that we are talking about the perceived world and not a metaphysical world without a knower. What kinds of attributes *can* be perceived are, of course, species-specific. A dog's sense of smell is more highly differentiated than a human's, and the structure of the world for a dog must surely include attributes of smell that we, as a species, are incapable of perceiving. Furthermore, because a dog's body is constructed differently from a human's, its motor interactions with objects are necessarily differently structured. The "out there" of a bat, a frog, or a bee is surely more different still from that of a human. What attributes *will* be perceived given the ability to perceive them is undoubtedly determined by many factors having to do with the functional needs of the knower interacting with the physical and social environment. One influence on how attributes will be defined by humans is clearly the category system already existent in the culture at a given time. Thus, our segmentation of a bird's body such that there is an attribute called "wings" may be influenced not only by perceptual factors such as the gestalt laws of form that would lead us to consider the wings as a separate part (Palmer, 1977) but also by the fact that at present we already have a cultural and linguistic category called "birds." Viewing attributes as, at least in part, constructs of the perceiver does not negate the higher-order structural fact about attributes at issue, namely that the attributes of wings and that of feathers do co-occur in the perceived world.

These two basic principles of categorization, a drive toward cognitive economy combined with structure in the perceived world, have implications both for the level of abstraction of categories formed in a culture and for the internal structure of those categories once formed.

For purposes of explication, we may conceive of category systems as having both a vertical and horizontal dimension. The vertical dimension concerns the level of inclusiveness of the category—the dimension along which the terms collie, dog, mammal, animal, and living thing vary. The horizontal dimension concerns the segmentation of categories at the same level of inclusiveness—the dimension on which dog, cat, car, bus, chair, and sofa vary. The implication of the two principles of categorization for the vertical dimension is that not all possible levels of categorization are equally good or useful; rather, the most basic level of categorization will be the most inclusive (abstract) level at which the categories can mirror the structure of attributes perceived in the world. The implication of the principles of categorization for the horizontal dimension is that to increase the distinctiveness and flexibility of categories, categories tend to become defined in terms of prototypes or prototypical instances that contain the attributes most representative of items inside and least representative of items outside the category.

THE VERTICAL DIMENSION OF CATEGORIES: BASIC-LEVEL OBJECTS

In a programmatic series of experiments, we have attempted to argue that categories within taxonomies of concrete objects are structured such that there is generally one level of abstraction at which the most basic category cuts can be made (Rosch et al., 1976a). By *category* is meant a number of objects that are considered equivalent. Categories are generally designated by names (e.g., *dog*, *animal*). A *taxonomy* is a system by which categories are related to one another by means of class inclusion. The greater the inclusiveness of a category within a taxonomy, the higher the level of abstraction. Each category within a taxonomy is entirely included within one other category (unless it is the highest-level category) but is not exhaustive of that more inclusive category (see Kay, 1971). Thus the term *level of abstraction* within a taxonomy refers to a particular level of inclusiveness. A familiar taxonomy is the Linnean system for the classification of animals.

Our claims concerning a basic level of abstraction can be formalized in terms of cue validity (Rosch et al., 1976a) or in terms of the set theoretic representation of similarity provided by Tversky (1977). Cue validity is a probabilistic concept; the validity of a given cue x as a predictor of a given category y (the conditional probability of y/x) increases as the frequency with which cue *x* is associated with category *y* increases and decreases as the frequency with which cue *x* is associated with categories other than *y* increases (Beach, 1964a, 1964b; Reed, 1972). The cue validity of an entire category may be defined as the summation of the cue validities for that category of each of the attributes of the category. A category with high cue validity is, by definition, more differentiated from other categories than one of lower cue validity. The elegant formulization that Tversky (1978) provides in chapter 4 [not included] is in terms of the variable "category resemblance," which is defined as the weighted sum of the measures of all of the common features within a category minus the sum of the measures of all of the distinctive features. Distinctive features include those that belong to only some members of a given category as well as those belonging to contrasting categories. Thus Tversky's formalization does not weight the effect of contrast categories as much as does the cue validity formulation. Tversky suggests that two disjoint classes tend to be combined whenever the weight of the added common features exceeds the weight of the distinctive features.

A working assumption of the research on basic objects is that (1) in the perceived world, information-rich bundles of perceptual and functional attributes occur that form natural discontinuities, and that (2) basic cuts in categorization are made at these discontinuities. Suppose that basic objects (e.g., chair, car) are at the most inclusive level at which there are attributes common to all or most members of the category. Then both total cue validities and category resemblance are maximized at that level of abstraction at which basic objects are categorized. This is, categories one level more abstract will be superordinate categories (e.g., furniture, vehicle) whose members share only a few attributes among each other. Categories below the basic level will be bundles of common and, thus, predictable attributes and functions but contain many attributes that overlap with other categories (for example, kitchen chair shares most of its attributes with other kinds of chairs).

Superordinate categories have lower total cue validity and lower category resemblance than do basic-level categories, because they have fewer common attributes; in fact, the category resemblance measure of items within the superordinate can even be negative due to the high ratio of distinctive to common features. Subordinate categories have lower total cue validity than do basic categories, because they also share most attributes with contrasting subordinate categories; in Tversky's terms, they tend to be combined because the weight of the added common features tend to exceed the weight of the distinctive features. That basic objects are categories at the level of abstraction that maximizes cue validity and maximizes category resemblance is another way of asserting that basic objects are the categories that best mirror the correlational structure of the environment.

We chose to look at concrete objects because they appeared to be a domain that was at once an indisputable aspect of complex natural language classifications yet at the same time were amenable to methods of empirical analysis. In our investigations of basic categories, the correlational structure of concrete objects was considered to consist of a number of inseparable aspects of form and function, any one of which could serve as the starting point for analysis. Four investigations provided converging operational definitions of the basic level of abstraction: attributes in common, motor movements in common, objective similarity in shape, and identifiability of averaged shapes.

Common attributes

Ethnobiologists had suggested on the basis of linguistic criteria and field observation that the folk genus was the level of classification at which organisms had bundles of attributes in common and maximum discontinuity between classes. The purpose of our research was to

TABLE I   Examples of taxonomies used in basic object research

Superordinate	Basic level	Subordinate
Furniture	Chair	Kitchen chair
		Living-room chair
	Table	Kitchen table
		Dining-room table
	Lamp	Floor lamp
		Desk lamp
Tree	Oak	White oak
		Red oak
	Maple	Silver maple
		Sugar maple
	Birch	River birch
		White birch

provide a systematic empirical study of the co-occurrence of attributes in the most common taxonomies of biological and man-made objects in our own culture.

The hypothesis that basic level objects are the most inclusive level of classification at which objects have numbers of attributes in common was tested for categories at three levels of abstraction for nine taxonomies: tree, bird, fish, fruit, musical instruments, tool, clothing, furniture, and vehicle. Examples of the three levels for one biological and one nonbiological taxonomy are shown in Table 1. Criteria for choice of these specific items were that the taxonomies contain the most common (defined by word frequency) categories of concrete nouns in English, that the levels of abstraction bear simple class-inclusion relations to each other, and that those class-inclusion relations be generally known to our subjects (be agreed upon by a sample of native English speakers). The middle level of abstraction was the hypothesized basic level. For nonbiological taxonomies, this corresponded to the intuition of the experimenters (which also turned out to be consistent with Berlin's linguistic criteria); for biological categories, we assumed that the basic level would be the level of the folk generic.

Subjects received sets of words taken from these nine taxonomies; the subject's task was to list all of the attributes he could think of that were true of the items included in the class of things designated by each object name. Thus, for purposes of this study, attributes were defined operationally as whatever subjects agreed them to be with no implications for whether such analysis of an object could or could not be perceptually considered prior to knowledge of the object itself. Results of the study were as predicted: very few attributes were listed for the superordinate categories, a significantly greater number listed for the supposed basic-level objects, and not significantly more attributes listed for subordinate-level objects than for basic-level. An additional study showed essentially the same attributes listed for visually present objects as for the object names. The single unpredicted result was that for the three biological taxonomies, the basic level, as defined by numbers of attributes in common, did not occur at the level of the folk generic but appeared at the level we had originally expected to be superordinate (e.g., *tree* rather than *oak*).

Motor movements

Inseparable from the perceived attributes of objects are the ways in which humans habitually use or interact with those objects. For concrete objects, such interactions take the form of motor movements. For example, when performing the action of sitting down on a chair, a sequence of body and muscle movements are typically made that are inseparable from the nature of the attributes of chairs—legs, seat, back, etc. This aspect of objects is particularly important in light of the role that sensory-motor interaction with the world appears to play in the development of thought (Bruner, Olver, and Greenfield, 1966; Nelson, 1974; Piaget, 1952).

In our study of motor movements, each of the sets of words used in the previous experiment was administered to new subjects. A subject was asked to describe, in as much finely analyzed detail as possible, the sequences of motor movements he made when using or interacting with the object. Tallies of agreed upon listings of the same movements of the same body part in the same part of the movement sequence formed the unit of analysis. Results were identical to those of the attribute listings; basic objects were the most general classes to have motor sequences in common. For example, there are few motor programs we carry out to items of furniture in general and several specific motor programs carried out in regard to sitting down on chairs, but we sit on kitchen and living-room chairs using essentially the same motor programs.

Similarity in shapes

Another aspect of the meaning of a class of objects is the appearance of the objects in the class. In order to be able to analyze correlational structures by different but converging methods, it was necessary to find a method of analyzing similarity in the visual aspects of the objects that was not dependent on subjects' descriptions, that was free from effects of the object's name (which would not have been the case for subjects' ratings of similarity), and that went beyond similarity of analyzable, listable attributes that had already been used in the first study described. For this purpose, outlines of the shape of two-dimensional representations of objects were used, an integral aspect of natural forms. Similarity in shape was measured by the amount of overlap of the two outlines when the outlines (normalized for size and orientation) were juxtaposed.

Results showed that the ratio of overlapped to nonoverlapped area when two objects from the same basic-level category (e.g., two cars) were superimposed was far greater than when two objects from the same superordinate category were superimposed (e.g., a car and a motorcycle). Although some gain in ratio of overlap to nonoverlap also occurred for sub-ordinate category objects (e.g., two sports cars), the gain obtained by shifting from basic-level to subordinate objects was significantly less than the gain obtained by shifting from super-ordinate to basic-level objects.

Identifiability of averaged shapes

If the basic level is the most inclusive level at which shapes of objects of a class are similar, a possible result of such similarity may be that the basic level is also the most inclusive level at which an averaged shape of an object can be recognized. To test this hypothesis, the same normalized superimposed shapes used in the previous experiment were used to draw an average outline of the overlapped figures. Subjects were then asked to identify both the superordinate category and the specific object depicted. Results showed that basic objects were the most general and inclusive categories at which the objects depicted could be identified. Furthermore, overlaps of subordinate objects were no more identifiable than objects at the basic level.

In summary, our four converging operational definitions of basic objects all indicated the same level of abstraction to be basic in our taxonomies. Admittedly, the basic level for biological objects was not that predicted by the folk genus; however, this fact appeared to be simply accounted for by our subjects' lack of knowledge of the additional depth of real-world attribute structure available at the level of the folk generic (see Rosch et al., 1976a).

IMPLICATIONS FOR OTHER FIELDS

The foregoing theory of categorization and basic objects has implications for several traditional areas of study in psychology; some of these have been tested.

Imagery

The fact that basic-level objects were the most inclusive categories at which an averaged member of the category could be identified suggested that basic objects might be the most inclusive categories for which it was possible to form a mental image isomorphic to the appearance of members of the class as a whole. Experiments using a signal-detection paradigm and a priming paradigm, both of which have been previously argued to be measures of imagery (Peterson and Graham, 1974; Rosch, 1975c), verified that, in so far as it was meaningful to use the term *imagery*, basic objects appeared to be the most abstract categories for which an image could be reasonably representative of the class as a whole.

Perception

From all that has been said of the nature of basic classifications, it would hardly be reasonable to suppose that in perception of the world, objects were first categorized either at the most abstract or at the most concrete level possible. Two separate studies of picture verification (Rosch et al., 1976a; Smith, Balzano, and Walker, 1978) indicate that, in fact, objects may be first seen or recognized as members of their basic category, and that only with the aid of additional processing can they be identified as members of their superordinate or subordinate category.

Development

We have argued that classification into categories at the basic level is overdetermined because perception, motor movements, functions, and iconic images would all lead to the same level of categorization. Thus basic objects should be the first categorizations of concrete objects made by children. In fact, for our nine taxonomies, the basic level was the first named. And even when naming was controlled, pictures of several basic-level objects were sorted into groups "because they were the same type of thing" long before such a technique of sorting has become general in children.

Language

From all that has been said, we would expect the most useful and, thus, most used name for an item to be the basic-level name. In fact, we found that adults almost invariably named pictures of the subordinate items of the nine taxonomies at the basic level, although they knew the correct superordinate and subordinate names for the objects. On a more speculative level, in the evolution of languages, one would expect names to evolve first for basic-level objects, spreading both upward and downward as taxonomies increased in depth. Of great relevance for this hypothesis are Berlin's (1972) claims for such a pattern for the evolution of plant names, and our own (Rosch et al., 1976a) and Newport and Bellugi's (1978) finding for American Sign Language of the Deaf, that it was the basic-level categories that were most often coded by single signs and super- and subordinate categories that were likely to be missing. Thus a wide range of converging operations verify as basic the same levels of abstraction.

THE HORIZONTAL DIMENSION: INTERNAL STRUCTURE OF CATEGORIES: PROTOTYPES

Most, if not all, categories do not have clear-cut boundaries. To argue that basic object categories follow clusters of perceived attributes is not to say that such attribute clusters are necessarily discontinuous.

In terms of the principles of categorization proposed earlier, cognitive economy dictates that categories tend to be viewed as being as separate from each other and as clear-cut as possible. One way to achieve this is by means of formal, necessary and sufficient criteria for category membership. The attempt to impose such criteria on categories marks virtually all definitions in the tradition of Western reason. The psychological treatment of categories in the standard concept-identification paradigm lies within this tradition. Another way to achieve separateness and clarity of actually continuous categories is by conceiving of each category in terms of its clear cases rather than its boundaries. As Wittgenstein (1953) has pointed out, categorical judgments become a problem only if one is concerned with boundaries—in the normal course of life, two neighbors know on whose property they are standing without exact demarcation of the boundary line. Categories can be viewed in terms of their clear cases if the perceiver places emphasis on the correlational structure of perceived attributes such that the categories are represented by their most structured portions.

By prototypes of categories we have generally meant the clearest cases of category membership defined operationally by people's judgments of goodness of membership in the category. A great deal of confusion in the discussion of prototypes has arisen from two sources. First, the notion of prototypes has tended to become reified as though it meant a specific category member or mental structure. Questions are then asked in an either–or fashion about whether something is or is not the prototype or part of the prototype in exactly the same way in which the question would previously have been asked about the category boundary. Such thinking precisely violates the Wittgensteinian insight that we can judge how clear a case something is and deal with categories on the basis of clear cases in the total absence of information about boundaries. Second, the empirical findings about prototypicality have been confused with theories of processing—that is, there has been a failure to distinguish the structure of categories from theories concerning the use of that structure in processing. Therefore, let us first attempt to look at prototypes in as purely structural a fashion as possible. We will focus on what may be said about prototypes based on operational definitions and empirical findings alone without the addition of processing assumptions.

Perception of typicality differences is, in the first place, an empirical fact of people's judgments about category membership. It is by now a well-documented finding that subjects overwhelmingly agree in their judgments of how good an example or clear a case members are of a category, even for categories about whose boundaries they disagree (Rosch, 1974, 1975b). Such judgments are reliable even under changes of instructions and items (Rips, Shoben, and Smith, 1973; Rosch, 1975b, 1975c; Rosch and Mervis, 1975). Were such agreement and reliability in judgment not to have been obtained, there would be no further point in discussion or investigation of the issue. However, given the empirical verification of degree of prototypicality, we can proceed to ask what principles determine which items will be judged the more prototypical and what other variables might be affected by prototypicality.

In terms of the basic principles of category formation, the formation of category prototypes should, like basic levels of abstraction, be determinate and be closely related to the initial formation of categories. For categories of concrete objects (which do not have a physiological basis, as categories such as colors and forms apparently do—Rosch, 1974), a reasonable hypothesis is that prototypes develop through the same principles such as maximization of cue validity and maximization of category resemblance[1] as those principles governing the formation of the categories themselves.

In support of such a hypothesis, Rosch and Mervis (1975) have shown that the more prototypical a category a member is rated, the more attributes it has in common with other members of the category and the fewer attributes in common with members of the contrasting categories. This finding was demonstrated for natural language superordinate categories, for natural language basic-level categories, and for artificial categories in which the definition of attributes and the amount of experience with items was completely specified and controlled. The same basic principles can be represented in ways other than through attributes in common. Because the present theory is a structural theory, one aspect of it is that centrality shares the mathematical notions inherent in measures like the mean and mode. Prototypical category members have been found to represent the means of attributes that have a metric, such as size (Reed, 1972; Rosch, Simpson, and Miller, 1976).

In short, prototypes appear to be just those members of a category that most reflect the redundancy structure of the category as a whole. That is, if categories form to maximize the information-rich cluster of attributes in the environment and, thus, the cue validity or category resemblance of the attributes of categories, prototypes of categories appear to form in such a manner as to maximize such clusters and such cue validity still further within categories.

It is important to note that for natural language categories both at the superordinate and basic levels, the extent to which items have attributes common to the category was highly negatively correlated with the extent to which they have attributes belonging to members of contrast categories. This appears to be part of the structure of real-world categories. It may be that such structure is given by the correlated clusters of attributes of the real world. Or such structure may be a result of the human tendency once a contrast exists to define attributes for contrasting categories so that the categories will be maximally distinctive. In either case, it is a fact that both representativeness within a category and distinctiveness from contrast categories are correlated with prototypicality in real categories. For artificial categories, either principle alone will produce prototype effects (Rosch et al., 1976b; Smith and Balzano, personal communication) depending on the structure of the stimulus set. Thus to perform experiments to try to distinguish which principle is the *one* that determines prototype formation and category processing appears to be an artificial exercise.

---

[1] Tversky formalizes prototypicality as the member or members of the category with the highest summed similarity to all members of the category. This measure, although formally more tractable than that of cue validity, does not take account, as cue validity does, of an item's dissimilarity to contrast categories. This issue is discussed further later.

EFFECTS OF PROTOTYPICALITY ON PSYCHOLOGICAL DEPENDENT VARIABLES

The fact that prototypicality is reliably rated and is correlated with category structure does not have clear implications for particular processing models nor for a theory of cognitive representations of categories (see the introduction to Part III and Chapter 9 [not included]). What is very clear from the extant research is that the prototypicality of items within a category can be shown to affect virtually all of the major dependent variables used as measures in psychological research.

Speed of processing: reaction time

The speed with which subjects can judge statements about category membership is one of the most widely used measures of processing in semantic memory research within the human information-processing framework. Subjects typically are required to respond true or false to statements of the form: *X* item is a member of *Y* category, where the dependent variable of interest is reaction time. In such tasks, for natural language categories, responses of true are invariably faster for the items that have been rated more prototypical. Furthermore, Rosch et al. (1976b) had subjects learn artificial categories where prototypicality was defined structurally for some subjects in terms of distance of a gestalt configuration from a prototype, for others in terms of means of attributes, and for still others in terms of family resemblance between attributes. Factors other than the structure of the category, such as frequency, were controlled. After learning was completed, reaction time in a category membership verification task proved to be a function of structural prototypicality.

Speed of learning of artificial categories (errors) and order of development in children

Rate of learning of new material and the naturally obtainable measure of learning (combined with maturation) reflected in developmental order are two of the most pervasive dependent variables in psychological research. In the artificial categories used by Rosch et al. (1976b), prototypicality for all three types of stimulus material predicted speed of learning of the categories. Developmentally, Anglin (1976) obtained evidence that young children learn category membership of good examples of categories before that of poor examples. Using a category-membership verification technique, Rosch (1973) found that the differences in reaction time to verify good and poor members were far more extreme for 10-year-old children than for adults, indicating that the children had learned the category membership of the prototypical members earlier than that of other members.

Order and probability of item output

Item output is normally taken to reflect some aspect of storage, retrieval, or category search. Battig and Montague (1969) provided a normative study of the probability with which college students listed instances of superordinate semantic categories. The order is correlated with prototypicality ratings (Rosch, 1975b). Furthermore, using the artificial categories in which frequency of experience with all items was controlled, Rosch et al. (1976b) demonstrated that the most prototypical items were the first and most frequently produced items when subjects were asked to list the members of the category.

Effects of advance information on performance: set, priming

For colors (Rosch, 1975c), for natural superordinate semantic categories (Rosch, 1975b), and for artificial categories (Rosch et al., 1976b), it has been shown that degree of prototypicality determines whether advance information about the category name facilitates or inhibits responses in a matching task.

The logic of natural language use of category terms: hedges, substitutability into sentences, superordination in ASL

Although logic may treat categories as though membership is all or none, natural languages themselves possess linguistic mechanisms for coding and coping with gradients of category membership.

Hedges
In English there are qualifying terms such as "almost" and "virtually," which Lakoff (1972) calls "hedges." Even those who insist that statements such as "A robin is a bird" and "A penguin is a bird" are equally true, have to admit different hedges applicable to statements of category membership. Thus it is correct to say that a penguin is technically a bird but not that a robin is technically a bird, because a robin is more than just technically a bird; it is a real bird, a bird par excellence. Rosch (1975a) showed that when subjects were given sentence frames such as "X is virtually Y," they reliably placed the more prototypical member of a pair of items into the referent slot, a finding which is isomorphic to Tversky's work on asymmetry of similarity relations (1978).

Substitutability into sentences
The meaning of words is intimately tied to their use in sentences. Rosch (1977) has shown that prototypicality ratings for members of superordinate categories predicts the extent to which the member term is substitutable for the superordinate word in sentences. Thus, in the sentence "Twenty or so birds often perch on the telephone wires outside my window and twitter in the morning," the term "sparrow" may readily be substituted for "bird" but the result turns ludicrous by substitution of "turkey," an effect which is not simply a matter of frequency (Rosch, 1975d).

Productive superordinates in ASL
Newport and Bellugi (1978) demonstrate that when superordinates in ASL are generated by means of a partial fixed list of category members, those members are the more prototypical items in the category.

In summary, evidence has been presented that prototypes of categories are related to the major dependent variables with which psychological processes are typically measured. What the work summarized does not tell us, however, is considerably more than it tells us. The pervasiveness of prototypes in real-world categories and of prototypicality as a variable indicates that prototypes must have some place in psychological theories of representation, processing, and learning. However, prototypes themselves do not constitute any particular model of processes, representations, or learning. This point is so often misunderstood that it requires discussion:

1.   To speak of *a prototype* at all is simply a convenient grammatical fiction; what is really referred to are judgments of degree of prototypicality. Only in some artificial categories is there by definition a literal single prototype (for example, Posner, Goldsmith, and Welton,

1967; Reed, 1972; Rosch et al., 1976b). For natural-language categories, to speak of a single entity that is the prototype is either a gross misunderstanding of the empirical data or a covert theory of mental representation.

2.   Prototypes do not constitute any particular processing model for categories. For example, in pattern recognition, as Palmer (1978) points out, a prototype can be described as well by feature lists or structural descriptions as by templates. And many different types of matching operations can be conceived for matching to a prototype given any of these three modes of representation of the prototype. Other cognitive processes performed on categories such as verifying the membership of an instance in a category, searching the exemplars of a category for the member with a particular attribute, or understanding the meaning of a paragraph containing the category name are not bound to any single process model by the fact that we may acknowledge prototypes. What the facts about prototypicality do contribute to processing notions is a constraint—process models should not be inconsistent with the known facts about prototypes. For example, a model should not be such as to predict equal verification times for good and bad examples of categories nor predict completely random search through a category.

3.   Prototypes do not constitute a theory of representation of categories. Although we have suggested elsewhere that it would be reasonable in light of the basic principles of categorization, if categories were represented by prototypes that were most representative of the items in the category and least representative of items outside the category (Rosch and Mervis, 1975; Rosch, 1977), such a statement remains an unspecified formula until it is made concrete by inclusion in some specific theory of representation. For example, different theories of semantic memory can contain the notion of prototypes in different fashions (Smith, 1978). Prototypes can be represented either by propositional or image systems. As with processing models, the facts about prototypes can only constrain, but do not determine, models of representation. A representation of categories in terms of conjoined necessary and sufficient attributes alone would probably be incapable of handling all of the presently known facts, but there are many representations other than necessary and sufficient attributes that are possible.

4.   Although prototypes must be learned, they do not constitute any particular theory of category learning. For example, learning of prototypicality in the types of categories examined in Rosch and Mervis (1975) could be represented in terms of counting attribute frequency (as in Neuman, 1974), in terms of storage of a set of exemplars to which one later matched the input, or in terms of explicit teaching of the prototypes once prototypicality within a category is established in a culture (e.g., "Now that's a *real* coat.")

In short, prototypes only constrain but do not specify representation and process models. In addition, such models further constrain each other. For example, one could not argue for a frequency count of attributes in children's learning of prototypes of categories if one had reason to believe that children's representation of attributes did not allow for separability and selective attention to each attribute.

TWO PROBLEMATICAL ISSUES

The nature of perceived attributes

The derivations of basic objects and of prototypes from the basic principles of categorization have depended on the notion of a structure in the perceived world—bundles of perceived world attributes that formed natural discontinuities. When the research on basic objects and their prototypes was initially conceived (Rosch et al., 1976a), I thought of such attributes as inherent in the real world. Thus, given an organism that had sensory equipment capable of perceiving attributes such as wings and feathers, it was a fact in the real world that wings and feathers co-occurred. The state of knowledge of a person might be ignorant of (or indifferent or inattentive to) the attributes or might know of the attributes but be ignorant concerning their correlation. Conversely, a person might know of the attributes and their correlational structure but exaggerate that structure, turning partial into complete correlations (as when attributes true only of many members of a category are thought of as true of all members). However, the environment was thought to constrain categorizations in that human knowledge could not provide correlational structure where there was none at all. For purposes of the basic object experiments, perceived attributes were operationally defined as those attributes listed by our subjects. Shape was defined as measured by our computer programs. We thus seemed to have our system grounded comfortably in the real world.

On contemplation of the nature of many of the attributes listed by our subjects, however, it appeared that three types of attributes presented a problem for such a realistic view: (1) some attributes, such as "seat" for the object "chair," appeared to have names that showed them not to be meaningful prior to knowledge of the object as chair; (2) some attributes such as "large" for the object "piano" seemed to have meaning only in relation to categorization of the object in terms of a superordinate category—piano is large for furniture but small for other kinds of objects such as buildings; (3) some attributes such as "you eat on it" for the object "table" were functional attributes that seemed to require knowledge about humans, their activities, and the real world in order to be understood. That is, it appeared that the analysis of objects into attributes was a rather sophisticated activity that our subjects (and indeed a system of cultural knowledge) might well be considered to be able to impose only *after* the development of the category system.

In fact, the same laws of cognitive economy leading to the push toward basic-level categories and prototypes might also lead to the definition of attributes of categories such that the categories once given would appear maximally distinctive from one another and such that the more prototypical items would appear even more representative of their own and less representative of contrastive categories. Actually, in the evolution of the meaning of terms in languages, probably both the constraint of real-world factors and the construction and reconstruction of attributes are continually present. Thus, given a particular category system, attributes are defined such as to make the system appear as logical and economical as possible. However, if such a system becomes markedly out of phase with real-world constraints, it will probably tend to evolve to be more in line with those constraints—with redefinition of attributes ensuing if necessary. Unfortunately, to state the matter in such a way is to provide no clear place at which we can enter the system as analytical scientists. What is the unit with which to start our analysis? Partly in order to find a more basic real-world unit for analysis than attributes, we have turned our attention to the contexts in which objects occur—that is, to the culturally defined events in which objects serve as props.

The role of context in basic-level objects and prototypes

It is obvious, even in the absence of controlled experimentation, that a man about to buy a chair who is standing in a furniture store surrounded by different chairs among which he must choose will think and speak about chairs at other than the basic level of "chair." Similarly, in regard to prototypes, it is obvious that if asked for the most typical African animal, people of any age will not name the same animal as when asked for the most typical American pet animal. Because interest in context is only beginning, it is not yet clear just what experimentally defined contexts will affect what dependent variables for what categories. But it is predetermined that there will be context effects for both the level of abstraction at which an object is considered and for which items are named, learned, listed, or expected in a category. Does this mean that our findings in regard to basic levels and prototypes are relevant only to the artificial situation of the laboratory in which a context is not specified?

Actually, both basic levels and prototypes are, in a sense, theories about context itself. The basic level of abstraction is that level of abstraction that is appropriate for using, thinking about, or naming an object in most situations in which the object occurs (Rosch et al., 1976a). And when a context is not specified in an experiment, people must contribute their own context.

Presumably, they do not do so randomly. Indeed, it seems likely that, in the absence of a specified context, subjects assume what they consider the normal context or situation for occurrence of that object. To make such claims about categories appears to demand an analysis of the actual events in daily life in which objects occur.

THE ROLE OF OBJECTS IN EVENTS

The attempt we have made to answer the issues of the origin of attributes and the role of context has been in terms of the use of objects in the events of daily human life. The study of events grew out of an interest in categorizations of the flow of experience. That is, our initial interest was in the question of whether any of the principles of categorization we had found useful for understanding concrete objects appeared to apply to the cutting up of the continuity of experience into the discrete bounded temporal units that we call *events*.

Previously, events have been studied primarily from two perspectives in psychology. Within ecological and social psychology, an observer records and attempts to segment the stream of another person's behavior into event sequences (for example, Barker and Wright, 1955; Newtson, 1976). And within the artificial intelligence tradition, Story Understanders are being constructed that can "comprehend," by means of event scripts, statements about simple, culturally predictable sequences such as going to a restaurant (Schank, 1975).

The unit of the event would appear to be a particularly important unit for analysis. Events stand at the interface between an analysis of social structure and culture and an analysis of individual psychology. It may be useful to think of scripts for events as the level of theory at which we can specify how culture and social structure enter the individual mind. Could we use events as the basic unit from which to derive an understanding of objects? Could we view objects as props for the carrying out of events and have the functions, perceptual attributes, and levels of abstraction of objects fall out of their role in such events?

Our research to date has been a study rather than an experiment and more like a pilot study at that. Events were defined neither by observation of others nor by a priori units for scripts but introspectively in the following fashion. Students in a seminar on events were asked to choose a particular evening on which to list the events that they remembered of that day—e.g., to answer the question what did I do? (or what happened to me?) that day by means of a list of the names of the events. They were to begin in the morning. The students were aware of the nature of the inquiry and that the focus of interest was on the units that they would perceive as the appropriate units into which to chunk the days' happenings. After completing the list for that day, they were to do the same sort of lists for events remembered from the previous day, and thus to continue backwards to preceding days until they could remember no more day's events. They also listed events for units smaller and larger than a day: for example, the hour immediately preceding writing and the previous school quarter.

The results were somewhat encouraging concerning the tractability of such a means of study. There was considerable agreement on the kinds of units into which a day should be broken—units such as making coffee, taking a shower, and going to statistics class. No one used much smaller units: that is, units such as picking up the toothpaste tube, squeezing toothpaste onto the brush, etc., never occurred. Nor did people use larger units such as "got myself out of the house in the morning" or "went to all my afternoon classes." Furthermore, the units that were listed did not change in size or type with their recency or remoteness in time to the writing. Thus, for the time unit of the hour preceding writing, components of events were not listed. Nor were larger units of time given for a day a week past than for the day on which the list was composed. Indeed, it was dramatic how, as days further and further in the past appeared, fewer and fewer events were remembered although the type of unit for those that were remembered remained the same. That is, for a day a week past, a student would not say that he now only remembered getting himself out of the house in the morning (though such "summarizing" events could be inferred); rather he either did or did not remember feeding the cat that day (an occurrence that could also be inferred but for which inference and memory were introspectively clearly distinguishable). Indeed, it appeared that events such as "all the morning chores" as a whole do not have a memory representation separate from memory of doing the individual chores—perhaps in the way that superordinate categories, such as furniture, do not appear to be imageable per se apart from imaging individual items in the category. It should be noted that event boundaries appeared to be marked in a reasonable way by factors such as changes of the actors participating with ego, changes in the objects ego interacts with, changes in place, and changes in the type or rate of activity with an object, and by notable gaps in time between two reported events.

A good candidate for the basic level of abstraction for events is the type of unit into which the students broke their days. The events they listed were just those kinds of events for which Schank (1975) has provided scripts. Scripts of events analyze the event into individual units of action; these typically occur in a predictable order. For example, the script for going to a restaurant contains script elements such as entering, going to a table, ordering, eating, and paying. Some recent research has provided evidence for the psychological reality of scripts and their elements (Bower, 1976).

Our present concern is with the role of concrete objects in events. What categories of objects are required to serve as props for events at the level of abstraction of those listed by the students? In general, we found that the event name itself combined most readily with superordinate noun categories; thus, one gets dressed with clothes and needs various kitchen utensils to make breakfast. When such activities were analyzed into their script elements, the basic level appeared as the level of abstraction of objects necessary to script the events; e.g., in getting dressed, one puts on pants, sweater, and shoes, and in making breakfast, one cooks eggs in a frying pan.

With respect to prototypes, it appears to be those category members judged the more prototypical that have attributes that enable them to fit into the typical and agreed upon script elements. We are presently collecting normative data on the intersection of common events, the objects associated with those events and the other sets of events associated with those objects.[2] In addition, object names for eliciting events are varied in level of abstraction and in known prototypicality in given categories. Initial results show a similar pattern to that obtained in the earlier research in which it was found that the more typical members of

---

[2] This work is being done by Elizabeth Kreusi.

superordinate categories could replace the superordinate in sentence frames generated by subjects told to "make up a sentence" that used the superordinate (Rosch, 1977). That is, the task of using a given concrete noun in a sentence appears to be an indirect method of eliciting a statement about the events in which objects play a part; that indirect method showed clearly that prototypical category members are those that can play the role in events expected of members of that category.

The use of deviant forms of object names in narratives accounts for several recently explored effects in the psychological literature. Substituting object names at other than the basic level within scripts results in obviously deviant descriptions. Substitution of superordinates produces just those types of narrative that Bransford and Johnson (1973) have claimed are not comprehended; for example, "The procedure is actually quite simple. First you arrange things into different groups. Of course, one pile may be sufficient [p. 400]." It should be noted in the present context that what Bransford and Johnson call context cues are actually names of basic-level events (e.g., washing clothes) and that one function of hearing the event name is to enable the reader to translate the superordinate terms into basic-level objects and actions. Such a translation appears to be a necessary aspect of our ability to match linguistic descriptions to world knowledge in a way that produces the "click of comprehension."

On the other hand, substitution of subordinate terms for basic-level object names in scripts gives the effect of satire or snobbery. For example, a review (Garis, 1975) of a pretentious novel accused of actually being about nothing more than brand-name snobbery concludes, "And so, after putting away my 10-year-old Royal 470 manual and lining up my Mongol number 3 pencils on my Goldsmith Brothers Formica imitation-wood desk, I slide into my oversize squirrel-skin L. L. Bean slippers and shuffle off to the kitchen. There, holding *Decades* in my trembling right hand, I drop it, *plunk*, into my new Sears 20-gallon, celadon-green Permanex trash can [p. 48]."

Analysis of events is still in its initial stages. It is hoped that further understanding of the functions and attributes of objects can be derived from such an analysis.

SUMMARY

The first part of this chapter showed how the same principles of categorization could account for the taxonomic structure of a category system organized around a basic level and also for the formation of the categories that occur within this basic level. Thus the principles described accounted for both the vertical and horizontal structure of category systems. Four converging operations were employed to establish the claim that the basic level provides the cornerstone of a taxonomy. The section on prototypes distinguished the empirical evidence for prototypes as structural facts about categories from the possible role of prototypes in cognitive processing, representation, and learning. Then we considered assumptions about the nature of the attributes of real-world objects and assumptions about context—insofar as attributes and contexts underlie the claim that there is structure in the world. Finally, a highly tentative pilot study of attributes and functions of objects as props in culturally defined events was presented.

REFERENCES

Anglin, J. (1976). 'Les premiers termes de référence de l'enfant'. In S. Ehrlich and E. Tulving (eds.), *La Mémoire sémantique*. Paris: Bulletin de Psychologie.

Barker, R., and H. Wright (1955). *Midwest and its Children*. Evanston, Ill.: Row-Peterson.

Battig, W. F., and W. E. Montague. 'Category norms for verbal items in 56 categories: a replication and extension of the Connecticut category norms'. *Journal of Experimental Psychology Monograph* 80 (3, pt. 2).

Beach, L. R. (1964a). 'Cue probabilism and inference behavior'. *Psychological Monographs* 78 (whole No. 582).

——(1964b). 'Recognition, assimilation, and identification of objects'. *Psychological Monographs* 78 (whole No. 583).

Berlin, B. (1972). 'Speculations on the growth of ethnobotanical nomenclature'. *Language in Society* 1: 51–86.

Borges, J. L. (1966). *Other Inquisitions, 1937–1952*. New York: Washington Square Press.

Bower, G. (1976). 'Comprehending and Recalling stories'. Paper presented as Division 3 presidential address to the American Psychological Association, Washington, DC, Sept.

Bransford, J. D., and M. K. Johnson (1973). 'Considerations of some problems of comprehension'. In W. Chase (ed.), *Visual Information Processing*. New York: Academic Press.

Bruner, J. S., R. R. Oliver, and P. M. Greenfield (1966). *Studies in cognitive growth*. New York: Wiley.

Garis, L. (1975). 'The Margaret Mead of Madison Avenue'. MS (Mar.), 47–8.

Garner, W. R. (1974). *The Processing of Information and Structure*. New York: Wiley.

Kay, P. (1971). 'Taxonomy and semantic contrast'. *Language* 47: 866–87.

Lakoff, G. (1972). 'Hedges: a study in meaning criteria and the logic of fuzzy concepts'. In *Papers from the Eighth Regional Meeting of the Chicago Linguistics Society*.

Nelson, K. (1974). 'Concept, word and sentence: interrelations in acquisition and development'. *Psychological Review* 81: 267–85.

Neuman, P. G. (1974). 'An attribute frequency model for the abstraction of prototypes'. *Memory and Cognition* 2: 241–8.

Newport, E. L., and V. Bellugi (1978). 'Linguistic expression of category levels in a visual-gestural language: a flower is a flower is a flower'. In E. Rosch and B. B. Lloyd (eds.), *Cognition and Categorization*. Hillsdale, NJ: Erlbaum.

Newtson, D. (1976). 'Foundations of attribution: the perception of ongoing behavior'. In J. Harvey, W. Ickes, and R. Kidd (eds.), *New Directions in Attribution Research*. Hillsdale, NJ: Erlbaum.

Palmer, S. E. (1977). 'Hierarchical structure in perceptual representation'. *Cognitive Psychology* 9: 441–74.

——(1978). 'Fundamental aspects of cognitive representation'. In E. Rosch and B. B. Lloyd (eds.), *Cognition and Categorization*. Hillsdale, NJ: Erlbaum.

Peterson, M. J., and S. E. Graham (1974). 'Visual detection and visual imagery'. *Journal of Experimental Psychology* 103: 509–14.

Piaget, J. (1952). *The Origins of Intelligence in Children*. New York: International Universities Press.

Posner, M. I., R. Goldsmith, and K. E. Welton (1967). 'Perceived distance and the classification of distorted patterns'. *Journal of Experimental Psychology* 73: 28–38.

Reed, S. K. (1972). 'Pattern recognition and categorization'. *Cognitive Psychology* 3: 382–407.

Rips, L. J., E. J. Shoben, and E. E. Smith (1973). 'Semantic distance and the verification of semantic relations'. *Journal of Verbal Learning and Verbal Behavior* 12: 1–20.

Rosch, E. (1973). 'On the internal structure of perceptual and semantic categories'. In T. E. Moore (ed.), *Cognitive Development and the Acquisition of Language*. New York: Academic Press.

——(1974). 'Linguistic relativity'. In A. Silverstein (ed.), *Human Communication: Theoretical Perspectives*. New York: Halsted Press.

——(1975a). 'Cognitive reference points'. *Cognitive Psychology* 7: 532–47.

——(1975b). 'Cognitive representations of semantic categories'. *Journal of Experimental Psychology: General* 104: 192–233.

——(1975c). 'The nature of mental codes for color categories'. *Journal of Experimental Psychology: Human Perception and Performance* 1: 303–22.

Rosch, E. (1975d). 'Universals and cultural specifics in human categorization'. In R. Brislin, S. Bochner, and W. Lonner (eds.), *Cross-Cultural Perspectives On Learning*. New York: Halsted Press.

Rosch, E. (1975e). 'Human categorization'. In N. Warren (ed.), *Advances in Cross-Cultural Psychology*, vol. i. London: Academic Press.

——and C. B. Mervis (1975). 'Family resemblances: studies in the internal structure of categories'. *Cognitive Psychology* 7: 573–605.

——Gray, W. D., D. M. Johnson, and P. Boyes-Braem (1976). 'Basic objects in natural categories'. *Cognitive Psychology* 8: 382–439.

——Simpson, C., and R. S. Miller (1976). 'Structural bases of typicality effects'. *Journal of Experimental Psychology: Human Perception and Performance* 2: 491–502.

Schank, R. C. (1975). 'The structure of episodes in memory'. In D. G. Bobrow and A. Collins (eds.), *Representation and Understanding: Studies in Cognitive Science*. New York: Academic Press.

Smith, E. E. (1978). 'Theories of semantic memory'. In W. K. Estes (ed.), *Handbook of Learning and Cognitive Processes*, vol. v. Hillsdale, NJ: Erlbaum.

——and G. J. Balzano (1977). Personal communication.

——and J. H. Walker (1978). 'Nominal, perceptual, and semantic codes in picture categorization'. In J. Cotton and R. Klatzky (eds.), *Semantic Factors in Cognition*. Hillsdale, NJ: Erlbaum.

Tversky, A. (1977). 'Features of similarity'. *Psychological Review* 84: 327–52.

——and I. Gati (1978). 'Studies of similarity'. In E. Rosch and B. B. Lloyd (eds.), *Cognition and Categorization*. Hillsdale, NJ: Erlbaum.

Wittgenstein, L. (1953). *Philosophical Investigations*. New York: Macmillan.

8

Categorization, Fuzziness, and Family Resemblances

RAY JACKENDOFF

CATEGORIZATION

An essential aspect of cognition is the ability to categorize: to judge that a particular thing is or is not an instance of a particular category. A categorization judgment is expressed most simply in English by a predicative sentence such as "*a* is a dog" and represented in first order logic by an atomic sentence such as "D*a*." This chapter will develop the basic elements of conceptual structure necessary to represent categorization.

We should note at the outset that categorization judgments need not involve the use of language: they are fundamental to any sort of discrimination task performed by dogs or rats or babies. In order to reliably press one lever when presented with a square and another when presented with a circle, an animal must make a judgment about the proper categorization of the newly presented stimulus. It must also distinguish experimental stimuli from food, other animals, the bars of the cage, and so forth. More generally, the ability to categorize is indispensable in using previous experience to guide the interpretation of new experience: without categorization, memory is virtually useless.[1] Thus an account of the organism's ability to categorize transcends linguistic theory. It is central to all of cognitive psychology.

* Ray Jackendoff, 'Categorization', ch. 5 of *Semantics and Cognition* (Cambridge, Mass.: MIT Press, 1983). © 1983 The Massachusetts Institute of Technology. Reprinted by permission.

[1] If I may be permitted a speculation here, it seems plausible to attribute the bizarre behavior of autism to a severe limitation in the ability to form categories and to make sufficiently general categorization judgments. Such a view would account for three important characteristics of this disability. First, if one could not go beyond #individual tokens# to the #similarities# among them, one could neither form stable categories of #objects in the world# nor categorize #utterances# as sequences of repeated #words#. Thus language would be extremely difficult at both the semantic and the phonological level. Second, since only small differences among #tokens# could be accommodated in the categorization process, stabilization of the projected #world# could be achieved only under very limited conditions of variation. Hence the autistic would be badly confused by even moderate changes in the environment. Third, since [TOKENS] would be subject to only minimal categorization, their internal structure would be left basically at the initial level of perception, accounting for the autistic's quasi-eidetic memory.

These speculations seem to be supported by recent research, which suggests that autism is not merely a social or linguistic deficit but in fact a central cognitive one:

It has been suggested . . . that the autistic child's stereotyped behavior and insistence on sameness in his environment may reflect the same underlying deficit as is revealed in echolalia, namely an inability to segment or break down patterns . . . When given a list of items to recall, normals will tend to group these into semantic categories, whereas the autistic children failed to do this. (Baker et al. 1976, p. 144) (*continues*)

PRELIMINARY FORMALIZATION

The usual logical metalanguages explicate atomic sentences in terms of the conditions under which they are true:

$$(5.1) \quad \text{"D}a\text{" is true iff} \begin{cases} \text{a.} & \text{D}a \text{ (Tarski)} \\ \text{b.} & \text{The extension of "}a\text{" is a member} \\ & \text{of the extension of "D" (set-theoretic} \\ & \text{semantics)} \\ \text{c.} & \text{What "}a\text{" maps into in some model} \\ & \text{is a member of the set that "D" maps} \\ & \text{into (model-theoretic semantics)} \\ \text{d.} & \text{Among the semantic markers of "}a\text{" is} \\ & \text{the marker [+D] (Katz)}^2 \end{cases}$$

These treatments all make an assumption that we rejected in chapter 2 [not included in this volume]: a fixed, preestablished connection of truth between sentences and the real world.[3] By contrast, we are concerned with how the organism makes the judgment, or with what is involved in *grasping* an atomic sentence. We thus take the theory of categorization to concern not whether a particular categorization is true, but what information and processing must be ascribed to an organism to account for its categorization judgments.

Since there can be no judgment without representation, categorization cannot be treated simply as the organism's comparison of some component of reality "*a*" to a preexisting category of dogs. Rather, the comparison must be made between the internal representations of *a* and of the category of dogs. Moreover, categorization can involve input through any combination of sensory media —vision, language, smell, and so forth. Thus the mechanism of categorization must be assigned to the level of conceptual structure, where all these types of information are available. In short, *a categorization judgment is the outcome of the juxtaposition of two conceptual structures.*

We will refer to the representation of the thing being categorized as a [TOKEN] concept and that of the category as a [TYPE] concept. The [TOKEN], corresponding to the constant of a first-order logic atomic sentence, is a concept of the sort discussed in chapter 3: a mental construct of potentially elaborate internal structure, which can be projected into awareness as a unified #entity#. Chapter 3 [not included in this volume] showed that [TOKENS] exist across a wide

---

No abnormalities were found in primary perceptual processing per se; the data suggested, however, that the autistic children were unable to generate modality-independent rules by which features of external stimuli were processed or "understood." This deficit in creating rules for dealing with perceptual information is a useful explanation for many of the apparent incongruities and discrepancies revealed during psychological testing of autistic children...Persistent rejection of external sensory stimulation implies, not inability to perceive stimuli, but, rather, abnormal processing and impaired coding...The autistic children's failure in social development may be seen, in some ways, as a symptom of their inability to make sense of the world and the people in it. (Caparulo and Cohen 1977, pp. 625–6, p. 630, p. 641) (I am grateful to Laura Meyers for her help with this note.)

[2] Strictly speaking, this is Katz's account of *analytic* truth; he consigns synthetic truth to the theory of pragmatics, which is none of his concern. However, the inclusion of markers (or attributes) is a characteristic conception of the criterion for categorization within decompositional theories of meaning such as Katz's.

[3] Or, in possible worlds semantics, between sentences and the set of possible worlds, one of which is the real world. The same objections obtain.

range of major ontological categories; we may thus speak of [THING TOKENS], [PLACE TOKENS], [EVENT TOKENS], and so forth.

A [TYPE] concept is the information that the organism creates and stores when it learns a category. Since #entities# of different ontological categories can be categorized, [TYPES] likewise divide into [THING TYPES], [PLACE TYPES], [EVENT TYPES], etc.

A categorization judgment might be represented formally in two ways. The first resembles first-order logical notation, in that the [TYPE] concept is treated as a one-place predicate whose argument is a [TOKEN]. This gives a representation like (5.2) for "*a* is a dog."

$$(5.2) \quad \begin{bmatrix} \text{THING TYPE} \\ \text{DOG} \end{bmatrix} \left(\begin{bmatrix} \text{THING TOKEN} \\ a \end{bmatrix} \right)$$

Alternatively, the [TOKEN] and the [TYPE] may both be variable-free structures that are compared by a two-place function. Such a formalization resembles the set-theoretic notation "$a \in D$," with the two-place function playing the role of the relation "$\in$":

$$(5.3) \quad \text{IS AN INSTANCE OF} \left(\begin{bmatrix} \text{THING TOKEN} \\ a \end{bmatrix}, \right.$$
$$\left. \begin{bmatrix} \text{THING TYPE} \\ \text{DOG} \end{bmatrix} \right)$$

The theory of syntax-semantics correspondence developed in chapter 4 [not included in this volume] provides preliminary evidence in favor of the latter formalization. In that theory, NPs correspond to variable-free conceptual constituents, and verbs correspond to functions whose argument places are filled by strictly subcategorized syntactic categories. The typical categorization sentence "*a* is a dog" contains two NPs connected by the verb "be." Thus (5.3) corresponds in the proper way: the subject and predicate NPs correspond to the two arguments, and the verb "be" translates into the function IS AN INSTANCE OF (x, y). By contrast, (5.2) is a version of the theory of common nouns as predicates, which section 4.1 rejected.

However, (5.3) does not specify what the two-place function comparing the two relata maps into. In predicate logic or set theory, the answer would be a truth value; the categorization would be either true or false. But truth values are not part of our metalanguage. Rather, according to the correspondence principles of chapter 4, the function must map into a conceptual constituent belonging to a major ontological category.

The proper category would appear to be [STATE TOKEN]. Just in case a [STATE TOKEN] with internal structure (5.3) turns out to be projectable, the organism experiences it as #a state that obtains in the world#—in other words, it makes a positive categorization judgment. Thus "(5.4) is projectable" is our metalanguage's counterpart of the expression " 'Da' is true" in the metalanguage of logic.

$$(5.4) \quad \begin{bmatrix} \text{STATE TOKEN} \\ \text{IS AN INSTANCE OF} \left(\begin{bmatrix} \text{THING TOKEN} \\ a \end{bmatrix}, \right. \\ \left. \begin{bmatrix} \text{THING TYPE} \\ \text{DOG} \end{bmatrix} \right) \end{bmatrix}$$

Notice that in this formalism it is just as easy to categorize [TOKENS] of other major ontological categories. For example, (5.5) asserts that *a* is a case of Max sleeping.

$$(5.5) \quad \begin{bmatrix} \text{STATE TOKEN} \\ \text{IS AN INSTANCE OF } (\begin{bmatrix} \text{EVENT TOKEN} \\ a \end{bmatrix} \end{bmatrix},$$

$$\begin{bmatrix} \text{EVENT TYPE} \\ \text{SLEEP } (\begin{bmatrix} \text{THING TOKEN} \\ \text{MAX} \end{bmatrix}) \end{bmatrix})\end{bmatrix}$$

In addition to the function IS AN INSTANCE OF, we need an operator that I will call INSTANCE OF, which maps a [TYPE] constituent into a feature of a [TOKEN] constituent. This feature encodes the presupposed category membership(s) of the [TOKEN]. For example, (5.6) is a [TOKEN] that has previously been judged to be an instance of [TYPE DOG].

$$(5.6) \quad \begin{bmatrix} \text{THING TOKEN} \\ \text{INSTANCE OF } (\begin{bmatrix} \text{THING TYPE} \\ \text{DOG} \end{bmatrix}) \end{bmatrix}$$

The kinship of the operator INSTANCE OF and the function IS AN INSTANCE OF is intuitively obvious. Formally, the operator could be treated as an abstraction operator that binds the first argument of the function, e.g., λx(IS AN INSTANCE OF $(x, $ [TYPE])). Since for the moment nothing hangs on the exact formalization, though, I leave it in the simple form shown in (5.6).

The relation between the categorization judgment (5.4) and the presupposed categorization (5.6) can be expressed by inference rule (5.7), a mapping from one class of conceptual structures into another.

$$(5.7) \quad \begin{bmatrix} \text{STATE TOKEN} \\ \text{IS AN INSTANCE OF } ([\text{TOKEN}]_i, [\text{TYPE }]_j) \end{bmatrix} \leftrightarrow$$

$$\begin{bmatrix} \text{TOKEN} \\ \text{INSTANCE OF } ([\text{TYPE }]_j) \end{bmatrix}_i$$

Using this inference rule, an organism that has made a categorization judgment about [TOKEN]$_i$ can incorporate the information about [TYPE]$_j$ into [TOKEN]$_i$ itself; or, using the rule in reverse, it can extract explicit categorization information from within [TOKEN]$_i$ into the form of a categorization judgment.

A converse operator, which I will call EXEMPLIFIED BY, maps a [TOKEN] into a feature of a [TYPE] that it is an instance of. This operator is used for incorporating examples of a [TYPE] into the information listed in the [TYPE] concept itself, should one wish to do so. (5.8) shows the effect of incorporating the information that a is a dog into [TYPE DOG].

$$(5.8) \quad \begin{bmatrix} \text{THING TYPE} \\ \text{DOG} \\ \text{EXEMPLIFIED BY } (\begin{bmatrix} \text{THING TOKEN} \\ a \end{bmatrix}) \end{bmatrix}$$

Parallel to (5.7), we can state an inference rule (5.9) that relates the operator EXEMPLIFIED BY to categorization judgments.

$$(5.9) \begin{bmatrix} \text{STATE TOKEN} \\ \text{IS AN INSTANCE OF } ([\text{TOKEN}]_i, [\text{TYPE}]_j) \end{bmatrix} \leftrightarrow \\ \begin{bmatrix} \text{TYPE} \\ \text{EXEMPLIFIED BY}([\text{TOKEN}]_i) \end{bmatrix}_j$$

An interesting hypothesis emerges from this formalization of categorization judgments. In the first-order logic and set-theoretic notations, tokens and categories are treated syntactically as entirely distinct: constants vs. predicates and elements vs. sets. In the present formalization, though, [TOKENS] and [TYPES] are less differentiated: they are both variable-free conceptual constituents, marked in similar fashion for major ontological category.

Let us push this formal similarity further. We will claim that, aside from the distinction expressed by the TOKEN/TYPE feature opposition, the internal structures of [TOKEN] and [TYPE] concepts are organized by exactly the same principles; in other words, the conceptual well-formedness rules are not bifurcated into rules specific to [TOKENS] and rules specific to [TYPES]. As a consequence, many if not all of the formal relations and processes that apply to [TOKENS] will also apply to [TYPES]. From this claim we will develop an important and unexpected consequence about the nature of logical inference.

The next two sections will provide some evidence for the formal similarity of [TOKENS] and [TYPES], on cognitive and grammatical grounds, respectively.

THE CREATIVITY OF CATEGORIZATION

[TYPES] contain rules

First note that one can in general identify novel #things# as #instances of a known type#, such as #another chrysanthemum# or #another piano concerto#. This means that the internal structure of a [TYPE] cannot consist merely of a list of all the [TOKENS] one has encountered that instantiate it. A [TYPE] may of course list some prominent examples, as provided for in our theory with the operator EXEMPLIFIED BY. But the categorization process must also include a set of principles that may be used creatively to categorize arbitrary new [TOKENS].

Moreover, one can create new [TYPE] concepts at will. One of the simplest ways to do this is to construct, for an arbitrary [TOKEN]$_i$, a [TYPE] of THINGS LIKE [TOKEN]$_i$, where likeness can be determined along any arbitrary class of dimensions. For each of the indefinitely many [TOKENS] that one can construct in response to environmental stimulation, there are any number of such [TYPES]. These in turn can be used to categorize arbitrary [TOKENS].

The creativity of [TYPE]-formation shows that a [TOKEN] concept cannot consist merely of a list of all the [TYPES] it is an instance of, since there may be indefinitely many of these.[4] Some [TYPE]-inclusions may be explicitly encoded within the [TOKEN], by use of the operator INSTANCE OF —but by no means all.

Now consider the function IS AN INSTANCE OF ([TOKEN], [TYPE]). Since a [TOKEN] is not a list of [TYPES], the function cannot simply examine the [TOKEN] to see if the [TYPE] is included in it. Conversely, since a [TYPE] is not a list of [TOKENS], the function cannot simply examine the [TYPE] to see if the [TOKEN] is included. Such lookup functions, which relate categorization judgments to internal lists in the [TOKEN] and [TYPE], are present in the theory as inference rules (5.7) and (5.9). However, because of the creativity of categorization and of [TOKEN] and

---

[4] Such an account of [TOKENS] is assumed by Montague semantics. See Partee (1975).

[TYPE] formation they alone are not enough. The function IS AN INSTANCE OF must examine the internal structures of both relata for compatibility.

The discussion so far already provides two arguments for the claim that the internal organization of [TOKENS] and [TYPES] is the same. First, such parallel organization would facilitate the operation of the function IS AN INSTANCE OF, which must make a comparison of the internal structures of a [TOKEN] and a [TYPE]. Second, the easiest formal way to derive a [TYPE]$_j$ of THINGS LIKE [TOKEN]$_i$ would be to copy internal information from [TOKEN]$_i$ into [TYPE]$_j$ intact. This is only possible if a [TYPE] can be organized along the same lines as a [TOKEN].

We also have reason to reject Fodor's (1975) theory that all possible [TYPES] are innately given as unanalyzed monads: a [TYPE] without internal structure cannot be compared with novel [TOKENS] to yield categorization judgments. Moreover, Fodor's theory entails that there is only a finite number of [TYPES], since there is only a finite space in the brain for storing them all. This consequence Fodor seems willing to live with. But if one can generate new [TYPES] at will on the basis of given [TOKENS], then either the set of [TYPES] must be infinite, contra Fodor, or else the set of [TOKENS] must be finite and innate, a totally implausible conclusion. For the moment we note that it is impossible to maintain such a theory in the face of the creativity of categorization.

The character of rules within [TYPES]

We conclude therefore that [TYPE] concepts contain as part of their internal structure a set of principles, rules, or conditions that make creative categorization possible. These principles are not generally projectable; that is, they are not accessible to introspection. However, the unconscious character of rules for [TYPES] has been more widely remarked, and it is worth giving some representative quotations to illustrate the scope of the phenomenon.

What does it mean to know what a game is? What does it mean, to know it and not be able to say it?...Compare *knowing* and *saying*:

  how many feet high Mont Blanc is—
  how the word "game" is used—
  how a clarinet sounds.

If you are surprised that one can know something and not be able to say it, you are perhaps thinking of a case like the first. Certainly not of one like the third. (Wittgenstein 1953, pp. 35–6)

Everyone has perceived such traits as suppressed anger in a face, gaiety in a movement, or peaceful harmony in a picture. Often these perceptions seem very direct. We do not first notice the tightness of the jaw and then infer the anger; more often it is the other way around. Such reactions are not so rare that cognitive psychology can afford to ignore them. According to many developmental psychologists, they are the rule rather than the exception in children. (Neisser 1967, p. 96)

Although the expert diagnostician, taxonomist and cotton-classer can indicate their clues and formulate their maxims, they know many more things than they can tell, knowing them only in practice, as instrumental particulars, and not explicitly, as objects. The knowledge of such particulars is therefore ineffable, and the pondering of a judgment in terms of such particulars is an ineffable process of thought. This applies equally to connoisseurship as the art of knowing and to skills as the art of doing, wherefore both can be taught only by aid of practical example and never solely by precept. (Polanyi 1958, p. 88)

Obviously, every speaker of a language has mastered and internalized a generative grammar that expresses his knowledge of his language [i.e., the category [SENTENCE OF LANGUAGE L]—RJ]. This is not to say that he is aware of the rules of the grammar or even that he can become aware of them or that his statements about his intuitive knowledge of the language are necessarily accurate. (Chomsky 1965, p. 8)[5]

What are the unconscious principles encoded in a [TYPE] concept like? Recalling that (5.4) is the conceptual equivalent of an atomic sentence "*Da*" of logic, we might be tempted to think of these rules as necessary and sufficient conditions, like Tarski's. But this cannot be the case: as we will see, categorization judgments follow the same yes/no/not-sure distribution that we encountered with #things# in section 3.1. Since necessary and sufficient conditions cannot produce such a distribution, we have a preliminary argument against them. Here we will examine only two simple cases.

Consider an operant conditioning experiment in which an animal is trained to signal discrimination between two types of stimuli. In learning the task, the animal has had to construct two [TYPE] concepts. If it does not respond at all, it has not perceived an #instance of either type#; if it responds in one way or the other, the presented stimulus has been perceived as an #instance of one type and not the other#. Suppose, however, that the animal is trained on two different colors or pitches and tested on an intermediate one; or suppose that it is trained on red squares and blue circles and then presented with a red circle. In various situations of this sort, the animal may be unsure, and rightly so —we would be, too. (Pavlov apparently claimed he could induce neurosis in his animals if he set the tasks up right.) Moreover, it misses the point to ask which [TYPE] the novel stimulus is *truly* an instance of: these experiments are designed to explore the animal's capabilities for forming [TYPES], not to find out how good the animal is at ascertaining the truth. The latter goal hardly makes sense.

Similarly, Labov (1973 [included in this volume]) presented human subjects with pictures of containers that differed in the ratio of width to height, asking them to label the pictures "vase," "cup," or "bowl."

(5.10)

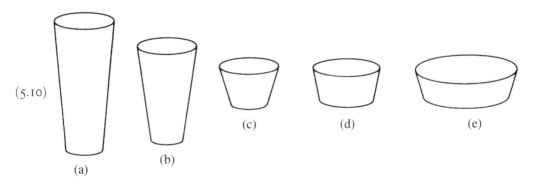

At certain ratios such as (5.10a,c,e), the responses were relatively uniform; but at intermediate ratios such as (5.10b,d), two different responses were equally probable. At these ratios, the choice is highly sensitive to context effects such as the exact form of the question or the immediately preceding examples. Such a graded response pattern shows that the boundaries of "vase," "cup," and "bowl" are not precisely defined, as they would be if the [TYPES] were necessary and sufficient conditions. And again, the *truth* of the categorization judgment in

---

[5] It is interesting to compare these statements with Katz's (1972) discussion of effability. Citing principles of Frege, Searle, and Tarski as antecedents, Katz says (p. 19), " ... anything which is thinkable is communicable through some sentence of a natural language. ... It would clearly be absurd for anyone to assert that he cannot communicate one of his thoughts because English has no sentence that expresses it. ..." As the quotations above show, it is not absurd at all. At best, one might claim that anything which is *projectable* is communicable through some sentence of a natural language. But even this is doubtful if we consider thoughts about, say, music, dance, or art, particularly from the point of view of creation or production rather than merely appreciation.

these intermediate cases is not at issue: (5.10b) is what it is, and if one person chooses to call it "a vase" and another "a cup," is either of them *wrong*?

We thus can identify four important characteristics both in nonverbal categorization tasks such as discrimination and in verbal categorization tasks such as labeling: (1) judgments are made creatively and hence must be governed by a set of rules; (2) the rules are generally unconscious; (3) the judgments are distributed in a yes/no/not-sure pattern and hence cannot be formalized by necessary and sufficient conditions; (4) it is odd to talk about the truth of the judgments in the borderline cases. The interchangeability of these two sorts of tasks is pointed out in studies such as Rosch and Mervis (1975) and Rosch et al. (1976). Their similarity is a central argument for the position that categorization sentences are evaluated at the level of conceptual structure, where inputs can be compared independent of modality.

Moreover, these four characteristics of categorization are qualitatively entirely parallel to the characteristics of #thing#-perception discussed in section 3.1. (In particular, compare paradigm (5.10) to (3.5) of section 3.1.) In other words, we seem to be dealing with systems whose formal properties lead to the same sort of judgmental results. Although many different theories of the organization of [TOKENS] and [TYPES] might be made consistent with this generalization, it is in fact a *consequence* of the theory we are proposing here: if [TOKENS] and [TYPES] have the same principles of internal organization, then individuation and categorization judgments cannot help but have similar qualitative characteristics.

Acquisition of [TYPES] through ostensive definition

Since in general the rules encoded in a [TYPE] are not available to consciousness, they cannot be explicitly taught. Rather, as Polanyi points out in the passage just quoted, a good proportion of [TYPE] teaching is necessarily limited to the presentation of examples, leaving the student to figure out the principles. That is, much [TYPE] learning (and *all* of it in nonverbal organisms) takes place at best through the examination of a number of #things# stipulated to be #instances# or #noninstances# of the type in question. Wittgenstein (1953) exercises himself a great deal over how such learning could possibly take place at all, in the face of underdetermination of the rules by any given amount of evidence. The trouble is that it does indeed occur.[6]

In order to account for [TYPE] acquisition on the basis of such ostensive definition, we must presuppose an active, unconscious mental process that can construct [TYPES] from the information in the [TOKENS] given as examples and nonexamples. I am inclined to consider the theory of this process to be about the most fundamental problem of cognitive psychology. At the very least it is responsible for all generalization of experience into a form usable as a guide

---

[6] Most studies of [TYPE] acquisition have involved perception, where the output of the acquisition process can be studied only through further categorization judgments. However, Polanyi (1958, ch. 4) emphasizes the strict cognitive parity between perceptual [TYPES] and motor skill [TYPES]. The latter are learned by following someone's example and practicing. Think of how inadequate verbal instructions alone would be for teaching someone to drive a car or play the piano or paint; one cannot learn these skills by merely reading a book or seeing someone else perform them. If the skill is not too hard, there is a point where practice pays off and we "get it"—we have formed a motor skill [TYPE] for which we can summon up exemplars at will.

If Polanyi's argument is correct (and I see no reason to doubt it), the unconscious processes behind motor skill acquisition are very much like those behind learning perceptual [TYPES] from exemplars. In the case of motor skills, though, we have a highly structured motor output to study during the acquisition process—potentially a much richer source of information than perceptual judgments. Thus Polanyi's hypothesis suggests that the study of motor skills is of great importance to cognitive theory and, in the present framework, to semantics as well.

to future action. In a grander guise, it is the unconscious force behind creativity in science and art, the "ripening" of unattended ideas that eventually spring into awareness fully formed.

Miller and Johnson-Laird (1976, p. 215) discuss this process basically in despair: ". . . we do not know how perceptual paradigms develop from perception of a finite number of exemplars. Conditions affecting the rate and accuracy of inductive learning have been studied in psychological experiments, but the process itself remains a mystery."

In the present formalism, the problem can be stated as follows. On the basis of stipulated examples, inference rule (5.9) can be invoked repeatedly to construct a [TYPE] concept that consists of a list of the presented [TOKENS], like (5.11).

$$(5.11) \quad \begin{bmatrix} \text{TYPE} \\ \text{EXEMPLIFIED BY [TOKEN]}i \\ \text{EXEMPLIFIED BY [TOKEN]}j \\ \text{EXEMPLIFIED BY [TOKEN]}k \\ \vdots \end{bmatrix}$$

For creative categorization, though, the information within the [TOKENS] must be extracted and generalized into a [TOKEN]-independent set of principles. The problem of learning from ostensive definition can thus be restated in terms of asking what happens to the [TOKEN] information in the extraction process.[7]

It would obviously be a formal advantage for the acquisition process if the information extracted from [TOKENS] and the resulting information in [TYPES] were of essentially the same organization—especially since once the principles are constructed, they will be turned around and compared with information in new [TOKENS]. In fact, in all the attempts I have seen to characterize aspects of perceptual learning (e.g., Winston 1970, Rosch and Mervis 1975, Miller and Johnson-Laird 1976), such a relationship of [TOKEN] and [TYPE] information is taken for granted. In general, [TYPE] information may be less highly specified in some respects and more highly specified in others (see chapter 8, [not included]), but the two kinds of information are easily interchangeable.[8]

LINGUISTIC TREATMENT OF [TOKENS] AND [TYPES]

We turn now to evidence from the Grammatical Constraint that [TOKENS] and [TYPES] have parallel internal structure. The fundamental fact here is that [TOKENS] and [TYPES] of a given *ontological* category are expressed by the same *syntactic* category, and may have the same range of internal syntactic structure. For instance, both [THING TOKENS] and [THING TYPES] are expressed by NPs, not by nouns and verbs respectively, as predicate logic might lead one to expect.

---

[7] This is not the problem of learning in general, where one is not even presented with discrete stipulated examples. The general case involves the prior (and probably even more serious) problem of noticing that there is a generalization to be made, hence deciding to construct a [TYPE] in the first place.

[8] The theory of language acquisition would by contrast appear not to conform to this generalization, since rules of grammar, the output of the acquisition process, are not apparently of the same formal nature as sentences, the #tokens# from which the rules are constructed. However, I think this appearance is merely a consequence of common notational practice in linguistics. For example, phrase structure rules and the trees they describe look entirely different. When treated formally, however, both are descriptions of structures whose elements are syntactic categories and whose principles of combination are daughter-dependency and linear order. It is simply that the internal structure of particular [SENTENCE TOKENS] is much more specific than [SENTENCE TYPE] (the phrase structure grammar) about the relationships among its syntactic categories. A similar construal can be placed on the relationship of transformations to transformational derivations and on the relationship of phonological rules to phonological derivations—though perhaps less transparently. If this is so, the generalization stands that the internal structure of [TYPES] is in large part formally undistinguished from that of [TOKENS].

To elaborate this argument, notice the semantic effect of different choices for the NP after "be" in (5.12).

(5.12) a. Clark Kent is a reporter.
　　　　 b. Clark Kent is Superman.
　　　　 c. Clark Kent is the man drinking a martini.

(5.12a) expresses a categorization judgment of the form (5.13a). (5.12b), however, expresses the identity of two [TOKENS], so its semantic structure (5.13b) involves a different relationship between the two relata, which I will call IS TOKEN-IDENTICAL TO.

(5.13)

a.
$$\begin{bmatrix} \text{STATE TOKEN} \\ \text{IS AN INSTANCE OF } (\begin{bmatrix} \text{THING TOKEN} \\ \text{CLARK KENT} \end{bmatrix}, \\ \begin{bmatrix} \text{THING TYPE} \\ \text{REPORTER} \end{bmatrix}) \end{bmatrix}$$

b.
$$\begin{bmatrix} \text{STATE TOKEN} \\ \text{IS TOKEN-IDENTICAL TO } (\begin{bmatrix} \text{THING TOKEN} \\ \text{CLARK KENT} \end{bmatrix}, \\ \begin{bmatrix} \text{THING TOKEN} \\ \text{SUPERMAN} \end{bmatrix}) \end{bmatrix}$$

(5.12c) is ambiguous between these two readings.[9] On the token-identity reading the definite article serves as a demonstrative—"that one over there, the man drinking a martini." On the categorization reading, the definite article expresses uniqueness of the categorized [TOKEN] within its [TYPE]: "Here's how you can tell which is Clark Kent: he will be the (only) man drinking a martini." In general, an indefinite NP in predicate position leads to a [TYPE] reading like (5.13a); a proper noun leads to a [TOKEN] reading like (5.13b); a definite NP may lead to either, but various modifiers such as demonstratives and "only" may restrict the choice. (Note that the modifiers that explicitly distinguish the two readings are mutually incompatible: "that only man drinking a martini" is unacceptable.)

The possibility of both [TOKEN] and [TYPE] readings in (5.12) is a property of this particular syntactic position and this choice of verb. In other positions, such as the subject of "walk in" or the object of "buy," all NPs express [TOKENS], regardless of definiteness.[10]

(5.14) a.
$$\left\{ \begin{array}{l} \text{A reporter} \\ \text{The man drinking a martini} \\ \text{Clark Kent} \end{array} \right\} \text{walked in.}$$

　　　　 b. Max bought
$$\left\{ \begin{array}{l} \text{a dog} \\ \text{the dog in the store.} \\ \text{Snoopy.} \end{array} \right\}$$

---

[9] (5.12c) is deliberately reminiscent of Donnellan's (1966) much-discussed distinction between *referential* (here, token-identity) and *attributive* (categorization) readings for definite NPs. Kripke (1977) shows that this distinction cannot be expressed by quantifier scope, and that the choice between the two readings is pragmatic. Such an analysis seems appropriate to the treatment here. The referential-attributive distinction does not always lead to a [TOKEN]-[TYPE] difference, as it does in (5.12), but it will in many of the examples to follow in this section.

[10] That is, there are specific individuals picked out by these NPs. However, it may be (as Donnellan believed) that the definite NPs here still display the referential-attributive distinction (see note 9).

In other words, it is the verb "be" that is responsible for the choice of readings for the NPs in (5.12).[11]

Now consider the two functions IS TOKEN-IDENTICAL TO and IS AN INSTANCE OF. In set-theoretic semantics, these would be entirely unrelated: the former is "$=$" and the latter "$\in$". Similarly, in predicate logic, token-identity is expressed by "$=$" and categorization by predicate-argument structure. These analyses seem to suggest that the verb "be" has two unrelated readings; it is just coincidence that a single morphological form expresses both token-identity and categorization.

In the present theory, though, these two functions are not so different. IS AN INSTANCE OF must compare the structure of its first argument with that of a [TYPE] in the second argument. IS TOKEN-IDENTICAL TO must compare the structure of the first argument with that of a [TOKEN] in the second argument—which may include [TYPE]-information embedded under the operator INSTANCE OF. Since there is no reason to believe that the two functions make any different use of the [TYPE] information in the second argument, IS TOKEN-IDENTICAL TO must do all the work of IS AN INSTANCE OF, and more.

Suppose, as we have been claiming, that [TOKEN] and [TYPE] structures are not internally distinguished. Then it is possible for there to be a function one of whose argument places is indifferently a [TOKEN] or a [TYPE]. Such a function need not be a disjunction of unrelated functions, as it would have to be in predicate logic or set-theoretic semantics; it can simply be insensitive to the feature opposition TOKEN/TYPE. In this case, it can be claimed that IS TOKEN-IDENTICAL TO and IS AN INSTANCE OF are not only related, but in fact the *very same function*. That is, the verb "be" surrounded by two NPs has only a single reading, which we may call BE (x, y), capable of comparing either two [TOKENS] or a [TOKEN] and a [TYPE]. This is just the sort of explanatory advantage that the Grammatical Constraint leads us to seek.[12]

If "be" were an isolated example, we might be able to live with the position that it expresses two distinct functions, one for [TOKENS] and one for [TYPES]. However, a variety of verbs display similar behavior, and under this hypothesis all of them would have to be lexically split. Here are three cases.

(5.15) Clark $\left\{ \begin{array}{l} \text{looks like} \\ \text{resembles} \end{array} \right\}$ $\left\{ \begin{array}{l} \text{a. President Roosevelt.} \\ \text{b. a famous politician.} \\ \text{c. a turtle.} \end{array} \right\}$

(5.16) Max $\left\{ \begin{array}{l} \text{is looking for} \\ \text{is seeking} \end{array} \right\}$ $\left\{ \begin{array}{l} \text{a. Charlie.} \\ \text{b. a friend of mine.} \\ \text{c. an honest politician.} \end{array} \right\}$

(5.17) This suit fits $\left\{ \begin{array}{l} \text{a. Clark.} \\ \text{b. a seven-year-old boy.} \end{array} \right\}$

---

[11] This sort of interaction is explicitly denied in the traditional logical approach to reference, where scope differences of various sorts are the only source of nonreferentiality. In a critique of Jackendoff (1975), Abbott (1979) takes the verb's lack of influence on referentiality as a virtue of the traditional scope analysis of belief-contexts; Jackendoff (1980) argues that in fact it is a liability. Similarly, Aune (1975) expresses amazement that Vendler (1975) could propose that subordinate clauses have different referential properties depending on what verb they are subordinate to. I agree with Vendler in seeing this interaction as an inescapable fact.

[12] It might be objected that these functions cannot be identical, since IS TOKEN-IDENTICAL TO is symmetrical and IS AN INSTANCE OF is not. But I think the symmetry of IS TOKEN-IDENTICAL TO is an artifact of comparing two [TOKENS]: identity is the only way for one [TOKEN] to be "included in" another in the requisite sense.

In the (a) cases, the second NP clearly expresses a [TOKEN]. In the (c) cases, though, it expresses a [TYPE], and the (b) cases are ambiguous. In the [TYPE] reading, there is no particular turtle that Max resembles, Max would be satisfied with any old honest politician, and the suit is seven-year-old-boy size.[13]

But do we want to say that comparing Clark on the basis of [TOKEN] criteria is essentially a different process from comparing him on [TYPE] criteria? Or that Max's quest is different if [TOKEN] rather than [TYPE] features are his criteria for success? Or that one is making an essentially different assertion about the size of the suit in the two cases? My intuition is that these are not distinct senses, and that a lexical split in these verbs would serve no purpose other than formal necessity. It would be far better to explain the morphological unity of these verbs by claiming that they express a single function, and that only the TOKEN/TYPE feature of the second argument varies. Under the theory that [TOKENS] and [TYPES] are structurally compatible conceptual constituents, this is the most natural account. By contrast, it is not an account especially congenial to the predicate logic or set-theoretic notations for categorization. Thus these verbs provide further confirmation for the unification of [TOKEN] and [TYPE] structure and for the conceptual unity of the verb "be."

THE NONPROJECTABILITY OF [TYPES]

The reader may have noticed my careful avoidance of the issue of reference in the previous section. The time has now come to ask the fateful question: what is the reference of an NP that expresses a [TYPE]?

According to the view of reference developed in chapter 2 [not included], the reference of a linguistic expression must be an #entity# projected from the conceptual structure the phrase expresses. Considerable effort was spent in chapter 3 [not included] to demonstrate that [TOKENS] of many major ontological categories are projectable into visual experience, and hence that many more linguistic expressions refer than are usually assumed to. This section, by contrast, will claim that [TYPES] as such have *no* projection, and hence that phrases expressing [TYPES] are nonreferring.

Let us see what such a claim would mean. It does not deny the existence of [TYPES]; the conceptual processing involved in making categorization judgments must go on whether or not [TYPES] have projections. The claim is simply that [TYPES] do not correspond directly to experience. We can't point to a #type# but only to #instances of a type#, which is why one must learn [TYPES] indirectly, on the basis of ostensive definition.

Without being projected, [TYPES] can still contribute vitally to the character of experience. For example, when we see #something# as #a dog# ("Lo! A dog!"), we are seeing #it# as #an instance of a type#, and this is a different experience from seeing #it# as #Rover# (i.e., simply as a #token#) or as #a brown physical object# (i.e., #instance of a different type#). We can even use pragmatic anaphora to signal that a #token# is to be seen in the role of #instance of a type#, as in (5.18).

(5.18) Those [*pointing to a single Cadillac*] are expensive.

But is one seeing a #type# under these conditions? I don't think so. The #token# has not disappeared, as for instance #the faces# do when one is seeing #the vase# in (2.2). At most the

---

[13] It is interesting that the division between [TOKEN] and [TYPE] readings falls at a different point with these than with "be": here indefinite NPs are ambiguous, rather than expressing only [TYPES]. Moreover, my intuition is that definite NPs in the object of "resemble" allow only a [TOKEN] reading, but are ambiguous in the object of "seek." I have no explanation for these differences, but they make impossible any simple-minded reduction of one of these classes of verbs to another. The ambiguity with "seek" is usually attributed to differences in quantifier scope; for arguments against this, see Jackendoff (1972, ch. 7; 1980).

character of the #token# changes as different categorizations are attended to. One experiences the [TYPE] only through the character of its projected #instance#.

Many previous semantic theories have been hampered by regarding a categorization judgment as the grasping of something true about the real world. This inevitably leads one to search for something in the real world that the categorization judgment is about: a category to which things may belong.

But theories of reference for category terms have been notably unsuccessful. Among the more popular have been (1) a stereotypical instance; (2) a mental image of a stereotypical instance; (3) the good old Platonic essence (e.g., of "dogness"); (4) the extension of the predicate (e.g., the set of all dogs). Stereotypes have well-known problems. For example, does the stereotypical animal have any particular number of legs? If so, how can it be representative of animals with a different number? If not, how can it be representative of animals at all, since surely every instance does have a particular number of legs? (See Fodor et al.'s (1974, pp. 152–62) summary of these arguments.) The Platonic essential animal suffers from the same problems, not to mention the difficulty many of us have with the idea of Platonic essences out there somewhere, just waiting to be grasped.

Thus, most theorists seem to have settled on the notion of *extension* as the proper explication of categories; it looks nice and objective. But in fact it too leads to serious trouble. Putnam (1975) constructs an argument that senses and extensions cannot be related in the way they are supposed to be. According to the usual assumptions, the language user grasps the senses of the words he uses, and the sense of a word determines its reference (i.e., its extension). However, Putnam argues in detail that what one knows cannot in general determine the extension of the word.[14] For instance, the things that one judges to be gold may or may not really be gold, and it may be that only an expert can tell, or maybe only an expert two centuries from now or on another planet. Thus the sense of the word "gold"—that is, the knowledge on which one supposedly bases judgments—does not determine the extension.

Putnam concludes from this that one does not know what "gold" really means. But where else is there to put word meanings but in people's minds?[15] One must either deny that there are such things as word meanings or else (like Katz 1980) treat meanings as Platonic entities that we humans grasp only imperfectly. Such tactics, however, totally remove semantics from the domain of psychology; it is not the semanticist's business anymore to ask how people internalize language. Inasmuch as our central concern here is human linguistic and cognitive ability, we must find a different way out of Putnam's argument. I vote for giving up the assumption that reference equals real-world extension.

Chapter 2 [not included] argued that, in the case of [TOKENS], the theory should substitute projected-world extension for real-world extension. In this way, sense still determines reference—almost trivially so, since projected-world #entities# are mental constructs isomorphic to a subset of conceptual structures. But consider a parallel substitution (e.g., the set of all #dogs#) for the extension of [TYPE] concepts. One cannot experience the set of all #dogs# as one experiences an individual #dog#, especially when we include not only all past and future #dogs# but all *possible* #dogs#, whatever *they* are. In fact, it is not even clear that the notion of the set of all #dogs# is coherent. Such an attempt to provide an extension for [TYPE] concepts seems to account for little besides the theorist's desire to provide extension equally for

---

[14] This point is already recognized by Frege (1892), who unlike Putnam is not disturbed by it:

The sense of a proper name is grasped by everybody who is sufficiently familiar with the language. . . . Comprehensive knowledge of the reference would require us to be able to say immediately whether any given sense belongs to it. To such knowledge we never attain.

[15] To say with Putnam that word meanings are spread over the society won't work either—they still must be in somebody's mind.

[TOKENS] and [TYPES]: it does not correspond to anything in experience, and it does no computational work.

In the absence of a viable candidate for the projection of [TYPE] concepts, then, we may conclude that [TYPES] have no projection.

Turning back to issues of language, this means that "a dog" in "That is a dog" is a non-referring expression, since it expresses a [TYPE]. It therefore contrasts with the same NP used in "A dog bit me," which expresses a [TOKEN] and so refers to a particular #dog#. As observed in the previous section, the difference is due to the semantic structure of the verb "be," which specifies that its second NP, if indefinite (or under various other conditions), expresses a [TYPE]. This property of "be" is what gives the NP after it the special characteristics of a predicate nominal; a similar marking is present in all verbs such as "become" and "resemble" that condition the predicate nominal construction.

This conclusion prompts a revision to the Referentiality Principle, which did not distinguish between [TOKEN] and [TYPE] constituents. An appropriate restatement for the moment is as follows:

Referentiality Principle II
  Unless there is a linguistic marking to the contrary, all phrases that express [TOKEN] constituents are referential; phrases that express [TYPE] constituents are nonreferential.

The evident analogy between designation by pointing and designation by use of clearly referential expressions like "Clark Kent" fuels an illusion that the purpose of language is to describe the world. Such a view, however, leaves mysterious the function of nonreferential expressions such as predicate nominals—unless one posits notions like extension or Platonic essence for them to refer to. If, on the other hand, one takes the view that the purpose of language is to make one's internal structures projectable to others as #sounds#—i.e., to express thought—then there is nothing at all puzzling about nonreferential expressions. It is just that some internal structures correspond directly to experience and some do not, a conclusion that should come as no surprise in any contemporary theory of mind.

REFERENCES

Abbott, B. (1979). 'Remarks on "On belief-contexts" '. *Linguistic Inquiry* 10(1): 143–9.

Aune, B. (1975). 'Vendler on knowledge and belief'. In Gunderson (1975: 391–9).

Baker, L., D. Cantwell, M. Rutter, and L. Bartak (1976). 'Language and autism'. In E. Ritvo (ed.), *Autism: Diagnosis, Current Research, and Management*. New York: Spectrum, 121–49.

Caparulo, B. K., and D. J. Cohen (1977). 'Cognitive structures, language, and emerging social competence in autistic and aphasic children'. *Journal of Child Psychiatry* 16(4): 620–45.

Chomsky, N. (1965). *Aspects of the Theory of Syntax*. Cambridge, Mass.: MIT Press.

Davidson, D., and G. Harman (eds.) (1975). *The Logic of Grammar*. Encino, Calif.: Dickenson.

Donnellan, K. (1966). 'Reference and definite descriptions'. *Philosophical Review* 75: 281–304.

Fodor, J. A. (1975). *The Language of Thought*. Cambridge, Mass.: Harvard University Press.

——T. Bever, and M. Garrett (1974). *The Psychology of Language*. New York: McGraw-Hill.

Frege, G. (1892). 'On sense and reference'. Repr. in Davidson and Harman (1975: 116–28).

Gunderson, K. (ed.) (1975). *Language, Mind, and Knowledge*. Minneapolis: University of Minnesota Press.

Jackendoff, R. (1972). *Semantic Interpretation in Generative Grammar*. Cambridge, Mass.: MIT Press.

——(1975). 'On belief-contexts'. *Linguistic Inquiry* 6(1): 53–93.

——(1980). 'Belief-contexts revisited'. *Linguistic Inquiry* 11(2): 395–414.

Katz, Jerrold J. (1972). *Semantic Theory*. New York: Harper & Row.

——(1980). 'Chomsky on meaning'. *Language* 56(1): 1–41.

Kripke, S. (1977). 'Speaker's reference and semantic reference'. *Midwest Studies in Philosophy* 2: 28–41.

Miller, G., and P. Johnson-Laird (1976). *Language and Perception*. Cambridge, Mass.: Harvard University Press.

Neisser, U. (1967). *Cognitive Psychology*. Englewood Cliffs, NJ: Prentice-Hall.

Partee, B. (1975). 'Montague Grammar and Transformational Grammar'. *Linguistic Inquiry* 6(2): 203–300.

Polanyi, M. (1958). *Personal Knowledge*. Chicago: University of Chicago Press.

Putnam, H. (1975). 'The meaning of "Meaning"'. In Gunderson (1975: 131–93).

Rosch, E., and C. Mervis (1975). 'Family resemblances: Studies in the internal structure of categories'. *Cognitive Psychology* 7: 573–605.

——W. Gray, D. Johnson, and P. Boyes-Braem (1976). 'Basic objects in natural categories'. *Cognitive Psychology* 8: 382–439.

Vendler, Z. (1975). 'On what we know'. In Gunderson (1975: 370–90).

Winston, P. (1970). *Learning Structural Descriptions from Examples*. Cambridge, Mass.: MIT Project MAC.

Wittgenstein, L. (1953). *Philosophical Investigations*. Oxford: Blackwell.

FUZZINESS

The objection to necessary and sufficient conditions that played a major role in chapters 3 [not included] and 5 is that they predict secure yes or no judgments for categorization. If some object meets all the conditions, it is judged an instance of the category; if it fails to meet one or more, it is judged a nonmember, and that's that. But for many if not most categories this is not the case. Rather, as Putnam (1975, p. 133) observes,

> . . . words in a natural language are not generally "yes–no": there are things of which the description "tree" is clearly true and things of which the description "tree" is clearly false, to be sure, but there are a host of borderline cases. Worse, the line between the clear cases and the borderline cases is itself fuzzy.

We saw this in the case of vases, cups, and bowls in section 5.2, for example.

Three responses to this problem have emerged in the literature. One is Searle's (1958) idea of a collection of criterial attributes, some large enough number of which is sufficient for category membership. Strictly speaking, this does not account for fuzziness without further refinement, for it still predicts a yes answer if "enough" criteria are met and a no otherwise. If a scale could be defined on "enough," though, one could presumably elicit a gradation of judgments. Even so, Searle's proposal still does not account for gradations of judgment that involve variation in only one criterial attribute, such as the height–width ratio in the cup–bowl paradigm and hue in color judgment. Thus this suggestion alone is insufficient.

Another response is to use the notion of "fuzzy set"—a set whose membership is defined not categorically, but in terms of degree or probability of membership. For instance, one might think of a typical bird such as a robin as 100% bird, but a penguin as perhaps only 71% bird and a bat as 45% bird. According to this view, the gradation of judgments is a consequence of the gradation of degree of membership, with values in the neighborhood of 50% resulting in the most difficult judgments. (The mathematics of fuzzy sets is developed in Zadeh 1965; the notion was popularized in linguistics by Lakoff 1972.)

* Ray Jackendoff, 'Fuzziness and "family resemblances"', sections 7.3 and 7.4 of *Semantics and Cognition* (Cambridge, Mass.: MIT Press, 1983). © 1983 The Massachusetts Institute of Technology. Reprinted by permission.

One difficulty with this view (pointed out to me by John Macnamara) is that a penguin is not 71% bird and 29% something else, it just *is* a bird. It may not be a typical bird, but it is still no less a bird than a robin or a sparrow is. One might respond by trying to interpret the percentages in terms of degree of confidence of judgment. But this makes the second objection only more patent: the theory provides no account of where the percentages might have come from. To derive the one-dimensional degree of membership, one needs a theory of the internal structure of the concepts in question—which is what we are trying to develop in the first place. Fuzzy set theory at best gives only a crude way to describe observations about category judgments; it does not even purport to address the mechanism behind them.[1]

Both Searle's proposal and fuzzy set theory have abandoned necessary and sufficient conditions in favor of a less rigid sort of condition, an approach that appears to me to be on the right track. A third possible response appears in Katz (1977): to make a distinction between "dictionary" and "encyclopedia" information associated with a lexical item, and to claim that factors leading to graded judgments are of the latter sort and hence not the responsibility of semantics. Such a move attempts by definition to preserve necessary and sufficient conditions as the semantic structures of lexical items.

However, Katz's position entails that the distinctions among color names must be non-semantic, since hue information is graded. This means that in this theory (7.3a) is contra-dictory (false by virtue of its semantic structure) but (7.3b) is not; rather, (7.3b) is only false by virtue of encyclopedia information.

(7.3) a. Green things are not colored.
     b. Green things are blue.

To say that semantic theory, thus narrowly understood, should be responsible for (7.3a) but not for (7.3b) strikes me as an arbitrary bifurcation of the data whose only purpose is to save the theory.[2]

It is perhaps instructive to follow this point a little further. Katz (1974; 1975, section 4) devotes some effort to a reply to Tarski's (1956a) and Quine's (1953) observations that analyticity (truth by virtue of semantic structure) seems to be subject to unclear judgments. Quine concludes from such observations that the analytic-synthetic distinction is incoherent. Katz apparently accepts the validity of Quine's conclusion, granted the premises, for he attacks only the premises, namely, that there are unclear judgments of analyticity. It seems not to occur to either him or Quine that "analytic" is just like almost every other word. Unclear cases of doors and tigers do not make the distinction between doors and nondoors or between tigers and nontigers incoherent; why then should such cases be grounds for rejecting the analytic-synthetic distinction?[3]

Thus an apparently important philosophical dispute has arisen pointlessly, out of a failure to recognize the ubiquity of fuzziness in word meanings. The moral is that fuzziness must not

---

[1] In fact, Mervis and Roth (1981) argue that fuzzy set theory does not provide an adequate account of the *observations*, even in so elementary a domain as color terms.

[2] Katz (1977) purports specifically to address Labov's cup–bowl case. He claims that one of Labov's factors, having a handle, is encyclopedia information and hence nonsemantic. However, he deals with the height–width ratio by specifying a semantic marker "height about equal to top diameter," and it is precisely the interpretation of "about equal" that gives rise to the gradation of judgments we are concerned with here. Since Katz proposes this marker without comment, I cannot evaluate the degree to which he appreciates the significance of this implicit concession.

[3] I cannot resist quoting Wittgenstein (1953, p. 44): 'We are under the illusion that what is peculiar, profound, essential, in our investigation, resides in its trying to grasp the incomparable essence of language. That is, the order existing between the concepts of proposition, word, proof, truth, experience, and so on. . . . Whereas, of course, if the words "language," "experience," "world," have a use, it must be as humble a one as that of the words "table," "lamp," "door."'

be treated as a defect in language; nor is a theory of language defective that countenances it. Rather, fuzziness is an inescapable characteristic of the concepts that language expresses. To attempt to define it out of semantics is only evasion.

FAMILY RESEMBLANCES

The gradation of height–width ratio in cups and bowls and the gradation of hues in color judgments both represent one sort of problem for necessary and sufficient conditions: the existence of graded attributes along which it is impossible to draw sharp boundaries. A different sort of problem arises with attributes that are subject to discrete exceptions. If it is a necessary part of being human to have two legs or high intelligence, then are one-legged people and imbeciles not human? If having stripes is criterial for tigers, are albino tigers tigers? And so forth. One response to this difficulty is to allow conditions that incorporate the notion of normality (a *normal* tiger has stripes, etc.). However, this solution rests on an adequate treatment of "normal," and many apparently agree with Katz (1975, p. 99) that a definition involving normality is little better than no definition at all. Nonetheless, there is appeal in this idea.

Those who reject the use of normality in definitions must adopt the tactic that only exceptionless conditions can be part of a word's meaning; if we haven't yet found the necessary conditions, we just have to look harder. Putnam (1975), for instance, places his faith in science to determine the extension of natural kind terms like "water" and "gold"; similarly, one might try to explicate "human" and "tiger" in terms of conditions on DNA. But there are two serious objections. First, what we are interested in is the prescientific, intuitive, and probably unconscious theory which people carry around in their heads, and which may lead to the questions that motivate scientific inquiry. People had a meaning for "tiger" long before DNA was dreamed of. (Katz (1974) makes this objection.) Second, even from Putnam's point of view, such a faith in science is only sensible when dealing with words for which there might conceivably be a scientific theory. How could there be (and why would anyone be tempted to seek) a science explicating what is necessary for something to be an instance of "pebble" or "puddle" or "giggle" or "snort" or "cute"? But a theory of word meanings must encompass these words too.

What of the alternative that it is the semanticist rather than the natural scientist to whom the responsibility for necessary and sufficient conditions is to be entrusted? Wittgenstein (1953, pp. 31–2) dashes these hopes in a passage that it is almost a cliché to quote:

66. Consider for example the proceedings that we call "games". I mean board-games, card-games, ball-games, Olympic games, and so on. What is common to them all?—Don't say. "There must be something common, or they would not be called 'games' "—but *look and see* whether there is anything common to all.—For if you look at them you will not see something that is common to *all*, but similarities, relationships, and a whole series of them at that. To repeat: don't think, but look!...Are they all "amusing"? Compare chess with noughts and crosses. Or is there always winning and losing, or competition between players? Think of patience. In ball games there is winning and losing, but when a child throws his ball at the wall and catches it again, this feature has disappeared. [This example is better

---

Katz's attack on Quine's premises again appeals to the distinction between dictionary and encyclopedia information. He claims that analyticity can be defined precisely, in terms of inclusion of semantic (dictionary) markers in lexical entries, whereas encyclopedia information is synthetic. Katz's criterion for an attribute to be a semantic marker is that semantic properties of the lexical item depend on it. However, since all the semantic properties are interdependent (as Katz himself works out), Katz begs the question. See Bar-Hillel (1970, chs 15 and 31) for further discussion of Katz's views on analyticity.

in the original German, where the term is "Ballspiel."—R.J.] Look at the parts played by skill and luck; and at the difference between skill in chess and skill in tennis. Think now of games like ring-a-ring-a-roses; here is the element of amusement, but how many other characteristic features have disappeared! And we can go through the many, many other groups of games in the same way; we can see how similarities crop up and disappear.

And the result of this examination is: we see a complicated network of similarities overlapping and criss-crossing: sometimes overall similarities, sometimes similarity of detail.

67. I can think of no better expression to characterize these similarities than "family resemblances"; for the various resemblances between members of a family: build, features, colour of eyes, gait, temperament, etc. etc. overlap and criss-cross in the same way.—And I shall say: 'games' form a family.

In short, necessary and sufficient conditions (even graded ones) are inadequate to characterize the word "game"; and it is clear from the context of the passage that Wittgenstein considers this not an isolated counterexample but a typical instance of how words are understood.

Wittgenstein's point has been widely appreciated for noun meanings, but in general, faith in decomposition for verbs has remained unshaken. However, section 8.6 [not included] will show that the verb "see" has this "family resemblance" character, suggesting that necessary and sufficient conditions are inadequate for any interesting part of the lexicon.

There have been various reactions to Wittgenstein's argument. In the last section we encountered Searle's (1958) suggestion that the totality of conditions in a definition need not be fulfilled—only a sufficiently large number of them. In the case of the single graded conditions under discussion there, this suggestion was inappropriate, but it does apply nicely to the family resemblance problem.

A related suggestion appears in the work of Smith, Shoben, and Rips (1974), who place on each condition a degree of "definingness." Conditions of lesser degree are permitted to have exceptions, and in cases of doubt, the more highly defining conditions are to be relied upon. However, Smith, Shoben, and Rips assume there is a central core of most essential conditions that serve as a "dictionary" definition. Since this is just what Wittgenstein denies, they have not really solved the problem.

The same difficulty appears in Katz's (1977) attempt to separate out dictionary definitions of necessary and sufficient conditions from an encyclopedia entry that is subject to exceptions. Though he cites Labov in this connection, Katz surprisingly does not mention Wittgenstein (see note 2).

Finally, Rosch and Mervis (1975) and Mervis and Pani (1980) develop a theory of categories in which family resemblance phenomena play an essential part. They show experimentally how artificial categories of objects can be learned whose defining conditions are subject to exceptions. Those instances that satisfy all or most defining conditions are perceived as more central instances and are more easily learned and remembered. This confirms Wittgenstein's argument and extends it beyond word meanings to perceptual concepts.[4]

All of these responses again enrich the narrow theory of necessary and sufficient conditions into something more flexible. Katz (1966, pp. 72–3), on the other hand, attempts to defend it

---

[4] Armstrong, Gleitman, and Gleitman (AGG) (1983) present evidence that has been widely interpreted as vitiating Rosch's arguments for family resemblance ("cluster") concepts. They show that certain of Rosch's typicality effects appear even with concepts like "even number" and "female" that should be absolutely categorical: subjects judge 18 and 42 more typical even numbers than 34 and 106, and mothers and sisters more typical females than comediennes and cowgirls. Moreover, verification times for "better" exemplars are faster than for "poorer" exemplars, just as with Rosch's alleged cluster categories such as "fruit" and "vehicle." The conclusion that AGG draw is that category exemplariness is not psychologically equivalent to category membership, as has generally been assumed. Hence experimental results that bear on exemplariness reveal nothing about the mental representation of category membership.

against Wittgenstein's objection. His argument consists essentially of two points. The first is that Wittgenstein has not *proven* that there are no necessary and sufficient conditions for "game"; he has merely been unable to find any. Moreover, there *are* necessary and sufficient conditions for words like "brother" ("male sibling") and "highball" ("drink of diluted spirits served with ice in a tall glass"), and Wittgenstein has not given any principled distinction between these cases and "game." Without such a distinction, Katz says, Wittgenstein has no case.

But clearly it is not up to Wittgenstein to prove that necessary and sufficient conditions never work; it is up to Katz to prove that they *always* work. As Fodor, Garrett, Walker, and Parkes (1980) observe, practically all the plausible examples of necessary and sufficient conditions come from jargon vocabularies ("ketch," "highball"), kinship vocabularies ("grandmother," "bachelor"), and axiomatized systems ("triangle"). Thus Wittgenstein appears closer to the truth than Katz.

Katz's second point is that if "game" turns out not to have necessary and sufficient conditions, we can treat it as an ambiguous lexical item, picking apart the family resemblances into different senses, each of which is a bundle of necessary and sufficient conditions. Even if this move succeeds technically, though, it evades an important issue: is "game" really ambiguous? Katz's proposal treats the varieties of games as being as distinct as a river bank and the Bank of England, which hardly seems correct. Of course, it is not logically necessary that all these diverse activities should be called games, as witness the difference between German "Spiel" of Wittgenstein's original and "game" of the translation; but it does not by any stretch of the imagination seem to be mere coincidence either. The degree to which the collection of activities called "games" is *not* fortuitous is captured by Wittgenstein's notion of family resemblances among them. It is not captured by splitting "game" into a number of separate lexical readings. Thus Katz has failed really to address Wittgenstein's point.

In closing this discussion, I should emphasize that all the objections raised in this section and the past two apply equally to any of the decomposition theories that assume (7.1) and (7.2) [not included]. I have singled out Katz's work for discussion only because no one else to my knowledge has explicitly defended necessary and sufficient conditions rather than simply assuming them.

The treatment of categorization in the present study is, I believe, immune to AGG's objection to Rosch. The crucial issue here has not been gradation of typicality, but the gradation of uncertain category judgments, which involves a narrower class of cases. For instance, "even number," while subject to typicality effects, does not produce uncertain judgments. By contrast, "fruit" not only has gradations in typicality, from cases like "apple" (most typical) to cases like "fig" (less typical), but also has uncertain cases like "tomato," which is conflicted between "fruit" and "vegetable" (would a tomato go in a fruit bowl?). Even "female," which AGG treat as well defined, has its uncertain cases. To be sure, "comedienne" unquestionably is a subcategory of "female," though an atypical exemplar. But "transsexual" presents real conflicts of judgment, which may be resolved differently depending on one's purpose: apparently, transsexuals count as females for legal marriage, but not for competition on the women's professional tennis circuit. It is this narrower class of cases, those that produce uncertain or conflicted judgments, that is crucial to the argument against necessary and sufficient conditions for category membership. The value of AGG's results, therefore, is in showing the importance of distinguishing this class of cases from the wider class of atypical exemplars. That is, the argument against necessary and sufficient conditions must be pursued more carefully than it often has been in the literature.

One further remark on AGG's analysis. They observe that a theory of cluster concepts makes the process of semantic composition far more difficult computationally: how is one to construe the combination of the two cluster concepts "foolish" and "bird" into a single cluster concept "foolish bird"? They take this complexity as reason to avoid a theory of cluster concepts if at all possible. While this observation is methodologically sound, it lacks empirical force. The formidable problems of semantic composition in a cluster theory in no way diminish the weight of evidence against necessary and sufficient conditions. Rather, this just seems to be one of those times when the theorist has to bite the bullet.

To sum up, it appears that at least three sorts of conditions are needed to adequately specify word meanings. First, we cannot do without *necessary* conditions: e.g., "red" must contain the necessary condition COLOR and "tiger" must contain at least THING. Second, we need graded conditions to designate hue in color concepts and the height–width ratio of cups, for example. These conditions specify a focal or central value for a continuously variable attribute; the most secure positive judgments are for those examples that lie relatively close to the focal value of the attribute in question. I will call such conditions *centrality* conditions. Third, we need conditions that are typical but subject to exceptions—for instance, the element of competition in games or a tiger's stripedness. Bundles of such *typicality* conditions lead to the family resemblance phenomena pointed out by Wittgenstein. Words can differ widely in which kinds of conditions are most prominent. Kinship terms, for example, are among the purest cases involving necessary conditions; in color names, centrality conditions play the most crucial role.

As an illustration of the difference between centrality and typicality conditions, contrast redness as such with the redness of apples. The former is a continuously graded notion; as examples get farther from focal red, they are judged to be worse instances of red. There is no "exceptional red" that is close to focal green. On the other hand, since there are yellow and green apples, the redness of apples is a typicality condition. The exceptions are discrete; there is no gradation from red apples through orange apples to yellow and green, with green being the least typical case. Rather, the typicality conditions for apple color specify a number of focal values, with red being most typical or highest valued. (I am indebted to Richard McGinn for this example.)

We cannot go further into centrality and typicality conditions without talking about how multiple conditions interact. I defer this to the next chapter, finishing this one with a discussion of the other most popular candidate for the theory of word meanings: meaning postulates or semantic networks.

REFERENCES

Armstrong, S. L., L. R. Gleitman, and H. Gleitman (1983). 'On what some concepts might not be'. *Cognition* 13: 263–308.

Bar-Hillel, Y. (1970). *Aspects of Language*. Jerusalem: Magnes Press.

Dougherty, J. W. D. (1978). 'Saliency and relativity in classification'. *American Ethnologist* 15: 66–80. Repr. in R. Casson (ed.) (1981), *Language, Culture and Cognition: Anthropological Perspectives*. New York: Macmillan.

Fodor, J. A., M. Garrett, E. Walker, and C. Parkes (1980). 'Against definitions'. *Cognition* 8: 263–367.

Gunderson, Keith (ed.) (1975). *Language, Mind, and Knowledge*. Minneapolis: University of Minnesota Press.

Katz, J. J. (1966). *The Philosophy of Language*. New York: Harper & Row.

——(1974). 'Where things stand with the analytic-synthetic distinction'. *Synthese* 28: 283–319.

——(1975). 'Logic and language: an examination of recent criticisms of intensionalism'. In Gunderson (1975: 36–130).

——(1977). 'A proper theory of names'. *Philosophical Studies* 31(1): 1–80.

Lakoff, G. (1972). 'Hedges: a study in meaning criteria and the logic of fuzzy concepts'. In P. Peranteau, J. Levi, and G. Phares (eds.), *Papers from the Eighth Regional Meeting of the Chicago Linguistic Society*.

Mervis, C., and J. Pani (1980). 'Acquisition of basic object categories'. *Cognitive Psychology* 12: 496–522.

——and E. M. Roth (1981). 'The internal structure of basic and non-basic color categories'. *Language* 57(2): 383–405.

Putnam, H. (1975). 'The meaning of "Meaning"'. In Gunderson (1975: 131–93).

Rosch, E., and C. Mervis (1975). 'Family resemblances: studies in the internal structure of categories'. *Cognitive Psychology* 7: 573–605.

Searle, J. (1958). 'Proper names'. *Mind* 67: 166–73.

Smith, E., E. Shoben, and L. J. Rips (1974). 'Structure and process in semantic memory: a featural model for semantic decisions'. *Psychological Review* 81(3): 214–41.

Tarski, A. (1956). *Logic, Semantics, and Metamathematics*. Oxford: Oxford University Press.

Wittgenstein, L. (1953). *Philosophical Investigations*. Oxford: Blackwell.

Zadeh, L. (1965). 'Fuzzy sets'. *Information and Control* 8: 338–53.

9

Discreteness

RONALD W. LANGACKER

DISCRETENESS

Much in language is a matter of degree. Linguistic relationships are not invariably all-or-nothing affairs, nor are linguistic categories always sharply defined and never fuzzy around the edges. This is perhaps unfortunate from the analytical standpoint—discrete entities are easier to manipulate, require simpler descriptive tools, lend themselves to stronger claims, and yield esthetically more pleasing analyses—but it is true nonetheless. Eventually the predilections of the analyst must give way to the actual complexity of the empirical data. Nondiscrete aspects of language structure must be accommodated organically in the basic design of an adequate linguistic theory.

The issue of discreteness has a number of interrelated dimensions. Four merit a closer look here. The first of these is the adequacy of simple, categorical judgments. The second is whether the **criterial-attribute model** or the **prototype model** offers a better account of linguistic categorization. The third dimension is the appropriateness of imposing a sharply dichotomous organization on gradient phenomena. The final dimension is whether an integrated system is adequately described componentially (as a bundle of features), or whether some type of holistic representation might also be required.

Simple categorical judgments

A simple plus/minus value or yes/no answer is not always sufficient in specifying whether a linguistic structure has a certain property, belongs to a particular category, or participates in a given relationship. These conditions are often matters of degree, and we must devise some means of accommodating the complete range of possibilities. A few examples will suffice at present. A familiar one is the generally recognized inadequacy of the simple grammatical/ ungrammatical dichotomy for dealing with the well-formedness of sentences. For the most part linguists merely note this inadequacy through a variety of ad hoc and ill-defined notations, e.g. the following, to indicate progressively greater degrees of deviance: ?, ??, ???, ?*, *, **, ***; I will use such notations myself for expository purposes. More to be desired, however, is a unified conception of linguistic organization that intrinsically accommodates assessments of well-formedness along a continuous scale of values.

A second example pertains to the relatedness of lexical items. Almost everyone would agree that the *drive* of *drive a nail* and *drive a golf ball* are related, but what about *drive a car*? Is the use of *cat* to designate a small, furry domesticated mammal connected in any significant way to its use in referring to a spiteful woman or a type of whip? Is there any relation between *ear*,

* Ronald W. Langacker, 'Discreteness', section 1.1.4 of *Foundations of Cognitive Grammar*, vol. i: *Theoretical Prerequisites* (Stanford: Stanford University Press, 1987). © 1987 Stanford University Press. Reprinted by permission.

a body part, and *ear*, a corn cob?[1] What about *ring* as a sound, as a boxing arena, and as a piece of jewelry? Intuition argues strongly that a simple yes/no answer would drastically oversimplify matters. The expressions in each of these sets are related to different degrees and in different ways, with the connections between the various uses of *cat*, for instance, being more tenuous and more metaphorical than those uniting the different uses of *drive*. We need straightforward constructs for dealing with the full spectrum of possibilities.

As a final example, consider the relation between a complex lexical item, e.g. *stapler*, and a productive derivational pattern that it apparently instantiates, in this case the V (verb) + *-er* (suffix) pattern for subject nominalization. The question is simple—is *stapler* derived by the V + *-er* rule?—but certain commonly made assumptions prevent a fully satisfactory answer. *Stapler* cannot be rule-derived, it might be argued, since the meaning of this form is far more specific and elaborate than just 'something that staples'; yet merely listing *stapler* in the lexicon stretches credibility in failing to accord it any relation at all to the V + *-er* pattern. One of the erroneous assumptions leading to this dilemma is that a form either is or is not derived by rule, that it either does or does not instantiate a given pattern. This is simplistic. What we want to say instead is that *stapler* does instantiate the V + *-er* pattern, i.e. that its organization and meaning are determined in large measure by the rule, even though it has properties above and beyond those the rule itself specifies.

Models for categorization

A related issue is the choice between the standard criterial-attribute model of linguistic categorization and a conception based on prototypes. The criterial-attribute model characterizes a class by means of a list of defining features; in its strict form, it requires that every member of the class fully possess every property on this list, and that no nonmember possess all of the listed properties. Class membership is thus an all-or-nothing affair; a sharp distinction is presumed between those entities that are in the class and those that are not.

This conception leads to a number of well-known problems. It often happens, for example, that certain class members lack a property so fundamental (on intuitive grounds) that it can hardly be denied criterial status: flightless birds and egg-laying mammals are familiar illustrations.[2] Another difficulty is that a set of properties sufficient to pick out all and only the members of a class might still be incomplete and inadequate as a **characterization** of that class. Thus, if the semantic specifications [FEATHERLESS] and [BIPED] were in fact adequate as criterial features for defining the class of humans, we would nevertheless hesitate to accept these two features as a comprehensive or revealing description of our species. Yet another problem is that speakers do not adhere rigidly to criterial attributes in judging class membership. Consider the sentences in (1).

(1) a. *I've never seen an orange baseball before!*
    b. *Look at that giant baseball!*
    c. *This tennis ball is a good baseball.*

---

[1] It is not etymological relationship that is at issue here, but rather the connections established by contemporary speakers.

[2] For an example from another domain, consider voiceless vowels and syllabic resonants. Both are classed as vowels for many purposes, but an adequate description of this category must surely refer to properties they lack (voicing; absence of a significant obstruction in the oral tract).

    d. *Who tore the cover off my baseball?*
    e. *My baseball just exploded!*

A speaker will not hesitate to call something a baseball even if it happens to be (a) the wrong color, (b) the wrong size, or (c) wrong in virtually all criterial properties. He will also use the term to designate (d) a baseball that has been drastically deformed, or even (e) a baseball that has ceased to exist. Unless one alters its basic character, the criterial-attribute model is not equipped to handle such expressions. It can do so only if one loosens the defining criteria, but then there is no nonarbitrary stopping point, and the relaxed criteria will hardly serve to distinguish class members from other entities.

The cognitive validity of the criterial-attribute model can therefore be doubted, despite its entrenchment in our intellectual tradition, and the prototype model suggests itself as a viable alternative. Experimental work in cognitive psychology (pioneered by Rosch, e.g. 1973, 1975, 1977, 1978) has demonstrated that categories are often organized around prototypical instances. These are the instances people accept as common, run-of-the-mill, garden-variety members of the category. They generally occur the most frequently in our experience, tend to be learned the earliest, and can be identified experimentally in a variety of ways (e.g. respondents accept them as class members with the shortest response latencies). Non-prototypical instances are assimilated to a class or category to the extent that they can be construed as matching or approximating the prototype. Membership is therefore a matter of degree: prototypical instances are full, central members of the category, whereas other instances form a gradation from central to peripheral depending on how far and in what ways they deviate from the prototype. Moreover, the members are not necessarily a uniquely defined set, since there is no specific degree of departure from the prototype beyond which a person is absolutely incapable of perceiving a similarity. The best we can say, as a general matter, is that substantial dissimilarity to the prototype greatly diminishes the probability that a person will make that categorization.

The prototype model thus avoids the problems inherent in the criterial-attribute model. First, it does not require that every member of a category possess a given feature (or even that there be any salient property shared by all members). Flightless birds, egg-laying mammals, and voiceless vowels are thus unproblematic; the absence of an obviously essential property does not force their removal from a category, but merely renders them nonprototypical. Second, the characterization problem is avoided because the prototype model is not inherently minimalist in spirit; instead it encourages the fullest possible characterization of prototypical instances, if only to specify the basis for assimilating the full range of nonprototypical instances to the category. Finally, the prototype model allows an entity to be assimilated to a category if a person finds any plausible rationale for relating it to prototypical members; the term *baseball* can therefore be applied to a ball that is orange, a tennis ball hit with a bat, a ball that has lost its cover, or even a ball that has ceased to exist.

I conclude, then, that the prototype model has considerable linguistic and cognitive plausibility. Its acceptance permits a revealing account of certain linguistic phenomena and the avoidance of descriptive and conceptual difficulties (cf. Brugman 1981; Lakoff 1982; Hawkins 1984). In adopting it over the more discrete criterial-attribute model, we do not forsake the possibility of either precise description or strong empirical claims.[3] The choice is not an a priori matter of preference or scientific rigor, but a factual one pertaining to the organization and complexity of the linguistic data.

---

[3] There are, however, consequences for the nature of descriptions and the types of predictions they afford. For instance, the prototype model allows statistical predictions to the effect that a class member is more likely to behave in a particular way the more central it is to the category.

Dichotomous organization

A third dimension of the discreteness issue concerns the propriety of positing sharp distinctions between certain broad classes of linguistic phenomena, thereby implying that the classes are fundamentally different in character and in large measure separately describable. The nondiscrete alternative regards these classes as grading into one another along various parameters. They form a continuous spectrum (or field) of possibilities, whose segregation into distinct blocks is necessarily artifactual.

Linguists are particularly fond of positing sharp dichotomies. Sometimes the practice serves well initially, allowing the analyst to differentiate a complex mass of data and fix attention on certain variable features. It may even be descriptively appropriate. Not infrequently, though, it leads to the reification of working distinctions into disjoint categories, which are then taken as "established" and accorded a theoretical status quite unjustified by the facts. Among the many distinctions commonly treated by investigators as rigid dichotomies are the following: synchrony vs. diachrony, competence vs. performance, grammar vs. lexicon, morphology vs. syntax, semantics vs. pragmatics, rule vs. analogy, grammatical vs. ungrammatical sentences, homonymy vs. polysemy, connotation vs. denotation, morphophonemic vs. phonological (or phonological vs. phonetic) rules, derivational vs. inflectional morphology, vagueness vs. ambiguity, and literal vs. figurative language. I regard all of these as false dichotomies (most will be examined later). Strict adherence to them results in conceptual problems and the neglect of transitional examples.

One way to produce a false dichotomy is to focus solely on representative examples from the two extremes of a continuum: by overlooking intermediate cases, one readily observes discrete classes with sharply contrasting properties. A good illustration is the traditional distinction between lexical and grammatical morphemes (or content words vs. function words). If we restrict our attention to forms like *giraffe, encyclopedia, upholster, inquisitive*, and *fastidiously* on the one hand, and on the other hand to forms like *-ing, of, be, it* (e.g. *It's raining*), and *that* (e.g. *I know that she left*), the differences are of course striking. The lexical vs. grammatical distinction seems clear on the basis of concreteness of sense, amount of semantic content, whether the choice of a particular form is free or is determined by the grammatical environment, and whether or not a subclass accepts new members.

All these differences are nevertheless matters of degree, and intermediate examples are easily found. Content words vary enormously in concreteness of meaning (as in the ordered sequence *kick > talk > think > live > exist*) and also in semantic specificity (*giraffe > mammal > animal > organism > thing*). I will argue that most (if not all) grammatical morphemes are meaningful, and some are at least as elaborate semantically as numerous content words. It would be hard to claim that modals, quantifiers, and prepositions have less semantic content than such lexical morphemes as *thing* or *have*, nor are they obviously more abstract than *entity, exist, proximity*, etc. I will further argue that grammatical morphemes contribute semantically to the constructions they appear in, and that their occurrence has a semantic rationale even when conventionally determined (cf. Langacker 1982a). Moreover, the speaker is often free to choose from among grammatical morphemes that structure the conceived situation through alternate images (e.g. *try to complain* vs. *try complaining*; *surprised at* vs. *surprised by*). At the same time, the choice among lexical morphemes is often highly constrained (consider idioms, standard collocations, and formulaic expressions). Finally, certain classes of function words readily accept new members. Quantifiers, prepositions/ postpositions, conjunctions, and subordinators are commonly innovated, and in some languages are essentially open-ended classes. It is doubtful that any class, even personal pronouns, is ever definitively closed.[4]

But to posit a continuum is not to abandon the goal of rigorous description: we must still describe the individual structures in explicit detail, even as we articulate their parameters of gradation. Nor does recognizing a continuum render us impotent to make valid distinctions or interesting claims. It is perfectly reasonable, for instance, to speak of lexical morphemes or grammatical morphemes as a group, so long as we avoid pointless questions deriving from the erroneous presupposition that they constitute disjoint sets (e.g. whether prepositions are lexical or grammatical). Rules and generalizations can perfectly well refer to such categories; we need only realize that predictions inspired by representative instances of a category, found near one pole of a continuum, hold with progressively less force as one moves away from that pole towards the opposite extreme.

Integrated systems

Most linguistic units are highly integrated structural complexes, or **systems**, which are more than just the sum of their recognizable parts. It is nevertheless common for linguists to impose a componential analysis on these systems, representing them as unordered bundles of discrete features. The vowel sound [i], for instance, is a phonological structure resolvable into the features [− CONSONANTAL, +VOCALIC, + HIGH, + FRONT, − ROUNDED], and the concept [UNCLE] is resolvable into the semantic components [MALE, COLLATERAL, ASCENDING GEN- ERATION]. We are not concerned here with the choice of features, nor with the nature of their values (binary or multivalued, discrete or continuous, etc.); we will consider instead the implications of the feature conception per se. I suggest that a feature representation is per- fectly legitimate (if properly interpreted), but does not in itself fully reconstruct the systemic nature of the actual phenomenon. For a description to be complete, the feature representation of a structural complex must be supplemented by a more holistic account that accommodates its integrated nature. Such an account is in fact essential to a substantive characterization of the features themselves.

What do I have in mind in saying that a sound such as [i] constitutes an integrated system not reducible to its parts? After all, we *can* decompose its articulation into a number of components, as reflected in a typical feature analysis: vibration of the vocal cords, raising of the tongue towards the palate (without contact or constriction sufficient to cause turbulence), advancement of the tongue towards the front of the palate, spreading and retraction of the lips, and so on. If [i] were merely the sum of these components, I could pronounce it by carrying out these articulatory gestures sequentially: first vibrating my vocal cords, then raising my tongue, then fronting my tongue, and so on. But of course I cannot. The sound is not the mere sum of these components, but rather a matter of blending them into a smooth, coordinated articulatory routine. A complete description of the sound therefore requires more than a separate account of each individual component. It must additionally—and crucially— specify such matters as their relative timing and how they influence and accommodate one another. These are the specifications of the sound's essential systemic character.

Similar remarks hold for concepts. In its narrowest genealogical construal, [UNCLE] makes internal reference to three conceived persons: ego, a linking relative, and the person referred to by the notion. It also invokes (among others) the sibling and offspring relationships. But if the

---

[4] Witness the innovation and spread of *youall* as the plural of *you*, which I sometimes find even in my own non-Southern speech.

notion were only the sum of these persons and relationships, there would be no difference between, say, [UNCLE] and [NEPHEW]. We must further specify how these entities are connected to form a coherent, integrated structure. More precisely, particular persons are assigned to particular roles in the relationships: the person identified as the uncle is joined through the sibling relationship to the linking relative, and the latter is joined to ego as the parent in a parent/offspring relationship. Normally, of course, we do not focus our attention on these separate specifications; when employing the concept [UNCLE] we generally manipulate the configuration holistically, as a kind of gestalt.

If it is admitted that a sound or a concept must be characterized as an integrated system at some level of description, what is the function of a feature representation? Its motivation is primarily classificatory: a feature like [+ HIGH] is posited to group together a set of sounds on the basis of a systematically exploited property that they share; in the same manner, the feature [MALE] unites a set of concepts. The utility and essential correctness of this type of classification is beyond dispute. We can justify the phonological feature [+ HIGH] by showing that the class of sounds function alike in various ways to the exclusion of other sounds. Similarly, we can show that the semantic feature [MALE] is not arbitrary, but rather a property of systematic relevance to the language, by citing the numerous contrastive pairs that depend on it: *uncle/aunt, boy/girl, man/woman, stallion/mare, buck/doe*, etc.

The features used to represent a sound or a concept can therefore be regarded as diacritics specifying class co-membership with other units. However, a list of class memberships is not per se a full characterization of the categorized entities, and is only minimally revealing if the defining properties are left unexplicated. Moreover, few analysts would accept the claim that the phonological or semantic features they postulate have only a diacritic function. For a feature analysis to be truly substantive, the features must be attributed intrinsic phonological or semantic content, described as precisely and explicitly as possible.[5]

If these points are accepted, how do we characterize the intrinsic phonological or semantic content of the features we postulate? I suggest that autonomous descriptions of individual features will generally prove inadequate, precisely because sounds and concepts are systemic in nature. Features correspond to properties discernible within an integrated system, and are properly describable only in the context of that system.

Consider the articulatory feature [+ HIGH]. We cannot characterize it with full precision as an isolated entity, for its specific value depends on other properties of the sound it occurs in. For example, a different region of the tongue is raised depending on whether the vowel is front or back. More crucially, the height specification can only be understood relative to the matrix of a vocalic articulation. If, while I am eating, my tongue accidentally assumes the shape and position that would be appropriate for the sound [i], I cannot claim to have thereby implemented the phonological feature [+ HIGH] (or [+ FRONT]) in the sense that linguists understand the term. I can properly be said to have implemented the [+ HIGH] feature only when my tongue achieves the requisite configuration by virtue of specific neuromuscular actions synergistically related to those of other speech organs as an integral part of a coordinated articulatory gesture. The feature exists only in the context of a system providing the conditions for its manifestation, where it serves a specific function.[6]

---

[5] It would be pointless for linguists to abjure responsibility for describing linguistic constructs as integrated systems, or for specifying the content of classificatory features. We will not solve these problems by bequeathing them to other disciplines (e.g. experimental phonetics or cognitive psychology) whose separation from our own is essentially arbitrary. Moreover, the systemic character of linguistic units is fundamental to understanding their behavior.

[6] Relevant here are Sapir's remarks (1925) on the difference between the speech sound [w] and the sound made in blowing out a candle.

The same is true for semantic structure. The componential analysis of [UNCLE] into [MALE], [COLLATERAL], and [ASCENDING GENERATION] does not eliminate its systemic character, for these features must themselves be defined configurationally. [COLLATERAL] and [ASCENDING GENERATION] indicate relative position within a kinship network, hence presuppose the conception of such an entity. The feature [MALE] perhaps does not, but its value must nevertheless be construed in systemic terms: the collection of properties subsumed by [MALE] do not float about unattached within the confines of the [UNCLE] concept; instead they are understood as pertaining to a specific person, who occupies a particular place within the system of relationships. The unstructured feature bundle [MALE, COLLATERAL, ASCENDING GENERATION] therefore conceals behind its digital facade a highly integrated conceptualization providing a necessary context for the interpretation of each component.

The program I advocate is not reductionist. In arguing for the necessity and priority of a systemic view of semantic and phonological units I am not thereby denying either the descriptive utility or the cognitive reality of classificatory features. I contend that speakers extract these features to embody the commonality they perceive in arrays of fully specified, integrated units, and that these features consequently make intrinsic (though schematic) reference to the overall systemic units relative to which they are characterized. But the features do not obviate the need for a systemic representation; they coexist with it as an additional dimension of linguistic organization.

REFERENCES

Brugman, C. (1981). 'The story of *over*'. M.A. thesis, University of California, Berkeley.
Hawkins, B. W. (1984). 'The Semantics of English Spatial Prepositions'. Ph.D. dissertation, University of California, San Diego.
Lakoff, G. (1982). 'Categories: an essay in cognitive linguistics'. In Linguistic Society of Korea (ed.), *Linguistics in the Morning Calm*. Seoul: Hanshin, 139–93.
Langacker, R. W. (1982a). 'Space grammar, analysability, and the English passive'. *Language* 58: 22–80.
Rosch, E. (1973). 'On the internal structure of perceptual and semantic categories'. In T. E. Moore (ed.), *Cognitive Development and the Acquisition of Language*. New York: Academic Press, 111–44.
——(1975). 'Cognitive representations of semantic categories'. *Journal of Experimental Psychology: General* 104: 192–233.
——(1977). 'Human categorization'. In N. Warren (ed.), *Studies in Crosscultural Psychology*. London: Academic Press, 1–49.
——(1978). 'Principles of categorization'. In E. Rosch and B. B. Lloyd (eds.), *Cognition and Categorization*. Hillsdale, NJ: Erlbaum, 27–47.
Sapir, E. (1925). 'Sound patterns in language'. *Language* 1: 37–51. Repr. in D. G. Mandelbaum (ed.) (1963), *Selected Writings of Edward Sapir in Language, Culture and Personality*. Berkeley: University of California Press, 33–45.

10

The Importance of Categorization

GEORGE LAKOFF

The importance of categorization

Many readers, I suspect, will take the title of this book as suggesting that women, fire, and dangerous things have something in common—say, that women are fiery and dangerous. Most feminists I've mentioned it to have loved the title for that reason, though some have hated it for the same reason. But the chain of inference—from conjunction to categorization to commonality—is the norm. The inference is based on the common idea of what it means to be in the same category: things are categorized together on the basis of what they have in common. The idea that categories are defined by common properties is not only our everyday folk theory of what a category is, it is also the principal technical theory—one that has been with us for more than two thousand years.

The classical view that categories are based on shared properties is not entirely wrong. We often do categorize things on that basis. But that is only a small part of the story. In recent years it has become clear that categorization is far more complex than that. A new theory of categorization, called *prototype theory*, has emerged. It shows that human categorization is based on principles that extend far beyond those envisioned in the classical theory. One of our goals is to survey the complexities of the way people really categorize. For example, the title of this book was inspired by the Australian aboriginal language Dyirbal, which has a category, *balan*, that actually includes women, fire, and dangerous things. It also includes birds that are *not* dangerous, as well as exceptional animals, such as the platypus, bandicoot, and echidna. This is not simply a matter of categorization by common properties, as we shall see when we discuss Dyirbal classification in detail.

Categorization is not a matter to be taken lightly. There is nothing more basic than categorization to our thought, perception, action, and speech. Every time we see something as a *kind* of thing, for example, a tree, we are categorizing. Whenever we reason about *kinds* of things—chairs, nations, illnesses, emotions, any kind of thing at all—we are employing categories. Whenever we intentionally perform any *kind* of action, say something as mundane as writing with a pencil, hammering with a hammer, or ironing clothes, we are using categories. The particular action we perform on that occasion is a *kind* of motor activity (e.g., writing, hammering, ironing), that is, it is in a particular category of motor actions. They are never done in exactly the same way, yet despite the differences in particular movements, they are all movements of a kind, and we know how to make movements of that kind. And any time we either produce or understand any utterance of any reasonable length,

* George Lakoff, 'The importance of characterization', ch. 1 of *Women, Fire and Dangerous Things: What Categories Reveal about the Mind* (Chicago and London: The University of Chicago Press, 1987). © 1987 The University of Chicago. Reprinted by permission.

we are employing dozens if not hundreds of categories: categories of speech sounds, of words, of phrases and clauses, as well as conceptual categories. Without the ability to categorize, we could not function at all, either in the physical world or in our social and intellectual lives. An understånding of how we categorize is central to any understanding of how we think and how we function, and therefore central to an understanding of what makes us human.

Most categorization is automatic and unconscious, and if we become aware of it at all, it is only in problematic cases. In moving about the world, we automatically categorize people, animals, and physical objects, both natural and man-made. This sometimes leads to the impression that we just categorize things as they are, that things come in natural kinds, and that our categories of mind naturally fit the kinds of things there are in the world. But a large proportion of our categories are not categories of *things;* they are categories of abstract entities. We categorize events, actions, emotions, spatial relationships, social relationships, and abstract entities of an enormous range: governments, illnesses, and entities in both scientific and folk theories, like electrons and colds. Any adequate account of human thought must provide an accurate theory for *all* our categories, both concrete and abstract.

From the time of Aristotle to the later work of Wittgenstein, categories were thought be well understood and unproblematic. They were assumed to be abstract containers, with things either inside or outside the category. Things were assumed to be in the same category if and only if they had certain properties in common. And the properties they had in common were taken as defining the category.

This classical theory was not the result of empirical study. It was not even a subject of major debate. It was a philosophical position arrived at on the basis of a priori speculation. Over the centuries it simply became part of the background assumptions taken for granted in most scholarly disciplines. In fact, until very recently, the classical theory of categories was not even thought of as a *theory*. It was taught in most disciplines not as an empirical hypothesis but as an unquestionable, definitional truth.

In a remarkably short time, all that has changed. Categorization has moved from the background to center stage because of empirical studies in a wide range of disciplines. Within cognitive psychology, categorization has become a major field of study, thanks primarily to the pioneering work of Eleanor Rosch, who made categorization an issue. She focused on two implications of the classical theory:

First, if categories are defined only by properties that all members share, then no members should be better examples of the category than any other members. Second, if categories are defined only by properties inherent in the members, then categories should be independent of the peculiarities of any beings doing the categorizing; that is, they should not involve such matters as human neurophysiology, human body movement, and specific human capacities to perceive, to form mental images, to learn and remember, to organize the things learned, and to communicate efficiently.

Rosch observed that studies by herself and others demonstrated that categories, in general, have best examples (called "prototypes") and that all of the specifically human capacities just mentioned do play a role in categorization.

In retrospect, such results should not have been all that surprising. Yet the specific details sent shock waves throughout the cognitive sciences, and many of the reverberations are still to be felt. Prototype theory, as it is evolving, is changing our idea of the most fundamental of human capacities—the capacity to categorize—and with it, our idea of what the human mind and human reason are like. Reason, in the West, has long been assumed to be disembodied and abstract—distinct on the one hand from perception and the body and culture, and on the other hand from the mechanisms of imagination, for example, metaphor and mental imagery.

In this century, reason has been understood by many philosophers, psychologists, and others as roughly fitting the model of formal deductive logic:

Reason is the mechanical manipulation of abstract symbols which are meaningless in themselves, but can be given meaning by virtue of their capacity to refer to things either in the actual world or in possible states of the world.

Since the digital computer works by symbol manipulation and since its symbols can be interpreted in terms of a data base, which is often viewed as a partial model of reality, the computer has been taken by many as essentially possessing the capacity to reason. This is the basis of the contemporary mind-as-computer metaphor, which has spread from computer science and cognitive psychology to the culture at large.

Since we reason not just about individual things or people but about categories of things and people, categorization is crucial to every view of reason. Every view of reason must have an associated account of categorization. The view of reason as the *disembodied* manipulation of abstract symbols comes with an implicit theory of categorization. It is a version of the classical theory in which categories are represented by sets, which are in turn defined by the properties shared by their members.

There is a good reason why the view of reason as disembodied symbol-manipulation makes use of the classical theory of categories. If symbols in general can get their meaning only through their capacity to correspond to things, then *category* symbols can get their meaning only through a capacity to correspond to *categories* in the world (the real world or some possible world). Since the symbol-to-object correspondence that defines meaning in general must be independent of the peculiarities of the human mind and body, it follows that the symbol-to-category correspondence that defines meaning for category symbols must also be independent of the peculiarities of the human mind and body. To accomplish this, categories must be seen as existing in the world independent of people and defined only by the characteristics of their members and not in terms of any characteristics of the human. The classical theory is just what is needed, since it defines categories only in terms of shared properties of the *members* and not in terms of the peculiarities of human understanding.

To question the classical view of categories in a fundamental way is thus to question the view of reason as disembodied symbol-manipulation and correspondingly to question the most popular version of the mind-as-computer metaphor. Contemporary prototype theory does just that—through detailed empirical research in anthropology, linguistics, and psychology.

The approach to prototype theory that we will be presenting here suggests that human categorization is essentially a matter of both human experience and imagination—of perception, motor activity, and culture on the one hand, and of metaphor, metonymy, and mental imagery on the other. As a consequence, human reason crucially depends on the same factors, and therefore cannot be characterized merely in terms of the manipulation of abstract symbols. Of course, certain aspects of human reason can be isolated artificially and modeled by abstract symbol-manipulation, just as some part of human categorization does fit the classical theory. But we are interested not merely in some artificially isolatable subpart of the human capacity to categorize and reason, but in the full range of that capacity. As we shall see, those aspects of categorization that do fit the classical theory are special cases of a general theory of cognitive models, one that permits us to characterize the experiential and imaginative aspects of reason as well.

To change the very concept of a category is to change not only our concept of the mind, but also our understanding of the world. Categories are categories *of* things. Since we understand the world not only in terms of individual things but also in terms of *categories* of things, we tend to attribute a real existence to those categories. We have categories for biological species, physical substances, artifacts, colors, kinsmen, and emotions and even categories of sentences, words, and meanings. We have categories for everything we can think about. To change the concept of *category* itself is to change our understanding of the world. At stake is our understanding of everything from what a biological species is to what a word is.

The evidence we will be considering suggests a shift from classical categories to prototype-based categories defined by cognitive models. It is a change that implies other changes: changes in the concepts of truth, knowledge, meaning, rationality—even grammar. A number of familiar ideas will fall by the wayside. Here are some that will have to be left behind:

- Meaning is based on truth and reference; it concerns the relationship between symbols and things in the world.
- Biological species are natural kinds, defined by common essential properties.
- The mind is separate from, and independent of, the body.
- Emotion has no conceptual content.
- Grammar is a matter of pure form.
- Reason is transcendental, in that it transcends—goes beyond—the way human beings, or any other kinds of beings, happen to think. It concerns the inferential relationships among all possible concepts in this universe or any other. Mathematics is a form of transcendental reason.
- There is a correct, God's eye view of the world—a single correct way of understanding what is and is not true.
- All people think using the same conceptual system.

These ideas have been part of the superstructure of Western intellectual life for two thousand years. They are tied, in one way or another, to the classical concept of a category. When that concept is left behind, the others will be too. They need to be replaced by ideas that are not only more accurate, but more humane.

Many of the ideas we will be arguing against, on empirical grounds, have been taken as part of what *defines* science. One consequence of this study will be that certain common views of science will seem too narrow. Consider, for example, scientific rigor. There is a narrow view of science that considers as rigorous only hypotheses framed in first-order predicate calculus with a standard model-theoretic interpretation, or some equivalent system, say a computer program using primitives that are taken as corresponding to an external reality. Let us call this the predicate calculus (or "PC") view of scientific theorizing. The PC view characterizes explanations only in terms of deductions from hypotheses, or correspondingly, in terms of computations. Such a methodology not only claims to be rigorous in itself, it also claims that no other approach can be sufficiently precise to be called scientific. The PC view is prevalent in certain communities of linguists and cognitive psychologists and enters into many investigations in the cognitive sciences.

Such a view of science has long been discredited among philosophers of science (for example, see Hanson 1961, Hesse 1963, Kuhn 1970, 1977, and Feyerabend 1975). The PC view is especially inappropriate in the cognitive sciences since it *assumes* an a priori view of categorization, namely, the classical theory that categories are sets defined by common properties of objects. Such an assumption makes it impossible to ask, as an empirical question, whether the classical view of categorization is correct. The classical view is assumed to be correct, because it is built into classical logic, and hence into the PC view. Thus, we sometimes find circular arguments about the nature of categorization that are of the following form:

Premise (often hidden): The PC view of scientific rigor is correct.

. . .

. . .

. . .

Conclusion: Categories are classical.

The conclusion is, of course, presupposed by the premise. To avoid vacuity, the empirical study of categorization cannot take the PC view of scientific rigor for granted.

A central goal of cognitive science is to discover what reason is like and, correspondingly, what categories are like. It is therefore especially important for the study of cognitive science not to assume the PC view, which presupposes an a priori answer to such empirical questions. This, of course, does not mean that one cannot be rigorous or precise. It only means that rigor and precision must be characterized in another way—a way that does not stifle the empirical study of the mind.

The PC view of rigor leads to rigor mortis in the study of categorization. It leads to a view of the sort proposed by Osherson and Smith (1981) and Armstrong, Gleitman, and Gleitman (1983), namely, that the classical view of categorization is correct and the enormous number of phenomena that do not accord with it are either due to an "identification" mechanism that has nothing to do with reason or are minor "recalcitrant" phenomena. As we go through this book, we will see that there seem to be more so-called recalcitrant phenomena than there are phenomena that work by the classical view.

This book surveys a wide variety of rigorous empirical studies of the nature of human categorization. In concluding that categorization is not classical, the book implicitly suggests that the PC view of scientific rigor is itself not scientifically valid. The result is not chaos, but an expanded perspective on human reason, one which by no means requires imprecision or vagueness in scientific inquiry. The studies cited, for example, those by Berlin, Kay, Ekman, Rosch, Tversky, Dixon, and many others, more than meet the prevailing standards of scientific rigor and accuracy, while challenging the conception of categories presupposed by the PC view of rigor. In addition, the case studies presented below in Book II are intended as examples of empirical research that meet or exceed the prevailing standards. In correcting the classical view of categorization, such studies serve to raise the general standards of scientific accuracy in the cognitive sciences.

The view of categorization that I will be presenting has not arisen all at once. It has developed through a number of intermediate stages that lead up to the cognitive model approach. An account of those intermediate steps begins with the later philosophy of Ludwig Wittgenstein and goes up through the psychological research of Eleanor Rosch and her associates.

REFERENCES

Armstrong, S. L., L. Gleitman, and H. Gleitman (1983). 'What some concepts might not be'. *Cognition* 13: 263–308.

Feyerabend, P. (1975). *Against Method: Outline of an Anarchistic Theory of Knowledge*. London: New Left Books.

Hanson, N. R. (1961). *Patterns of Discovery: An Inquiry into the Conceptual Foundations of Science*. Cambridge: Cambridge University Press.

Hesse, M. (1963). *Models and Analogies in Science*. London: Sheed & Ward.

Kuhn, T. (1970). *The Structure of Scientific Revolutions*, 2nd edn. Chicago: University of Chicago Press.

Kuhn, T. (1977). *The Essential Tension*. Chicago: University of Chicago Press.
Osherson, D., and E. Smith, (1981). 'On the adequacy of prototype theory as a theory of concepts'. *Cognition* 9(1): 35–58.

From Wittgenstein to Rosch

The short history I am about to give is not intended to be exhaustive. Its purpose, instead, is to give some sense of the development of the major themes I will be discussing. Here are some of those themes.

Family resemblances: The idea that members of a category may be related to one another without all members having any properties in common that define the category.

Centrality: The idea that some members of a category may be "better examples" of that category than others.

Polysemy as categorization: The idea that related meanings of words form categories and that the meanings bear family resemblances to one another.

Generativity as a prototype phenomenon: This idea concerns categories that are defined by a generator (a particular member or subcategory) plus rules (or a general principle such as similarity). In such cases, the generator has the status of a central, or "prototypical," category member.

Membership gradience: The idea that at least some categories have degrees of membership and no clear boundaries.

Centrality gradience: The idea that members (or subcategories) which are clearly within the category boundaries may still be more or less central.

Conceptual embodiment: The idea that the properties of certain categories are a consequence of the nature of human biological capacities and of the experience of functioning in a physical and social environment. It is contrasted with the idea that concepts exist independent of the bodily nature of any thinking beings and independent of their experience.

Functional embodiment: The idea that certain concepts are not merely *understood intellectually*; rather, they are *used* automatically, unconsciously, and without noticeable effort as part of normal functioning. Concepts used in this way have a different, and more important, psychological status than those that are only thought about consciously.

Basic-level categorization: The idea that categories are not merely organized in a hierarchy from the most general to the most specific, but are also organized so that the categories that are cognitively basic are "in the middle" of a general-to-specific hierarchy. Generalization proceeds "upward" from the basic level and specialization proceeds "downward."

Basic-level primacy: The idea that basic-level categories are functionally and epistemologically primary with respect to the following factors: gestalt perception, image formation, motor movement, knowledge organization, ease of cognitive processing (learning, recognition, memory, etc.), and ease of linguistic expression.

Reference-point, or "metonymic," reasoning: The idea that a part of a category (that is, a member or subcategory) can stand for the whole category in certain reasoning processes.

* George Lakoff, 'From Wittgenstein to Rosch', ch. 2 of *Women, Fire and Dangerous Things: What Categories Reveal about the Mind* (Chicago and London: The University of Chicago Press, 1987). © 1987 The University of Chicago. Reprinted by permission.

What unites these themes is the idea of a cognitive model:

- Cognitive models are directly *embodied* with respect to their content, or else they are systematically linked to directly embodied models. Cognitive models structure thought and are used in forming categories and in reasoning. Concepts characterized by cognitive models are understood via the embodiment of the models.
- Most cognitive models are embodied with respect to use. Those that are not are only used consciously and with noticeable effort.
- The nature of conceptual embodiment leads to *basic-level categorization* and *basic-level primacy*.
- Cognitive models are used in *reference-point, or "metonymic," reasoning*.
- *Membership gradience* arises when the cognitive model characterizing a concept contains a scale.
- *Centrality gradience* arises through the interaction of cognitive models.
- *Family resemblances* involve resemblances among models.
- *Polysemy* arises from the fact that there are systematic relationships between different cognitive models and between elements of the same model. The same word is often used for elements that stand in such cognitive relations to one another.

Thus it is the concept of a cognitive model, which we will discuss in the remainder of the book, that ties together the themes of this section.

The scholars we will be discussing in this section are those I take to be most representative of the development of these themes:

- Ludwig Wittgenstein is associated with the ideas of family resemblance, centrality, and gradience.
- J. L. Austin's views on the relationships among meanings of words are both a crystalization of earlier ideas in lexicography and historical semantics and a precursor of the contemporary view of polysemy as involving family resemblances among meanings.
- Lotfi Zadeh began the technical study of categories with fuzzy boundaries by conceiving of a theory of fuzzy sets as a generalization of standard set theory.
- Floyd Lounsbury's generative analysis of kinship categories is an important link between the idea that a category can be generated by a generator plus rules and the idea that a category has central members (and subcategories).
- Brent Berlin and Paul Kay are perhaps best known for their research on color categories, which empirically established the ideas of centrality and gradience.
- Paul Kay and Chad McDaniel put together color research from anthropology and neurophysiology and established the importance of the embodiment of concepts and the role that embodiment plays in determining centrality.
- Roger Brown began the study of what later became known as "basic-level categories." He observed that there is a "first level" at which children learn object categories and name objects, which is neither the most general nor most specific level. This level is characterized by distinctive actions, as well as by shorter and more frequently used names. He saw this level of categorization as "natural," whereas he viewed higher-level and lower-level categorization as "achievements of the imagination."
- Brent Berlin and his associates, in research on plant and animal naming, empirically established for these domains many of the fundamental ideas associated with basic-level categorization and basic-level primacy. They thereby demonstrated that embodiment determines some of the most significant properties of human categories.

– Paul Ekman and his co-workers have shown that there are universal basic human emotions that have physical correlates in facial expressions and the autonomic nervous system. He thereby confirmed such ideas as basic-level concepts, basic-level primacy, and centrality while demonstrating that emotional concepts are embodied.
– Eleanor Rosch saw the generalizations behind such studies of particular cases and proposed that thought in general is organized in terms of prototypes and basic-level structures. It was Rosch who saw categorization itself as one of the most important issues in cognition. Together with Carolyn Mervis and other co-workers, Rosch established research paradigms in cognitive psychology for demonstrating centrality, family resemblance, basic-level categorization, basic-level primacy, and reference-point reasoning, as well as certain kinds of embodiment. Rosch is perhaps best known for developing experimental paradigms for determining subjects' ratings of how good an example of a category a member is judged to be. Rosch ultimately realized that these ratings do not in themselves constitute models for representing category structure. They are effects that are inconsistent with the classical theory and that place significant constraints on what an adequate account of categorization must be.

These scholars all played a significant role in the history of the paradigm we will be presenting. The theory of cognitive models, which we will discuss later, attempts to bring their contributions into a coherent paradigm.

There are some notable omissions from our short survey. Since graded categories will be of only passing interest to us, I will not be mentioning much of the excellent work in that area. Graded categories are real. To my knowledge, the most detailed empirical study of graded categories is Kempton's thoroughly documented book on cognitive prototypes with graded extensions (Kempton 1981). It is based on field research in Mexico on the categorization of pottery. I refer the interested reader to that superb work, as well as to Labov's classic 1973 paper. I will also have relatively little to say about fuzzy set theory, since it is also tangential to our concerns here. Readers interested in the extensive literature that has developed on the theory of fuzzy sets and systems should consult Dubois and Prade (1980). There is also a tradition of research in cognitive psychology that will not be surveyed here. Despite Rosch's ultimate refusal to interpret her goodness-of-example ratings as constituting a representation of category structure, other psychologists have taken that path and have given what I call an EFFECTS = STRUCTURE INTERPRETATION to Rosch's results. Smith and Medin (1980) have done an excellent survey of research in cognitive psychology that is based on this interpretation. In chapter 9 below, I will argue that the EFFECTS = STRUCTURE INTERPRETATION is in general inadequate.

Let us now turn to our survey.

WITTGENSTEIN

Family resemblances

The first major crack in the classical theory is generally acknowledged to have been noticed by Wittgenstein (1953, 1: 66–71). The classical category has *clear boundaries*, which are defined by *common properties*. Wittgenstein pointed out that a category like *game* does not fit the classical mold, since there are no common properties shared by all games. Some games involve mere amusement, like ring-around-the-rosy. Here there is no competition—no winning or losing—though in other games there is. Some games involve luck, like board games where a throw of the dice determines each move. Others, like chess, involve skill. Still others, like gin rummy, involve both.

Though there is no single collection of properties that all games share, the category of games is united by what Wittgenstein calls *family resemblances*. Members of a family resemble one another in various ways: they may share the same build or the same facial features, the same hair color, eye color, or temperament, and the like. But there need be no single collection of properties shared by everyone in a family. Games, in this respect, are like families. Chess and go both involve competition, skill, and the use of long-term strategies. Chess and poker both involve competition. Poker and old maid are both card games. In short, games, like family members, are similar to one another in a wide variety of ways. That, and not a single, well-defined collection of common properties, is what makes *game* a category.

Extendable boundaries

Wittgenstein also observed that there was no fixed boundary to the category *game*. The category could be extended and new kinds of games introduced, provided that they resembled previous games in appropriate ways. The introduction of video games in the 1970s was a recent case in history where the boundaries of the *game* category were extended on a large scale. One can always impose an artificial boundary for some purpose; what is important for his point is that extensions are possible, as well as artificial limitations. Wittgenstein cites the example of the category *number*. Historically, numbers were first taken to be integers and were then extended successively to rational numbers, real numbers, complex numbers, transfinite numbers, and all sorts of other kinds of numbers invented by mathematicians. One can for some purpose limit the category *number* to integers only, or rational numbers only, or real numbers only. But the category *number is* not bounded in any natural way, and it can be limited or extended depending on one's purposes.

In mathematics, intuitive human concepts like *number* must receive precise definitions. Wittgenstein's point is that different mathematicians give different precise definitions, depending on their goals. One can define *number* to include or exclude transfinite numbers, infinitesimals, inaccessible ordinals, and the like. The same is true of the concept of a *polyhedron*. Lakatos (1976) describes a long history of disputes within mathematics about the properties of polyhedra, beginning with Euler's conjecture that the number of vertices minus the number of edges plus the number of faces equals two. Mathematicians over the years have come up with counterexamples to Euler's conjecture, only to have other mathematicians claim that they had used the "wrong" definition of *polyhedron*. Mathematicians have defined and redefined *polyhedron* repeatedly to fit their goals. The point again is that there is no single well-defined intuitive category *polyhedron* that includes tetrahedra and cubes and some fixed range of other constructs. The category *polyhedron* can be given precise boundaries in many ways, but the intuitive concept is not limited in any of those ways; rather, it is open to both limitations and extensions.

Central and noncentral members

According to the classical theory, categories are uniform in the following respect: they are defined by a collection of properties that the category members share. Thus, no members should be more central than other members. Yet Wittgenstein's example of *number* suggests that integers are central, that they have a status as numbers that, say, complex numbers or transfinite numbers do not have. Every precise definition of *number* must include the integers;

not every definition must include transfinite numbers. If anything is a number, the integers are numbers; that is not true of transfinite numbers. Similarly, any definition of polyhedra had better include tetrahedra and cubes. The more exotic polyhedra can be included or excluded, depending on your purposes. Wittgenstein suggests that the same is true of games. "Someone says to me: 'Show the children a game.' I teach them gaming with dice, and the other says 'I didn't mean that sort of game'" (1: 70). Dice is just not a very good example of a game. The fact that there can be good and bad examples of a category does not follow from the classical theory. Somehow the goodness-of-example structure needs to be accounted for.

AUSTIN

Wittgenstein assumed that there is a single category named by the word *game*, and he proposed that that category and other categories are structured by family resemblances and good and bad examples. Philosopher J. L. Austin extended this sort of analysis to the study of words themselves. In his celebrated paper, "The Meaning of a Word," written in 1940 and published in 1961, Austin asked, "Why do we call different [kinds of] things by the same name?" The traditional answer is that the kinds of things named are similar, where "similar" means "partially identical." This answer relies on the classical theory of categories. If there are common properties, those properties form a classical category, and the name applies to this category. Austin argued that this account is not accurate. He cited several classes of cases. As we will see in the remainder of this book, Austin's analysis prefigured much of contemporary cognitive semantics—especially the application of prototype theory to the study of word meaning.

If we translate Austin's remarks into contemporary terms, we can see the relationship between Austin's observation and Wittgenstein's: the senses of a word can be seen as forming a category, with each sense being a member of that category. Since the senses often do not have properties in common, there is no classical category of senses that the word could be naming. However, the senses can be viewed as forming a category of the kind Wittgenstein described. There are central senses and noncentral senses. The senses may not be similar (in the sense of sharing properties), but instead are related to one another in other specifiable ways. It is such relationships among the senses that enable those senses to be viewed as constituting a single category: the relationships provide an explanation of why a single word is used to express those particular senses. This idea is far from new. Part of the job of traditional historical semanticists, as well as lexicographers, has been to speculate on such relationships. Recent research has taken up this question again in a systematic way. The most detailed contemporary study along these lines has been done by Brugman (1981).

Let us now turn to Austin's examples:

The adjective 'healthy': when I talk of a healthy body, and again of a healthy complexion, of healthy exercise: the word is *not* just being used *equivocally*... there is what we may call a *primary nuclear sense* of 'healthy': the sense in which 'healthy' is used of a healthy body: I call this *nuclear* because it is 'contained as a part' in the other two senses which may be set out as 'productive of healthy bodies' and 'resulting from a healthy body'.... Now are we content to say that the exercise, the complexion, and the body are all called 'healthy' because they are similar? Such a remark cannot fail to be misleading. Why make it? (p. 71)

Austin's *primary nuclear sense* corresponds to what contemporary linguists call *central* or *prototypical* senses. The contained-as-a-part relationship is an instance of what we will refer to below as metonymy—where the part stands for the whole. Thus, given the relationships "productive of" and "resulting from," Austin's examples can be viewed in the following way:

Exercise of type *B* is productive of bodies of type *A*.
Complexion of type *C* results from bodies of type *A*.
The word *healthy* names *A*.
With respect to naming, *A* stands for *B*. (Metonymy)
With respect to naming, *A* stands for *C*. (Metonymy)

Thus, the word "healthy" has senses *A*, *B*, and *C*. *A*, *B*, and *C* form a category whose members are related in the above way. *A* is the central member of this category of senses (Austin's *primary nuclear sense*). *B* and *C* are extended senses, where metonymy is the principle of extension.

I am interpreting Austin as making an implicit psychological claim about categorization. In the very act of pointing out and analyzing the *differences* among the senses, Austin is presupposing that these senses form a natural collection for speakers—so natural that the senses have to be differentiated by an analyst. No such analysis would be needed for true homonyms, say, *bank* (where you put your money) and *bank* (of a river), which are not part of a natural collection (or category) of senses. In pointing out the existence of a small number of mechanisms by which senses are related to one another, Austin is implicitly suggesting that those mechanisms are psychologically real (rather than being just the arbitrary machinations of a clever analyst). He is, after all, trying to explain why people naturally use the same words for different senses. His implicit claim is that these mechanisms are *principles* which provide a "good reason" for grouping the senses together by the use of the same word. What I have referred to as "metonymy" is just one such mechanism.

From metonymy, Austin turns to what Johnson and I (Lakoff and Johnson 1980) refer to as metaphor, but which Austin, following Aristotle, terms "analogy."

When *A:B::X:Y* then *A* and *X* are often called by the same name, e.g., the foot of a mountain and the foot of a list. Here there is a good reason for calling the things both "feet" but are we to say they are "similar"? Not in any ordinary sense. We may say that the relations in which they stand to *B* and *Y* are similar relations. Well and good: but *A* and *X* are not the relations in which they stand. (pp. 71–2)

Austin isn't explicit here, but what seems to be going on is that both mountains and lists are being structured in terms of a metaphorical projection of the human body onto them. Expanding somewhat on Austin's analysis and translating it into contemporary terminology, we have:

A is the bottom-most part of the body.
X is the bottom-most part of the mountain.
X' is the bottom-most part of a list.
Body is projected onto mountain, with *A* projected onto *X'*. (Metaphor)
Body is projected onto list, with *A* projected onto *X'*. (Metaphor)
The word "foot" names *A*.
A, *X'*, and *X'* form a category, with *A* as central member. *X* and *X'* are noncentral members related to *A* by metaphor.

Austin also notes examples of what we will refer to below as *chaining* within a category.

Another case is where I call *B* by the same name as *A*, because it resembles *A*, *C* by the same name because it resembles *B*, *D* . . . and so on. But ultimately *A* and, say *D* do not resemble each other in any recognizable sense at all. This is a very common case: and the dangers are obvious when we search for something 'identical' in all of them! (p. 72)

Here A is the *primary nuclear sense*, and B, C, and D are extended senses forming a chain. *A*, *B*, *C*, and *D* are all members of the same category of senses, with A as the central member.

Take a word like 'fascist': this originally connotes a great many characteristics at once: say, *x*, *y*, and *z*. Now we will use 'fascist' subsequently of things which possess only *one* of these striking characteristics. So that things called 'fascist' in these senses, which we may call 'incomplete' senses, need not be similar at all to each other. (p. 72)

This example is very much like one Fillmore (1982) has recently given in support of the use of prototype theory in lexical semantics. Fillmore takes the verb *climb*, as in

– John climbed the ladder.

Here, "climbing" includes both motion upward and the use of the hands to grasp onto the thing climbed. However, climbing can involve just motion upwards and no use of the hands, as in

– The airplane climbed to 20,000 feet.

Or the motion upward may be eliminated if there is grasping of the appropriate sort, as in

– He climbed out onto the ledge.

Such contemporary semantic analyses using prototype theory are very much in the spirit of Austin.
    Fillmore's frame semantics is also prefigured by Austin.

Take the sense in which I talk of a cricket bat and a cricket ball and a cricket umpire. The reason that all are called by the same name is perhaps that each has its part—its *own special* part—to play in the activity called cricketing: it is no good to say that *cricket* means simply 'used in cricket': for we cannot explain what we mean by 'cricket' *except* by explaining the special parts played in cricketing by the bat, ball, etc. (p. 73)

Austin here is discussing a holistic structure—a gestalt—governing our understanding of activities like cricket. Such activities are structured by what we call a cognitive model, an overall structure which is more than merely a composite of its parts. A modifier like *cricket* in *cricket bat, cricket ball, cricket umpire*, and so on does not pick out any common property or similarity shared by bats, balls, and umpires. It refers to the structured activity as a whole. And the nouns that *cricket* can modify form a category, but not a category based on shared properties. Rather it is a category based on the structure of the activity of cricket and on those things that are part of the activity. The entities characterized by the cognitive model of cricket are those that are in the category. What defines the category is our structured understanding of the activity.
    Cognitive psychologists have recently begun to study categories based on such holistically structured activities. Barsalou (1983, 1984) has studied such categories as *things to take on a camping trip, foods not to eat on a diet, clothes to wear in the snow*, and the like. Such categories, among their other properties, do not show family resemblances among their members.
    Like Wittgenstein, Austin was dedicated to showing the inadequacies of traditional philosophical views of language and mind—views that are still widely held. His contribution to prototype theory was to notice for words the kinds of things that Wittgenstein noticed for conceptual categories. Language is, after all, an aspect of cognition. Following Austin's lead, we will try to show how prototype theory generalizes to the linguistic as well as the non-linguistic aspects of mind.

ZADEH

Some categories do not have gradations of membership, while others do. The category *U.S. Senator* is well defined. One either is or is not a senator. On the other hand, categories like *rich people* or *tall men* are graded, simply because there are gradations of richness and tallness. Lotfi Zadeh (1965) devised a form of set theory to model graded categories. He called it *fuzzy set theory*. In a classical set, everything is either in the set (has membership value 1) or is outside the set (has membership value 0). In a fuzzy set, as Zadeh defined it, additional values are allowed between 0 and 1. This corresponds to Zadeh's intuition that some men are neither clearly tall nor clearly short, but rather in the middle—tall to some degree.

In the original version of fuzzy set theory, operations on fuzzy sets are simple generalizations of operations on ordinary sets:

Suppose element x has membership value v in fuzzy set A and membership value w in fuzzy set B.

Intersection: The value of x in $A \cap B$ is the minimum of v and w.
Union: The value of x in $A \cup B$ is the maximum of v and w.
Complement: The value of x in the complement of A is $1 - v$.

It is a natural and ingenious extension of the classical theory of sets.

Since Zadeh's original paper, other definitions for union and intersection have been suggested. For an example, see Goguen 1969. The best discussion of attempts to apply fuzzy logic to natural language is in McCawley 1981.

LOUNSBURY

Cognitive anthropology has had an important effect on the development of prototype theory, beginning with Floyd Lounsbury's (1964) studies of American Indian kinship systems. Take the example of Fox, in which the word *nehcihsähA is* used not only to refer to one's maternal uncle—that is, one's mother's mother's son—but also to one's mother's mother's son's son, one's mother's mother's father's son's son, one's mother's brother's son, one's mother's brother's son's son, and a host of other relatives. The same sort of treatment also occurs for other kinship categories. There are categories of "fathers," "mothers," "sons," and "daughters" with just as diverse a membership.

The Fox can, of course, distinguish uncles from great-uncles from nephews. But they are all part of the same kinship category, and thus are named the same. Lounsbury discovered that such categories were structured in terms of a "focal member" and a small set of general rules extending each category to nonfocal members. The same rules apply across all the categories. The rules applying in Fox are what Lounsbury called the "Omaha type":

Skewing rule: Anyone's father's sister, as a linking relative, is equivalent to that person's sister.
Merging rule: Any person's sibling of the same sex, as a linking relative, is equivalent to that person himself.
Half-sibling rule: Any child of one of one's parents is one's sibling.

The condition "as a linking relative" is to prevent the rule from applying directly; instead, there must be an intermediate relative between ego (the reference point) and the person being described. For example, the skewing rule does not say that a person's paternal aunt is equivalent to his sister. But it does say, for example, that his father's paternal aunt is equivalent to his father's sister. In this case, the intermediate relative is the father.

These rules have corollaries. For example,

> Skewing corollary: The brother's child of any female linking relative is equivalent to the sibling of that female linking relative. (For example, a mother's brother's daughter is equivalent to a mother's sister.)

Lounsbury illustrates how such rules would work for the Fox maternal uncle category. We will use the following abbreviations: M: mother, F: father, B: brother, S: sister, d: daughter, s: son. Let us consider the following examples of the *nehcihsähA* (mother's brother) category, and the equivalence rules that make them part of this category. Lounsbury's point in these examples is to take a very distant relative and show precisely how the same general rules place that relative in the MB (mother's brother) category. Incidentally, all the intermediate relatives in the following cases are also in the MB category—e.g., MMSs, that is, mother's mother's sister's son, etc. Let "→" stand for "is equivalent to."

1. Mother's mother's father's sister's son: MMFSs
   MMFSs → MMSs [by the skewing rule]
   MMSs   → MMs   [by the merging rule]
   MMs   → MB   [by the half-sibling rule]
2. Mother's mother's sister's son's son: MMSss
   MMSss → MMss [by the merging rule]
   MMss   → MBs   [by the half-sibling rule]
   MBs   → MB   [by the skewing corollary]
3. Mother's brother's son's son's son: MBsss
   MBsss → MBss [by the skewing corollary]
   MBss   → MBs   [by the skewing corollary]
   MBs   → MB   [by the skewing corollary]

Similarly, the other "uncles" in Fox are equivalent to MB.

Not all conceptual systems for categorizing kinsmen have the same skewing rules. Lounsbury also cites the Crow version of the skewing rule:

> Skewing rule: Any woman's brother, as a linking relative, is equivalent to that woman's son, as a linking relative.
>
> Skewing corollary: The sister of any male linking relative is equivalent to the mother of that male linking relative.

These rules are responsible for some remarkable categorizations. One's paternal aunt's son is classified as one's "father." But one's paternal aunt's daughter is classified as one's "grandmother"! Here are the derivations:

Father's sister's son: FSs
FSs → FMs [by skewing corollary]
FMs → FB   [by half-sibling rule]
FB   → F   [by merging rule]
Father's sister's daughter: FSd
FSd → FMd [by skewing corollary]
FMd → FS   [by half-sibling rule]
FS   → FM   [by skewing corollary]

Moreover, Lounsbury observed that these categories were not mere matters of naming. Such things as inheritance and social responsibilities follow category lines.

Categories of this sort—with a central member plus general rules—are by no means the norm in language, as we shall see. Yet they do occur. We will refer to such a category as a *generative* category and to its central member as a *generator*. A generative category is characterized by at least one generator plus something else: it is the "something else" that takes the generator as input and yields the entire category as output. It may be either a general principle like similarity or general rules that apply elsewhere in the system or specific rules that apply only in that category. In Lounsbury's cases, the "something else" is a set of rules that apply throughout the kinship system. The generator plus the rules generate the category.

In such a category, the generator has a special status. It is the best example of the category, the model on which the category as a whole is built. It is a special case of a prototype.

BERLIN AND KAY

The next major contribution of cognitive anthropology to prototype theory was the color research of Brent Berlin and Paul Kay. In their classic, *Basic Color Terms* (Berlin and Kay 1969), they took on the traditional view that different languages could carve up the color spectrum in arbitrary ways. The first regularity they found was in what they called *basic color terms*. For a color term to be basic,

- It must consist of only one morpheme, like *green*, rather than more than one, as in *dark green* or *grass-colored*.
- The color referred to by the term must not be contained within another color. *Scarlet* is, for example, contained within *red*.
- It must not be restricted to a small number of objects. *Blond*, for example, is restricted to hair, wood, and perhaps a few other things.
- It must be common and generally known, like *yellow* as opposed to *saffron*.

Once one distinguishes basic from nonbasic color terms, generalizations appear.

- Basic color terms name basic color *categories*, whose central members are the same universally. For example, there is always a psychologically real category RED, with focal red as the best, or "purest," example.
- The color categories that basic color *terms* can attach to are the equivalents of the English color categories named by the terms *black, white, red, yellow, green, blue, brown, purple, pink, orange*, and *gray*.
- Although people can *conceptually* differentiate all these color categories, it is not the case that all languages make all of those differentiations. Many languages have fewer basic categories. Those categories include *unions* of the basic categories; for example, BLUE + GREEN, RED + ORANGE + YELLOW, etc. When there are fewer than eleven basic color terms in a language, one basic term, or more, names such a union.
- Languages form a hierarchy based on the number of basic color terms they have and the color categories those terms refer to.

Some languages, like English, use all eleven, while others use as few as two. When a language has only two basic color terms, they are *black* and *white*—which might more appropriately be called *cool* (covering black, blue, green, and gray) and *warm* (covering white, yellow, orange, and red). When a language has three basic color terms, they are *black, white*, and *red*. When a language has four basic color terms, the fourth is one of the following: *yellow, blue*, or *green*. The possibilities for four-color-term languages are thus: *black, white, red, yellow; black, white, red, blue*; and *black, white, red, green.* And so on, down the following hierarchy:

black, white
red
yellow, blue, green
brown
purple, pink, orange, gray

What made it possible for Berlin and Kay to find these regularities was their discovery of *focal colors.* If one simply asks speakers around the world to pick out the portions of the spectrum that their basic color terms refer to, there seem to be no significant regularities. The boundaries between the color ranges differ from language to language. The regularities appear only when one asks for the *best example* of a basic color term given a standardized chart of 320 small color chips. Virtually the same best examples are chosen for the basic color terms by speakers in language after language. For example, in languages that have a basic term for colors in the blue range, the best example is the same focal blue for all speakers no matter what language they speak. Suppose a language has a basic color term that covers the range of both *blue* and *green*; let us call that color *grue.* The best example of grue, they claim, will not be turquoise, which is in the middle of the blue-to-green spectrum. Instead the best example of grue will be either focal blue or focal green. The focal colors therefore allow for comparison of terms across languages.

The existence of focal colors shows that color categories are not uniform. Some members of the category RED are better examples of the category than others. Focal red is the best example. Color categories thus have central members. There is no general principle, however, for predicting the boundaries from the central members. They seem to vary, somewhat arbitrarily, from language to language.

KAY AND McDANIEL

The Berlin–Kay color research raised questions that were left unanswered. What determines the collection of universal focal colors? Why should the basic color terms pick out just those colors? Kay and McDaniel (1978) provided an answer to these questions that depended jointly on research on the neurophysiology of color vision by DeValois and his associates and on a slightly revised version of Zadeh's fuzzy set theory.

DeValois and his associates (DeValois, Abramov, and Jacobs 1966; DeValois and Jacobs 1968) had investigated the neurophysiology of color vision in the macaque, a monkey with a visual system similar to man's. Their research concentrated on the neural pathways between the eye and the brain. They found six types of cell. Four of these, called *opponent response cells*, determine hue, while the other two determine brightness. The opponent response cells are grouped into two pairs, one having to do with the perception of blue and yellow, the other having to do with the perception of red and green. Each opponent response cell has a spontaneous rate of firing—a base response rate that it maintains without any external stimulation. There are two types of blue-yellow cells. The $+B-Y$ cells fire above their base rate in response to a blue stimulus, and below their base rate in response to a yellow stimulus. The $+Y-B$ cells do the reverse: they fire above their base rate in response to yellow and below their base rate in response to blue. Similarly, there are two types of red-green cells: $+G-R$ cells fire above their base rate in response to green and below in response to red, while $+R-G$ cells fire above in response to red and below in response to green. The two types of blue-yellow cells jointly determine a blue-yellow response, while the two kinds of red-green cells jointly determine a red-green response.

Focal blue is perceived when the blue-yellow cells show a blue response and when the red-green cells are firing at the neutral base rate. Purple is a combination of blue and red; it is perceived when the blue-yellow cells show a blue response and the red-green cells show a red response. Turquoise is perceived when the blue-yellow cells show a blue response and the red-green cells show a green response. Pure primary colors—blue, yellow, red, and green—are perceived when either the blue-yellow or red-green cells are firing at their neutral base rates. Nonprimary colors correspond to cases where no opponent cells are firing at neutral base rates.

The remaining two kinds of cells are light- and darkness-sensitive. Pure black, white, and gray are perceived when the blue-yellow and red-green cells are all firing at their neutral base rates and making no color contribution. Pure black occurs when the darkness-sensitive cells are firing at their maximum rate and the light-sensitive cells are firing at their minimum rates. Pure white is the reverse.

Given these results from neurophysiological studies, Kay and McDaniel apply a version of fuzzy set theory to make sense of the Berlin–Kay results. For example, they define degree of membership in the category *blue* as the proportion of blue response on the part of the blue-yellow cells. Pure blue (degree of membership $= 1$) occurs when the red-green response is neutral. Blues in the direction of purple or green or white have an intermediate degree of membership in the blue category. Corresponding definitions are given for other primary colors. The accompanying diagrams give curves that correlate degree of membership in color categories with wavelengths in nanometers for hues and percentage of reflectance for black and white.

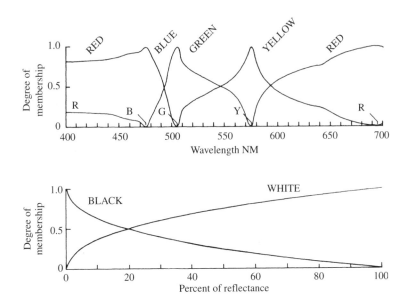

The neurophysiological account only characterizes the primary colors: black, white, red, yellow, blue, and green. What allows us to "see" other colors as being members of color categories? What about orange, brown, purple, etc.? Some cognitive mechanism in addition to the neurophysiology is needed to account for those. Kay and McDaniel suggested that such a mechanism would make use of something akin to fuzzy set theory.

The postulation of a cognitive mechanism that has some of the effects of fuzzy set theory enables Kay and McDaniel to do two things that the neurophysiological account alone could not do. First, it enables them to characterize focal nonprimary colors (orange, purple, pink, brown, gray, etc.) in the following intuitive way:

ORANGE = RED and YELLOW
PURPLE = BLUE and RED
PINK = RED and WHITE
BROWN = BLACK and YELLOW
GRAY = BLACK and WHITE

Thus, ORANGE is characterized in terms of the fuzzy set intersection of the RED and YELLOW curves. (Actually, for technical reasons the definition is twice the fuzzy-set intersection value. See Kay and McDaniel 1978, pp. 634–5, for details.) Correspondingly, PURPLE is defined in terms of the fuzzy set intersection of BLUE and RED, and GRAY in terms of the fuzzy set intersection for BLACK and WHITE. PINK and BROWN require somewhat different functions based on fuzzy set intersections.

The second advantage of fuzzy set theory is that it permits an intuitive account of basic color categories that include more than one focal color. Dani, for example, has only two basic color terms: *mili* contains black and all the cool colors, the greens and blues; *mola* contains white and all the warm colors, the reds, oranges, yellows, pinks, and red-purples. Some languages have basic color categories containing both blues and greens, while others have basic color categories containing both reds and yellows. Such cases can be accounted for intuitively by using fuzzy set union.

DARK-COOL = BLACK or GREEN or BLUE
LIGHT-WARM = WHITE or RED or YELLOW
COOL = GREEN or BLUE
WARM = RED or YELLOW

Thus, Kay and McDaniel make the claim that basic color categories are a product of both neurophysiology and cognitively real operations that can be partially modelled by fuzzy set intersection and union.

At present, this is the only plausible account we have of why the facts of basic color categories should be as they are. The Kay–McDaniel theory has important consequences for human categorization in general. It claims that colors are not objectively "out there in the world" independent of any beings. Color concepts are *embodied* in that focal colors are partly determined by human biology. Color categorization makes use of human biology, but color categories are more than merely a consequence of the nature of the world plus human biology. Color categories result from the world plus human biology plus a cognitive mechanism that has some of the characteristics of fuzzy set theory plus a culture-specific choice of which basic color categories there are.

The Kay–McDaniel theory seems to work well for characterizing the focal colors corresponding to basic color categories. But it does not work as well at the boundaries between colors. According to the Kay–McDaniel account, the boundaries, as well as the focal colors, should be uniform across languages. But this is simply not the case. The most detailed work on the detailed mapping of color categories, especially in nonfocal areas, has been done by MacLaury (1986). Among the test cases for the Kay–McDaniel theory are cases where a language does not have a separate color category for nonprimary focal colors, like purple and orange, colors that, in the Kay–McDaniel account, are "computed" on the basis of fuzzy set theory plus the response curves for the primary colors. The Kay–McDaniel theory predicts that colors like purple and orange should be treated uniformly across languages and that they should always be on the boundaries between basic color categories in languages that do not have separate categories for them.

But MacLaury has found cases where purple is entirely within the cool color range (a single color with focal points at blue and green) and other cases where purple is on the boundary between cool and red. He has also found cases where brown is subsumed by yellow and other cases where it is subsumed by black. That is, what we call "brown" falls within the range of a category with a center at pure yellow in some languages, and it falls within the range of a category with a center at pure black in other languages.

In Kay–McDaniel terms, this means that the fuzzy-set-theoretical functions that compute conjunctions and disjunctions for color categories are not exactly the same for all people; rather they vary in their boundary conditions from culture to culture. They are thus at least partly conventional, and not completely a matter of universal neurophysiology and cognition. What this requires is a revision of the Kay–McDaniel theory to permit conceptual systems for color to vary at the boundaries, by having the exact nature of the disjunction function be somewhat different in different systems. Such differences may not only be at the boundaries but at the focal peaks. Kay and McDaniel's theory implied that each binary disjunctive color category (e.g., COOL = BLUE or GREEN) should have two focal peaks (e.g., both focal blue and focal green). MacLaury has found cases where there is a cool category covering blue and green, but where there is a skewing effect such that the center of the category is at pure green alone or pure blue alone. Thus, in Kay–McDaniel terms, conceptual systems seem to have disjunction functions that take the blue and green response curves as input and yield an output curve with only one focal center. This would require a cognitive mechanism with more than just something akin to the operation of union in fuzzy set theory.

Color categories, thus, are generative categories in the same sense in which kinship categories characterized by Lounsbury are. They have generators plus something else. The generators are the neurophysiologically determined distribution functions, which have peaks where the primary colors are pure: black, white, red, yellow, blue, and green. These generators are universal; they are part of human neurophysiology. The "something else" needed to generate a system of basic color categories consists of a complex cognitive mechanism incorporating some of the characteristics of fuzzy set theory union and intersection. This cognitive mechanism has a small number of parameters that may take on different values in different cultures.

It is important to bear in mind that it is not just the names for colors that vary. The color names do not just attach to the neurophysiologically determined distribution functions directly. Cognitive mechanisms of the sort described above must be postulated in addition. There are general characteristics of the cognitive mechanisms, for example, the use of something like fuzzy set theory union and intersection. But, as MacLaury shows, color cognition is by no means all the same across cultures. Nor is it by any means arbitrarily different across cultures. The possible color ranges depend upon limited parameters within the cognitive mechanism.

BROWN AND BERLIN: GLIMPSES OF THE BASIC LEVEL

The study of basic-level categories is usually traced to Roger Brown's classic paper, "How Shall a Thing Be Called?" (1958), and his textbook, *Social Psychology* (1965, pp. 317–21). Brown observed that objects have many names: "The dime in my pocket is not only a *dime*. It is also *money*, a *metal object*, a *thing*, and, moving to subordinates, it is a 1952 dime, in fact, a *particular* 1952 *dime* with a unique pattern of scratches, discolorations, and smooth places. The dog on the lawn is not only a *dog* but is also a *boxer*, a *quadruped*, an *animate being*"

(Brown 1958, p. 14). Brown also observed that of all the possible names for something in a category hierarchy, a particular name, at a particular level of categorization, "has a superior status." "While a dime *can* be called a coin or *money* or *a* 1952 *dime*, we somehow feel that *dime is* its real name. The other categorizations seem like achievements of the imagination" (Brown 1965, p. 320). Such "real names," Brown observed, seem to be shorter and to be used more frequently. They also seem to correlate with nonlinguistic actions.

When Lewis' son first looked upon the yellow jonquils in a bowl and heard them named flowers he was also enjoined to smell them and we may guess that his mother leaned over and did just that. When a ball is named *ball* it is also likely to be bounced. When a cat is named *kitty* it is also likely to be petted. Smelling and bouncing and petting are actions distinctively linked to certain categories. We can be sure they are distinctive because they are able to function as symbols of these categories. In a game of charades one might symbolize *cat* by stroking the air at a suitable height in a certain fashion, or symbolize *flower* by inclining forward and sniffing.

Flowers are marked by sniffing actions, but there are no actions that distinguish one species of flower from another. The first names given to things fall at the level of distinctive action but names go on to code the world at every level; non-linguistic actions do not.

When something is categorized it is regarded as equivalent to certain other things. For what purposes equivalent? How are all dimes equivalent or all flowers or all cats? ... Dimes are equivalent in that they can be exchanged for certain newspapers or cigars or ice cream cones or for any two nickels. In fact, they are equivalent for all purposes of economic exchange. Flowers are equivalent in that they are agreeable to smell and are pickable. Cats are equivalent in that they are to be petted, but gently, so that they do not claw. (Brown 1965, pp. 318–19)

The picture Brown gives is that categorization, for a child, begins "at the level of distinctive action," the level of flowers and cats and dimes, and then proceeds upward to superordinate categories (like *plant* and *animal*) and downward to subordinate categories (like *jonquil* and *Siamese*) by "achievements of the imagination." "For these latter categories there seem to be no characterizing actions" (Brown 1965, p. 321). This "first level" of categorization was seen by Brown as having the following converging properties:

- It is the level of distinctive actions.
- It is the level which is learned earliest and at which things are first named.
- It is the level at which names are shortest and used most frequently.
- It is a natural level of categorization, as opposed to a level created by "achievements of the imagination."

The next important impetus to the study of basic-level categories came from the work of Brent Berlin and his associates. Berlin's research can be viewed as a response to the classical philosophical view that THE CATEGORIES OF MIND FIT THE CATEGORIES OF THE WORLD, and to a linguistic version of this, THE DOCTRINE OF NATURAL KIND TERMS. That doctrine states that the world consists very largely of natural kinds of things and that natural languages contain names (called "natural kind terms") that fit those natural kinds. Typical examples of natural kinds are cows, dogs, tigers, gold, silver, water, etc.

Berlin takes these philosophical doctrines as empirically testable issues and asks: To what extent do the categories of mind (as expressed in language) fit the categories of the world? In particular, Berlin considers domains in which there *are* natural kinds of things: the domains of plants and animals. Moreover, botany and zoology can reasonably be taken to have determined to a high degree of scientific accuracy just what kinds of plants and animals there are. Since Berlin is an anthropologist who studies people who live close to nature and who know an awful lot about plants and animals, he is in an excellent position to test such philosophical doctrines empirically.

Berlin and his students and associates have studied folk classification of plants and animals in incredibly minute detail and compared those classifications with scientific classifications. Most of the research has been carried out with speakers of Tzeltal living in Tenejapa in the Chiapas region of Mexico. This enormous undertaking has been documented meticulously in *Principles of Tzeltal Plant Classification* (Berlin, Breedlove, and Raven 1974), *Tzeltal Folk Zoology* (Hunn 1977), and 'Language Acquisition by Tenejapa Tzeltal Children' (Stross 1969). The results to date have been surprising and have formed the basis for the psychological research on basic-level categorization.

What Berlin and his co-workers discovered was that a single level of classification—the genus—was for Tzeltal speakers psychologically basic in a certain number of ways. Examples of plants and animals at the genus level are *oak, maple, rabbit, racoon*, etc. The first way that the priority of the genus manifested itself was in a simple naming task. Berlin went out into the jungle with a native consultant, stopped on the path, and asked the consultant to name the plants he could see. The consultant could easily name forty or fifty, but he tended to name them at the level of the genus (oak, maple, etc.) instead of the level of the species (sugar maple, live oak), even though further study showed he could distinguish the species and had names for them. Nor did he name them at the level of the life form (tree), nor at an intermediate level (needle-bearing tree). The level of the genus is, incidentally, "in the middle" of the folk classification hierarchy, the levels being:

UNIQUE BEGINNER (plant, animal)
LIFE FORM (tree, bush, bird, fish)
INTERMEDIATE (leaf-bearing tree, needle-bearing tree)
GENUS (oak, maple)
SPECIES (sugar maple, white oak)
VARIETY (cutleaf staghorn sumac)

Further study revealed that this was no accident and that the level of the genus (what Berlin called the "folk-generic level") seems to be a psychologically basic level in the following respects:

- People name things more readily at that level.
- Languages have simpler names for things at that level.
- Categories at that level have greater cultural significance.
- Things are remembered more readily at that level.
- At that level, things are perceived holistically, as a single gestalt, while for identification at a lower level, specific details (called *distinctive features*) have to be picked out to distinguish, for example, among the kinds of oak.

In addition, Stross (1969), in a study of Tzeltal language acquisition, discovered that "the bulk of the child's first-learned plant names are generic names and that from this starting point he continues to differentiate nomenclaturally, while cognitively he continues to differentiate and generalize plants simultaneously." In other words, the basic-level (or generic) categories, which are in the middle of the taxonomic hierarchy, are learned first; then children work up the hierarchy generalizing, and down the hierarchy specializing. Thus, we can add the finding:

- Children learn the names for things at that level earlier.

But perhaps the most remarkable finding of all was this:

- Folk categories correspond to scientific categories extremely accurately at this level, but not very accurately at other levels.

This says something very remarkable about THE DOCTRINE OF NATURAL KIND TERMS: For the Tzeltal, this doctrine works very well at the level of the genus, but not very well at other levels of classification, e.g., the intermediate, the species, and the variety levels.

But now if one considers philosophical discussions of natural kinds, it turns out that this is not such a surprising result after all. In the literature on natural kinds, one finds that the usual examples of natural kinds are animals like *dog, cow, tiger*, and substances like *gold* and *water*. As it happens, they are all basic-level categories! In short, the examples on which the doctrine of natural kinds was based were all basic level, which is the level of the genus among plants and animals. At least for the Tzeltal, the doctrine works well for the kinds of examples that philosophers had in mind when they espoused the doctrine. For other kinds of examples, it does not work very well.

But if THE DOCTRINE OF NATURAL KIND TERMS fits well for the Tzeltal at even one level of categorization, it still seems to be quite a remarkable result. It suggests that there is one psychologically relevant level at which THE CATEGORIES OF THE MIND FIT THE CATEGORIES OF THE WORLD. However, Berlin's research into the history of biological classification shows this result to be much less remarkable. Scientific classification in biology grew out of folk classification. And when Linnaeus classified the living things of the world, he specifically made use of psychological criteria in establishing the level of the genus. This comes across particularly clearly in A. J. Cain's 1958 essay 'Logic and Memory in Linnaeus's System of Taxonomy' (1958). The heart of the Linnaean system was the genus, not the species. It is the genus that gives the *general* characteristics and the species that is defined in terms of differentiating characteristics. But what is a *general* characteristic? As Cain observes, "The *Essential Character* of a genus is that which gives some characteristic peculiar to it, if there is one such, which will instantly serve to distinguish it from all others in the natural order" (p. 148). This is a psychologically defined notion of an "essential character"; which characteristics can be instantly distinguished depends on the perceptual systems of the beings doing the distinguishing. As Linnaeus's son writes,

My Father's secret art of determining (delimiting) genera in such a way the Species should not become genera? This was no other than his practice in knowing a plant from its external appearance (externa facie). Therefore he often deviated from his own principles in such a way that variation as to the number of parts... did not disturb him, if only the character of the genus... could be preserved. Foreigners don't do so, but as soon as a plant has a different splitting (cleavage) of the corolla and calyx, or if the number of stamens and pistils... varies, they make a new genus. . . . If possible he [Linnaeus] tried to build the character genericus on the cleavage of the fruit so that all species that constitute a genus should have the same shape of their fruit. (Cain, p. 159)

Why did Linnaeus use the shape of the fruit as a basis for defining the genus? As Cain observes, "The characters chosen from the fructification were clearly marked, readily appreciated, easily described in words, and usually determinable on herbarium specimens" (p. 152). In other words, the shape of the fruit was easy to perceive and describe. Genera, as Linnaeus conceived of them, were "practical units of classification" upon which all biologists should be able to agree; it was important that they should "not become confused and indistinct in the mind" (Cain, p. 156). Most of Linnaeus's rules of nomenclature "follow directly from [the] requirement that the botanist must know and remember all genera" (Cain, p. 162)—again a psychological requirement. "Linnaeus states explicitly and repeatedly that the botanist... [and] the zoologist too must know all genera and commit their names to memory"

(Cain, p. 156). Linnaeus also assumed, of course, that this practical system would also be "natural," in short, a convergence between nature and psychology could be taken for granted at this level.

In short, the genus was established as that level of biological discontinuity at which human beings could most easily perceive, agree on, learn, remember, and name the discontinuities. The genus, as a scientific level of classification, was set up because it was the most psychologically basic level for the purposes of the study of taxonomic biology by human beings. It was assumed that this would also fit certain real discontinuities in nature. Berlin found that there is a close fit at this level between the categories of Linnaean biology and basic-level categories in folk biology. This fit follows in part from the criteria used to set up the level of the genus in Linnaean biology; those criteria correspond to the psychological criteria that characterize the basic level in folk biology.

At the level of the genus, the categories of mind of the biologists who set up the level of the genus correspond closely to the basic-level categories of mind of Tzeltal speakers. But this is not merely a fact about psychology. It is a fact about both psychology and biology. Here is the reason: Within scientific biology, the genus is one level above the species—the level defined by interbreeding possibilities: two populations that are members of the same species can breed and produce fertile offspring. Typically, members of two populations that can interbreed have pretty much the same overall shape. In the course of evolution, two populations of the same species may change sufficiently so that interbreeding is no longer possible. At the point at which they cease to be able to interbreed, they become different species. But at this point they may still have pretty much the same overall shape. They will no longer be members of the same species, but they will be members of the same genus—the category one level up. Thus, one level up from the species in scientific biology, it is common to find certain general shape similarities. It may not always happen, but it is common.

Now overall shape is a major determinant of the basic level in folk biology. The basic level is primarily characterized by gestalt perception (the perception of overall shape), by imaging capacity (which depends on overall shape), and by motor interaction (the possibilities for which are also determined by overall shape). It is anything but an accident that the level of the genus in scientific biology should correspond so well to the basic level in folk biology.

Moreover, given the experience of people like the Tzeltal, who are indigenous to a circumscribed geographical area, there is a good reason why divisions in nature at the level of the genus should be particularly striking. In the course of evolution, the species that survive in a particular geographical region are those that adapt most successfully to the local environment. Thus, for each genus, it is common for there to be only one species representing the genus locally. This does not always happen, but it does happen frequently. Thus, there tend to be genus-sized gaps among the *species* that occur locally—and these are very striking and perceptible gaps. Thus, divisions at the basic level in folk biology correspond to very striking discontinuities in nature for people in a circumscribed geographical area.

In summary, ethnobiological research has established that there is, at least for biological categories, a basic level of categorization. Among the Tzeltal, who have an intimate familiarity with a large range of plants and animals, the categories of the mind fit discontinuities in the world very well at the level of the genus, though not very well at other levels. The reason for this is partly because the level of the genus, as a fundamental level used in scientific biology, is a psychologically based level of categorization. But there are equally important biological reasons.

Basic-level categorization depends upon experiential aspects of human psychology: gestalt perception, mental imagery, motor activities, social function, and memory. (What I call "memory" here is the ability of a subject in a psychological test to recall on demand particular presented instances of the category.) To what extent is basic-level categorization universal? If we assume that human physiology and psychology are pretty much the same around the world, then any variation would most likely be due to culture and context. But how much variation would there be and what kind would it be?

Berlin has suggested (personal communication) that a distinction be made between a general human capacity for basic-level categorization (due to general physiological and psychological factors) and functional basic-level categorization, which adds in factors having to do with culture and specialized training. Berlin suggests that a given culture may underutilize certain human capacities used in basic-level categorization, for example, the capacity for gestalt perception. Thus, in urban cultures, people may treat the category *tree* as basic level. Such cases have been documented by Dougherty (1978). Moreover, there may be subpopulations of specialists in a culture who, through training, may achieve a more finely honed gestalt perception for a limited range of domains, e.g., breeds of horses, types of cars, etc. But this should be possible only in a limited number of domains, even for trained specialists. Berlin thus hypothesizes two kinds of nonuniversality: (*a*) one kind due to cultural underutilization of general human capacities, with the result that certain higher-level categories (e.g., tree) may be treated as basic, and (*b*) another kind due to special training, limited to subpopulations of experts who may treat a slightly more specific level as basic in some domains of expertise.

Berlin's hypothesis makes the following prediction: People from, say, an urban culture that treats trees as basic level should still have the general human capacity for gestalt perception and should thus be capable of learning to discriminate among trees readily at the level of the genus, but not so readily at the level of the species or variety. Berlin's hypothesis also predicts that there will be no whole cultures that will treat the level of the species or variety as basic, but that individuals may have a capacity for expertise in a limited range of domains and thus may be able to treat a small number of more specific categories as basic.

Berlin also predicts that there will be no culture where all the levels of categorization are different from ours or from the Tzeltal. In most domains, levels of categorization will be the same for all human beings, simply because human beings share the same general capacities for gestalt perception and for holistic motor movement. It is these capacities that have the major role in determining basic-level categorization.

Basicness in categorization has to do with matters of human psychology: ease of perception, memory, learning, naming, and use. Basicness of level has no objective status external to human beings. It is constant only to the extent that the relevant human capacities are utilized in the same way. Basicness varies when those capacities either are underutilized in a culture or are specially developed to a level of expertise.

As we shall see below, Berlin's results have a special philosophical importance. Berlin showed that human categorizations based on interactions with the environment are extremely accurate at the basic level. Basic-level interactions thus provide a crucial link between cognitive structure and real knowledge of the world. We will argue in chapter 17 [not included] that basic-level interactions can therefore form the basis of an epistemology for a philosophy of mind and language that is consistent with the results of prototype theory.

EKMAN

In research spanning more than two decades, Paul Ekman and his associates have studied in detail the physiological correlates of emotions (Ekman 1971; Ekman, Friesen, and Ellsworth 1972). In a major crosscultural study of facial gestures expressing emotion, Ekman and his associates discovered that there were basic emotions that seem to correlate universally with facial gestures: happiness, sadness, anger, fear, surprise, and interest. Of all the subtle emotions that people feel and have words and concepts for around the world, only these have consistent correlates in facial expressions across cultures.

Although Ekman was by no means a prototype theorist, his research fits prototype research in the following way. The seven basic emotions appear to have prototype status. There are many shades and varieties of happiness, sadness, anger, etc. These form categories of emotions. Rage and annoyance, for example, are in the anger category. Basic happiness, anger, etc.—the emotions that correlate with the universal facial gestures—seem to function as central members of those categories. These emotions also appear to have basic-level status. They are readily recognizable by gestalt perception around the world. We have facial images and motor movements for them that represent the entire emotional category.

Emotional concepts are embodied, in that the physiology corresponding to each emotion has a great deal to do with how the emotion is conceptualized. For example, anger is metaphorically understood in terms of heat and internal pressure. Ekman, Levenson, and Friesen (1983) have shown that there is autonomic nervous system (ANS) activity that corresponds to the basic emotions. The ANS activity that corresponds to anger is an increase in skin temperature and an increase in heart rate (experienced as internal pressure).

The experiments that demonstrated this involved two tasks. In the first, subjects were instructed to change their facial expressions, muscle by muscle, until their expressions matched the facial prototypes of emotions. In the second, subjects were asked to relive emotional experiences. Heart rate and left- and right-finger temperatures were recorded.

Two findings were consistent across tasks:

> (i) Heart rate increased more in anger (mean calculated across tasks $\pm$ standard error, $+8.0 \pm 1.8$ beats per minute) and fear ($+8.0 \pm 1.6$ beats per minute) than in happiness ($+2.6 \pm 1.0$ beat per minute).
>
> (ii) Left- and right-finger temperatures increased more in anger (left, $+0.10\,^{\circ}\mathrm{C} \pm 0.009^{\circ}$; right, $+0.08^{\circ} \pm 0.008\,^{\circ}\mathrm{C}$) than in happiness (left, $-0.07\,^{\circ}\mathrm{C} \pm 0.002^{\circ}$; right, $-0.03^{\circ} \pm 0.002\,^{\circ}\mathrm{C}$). (Ekman, Levenson, and Friesen 1983, p. 1209)

Thus the metaphorical conceptualization of anger that we will explore in case study 1 is actually embodied in the autonomic nervous system, in that it is motivated by ANS activity that corresponds to the emotions as felt.

ROSCH

The studies cited above are all special cases. It was Eleanor Rosch who first provided a general perspective on all these problems. She developed what has since come to be called "the theory of prototypes and basic-level categories," or "prototype theory." In doing so, she provided a full-scale challenge to the classical theory and did more than anyone else to establish categorization as a subfield of cognitive psychology. Before her work, the classical theory was taken for granted, not only in psychology, but in linguistics, anthropology, and philosophy, as well as other disciplines. In a series of electrifying papers, Rosch and her associates presented an overwhelming array of empirical studies that challenged the classical view.

The experimental contributions of Rosch and her associates are generally and justly recognized by cognitive psychologists as having revolutionized the study of categorization within experimental psychology. Rosch's experimental results fall into two categories: prototype effects, which extend the Berlin–Kay color research, and basic-level effects, which generalize Brown's observations and Berlin's results.

Prototype effects

If the classical theory were both correct and complete, no member of a càtegory would have any special status. The reason is that, in the classical theory, the properties defining the category are shared by all members, and so all members have equal status as category members. Rosch's research on prototype effects has been aimed at showing asymmetries among category members and asymmetric structures within categories. Since the classical theory does not predict such asymmetries, either something more or something different must be going on.

Rosch's early studies were on color. She learned of the Berlin–Kay color research midway through her own research and found that their results meshed with her own work on Dani, a New Guinea language that has only two basic color categories: *mili* (dark-cool, including black, green, and blue) and *mola* (light-warm, including white, red, yellow). Berlin and Kay had shown that focal colors had a special status within color categories—that of the best example of the category. Rosch found that Dani speakers, when asked for the best examples of their two color categories, chose focal colors, for example, white, red, or yellow for *mola* with different speakers making different choices.

In a remarkable set of experiments, Rosch set out to show that primary color categories were psychologically real for speakers of Dani, even though they were not named. She set out to challenge one of Whorf's hypotheses, namely, that language determines one's conceptual system. If Whorf were right on this matter, the Dani's two *words* for colors would determine two and only two *conceptual categories* of colors. Rosch reasoned that if it was language alone that determined color categorization, then the Dani should have equal difficulty learning new words for colors, no matter whether the color ranges had a primary color at the center or a nonprimary color. She then went about studying how Dani speakers would learn new, made-up color terms. One group was taught arbitrary names for eight focal colors, and another group, arbitrary names for eight nonfocal colors (Rosch 1973). The names for focal colors were learned more easily. Dani speakers were also found (like English speakers) to be able to remember focal colors better than nonfocal colors (Heider 1972). In an experiment in which speakers judged color similarity, the Dani were shown to represent colors in memory the same way English speakers do (Heider and Olivier 1972). Rosch's color research also extended to children. When three-year-olds were presented with an array of color chips, and the experimenter turned her back and said "Show me a color," the children picked focal colors overwhelmingly over nonfocal colors (Heider 1971). And when four-year-olds were given a color chip and asked to pick from an assortment of chips the one that matched best, the children did best with focal colors.

Focal colors correspond to what Rosch in her later research called *cognitive reference points* and *prototypes*—subcategories or category members that have a special cognitive status—that of being a "best example." Rosch showed that a variety of experimental techniques involving learning, matching, memory, and judgments of similarity converged on cognitive reference points. And she extended the results from colors to other categories, primarily categories of physical objects. She developed other experimental paradigms for investigating categories of physical objects. In each case, asymmetries (called prototype *effects*) were found: subjects judged certain members of the categories as being more representative of the category than other members. For example, robins are judged to be more representative of the category BIRD than are chickens, penguins, and ostriches, and desk chairs are judged to be more representative of the category CHAIR than are rocking chairs, barber chairs, beanbag chairs, or electric chairs. The most representative members of a category are called "prototypical" members. Here are some of the experimental paradigms used in studying categories of physical objects. Subjects give consistent goodness-of-example ratings across these experimental paradigms.

Direct rating: Subjects are asked to rate, say on a scale from one to seven, how good an example of a category (e.g., BIRD) various members are (e.g., a robin, a chicken, etc.).

Reaction time: Subjects are asked to press a button to indicate true or false in response to a statement of the form "An [example] is a [category name]" (e.g., "A chicken is a bird"). Response times are shorter for representative examples.

Production of examples: When asked to list or draw examples of category members, subjects were more likely to list or draw more representative examples.

Asymmetry in similarity ratings: Less representative examples are often considered to be more similar to more representative examples than the converse. Not surprisingly, Americans consider the United States to be a highly representative example of a country. In experiments where subjects were asked to give similarity ratings for pairs of countries, the following asymmetry arose. Subjects considered Mexico to be more similar to the United States than the United States is to Mexico. See Rosch 1975a and Tversky and Gati 1978.

Asymmetry in generalization: New information about a representative category member is more likely to be generalized to nonrepresentative members than the reverse. For example, it was shown that subjects believed that a disease was more likely to spread from robins to ducks on an island, than from ducks to robins. (This result is from Rips 1975.)

Family resemblances: Wittgenstein had speculated that categories were structured by what he called "family resemblances." Rosch showed that what philosophers took as a matter for a priori speculation could be demonstrated empirically. Characterizing "family resemblances" as perceived similarities between representative and nonrepresentative members of categories, Rosch showed that there was a correlation between family resemblances and numerical ratings of best examples derived from the above experiments. (See Rosch and Mervis 1975 and Rosch, Simpson, and Miller 1976.)

Such studies have been replicated often by other experimenters. There is no doubt that prototype effects of this sort are real. However, there have been some misunderstandings and debates concerning the interpretation of these results. Some of the debates will be discussed in detail below. But before we go on, we ought to clear up some of the common misunderstandings.

Rosch's genius has two aspects: she both launched a general challenge to the classical theory and devised, with her co-workers, replicable experiments demonstrating prototype effects, as well as basic-level effects. These experiments demonstrate the inadequacy of the classical theory; the classical theory cannot account for such results. But prototype effects, in themselves, do not provide any specific alternative theory of mental representation. And, as a responsible experimenter, Rosch has consistently distinguished between what her experimental results show and any theories that might account for those results.

Rosch went through three phases in her thinking about categorization.

– Phase I (late 1960s to early 1970s): Because she was studying color, shape, and emotions, she assumed prototypes were primarily a matter of (*a*) perceptual salience, or which things are most readily noticed by people; (*b*) memorability, or which things are easiest for people to remember; and (*c*) stimulus generalization, or the ability of people to generalize from one thing to something else that is physically similar to it. As she says (Rosch 1988): "Suppose that there are perceptually salient colors which more readily attract attention and are more easily remembered than other colors. When category names are learned, they tend to become attached first to the salient stimuli; then, by means of the principle of stimulus generalization, they generalize to other, physically similar instances."

- Phase II (early to mid 1970s): Under the influence of information-processing psychology, Rosch considered the possibility that prototype effects, as operationalized by the experiments cited above, might provide a characterization of the internal structure of the category. Thus, for example, the goodness-of-example ratings might directly reflect the internal structure of the category in mental representation. Two natural questions arose:

  1. Do the EFFECTS, defined operationally, characterize the STRUCTURE of the category as it is represented in the mind?
  2. Do the PROTOTYPES constitute mental REPRESENTATIONS?
     Given the assumptions of information-processing psychology, the experimental data can be interpreted most straightforwardly by answering yes to both questions. Rosch (1975b) initially interpreted her data in just this way.

- Phase III (late 1970s): Rosch eventually gave up on these interpretations of her experimental results. Such interpretations were artifacts of an overly narrow view of information-processing psychology. She came to the conclusion that prototype effects, defined operationally by experiment, underdetermined mental representations. The effects constrained the possibilities for what representations might be, but there was no one-to-one correspondence between the effects and mental representations. The effects had "sources," but one could not determine the sources given the effects. As she says of the research in Phase II (Rosch 1988): "The type of conclusions generated by this approach were, however, very general; e.g., that the representation evoked by the category name was more like good examples than poor examples of the category; that it was in a form more general than either words or pictures, etc. On the whole other information-processing researchers have considered the concepts of prototypes and typicality functions underspecified and have provided a variety of precise models, mini-models, and distinctions to be tested."

It is often the case that positions taken early in one's career tend to be associated with a researcher long after he or she has given up those positions. Many of those who read Rosch's early works did not read her later works, where she gave up on her early interpretations of the experimental results. Consequently, it is not widely known that Rosch abandoned the ideas that prototype effects directly mirror category structure and that prototypes constitute representations of categories. Because of this, Rosch has had to provide explicit admonitions against overly simplistic interpretations of prototype effects-interpretations of the sort that she herself made in Phase II of her research. For example, she states:

The pervasiveness of prototypes in real-world categories and of prototypicality as a variable indicates that prototypes must have some place in psychological theories of representation, processing, and learning. However, prototypes themselves do not constitute any particular model of processes, representations, or learning. This point is so often misunderstood that it requires discussion:

  1. To speak of a prototype at all is simply a convenient grammatical fiction; what is really referred to are judgments of degree of prototypicality. . . . For natural-language categories, to speak of a

single entity that is the prototype is either a gross misunderstanding of the empirical data or a covert theory of mental representation.

2. Prototypes do not constitute any particular processing model for categories. . . . What facts about prototypicality do contribute to processing notions is a constraint—processing models should not be inconsistent with the known facts about prototypes. For example, a model should not be such as to predict equal verification times for good and bad examples of categories nor predict completely random search through a category.

3. Prototypes do not constitute a theory of representation for categories. . . . Prototypes can be represented either by propositional or image systems. . . . As with processing models, the facts about prototypes can only constrain, but do not determine, models of representation. A representation of categories in terms of conjoined necessary and sufficient attributes alone would probably be incapable of handling all of the presently known facts, but there are many representations other than necessary and sufficient attributes that are possible.

4. Although prototypes must be learned, they do not constitute any particular theory of category learning. (Rosch 1978, pp. 40–1)

Despite Rosch's admonitions to the contrary, and despite her minimal theorizing concerning the sources of prototype effects, her results on prototype effects are still sometimes interpreted as constituting a prima facie theory of representation of category structure, as she thought was possible during Phase II of her research.

For example, take her results showing prototype effects within the category *bird*. Her experimental ranking shows that subjects view robins and sparrows as the best examples of birds, with owls and eagles lower down in the rankings and ostriches, emus, and penguins among the worst examples. In the early to mid-1970s, during Phase II of Rosch's research, such empirical goodness-of-example ratings were commonly taken as constituting a claim to the effect that membership in the category *bird* is graded and that owls and penguins are less members of the *bird* category than robins. (See Lakoff 1972 for a typical example.) It later became clear that that was a mistaken interpretation of the data. Rosch's ratings make no such claim; they are just ratings and do not make any claims at all. They are consistent with the interpretation that the category *bird* has strict boundaries and that robins, owls, and penguins are all 100 percent members of that category. However, that category must have additional internal structure of some sort that produces these goodness-of-example ratings. Moreover, that internal structure must be part of our concept of what a bird is, since it results in asymmetric inferences of the sort discussed above, described by Rips (1975).

This point is extremely important. Category structure plays a role in reasoning. In many cases, prototypes act as *cognitive reference points* of various sorts and form the basis for inferences (Rosch 1975a, 1981). The study of human inference is part of the study of human reasoning and conceptual structure; hence, those prototypes used in making inferences must be part of conceptual structure.

It is important to bear in mind that prototype effects are superficial. They may result from many factors. In the case of a graded category like *tall man*, which is fuzzy and does not have rigid boundaries, prototype effects may result from degree of category membership, while in the case of *bird*, which does have rigid boundaries, the prototype effects must result from some other aspect of internal category structure.

One of the goals of this book is to outline a general approach to the theory of categorization and to sketch the range of sources for superficial prototype effects. Our basic claim will be that prototype effects result from the nature of cognitive models, which can be viewed as "theories" of some subject matter.

One of the most interesting confirmations of this hypothesis has come through the work of Barsalou (1983, 1984). Barsalou has studied what he calls "ad hoc categories"—categories that are not conventional or fixed, but rather are made up on the fly for some immediate purpose. Such categories must be constructed on the basis of one's cognitive models of the subject matter under consideration. Examples of such categories are *things to take from one's home during a fire, what to get for a birthday present, what to do for entertainment on a weekend,* etc. Barsalou observes that such categories have prototype structure—structure that does not exist in advance, since the category is not conventional and does not exist in advance. Barsalou argues that in such cases, the nature of the category is principally determined by goals and that such goal structure is a function of one's cognitive models. Such a view has also been advocated by Murphy and Medin (1984).

Basic-level effects

The classical theory of categories gives no special importance to categories in the middle of a taxonomic hierarchy. Yet, as Berlin (Berlin, Breedlove, and Raven 1974) and Hunn (1977) have shown for Tzeltal plant and animal taxonomies, the level of the biological genus is psychologically basic. The genus stands in the middle of the hierarchy that goes from UNIQUE BEGINNER to LIFE FORM to INTERMEDIATE to GENUS to SPECIES to VARIETY. Their results show a discrepancy between the classical theory of categories and a cognitively adequate theory of categories.

Rosch and her associates have extended the study of basic-level effects from cognitive anthropology to the experimental paradigm of cognitive psychology. Like Berlin, they found that the psychologically most basic level was in the middle of the taxonomic hierarchies:

SUPERORDINATE	ANIMAL	FURNITURE
BASIC LEVEL	DOG	CHAIR
SUBORDINATE	RETRIEVER	ROCKER

Just as Hunn (1975) argued that the basic level for animal categories is the only level at which categorization is determined by overall gestalt perception (without distinctive feature analysis), so Rosch and others (1976) have found that the basic level is:

– The highest level at which category members have similarly perceived overall shapes.
– The highest level at which a single mental image can reflect the entire category.
– The highest level at which a person uses similar motor actions for interacting with category members.
– The level at which subjects are fastest at identifying category members.
– The level with the most commonly used labels for category members.
– The first level named and understood by children.
– The first level to enter the lexicon of a language.
– The level with the shortest primary lexemes.
– The level at which terms are used in neutral contexts. For example, *There's a dog on the porch* can be used in a neutral context, whereas special contexts are needed for *There's a mammal on the porch* or *There's a wire-haired terrier on the porch*. (See Cruse 1977.)
– The level at which most of our knowledge is organized.

Thus basic-level categories are basic in four respects:

Perception: Overall perceived shape; single mental image; fast identification.
Function: General motor program.

Communication: Shortest, most commonly used and contextually neutral words, first learned by children and first to enter the lexicon.

Knowledge Organization: Most attributes of category members are stored at this level.

The fact that knowledge is mainly organized at the basic level is determined in the following way: When subjects are asked to list attributes of categories, they list very few attributes of category members at the superordinate level (furniture, vehicle, mammal); they list most of what they know at the basic level (chair, car, dog); and at the subordinate level (rocking chair, sports car, retriever) there is virtually no increase in knowledge over the basic level.

Why should most information be organized at a single conceptual level and why should it be this level in particular? To me, the most convincing hypothesis to date comes from the research of Tversky and Hemenway (1984). Berlin (Berlin, Breedlove, and Raven 1974) and Hunn (1977) had suggested that gestalt perception—perception of overall part-whole configuration—is the fundamental determinant of the basic level. The experimental evidence accumulated by Tversky and Hemenway supports the Berlin–Hunn hypothesis. Their basic observation is that the basic level is distinguished from other levels on the basis of the type of attributes people associate with a category at that level, in particular, attributes concerned with *parts*. Our knowledge at the basic level is mainly organized around part-whole divisions. The reason is that the way an object is divided into parts determines many things. First, parts are usually correlated with functions, and hence our knowledge about functions is usually associated with knowledge about parts. Second, parts determine shape, and hence the way that an object will be perceived and imaged. Third, we usually interact with things via their parts, and hence part-whole divisions play a major role in determining what motor programs we can use to interact with an object. Thus, a handle is not just long and thin, but it can be grasped by the human hand. As Tversky and Hemenway say, "We sit on the *seat* of a chair and lean against the *back*, we remove the *peel* of a banana and eat the *pulp*."

Tversky and Hemenway also suggest that we impose part-whole structure on events and that our knowledge of event categories is structured very much the way our knowledge of physical object categories is. Their suggestion is in the same spirit as Lakoff and Johnson (1980), where it is suggested that event categories and other abstract categories are structured metaphorically on the basis of structures from the realm of physical experience.

Acquisition

One of the most striking results about basic-level categorization concerns the acquisition of concepts by children. If the classical theory of categorization were correct, then there should be no more to categorization than what one finds in the logic of classes: hierarchical categorization based on shared properties of the members of the categories. Before the work of Rosch and Mervis (Rosch et al. 1976), research on child development had not been informed by the idea of basic-level categorization. It had been concluded that, for example, three-year-old children had not mastered categorization, which was taken to be taxonomic categorization defined by the logic of classes. This conclusion was based on the performance of children in "sorting tasks," where subjects are asked to "put together the things that go together." Rosch and her associates observed that such studies tended to involve categorization at the *superordinate* level.

The stimuli used in sorting tasks have tended to be of two types: If abstract (e.g., geometric forms varying in dimensions such as form, color, and size), they are typically presented in a set which has no structure (e.g., each attribute occurs with all combinations of all others); if representational (e.g., toy versions or pictures of real-world objects), the arrays are such that they can be grouped taxonomically only at the superordinate level. Thus, the representational stimuli used in sorting tasks are such that if the child were to sort the objects into those of like taxonomic category, he would have to put together such items as socks and shirt, dog and cow. Children do not seem to have been asked to sort together objects belonging to the same basic level category (e.g., several shoes or several dogs). We suspect this results from the fact that basic objects are so obviously the "same object" to adults that a task does not seem to be a problem of categorization to an adult experimenter unless objects are taken from different basic level categories. (Rosch et al. 1976, pp. 414–15)

Rosch and Mervis then compared sorting tasks for basic-level and superordinate categories. Basic-level sorting required being able to put together pictures of two different kinds of cows (compared to an airplane, say) or two different kinds of cars (compared to, say, a dog). Superordinate sorting required, for example, being able to put together a cow and a dog (compared to an airplane), or a motorcycle and an airplane (compared to a cow). At all age levels, from three years old up, subjects were virtually perfect on basic-level sorting. But, as had been well-known, the three-year-olds had trouble with superordinate sorting. They were only 55 percent correct, while the four-year-olds were 96 percent correct.

It is not true that three-year-olds have not mastered categorization. They have mastered *basic-level* categorization perfectly. It is *superordinate* categorization that is not mastered till later. The ability to categorize at the basic level comes first; the general logic of classes is learned later. Learning to categorize is thus something rather different from learning to use the logic of classes. Therefore, categorization itself is not merely the use of classical taxonomies.

It is important to bear these results in mind throughout the remainder of the book. The reason is this: It is sometimes claimed that basic-level categorization is merely classical taxonomic classification with additional constraints on cognitive processing added (e.g., perceptual and motor constraints). The Rosch–Mervis acquisition results show that this is not the case. Basic-level categories develop prior to classical taxonomic categories. They therefore cannot be the result of classical taxonomic categories *plus* something of a sensory-motor nature. Basic-level categories have an integrity of their own. They are our earliest and most natural form of categorization. Classical taxonomic categories are later "achievements of the imagination," in Roger Brown's words.

As Rosch and her co-workers observe, basic-level distinctions are "the generally most useful distinctions to make in the world," since they are characterized by overall shape and motor interaction and are at the most general level at which one can form a mental image. Basic-level categorization is mastered by the age of three. But what about children at earlier ages? It is known, for example, that two-year-olds have different categories from adults. Lions and tigers as well as cats are commonly called "kitty" by two-year-olds. Round candles and banks are commonly called "ball." And some things that we call "chair" may not be chairs for two-year-olds, e.g., beanbag chairs. The categories of two-year-olds may be broader than adult categories, or narrower, or overlapping. Does this mean that two-year-olds have not mastered the ability to form basic-level categories?

Not at all. Mervis (1984) has shown that although two-year-olds may have different categories than adults have, those categories are determined by the same principles that determine adult basic-level categories. In short, two-year-olds have mastered basic-level categorization, but have come up with different categories than adults—for very good reasons.

The difference is determined by three factors:

1. The child may not know about culturally significant attributes. Thus, not knowing that a bank is used for storing money, the child may attend to its round shape and classify it as a *ball*.

2. The salience of particular attributes may be different for a child than for an adult. Thus, a child may know that a bank is for storing money, but may attend to its round shape more than

to the slot and keyhole, and still call it a ball. Or the child may attend to both and classify it as both a *bank* and a *ball*.

3. The child may include false attributes in the decision process. Thus, if the child thinks a leopard says "meow," he or she may classify leopards as *kitties*.

The point is that the level of categorization is not independent of who is doing the categorizing and on what basis. Though the same principles may determine the basic level, the circumstances under which those principles are employed determine what system of categories results.

Clusters of interactional properties

What determines basic-level structure is a matter of correlations: the overall perceived part-whole structure of an object correlates with our motor interaction with that object and with the functions of the parts (and our knowledge of those functions). It is important to realize that these are not purely objective and "in the world"; rather they have to do with the world as we interact with it: as we perceive it, image it, affect it with our bodies, and gain knowledge about it.

This is, again, a matter which has often been misunderstood, and Rosch has written at length on the nature of the misunderstanding. "It should be emphasized that we are talking about a perceived world and not a metaphysical world without a knower" (Rosch 1978, p. 29). She continues:

When research on basic objects and their prototypes was initially conceived (Rosch et al. 1976), I thought of such attributes as inherent in the real world. Thus, given an organism that had sensory equipment capable of perceiving attributes such as wings and feathers, it was a fact in the real world that wings and feathers co-occurred. The state of knowledge of a person might be ignorant of (or indifferent or inattentive to) the attributes or might know the attributes but be ignorant concerning their correlation. Conversely, a person might know of the attributes and their correlational structure but exaggerate that structure, turning partial into complete correlations (as when attributes true of only many members of a category are thought of as true of all members). However, the environment was thought to constrain categorizations in that human knowledge could not provide correlational structure where there was none at all. For purposes of the basic object experiments, perceived attributes were operationally defined as those attributes listed by our subjects. Shape was defined as measured by our computer programs. We thus seemed to have our system grounded comfortably in the real world.

On contemplation of the nature of many of our attributes listed by our subjects, however, it appeared that three types of attributes presented a problem for such a realistic view: (1) some attributes, such as "seat" for the object "chair," appeared to have names that showed them not to be meaningful prior to the knowledge of the object as chair; (2) some attributes such as "large" for the object "piano" seemed to have meaning only in relation to categorization of the object in terms of a superordinate category—piano is large for furniture but small for other kinds of objects such as buildings; (3) some attributes such as "you eat on it" for the object "table" were functional attributes that seemed to require knowledge about humans, their activities, and the real world in order to be understood. That is, it appeared that the analysis of objects into attributes was a rather sophisticated activity that our subjects (and indeed a system of cultural knowledge) might be considered to be able to impose only *after* the development of a system of categories. (Rosch 1978, pp. 41–2)

Thus the relevant notion of a "property" is not something objectively in the world independent of any being; it is rather what we will refer to as an *interactional property*—the result of our interactions as part of our physical and cultural environments given our bodies and our cognitive apparatus. Such interactional properties form *clusters* in our experience, and prototype and basic-level structure can reflect such clusterings.

As Berlin has observed, interactional properties and the categories they determine seem objective in the case of properties of basic-level categories—categories like *chair*, *elephant*, and *water*. The reason is that, given our bodies, we perceive certain aspects of our external environment very accurately at the basic level, though not so accurately at other levels. As long as we are talking about properties of basic-level objects, interactional properties will seem objective.

Perhaps the best way of thinking about basic-level categories is that they are "human-sized." They depend not on objects themselves, independent of people, but on the way people interact with objects: the way they perceive them, image them, organize information about them, and behave toward them with their bodies. The relevant properties clustering together to define such categories are not inherent to the objects, but are interactional properties, having to do with the way people interact with objects.

Basic-level categories thus have different properties than superordinate categories. For example, superordinate categories seem not to be characterized by images or motor actions. For example, we have mental images of chairs—abstract images that don't fit any particular chair—and we have general motor actions for sitting in chairs. But if we go from the basic-level category CHAIR to the superordinate category FURNITURE, a difference emerges. We have no abstract mental images of furniture that are not images of basic-level objects like chairs, tables, beds, etc. Try to imagine a piece of furniture that doesn't look like a chair, or table, or bed, etc., but is more abstract. People seem not to be able to do so. Moreover, we do not have motor actions for interacting with furniture in general that are not motor actions for interacting with some basic-level object—chairs, tables, beds, etc. But superordinate categories do have other human-based attributes—like purposes and functions.

In addition, the complements of basic-level categories are not basic level. They do not have the kinds of properties that basic-level categories have. For example, consider nonchairs, that is, those things that are not chairs. What do they look like? Do you have a mental image of a general or an abstract nonchair? People seem not to. How do you interact with a nonchair? Is there some general motor action one performs with nonchairs? Apparently not. What is a nonchair used for? Do nonchairs have general functions? Apparently not.

In the classical theory, the complement of a set that is defined by necessary and sufficient conditions is another set that is defined by necessary and sufficient conditions. But the complement of a basic-level category is not itself a basic-level category.

Cue validity

One of the ideas that Rosch has regularly stressed is that categories occur in systems, and such systems include contrasting categories. Categorization depends to a large extent on the nature of the system in which a category is embedded. For example, within the superordinate category of things-to-sit-on, *chair* contrasts with *stool*, *sofa*, *bench*, etc. *Chair* would no doubt cover a very different range if one of the contrasting categories, say, *stool* or *sofa*, were not present.

Rosch has made use of contrasting categories in trying to give a theory of basic-level categorization. At the basic level, Rosch has claimed, categories are maximally distinct—that is, they maximize perceived similarity among category members and minimize perceived similarities across contrasting categories. Rosch and others (1976) attempted to capture this intuition by means of a quantitative measure of what they called *category cue validity*.

Cue validity is the conditional probability that an object is in a particular category given its possession of some feature (or "cue"). The best cues are those that work all of the time for categories at a given level. For example, if you see a living thing with gills, you can be certain it is a fish. Gills thus has a cue validity of 1.0 for the category fish, and a cue validity of 0 for other categories. Rosch and her associates suggested that one could extend this definition of cue validity to characterize basic-level categories. They defined *category cue validity* as the sum of all the individual cue validities of the features associated with a category.

The highest cue validities in a taxonomic hierarchy, they reasoned, should occur at the basic level. For example, subordinate categories like *kitchen chair* should have a low category cue validity because most of the attributes of kitchen chairs would be shared with other kinds of chairs and only a few attributes would differentiate kitchen chairs from other chairs. The individual attributes shared across categories would have low cue validities for the kitchen chair category; thus, seeing a chair with a back doesn't give you much reason for thinking it's a kitchen chair rather than some other kind of chair. Since most of the individual cue validities for attributes would be low, the sum should be low.

Correspondingly, they reasoned that category cue validity would be low for superordinate categories like *furniture*, since they would have few or no common attributes. Since basic-level categories have many properties in common among their members and few across categories, their category cue validities should be highest.

This idea was put forth during the earlier phase of Rosch's career when she still believed that the relevant attributes for characterizing basic-level categories were objectively existing attributes "in the world." Murphy (1982) has shown, however, that if category cue validity is defined for objectively existing attributes, then that measure cannot pick out basic-level categories. Murphy observes that individual cue validities for a superordinate category are always greater than or equal to those for a basic-level category; the same must be true for their sums. For example,

(a) if people know that some trucks [basic-level] have air brakes, they know that having air brakes is a possible cue for being a vehicle [superordinate].
(b) People know that some animals [superordinate] have beaks, but that fish [basic-level] do not (thereby giving animal a valid cue that the basic category does not have). (Murphy 1982, p. 176)

Murphy observes that his objection could be gotten around under the assumption that most attributes are not directly linked to superordinate categories in memory. This would be true, for example, given Tversky and Hemenway's characterization of the basic level as that level at which most knowledge is organized. But this would require a psychological definition of attribute (equivalent to our *interactional properties*), not a notion of attributes as existing objectively in the external world. But such a notion would presuppose a prior characterization of basic-level category—that level at which most knowledge is organized. Category cue validity defined for such psychological (or interactional) attributes might *correlate* with basic-level categorization, but it would not *pick out* basic-level categories; they would already have to have been picked out in order to apply the definition of category cue validity so that there was such a correlation. Thus, it seems reasonable to conclude that basic-level categories are, in fact, most differentiated in people's minds; but they are most differentiated because of their other properties, especially because most knowledge is organized at that level.

Clustering and causation

Two of the themes that emerge from the research just discussed are the clustering of properties and the nonobjective, or interactional, character of properties relevant to human categorization. One of the most interesting of human categories from a philosophical point of view is the category of causes. Causation is represented in the grammar of most languages—and usually not just one kind of causation, but a variety of kinds. I have suggested elsewhere (Lakoff 1977) that the category of kinds of causation shows prototype effects in the ways that they are represented in natural languages. These effects are relatively uniform across languages.

We can account for these effects if we assume that prototypical causation is understood in terms of a cluster of interactional properties. This hypothesis appears to account best for the relation between language and conceptual structure, as well as for the relationships among the varieties of causation. The cluster seems to define a prototypical causation, and non-prototypical varieties of causation seem to be best characterizable in terms of deviations from that cluster.

Prototypical causation appears to be direct manipulation, which is characterized most typically by the following cluster of interactional properties:

1. There is an agent that does something.
2. There is a patient that undergoes a change to a new state.
3. Properties 1 and 2 constitute a single event; they overlap in time and space; the agent comes in contact with the patient.
4. Part of what the agent does (either the motion or the exercise of will) precedes the change in the patient. .
5. The agent is the energy source; the patient is the energy goal; there is a transfer of energy from agent to patient.
6. There is a single definite agent and a single definite patient.
7. The agent is human.
8. a. The agent wills his action.
   b. The agent is in control of his action.
   c. The agent bears primary responsibility for both his action and the change.
9. The agent uses his hands, body, or some instrument.
10. The agent is looking at the patient, the change in the patient is perceptible, and the agent perceives the change.

The most representative examples of humanly relevant causation have all ten of these properties. This is the case in the most typical kinds of examples in the linguistics literature: Max broke the window, Brutus killed Caesar, etc. Billiard-ball causation, of the kind most discussed in the natural sciences, has properties 1 through 6. Indirect causation is not prototypical, since it fails in number 3, and possibly other conditions. According to this account, indirect causes are less representative examples of causation than direct causes. Multiple causes are less representative than single causes. Involuntary causation is less representative than voluntary causation. Many languages of the world meet the following generalization: The more direct the causation, the closer the morphemes expressing the cause and the result. This accounts for the distinction between *kill* and *cause to die*. *Kill* expresses direct causation, with cause and result expressed in a single morpheme—the closest possible connection. When would anyone ever say "cause to die"? In general, when there is no direct causation, when there is causation at a distance or accidental causation. Hinton (1982) gives a similar case from Mixtec, an Otomanguean language of Mexico. Mixtec has three causative morphemes: the word *sáʔà*, and the prefixes *sá-* and *s-*. The longest of these corresponds to the most indirect causation, and the shortest to the most direct causation. An explanation of this fact about the linguistic expression of kinds of causation is provided by Lakoff and Johnson (1980, ch. 20).

What is particularly interesting about this state of affairs is that the best example of the *conceptual category* of causation is typically marked by a grammatical construction or a morpheme and that the word *cause* is reserved for noncentral members of the conceptual .

category. There is a good reason for this. The concept of causation—prototypical causation—is one of the most fundamental of human concepts. It is a concept that people around the world use in thought. It is used spontaneously, automatically, effortlessly, and often. Such concepts are usually coded right into the grammar of languages—either via grammatical constructions or grammatical morphemes. For this reason, the prototypical concept of causation is built into the grammar of the language, and the word *cause* is relegated to characterizing non-central causation.

SUMMARY

The basic results of prototype theory leading up to the cognitive models approach can be summarized as follows:

- Some categories, like *tall man* or *red*, are graded; that is, they have inherent degrees of membership, fuzzy boundaries, and central members whose degree of membership (on a scale from zero to one) is one.
- Other categories, like *bird*, have clear boundaries; but within those boundaries there are graded prototype effects—some category members are better examples of the category than others.
- Categories are not organized just in terms of simple taxonomic hierarchies. Instead, categories "in the middle" of a hierarchy are the most *basic*, relative to a variety of psychological criteria: gestalt perception, the ability to form a mental image, motor interactions, and ease of learning, remembering, and use. Most knowledge is organized at this level.
- The basic level depends upon perceived part-whole structure and corresponding knowledge about how the parts function relative to the whole.
- Categories are organized into systems with contrasting elements.
- Human categories are not objectively "in the world," external to human beings. At least some categories are *embodied*. Color categories, for example, are determined jointly by the external physical world, human biology, the human mind, plus cultural considerations. Basic-level structure depends on human perception, imaging capacity, motor capabilities, etc.
- The properties relevant to the description of categories are *interactional properties*, properties characterizable only in terms of the interaction of human beings as part of their environment. Prototypical members of categories are sometimes describable in terms of *clusters* of such interactional properties. These clusters act as gestalts: the cluster as a whole is psychologically simpler than its parts.
- Prototype effects, that is, asymmetries among category members such as goodness-of-example judgments, are superficial phenomena which may have many sources.

The cognitive models approach to categorization is an attempt to make sense of all these observations. It is motivated by

- a need to understand what kinds of prototype effects there are and what their sources are
- a need to account for categorization not merely for physical objects but in abstract conceptual domains—emotions, spatial relations, social relationships, language, etc.
- a need for empirical study of the nature of cognitive models
- a need for appropriate theoretical and philosophical underpinnings for prototype theory.

These needs will be addressed below. But before we begin, it is important to see that prototype effects occur not only in nonlinguistic conceptual structure, but in linguistic structure as well. The reason is that linguistic structure makes use of general cognitive apparatus, such as category structure. Linguistic categories are kinds of cognitive categories.

REFERENCES

Austin, J. L. (1961). *Philosophical Papers*. Oxford: Oxford University Press.

Barsalou, L. W. (1983). 'Ad-hoc categories'. *Memory and Cognition* 11: 211–27.

——(1984). 'Determinants of graded structure in categories'. Atlanta, Ga.: Psychology Department, Emory University.

Berlin, B., D. E. Breedlove, and P. H. Raven (1974). *Principles of Tzeltal Plant Classification*. New York: Academic Press.

——and P. Kay (1969). *Basic Color Terms: Their Universality and Evolution*. Berkeley: University of California Press.

Brown, R. (1958). 'How shall a thing be called?' *Psychological Review* 65: 14–21.

——(1965). *Social Psychology*. New York: Free Press.

Brugman, C. (1981). 'The story of *over*'. M.A. thesis, University of California, Berkeley.

Cain, A. J. (1958). 'Logic and memory in Linnaeus's system of taxonomy'. *Proceedings of the Linnaean Society of London* 169: 144–63.

Cruse, D. A. (1977). 'The pragmatics of lexical specificity'. *Journal of Linguistics* 13: 153–64.

DeValois, R. L., I. Abramov, and G. H. Jacobs (1966). 'Analysis of response patterns of LGN cells'. *Journal of the Optical Society of America* 56: 966–77.

——and G. H. Jacobs. (1968). 'Primate color vision'. *Science* 162: 533–40.

Dubois, D., and H. Prade (1980). *Fuzzy Sets and Systems: Theory and Applications*. New York: Academic Press.

Ekman, P. (1971). *Universals and Cultural Differences in Facial Expressions of Emotions*. Lincoln: University of Nebraska Press.

——W. V. Friesen, and R. Ellsworth (1972). *Emotion in the Human Face*. Elmsford, NY: Pergamon Press.

——R. W. Levenson, and W. V. Friesen (1983). 'Autonomic nervous system activity distinguishes among emotions'. *Science* 221: 1208–10.

Fillmore, C. (1982). 'Towards a descriptive framework for spatial deixis'. In R. J. Jarvella and W. Klein (eds.), *Speech, Place, and Action*, London: Wiley, 31–59.

Goguen, J. A. (1969). 'The logic of inexact concepts'. *Synthese* 19: 325–73.

Heider, E. (E. Rosch) (1971). ' "Focal" color areas and the development of color names'. *Developmental Psychology* 4: 447–55.

——and D. Olivier (1972). 'The structure of the color space in naming and memory for two languages'. *Cognitive Psychology* 3: 337–54.

Hinton, L. (1982). 'How to cause in Mixtec'. In *Proceedings of the Eighth Annual Meeting of the Berkeley Linguistics Society*, 354–63.

Hunn, E. S. (1975). 'A measure of the degree of correspondence of folk to scientific biological classification'. *American Ethnologist* 2(2): 309–27.

——(1977). *Tzeltal Folk Zoology: The Classification of Discontinuities in Nature*. New York: Academic Press.

Kay, P., and C. McDaniel (1978). 'The linguistic significance of the meanings of basic color terms'. *Language* 54(3): 610–46.

Kempton, W. (1981). *The Folk Classification of Ceramics: A Study of Cognitive Prototypes*. New York: Academic Press.

Labov, W. (1973). 'The boundaries of words and their meanings'. In J. Fishman (ed.), *New Ways of Analyzing Variation in English*, Washington, DC: Georgetown University Press.

Lakatos, I. (1976). *Proofs and Refutations*. Cambridge: Cambridge University Press.

Lakoff, G. (1972). 'Hedges: a study in meaning criteria and the logic of fuzzy concepts'. In *Papers from the Eighth Regional Meeting of the Chicago Linguistic Society*, 183–228. Repr. in *Journal of Philosophical Logic* 2 (1973): 458–508.

——(1977). 'Linguistic gestalts'. In *Papers from the Thirteenth Regional Meeting of the Chicago Linguistic Society*, 236–87.

—— and M. Johnson (1980). *Metaphors We Live By*. Chicago: University of Chicago Press.

Lounsbury, F. (1964). 'A formal account of the Crow- and Omaha-type kinship terminologies'. In W. H. Goodenough (ed.), *Explorations in Cultural Anthropology*. New York: McGraw-Hill, 351–94. Repr. in S. A. Tyler (ed.), *Cognitive Anthropology*. New York: Holt, Rinehart & Winston, 212–54.

McCawley, J. D. (1981). *Everything That Linguists Have Always Wanted to Know about Logic—But Were Ashamed to Ask*. Chicago: University of Chicago Press.

MacLaury, R. (1986). 'Color in Mesoamerica, A theory of composite categorization'. Doctoral dissertation, Berkeley, University of California.

Mervis, C. (1984). 'Early lexical development: the contributions of mother and child'. In C. Sophian (ed.), *Origins of Cognitive Skills*. Hillsdale, NJ: Erlbaum.

Murphy, G. L. (1982). 'Cue validity and levels of categorization'. *Psychological Bulletin* 91(1): 174–7.

—— and D. L. Medin (1984). 'The role of theories in conceptual coherence'. Providence, RI: Psychology Department, Brown University.

Rips, L. J. (1975). 'Inductive judgments about natural categories'. *Journal of Verbal Learning and Verbal Behavior* 14: 665–81.

Rosch, E. (1975a). 'Cognitive reference points'. *Cognitive Psychology* 7: 532–47.

——(1975b). 'Cognitive representations of semantic categories'. *Journal of Experimental Psychology: General*, 104: 192–233.

——(1978). 'Principles of categorization'. In E. Rosch and B. B. Lloyd (eds.), *Cognition and Categories*. Hillsdale, NJ: Erlbaum, 27–48.

——(1981). 'Prototype classification and logical classification: the two systems'. In E. Scholnick (ed.), *New Trends in Cognitive Representation: Challenges to Piaget's Theory*. Hillsdale, NJ: Erlbaum, 73–86.

——(1988). 'Coherences and categorization: a historical view'. In F. S. Kessel (ed.), *The Development of Language and Language Researchers: Essays in honor of Roger Brown*. Hillsdale, NJ: Erlbaum, 379–92.

—— and B. B. Lloyd (eds.) (1978). *Cognition and Categorization*. Hillsdale, NJ: Erlbaum.

—— and C. Mervis (1975). 'Family resemblances: studies in the internal structure of categories'. *Cognitive Psychology* 7: 573–605.

—— C. Simpson, and R. S. Miller (1976). 'Structural bases of typicality effects'. *Journal of Experimental Psychology: Human Perception and Performance* 2: 491–502.

Smith, E. E., and D. L. Medin (1981). *Categories and Concepts*. Cambridge, Mass.: Harvard University Press.

Stross, B. (1969). 'Language acquisition by Tenejapa Tzeltal children'. Ph.D. dissertation, University of California, Berkeley.

Tversky, A., and I. Gati (1978). 'Studies of similarity'. In E. Rosch and B. B. Lloyd (eds.), *Cognition and Categories*. Hillsdale, NJ: Erlbaum, 79–98.

Tversky, B., and K. Hemenway (1984). 'Objects, parts, and categories'. *Journal of Experimental Psychology: General* 113: 169–93.

Wittgenstein, L. (1953). *Philosophical Investigations*. New York: Macmillan.

Zadeh, L. (1965). 'Fuzzy Sets'. *Information and Control* 8: 338–53.

PART III
Categories in Grammar

11

Parts of Speech

OTTO JESPERSEN

It is customary to begin the teaching of grammar by dividing words into certain classes, generally called "parts of speech"—substantives, adjectives, verbs, etc.—and by giving definitions of these classes. The division in the main goes back to the Greek and Latin grammarians with a few additions and modifications, but the definitions are very far from having attained the degree of exactitude found in Euclidean geometry. Most of the definitions given even in recent books are little better than sham definitions in which it is extremely easy to pick holes; nor has it been possible to come to a general arrangement as to what the distinction is to be based on—whether on form (and form-changes) or on meaning or on function in the sentence, or on all of these combined.

The most ingenious system in this respect is certainly that of Varro, who distinguishes four parts of speech, one which has cases (nouns, nomina), one which has tenses (verbs), one which has both cases and tenses (participles), and one which has neither (particles). If this scheme is now generally abandoned, the reason evidently is that it is so manifestly made to fit Latin (and Greek) only and that it is not suitable either to modern languages evolved out of a linguistic structure similar to Latin (English, for instance) or to languages of a totally different type, such as Eskimo.

A mathematical regularity similar to that in Varro's scheme is found in the following system: some nouns distinguish tense like verbs and distinguish gender like ordinary nouns (participles), others distinguish neither gender nor tense (personal pronoun). Verbs are the only words combining tense distinction with lack of genders. Thus we have:

nouns	ordinary:	with gender, without tense
	personal pronouns:	with gender, without tense
	participles:	with gender, without tense
verbs:		without gender, with tense.[1]

This system, again, fits only the ancient languages of our family, and differs mainly from Varro's scheme in being based on gender instead of case distinction. Both are equally arbitrary. In both tense is made the really distinctive feature of verbs, a conception which has found expression in the German rendering of *verb* by *zeitwort*: but on that showing Chinese has no verbs, while on the other hand we shall see later that nouns sometimes distinguish

---

* Otto Jespersen, 'Parts of speech', ch. 4 of *The Philosophy of Grammar* (London: George Allen & Unwin, 1924), 58–71. © Taylor & Francis. Reprinted by permission.

[1] Schroeder, *Die formelle Unterscheidung der Redetheile im griech. u. lat.* (Leipzig, 1874).

tenses. Other grammarians think that the distinctive feature of verbs is the personal endings (Steinthal, etc.). But this criterion would also exclude the Chinese verb from that denomination; in Danish, again, verbs do not distinguish persons, and it is no help out of the difficulty to say, as Schleicher does (NV 509) that "verbs are words which have or have had personal endings," for it should not be necessary to know linguistic history to determine what part of speech a word belongs to.

DEFINITIONS

Let us now cast a glance at some of the definitions found in J. Hall and E. A. Sonnenschein's *Grammar* (London, 1902). "Nouns name. Pronouns identify without naming." I cannot see that *who* in *Who killed Cock Robin?* identifies; it rather asks some one else to identify. And *none* in *Then none was for a party*—whose identity is established by that pronoun? "Adjectives are used with Nouns, to describe, identify or enumerate."[2] But cannot adjectives be used without nouns? (*the absent* are always at fault. He was *angry*). On the other hand, is *poet* in *Browning the poet* an adjective? "By means of Verbs something is said about something or somebody": *You scoundrel*—here something is said about "you" just as much as in *You are a scoundrel*, and in the latter sentence it is not the verb *are*, but the predicative that says something. "Conjunctions connect groups of words or single words"—but so does *of* in *a man of honour* without being on that account a conjunction. Not a single one of these definitions is either exhaustive or cogent.[3]

THE BASIS OF CLASSIFICATION

Some grammarians, feeling the failure of such definitions as those just given have been led to despair of solving the difficulty by the method of examining the meaning of words belonging to the various classes: and therefore maintain that the only criterion should be the *form* of words. This is the line taken, for instance, by J. Zeitlin ('On the Parts of Speech. The Noun,' in *The English Journal*, March 1914), though unfortunately he deals only with nouns. He takes "form" in rather a wide sense, and says that "in English the noun does still possess certain formal characteristics which attach to no other class of words. These are the prefixing of an article or demonstrative, the use of an inflexional sign to denote possession and plurality, and union with prepositions to mark relations originally indicated by inflexional endings." He is careful to add that the absence of all the features enumerated should not exclude a word from

---

[2] "Enumerate" seems to be used here in a sense unknown to dictionaries. If we take it in the usual signification, then, according to the definition *coat*, etc., would be adjectives in "All his garments, coat, waistcoat, shirt and trousers, were wet."

[3] Long after this was written in the first draft of my book, I became acquainted with Sonnenschein's *New English Grammar* (Oxford, 1921—in many ways an excellent book, though I shall sometimes have occasion to take exception to it). Here some of the definitions have been improved. "A pronoun is a word used in place of a noun, to indicate or enumerate persons or things, without naming them." *Indicate* is much better than *identify*, but the difficulty about *none* and *who* persists. "A co-ordinating conjunction is a word used to connect parts of a sentence which are of equal rank. A subordinating conjunction is a word used to connect an adverb clause or a noun-clause with the rest of a complex sentence." A co-ordinating conjunction may also be used to connect whole sentences (Sonnenschein, § 59). The definition is rather complicated, and presupposes many other grammatical terms; it really gives no answer to the question, what is a conjunction? What is common to the two classes?

being a noun, for this should be described "as a word which has, or in any given usage may have" those formal signs.

If form in the strictest sense were taken as the sole test, we should arrive at the absurd result that *must* in English, being indeclinable, belonged to the same class as *the, then, for, as, enough*, etc. Our only justification for classing *must* as a verb is that we recognize its use in combinations like *I must (go), must we (go)?* as parallel to that of *I shall (go), shall we (go)?*—in other words, that we take into consideration its meaning and function in the sentence. And if Zeitlin were to say that the use of *must* with a nominative like *I* is "formal" (in the same way as "union with prepositions" was one of the "formal" tests by which he recognized a noun), I should not quarrel with him for taking such things into account, but perhaps for calling them formal considerations.

In my opinion everything should be kept in view, form, function, and meaning, but it should be particularly emphasized that form, which is the most obvious test, may lead to our recognizing some word-classes in one language which are not distinct classes in other languages, and that meaning, though very important, is most difficult to deal with, and especially that it is not possible to base a classification on short and easily applicable definitions.

We may imagine two extreme types of language structure, one in which there is always one definite formal criterion in each word-class, and one in which there are no such outward signs in any class. The nearest approach to the former state is found, not in any of our natural languages, but in an artificial language such as Esperanto or, still better, Ido, where every common substantive ends in -*o* (in the plural in -*i*), every adjective in -*a*, every (derived) adverb in -*e*, every verb in -*r*, -*s*, or -*z* according to its mood. The opposite state in which there are no formal signs to show word-classes is found in Chinese, in which some words can only be used in certain applications, while others without any outward change may function now as substantives, now as verbs, now as adverbs, etc., the value in each case being shown by syntactic rules and the context.

English here steers a middle course though inclining more and more to the Chinese system. Take the form *round*: this is a substantive in "a round of a ladder," "he took his daily round," an adjective in "a round table," a verb in "he failed to round the lamp-post," an adverb in "come round to-morrow," and a preposition in "he walked round the house." *While* similarly may be a substantive (he stayed here for a while), a verb (to while away time), and a conjunction (while he was away). *Move* may be a substantive or a verb, *after* a preposition, an adverb, or a conjunction,[4] etc.

On the other hand, we have a great many words which can belong to one word-class only; *admiration, society, life* can only be substantives, *polite* only an adjective, *was, comprehend* only verbs, *at* only a preposition.

To find out what particular class a given word belongs to, it is generally of little avail to look at one isolated form. Nor is there any flexional ending that is the exclusive property of any single part of speech. The ending -*ed* (-*d*) is chiefly found in verbs (*ended, opened*, etc.), but it may be also added to substantives to form adjectives (*blue-eyed, moneyed, talented*, etc.). Some endings may be used as tests if we take the meaning of the ending also into account; thus if an added -*s* changes the word into a plural, the word is a substantive, and if it is found in the third person singular, the word is a verb: this, then, is one of the tests for keeping the substantive and the verb *round* apart (many rounds of the ladder; he rounds the lamp-post). In other cases the use of certain words in combinations is decisive, thus *my* and *the* in "my love for her" and "the love I bear her," as against "I love her," show that *love* is a substantive and not a verb as

---

[4] We shall discuss later whether these are really different parts of speech.

in the last combination (cf. *my admiration, the admiration* as against *I admire*, where *admiration* and *admire* are unambiguous).[5]

It is, however, very important to remark that even if *round* and *love* and a great many other English words belong to more than one word-class, this is true of the isolated form only: in each separate case in which the word is used in actual speech it belongs definitely to one class and to no other. But this is often overlooked by writers who will say that in the sentence "we tead at the vicarage" we have a case of a substantive used as a verb. The truth is that we have a real verb, just as real as *dine* or *eat*, though derived from the substantive *tea*—and derived without any distinctive ending in the infinitive. To form a verb from another word is not the same thing as using a substantive as a verb, which is impossible. Dictionaries therefore must recognize *love* sb. and *love* v. as two words, and in the same way *tea* sb. and *tea* v. In such a case as *wire* they should even recognize three words, (1) sb. 'metallic thread,' (2) 'to send a message by wire, to telegraph'—a verb formed from the first word without any derivative ending, (3) 'message, telegram'—a sb. formed from the verb without any ending.

In teaching elementary grammar I should not begin with defining the several parts of speech, least of all by means of the ordinary definitions, which say so little though seeming to say so much, but in a more practical way. As a matter of fact the trained grammarian knows whether a given word is an adjective or a verb not by referring to such definitions, but in practically the same way in which we all on seeing an animal know whether it is a cow or a cat, and children can learn it much as they learn to distinguish familiar animals, by practice, being shown a sufficient number of specimens and having their attention drawn successively now to this and now to that distinguishing feature. I should take a piece of connected text, a short story for instance, and first give it with all the substantives printed in italics. After these have been pointed out and briefly discussed the pupil will probably have little difficulty in recognizing a certain number of substantives of similar meaning and form in another piece in which they are not marked as such, and may now turn his attention to adjectives, using the same text as before, this time with the adjectives italicized. By proceeding in this way through the various classes he will gradually acquire enough of the "grammatical instinct" to be able to understand further lessons in accidence and syntax in his own and foreign languages.

It is not, however, my purpose here to give advice on elementary grammatical teaching, but to try to arrive at some scientific understanding of the logical basis of grammar. This will be best attained, I think, if we consider what it is that really happens when we talk of something, and if we examine the relation between the real world and the way in which we are able to express its phenomena in language.

LANGUAGE AND REAL LIFE

Real life everywhere offers us only *concretissima*: you see this definite apple, definitely red in one part and yellowish in that other part, of this definite size and shape and weight and degree of ripeness, with these definite spots and ruggednesses, in one definite light and place at this definite moment of this particular day, etc. As language is totally unable to express all this in corresponding concreteness, we are obliged for the purpose of communication to ignore many

---

[5] See the detailed discussion in *A Modern English Grammar on historical principles* II, Chs. VIII and IX, on the question whether we have real substantives in combinations like "Motion requires a *here* and a *there*, "a *he*," "a *pick-pocket*," "*my Spanish* is not very good," etc. A specially interesting case in which one may be in doubt as to the class of words is dealt with in *A Modern English Grammar on historical principles* II, Ch. XIII: have first-words in English compounds become adjectives? (See there instances like: intimate and *bosom* friends | the *London* and American publishers | a *Boston* young lady | his own umbrella—the *cotton* one | much purely *class* legislation | the most *everyday* occurrences | the roads which are all *turnpike* | her *chiefest* friend | *matter-of-factly, matter-of-factness*.)

of these individual and concrete characteristics: the word "apple" is not only applied to the same apple under other circumstances, at another time and in another light, but to a great many other objects as well, which it is convenient to comprise under the same name because otherwise we should have an infinite number of individual names and should have to invent particular names for new objects at every moment of the day. The world is in constant flux around us and in us, but in order to grapple with the fleeting reality we create in our thought, or at any rate in our language, certain more or less fixed points, certain averages. Reality never presents us with an average object, but language does, for instead of denoting one actually given thing a word like *apple* represents the average of a great many objects that have something, but of course not everything, in common. It is, in other words, absolutely necessary for us, if we want to communicate our impressions and ideas, to have more or less abstract[6] denominations for class-concepts: *apple* is abstract in comparison with any individual apple that comes within our ken, and so is *fruit* to an even higher degree, and the same is still more true of such words as *red* or *yellow* and so on: language everywhere moves in abstract words, only the degree of abstraction varies infinitely.

Now, if you want to call up a very definite idea in the mind of your interlocutor you will find that the idea is in itself very complex, and consists of a great many traits, really more than you would be able to enumerate, even if you were to continue to the end of time. You have to make a selection, and you naturally select those traits that according to the best of your belief will be best fitted to call up exactly the same idea in the other man's mind. More than that, you select also those that will do it in the easiest way to yourself and to your hearer, and will spare both of you the trouble of long circuitous expressions. Therefore instead of *a timid gregarious woolly ruminant mammal* you say *sheep*, instead of *male ruler of independent state* you say *king*, etc. Thus wherever you can, you use single special terms instead of composite ones. But as special terms are not available for all composite ideas, you often have to piece together expressions by means of words each of which renders one of the component traits of the idea in your mind. Even so, the designation is never exhaustive. Hence the same man may under various circumstances be spoken of in totally different ways, and yet the speaker is in each case understood to refer to the same individual: as "James Armitage" or simply "Armitage" or "James," or else as "the little man in a suit of grey whom we met on the bridge," or as "the principal physician at the hospital for women's diseases," as "the old Doctor," as "the Doctor," as "Her husband," as "Uncle James," as "Uncle," or simply as "he." In each case the hearer supplies from the situation (or context), i.e. from his previous knowledge, a great many distinctive traits that find no linguistic expression—most of all in the last-mentioned case, where the pronoun "he" is the only designation.

Among these designations for the same individual there are some which are easily seen to have a character of their own, and we at once single out *James* and *Armitage* (and, of course, the combination *James Armitage*) as *proper names*, while we call such words as *man, physician, doctor, husband, uncle*, which enter into some of the other designations, *common names*, because they are common to many individuals, or at least to many more, than are the proper names. Let us now try to consider more closely what is the essence of proper names.

PROPER NAMES

A proper name would naturally seem to be a name that can only be used in speaking of one individual. It is no objection to this definition that *the Pyrenees* or *the United States* are proper

---

[6] "Abstract" is used here in a more popular sense than in the logico-grammatical terminology.

names, for in spite of the plural form by which they are designated this range of mountains and this political body are looked upon as units, as individuals: it is not possible to speak of *one Pyrenee* or of *one United State*, but only of *one of the Pyrenees, one of the United States.*

A more serious difficulty encounters us when we reflect that *John* and *Smith* by common consent are reckoned among proper names, and yet it is indubitable that there are many individuals that are called *John*, and many that are called *Smith*, and even a considerable number that are called *John Smith. Rome* similarly is a proper name, yet there are at least five towns of that name in North America besides the original Rome in Italy. How then are we to keep up the distinction between proper and common names?

A well-known attempt at a solution is that of John Stuart Mill (*System of Logic*, I, Ch. II). According to him proper names are not *connotative*; they *denote* the individuals who are called by them; but they do not indicate or imply any attributes as belonging to those individuals, they answer the purpose of showing what thing it is we are talking about, but not of telling anything about it. On the other hand, such a name as *man*, besides *denoting* Peter, James, John, and an indefinite number of other individuals, *connotes* certain attributes, corporeity, animal life, rationality, and a certain external form, which for distinction we call the human. Whenever, therefore, the names given to objects convey any information, that is, whenever they have any meaning, the meaning resides not in what they *denote*, but in what they *connote*. The only names of objects which connote nothing are proper names; and these have, strictly speaking, no signification.

Similarly a recent Danish writer (H. Bertelsen, *Fællesnavne og egennavne*, 1911) says that John is a proper name, because there is nothing else besides the name that is common to all John's in contradistinction to Henry's and Richard's, and that while a common name indicates by singling out something that is peculiar to the individual persons or things to whom the name is applied, the opposite is true of a proper name. Accordingly, the distinction has nothing to do with, or at any rate has no definite relation to, the number of individuals to whom a name is given. I do not think, however, that this view gets to the bottom of the problem.

ACTUAL MEANING OF PROPER NAMES

What in my view is of prime importance is the way in which names are actually employed by speakers and understood by hearers. Now, every time a proper name is used in actual speech its value to both speaker and hearer is that of denoting one individual only, and being restricted to that one definite being. To-day, in talking to one group of my friends, I may use the name John about a particular man of that name, but that does not prevent me from using it to-morrow in different company of a totally different individual; in both cases, however, the name fulfils its purpose of calling up in the mind of the hearer the exact meaning which I intend. Mill and his followers lay too much stress on what might be called the dictionary value of the name, and too little on its contextual value in the particular situation in which it is spoken or written. It is true that it is quite impossible to tell the meaning of *John* when nothing but the name is before us, but much the same thing may be said of a great many "common names." If I am asked to give the meaning of *jar* or *sound* or *palm* or *tract*, the only honest answer is, Show me the context, and I will tell you the meaning. In one connexion *pipe* is understood to mean a tobacco-pipe, in another a water-pipe, in a third a boatswain's whistle, in another one of the tubes of an organ, and in the same way John, in each separate sentence in which it is used, has one distinct meaning, which is shown by the context and situation; and if this meaning is more special in each case than that of *pipe* or the other words mentioned, this is only another side of the important fact that the number of characteristic traits is greater in the case of a proper name than in the case of a common name. In Mill's terminology, but in absolute contrast to his view, I should venture to say that proper names (as actually used) "connote" the greatest number of attributes.

The first time you hear of a person or read his name in a newspaper, he is "a mere name" to you, but the more you hear and see of him the more will the name mean to you. Observe also the way in which your familiarity with a person in a novel grows the farther you read. But exactly the same thing happens with a "common name" that is new to you, say *ichneumon*: here again, the meaning or connotation grows along with the growth of your knowledge. This can only be denied on the assumption that the connotation of a name is something inherent in the name, something with an existence independent of any human mind knowing and using the name: but that is surely absurd and contrary to all right ideas of the essence of language and human psychology.

If proper names as actually understood did not connote many attributes, we should be at a loss to understand or explain the everyday phenomenon of a proper name becoming a common name. A young Danish girl was asked by a Frenchman what her father was, and in her ignorance of the French word for 'sculptor' got out of the difficulty by saying: "Il est un *Thorvaldsen* en miniature." Oscar Wilde writes: "Every great man nowadays has his disciples, and it is always *Judas* who writes the biography" (*Intentions*, 81)—a transition to speaking of *a Judas*. Walter Pater says that France was about to become *an Italy* more Italian than Italy itself (*Renaissance*, 133). In this way *Cæsar* became the general name for Roman emperors, German Kaisers and Russian tsars (in Shakespeare's tragedy III.2.55, the rabble shouts: "Liue Brutus, liue, liue.... Let him be Cæsar")—to mention only a few examples.[7]

Logicians, of course, see this, but they dismiss it with some remark like this (Keynes 1906, p. 45): "Proper names, of course, become connotative when they are used to designate a certain type of person; for example, a Diogenes, a Thomas, a Don Quixote, a Paul Pry, a Benedick, a Socrates. But, when so used, such names have really ceased to be proper names at all; they have come to possess all the characteristics of general names." The logician as such with his predilection for water-tight compartments in the realm of ideas, is not concerned with what to me as a linguist seems a most important question, viz. how is it to be explained that a sequence of sounds with no meaning at all suddenly from non-connotative becomes connotative, and that this new full meaning is at once accepted by the whole speaking community?

If we take the view suggested above, this difficulty vanishes at once. For what has happened is simply this, that out of the complex of qualities characteristic of the bearer of the name concerned (and, as I should say, really connoted by the name) one quality is selected as the best known, and used to characterize some other being or thing possessed of the same quality. But this is exactly the same process that we see so very often in common names, as when a bell-shaped flower is called a bell, however different it is in other respects from a real bell, or when some politician is called an old *fox*, or when we say that *pearl*, or *jewel*, of a woman. The transference in the case of original proper names is due to the same cause as in the case of common names, viz. their connotativeness, and the difference between the two classes is thus seen to be one of degree only.

The difference between *Cræsus* as applied to the one individual and as used for a very rich man may be compared to that between *human* (connoting everything belonging to man) and *humane* (selecting one particular quality).

---

[7] The Lithuanian word for 'king,' *karalius*, is derived from *Carolus* (Charlemagne); so also Russ. *korol*, Pol. *król*, Magy. *király*.

With our modern European system of composite personal names we have a transference of names of a somewhat different kind, when a child through the mere fact of his birth acquires his father's family name. Here it would be rash to assert that Tymperleys, for instance, of the same family have nothing in common but their name; they may sometimes be recognized by their nose or by their gait, but their common inheritance, physical and psychical, may be much more extensive, and so the name Tymperley may get a sense not essentially different from that of such "common names" as *Yorkshireman*, or *Frenchman*, or *negro*, or *dog*. In some of the latter cases it is difficult to define exactly what the name "connotes" or by what characteristics we are able to tell that a person belongs to this or the other class, yet logicians agree that all these names are connotative. Then why not *Tymperley?*

It is different, of course, with Christian names, which are given in a much more arbitrary way. One Maud may have been so called "after" a rich aunt, and another simply because her parents thought the name pretty, and the two thus have nothing but the name in common. The *temple* of worship and the *temple* of the head are in much the same case. (The two Mauds have really more in common than the two temples, for they are both female human beings.[8]) But that does not affect the main point in my argument, which is that whenever the name Maud is naturally used it makes the hearer think of a whole complex of distinctive qualities or characteristics.

Now it will be said against this view that "the connotation of a name is not the quality or qualities by which I or anyone else may happen to recognize the class which it denotes. For example, I may recognize an Englishman abroad by the cut of his clothes, or a Frenchman by his pronunciation, or a proctor by his bands, or a barrister by his wig; but I do not *mean* any of these things by these names, nor do they (in Mill's sense) form any part of the connotation of the names" (Keynes 1906, p. 43). This seems to establish a distinction between essential characteristics comprised in the "connotation"[9] and unessential or accidental qualities. But surely no sharp line can be drawn. If I want to know what is connoted by the names *salt* and *sugar* respectively, is it necessary to apply chemical tests and give the chem-ical formula of these two substances, or am I permitted to apply the popular criterion of tasting them? What qualities are connoted by the word "dog"? In this and in a great many other cases we apply class-names without hesitation, though very often we should be embarrassed if asked what we "mean" by this or that name or why we apply it in particular instances. Sometimes we recognize a dog by this, and sometimes by that characteristic, or group of characteristics, and if we apply the name "dog" to a particular animal, it means that we feel confident that it possesses the rest of that complex of traits which together make up dog-nature.[10]

The use of proper names in the plural (cf. *A Modern English Grammar on historical principles*, volume II, 4.4) is made intelligible by the theory we have here defended. In the strictest sense no proper name can have a plural, it is just as unthinkable as a plural of the pronoun "I": there is only one "I" in existence, and there is only one "John" and one "Rome," if by these names we understand the individual person or city that we are speaking of at the moment. But in the above-mentioned modified senses it is possible for proper names to form a plural in the

---

[8] A further method of transference of proper names is seen in the case of married women, when Mary Brown by marrying Henry Taylor becomes Mrs Taylor, Mrs Mary Taylor, or even Mrs Henry Taylor.

[9] Cf. ib. 24, "we include in the connotation of a class-name only those attributes upon which the classification is based."

[10] The best definition of a dog probably is the humorous one that a dog is that animal which another dog will instinctively recognize as such.

usual way. Take the following classes:

1. individuals which have more or less arbitrarily been designated by the same name: in the party there were three *Johns* and four *Marys* | I have not visited any of the *Romes* in America;
2. members of the same family: all the *Tymperleys* have long noses | in the days of the *Stuarts* | the *Henry Spinkers*;
3. people or things like the individual denoted by the name: *Edisons* and *Marconis* may thrill the world with astounding novelties | *Judases* | *King-Henrys, Queen-Elizabeths* go their way (Carlyle) | the Canadian Rockies are advertised as "fifty *Switzerlands* in one";
4. by metonymy, a proper name may stand for a work of the individual denoted by the name: there are two *Rembrandts* in this gallery.

It should also be remembered that what we designate by an individual name is, if we look very closely into it, merely an abstraction. Each individual is constantly changing from moment to moment, and the name serves to comprehend and fix the permanent elements of the fleeting apparitions, or as it were, reduce them to a common denominator. Thus we understand sentences like the following, which are very hard to account for under the assumption that proper names are strictly non-connotative: he felt convinced that Jonas was again the Jonas he had known a week ago, and not the Jonas of the intervening time (Dickens) | there were days when Sophia was the old Sophia—the forbidding, difficult Sophia (Bennett) | Anna was astounded by the contrast between the Titus of Sunday and the Titus of Monday (id.) | The Grasmere before and after this outrage were two different vales (de Quincey). In this way, too, we may have a plural of a proper name: Darius had known England before and after the repeal of the Corn Laws, and the difference between the two *Englands* was so strikingly dramatic... (Bennett).

Linguistically it is utterly impossible to draw a sharp line of demarcation between proper names and common names. We have seen transitions from the former to the latter, but the opposite transition is equally frequent. Only very few proper names have always been such (e.g. *Rasselas*), most of them have originated, totally or partially, in common names specialized. Is "the Union" as applied to one particular students' union at Oxford or Cambridge a proper name? Or the "British Academy" or the "Royal Insurance Company," or—from another sphere—"Men and Women" or "Outspoken Essays" or "Essays and Reviews" as book-titles? The more arbitrary the name is, the more inclined we are to recognize it at once as a proper name, but it is no indispensable condition. The Dover road (meaning 'the road that leads to Dover') is not originally a proper name, while *Dover Street* which has no connexion with Dover and might just as well have been baptized *Lincoln Street*, is a proper name from the first. But the *Dover Road* may in course of time become a proper name, if the original reason for the name is forgotten and the road has become an ordinary street; and the transition may to some extent be marked linguistically by the dropping of the definite article. One of the London parks is still by many called "the Green Park," but others omit the article, and then *Green Park* is frankly a proper name; compare also *Central Park* in New York, *New College, Newcastle*. Thus, the absence of the article in English (though not in Italian or German) becomes one of the exterior marks by which we may know proper from common names.

In the familiar use of such words as *father, mother, cook, nurse* without the article we accordingly have an approximation to proper names; no doubt they are felt as such by children up to a certain age, and this is justified if the mother or an aunt in speaking to the child says *father* not of her own, but of the child's father.

The specialization which takes place when a common name becomes a proper name is not different in kind, but only in degree, from specializations to be observed within the world of common names. Thus when *the Black Forest* (or, still more distinctly, the German name *Schwarzwald*) has become the name of a particular mountain range, the relation between this name and the combination "the black forest" which might be applied as a common name to some other forest is similar to that between *the blackbird* and the *black bird*.[11]

Our inquiry, therefore, has reached this conclusion, that no sharp line can be drawn between proper and common names, the difference being one of degree rather than of kind. A name always connotes the quality or qualities by which the bearer or bearers of the name are known, i.e. distinguished from other beings or things. The more special or specific the thing denoted is, the more probable is it that the name is chosen arbitrarily, and so much the more does it approach to, or become, a proper name. If a speaker wants to call up the idea of some person or thing, he has at his command in some cases a name specially applied to the individual concerned, that is, a name which in this particular situation will be understood as referring to it, or else he has to piece together by means of other words a composite denomination which is sufficiently precise for his purpose.

REFERENCES

Keynes, J. N. (1906). *Studies and Exercises in Formal Logic*, 4th edn. London.

Schleicher, A. (1865). *Nomen und Verbum*. Leipzig.

Steinthal, H. (1860). *Charakteristik der haupsächl: Typen des Sprachbaues*. Berlin.

[11] One final example may be given to illustrate the continual oscillations between common and proper names. When musicians speak of the Ninth Symphony they always mean Beethoven's famous work. It thus becomes a proper name; but Romain Rolland makes that again into a common name by using it in the plural (marked by the article, while the singular form of the noun and the capital letters show it to be apprehended as a proper name) when writing about some French composers: 'ils faisaient des *Neuvième Symphonie* et des *Quatuor* de Franck, mais beaucoup plus difficiles' (Jean Chr. 5. 83).

12

English Word Classes

DAVID CRYSTAL

I

The word classes of English have probably been studied more thoroughly, and from more different viewpoints, than those of any other language: apart from English grammars, English is usually the language of exemplification in most theoretical linguistic discussion of the subject. One almost unnoticed result of this lengthy tradition, however, has been the development of an extremely unhealthy complacency, in both a theoretical and descriptive context, which manifests itself in a number of ways. The surface structure of this complacency is readily identifiable with the terminological vagueness seemingly endemic in this subject: familiar terms, like 'partial conversion', 'full word', 'adverb', or 'particle' have been bandied about in a cavalier way, with little attention being paid to the extent of their intelligibility. This point needs (and will get, below) further discussion: clearly, to say that a word is an adverb, for example, explains little and confuses much, when one thinks that by 'adverb' one could be taken to be referring to the range of words in which such disparate items as 'the', 'however', 'yes', 'slowly', 'very', 'well', and 'who' have been yoked together. The near-universal use of a very small number of labels has obscured the existence of deeper problems, and has meant that people can rarely be sure of where they stand in any debate involving such labels. One person's use of a term like 'function word' or 'adverb' (even, at times, 'noun' and 'verb') is likely to be significantly distinct from another's, because its descriptive basis and theoretical status will hardly ever have been defined before discussion begins. Nor can one readily judge whether the word class discrimination of an adult is due to his perception of gross similarities in form and function of a group of words, or whether he is (unconsciously or otherwise) paying lip-service to a familiar label. And as no one seems to be able to do without these terms, nor the general concept of word class, in talking about English, whether this be in a generative context, in the context of pattern classification within a corpus, or in teaching-grammars, it is all the more unfortunate that the existence of terminological shortcomings is rarely acknowledged.

More worrying than this is the misdirected emphasis on word classes per se, seen in isolation from the rest of the grammar, and in textbooks usually given separate discussion towards the beginning.[1] It is frequently assumed that one can satisfactorily describe the word classes of (say) English before going on to the 'meaty' part of a grammar, for which the classes are seen merely as a kind of grammatical shorthand. This is complacency, because to isolate word classes in such a way is both misleading and distorting: word classes should not

* David Crystal, 'English', *Lingua* 17 (1967): 24–56. © 1967 David Crystal. Reprinted by kind permission of the author.

[1] A recent example is B. Ilyish, *The Structure of Modern English* (Moscow, 1965), where Part One ('Morphology') covers the parts of speech, first in general, then in individual detail; Part Two covers 'Syntax'.

be taken as being in some way part of a terminological preamble to grammar, because in a real sense they assume a grammar before one can begin to talk about them. Their definition is an abstraction from grammatical and other criteria—not directly from data—and their purpose is ultimately to act as the constituents of a grammatical meta-language, which one manipulates to display more interesting syntactic relations. It is the interrelationships between word classes, and their function in helping to formalise transformational and other relations, which is the really important issue arising out of a consideration of word classes— and not the establishment of a set of isolated classes as an end in itself. Again, the distinction between establishing and describing the word classes of English is still often confused and unnoticed. This too is worth stressing here and now. The problem of setting-up word classes is basically a question of discovery procedures, and the issues arising here are very different from the purely descriptive problem, where word class criteria are verified against an independently-verifiable grammar. Nor are procedural issues relevant to the descriptive task: for example, given that all word class definitions in English were to be syntactic, to criticise this as being 'circular in a way that vitiates all the definitions'[2] is to confuse procedural with descriptive method. Syntactic criteria may not be the best criteria for all classes, but there is no necessary circularity. Problems of 'where to start' are not of descriptive or explanatory interest, and defining X by Y and Y by X is from the viewpoint of descriptive grammar quite permissible.

There are other issues which have hardly been raised. Very little attempt has been made to evaluate systematically the multiplicity of different analyses which have been made of English word classes (apart from the familiar, and usually rather superficial remarks about the unreliability (unqualified) of notional criteria.[3] This of course relates to the general question of evaluating a grammar, which is only beginning to be explored. Again, the relationship of word classes to considerations of language typology is a useful approach to the whole concept, which has largely been overlooked:[4] what are the problems facing the word class analyst which are characteristically English? This in turn is a question which can only be answered by relating it to the more fundamental matter of the nature of linguistic universals. The presence of such issues,[5] makes it quite clear that any complacency about word classes in English is unfounded; and this paper, consequently, is a discussion of some neglected points of principle within this context. It is not an academic review of past work, nor a systematic description, for the first would produce an encyclopedia of territory well-charted already, while the second could only result in a complete English grammar. Its main aim is to stimulate further discussion on the matter by looking 'meta-meta-linguistically' at familiar descriptive concepts in a critical light, to see how far familiarity has bred too great a content, and obscured some real problems.

2

To begin near the beginning: word classes, it is agreed, do 'simplify our description of the structure of the language',[6] and are an essential stage in the construction of an adequate grammar of a language. It is important to be able to make statements about the grammatical

---

[2] H. A. Gleason Jr., *Linguistics and English Grammar* (New York: Holt, Rinehart and Winston, 1965) p. 115, footnote.   [3] Cf. below p. 202.

[4] But cf. C. E. Bazell, *Linguistic Typology* (University of London Inaugural Lecture) 1958.

[5] Discussed, for example in N. Chomsky, *Aspects of the Theory of Syntax* (Cambridge, Mass.: MIT, 1965).

[6] H. A. Gleason, Jr., *An Introduction to Descriptive Linguistics* (New York: Holt, Rinehart and Winston, 1961) p. 93.

relationships and restrictions exercised by groups of items upon each other than by individual items, for only in this way can one successfully achieve any notion of 'generality'—a notion which is inherent in the concept of 'rule' (generative, pedagogical, or any other). This implies, as already mentioned, that one cannot isolate word classes, giving them an identity of their own apart from the grammar. The proper emphasis in establishing or describing them does not allow them to be disassociated from the grammar at all: the concept word class implies the prior establishment of a grammar, and explicating the word classes of a language involves explicating its grammar. This is because the important and interesting aspect of the problem (as is now generally recognised) lies in the nature of the *criteria* which are used in defining the classes. 'The definition of a class, and its membership, can only arise from the criteria used to establish it in the first place'.[7] In the past, while the role of criteria was usually implicit in the definition of classes (e.g. a label like 'defective form' implied a ranking of criteria of some kind—defective and regular in what respects?), these criteria were rarely investigated explicitly, which accounts for much of the arbitrariness in description.[8] These days the shift in attention is clear: 'as many classes are set up as words of different formal behaviour are found'.[9] This as it stands, of course, is not satisfactory, for a criterion of formal difference, without further qualification, is going to take us too far. For example, one has to allow in the co-occurrence restrictions which exist between grosser classes, and which tend to reduce English to a very large number of very small classes. If one only considers the restrictions governing the 'behaviour' of verbal tense-forms in relation to temporal adverbials, this being a fairly easily definable field, the intuitive homogeneity of the class 'temporal adverbial' in English is shown to be clearly superficial, a number of important sub-classes becoming apparent immediately;[10] and one wonders what would happen if other co-occurrences of this general type were examined. Again, 'different formal behaviour' would attribute undue significance to morphological characteristics, which would result in the unsatisfactory situation of 'house', 'say', and other morphologically unique forms in English being set up as 'classes' of their own. The reductio of this approach, however, is to consider the restrictions exercised by collocability on individual lexical items, which suggest that very few words have an identical overall formal behaviour, even in a given restricted grammatical environment.[11] One would end up with a multitude of single member classes—ignoring the point, for the moment, that the phrase 'single member class' is usually taken to be a contradiction in terms (though this is an unnecessary conclusion, as it depends on one's definition of 'class' in the first place)— and the purpose of the exercise would have backfired. The requirement that classes be distinguished by different formal behaviour is clearly too absolute for the linguist, who wishes to set up a fairly small number of word classes if it is to be worth his while (as far as descriptive 'economy' is concerned).

An alternative and more careful formulation of the problem is therefore more reasonable, while retaining the emphasis on criteria suggested above, e.g. 'we must class together words which play essentially identical roles in the structure of the language';[12] 'the aim must be a

---

[7] R. H. Robins, *General Linguistics: An Introductory Survey* (London: Longmans, 1964) p. 228.
[8] An early exception is O. Jespersen, *Essentials of English Grammar* (London: Allen and Unwin, 1933) §7.7₁: 'in order to find out what class a word belongs to it is not enough to consider its form in itself; what is decisive is the way in which the word in connected speech "behaves" towards other words, and in which other words behave towards it'.
[9] Robins, op. cit., p. 229.
[10] Cf. D. Crystal 'Specification and English tenses', *Journal of Linguistics* 3 (1966) pp. 1–34.
[11] Cf. below, p. 195, for an instance of this, by no means maximal in depth of detail.
[12] Gleason, 1961, p. 93.

system of word classes characterized by maximum homogeneity within the classes';[13] 'a class of forms which have similar privileges of occurrence in building larger forms is a form class' ... 'a part of speech is a form class of stems which show similar behaviour in inflection, in syntax, or both';[14] form classes are treated as separate when they show 'enough difference' from other classes.[15] As they stand, of course, such statements only postpone the central issue, namely, How can notions of 'identity of role', 'maximum homogeneity', 'similarity of behaviour', and 'enough difference' be precisely defined? This question does not seem to have been answered. If the decision is arbitrary, as Bloomfield[16] thought,[17] then perhaps there is no one answer—but people should at least be aware of this weakness and limitation of the word class concept, and note the extent to which decisions become little more than a matter of linguistically sophisticated taste. This problem is acute for English, because there is no obvious single criterion, such as inflectional type, or fairly self-evident combination of criteria, which could be used to classify all, or even most words. One needs an aggregate of criteria of various degrees of generality, and hence some further criteria of selection and evaluation. A technique for assessing the relevance of all potential criteria is required to make any notion of 'maximum internal homogeneity' workable, to avoid introducing unimportant and irrelevant criteria into one's description, to allow judgements about 'exceptions', 'overlapping classes', and so on. But before looking in more detail at the criteria relevant for English (cf. section 4 below), we need to consider further the implications of the requirement of 'simplicity' or 'economy' which seems to lie behind most word classifications.

An ideal situation seems to exist if one can assign all words of a language to a very few classes by applying a very few general criteria—a balance between the number of classes, and the number and degree of complexity of the criteria. This is as near as one can get to maximal generality without overburdensome explanation. On the whole, there is a ratio between number of criteria and classes: the more criteria one introduces, the more classes will be established, with each class having fewer members. The current tendency is towards a more delicate or refined subclassification,[18] and while this is certainly the right direction in which to be moving (accurate general statements being more desirable as a first end than simple ones), it should also be remembered that the more subclassification one allows, the more points of general similarity become less clear: one begins to see some new trees that had not been visible previously, but one also begins to lose sight of the wood. And ultimately there is the danger of finding oneself with such small classes of items that general statement becomes impossible, and listing of members becomes the only simple descriptive solution, which is hardly an explanation. On the other hand, too few criteria produce the alternative danger of underclassification—major classes, e.g. bipartite (e.g. noun vs. non-noun), tripartite, with a very uncertain and miscellaneous constitution, lacking any readily perceivable homogeneity.[19] For English, this has usually taken the form of a Noun-class, a Verb-class, and a mixed bag. With very general classes of this kind, it is extremely difficult to define conditions of membership precisely: all one can usefully do is characterise the classes with reference to the most 'general'

---

[13] Gleason, 1965, p. 130.

[14] Cf. Hockett, *Course in General Linguistics* (New York: Macmillan, 1958) pp. 162, 221.

[15] Cf. R. A. Hall, Jr., *Introductory Linguistics* (New York: Chilton Books, 1964) p. 163. Any potential distinction between 'word-' and 'form-' class is irrelevant for this paper.

[16] L. Bloomfield, *Language* (New York: Holt, 1933) p. 269.

[17] Cf. Gleason, 1961, p. 92.

[18] The difference between 'class' and 'sub-class' is clearly one of degree, but in the absence of any satisfactory definition of the former, the distinction between them has unfortunately become extremely tenuous, and the same group of words (e.g. adverbs of manner, colour adjectives) has at times been referred to as a class, at times a sub-class.

[19] Cf. Hockett, op. cit. p. 221 ff.

criteria, and list (usually a large number of) exceptions.[20] There are, however, other general classifications of a different type from these, whose widespread use and usually unquestioned status warrant separate discussion.

3

There have been a number of attempts to find a major binary division in English words, at least four dichotomies being very familiar (and not, of course, being restricted to a context of English): 'full/empty', 'open/closed', 'variable/invariable', and 'lexical/grammatical'. Reference to these classifications seems to be made more often than any other;[20a] so it is a pity that there has been little attempt to define these terms clearly, to see how far they are meaningful or can be consistently applied in any exhaustive study of English words. It is often assumed that their meaning and definition is self-evident, and (more worryingly) that there is a parallelism between the pairs: 'full', 'lexical', and 'open' seem to be treated as synonymous very frequently, and similarly 'empty', 'grammatical', and 'closed'. Also one comes across unhelpful 'definitions', of the extreme form 'function words are grammatical words are lexically empty words are words functioning in a closed system . . . ', phrased more subtly, all too often. A look at what is involved in these dichotomies would thus seem to be called for, to see what help, if any, these classifications are in defining word classes for English.

(a) Variable vs. invariable words (inflectional vs. non-inflectional)

This is a dichotomy which is clearly distinct from the others, and which has often been taken as an obvious and potentially useful starting-point in word classification.[21] The inflected words are usually listed as nouns, verbs, adjectives, pronouns and a few adverbs;[22] invariable words, having little internal coherence, are most easily described as everything other than these. Having said this, the poverty of the classification should be apparent, for it is hardly a classification in any useful sense. The invariable group is merely a convenience; and within the variable fold, there are different types of inflection and degrees of variability which one would expect to see distinguished. Neither has a coherence supported throughout by any other (e.g. distributional) criterion. The major difficulty, however, is that the rigid division implies a naturalistic view of word class membership, and fails to provide a satisfactory account of words which can occur in different types of syntactic environment, and thus 'belong to more than one class', as it is traditionally put. There is no problem if such words inflect through their *whole* range of occurrence (e.g. words which occur as both nouns and verbs), or if neither inflect at all (e.g. as prepositions and adverbs); but if this does not happen, then one has words

---

[20] One danger of this is that it tempts people to talk in terms of a class having a 'central core' of regular members, and a 'periphery' of uncertain members, or some such metaphor—a pseudo-statistical priority which is based on size of membership alone, and ignores considerations of overall frequency of a word's occurrence and the crucial question of the ordering of criteria. cf. below, p. 204.

[20a] E.g., classification in terms of monomorphemic and polymorphemic words, whose analysis and classification in any case belongs primarily to the lexicon of the language (cf. Robins, 'In defence of WP', *Transactions of the Philological Society*, 1959, pp. 121–2).

[21] Cf. Robins, 1959, p. 121.

[22] Apart from 'more/most', 'worse/worst', and other familiar 'irregulars', one would have to list 'closer/-est', 'faster/-est', 'nearer/-est', 'oftener/-est', etc.

which are variable or invariable depending on the point of view, e.g. 'out', which may inflect as a noun ('ins and outs', etc.), and many more. Of course one can and does distinguish such cases syntactically, but this is at once to go beyond the basis of the variability criterion. Another criticism of this criterion, also, is that it does cut across certain other (intuitively important) classifications. Invariable nouns would be cut off from the main class, for example—such as in the case of some uncountable nouns (like 'tolerance' or 'perseverance') which do not inflect for number, and hardly ever for case (the nouns taking the postmodifying genitive instead).[23] Finally, the term 'variable' has also to be related to 'clusters' of the kind 'in-inside-into-within', where there is no obvious reason why these could not be seen as variable forms of 'in'.

(b) Full (content) vs. empty words

It perhaps needs stressing these days that 'empty' here really does (or at least did) mean words which have no meaning at all. Sweet, the founder, used 'empty' to refer only to form-words (words like 'the' and 'is', as he puts it) which are 'entirely devoid of meaning'.[24] This point needs to be made because a scepticism about the existence in English of truly empty words has now become so general, that there has developed a retrospective doubt that the term could ever have been seriously used in this absolute way. Even Sweet had trouble with the division, of course, and had to coin the phrase 'full form-words' to cope with words like 'became' in 'he became Prime Minister', and his vague definition here reflects his basic dissatisfaction: 'a word combines the function of a form-word with something of the independent meaning of a full word' (§59); cf. §61, 'It will, of course, be understood that it is not always easy—or even possible—to draw a definite line between full-words and form-words'. It is now generally accepted that the absolute terms and the rigid division of the dichotomy are misleading: on the one hand, there is no agreed way of quantifying the degrees of fulness which exist; on the other hand, the only words which seem to qualify as empty are the forms of 'be', 'to', 'there', and 'it'—but only in certain of their uses, of course, viz. 'be' as copula, infinitival 'to', 'there', and 'it' as unstressed subject 'props'. It is not difficult to produce examples of these words being used with important contrastive function in other contexts, e.g. the existential use of 'be', all other uses of 'to' (and also cf. 'I'd like to go' vs. 'I'd like a go'). Most of the words commonly adduced as empty (e.g. 'of', 'the') can be shown to contain meaning, definable in terms other than stating grammatical contexts, particularly when one considers them, as one must, in a full prosodic context: 'of' contrasts readily with other prepositions (e.g. 'the material of/by/ near . . . that book is . . .') and the *OED* takes many column-inches giving the referential meanings of 'the'. Most of what people normally label 'grammatical words' (cf. below) have referential relevance, in fact. All prepositions, for example, are definable literally, in terms of spatial-temporal dimensions: only when they are used as parts of idioms may they be strictly meaningless, and only then because the meaning is now being carried by the larger lexical unit (cf. the use of 'the' in proper names, etc.). Finally, the inadequacy of the dichotomy's semantic basis is pointed by its restriction to cognitive meaning: 'full' is usually explicated empirically. But this is to ignore the meaningfulness imposed on words by connotation, as well as the

---

[23] Cf. Jespersen, op. cit., 142 ff., B. M. H. Strang, *Modern English Structure* (London: Arnold, 1962) p. 93. I am excluding humorous and poetic licence, where these contrasts do exist, as this licence also applies, though not always in the same degree, to the majority of invariable words.

[24] H. Sweet, *A New English Grammar* (Oxford: Clarendon, 1892) §58. cf. Jespersen, op. cit., §36.6.

relevance of non-idiosyncratic attitudinal meaning deriving from the use of prosodic features of utterances,[25] which affect 'grammatical' words as well as 'lexical'.

The 'full-empty' opposition, then, is not a realistic classification. To salvage anything, one has to substitute a scale or continuum between the two poles, between words which have a complex metaphysical, attitudinal, and empirical relevance and words which have very little of this, but which nevertheless have a meaning of some kind independent of grammatical considerations. The difference is one of degree: exactly how many places along this continuum there are is an open question, which is unlikely to be answered until techniques of measuring meaning become more sophisticated. Meanwhile, it is worthwhile remembering that the full-empty distinction as it stands is of little theoretical or practical value in the definition of English word classes.[26]

(c) Lexical vs. grammatical (form or function) words (or functors)[27]

This division is usually taken as paralleling the full-empty classification. Again, there is mutual exclusiveness: lexical words imply absence of grammatical meaning and vice versa. It is difficult to say just what 'lexical' refers to: an expansion of the form, 'words about which statements of meaning are made in a lexicon' is unsatisfactory, because most 'grammatical words' have non-grammatical meanings which would also have to be listed there. 'Lexical' must not be seen as incompatible with 'grammatical', and it is not difficult to show that the dichotomy is unreal at both ends. On the one hand, there are numerous words usually called 'lexical' which have grammatical meaning 'built-in', as it were, due to the presence of a morphologically-identifying suffix, e.g. '-ance', '-tion', '-less', '-able', '-ize', '-wise', and many more. (This of course implies a prior morphological analysis, so that 'station' and 'interrogation', for example, may be distinguished.) On the other hand, as stated in the discussion of (b) above, all of what are usually called 'grammatical words' have a function or meaning which is clearly not grammatical (*ergo* lexical?) as well as their undeniably grammatical function. The article system, for example, may be discussed in terms of co-occurrence, substitutability, place in the system of determiners, and so on; but it may also be discussed in terms which are of empirical relevance. The auxiliary verbs and prepositions in English are even clearer examples of the impossibility of any kind of rigid division. And there is the further case of idioms which makes the division seem unreal: whatever the grammatical meaning of a word, it stands to resign this by becoming part of a larger lexical unit, e.g. 'in' in 'in case', 'out' in 'eke out', 'the' in 'the Thames'. Idioms clearly have to be taken as a separate class in this context. As with 'full-empty', then, there seem to be degrees of both 'lexicalness' and 'grammaticalness' in English, and a scale

+LEXICAL	−LEXICAL
−GRAMMATICAL	+GRAMMATICAL

would really be the only way to retain these terms usefully.

---

[25] D. Crystal, 'The linguistic status of prosodic and paralinguistic features' (University of Newcastle-upon-Tyne Philosophical Society) 1966.

[26] Cf. Robins, 1964, p. 277.

[27] Chomsky's distinction between lexical and grammatical formatives op. cit. p. 65 ff.) seems to be similar in principle, but the latter are defined in a different way from that discussed here: as non-lexical constituents of a terminal string, they include formatives like *Perfect, Possessive* and # (boundary symbol) as well as 'the', etc.

For 'function words', cf. C. C. Fries, *The Structure of English* (New York: Harcourt Brace, 1952) and W. N. Francis, *The Structure of American English* (New York: Ronald Press, 1958) p. 231.

It is worth discussing the criteria which have been suggested for the definition of 'grammatical words' (henceforth, inverted commas understood) in more detail: such criteria, of course, are usually also relevant for the definition of (b) and (d). They bring particular difficulties, largely because there are different types of such words. Six main kinds of criterion seem to have been used in discussing this subject. (Tautologies of the kind 'grammatical = structural meaning' or 'form words indicate grammatical relationships' will not be commented on.) First, there is an appeal to phonological criteria, which can be briefly dismissed as being of little assistance. It is true that the majority of grammatical words have weak sentence stress,[28] and many of them have reduced forms, but in certain environments, such words are regularly stressed (e.g. 'do' in 'I do like it'), or given full form (e.g. prepositions at the end of sentences). Also, the position of stress as a factor in the definition of 'full' words and 'empty' or 'form' words is often unclear: Sweet[29] seems to have begun a circularity by implying in his examples that 'some' has stress because it is a full-word, whereas 'piece' and 'lump' are to be taken as (nearly) form-words partly because of their diminished stress. Secondly, grammatical words are usually said to be relatively 'small' and 'finite'. Assuming these terms to be distinct, and assuming one can give some definition to 'relatively', the only meaning one can give to the former (phonological or graphological length—'little words' is a familiar phrase) is readily disprovable. (One does not have to explain away the absence of long grammatical words but the presence of short lexical ones!) 'Finite' has been taken to mean countable, 'not open-ended', 'the whole range readily listable', or some such formulation—a requirement which becomes extremely difficult to follow when one considers the whole range of prepositions, for example. These must of course include 'complex prepositions' ('on account of', 'in accordance with', etc.) which have a very gradual shading-off into compound nominal groups (e.g. 'at the side of') and which are only beginning to be studied.[30] Thirdly, grammatical words are also said to be relatively permanent, to not have any continuous growth (*contra* lexical and 'open-class' words); but this is a statement which is only relatively true, over long historical periods (cf. the major changes between Old and Middle English, for example), and hence of little synchronic relevance. It is true that, within a given period of years, one can point to new lexical items having emerged and no new grammatical items; but apart from haphazard exemplification there is little information about this process or the variables involved in it (e.g. no information about different rates of lexical addition in different periods in different areas of vocabulary); and in any case one still needs a concept to explain the relative stability of the grammatical words (cf. (d) below).

A fourth point, which is frequently made, is that the 'meaning' of grammatical words is only demonstrable by exemplifying their use in sentences. This is not the case, as the comments on 'full–empty' have already suggested. Very few grammatical words are in fact predictable in sentence-frames. It is possible to predict the occurrence of *some* grammatical words in a few contexts (excluding occurrence in formulaic utterances, which are wholly predictable), but only under very favourable conditions: 'it' and 'the' are predictable in such contexts as '~ seems that' and '~ only way' respectively, but in most other contexts, e.g. '~ good men', 'the' is but one choice from a number of alternatives (though widening the context would probably reduce the number substantially).[31] Any criterion of predictability is clearly more of a scale than a polarity, and if applied would display many different types of word, differentiating

---

[28] Cf. Sweet, op. cit., §60.

[29] Op. cit. 61.

[30] Cf. R. Quirk and J. Mulholland, 'Complex prepositions and related sequences', *English Studies*, (1964), Supplement to volume 45, pp. 64–73, and below, pp. 206–7.

[31] But allowing in wider contexts would tend to reduce the lexical-grammatical distinction to nil on this point, as over long contexts, lexical words (except at the very beginning) would also become highly predictable.

the high degree of unpredictability of prepositions from the more restricted auxiliary verbs and conjunctions: there would certainly be no nice parallel between what is predictable and what is grammatical. Again, some lexical items are largely or wholly predictable in certain contexts, e.g. 'better' in 'I think we'd ~ get off this bus', or 'never' in '/John'll !nèver agrée with you# / will he#'. To make such a criterion work would also involve considering such problems as the evaluation of the frames within which an item may be said to be predictable, the structure of 'units' higher than the sentence, and the distinction between notional and grammatical predictability—problems which have hardly been faced as yet. But while this makes the notion of predictability of little value in the context of word-classification, it is still possible to salvage something from this approach, at a fairly practical level. A good case could be made for seeing as grammatical words those about which statements of their use have to be made individually: they are unique in most or all respects. If this is taken to imply 'at a relatively surface level' (and not to enter into the question of collocability), then it is probably a helpful way of looking at them—as long as one remembers that there are liable to be quite a few more than one thought,[32] and that the resultant grammatical words will not coincide with the traditional views—many prepositions would be excluded, for example. By definition, of course, all these words would not be eligible for inclusion in classes at a more general level.

Fifthly, 'another practical test of form-words is that they may often be omitted with a slight change in the form of the sentence—sometimes without any change at all—or in translating into some other language. Thus *of* in *man of honour* is omitted in the synonymous expression *honourable man*, and *the earth is round* may be expressed in Latin by *terra rotunda*, literally 'earth round', where both form-words are omitted. So also *some* in *some people think differently*, being a full word has strong stress and cannot be omitted; while in *give me some more bread* it has weak stress, and might be omitted without loss of clearness'.[33] He compares French *du*, and continues: 'Even such words as *piece* and *lump* are used nearly as form-words in such groups as *a piece of bread, a lump of lead*, as is shown by their diminished stress, and by their having practically almost the same meaning as the weak *some* in *some bread*'. The tentative nature of this criterion is clear from such qualifying vagueness as 'may often', 'slight change', 'might be omitted', 'nearly as', and so on; but it is of little value for other reasons also. Apart from the irrelevance of the appeal to translation, one can easily think up counter-examples of uses of form-words which are non-omissible because there is no permissible attributive or other transformation; and there is usually more than a 'slight change' in the form and synonymity of the sentence when prosodic considerations are brought in. The implied circularity in the mention of stress has already been referred to. There is also an obvious danger in relying too heavily on any criterion of near-synonymity, and an equally undesirable flexibility enters in with the reference to such an indefinable stylistic consideration as clearness—on such grounds *full*-words may at times be omitted. Sixthly, and finally, it is said that grammatical words transcend distinctions in register—that all varieties of English will exemplify their use. This is a criterion which it should be possible to prove statistically: the frequency of grammatical words in any corpus should be far above that of any lexical words, and there should be a clear break in relative frequencies of occurrence. But of course as a statistical definition, it would have no necessary linguistic relevance, to prove which we are back where we started.

---

[32] The Survey of English Usage at University College London (cf. R. Quirk, 'Towards a description of English usage', *Transactions of the Philological Society*, 1960, pp. 40–61), has a separate file of 'closed system words'. These are words which have been set aside as belonging to small finite groups (such as the 'personal pronouns') or about which it is assumed that individual statements are necessary (such as *all, enough*). There are about 400 of these.

[33] Cf. Sweet, op. cit., §61.

(d) Open-class(-set) words vs. closed-system(-class) words

This is a more valuable dichotomy, which again runs only partially parallel to (b) and (c). The concept of system, first, is one which has received fairly clear exposition through analogies with cybernetics, and other fields, though there are nonetheless dangers in its uncritical linguistic use. If a system is an organised complex of a finite number of inter-related components (or some similar definition), then it is readily demonstrable that the components will have a stability of function (a definable positive and negative value) which would not be found in an inventory. In language, this seems to be true for relatively small closed systems of items, at any rate: with such cases as the personal pronouns, articles and other determiners, the internal contrasts are clear; there is the absence of synonymous terms; and there is homeostasis, so that to alter the value of one component is to alter the values of the others, such 'movements' being clearly identifiable and discussable at a practical as well as a theoretical level.[34] It is doubtful whether this notion is very helpful for systems with a finite, but relatively large membership, however, e.g. conjunctions, prepositions: here, to say there is a formal 'balance' between items is only true in an extremely theoretical sense, the implications of which linguists ignore in practice. One may discuss corners of the prepositional system, for example—or even the tense system—without feeling bound to refer to what would be inordinately complex sets of internal contrasts; and ignoring the whole network of formal relations seems to have no ill effects. If one artificially 'omits' the pluperfect tense from English, for example, there does not seem to be any difference in one's discussion of the present tense; its formal status has only 'altered' in a rather pickwickian sense, and to try to formalise the alteration seems pointless. This argues, then, that the notion of system has been stretched too widely, and that not everything which we may wish to call grammatical is systematic in the same (closed) sense throughout.

The weakness in the term 'system' is underlined by its being opposed to open-set words, which, it is claimed, are potentially infinite in number, display synonymity, and can have changes in number and—more important—meaning of single words take place without this affecting the whole. The distinction is not as clear-cut as this, however, for it is not true that there is no interdependence between open-class words. There are groups of open-class words which have a clear systematic function in relation to each other, either defining each other, or being ordered in some way. This is implied by such terms as the 'logic' of a particular use or discourse of language (though this is only common in a philosophical context), and by more specific cases, such as the numeral system, months of the year, and many other groups of proper names. One finds groups of mutually defining open-class words cutting up temporal-spatial dimensions,[35] and a relatively open-class prefixation working similarly (e.g. 'palaeo-lithic', 'neolithic', 'megalithic', etc.): all this beside the more familiar colour-spectrum and kinship-term vocabulary.[36] The establishment of these and other lexical subsystems on the basis of such semantic relations as incompatibility, hyponymy, and antonymy[37] is clearly going to have an important influence on the dichotomy of class v. system, and the evidence so far suggests that the division as it stands may well have to go. From the closed-system point of view, also, there is a great deal that has not been done: the systematic basis of many 'grammatical words' has often been assumed, and hardly studied at all (e.g. subordinating and

---

[34] Cf. Halliday (1961) pp. 246–7, who uses the notion of closed system as 'the crucial criterion for distinguishing grammar from lexis', though it is not clear how 'open set' and 'closed system' can be 'two distinct types of pattern' and at either ends of a cline at the same time. Cf. also Strang, op. cit., p. 77; Robins, 1964, p. 230.

[35] Cf. Crystal, *Journal of Linguistics* 3, for examples.

[36] Cf. J. Lyons, *Structural Semantics*. Publication of the Philological Society XX (Oxford: Blackwell, 1963) p. 38.

[37] Cf. Lyons, op. cit., p. 59 ff.

co-ordinating conjunctions,[38] or the predeterminers in the nominal group). Finally, some words are of unclear status in the light of the open-closed dichotomy: what are interjections, for instance?

One cannot but conclude that these four pairs of terms are not as valuable or as fundamental as has been implied by the frequency of their use, and are of very little relevance for word classification, as the resultant divisions are too general and ill-defined. Variable-invariable is clearly distinct from the others, and cuts across them to a large extent (there being so many grammatical words which inflect). And while the other pairs do have a partial parallelism (particularly at the lexical-full-open pole), the distinctions are largely vacuous because there is no actual rigid demarcation of this kind in language. The concept of 'closed-system' does, however, suggest lines of approach which could be useful; and it would be valuable if more attention were paid to refining the notion of 'grammatical word' along the lines suggested. There is also the general criticism that to set up dichotomies of this nature once again focuses attention too strongly on the concept of grammatically isolated word classes, whereas the needed emphasis, as already mentioned, is on the selection and grading of criteria. Finally, any further subclassification of these dichotomies would of course have to elicit further criteria of a completely different kind, and it is to a consideration of these that we must now return.

4

What is needed is a balance between the over-classification of words as mentioned in section 2, and their under-classification as described in section 3. The classes, to be useful to the linguist (or teacher) have to be few and fairly general, and have some degree of intuitive coherence. This ideal situation, however, can only be approached by in some way ranking the criteria which one considers relevant to the task of class definition.[39] As a first step in this direction, we may make use of the concept of 'levels' of linguistic analysis, and discriminate criteria as belonging to one or other of these levels.[40] Theoretically, criteria from any level are potentially relevant—phonological, grammatical, lexical, and semantic—so long as they are well-defined, and one avoids the correspondence fallacy of expecting all criteria used to produce identical results in classification. It cannot be aprioristically assumed that any one group of criteria is irrelevant. Moreover, one group of criteria at one level will not satisfactorily define all word classes for English, and recourse must be had to other levels, though as one might expect (the word being by definition a grammatical abstraction) the centre of interest does stay firmly at the syntactic level ((v) in the following discussion) for most purposes.

(i) *Phonological/graphological criteria.* While stress has occasionally been brought into the definition of some English word classes,[41] other types of sound-pattern (and their associated graphic representation), e.g. number of syllables or sounds, vowel harmony, segmental

---

[38] But cf. L. R. Gleitman, 'Co-ordinating conjunctions in English', *Language* 41 (1965) pp. 260–93, for an approach to the latter. A particularly tricky corner is how to relate conjunctions as they are discussed here to sentence-initiating optional 'conjunctions' as in: 'And there remains another point ...'.

[39] Which theoretically of course then means evaluating these other meta-meta-linguistic criteria as well: but we will not enter any further along this infinite regress.

[40] One must bear in mind throughout the need for an ultimately integrated statement of all the criteria discriminated, and not maintain a rigid division between (say) morphological and syntactic criteria, as in G. L. Trager and H. L. Smith, Jr., *An Outline of English Structure* (Norman, Okla.: Battenburg Press, 1951).

[41] E.g. by Strang, op. cit., p. 84.

structure, prosodic or paralinguistic characteristics, all seem to be grammatically irrelevant for English, providing no systematic information about word classification—though of course some intonational features are of relevance in plotting other grammatical relations (and cf. footnote 63 below). There are of course features like vowel-alternation in nouns and verbs, and morphophonological criteria of the type 'form the plural of the subclass of nouns ending in $/\theta/$ by $/\theta/ \rightarrow /\eth/ + /z/$, but only if a long vowel or diphthong precedes, and there is no intervening consonant' (i.e. to exclude 'breath', 'length', etc.); but these are only relevant for the description of very small classes, and are in any case better taken under the general heading of morphology.

(ii) *Morphological criteria.* In English, suffixation is the main criterion,[42] being of two types, inflectional (indicating plurality, possession, pastness, 3rd person, participiality and degree) and lexical (derivational): noun designators, e.g. '-phile', '-let', '-ence', '-dom', '-ism', '-ology', '-scopy'; adjective designators, e.g. '-ish', '-less', '-oid', '-ward'; verb-designators, e.g. '-ify', '-ize', '-ate'; and adverb-designators, e.g. '-wards', '-where', '-ly'. This is not an entirely satisfactory criterion, of course, because many suffixes (e.g. '-ly', '-en') can be added to other words which belong to one of a number of classes depending on syntactic position. For this reason, morphological criteria would seem to be clearly outranked by syntactic[43] (though procedurally one might well want to start with the clear-cut morphological distinctions in establishing some basic classes.[44]

(iii) *Lexical criteria.* This would involve defining classes in terms of similarity or identity of collocability, ranging from identity within a grammatically defined context to complete non-equivalence. So little work has been done in this field, however, that it is impossible to apply it to the present problem.

(iv) *Semantic or notional criteria.* There have been many objections made to defining word classes in English on a notional basis—difficulties of definition and delimitation of the referents of word classes, lack of parity between notional and grammatical categories, and so on—which are presumably too familiar to need discussion at this point, and are well covered elsewhere.[45] But bad definitions in the past are no justification for refusing to allow notional criteria any place in word classification at all. There are certain classes of words where notional definition would seem to provide obvious and intuitively most satisfactory information, e.g. certain types of time reference, the numeral system, some systems of proper names; and it is to be hoped that formally based classes will in any case have some notional coherence that can one day be defined.[46] Meanwhile, one must not rule out carefully formulated notional criteria as being wholly irrelevant in the definition of word classes, even though they may be secondary: to deny this is to invite a theoretical distortion comparable to that which was condemned when formal criteria were disregarded.

(v) *Syntactic criteria.* A discussion of criteria at the syntactic level has been left until last because of its central importance for word class description, although there has as yet been little done on the problem of grading. The main reason for this lies in the classification procedures used: for word classes, syntactic criteria generally come down to substitutability in frames, which is not entirely satisfactory. Not all the objections to this procedure are

[42] 'a-', commonly cited as an adverb-designator, is extremely dubious, cf. below, p. 208.
[43] Cf. Robins, 1964, p. 226.
[44] Cf. Hall, op. cit., p. 145.
[45] E.g. Gleason, 1965, Part One and ch. 6.
[46] Cf., for example, R. Brown, 'Linguistic determinism and the part of speech', *J. of Ab. and Soc. Psychol.* 55 (1957) 1–5, reprinted in *Psycholinguistics*, ed. S. Saporta (New York, 1961), and *Words and Things* (Glencoe: Free Press, 1958), on the perception of semantic properties shared by groups of words.

convincing, of course, e.g. criticising noun-establishing sentence-frames such as 'the ~ is good' on the grounds that many nouns are given uncertain status because of doubtful semantic/lexical relationship between them and 'good' ('the murder is good', 'the alacrity is good', etc.). This objection can usually be avoided, either by thinking up a genuine—if rare—context in which such utterances would be likely, or being more careful in the definition of the frame (e.g. by substituting a lexical 'prop' like 'such-and-such' for 'good' in these contexts). But substitutability does have other, unwanted results: taking just the above example, one is forced to omit many uncountable nouns which cannot co-occur with 'the' (unless the noun is also postmodified—in which case most proper nouns would be permitted). More generally, prosodic restrictions on occurrence and the environment of the sentence-frame as such are at times important considerations which are usually ignored; and there is no way for sentence-frames to reveal 'deeper' structural differences—they are restricted to defining classes on the basis of surface structural similarities. Quirk has criticised substitutability procedures on a number of other grounds, pointing out that the technique prejudices informant reactions by drawing too much attention to the feature being investigated; that it provides 'a proliferation of forms in a misleading guise of free variation';[47] and that the unsupplemented substitution test confuses idiomatic constructions with others, and tends to obscure the distinction between marginal and normal usage. A major objection, also, in the context of word classification, is that frames are only a temporary *deus ex machina* for the linguist, as they merely evade the evaluation question. He still has to decide how many and which frames to use.

The value of the sentence-frame technique is really that of an *ad hoc* measuring rod which can show at a glance whether two words are syntactically identical in respect of a particular criterion, though it does not help in providing an abstract definition of any frame or in relating frames to each other on the basis of their transformational relations. Thus all one has to do to show the superficial similarity between 'new' and 'railway' in 'new station' and 'railway station' is to point out that it is permissible to say 'this station is new' and not to say 'this station is railway'; and this process is presumably sufficiently familiar not to require any further exemplification. The point of present concern is: whether one takes them as belonging to different classes or not will depend on how many differences of a similar order one can find using other contexts. If two words are different in respect of every sentence-frame one can think up, then there is no problem. Likewise, if they are identical. The problem of grading comes when two words are identical for some frames and different for others. In assessing such similarities and differences, we are forced to rank criteria, and problems of the following type come to the fore: is the more important criterion for adjective class that a word may occur between determiner and noun or that it may occur directly after the verb 'to be' (attributive vs. predicative)? Or, more generally, should morphological criteria take precedence over syntactic in defining a class of nouns in English? And so on.

Any answer to such questions can only be reached in the light of some more general principle. Taking the second question, and using just four criteria as examples, how can one grade: number/case inflection in nouns, the ability of a noun to act as subject of a sentence, its ability to follow the article directly, and its being characterised derivationally? Constraints of different kinds come to mind for each criterion: not all nouns inflect for number and case, not all nouns have a clear non-inflectional morphological indication, not all are able to co-occur with the definite article, and other things beside nouns (phrases, clauses, pronouns) can be subject of a sentence. Here, the only realistic solution seems to be statistical: that criterion is ranked first which applies to most cases, and which least applies to other classes. The more

---

[47] R. Quirk, 'Substitutions and syntactic research', *Archivum Linguisticum* 10 (1958) p. 41.

words which fit a criterion, the more general the criterion; or, in the case of classes which are relatively 'open', the fewest words for which a criterion does not apply. One would always expect a coherent word class to have at least one criterion with 100% applicability, to justify one's intuition of coherence:[48] traditional classes which lack this (e.g. adverbs) would have no alternative but reclassification until this principle is met. Single words with a unique range of criteria would be defined independently as functors. In this way, the criterion of being subject would be clearly primary (the overlap with phrases and clauses not posing any problems in *word* classification), and the others could be rated accordingly—as soon as someone does the relevant work! One would expect, for example, number inflection to rank fairly high, and derivational morphological indication to be fairly low; or, taking the question of adjectives, attributive position would outrank predicative, because of the predicative slot's applicability to other words which never occur in attributive position and which differ from attributive words in all other morphosyntactic respects—predicativeness would be largely non-diagnostic for this problem.

The suggestion, then, is that some statistical approach along such lines could produce illuminating results over this question of the grading of criteria: what seems to us to be intuitively the most satisfactory solution should to a large extent reflect our unconscious awareness of proportions of frequencies. This approach would also seem to be the only way whereby one can give meaning to the notion of 'centrality' of membership of a word class. The technique is common to lexicography also, and illustratable through a series of overlapping circles (simplified here, as only certain criteria have been chosen, stylistic dimensions ignored, and the diagram is not to scale):

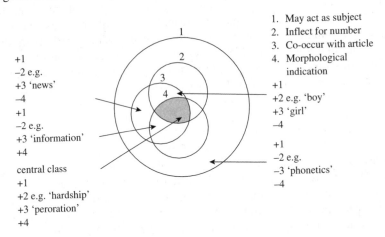

1. May act as subject
2. Inflect for number
3. Co-occur with article
4. Morphological indication

+1
−2 e.g.
+3 'news'
−4

+1
−2 e.g.
+3 'information'
+4

central class
+1
+2 e.g. 'hardship'
+3 'peroration'
+4

+1
+2 e.g. 'boy'
+3 'girl'
−4

+1
−2 e.g.
−3 'phonetics'
−4

A statistical rationale of the criteria for word classification seems to be the only alternative to the unqualified arbitrariness which Bloomfield stated was implicit in the definition of English word classes.[49] Arbitrariness cannot be eliminated, however, as there remain the questions of how many criteria to apply and how much sub-classification to allow. Where one draws the critical demarcation line between criteria which are deemed relevant to the definition of a word class and criteria which are not is a question which is better left open. There may not be an optimum level applicable to all word classes, a statistically definable boundary

---

[48] There is no reason why carefully selected negative criteria could not be introduced into the definition of a word class, though these will usually be the corollary of positive criteria used for the definition of other classes.

[49] But cf. his definition of 'categories' (p. 270): 'Large form classes which completely subdivide either the whole lexicon or some important form class into form classes *of approximately equal size*' (my italics).

beyond which the ratio of criteria to members of a class (or exceptions?) goes beyond a statistically significant point. And if this is so, then one is forced to conclude that word classes may be as broad or as narrow as there is need of in a particular situation, and that no one classification is absolutely better than any other. So long as the requirement of total accountability is kept in mind, there seems nothing wrong with this *laissez-faire* approach: different linguists for different purposes will make more or less detailed classifications; and teachers will presumably stay at a more general level, using the most widely applicable criteria, at least in the early stages of teaching English. In this way, one may produce results which are at once linguistically satisfactory and not too far removed from traditional classification: continuity of some kind seems to be essential, in view of the criticisms which were evoked by the merely terminological aspect of the innovations in Fries's *The Structure of English*. But it is difficult to avoid the conclusion that in English the problem of defining word classes ultimately resolves into no more than a question of taste.

5

A further issue which is often raised in connection with the definition of word classes in English is the problem of 'overlapping', in various forms. 'Form classes are not mutually exclusive', said Bloomfield[50] which meant, presumably, in respect of their members (not criteria) through the existence of homophones. In English, as one might expect, the paucity of inflection makes this a major problem, of typological significance, and a source of the language's productivity. How then should one take account of the presence of homophones in different classes? It is generally assumed that this is an important problem for word classification. Much of traditional grammar took a fundamentally naturalistic position on this question—once a part of speech, always a part of speech! They were defined on a notional basis (as in the noun or verb in English), given a pseudo-formal/functional definition (as with such terms as 'modifying' or 'qualifying' for adverb and adjective respectively), or characterised figuratively (as with the definition of interjection, very often);[51] consequently a main, if hidden, assumption was that each English word belonged to a single, specifiable part of speech. Words like 'punch', which could be used as different parts of speech, were regularly seen as having one function more 'basic' than the other: 'punch' was at bottom always a verb, except on those occasions when it 'acted' as a noun; or, within the noun class, abstract nouns could be used as common nouns or proper nouns, but not vice versa.[52] The basis of the implied priorities here (statistical? semantic? logical? etymological?) was never made explicit; and it is worth noting that an identical naturalistic implication lies behind such familiar terms as 'functional shift' or 'partial conversion', terms which without further qualification are not very helpful, as they too assume the existence of a 'basic' form from which the other is derived. This assumption of course needs to be justified, but it is doubtful whether it can be: is 'yesterday' a noun being used as an adverb, or an adverb being used as a noun? A statistical approach might again be feasible: if a word occurs more as a noun than an adverb, let us say, and this is statistically significant, then it is in this linguistically rather trivial sense 'basic'. The unfortunate point here is that for many pairs of homophones, frequency of occurrence is likely to be similar or indefinable; under which circumstances, the inadequacy of the approach should be clear.

---

[50] Bloomfield, op. cit., p. 269.
[51] E.g. L. Tipping, *A Higher English Grammar* (London: Macmillan, 1927). 'Interjections ... are of no grammatical importance and are akin to the cries uttered by the lower animals', p. 195.
[52] Cf. J. C. Nesfield, *English Grammar Past and Present* (London: Macmillan, 1898) pp. 10, 11.

Nor is it necessary to classify words into their homophonous potentialities, e.g. those words which only ever belong to a single class (noun only, adjective only, etc., e.g. 'icy'), and those which belong to groups of classes of different kinds, e.g. noun and adjective (e.g. 'German'), noun and verb ('walk'), adjective and verb ('dry'), noun and adjective and verb ('faint'), and so on.[53] Gleason[54] considers this classification bad because it is uncontrollable, with too many possible combinations, and because the repetition of criteria for each class set up would be too uneconomic (one would have to give the rules for plural formation each time a noun appeared, for example). There are other objections: it circularly takes for granted the prior establishment of the word classes of major interest; it ignores the problem of words occurring in a different class from normal once only (as in some idioms, e.g. 'he is *friends* with me', 'I feel *faint*'); and it is wholly performance orientated—one notes unanticipated extensions in usage all the time (e.g. 'German' as a verb) which would require a continuous reshuffling of membership.

These approaches raise more problems than they solve, which suggests that in a synchronic study to worry over homophones is generally wasted effort. The only way one is ever made aware of homophones, after all, is by noting their occurrence in two or more structurally dissimilar contexts. This fact may be described without reference to their phonetic identity, or to their semantic relationship, if this exists (as with noun-verb pairs like 'cut-cut', for example)—which is not to say that such correspondences are of no interest, only that they are better discussed in a context other than word classes, where the historical basis of the relationship has usually confused synchronic study.[55] What is relevant is to ensure that the criteria for distinguishing groups of homophones are explicit and non-overlapping: there are always clear contextual differences and paradigmatic relations to differentiate them. In short, homophones are a pseudo-problem in word classification, due to one's forgetting that the relevant issue is not in the words themselves, but in the criteria of their use. As these criteria do not overlap in homophones of different classes, by definition, there is never any confusion.

6

Apart from this matter of homophones, it is sometimes assumed that the word classes of English are fairly discrete. There are a number of important cases which suggest, however, that this is not the case; that there is a more genuine kind of 'overlapping' or shading-off between classes, and, no clear-cut dividing line. If syntactic and other criteria show some words to be clearly class X, for example, and others class Y, then it is the case that there are usually other words which share some of the characteristics of X and some of Y, forming a kind of 'bridge' class, assignable to neither. Moreover, it is typically the case that there is not one such class, but a number of partially-overlapping sub-classes. The situation, in fact, strongly resembles gradience phenomena, and suggests that the description of word classes in English might be usefully approached by displaying the serial relationship existing between single words or word-groups.[56] As the examples below indicate, it seems premature to be talking about 'classes' of words in relation to these bridge areas: what is primarily needed is facts about the function of the words in question, a survey of their distributional properties. This has already been begun for the class of prepositions in English, which, when extended to cover the complex prepositions (Preposition$_1$-Noun-Preposition$_2$, e.g. 'on account of'),

---

[53] Cf. Robins, 1964, p. 229.

[54] Gleason, 1965, p. 124.

[55] This confusion is often extreme, e.g. Nesfield, op. cit., pp. 118–121, where 'a' is referred to as both indefinite article and preposition (as in 'He has gone a hunting', where 'a' is a form of 'on' (cf. §230)).

[56] Cf. R. Quirk, 'Descriptive statement and serial relationship', *Language* 41 (1965) pp. 205–17.

displays a range of structures, at one pole there being structures nearest in type to what one has traditionally called prepositions (e.g. 'in lieu of'), at the other pole, structures which are closer to complex nominal groups than single prepositions (e.g. 'at the end of').[57] A similar situation exists between and within many of the other major word classes, however, and this has not been comparably studied.

As an example of shading-off between major classes, one might cite the boundary-line between adjective and adverb in English.[58] One first needs to define a set of criteria which will characterise these classes adequately for present purposes. 'Central' adjectives, then, may be defined as all words which satisfy all of the following criteria:

(1) ability to form adverb by adding '-ly'
(2) ability to inflect for degree (without '-ly' suffix) within nominal group functioning as subject (i.e. to exclude 'We seem to be more inside than outside', etc.)
(3) ability to take intensifiers,[59] especially 'very', within nominal group functioning as subject
(4) ability to occur in the slot 'a/the ~ *Noun*' (where 'Noun' stands for any of the central class of nouns)
(5) ability to occur in predicative position after the sub-class of verbs including 'be', 'seem' and 'become'.

In this way, adjectives like 'clear', 'interesting', 'red', 'regular', 'quick', 'nice', etc. would be positive in respect of these criteria and may be defined as central. One may now plot degrees of distributional divergence from this central class for words whose status as adjective is (however slightly) unclear.

	1	2	3	4	5
asleep	−	−	−	−	+
alike	−	?+[60]	−	−	+
one, two, etc.	−	−	−	+	+
inside, downstairs	−	−	−	+	+
top, bottom	−	−	+	+	+
old, young, fast, big, poorly, small	−	+	+	+	+
hard, kindly, low	?+	+	+	+	+

With the more marked degrees of deviation from the central pattern, one can hardly use the term 'adjective' to refer to them and retain any reasonably homogeneous definition for it (cf. the internal heterogeneity of the traditional adverb class). There remain two alternatives: either one finds that such words satisfy a list of predetermined criteria for some other word class fully, or they do not approximate to any other class, and consequently have to be set up as a class on their own (or a set of classes). The most frequently voiced suggestion has been that (apart from the numerals) they are better taken as adverbs; but even if one restricts oneself to three criteria, it is not at all clear (with the exception of 'asleep') that they are distributionally more alike:

(1) ability to occur immediately before or after verb, viz. Subject (Adverb) Verb (Adverb)
(2) ability to take intensifier without preceding determiner
(3) ability to occur initially (mobility criterion) in sentence.

---

[57] Cf. Quirk and Mulholland, op. cit.

[58] Assuming for the moment that these are distinct classes, and that adverbs are not 'positional variants' of adjectives.

[59] Cf. G. Kirchner, *Gradadverbien* (Halle: Max Niemeyer Verlag, 1955), esp. Alphabetische Liste der Intensivadverbien, pp. 13–86.

[60] 'Two more-alike people I've yet to see', etc.

Adverbs like 'gradually', 'usually', 'clearly', 'sadly', 'slowly', etc. would be positive in respect of these criteria and would be defined as central.

	1	2	3
asleep	+	+[61]	+
inside, downstairs	+	−	+
alike	+	+	? −
old, etc.	+	+	−
hard, etc.	+	+	−
top, bottom	−	−	−
one, two, etc.	−	−	−

Hence it seems better to take such words as constituting a peripheral area between the two classes, with an as yet undetermined number of sub-classes.

These words and criteria are only a sample, but already there is substantial distributional dissimilarity. It would thus seem premature to take all 'a-' words as a coherent class, whether labelled adverbs or anything else.[62] What is needed is a detailed examination of all the structures in which each 'a-' word can occur, not presupposing identity of distribution on the basis of morphological similarity; and similarly with the other words whose status is unclear. The degrees of difference from orthodox adjectives and adverbs might then be quantified in terms of the number and rank of criteria applicable and inapplicable, and these words said to be verifiably 'nearer' to one class than the other. Once descriptive adequacy is reached, the problem then becomes on a par with other 'higher-level' problems, such as whether to take two or more clearly distinct groups of words as separate classes, or as sub-classes within one major class (e.g. nouns and proper names, auxiliaries and lexical verbs, adjectives and numerals, even adjectives and adverbs): in each case, the descriptive differences are fairly well-known, and the problem is one of evaluating the alternative solutions in terms of the grammar as a whole. Meanwhile, until all the facts have been ascertained, the safest course seems to be to take these words as a series of overlapping 'bridge-classes', and not to force them into either the adjective or adverb class by turning a blind eye to important points of distributional dissimilarity. This solution clearly favours proliferation of word classes to meet the stringent demands of descriptive adequacy. This may involve overanalysis and lack of continuity from the pedagogical viewpoint, but the primary aim of descriptive accuracy can only be attained by allowing the data to suggest the number of classes, and by ignoring the preconceptions imposed by traditional definitions.[63]

Finally, as an example of partial identity of distribution at a quite detailed level within a major class, one could take the problems involved in classifying certain types of 'temporal' noun. An important question is the extent to which there are restrictions on the co-occurrence of such nouns with prepositions, to form temporal adverbial phrases. The following partial

---

[61] A more restricted but possible usage, e.g. ironically, seeing children playing, 'Very asleep, aren't they!'; or, 'They seemed very asleep'.

[62] Cf. N. Francis, op. cit., p. 284.

[63] It is an interesting point that linguistic realism sometimes produces a word class which has more relevance to a traditional definition than the traditional classification had! This is the case with the adverb, where the simple rule 'the adverb modifies the verb' can be accepted with very little qualification if one omits the 'exceptions' by handling them independently, i.e. 'the' (as in 'the happier we shall be'), 'not', intensifiers ('very', 'rather', etc.), unstressed 'there', interrogatives, sentence-modifiers ('however', 'frankly', etc.), interjections ('well', etc.), responses ('yes'), and the bridge-class words discussed above. Gleason seems in favour of this also (1965, p. 131). It is worth noting that the definition of many of these new classes involves detailed reference to prosodic criteria of juncture, pitch and prominence, e.g. sentence-modifiers have characteristic pitch movements, are usually separate tone-units, and so on: cf. P. F. R. Barnes and D. Crystal, *The analysis of English intonation: critique, theory and description* [never published].

sketch is instructive, as it displays the obstacles in the way of calling these nouns a coherent class at a more general level, as well as indicating the extent to which even a few criteria can produce an alarming degree of complexity and overlap. In my idiolect, the possibilities of co-occurrence,[64] which do not seem to be atypically irregular, are as follows:

	in a N or two	in that N	in the $N_{sg.}$ (no postmodification)[65]	in a N (no postmodification)[65]	in $\phi\, N_{pl.}$ (no postmodification)[65]	in $\phi\, N_{pl.}$	$\phi\, N_{pl.}$	on the $N_{sg.}$	on a $N_{sg.}$ (no postmodification)[65]	on $\phi\, N_{pl.}$ (no postmodification)[65]	on $\phi\, N_{sg.}$	at that N	at the $N_{sg.}$	at $\phi\, N_{sg.}$
afternoon	+	+	+	+	−	−	+	+	+	+	−	−	−	−
evening	+	+	+	+	−	−	+	+	?+	?+	−	−	−	−
weekend	+	+	?+	+	−	−	+	+	?+	+	−	−	−	−
night	+	+	+	?+	−	−	?−	+	−	−[66]	−	−	−	+
morning	+	+	+	+	−	−	+	+	−	−[66]	−	−	−	−
Monday...	+	−	−	−	−	−	+	+	+	+	+	−	−	−
January...	?+	+	+	+	−	+	−	−	−	−	−	−	−	−
hour	+	+	+	+	?−	−	−	+	−	−	−	+	+	−
minute	+	+	−	+	+	−	−	+	−	−	−	+	+	−
second	+	+	−	+	+	−	−	+	−	−	−	+	+	−
day	+	+	+	+	−	−	−	+	−	−[66]	−	−	−	−
summer	?+	+	+	?−	?−	+	?+	−	−	−	−	−	−	?+
winter	?+	+	+	?−	?−	+	?+	−	−	−	−	−	−	?+
spring	?+	+	+	?−	−	+	−	−	−	−	−	−	−	?+
autumn	?+	+	+	?−	−	+	−	−	−	−	−	−	−	?+
month	+	+	+	+	+	−	−	−	−	−	−	−	−	−
week	+	+	+	+	+	−	−	−	−	−	−	−	−	−
year	+	+	+	+	+	−	−	−	−	−	−	−	−	−
decade	+	+	−	+	?+	−	−	−	−	−	−	−	−	−
century	+	+	−	+	?−	−	−	−	−	−	−	−	−	−
fortnight	+	+	+	+	−	−	−	−	−	−	−	−	−	−
instant	+	?+	−	+	−	−	−	−	−	−	−	+	−	−
moment	+	?+	−	+	−	−	−	−	−	−	−	+	−	−
lifetime	−	?+	−	+	−	−	−	−	−	−	−	−	−	−
daytime	−	−	+	−	+	−	−	−	−	−	−	−	−	−
nighttime	−	−	+	−	−	+	−	−	−	−	−	−	−	−

[64] Excluding stylistically marked (e.g. humorous, nonce, poetic) uses.
[65] I.e., to exclude 'on a night like this', 'in the decade preceding the revolution', etc.
[66] Except in the restricted sense of 'morning-shifts', etc.

7

Throughout this paper, I have tried to underline two main points: that much of the terminology used in the discussion of word classes in English has been badly defined and used uncritically; and that the emphasis in word class analysis and definition should lie on the selection and ordering of criteria—which in turn means a great deal more detailed descriptive work than has yet been done. It is important not to let the familiarity of the traditional terms obscure these more important issues: words like 'verb', 'adverb', 'grammatical word', and so on, slip smoothly from the tongue, and for practical economy of reference one has just got to use them and hope for the best. But this should not be allowed to engender a false sense of security: each term has its weaknesses, and its validity must ultimately be assessed in the light of some general linguistic theory. If there is any conclusion at all that would not be premature from this turning-over of largely familiar ground, it is simply that word classes in English are more complex things than is still generally supposed;[67] and that before we can produce a set of satisfactory definitions, we need to examine the distribution of single words much more thoroughly.

REFERENCES

Barnes, P. F. R., and D. Crystal (never published). *The Analysis of English Intonation: Critique, Theory and Description.* [But see D. Crystal (1969). *Prosodic Systems and Intonation in English.* Cambridge: Cambridge University Press.]

Bazell, C. E. (1958). *Linguistic Typology.* University of London Inaugural Lecture.

Bloomfield, L. (1933). *Language.* New York: Holt.

Brown, R. W. (1957). 'Linguistic determinism and the part of speech'. *Journal of Abnormal and Social Psychology* 55: 1–5. Repr. in S. Saporta (ed.) (1961), *Psycholinguistics.* New York.

Brown, R. W. (1958). *Words and Things.* Glencoe, Ill.: Free Press.

Chomsky, N. (1965). *Aspects of the Theory of Syntax.* Cambridge, Mass.: MIT Press.

Crystal, D. (1966a). 'Specification and English tenses'. *Journal of Linguistics* 3: 1–34.

——(1966b). 'The linguistic status of prosodic and paralinguistic features'. In *Proceedings of the University of Newcastle upon Tyne Philosophical Society.*

Francis, W. N. (1958). *The Structure of American English.* New York: Ronald Press.

Fries, C. C. (1952). *The Structure of English.* New York: Harcourt Brace.

Gleason, H. A., Jr. (1961). *An Introduction to Descriptive Linguistics.* New York: Holt, Rinehart & Winston.

——(1965). *Linguistics and English Grammar.* New York: Holt, Rinehart & Winston.

Gleitman, L. R. (1965). 'Co-ordinating conjunctions in English'. *Language* 41: 260–93.

Hall, R. A., Jr. (1964). *Introductory Linguistics.* New York: Chilton Books.

Halliday, M. A. K. (1961). 'Categories of the theory of grammar'. *Word* 17: 241–92.

Hockett, C. F. (1958). *A Course in Modern Linguistics.* New York: Macmillan.

Ilysh, B. (1965). *The Structure of Modern English.* Moscow.

Jespersen, O. (1933). *Essentials of English Grammar.* London: Allen & Unwin.

Kirchner, G. (1955). *Gradadverbien.* Halle: Niemeyer.

Lyons, J. (1963). *Structural Semantics.* Oxford: Blackwell.

Nesfield, J. C. (1898). *English Grammar Past and Present.* London: Macmillan.

Quirk, R. (1958). 'Substitutions and syntactic research'. *Archivum Linguisticum* 10: 37–42.

---

[67] And there is no reason to suppose that English is any less complex than other partially inflected languages: as far as word classes are concerned, problemless or 'regular' hypotheses about little-known languages are always very suspicious!

—— (1960). 'Towards a description of English usage'. In *Transactions of the Philological Society*, 40–61.

—— (1965). 'Descriptive statement and serial relationship'. *Language* 41: 205–17.

—— and Mulholland, J. (1964). 'Complex prepositions and related sequences'. *English Studies*, supplement to vol. 45: 64–73.

Robins, R. H. (1959). 'In defence of WP'. In *Transactions of the Philological Society*, 116–44.

—— (1964). *General Linguistics: An Introductory Survey*. London: Longman.

Strang, B. M. H. (1962). *Modern English Structure*. London: Arnold.

Sweet, H. (1892). *A New English Grammar*. Oxford: Clarendon Press.

Tipping, L. (1927). *A Higher English Grammar*. London: Macmillan.

Trager, G. L., and Smith, H. L., Jr. (1951). *An Outline of English Structure*. Norman, Okla.: Battenburg Press.

13

A Notional Approach to the Parts of Speech

JOHN LYONS

ALLEGED CIRCULARITY OF TRADITIONAL DEFINITIONS

One of the criticisms most commonly made of the traditional definitions of the parts of speech is that they are circular. It is pointed out, for example, that, if the class of nouns is defined, in 'notional' terms, as that class of lexical items whose members denote persons, places and things (and this is one way in which the noun was defined in traditional grammar), the definition cannot be applied without circularity to determine the status of such English words as *truth, beauty, electricity*, etc. The circularity lies in the fact that the only reason we have for saying that truth, beauty and electricity are 'things' is that the words which refer to them in English are nouns.

The criticism of circularity loses its force as soon as we take into account the distinction between 'formal' and 'notional' definitions, and the possibility that the 'notional' definitions of the parts of speech may be used to determine the names, though not the membership, of the major syntactic classes of English and other languages. Let us assume that we have established for English a set of syntactic classes, *X, Y,* and *Z* (as well as a number of other classes) on 'formal', distributional grounds; and that the members of each of these classes are listed in the lexicon, or dictionary, associated with the grammar:

$X = \{boy, woman, grass, atom, tree, cow, truth, beauty, electricity, \ldots\}$
$Y = \{come, go, die, eat, love, exist, \ldots\}$
$Z = \{good, beautiful, red, hard, tall, \ldots\}$

By reference to the lexicon, we can decide for each word in the language to what syntactic class or classes it belongs. It is true that not all the members of class *X* denote persons, places and things (if 'thing' is interpreted as 'discrete, physical object'). However, it may still be true that all (or the vast majority) of the lexical items which refer to persons, places and things fall within the class *X*; and, if this is so, we may call *X* the class of nouns. In other words, we have the 'formal' class *X* and a 'notional' class *A*; they are not co-extensive, but, if *A* is wholly or mainly included in *X*, then *X* may be given the label suggested by the 'notional' definition of *A*. It is for this reason that the lexical class which has as its members, not only *boy, woman*, etc., but also *truth, beauty*, etc., is appropriately called the class of nouns in English. Whether there exists any language in which the noun cannot be defined in this way is an empirical question. Most of the statements made by linguists to the effect that the noun is not a universal category of human language are vitiated by the failure to take note of the distinction between the criteria for membership and the criteria for naming the classes. In practice, linguists seem

* John Lyons, 'The parts of speech', section 7.6 of *Introduction to Theoretical Linguistics* (Cambridge: Cambridge University Press, 1968), 317–33. © 1968 Cambridge University Press. Reprinted by permission.

to have had little difficulty in deciding that one class, rather than another, in a particular language, is correctly identified as the class of nouns. As we shall see, the situation is somewhat different with respect to the other parts of speech recognized in traditional grammar. But in principle the distinction between 'formal' and 'notional' definition is applicable there too.

It is a more serious criticism that the criteria incorporated in the definitions are obviously language-dependent (or 'glossocentric'), in the sense that they do not apply outside a very narrow range of languages (including Latin and Greek, for which they were primarily established). This point may be illustrated with reference to the definitions of the noun, verb and preposition given by Dionysius Thrax (and taken over by most of his successors in the mainstream of the Western grammatical tradition): 'The *noun* is a part of speech having case-inflexions, signifying a person or a thing'; 'The *verb* is a part of speech without case-inflexion, admitting inflexions of tense, person and number, signifying an activity or a being acted upon'; 'The *preposition* is a word placed before all other parts of speech in word-formation and syntactic constructions'. The noun and the verb are defined, not only 'notionally' in terms of what they 'signify', but also in terms of their inflexional characteristics; whereas the definition of the preposition invokes the quite different property of relative position (in both morphological and syntactic constructions). First of all, inflexion is far from being a universal feature of language; secondly, languages that have inflexion do not necessarily manifest the categories of case, number and tense; and the sharp distinction that is drawn between cases and prepositions in traditional grammar cannot be sustained in general syntactic theory. The question that the definitions of Dionysius Thrax were intended to answer may be put in the following terms: Given that the sentences of the language have been segmented into words, to what class would each word be assigned? And the grammatical criteria for classification were mainly based upon the surface-structure properties of words.

It may be taken for granted that any general theory of the parts of speech which is intended to apply to more than a narrow selection of the world's languages must give explicit recognition to the distinction between deep and surface structure and must define the parts of speech, not as classes of words in surface structure, but as deep-structure constituents of sentences. For the remainder of this section, we shall be concerned with the question whether any, or all, of the traditional parts of speech can be defined in this way.

SYNTACTIC FUNCTION OF MAJOR PARTS OF SPEECH

The distinction between deep and surface syntax was not made explicitly in traditional grammar. But it was implied, in part at least, by the assumption that all complex sentences, as well as various kinds of non-declarative sentences, clauses and phrases, were derived from simple, modally 'unmarked' sentences. Furthermore, the major parts of speech were associated with certain typical syntactic functions in simple sentences; and this was assumed by some grammarians to be a more important property of the parts of speech than their 'accidental', inflexional, characteristics in particular languages. It was asserted that every simple sentence is made up of two parts: a *subject* and a *predicate*. The subject was necessarily a noun (or a pronoun 'standing for' a noun). But the predicate fell into one of three types, according to the part of speech or parts of speech which occurred in it: (i) intransitive verb, (ii) transitive verb with its *object*, (iii) the 'verb *to be*' (or some other 'copula') with its *complement*. The object, like the subject, must be a noun. The complement must be either (*a*) an adjective, or (*b*) a noun.

The notions of 'subject', 'predicate', 'object', and 'complement' will be discussed in the following chapter. For the present, we will take them for granted; and we will assume that the statements made in the previous paragraph about their association with particular parts of speech are correct, for English at least. They may be illustrated by the following sentences:

(1) *Mary dances*
(2) *Mary cooks fish*
(3a) *Mary is beautiful*
(3b) *Mary is a child*

Omitting distinctions of tense, mood, aspect, countability, and definiteness, we can generate these sentences with the appropriate structural descriptions by means of the grammatical rules and associated lexicon shown in Table 1.

TABLE 1

	Grammar	Lexicon
(i)	$\Sigma \rightarrow A + X$	$A = \{Mary, fish, child, \ldots\}$
(ii)	$X \rightarrow \begin{cases} B \\ C + A \\ D + Y \end{cases}$	$B = \{dance, \ldots\}$ $C = \{cook, \ldots\}$ $D = \{be\}$
(iii)	$Y \rightarrow \begin{cases} E \\ A \end{cases}$	$E = \{beautiful, \ldots\}$

A diagrammatic representation of the underlying constituent-structure of these sentences is given in Fig. 1. It will be observed that X and Y are *auxiliary symbols*, the sole function of

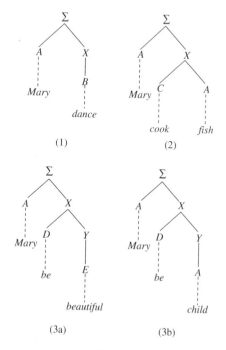

FIG. 1

which is to label the nodes and show that, whereas all four sentences are syntactically equivalent at the higher level, only (3a) and (3b) are equivalent at the lower level of constituent-structure. Apart from the fact that we have employed the arbitrary symbols A, B, C, D and E in place of the traditional names for the parts of speech, the rules that have just been proposed formalize the traditional statements quoted above about the structure of various types of simple, declarative sentences. The question that now arises is whether it is possible to determine the traditional parts of speech or their functions solely on the basis of the constituent-structure relations that hold between the four types of sentences.

The answer to this question is clearly 'yes'. The class A is the class of nouns, since it is the one constituent class which all sentences have in common at the highest level of constituent-structure; B is the only class which combines directly with nouns (under the auxiliary node X) to form sentences, and is therefore the class of intransitive verbs; since the members of C combine with nouns (A), and with no other class, to form predicates (X), C is the class of transitive verbs; and D is the copula-class, since it combines with both nouns and with E, which is therefore the class of adjectives.

This argument rests of course on the specific assumptions incorporated in the traditional view of the syntactic function of the parts of speech. In the construction of a more general theory of the parts of speech, at least two of these assumptions must be challenged: the first has to do with the status of the copula or 'verb *to be*'; the second with the universality of the distinction between verbs and adjectives.

THE 'VERB TO BE'

It is a well-known fact that in many languages the sentences (3a) *Mary is beautiful* and (3b) *Mary is a child* would take the form 'Mary beautiful' and 'Mary (a) child'; that is to say, the predicative adjective or noun would be combined directly with the subject-noun without a *copula*. Even in the Indo-European languages the copulative function of 'the verb *to be*' appears to be of secondary development. The 'original' state of affairs is illustrated by contemporary Russian: *Marija krasivaja* ('Mary is beautiful') and *Marija rebënok* ('Mary is a child'), where *krasivaja* is the feminine form of the adjective in concord with *Marija* and *rebënok* is a noun (in the nominative case). In Latin and Greek 'the verb to be' was optional in such sentences. However, if we put them in the past tense (or in some other mood than the indicative), they would necessarily have the appropriate form of the 'verb *to be*' in Russian (*byla*, *budet*, etc.), and also in Latin (*erat*, etc.) and Greek (*ên*, etc.).

This fact suggests that the principal function of the copulative 'verb *to be*' in Russian, Greek, and Latin is to serve as the *locus in* surface structure for the marking of tense, mood, and aspect. ('Locus' is not a standard technical term. It is introduced to refer to the surface-structure element which 'carries' the overt marking of some syntactic distinction.) In other words, '*to be*' is not itself a constituent of deep structure, but a semantically empty 'dummy verb' generated by the grammatical rules of Russian, Greek, and Latin for the specification of certain distinctions (usually 'carried' by the verb) when there is no other verbal element to carry these distinctions. Sentences that are temporally, modally and aspectually 'unmarked' (e.g. 'Mary is beautiful') do not need the 'dummy' carrier.

This account of the function of the copula in Russian, Greek, and Latin can be generalized for English and other languages, which have a 'verb *to be*' in sentences that are 'unmarked', as well as in those that are 'marked', for tense, mood, and aspect.

One of the advantages of regarding the copulative 'verb *to be*' as a purely grammatical 'dummy' in English (like the 'dummy auxiliary' *do* in such sentences as *Do they come regularly?, He doesn't eat fish*, etc.) is that such noun-phrases as *the tall man* can be transformationally derived from the phrase-markers underlying such sentences as *the man is tall* without the need to delete the copula. Grammars of English which introduce *be* into the deep structure of sentences will necessarily contain many transformational rules for the deletion of this element in a variety of positions in surface structure.

A more important point is that the 'verb *to be*' in such sentences as *Mary is beautiful* (unlike the verb *cook* in *Mary cooks fish*) is in contrast with only a limited set of other 'verbs', notably *become*. The occurrence of *become* rather than *be* depends upon the selection of the 'marked' rather than the 'unmarked' term in yet another grammatical opposition (of stative vs. non-stative aspect). We will return to this point presently. For the moment, it is sufficient to have made a general case for the elimination of the 'verb *to be*' from the underlying constituent-structure of English. There is no doubt that a similar case could be made for other languages with a copulative 'verb *to be*'. We may turn now to the distinction between verbs and adjectives in general syntactic theory.

VERB AND ADJECTIVE

As we have already observed, adjectives were regarded as a subclass of 'verbs' by Plato and Aristotle, but as a subclass of 'nouns' by the Alexandrians and their successors; the tripartite distinction of nouns, verbs and adjectives (as independent parts of speech) was not established until the medieval period. This difference of attitude towards the adjective in Greek and Latin is readily explained in terms of the distinction between deep and surface structure. The principal reason for grouping the adjective and the noun together in Greek and Latin is that they are both inflected for number and case. But the inflexion of the adjective is clearly a matter of surface structure: its number and case (and also its gender) are derived by the transformational rules of concord from the noun which it modifies. Otherwise the status of the adjective in Greek and Latin is not strikingly different from its status in English, where there is no concord between adjective and noun. Plato and Aristotle considered that the most typical function of both the adjective and the verb was that of predication, whereas the most characteristic function of the noun was that of naming the subject of the predication. It was for this reason that they grouped the adjective with the verb; and logicians have taken the same view. On the other hand, since the medieval period, most grammarians have drawn as sharp a distinction between the adjective and the verb as they have between the verb and the noun, We may therefore ask what, if anything, distinguishes the adjective from the verb in general syntactic theory? For simplicity, we will illustrate from English.

The two most obvious differences between the lexical classes in English traditionally referred to as adjectives and verbs both have to do with the surface phenomenon of inflexion. (1) The adjective, when it occurs in predicative position, does not take the verbal suffixes associated with distinctions of tense, mood and aspect; instead, a 'dummy verb' (*be, become*, etc.) is generated by the grammar to carry the necessary inflexional suffixes. Thus, *Mary is beautiful, Mary would have been beautiful: Mary dances, Mary would have danced*; but not **Mary beautiful-s* or **Mary would have beautiful-ed*, or **Mary is dance* or **Mary would have been dance*. (2) The verb is less freely transformed to the position of modifier in the noun-phrase; but when it does occur in this syntactic position, unlike the adjective, it bears the suffix *-ing*. Thus, *the beautiful girl: the singing girl*; but not **the beautiful-ing girl* or **the sing girl*.

In 'notional' treatments of the parts of speech, adjectives are frequently said to denote 'qualities', and verbs to denote either 'actions' or 'states'. But the difference between a 'quality' and a 'state' (if it is not entirely illusory) is less striking than the difference between an 'action' and a 'state'. One might well wonder, for example, whether *know, exist, happy, young,* etc. refer to 'states' or 'qualities'. There is no doubt, however, that *know* and *exist,* on the one hand, and *happy* and *young,* on the other, fall together grammatically. This question is decided for us by the criteria discussed in the previous paragraph. But there are many languages (e.g. Chinese) to which these criteria do not apply; and linguists tend to say that there is no adjective vs. verb distinction in such languages, but rather a distinction between stative verbs and verbs of action.

A distinction between *stative verbs* and *verbs of action* is also relevant to English. As we have already seen, there are certain stative verbs in English which do not normally occur in the progressive form: by contrast with these, the majority of English verbs, which occur freely in the progressive, may be called verbs of 'action'. This aspectual difference between stative verbs and verbs of action is matched by a similar difference in English adjectives. Most English adjectives are stative, in the sense that they do not normally take progressive aspect when they occur in predicative position (e.g. *Mary is beautiful,* not **Mary is being beautiful*). But there are a number of adjectives which occur freely with the progressive in the appropriate cir-cumstances (cf. *Mary is being silly now*). In other words, to be stative is normal for the class of adjectives, but abnormal for verbs; to be non-stative is normal for verbs, but abnormal for adjectives. The possibility of free combination with progressive aspect correlates with a number of other important features of English syntax: most notably, with the potentiality of occurrence in answer to a question like *What did she do? What is she doing?* Both *Mary danced (that's what she did)* and *Mary is being silly (that's what she's doing)* are possible answers to questions of this form, but not **Mary knows Greek (that's what she does)* or **Mary is beautiful (that's what she does)*.

We talk about 'stative verbs' in English (as distinct from adjectives) and 'non-stative adjectives' (as distinct from verbs) because the aspectual contrast of stative *v.* non-stative in general coincides with, but in particular instances is in conflict with, the inflexional differences traditionally regarded as being of greater importance in the definition of the parts of speech. It is, however, the aspectual contrast which correlates, if anything does, with the notional definition of the verb and the adjective in terms of 'action' and 'quality'.

THE ADVERB

A typical traditional definition of the adverb might run something like this: the adverb is a part of speech which serves as a modifier of a verb, an adjective or another adverb or adverbial phrase.

The first point to notice about this definition is the terminological one. The Latin prefix *ad-* (Greek *epi-*) may be translated as 'attached to and modifying'. But this is also the sense of 'adjective' (Greek *epithetos*). The adjective was the modifier *par excellence* of traditional grammar: it was 'attached to' and 'modified' the noun (and, for reasons that have already been discussed, it was regarded as a type of noun in the post-Aristotelian period). The adjective was therefore a nominal modifier (adnominal), and the adverb a verbal modifier (adverbial). But the definition given above makes reference to the 'modification' of adjectives as well as to the 'modification' of verbs. The point is that the traditional term 'adverb' (and indeed the definitions of Dionysius Thrax and Priscian) depended, implicitly, upon the earlier and wider sense of 'verb'. In other words, it presupposed that 'adjectives' and 'verbs' (in the narrower, more modern sense) were to be regarded as members of the same major syntactic class for the purpose of stating their combinatorial properties with respect to members of other major syntactic classes. We have already seen that 'adjectives' and 'verbs' have much in common, and that in many languages (including English) they are correctly brought together as members of the same deep-structure category.

The second point to notice about the definition of the adverb that we gave above is this: it implies that the adverb is a recursive category (more typically than the other parts of speech) in the sense that one adverb may modify another. For example, *extraordinarily* and *well* are both adverbs (of 'degree' and 'manner', respectively) in sentences like *Mary dances extraordinarily well* and *Mary cooks fish extraordinarily well*; and *extraordinarily* modifies *well* in the endocentric adverbial phrase *extraordinarily well*. It was on the basis of these combinatorial possibilities in simple sentences that both Jespersen and Hjelmslev constructed their theories of the parts of speech (independently of one another and with certain differences which, in the context of the present discussion, may be disregarded) some thirty years ago. We will give an outline of their views presently. But first we must say a little more about adverbs.

In traditional grammar, adverbs constitute a very heterogeneous class; and it is doubtful whether any general theory of syntax would bring together as members of the same syntactic class all the forms that are traditionally described as 'adverbs'. We will restrict our attention at this point to adverbs of 'manner' (as exemplified by *well* and *beautifully* in *Mary cooks fish well* and *Mary dances beautifully*).

Most adverbs of manner in English (and also in certain other languages) are distinct from, but morphologically related to, 'adjectives' (cf. *beautifully*: *beautiful*). Furthermore, they are transformationally related to the corresponding 'adjectives' in a variety of parallel constructions: cf. *Mary is a beautiful dancer*: *Mary dances beautifully*. Since there would seem to be no possibility of paradigmatic opposition between the 'adverb of manner' and the 'adjective', they are to be regarded as contextually-determined variants of the same 'part of speech'. The attachment of the adverbial suffix *-ly* (in English) to 'adjectives' like *beautiful* (and the 'rewriting' of *good* as *well*) is to be handled by the rules which convert the deep-structure analysis into the surface structure of sentences. In other words, 'adverbial' refers to the modification of one verb (in the wider sense of this term) by another verb, the modifying verb being typically, but not necessarily (cf. *smilingly*, etc.), an 'adjective'. Not all 'adjectives' occur in 'adverbial' positions: cf. **The light shone greenly*, etc. Conversely, others occur as modifiers of nouns only in constructions which are transformationally derived from structures in which the 'adjective' has an 'adverbial' function: cf. *a rapid movement* ← *move rapidly*. But the majority of 'adjectives' in English modify both nouns and verbs in deep structure.

A 'CATEGORIAL' INTERPRETATION OF THE PARTS OF SPEECH

In our discussion of the adverb, we made reference to the theories of the parts of speech put forward some years ago by Jespersen and Hjelmslev. These theories have tended to be neglected by most linguists in recent years (as part of the general lack of interest in 'notional' grammar). With the possibility of formalizing the distinction between deep structure and surface structure in transformational syntax, these theories have assumed a new importance in general syntactic theory. They have their roots in traditional grammar, and they were based on evidence from many languages.

We shall refer to Jespersen's formulation rather than Hjelmslev's (although, on points of detail, Hjelmslev's is somewhat subtler); but we will not use Jespersen's terminology, which is in conflict with the sense attached to particular terms elsewhere in this book and might lead to confusion. For Jespersen, nouns were categories of the *first degree*; verbs (including 'adjectives') were categories of the *second degree*; and adverbs categories of the *third degree*. This notion of what we are calling 'degree' is defined in terms of the combinatorial properties of the categories in question. Each category is modified, in the most typical simple structures, by a category of 'higher' degree. Nouns are modified by verbs (including 'adjectives'), which are therefore *adnominal* categories; verbs are modified by adverbs, which are therefore *ad-adnominal* categories; and adverbs are modified by other adverbs. No more than three degrees are required for the classification of the parts of speech (in any language referred to by either Jespersen or Hjelmslev), since there is no major category whose function it is to modify categories of the third degree.

It is worth pointing out here that this theory of 'degree' can be formalized very neatly in terms of categorial grammar: in fact, it was implicit in the early development of the notions of categorial grammar by Leśniewski and Ajdukiewicz. The noun is a fundamental category; all other parts of speech are derived, complex categories. Categories of the second degree combine with categories of the first degree (according to the principles of well-formedness which Ajdukiewicz called 'syntactic connectedness') to form sentences (or 'propositions'). Categories of the third degree combine with one another to form categories of the third degree.

For typographical simplicity, let us now introduce a numerical system of notation for the categorial representation of this notion of 'degree'. (The numerals may be defined to be equivalent to the 'fractional' expressions employed in our earlier references to categorial grammar.) We will use 0 (zero) for 'sentence', 1 for 'noun', 2 for 'verb' (including 'adjective'), and 3 for 'adverb'; and we will use 'primes' to indicate recursion, e.g. $3'$ ('three prime'), $3''$ ('three double-prime'), etc. The underlying constituent-structure of a sentence like *Mary dances extraordinarily well* is given in terms of these numerical conventions in Fig. 2. It may be represented, equivalently, as $0(1 + 2(2 + 3(3 + 3')))$. The reader will observe that the system is assumed to be *non-directional*: given a complex category x composed of a pair of fundamental or derived categories, we can 'cancel' the 'denominator' (in the 'fractional' representation) of x with another category y, whether x and y are adjacent to one another or not in the surface structure of the sentence, and independently of the relative sequence of x and y in surface structure. In terms of the numerical notation, $3'$ cancels with 3 to yield 3, 3 cancels with 2 to yield 2, and 2 cancels with 1 to yield 0.

We pointed out in an earlier section that (bidirectional) categorial grammars were weakly, but perhaps not strongly, equivalent to simple, context-free phrase-structure grammars. Neither categorial grammars nor simple phrase-structure grammars are sufficiently powerful for the total description of the syntax of any natural language. This has been proved by Chomsky (and others). So far no one has developed a transformational grammar with a

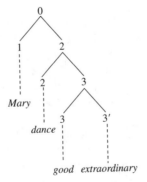

Mary dances extraordinarily well

FIG. 2   A categorial representation of underlying constituent-structure.

categorial, rather than a phrase-structure, base-component. (Shaumjan's theory comes closest to this conception; but it has certain other features which make it rather difficult to compare formally with Chomsky's theory of transformational syntax, and it has not yet been illustrated in detail.) Nevertheless, the notion of 'degree' has a good deal of support in the traditional theory of the parts of speech and in the application of this theory to the description of many languages throughout the world. It is noticeable that much of the work now being published by a number of linguists (Lakoff, Rosenbaum, Fillmore, and others), though not by Chomsky himself, assumes the 'categorial' identity of the 'verb' and the 'adjective' in the deep structure of English. It is not inconceivable that further developments will justify the view that the base-component of a more adequate transformational grammar of English than is yet available will include a 'sub-component', the rules of which can be more elegantly formulated in terms of categorial grammar. There are, however, other features of deep structure which cannot be formalized by categorial grammars. We shall turn to these presently, drawing upon our discussion of the secondary grammatical categories and the parts of speech in this chapter. But first we must refer to an alleged inadequacy of categorial grammars.

AN ALLEGED INADEQUACY OF CATEGORIAL GRAMMARS

It has been suggested that categorial grammars have one serious inadequacy by comparison with phrase-structure grammars. The criticism is this. A categorial grammar will identify 'adjectives' and 'intransitive verbs' as members of the same major category (e.g. *beautiful* and *dance* in such sentences as *Mary is beautiful* and *Mary dances*), but will fail to relate 'transitive verbs' and 'intransitive verbs'. At first sight, this is a damaging criticism. But the relationship between 'transitive verbs' and 'intransitive verbs' is by no means as straightforward as current transformational theory would suggest. We must leave that question for a later chapter. At this point we will draw attention to an equally serious inadequacy in the base-component formalized along the lines proposed by Chomsky in his most recent work. The point is that any theoretically satisfactory solution for phrase-structure grammar could be extended to categorial grammar; and it would automatically dispose of the criticism referred to above. Let us therefore turn our attention briefly to phrase-structure grammars, and the way in which they formalize the rules of the base-component of a transformational grammar.

AN INADEQUACY OF PHRASE-STRUCTURE GRAMMARS

Consider the following rules:

(1) $\Sigma \rightarrow NP + Aux + VP$
(2) $VP \rightarrow V + NP$
(3) $VP \rightarrow V$
(4) $NP \rightarrow T + N$

Assuming a lexicon of the following kind:

$N = \{man, doctor, \ldots\}$
$V = \{examine, leave, \ldots\}$
$T = \{the, a, \ldots\}$

and the necessary rules for the development of *Aux* (to handle tense, mood, and aspect), for the assignment of number to the nouns and for the subsequent handling of subject-verb concord, the above phrase-structure rules will generate such sentences as *The doctor examines the man* $(T+N+V+s+T+N)$ and *The man leaves* $(T+N+V+s)$. There are various ways in which the relationship between 'transitive' and 'intransitive' verbs can be formalized in a phrase-structure grammar. The above set of rules does so by making them both members of the same major category (V) and distinguishing particular members of V, we will assume, by marking them in the lexicon with a *feature* (not shown above) which indicates whether the verb in question may or must have a following *NP*: cf. rule (2). This is essentially the technique developed by Chomsky in *Aspects of the Theory of Syntax*. (The earlier system of *Syntactic Structures* formalized the relationship between 'transitive' and 'intransitive' verbs quite differently.)

The point we wish to make here is simply this: the rules given above fail to formalize the fact that there is an essential, language-independent, relationship between N and NP and between V and VP. As far as the formalization of phrase-structure grammars is concerned, it is a matter of 'accidental' coincidence that linguists will include in their grammars of different languages rules which always expand NP into a string of symbols containing N and rules which always expand VP into a string of symbols containing V. In other words, phrase-structure grammars fail to formalize the fact that NP and VP are not merely mnemonically convenient symbols, but stand for sentence-constituents which are necessarily nominal and verbal, respectively, because they have N and V as an obligatory major constituent. (Chomsky himself has recognized this particular inadequacy: he has indicated a possible solution, but this has not yet been developed in detail, and it is not referred to so far in the published literature.)

What is required, and what was assumed in traditional grammar, is some way of relating sentence-constituents of the form XP to X (where X is any major category: N, V, etc.). It would not only be perverse, but it should be theoretically impossible for any linguist to propose, for example, rules of the following form (for the base-component of English or of any other language):

(1a) $\Sigma \rightarrow VP + Aux + NP$
(2a) $NP \rightarrow V + VP$
(3a) $NP \rightarrow V$
(4a) $VP \rightarrow T + N$

The present system of formalization does not exclude rules like this; and they are equivalent, not only weakly, but perhaps also strongly, to the four rules given earlier. (This follows from the principles of phrase-structure grammar discussed in the previous chapter [not included here].)

If the problem can be solved for phrase-structure grammars, it can be solved also for categorial grammars. To take just the case of 'transitive' and 'intransitive' verbs: any lexical item with the categorial classification $(\Sigma n)/n$, e.g. a 'transitive' verb, would be defined by the general principles of the system to be the head of a phrase analysed by the grammar as Σn. Similarly for 'intransitive' verbs, which have the categorial classification Σn. However, as we have already remarked, the question of transitivity is more complex than we have so far indicated. No current system of transformational grammar handles all the facts correctly. We return to this point in the following chapter.

CATEGORIES AND FEATURES

The purpose of the above discussion of categorial and phrase-structure grammars was not merely to focus attention upon a rather important difference between the deep-structure combinatorial properties of the major parts of speech relative to one another, on the one hand, and their various inflexional and transformational characteristics, on the other.

We have seen that the difference between what are traditionally distinguished as 'verbs' and 'adjectives' in English is rather complex, involving differences of aspect ('state' vs. 'action') and differences of inflexion. But we have also seen that the inflexional and aspectual characteristics do not always coincide. 'Adjectives' and 'verbs' are similar in the way in which they combine with nouns to form bracketed strings of constituents in deep structure; and this might be appropriately referred to as their *categorial* function. The transformational, aspectual and inflexional differences associated with particular subclasses of this 'second-degree' category are more satisfactorily specified in the lexicon by means of *features* which differentiate the subclasses.

Current transformational grammars, formalized according to the system recently proposed by Chomsky, make use of such features, but only at the lowest level of constituent-structure. Our discussion of the minor parts of speech and the secondary grammatical categories in this chapter would suggest that tense, mood, aspect, number, definiteness, etc., are associated with constituents of various levels.

Such categories cannot be regarded as universal categories of human language (although they can be defined in universal terms within the general theory of syntax). Languages vary in respect of the 'selection' they make from the total set of secondary grammatical categories recognized in general syntactic theory: and the way in which the oppositions within these categories are realized in surface-structure also varies considerably from language to language. What may be universal in human language are the combinatorial properties of the major categories relative to one another (as suggested in the theories of Jespersen and Hjelmslev). If this is so, we can envisage the possibility that the base-component of a transformational grammar for any language will comprise two 'subcomponents'. The first (whether it is formalized in terms of rewrite rules or not) would be truly universal and would account for the categorial combination of lexical items. The second would contain rules associating features of tense, mood, aspect, number, definiteness, etc., at various levels of the constituent-structure generated by the categorial subcomponent.

GRAMMATICA EST UNA . . .

The suggestion that has just been made should be regarded as extremely tentative: it may not be technically feasible, and it may rest upon insufficient empirical evidence. But one point should be stressed. A few years ago the majority of linguists would have rejected the possibility of constructing a universal theory of grammatical categories. This is no longer so. As Chomsky has pointed out: 'modern work . . . has shown a great diversity in the surface structures of languages', but 'the deep structures for which universality is claimed may be quite distinct from the surface structures of sentences as they actually appear'. It follows that 'the findings of modern linguistics . . . are not inconsistent with the hypotheses of universal grammarians'. Once again Roger Bacon's famous statement about universal grammar is being quoted with approval by linguists: 'Grammar is substantially the same in all languages, even though it may vary accidentally'. The scholastic terms 'substantially' (*secundum substantiam*) and 'accidentally' (*accidentaliter*) may yet be given an acceptable syntactic interpretation in terms of the formalization of the distinction between deep and surface structure.

14

Syntactic Categories and Notional Features

JOHN M. ANDERSON

Givón (1979: §8.6; 1984: §1.3.4) relates the content of the noun/verb distinction to the 'time-stability scale', such that nouns denote stable phenomena, crucially concrete, physical, compact, and verbs denote rapid changes, events and adjectives, where distinct, are intermediate in this respect, denoting relatively stable physical qualities; in the terms of Anderson (1991), nouns are 'entity-specific', verbs 'event-specific'. It seems to me that this highlights, and only partially, only one aspect of differentiation, one which I shall associate, in the case of the noun/verb distinction, with the presence vs. absence of the notional feature **N**, or (perceived) referentiality, or rather referentiability, attribution of which to an element is supported not merely by relative stability but by relative independence (cf. Lyons' 'first-order entities' (1977: §11.3; 1989); also Hopper and Thompson 1984 [included in this volume]; Langacker 1987; Croft 1991).

Verbs are in addition inherently relational, they impose overt structure on (the perception of) events, either new or confirmatory structure—they are situation-defining. Nouns, on the other hand, typically label elements participating in situations, situations that are presented linguistically as (re-)structured primarily by verbal labelling; and nouns are thus potential undergoers of (non-constitutive) change, changes differentiated by verbs. I associate this difference, in the case of noun vs. verb, with the absence vs. presence of the notional feature **P**, or predicativity, or rather predicability.

The 'relational' character of **P** is reflected in one of the contrasting effects of verbalisation vs. nominalisation: verbalisation of a noun—say, *house*—creates an item—the verb *house*—with a complex 'argument structure' compared with the noun, as realised in *They housed the refugees in the barn*, for example; nominalisation of a verb either merely preserves such 'structure'—as with the derived noun of *Fred's abandonment of that principle*—or results in a reduction in complexity—as, for instance, with the English nouns in *-ee* derived from verbs (*deport* ⇒ *deportee* etc.). The 'stable' character of **N**, on the other hand, is reflected in the capacity of the derived noun, and of the basic *house*, to function as an argument.

The two aspects of content associated with **P** and **N** are related in a natural way: verbs denote time-dependent structurisations and nouns introduce autonomous (potential) referents. But the two aspects have different consequences: so that, as observed, verbs, as having **P**, so relation-inducing, can show a range of argument types, and, in lacking **N**, stability, are classified by event-type, or type of change, and are often associated with temporal deixis (which may be realised as the secondary category of Tense); nouns, in lacking **P**, are typically unsubcategorised, and, in having **N**, are classifiable in terms of stable properties, such as concreteness and animacy (possibly manifested as Gender). Further, we shall find (in §§2.3–6) that the notional characterisation of further categories involves the interaction of just these two features. Adjectives, for instance, combine **N** and **P**, and this is reflected in their syntax.

* John M. Anderson, 'Syntactic categories and notional features', section 2.1 of *A Notional Theory of Syntactic Categories* (Cambridge: Cambridge University Press, 1997). © 1997 Cambridge University Press. Reprinted by permission.

The word classes verb and noun are identified cross-linguistically as distributional classes with distinct membership whose members include respectively event- and entity-denoting items. We can distinguish **central** members whose status as one or the other is relatively transparent: thus, central nouns will denote first-order entities, basically 'persons, animals and other discrete physical entities' (Lyons 1989: 161; cf. again Lyons 1977: §11.3). Other members of a class are notionally more peripheral, as with nouns which are 'relational' (*stranger*, *opponent*) or 'abstract' (*lust*) or even 'actional' (*battle*). The extent to which the internal structure of the classes shows properties reflecting 'prototypicality' (e.g. Rosch and Lloyd 1978) is a distinct question whose resolution does not prejudice (though it might enhance) the viability of the idea of central members.

NOTIONAL FEATURES AS BASIC

The distribution of **N** and **P** is the ultimate basis for the construction of the predications which are realised as sentences. Nouns are optimal **arguments** (relatees) in the predications determined by the structures induced (optimally) by verbs, as **predicators**. (I adopt here Lyons' terminological suggestion (1977: 434), so that 'we can say that "play" in "Caroline plays the guitar" is a two-place predicator independently of whether we also say that "play the guitar" is a predicate'.) The nature of subcategorisation, or 'argument structure', and its role in the erection of syntactic structure, is explored in some detail in chapter 3 [not included here]. However, as a preliminary, I shall shortly have to somewhat refine upon the crude view of the syntactic roles of verbs and nouns just expressed in the light of the differentiation of further categories.

The notional features also correlate with discourse function (cf. again Hopper and Thompson 1984). Items with **N**, as stable referables, are optimal topics; items with **P**, as structure-inducing, are the nucleus of optimal comments. In a topic-free sentence, verbs may thus occur alone, as in the Greek (1):

(1) βrexi   'it rains/is raining'

However, clearly, the (possibly topic-free) structure induced by a verb may also include elements characterised as **N**:

(2) βrexi stin elaδa   'it rains/is raining in Greece'

And, more generally, discourse function cannot be regarded as a defining property of **N** and/or **P**, given the independence of categorial status and discourse function. So in (3):

(3) PADDY left

Paddy may be a comment on the topic of a 'leaving'. Such is familiar from the vast body of work on discourse functions.

The subject-predicate distinction is apparently a grammaticalisation of (the typical manifestation of) topic-comment. But another factor enters here. Languages typically accord a special status to animate, particularly human, and ultimately egocentric arguments and their properties (cognition, volition): cf. the 'animacy hierarchy' of Silverstein (1976) and others. Their preferential roles in predications are grammaticalised as **agent** (source of the action) and **experiencer** (location of the experience). On grounds of empathy (Kuno 1987), the human nouns associated with these roles (and particularly the source of the action) are preferred as topics. And thus the typical subject is seen as also agentive and human. Again, we return to a more careful consideration of this in chapter 3 (and cf. already e.g. Lyons 1968: §8.1). But we should further note at this point that such considerations also impinge on the character of the categories defined by **N** and **P**.

Within the set of noun denotata, humans have a special status; within the set of verbal notions, actions, particularly externally directed, or transitive actions. They are seen as epicentral to the class. It is not for nothing that (4):

(4)   The farmer killed the duckling

is perhaps the most familiar example in the discourse of linguistics. This special status of humans and (transitive) actions will be apparent in a number of places in what follows, not merely in relation to subjecthood.

N and **P** are **simplex** features (as proposed by Anderson and Jones 1974; Sanders 1974), either of which may be present or absent in the representation of a particular category. I shall also be assuming that in the representation of a particular category one feature may predominate over another—the combination may be asymmetrical—and that, further, this asymmetry is one manifestation of the **dependency** (head-modifier) relation that may hold between linguistic elements. We shall find that the invocation of simplex (and not *n*-ary-valued) features and of dependency is crucial not just to further elaboration of the range of categories allowed for, but also to the characterisation of markedness and other hierarchical relations between categories, and of the principle which governs the well-formedness of particular systems of categories.

From this, it may be apparent, too, that I do not envisage that all languages will necessarily share the same categories, or word classes. A basic, possibly universal core system is provided by the set of simple combinations of **N** and **P**—**N** alone, **P** alone, **N** and **P**, neither—but further elaborations, involving asymmetrical (dependency) combinations, are perhaps not necessarily universally attested, at least as constituting a system of word classes: see 'A minimal system', below. However, the elaboration of categories is strictly governed, and potentially upwardly bounded also, though the boundary must in our present state of knowledge be provisional only.

BASIC CATEGORIES

Let us provisionally represent the category **verb**, universally, as {P}: its categorial specification includes **P** alone. Nouns include **N** in their specification. But at this point it becomes urgent to introduce an important distinction thus far glossed over. Among the traditional 'naming' words only (proper) **names** qualify as belonging to a category whose specification contains only **N**. They are never predicative, i.e. predicators, unlike the (common) **nouns** in (5):

(5) a. Fred is a doctor
   b. Alphonse est médecin   'A. is a doctor'
   c. O Petros ine δikiγoros   'P. is a lawyer'

Notice in relation to this that I do not regard either of the post-copular elements in (6) as predicative:

(6) a. The man with the shakes is Fred
   b. The man with the shakes is the doctor

What is predicated in (6) is not 'Fred-ness' or 'doctorness' of 'the man with the shakes'; rather, what is predicated is (referential) identity between two arguments, 'the man with the shakes' and 'Fred'/'the doctor'. Unsurprisingly, (7) differ in interpretation from the respective sentences in (6):

(7) a. Fred is the man with the shakes
    b. The doctor is the man with the shakes

only in assignment of unmarked discourse function.

As illustrated by (5b and c), in many languages, such as French and Greek, it may be that no article accompanies a predicative noun, or some predicative nouns, even if, as in French, a noun is otherwise normally accompanied by a determiner. Bolinger notes that the article may be absent in English in 'intensifier' constructions, as *Is he farmer enough to face drought and pests?* or *That animal is only partly dog* (1972: 136, 108). Moreover, occurrence of the indefinite article in English does not ensure that a post-copular NP is predicative. Thus, (8a), on one interpretation, is equative, as, of course, is (b):

(8) a. Our teacher is a plumber from Yorkshire
    b. A plumber from Yorkshire is our teacher

The indefinites in (8) involve specific reference. Contrariwise, a nominal predicator may even bear a definite article: *Bertram is (the) president*. And, as this last example illustrates, 'relational' nouns in English are most likely to lack any determiner when predicative; cf. too e.g. Hugh Walpole's *He was now friend to all the valley* (*Rogue Herries*, part I, 'Christmas Feast'). This correlates with their non-central status as nouns.

In Classical Chinese (Graham 1967), for instance, predications of identity are distinguished by a special copula, *chi*. English and other languages show a common copula in locational, noun-predicative and identifying sentences; and elsewhere differences in copula correlate with 'aspectual' differences (Anderson 1973). Notice, however, that the question word with predicators in English is *what*, whether verbal, adjectival or nominal, no matter how the interrogatives involved may differ in other respects, as illustrated by (9i):

(9i) a. What happened (to Bill)? He died/Bert killed him
    b. What did Bert do? He left/killed Bill/was a butcher
    c. What is Bert like? He is charming
    d. What is Bert (like)? He's a Tory

(9ii) a. Who(m) did he kill? He killed Bill/a plumber from Yorkshire
    b. Who is he? He's our teacher/a plumber from Yorkshire

the one with animate arguments, as exemplified in (ii), is *who(m)*, and the latter may be answered with either a definite (including names) or indefinite nominal. Names are not predicators; and, as we shall see, nouns are arguments only in so far as they are potential names.

Given the notation developed so far, we can distinguish between names and nouns as in(10):

(10)   {N} {N,P}
      name noun

Elements with **P** are possible predicators; elements with **N** are possible **primary arguments**. Secondary arguments are the {P}s which are the heads of subordinate clauses. We can observe here already, however, that in English (for example) only primary arguments allow the full range of (predicator-) argument labels, or 'functors' (see below), to be expressed, as prepositions:

(11) a. Mary was surprised at John/the result
    b. Mary was surprised *at (that) John left

However, the partially predicative character of nouns renders them less optimal as stable labels for arguments, given that they are thus less referentially specific; they have inherent sense as set designators, they are classificatory rather than directly referential, while simple {N} elements differ only referentially rather than in sense (Lyons 1977: §7.5). The latter therefore also appear without restrictive attributives, as being (assumed to be) sufficient in themselves for identification of the referent of an argument: the adjective in *poor John* has no referential role, and that in *the younger Bill* involves recategorisation of *Bill* as a noun. (This is, of course, not to deny that names may themselves be e.g. denotationally gender-specific.)

Personal pronouns also are non-predicative: they too are simple {N}s. They are contextually determined names. Proper names are taken as stable labels for primary arguments; personal pronouns are shifting labels. Compare here Lyons (1977: 214–15; also Jespersen 1922: ch. 6, §7) on the personal pronouns as 'shifters'. Only non-central, 'relational' nouns, such as *father*, *enemy*, are in a sense 'shifters'. Of course, the reference of a name (such as *John*) may be context-dependent; but names, unlike pronouns, are not understood as inherently so. We might recall here that Latham describes the pronoun as 'a variable name' (1862: §646); whereas nouns ('common names') and ('proper') names are invariable but differ in whether they 'are applied to a whole class of objects' or 'are appropriated to certain individual objects' (1862: §633)—with pronouns sharing the latter property with (proper) names (§636). Like names, too, pronouns frequently distinguish gender (even when this is not overtly associated with the nouns in a language), as well as their characteristic deixis-based oppositions.

Definite determiners such as those in (6b) are transitive pronouns (cf. Anderson 1976); they take nouns as complements and render them in context name-like, 'terms', if you like. Compare here, again, on determiners in general, Latham 1862: part V, chs. 2–5. In this respect, too, a similar distinction to that I am drawing between names and nouns is embodied in e.g. unification categorial grammar (Zeevat 1988) and some of its antecedents. Given such observations, we might say that 'noun phrases' are more properly designated 'name phrases': determiners permit nouns to name. Such and related observations have led to analyses of pronouns as articles (e.g. Postal 1970) or determiners as the heads of the constructs traditionally termed 'noun phrases' (e.g. Abney 1987), renamed accordingly 'determiner phrases': for discussion, see e.g. Hudson 1990: §IIa. Given that nouns, names, pronouns and determiners are all nominal (in terms of the notation proposed here), the drastic categorial reinterpretations suggested by the above terms are unnecessary. Perhaps we can compromise on **nominal phrase** as the label for the construct.

Indefinite determiners, or 'quantifiers', such as those in *Fred adores a/some fan-dancer*, combine a kind of naming function with a 'presentative', ultimately predicative function. As with the corresponding 'intransitive' pronouns—such as French *on*, English *someone*—an entity is referred to, but not identified, by way of asserting its existence.

Here let us again note that the association of determiners and nouns is based on their respective notional properties: common nouns, as class labels, complement the closed class of determiners, transitive pronouns, to provide a more differentiated set of variable names. And I attribute, in turn, the properties that nouns share with names/pronouns to the presence of the feature **N**, just as the predicative role of nouns can be attributed to their also being **P**.

Names and verbs involve one-feature combinations; nouns combine two features. The final simple combination of **N** and **P** available is the null one, the empty set { }. These are items which are neither predicator nor argument; they simply provide an empty slot with which can be associated the label for the relation between predicator and argument. With primary arguments, they are typically realised as adpositions, as in (12):

(12) the destruction of the city by the Goths

or inflexionally. But, since the relation between predicator and argument is often clear from the character of the predicator, as when there is only one argument, as in *Mabel danced,* or from the predicator and the 'word order', such elements are frequently given no (other) overt expression. I have put 'word order' in 'scare' quotes to indicate awareness of the fact that this considerably oversimplifies the situation; the syntacticisation of argument-label expression is discussed more fully in §3.1 [not included], on the basis of the notion of dependency introduced in §2.2 [not included]. I shall term this category, viz. { }, the category of **functors**. As we shall see, the category includes, as well as the traditional (NP-introducing) prepositions and postpositions, other (secondary) argument-introducers ('subordinators') such as many complementisers (cf. e.g. Anderson 1972; 1977: 105, 161, 282 n. 31; Emonds 1985: especially ch. 7).

CATEGORIES AND DISTRIBUTION

Simple combinations of **N** and **P** provide for the range of distinctions in (13):

(13)   {P} {N}   {N,P} { }
  verb name noun functor

Let us suppose this at least constitutes a minimal categorial system, such that in particular languages, each category displays a distinctive distribution, attributable to its notional character, and not (totally) included in that of another category. Thus, for example, at a rather crude level, only verbs in English can be finite (i.e., for the moment, occur as the predicator of a simple clause)—names, nouns and functors require the 'support' of a copula:

(14) a. The plumber is Fred
 b. Fred is a plumber
 c. Fred is at the door/out

(where *out* in (c) is an 'intransitive' functor); only names, as the quintessential argument-type, inherent 'terms', can be the unmarked complement of an equative—'specific' nouns (nouns made 'name-like') only can also be such; only nouns are unmarkedly either predicator or argument; functors are neither, but label arguments with respect to their roles in the predication (even, I assume, in (14c), with *be* as a locative verb, in contrast e.g. with the equative *be* of (a)).

In terms of relations between the categories, we can say that the typical ('transitive') functor complements and is complemented by one of the other categories; the typical (non-impersonal) verb is complemented by functors; categories containing **N** typically complement functors. (This again assumes that functors are not necessarily expressed distinctively in the syntax, by adpositions.) Within the set of categories containing **N**, a noun, as opposed to name, may, like the verb, be subcategorized as to functor selection (*father of/to the bride, descendant of/*to Jonah*).

Here it could be objected that determiners (and functors—if we recognise some of them, such as that in (14c), as 'intransitive'), though lacking the **P** feature, also display subcategorisation (Roger Böhm, personal communication). But we should also observe that determiners and pronouns (and 'transitive' and 'intransitive' functors) are distinguished by presence vs. absence of a complement rather than in terms of the character of the complement(s), as in the functor selection of 'relational' nouns. We can then distinguish between **weak subcategorisation**, manifested by determiners, which is simply a consequence of complement structure and the fact that not all complements can be obligatory (with respect to a particular category), and **strong subcategorisation** of the differential character displayed by categories containing **P**. We refine upon this distinction in the following subsection; but there we preserve the essential distinction made here between the highly differentiated complementation of items with **P** compared with those without.

It might also be argued that names simply display a subpart of the distribution of nouns, in lacking the predicativity possibility, and are thus merely a restricted subclass of the latter; however, in suggesting that only names are quintessentially arguments, I am also claiming (to expand on the description above) that the occurrence of nouns as arguments is mediated by conversion to name/pronoun status, though such conversion is not always overtly signalled (by the presence of articles etc.). The basic idea is that even *vandals* in (15):

(15) The car was destroyed by vandals

is a converted noun, a derived name: it is associated with a determiner that is not given independent expression.

In some languages, names/pronouns and nouns show more gross distributional differences. Thus, in German only the genitives of names/pronouns can occur prenominally in the NP (*Jakobs Tod* 'J.'s death'), while noun genitives are restricted to postnominal position (*Der Tod des Freundes* 'the friend's death')—see Anderson 1987. Interestingly, as again pointed out to me by Roger Böhm, prenominal genitives include kinship terms used as names, as in *Opas Besuch* 'Granddad's visit. Let us note too, as another instance of a more overt differentiation of names, that in many of the Polynesian languages names are accompanied by a distinctive 'article' (cf. e.g. Krupa 1982: ch. 4).

One might similarly object, however, with respect to this scheme of categories, that in languages where a predicative noun does not need the support of a copula, as in the Russian (16)—cf (14b):

(16) Marija rebënok   'Mary (is a) child'   (Lyons 1968: §7.6.3)

the distribution of verbs is included in that of nouns, and the former are thus simply a subclass of the latter. But, again, nouns are not quintessential predicators. In Russian, this is reflected in the fact that in the past tense the presence of a copula is required. Curiously, Lyons, in arguing for the 'primitiveness' of structures such as (16), contends that 'there is no convincing syntactic or semantic reason for classifying "be" in English as a verb' (1977: 437). But its syntactic credentials are surely impeccable, and though as a verb it may not be notionally central, it nevertheless displays the relational, structure-inducing character I have attributed to **P**. Rather than regarding 'be' as simply a 'surface-structure element which "carries" the overt marking of some syntactic distinction' (here 'tense, mood, and aspect'—Lyons 1968: 322), with all the undesirable power that the idea of a purely 'surface-structure element' introduces, I take instead the presence of 'be' as an indication that nouns are, even in languages where its distribution is restricted, not preferred predicators. The kind of restrictions on absence of copula illustrated by Russian are not uncommon (cf. e.g. Ferguson 1972, on Bengali; Bhaskararao 1972, on Telugu). However, we return in a moment to issues raised by languages where predicative nouns are never accompanied by 'be'.

Nouns, {P,N}, are notionally intermediate between verbs, {P}, and names, {N}; conjunction of **P** and **N** 'dilutes' their individual characteristics. Syntactically, too, in a notionally based theory, they are expected to show a distribution shared with verbs and names, but attenuated. The (even partial) presence of copulas and articles is one indication of this, as is the intermediate capacity of nouns for complementation by distinct functors (strong subcategorisation).

On such grounds the potential word classes of English and many other languages associated with the representations in (13) are categorially distinct at a lexical level, in displaying distinct distributions for their members, and often association with a distinct set of secondary categories. In discussing, in particular, the noun/name distinction I have also endeavoured to show that, though their distributions may overlap, one is not simply included in the other. However, in many languages this is true only if the distributions are 'interpreted', in that e.g. nouns are associated with 'determiner' categories that may not be overtly expressed. And the non-inclusion requirement may not be necessary for the establishment of lexical categories; indeed, it is not clear how it is to be applied in the case of classes, such as the 'adverbs' discussed in the following section, which are categorially complex.

A MINIMAL SYSTEM?

A provisional general hypothesis might be that (13) represents the minimal system of word classes that needs to be attributed to any language. Thus, although Robins (1968), for instance, attributes to the 'basic structures' of Sundanese only the word classes 'N(ouns), V(erbs), and Particles', it is clear that pronouns (and names) are therein distinct from nouns in being nonpredicative, and potentially equative. And, more generally, although Schachter claims merely that 'in most languages some grammatical distinction is made between *common nouns*, which are used to refer to any member of a class of persons, etc. . . . and *proper nouns*, which are used to refer to specific persons, etc. . . .' (1985:8), such a conclusion seems to be generally applicable. It is not simply the case that, as noted in 'Categories and distribution' (above), in some languages there is a particular 'marker' of the distinction, either partially distinctive, as e.g. the typical absence of an article with names in English or the normal presence of a definite one in Greek (*Peter* vs. *o Petros*), or more generally, as e.g. in the selection of special 'articles' in many of the Polynesian languages (see again Krupa 1982: 64–8), or in terms of the differentiation of case/topic markers in Philippine languages (Llamzon 1979a: 115); names are apparently universally distinct with respect to their (non-)capacity for predicativity/equativity, reflecting their status as quintessential arguments or 'terms'.

Say, then, that (13) may not be reduced in particular languages to (17) as in (a):

(17)   {P}   {N}   { }
    a. *verb*   *name/noun*   *functor*
    b. *verb/noun*   *name*   *functor*

which has only unary or less combinations; (17a) is 'sub-minimal'. Schachter also discusses (1985: 11–13), however, suggestions that there are languages which reflect a system of categories that we might, in terms of the present notation, represent as (17b), with no verb/noun distinction, or even (18), a reduction of both of (17)—and thus in contradiction of what I have just concluded about (the universality of) the names/noun distinction:

(18)   {N}   { }
    verb/name/noun   *functor*

To allow for the construction of sentences in such putative systems, which requires a distinction between predicator and argument to be made, particular occurrences of the {P} class in (17b) (and the {N} class in (18), would be provided by redundancy with additional specification, so that arguments could be distinguished derivatively (non-lexically) as {N,P}. The choice of **N** rather than **P** for the non-functor class in (18) reflects the assumed primacy of naming.

A 'sub-minimal' system has been suggested for Salish: see e.g. Kuipers 1968; Kinkade 1983. The latter specifically argues for a system such as we have characterised in (18), in so far as (unlike Jacobsen 1979, on Makah) he proposes that names are not distinct from predicators; but the examples he offers (1983:29) show names as arguments in equative predications rather than functioning as predicators themselves: again names/pronouns are apparently distributionally distinct from other potential classes. In general, a system such as (18) has not been shown to be appropriate.

Swadesh's (1936–8) much cited description of Nootka would appear to warrant a characterisation such as (17b), as would Bloomfield's account of Ilocano (1942), wherein are recognised as word classes only 'pronouns', 'full words' and 'particles'. (Bloomfield also groups 'names' with 'full words' (1942: §6), on the basis of their requiring, like 'full words', special markers when they occur as arguments; but these seem to reflect differences in how functors are expressed rather than instantiating a fundamental difference in distribution between names and pronouns.) Swadesh sums up the Nootka situation as follows:

Normal words [vs. particles—*JMA*] do not fall into classes like noun, verb, adjective, preposition, but all sorts of ideas find their expression in the same general type of word, which is predicative or non-predicative according to its paradigmatic ending. (1936–8: 78)

and provides examples such as (19):

(19) a. Mamoʹkma   qoʹʔasʔi
       he-is-working the-man

  b. Qoʹʔasma   mamoʹkʔi
     he-is-a-man the-working

Cf. Sapir and Swadesh 1939: 235–6; Kuipers 1968: 625; more generally, Bloomfield 1933: 20; and, for references to other discussions, Thompson 1979: §4.2.4. Swadesh's 'particles' are a heterogeneous closed set, but include functors and adverbs.

Let us be clear that what is at issue is the **lexical** recognition of categorial distinctions: whether there are classes of words limited to one or other category. The claim being advanced in relation to Nootka and the like is that predicator and argument status is equally available to all 'full words'; we can contrast here the common situation, illustrated rather strikingly by Australian languages (e.g. Blake 1987: 9), wherein normally a 'noun used as a verb' will be derivationally marked. There is no doubt, however, as is recognised in Sapir's description, that the articulation of the morphosyntax of alleged 'sub-minimal' languages, characterisable in terms of (17b), requires, as with other languages, reference to a distinction between predicator and argument, and not all arguments are names/pronouns. In Ilocano, for instance, the formulation of word-order patterns depends on such, the basic pattern being: predicator (+argument(s)), where arguments are not limited to 'pronouns' but may involve members of the class of 'full words', whose members also occur as predicators. And, though Boas concludes, with respect to Kwakiutl, that, as concerns potential **P** and **P,N** words, 'all stems seem to be neutral' (1911a:441), he subsequently affirms that 'the classification of suffixes here given shows that a division of words into verbs and nouns has taken place' (p. 443), and the syntactic organisation of the sentence depends on the making of this distinction. See further, more generally, Lyons 1977: §11.2.

Discussion of this issue is bedevilled by a confusion of lexical class and syntactic category. Kinkade, for instance, seems to be unclear about (among other things) the distinction between category and word class when he concludes (1983: 32): 'as I have shown, Salish shows only predications, and there is thus no basis for claiming a distinction between nominal expressions and verbal expressions (Lyons' syntactic categories)' (cf. too Thompson 1979: 699). The evidence Kinkade presents suggests that there may be no lexical distinction between noun and verb categories (though the languages concerned deserve more detailed analysis in this respect—cf. van Eijk and Hess 1986); but it does not warrant the conclusion that the cat-egories predicator and argument (distinguishing, among other things, between the syntactic functions of 'full words') are irrelevant syntactically.

The members of a (lexical) word class may be assigned a range of categorial possibilities by redundancy. If there are languages whose set of word classes is limited to that defined by (17b), their syntax will nevertheless appeal to at least the system of (13), with the categorial distinctions being made available by a redundancy such as (20):

(20) $\{P\} \Rightarrow N$

i.e. predicates ($\{P\}$) may also be $\{P,N\}$, making them available to marking (with demonstratives etc.) as non-quintessential arguments and to the occupying of argument positions.

The existence and characterisation of such languages remains rather controversial. For instance, as concerns Nootka, Jacobsen (1979) has shown that of the set of 'full words' there are some which cannot occur as arguments unless suffixed, whereas others occur as such suffixed or unsuffixed; the former set includes items which universally are (otherwise) centrally **P** words. Now, one might say that this simply shows that such items have a more restricted distribution than other 'full words': we have a subclass rather than a class difference. (Cf. again Schachter 1985: 11–13, on both Nootka and Tagalog.) Alternatively, however, in view of the correlation with the primary categorial notional features, one could take the suffixation requirement as an indication that occurrence as an argument is not part of the basic distribution of the '**P**-words', with the suffix indicating nominalisation, as in other languages.

We can establish in general that (13) is appropriate for such a language as a system of lexical classes (rather than, in part, of subclasses) if we can show that '**P,N**-words', though showing a gross distribution that includes those of the '**P**-words' and the $\{N\}$-words, are neither preferred arguments nor preferred predicators (cf. above)—as would befit categor-isation as $\{P,N\}$. This seems relatively unproblematical in general in the case of their differ-entiation from names ($\{N\}$-words); but Kuipers, for instance, while dividing Squamish stems into those which are overtly marked (by affixes) as 'nominal' or 'verbal' and those which are not, concedes that even with the former 'difference in syntactic status', reflected in their combining with 'predicative' or 'possessive clitics', 'is statistical rather than absolute' (1967: 63–4). If a statistical correlation is rejected as the basis for a word-class distinction, one might conclude that, while (13) may define a set of minimal categories for the syntax of any language, it is possible that the minimal system of word classes is more restricted, as in (17b), with the potential of the $\{P\}$ class for argumenthood being allowed for by redundancy (20).

Even the suffixation phenomena of Nootka alluded to above are perhaps amenable to an analysis in terms of subclasses. In Nootka, verbs, in such terms, would be the subclass of $\{P\}$ marked as exceptional with respect to (20):

(21) *(20)

And only derived forms based on this subclass are arguments, along with items not marked as in (21). As noted above, only the correlation with the central verb/noun types in other languages would then offer some motivation for the elevation of this distinction among $\{P\}$ items in Nootka to word-class status.

However, even apart from such considerations, it may be that we have been looking for a verb/noun word-class distinction in the wrong place. Elsewhere, Kinkade (1976) discusses the syntax of what he calls the 'copula' in Inland Olympic Salish, where he reveals that, although the language is normally predicate-first, as shown in (22a):

(22) a. ʔit   qʷíl-əm   tat   n- čálš
        COMP   bleed-MIDDLE   COMP   my-arm
        ('My arm bled')

     b. Tit   qáʾʔ   wi   tit   pə́qʷ-l
        COMP   water   be   COMP   spill-INTRANS
        ('The water spilled')   (Kinkade 1976:17, 19)

the copula occurs with initial subject (apparently as some kind of focussing construction), as in (22b). Here we have a potential **P** item with a distinct distribution vis-à-vis other 'full words', one that is saliently predicative. This raises the possibility that the language may after all realise lexically the system of (13), but that almost all 'full words' are {P,N}, whereas the membership of {P} is very restricted indeed. (The status of, for instance, the negative /miɬta/, which is 'unclear' according to Kinkade (1976: 19), warrants further investigation in this regard.)

Now, such a suggestion departs from our normal assumptions concerning a class of verbs: here, it is closed, and its membership scarcely conforms to the usual notional type (denoting 'actions', etc.). But it may be that the two 'anomalies' are related. I shall be suggesting in §2.3.2 [not included] (and cf. e.g. Anderson 1990) that the membership of {P} in Wunambal and Ngäbére, for instance, is also closed, and also 'non-actional', consisting of the traditional 'auxiliaries'. These closed class {P}s nevertheless strongly manifest the relational property I attributed to **P**. It may be that retreat from the other aspects of notional typicality is something to be generally associated with closed class {P}s. Certainly, the corresponding simple class {N} is associated with a membership also limited, in this case in having members differing only referentially and not in sense, and, in the case of variable names (pronouns), also closed class.

This leaves at this point the question of the minimal set of word classes undecided, though evidence for 'sub-(13)' systems is, it seems to me, inconclusive. More work is warranted on such languages. For instance, apart from the considerations raised in the preceding paragraph, attention could be given to Kuipers' admission (1968: 625) that in Squamish 'the form /č'aw-at-c-as/ "he helps me" is the only finite form which cannot also occur in the positions X,Y' [i.e. as arguments]. In general, indeed, we lack systematic and explicit testing, in the context of a well-defined theory of categories, of the hypothesis that at least (13) is universally the minimal system of lexical classes, as well as being syntactically minimal. I shall take this to be the unmarked assumption.

CONCLUSION

In this section I have introduced the notional features whose combination defines syntactic categories; and, on the assumption that languages may vary in the set of categories that should be attributed to them, I have tentatively hypothesised a notion of minimal system of categories. In discussing this it is important to distinguish between the set of categories to be distinguished lexically as to their distribution, i.e. the word classes, and the set of categories distinguished by the syntax. Notably absent from the discussion has been mention of a further potential word class (or classes), the 'adverb'; and the realisational character of functors (as adpositions, morphological categories, etc.) has been left somewhat obscure. The following section [not included] will attempt to remedy these (related) lacks, in a preliminary way.

I approach this, however, via an endeavour to clarify another notion appealed to in the preceding, the notion of 'complement', invoked, for instance, in formulating (in 'Categories and distribution' above) the distributions of various categories in English. This will later prove fundamental to a formulation of the syntax induced by the categorial representations.

REFERENCES

Abney, S. (1987). 'The English noun phrase in its sentential aspect'. Ph.D. dissertation, Massachusetts Institute of Technology.

Anderson, J. M. (1972). 'Remarks on the hierarchy of quasi-predications'. *Revue roumaine de linguistique* 17: 23–44, 121–41, 193–202, 319–35.

——(1973). *An Essay concerning Aspect*. The Hague: Mouton.

——(1976). *Serialisation in English Syntax*. Ludwigsburg: Ludwigsburg Studies in Language and Linguistics 1.

——(1977). *On Case Grammar: Prolegomena to a Theory of Grammatical Relations*. London: Croom Helm.

——(1987). 'Invariance and linguistic variation: a case grammar characterisation'. In Melenk et al. (1987: 604–10).

——(1990). 'On the status of auxiliaries in notional grammar'. *Journal of Linguistics* 26: 241–62.

——(1991). 'Notional grammar and the redundancy of syntax'. *Studies in Language* 15: 301–33.

——and C. Jones (1974). 'Three theses concerning phonological representations'. *Journal of Linguistics* 10: 1–26

Arnold, D. J., M. Atkinson, J. Durand, C. Glover, and L. Sadler (eds.) (1989). *Essays on Grammatical Theory and Universal Grammar*. Oxford: Oxford University Press.

Bhaskararao, P. (1972). 'On the syntax of Telugu existential and copulative predications'. In Verhaar (1972: 153–206).

Blake, B. J. (1987). *Australian Aboriginal Grammar*. London: Croom Helm.

Bloomfield, L. (1933). *Language*. New York: Holt, Rinehart & Winston.

——(1942). 'Outline of Ilocano syntax'. *Language* 18: 193–200.

Boas, F. (1911a). 'Kwakiutl'. In Boas (1911b: 423–557).

——(ed.) (1911b). *Handbook of American Indian Languages*. Washington, DC: Bureau of American Ethnology, Smithsonian Institute.

Bolinger, D. L. (1972). *Degree Words*. The Hague: Mouton.

Campbell, L., and M. Mithun (eds.) (1979). *The Languages of Native America: Historical and Comparative Assessment*. Austin: University of Texas Press.

Croft, W. (1991). *Syntactic Categories and Grammatical Relations: The Cognitive Organization of Information*. Chicago Ill.: University of Chicago Press.

Dixon, R. M. W. (ed.) (1976). *Grammatical Categories in Australian Languages*. Canberra: Australian Institute for Aboriginal Studies/Atlantic Highlands, NJ: Humanities Press.

Efrat, B. S. (ed.) (1979). *The Victoria Conference on Northwestern Languages*. Victoria, BC: British Columbia Provincial Museum.

Eijk, J. P. van, and T. Hess (1986). 'Noun and verb in Salish'. *Lingua* 69: 319–31.

Emonds, J. E. (1985). *A Unified Theory of Syntactic Categories*. Dordrecht: Foris.

Ferguson, C. A. (1972). 'Verbs of "being" in Bengali, with a note on Amharic'. In Verhaar (1972: 74–114).

Givón, T. (1979). *On Understanding Grammar*. New York: Academic Press.

——(1984). *Syntax: A Functional-Typological Approach*, vol. i. Amsterdam: Benjamins.

Graham, A. C. (1967). '"Being" in Classical Chinese'. In Verhaar (1967: 1–39).

Hopper, P. J., and S. A. Thompson (1984). 'The discourse basis for lexical categories in universal grammar'. *Language* 60: 703–52.

Hudson, R. A. (1990). *A Word Grammar of English*. Oxford: Blackwell.

Jacobs, R. A., and P. S. Rosenbaum (eds.) (1970). *Readings in English Transformational Grammar*. Waltham, Mass.: Ginn.

Jacobsen, W. H. (1979). 'Noun and verb in Nootkan'. In Efrat (1979: 83–153).

Jespersen, O. (1922). *Language: Its Nature, Development and Origin*. London: Allen & Unwin.

Keenan, E. L. (ed.) (1975). *Formal Semantics of Natural Language*. Cambridge: Cambridge University Press.

Kinkade, M. D. (1976). 'The copula and negatives in Inland Olympic Salish'. *International Journal of American Linguistics* 42: 17–23.

——(1983). 'Salish evidence against the universality of noun and verb'. *Lingua* 60: 25–40.

Krupa, V. (1982). *The Polynesian Languages: A Guide*. London: Routledge & Kegan Paul.

Kuipers, A. H. (1967). *The Squamish Language*. The Hague: Mouton.

——(1968). 'The categories verb–noun and transitive–intransitive in English and Squamish'. *Lingua* 21: 610–26.

Kuno, S. (1987). *Functional Syntax: Anaphora, Discourse and Empathy*. Chicago, Ill.: University of Chicago Press.

Langacker, R. W. (1987). 'Nouns and verbs'. *Language* 63: 53–94.

Latham, R. G. (1862). *The English language*, 5th edn. London: Walton & Maberly.

Llamzon, T. A. (1979a). 'Languages of the Philippines: characteristic structures'. In Llamzon (1979b: 99–128).

——(ed.) (1979b). *Papers on Southeast Asian Languages*. Singapore: Singapore University Press.

Lyons, J. (1968). *Introduction to Theoretical Linguistics*. Cambridge: Cambridge University Press.

——(1977). *Semantics*, vols i and ii. Cambridge: Cambridge University Press.

——(1989). 'Semantic ascent'. In Arnold et al. (1989: 153–86).

Melenk, H., J. Firges, G. Nold, R. Strauch, and D. Zeh (eds.) (1987). *Fremdsprachendidaktiker-Kongreβ* 11. Tübingen: Narr.

Osgood, C. (ed.) (1946). *Linguistic Structures of Native America*. New York: Viking Fund.

Postal, P. M. (1970). 'On so-called pronouns in English'. In Jacobs and Rosenbaum (1970: 56–82).

Reyle, U., and C. Rohrer (eds.) (1988). *Natural Language Parsing and Linguistic Theory*. Dordrecht: Reidel.

Robins, R. H. (1968). 'Basic structures in Sundanese'. *Lingua* 21: 351–8.

Rosch, E., and B. B. Lloyd (eds.) (1978). *Cognition and Categorization*. Hillsdale, NJ: Erlbaum.

Sanders, G. (1974). 'The simplex feature hypothesis'. *Glossa* 8: 141–92.

Sapir, E., and M. Swadesh (1939). *Nootka Texts*. Philadelphia: Linguistic Society of America.

Schachter, P. (1985). 'Parts-of-speech systems'. In Shopen (1985: 3–61).

Shopen, T. (ed.) (1985). *Language Typology and Syntactic Description*, vol. i: *Clause Structure*. Cambridge: Cambridge University Press.

Silverstein, M. (1976). 'Hierarchy of features and ergativity'. In Dixon (1976: 112–71).

Swadesh, M. (1936–8). 'Nootka internal syntax'. *International Journal of American Linguistics* 9: 77–102.

Thompson, L. C. (1979). 'Salishan and the Northwest'. In Campbell and Mithun (1979: 692–765).

Verhaar, J. W. M. (ed.) (1967). *The Verb 'Be' and its Synonyms*, part i: *Classical Chinese/Athapaskan/Mundari*. Dordrecht: Reidel.

Zeevat, H. (1988). 'Combining categorial grammar and unification'. In Reyle and Rohrer (1988: 202–29).

15

Bounded Regions

RONALD W. LANGACKER

Counter to received wisdom, I claim that basic grammatical categories such as **noun, verb, adjective**, and **adverb** are semantically definable. The entities referred to as nouns, verbs, etc. are symbolic units, each with a semantic and a phonological pole, but it is the former that determines the categorization. All members of a given class share fundamental semantic properties, and their semantic poles thus instantiate a single abstract schema subject to reasonably explicit characterization. A noun, for example, is a symbolic structure whose semantic pole instantiates the schema [THING]; or to phrase it more simply, a noun designates a **thing**.[1] In similar fashion, a verb is said to designate a **process**, whereas adjectives and adverbs designate different kinds of **atemporal relations**. Our immediate task is to arrive at a motivated description of the [THING] category. I propose that a thing is properly characterized as a **region in some domain**, i.e. every nominal predication designates a region. Count nouns represent a special but prototypical case, in which the designated region is specifically construed as being **bounded** in a primary domain.

DOMAINS OF BOUNDING

Discussions of nouns as a possible semantic class generally focus on physical objects: witness the traditional definition of a noun as the name of a person, place, or "thing" (i.e. discrete, nonhuman object). This is understandable in view of the prototypicality of physical objects, but it dooms a notional definition to failure from the very outset. Most nouns do *not* designate physical objects, and by concentrating on those that do, the best one can offer for the remainder is the assertion that they constitute extensions from the prototype, often at such a distance that the basis for extension is not apparent (how does one get from *cup* to *exacerbation?*).[2] Categorization by prototype is essential to linguistic structure, and it is perfectly valid for the class of nouns (cf. Hopper and Thompson 1984 [included in this volume]). In this instance, however, I believe a schematic characterization (reflecting the commonality of all class members) to be both feasible and revealing.

* Ronald W. Langacker, 'Bounded regions', section 5.2 of *Foundations of Cognitive Grammar*, vol. i: *Theoretical Prerequisites* (Stanford: Stanford University Press, 1987). © 1987 Stanford University Press. Reprinted by permission.

[1] Possibly the schema [THING] can be equated with the semantic pole of the morpheme *thing* in its most general sense, as represented in *something*. The apparent problems with this equation may be resolvable; for instance, the existence of more specialized pro forms like *someone* and *someplace* explains why *something* is not easily used for people or locations.

[2] Thus Lyons (1968, p. 318) concludes that a notional definition is possible only for a subclass of nouns; the class as a whole must be identified by formal criteria. He suggests that a formally defined class may be identified as the noun class if all or the vast majority of lexical items referring to persons, places, and "things" fall within it.

The requisite schema is necessarily quite abstract. Note that the proffered definition of a thing (a region in some domain) does not refer specifically to either physical objects or three-dimensional space. Despite its cognitive salience, three-dimensional space is only one of the countless domains—basic and abstract—relative to which linguistic predications are made and regions delimited. As bounded regions in three-dimensional space, physical objects clearly satisfy the description, but many other kinds of entities also qualify as things. In fact, not even all bounded regions in three-dimensional space are physical objects: consider *sphere* (interpreted geometrically rather than concretely), or terms like *area*, *region*, and *location* (when construed in three dimensions rather than one or two). Strictly speaking, of course, a physical object *occupies* a bounded region in space but cannot be equated with that region per se.

Let us then consider some bounded regions in domains other than three-dimensional space. The objective is both to furnish enough examples of diverse character to establish the initial plausibility of this definition of count nouns, and also to note certain subtleties that arise in regard to bounding. Ultimately, the notions region and bounding require explicit description; the phrase **bounded region** must be interpreted abstractly enough to overcome the limitations of its spatial origin. For the moment, though, I will take this phrase to be self-explanatory and its import to be intuitively obvious, since our initial concern is with the domain in which bounding occurs.

To start with basic domains, nouns like *circle*, *point*, *line*, and *triangle* designate bounded regions in two-dimensional space. *Spot*, *dot*, *stripe*, and *streak* are not unreasonably analyzed as designating circumscribed impressions in the visual field, whereas *moment*, *instant*, and *period* are bounded regions in time. Color terms (when used as nouns) designate particular regions in color space; most are defined relative to the hue dimension primarily (*red*, *yellow*, *blue*, etc.), but a few are confined largely or solely to the brightness dimension (*black*, *white*, *gray*). The matrix for other nominal concepts is formed by coordinating basic domains. A *beep*, for instance, is bounded in both pitch and time: it must to some degree approximate a pure tone (white noise does not qualify) and be quite short in duration as well. Duration is also limited for a *blip* and a *flash*, which display an instructive contrast. A flash must be almost instantaneous, whereas a blip can persevere (though only for a short time). Moreover, a blip (like a dot) must constitute a highly restricted region in the visual field; a flash, though it occupies the visual field, need not be bounded in this domain (it can totally suffuse the field of vision). We see from this example that the profile of a count noun is not necessarily bounded in every domain with which it interacts, a point of some significance.

Abstract domains presuppose (and thus incorporate) more-basic domains. Bounding in an abstract domain is therefore compatible with bounding in an incorporated basic domain, though the former may be primary and the latter derivative. An *arc*, for example, is a bounded region within a circle, and a *hypotenuse*, one within a right triangle. Because a circle or triangle is a two-dimensional figure, a subpart of either one also occupies two-dimensional space and even constitutes a restricted region in this basic domain. Undifferentiated two-dimensional space is not, however, the place to begin for an optimal definition of terms like *arc* and *hypotenuse*. They are best characterized with respect to abstract domains at the appropriate level in hierarchies of conceptual complexity, and it is in these domains that their primary bounding occurs. Similar remarks are valid for a host of other relational nouns pertaining to two- and three-dimensional spatial entities. Terms for body parts were considered previously: a *knuckle* is a bounded region within a finger, a *finger* within a hand, a *hand* within an arm, etc. All these entities are also restricted regions within the body as a whole and in three-dimensional space, but these latter relations are derivative rather than fundamental. A *tip* is defined more schematically, being a bounded region within an elongated object (generally a thin one); the schematic conception of such an object constitutes the base for the predicate

[TIP], which designates its extremity and a vaguely delimited surrounding area. More schematic still in regard to the specification of their abstract domains are generalized relational expressions like *top*, *center*, *edge*, *surface*, and *end*.

Parallel observations can be made for examples farther up in hierarchies of conceptual complexity. A kinship network plots relations among people, so every node is equated with a person; a term like *uncle* therefore designates a person, hence a three-dimensional object, but I have suggested that this is derivative of the fact that it profiles a particular node (bounded region) in a kinship configuration. The relation of terms for musical notes (e.g. *C-sharp*, *B-flat*, *F*) to the basic domain of pitch is similarly indirect, for they designate positions on a musical scale, an abstract structure erected for the analysis and description of pitch. Expressions like *January*, *Tuesday*, *century*, *year*, *month*, *week*, and *hour* designate bounded regions within abstract constructs devised to track and calibrate the passage of time; their relation to time is consequently indirect, and they are classed linguistically as atemporal expressions (nouns rather than verbs). The terms *word*, *sentence*, *paragraph*, *section*, and *chapter* can all be used to designate bounded portions of a written work (regardless of whether it has physical instantiation). *Prolog*, *act*, *scene*, and *line* (not to mention *intermission*) indicate segments of a stage performance, and for portions of an athletic event we have words like *inning*, *period*, *quarter*, *half*, and *round*.

These examples afford some initial idea of the diversity of those entities reasonably construed as bounded regions in a domain. The viability of this characterization depends on the proper recognition of certain points, however. Typically a thing occupies or interacts with a variety of different domains, all of which are potentially included in the complex matrix of a predicate. These domains are not all on a par: they are ranked in terms of prominence and centrality, some presuppose (hence incorporate) more basic ones, and so on. There are some predicates that specifically require bounding in more than one domain (e.g. *beep* and *blip*). Others are bounded in only some of the domains central to their characterization (*flash*). Bounding in an abstract domain often implies bounding in a more basic domain that it incorporates (*arc*, *knuckle*, *tip*); but it can also happen that bounding inherited from an incorporated domain is crucial (rather than derivative) in establishing an entity as a thing. Consider deverbal agentive nouns like *painter*, *skier*, *complainer*, and so on. The base and primary domain for such nouns is the process designated by the verb stem: a *painter*, for instance, is someone who plays a specific role in the process of painting. Yet it seems implausible to say that a painter qualifies as a thing by virtue of being a bounded region within the process designated by *paint*. Indeed, the process itself presupposes the conception of a thing (prototypically a person) capable of acting in the appropriate fashion: suffixing -*er* to *paint* shifts the profile from the process as a whole to the actor specifically, but the process per se is not the domain in which the designated entity receives its primary bounding. In contrast, *arc*, *knuckle*, or *tip* itself establishes a bounded region (within a circle, finger, or elongated object) through the profile it imposes.[3]

A crucial point concerns the interaction between bounding and the scope of predication. The scope of a predication (its base) is the extension of its coverage within relevant domains. Though the limits of this extension are often rather flexible and vaguely defined, evidence has been adduced for the validity of the construct (see Casad and Langacker 1985). When a conceived entity "overflows" the scope of a predication, only restricted portions of the entity fall within its explicit coverage, but this implicit limitation due to scope must be distinguished

---

[3] *Uncle* can be analyzed either way, and the two alternatives are not mutually exclusive (profiling in the primary domain may simply add a dimension of bounding to that inherited from more basic domains). The inheritance of bounding is not limited to derived nouns like *painter*—note *friend*, enemy, chief, king, bachelor, etc.

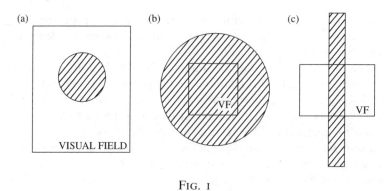

FIG. I

from bounding. We can properly speak of bounding only when an entity is fully included in the scope of predication (with respect to a particular domain), so that its outer limits are a specific matter of predication.

For example, the verb *see* establishes the visual field as a pertinent scope of predication for the characterization of its direct object, e.g. *spot* in the sentence *I see a dark spot*. A speaker could utter this sentence felicitously in the situation depicted in Fig. 1(a): the entire spot is included in his visual field (scope of predication), together with enough nondark background for the spot to stand out as the figure within the scene. The sentence would not be so felicitous in the situation of Fig. 1(b), where the speaker sees nothing but black. Because *spot* designates a bounded region contrasting visually with its surroundings, the outer perimeter—the line of visual contrast—is essential to its characterization and necessarily included in the scope of predication.[4] We can conclude that the limitation of coverage attributable to scope does not per se qualify as bounding.

Spot can instructively be compared to *stripe*. Since a spot is crucially bounded in two dimensions, but a stripe in only one, a speaker can properly say *I see a dark stripe* in the context of Fig. 1(c): the dark region is fully bounded with respect to the horizontal dimension of his visual field, though it overflows the scope boundaries along the vertical dimension. The speaker may know that the stripe extends vertically only a certain distance, but even so this bounding is not explicitly predicated in the sentence. We see, then, that a bounded region is not necessarily bounded in all dimensions of the primary domain. *Horizon* is similar to *stripe*, but more specific. Its base consists of whatever a person can see (or potentially see) in an outdoor setting, and its profile is the line between earth and sky at the limits of vision. This line is bounded along the axis of vision, but perpendicular to this axis (i.e. to either side) it is considered to extend indefinitely, overflowing the restricted visual field. The spatially non-bounded character of *flash* can perhaps now be better appreciated. A flash may be confined to a small region of an observer's visual field, as in Fig. 1(a), or it may overflow it, as in (b). In either case a person can say *I saw a flash* without strain or qualification, since a flash (a brief episode of light intensity) is crucially bounded in time rather than space.

STRUCTURING

Meaning is not objectively given, but constructed, even for expressions pertaining to objective reality. We therefore cannot account for meaning by describing objective reality, but only by

---

[4] *I see a dark spot* is felicitous in the context of diagram (b) if the speaker knows from other experience that what he is seeing is part of a larger bounded region and implicitly expands the scope of predication (beyond the limits implied by *see*) to include this region as a whole.

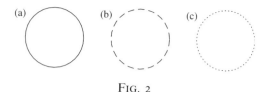

FIG. 2

describing the cognitive routines that constitute a person's understanding of it. The subject matter of semantic analysis is human conceptualization, and the structures of concern are those that a person imposes on his mental experience through active cognitive processing.

Coherent mental experience is structured with reference to previous experience. The activation of a previously established cognitive routine serves as standard (S) for an act of comparison in which some facet of current experience functions as target (T); to the extent that $S > T$ approximates zero, the overall event is one of recognition, and T is thereby interpreted as an instance of S. A great deal of variability is inherent in the process, however. For example, more than one established routine may be available to interpret T (or selected aspects of T), and there is no way to predict in absolute terms which one might be invoked on a given occasion. Recognition can operate at different levels of tolerance (i.e. the vector V_{ST} need not be precisely zero) and can be made sensitive to different parameters. Moreover, S is commonly schematic relative to T, with scanning made to assess only their compatibility (thus all of the specifications of S are recognized in T, even though T is more detailed); in this case recognition amounts to categorization.

This model accounts straightforwardly for the closure phenomenon, in which recognition is achieved despite the incomplete or degraded nature of the target structure. Consider the three diagrams in Fig. 2, any one of which is readily recognized as a circle. Objectively, diagrams (b) and (c) consist of separate line segments or points, yet it is very hard to perceive the separate elements independent of their organization. The concept of a circle is deeply entrenched and easily elicited. Through the activation of this concept as a standard of comparison, any of the configurations in Fig. 2 is categorized as a circle with a minimal amount of strain. The full, autonomous conceptualization of a circle therefore occurs and functions as standard within the recognition event, and it is through their correspondence to facets of this integrated autonomous conception that the line segments and points in diagrams (b) and (c) are united in a coherent perceptual experience. Their continuity is imposed rather than being objectively given.

Taken to its extreme, this process results in the imputation of boundaries where they have no objective existence at all, even in nondegraded instances. In such cases I will speak of a **virtual** boundary. Virtual boundaries are nicely illustrated by nouns like *bump* and *dent*, sketched in Fig. 3 [on p. 244]; they are represented diagrammatically by broken lines, but it must be understood that no boundary feature at all is objectively present (in contrast to Fig. 2(b)).[5] The domains for *bump* and *dent* are abstract, involving the conception of a three-dimensional object at least one surface of which has a canonical (typically smooth) shape. A bump or dent resides in the departure of the actual shape of the object from its expected shape; the latter therefore figures in the base of the predicates [BUMP] and [DENT] and contributes the virtual boundary to the designated entities. To see the importance of expectations, observe that the nose is not considered a bump in the middle of the face, nor is the depression in the

---

[5] Fig. 3 construes *bump* or *dent* as designating an entire enclosed area; an alternate construal profiles only the adjacent physical surface (indicated by the heavy solid line), relegating the virtual boundary and virtually enclosed area to the base. Comparable remarks hold for other examples, e.g. *circle*, which can be construed as designating either the curved line alone (a very thin bounded region) or else the entire area it encloses.

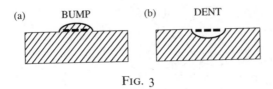

FIG. 3

head of a screw considered a dent. The role of expectations underscores the nonobjective nature of semantic structure.

Virtual bounding is far more prevalent than might be anticipated. Terms similar to *bump* and *dent* are not uncommon (*bulge, ridge, protrusion, hole, depression, cavity, cave*). The names of open containers (*jar, pot, box, tub, vat*) are often construed as designating the entire enclosed area, and not simply the physical object per se.[6] Nouns commonly designate parts of a larger whole that are not necessarily separated from the rest by any distinct objective boundary. Often, for example, there is no discontinuity of any kind between the *handle* of a baseball bat and its *barrel*. The body parts designated by *elbow, waist, shoulder*, and *side* are neither saliently nor sharply delimited. A boundary can be virtual in its entirety: the *middle* of a floor is typically not set off from the rest in any way, but though its extension is subject to highly variable interpretation, certainly it constitutes a bounded region. In the last analysis, then, something is a bounded region because a conceptualizer imposes a boundary in structuring a conceived situation, irrespective of how the requisite cognitive events are prompted. The perception of an objective line of demarcation greatly facilitates these events, but it is neither necessary nor sufficient for their occurrence.

By recognizing the importance of closure and virtual bounding, we can account for nouns designating collections of separate entities, for instance *swarm, archipelago*, and *forest*. The individual entities in the collection (bees, islands, or trees) are more or less contiguous, but nonetheless they are separated by appreciable gaps. Closure is responsible both for the association of peripheral members to form a largely virtual boundary delimiting the populated region from its surroundings, and also for the connection of internal members to provide a conception of continuity (even homogeneity) within the bounded area. Observe that the farther apart the bees, islands, or trees are (on a given scale, and in relation to other entities in the scope of predication), the more difficult it is to impose a virtual boundary and use the nouns in question to describe them. Space is therefore a primary domain for these nouns, and it is in this domain that their most salient bounding occurs. *Group, assembly*, and *collection* also incline towards a spatial construal, but they are more flexible in this regard, and specify their component members far more schematically, than *swarm, archipelago*, and *forest*.

Up to this point, the import of the term bounded region has been clear enough. Many illustrations have been spatial, and even for more-abstract examples it has been easy to conceive of the designated entity as a continuous region separated by a boundary from other portions of the domain. Matters become more difficult when we turn to nouns like *team*, or to more-abstract notions like *set* and *class*. At first they appear comparable to *archipelago, forest, group*, and *assembly* in that they designate an entity comprising an indeterminate number of component members that are not themselves separately profiled: the profiling is collective rather than individual. There is an important difference, however. The bounding in *archipelago* and the others pertains to space, where the nature of a boundary is fairly evident,

---

[6] This is so when we speak of the volume of a container; compare what is meant by the volume of a block of ice. The virtual boundary across the opening of a container also comes into play in determining whether something can be considered *in* it (see Herskovits 1982 and Vandeloise 1984 for sophisticated analysis).

even a virtual boundary imposed by closure. An *archipelago* or a spatially defined *group* also has some kind of shape determined by its peripheral members (though these predicates specify the shape of their designatum only in the most schematic terms). A *team, set,* or *class,* on the other hand, is apparently nonspatial in its bounding. We recognize a set of individuals as a *team* even if they are scattered all over a playing field and intermingled with members of the opposition; if relevant at all, spatial relations are less important than cooperative activity towards a common objective. Similarly, a *set* or *class* is defined by some kind of commonality regardless of where (and whether) its members are located in space. It is not obviously reasonable to speak of a boundary, and the concept of shape seems altogether inappropriate.

One might try to bridge the differences in profiling between *archipelago* and *team* by claiming that nouns like *team, set,* and *class* do indeed involve spatial (or quasi-spatial) bounding. In conceptualizing a team, for example, I tend to visualize them huddled together plotting strategy or posing for a team picture. Even for a class defined by an abstract property, e.g. the set of odd numbers, I can hardly avoid the image of the entities in question being extracted from a larger population of diverse objects and assembled into a compact spatial group whose peripheral members are linked by closure to form a virtual boundary (in the fashion of *archipelago*). Spatial metaphors and mental transformations of this kind are undeniably important to the semantics of the collective-noun class.

I doubt that spatial bounding tells the whole story, however. I have already suggested that abstract conceptions of motion, directionality, and distance are linguistically important, and are in fact presupposed by an explicit account of spatial metaphor. A semantic characterization of the collective-noun class requires comparably abstract definitions of bounding, and more fundamentally, of what constitutes a region. These definitions should accommodate regions in space and spatial bounding as prototypical instantiations, and yet be applicable to the full spectrum of abstract domains. We should not expect any direct analog of shape at this highly schematic level, inasmuch as shape is tied more closely to spatial domains.

REFERENCES

Casad, E. H., and R. W. Langacker (1985). '"Inside" and "outside" in Cora grammar'. *International Journal of American Linguistics* 51: 247–81.

Herskovits, A. H. (1982). 'Space and the prepositions in English: regularities and irregularities in a complex domain'. Ph.D. dissertation, Stanford University.

Hopper, P. J., and S. A. Thompson (1984). 'The discourse basis for lexical categories in universal grammar'. *Language* 60: 703–52.

Lyons, J. (1968). *Introduction to Theoretical Linguistics.* Cambridge: Cambridge University Press.

Vandeloise, C. (1984). 'Description of space in French'. Ph.D. dissertation, University of California, San Diego.

16

The Discourse Basis for Lexical Categories in Universal Grammar

PAUL J. HOPPER AND SANDRA A. THOMPSON

1. INTRODUCTION

The classification of the lexicon into categories or 'parts of speech' has been a concern of linguists since ancient times. This paper offers a new approach to the many problems raised when linguistic categories are considered from the aspect of universal grammar.

1.1. Categories

Over the centuries during which the Western grammatical tradition has evolved, the criteria for determining categories have shifted according to trends in linguistic thought as a whole. These criteria have included the following:

(a) MORPHOLOGICAL. This criterion takes the possibility of a form's combining with different types of inflectional morphemes as the basis for identifying categories.[1] A NOUN is thus defined as a form which is 'declined' according to case, number, and gender (case being primary, indeed to some extent synonymous with 'noun'); a VERB is a form which is 'conjugated' according to person, tense, and mood. This criterion clearly derives from a grammatical tradition within a classical Indo-European speech community; but in fact it extends remarkably well, as we shall see, to a wide range of non-IE languages.

(b) SEMANTIC. That the major categories are associated with fairly consistent semantic classes was recognized by the earliest grammarians. Thus Dionysius Thrax defined the noun (onoma) as 'a part of speech inflected for case, signifying a person or thing' (Robins 1979: 33). The difficulty of applying semantic or 'notional' criteria consistently has been a perennial problem; yet the broad correlation is so obvious that linguists have repeatedly returned to it in one form or another.

* Paul J. Hopper and Sandra A. Thompson, 'The discourse basis for lexical categories in Universal Grammar', *Language* (Journal of the Linguistic Society of America) 60 (1984): 703–52. © 1984 The Linguistic Society of America. Reprinted by permission.

Authors' note. We are grateful to several people whose comments have helped shape this study: Raimo Anttila, Joan Bybee, Wallace Chafe, Bernard Comrie, Jack Du Bois, John Haiman, Carol Lord, Francesca Merlan, Edith Moravcsik, Johanna Nichols, Michael Noonan, and Kenneth Whistler; and to Christian Matthiessen for help in preparing the manuscript. Authorship of this paper, as with all our joint work, is shared equally.

[1] However, Lyons (1966: 217) rejects the characterization 'morphological' for this approach.

(c) SYNTACTIC. Syntactic arguments for determining boundaries among word classes go back to earliest times; the distinction between 'subject' and 'predicate' was well known to the Hindu grammarians, and was equated by them with the noun/verb distinction (Lyons 1968: 19–20). Furthermore, the Greek term *rhêma* 'verb' appears originally to have referred to the predicate of the sentence (Robins 1979: 26–7), rather than to the (conjugated) verb. Purely syntactic arguments are also used by modern structural linguistics; thus, in the transformational/generative paradigm, the criteria for assigning forms to the major categories are linked to the usefulness of the classification to the formulation of rules:

> The way in which we have arrived at the particular decisions [about word classes]...is, in principle, irrelevant...What matters is whether one classification rather than another enables the grammarian to formulate a set of rules which will include the maximum number of acceptable sentences and the minimum number of unacceptable sentences among the total set of sentences which the grammar generates. (Lyons 1968: 151)

By this criterion, it is the abstract system of grammar which predetermines the membership of a form in its category: in essence, the system of syntactic rules 'defines' the categories. Hence 'ambiguous' forms do not exist, since potential ambiguities are automatically resolved by decisions about the postulated deep structures. Thus PARTICIPLES—which constitute a persistent problem in the drawing of category boundaries—are converted into underlying (finite?) verbs. The hybrid nature of participles, which have both structural and semantic features of Ns and Vs together, was noted by the ancient grammarians. But in a linguistic theory permitting deep structures, they are said to owe their N-like features to 'lower level' processes involving embedding and complementation. Such structuralist positions essentially declare that the semantic and grammatical congruences which exist in linguistic categories are beyond the domain of linguistics, and make no provision for them in formal grammar (see Lyons 1966, 1968: 317–33). Given the extraordinary significance of this possible link between language structure and cognition (cf. Brown 1958), it seems strange that discussion of it should be relegated to the periphery. We shall attempt here to restore the centrality of the phenomenon of categoriality by integrating the notional side of categories with their pragmatic function in language use.

1.2. History

During the development of linguistic thought, the number of basic categories postulated has varied, often in accordance with the practical requirements of a particular theory. Thus a theory whose needs were directed toward a single-language rhetoric could combine parts of speech (such as adjective and noun) which a more comprehensive theory would be forced to differentiate. The incorporation of a wider range of languages into the field of inquiry led eventually to a questioning by some researchers of the universality of any of the categories assumed by traditional grammar; the history of this question is discussed by Robins 1952, who concludes that the two nuclear categories N and V must be recognized as universal. Nearly three decades later, the question of the universality of the noun/verb distinction has been reopened, in the Amerindian languages of the Pacific Northwest: Jacobsen 1979 shows, we believe convincingly, that the distinction must be maintained, ultimately on grammatical grounds. (For a similar view, cf. Schachter 1983.) An argument along more general lines was made by Sapir (1921: 117–19), namely that ordinary discourse requires the differentiation of things talked about—which 'cluster about concrete concepts,' such as person or thing—from predications, which cluster about concepts of 'activity' (119).

1.3. Prototypes

That these functional and grammatical entities should have corresponding semantic properties has been an assumption held, as has been seen, since antiquity. The chief problem with positing such a correspondence as the basis of the distinction between categories is one of circularity. As Lyons notes (1968: 318), 'the only reason we have for saying that truth, beauty and electricity are "things" is that the words which refer to them in English are nouns.' A further problem is the lack of complete commensurability among languages in the assignment of percepts to grammatical categories. Although this lack is more obvious in less central categories such as adjective and preposition, the noun/verb distinction is not immune from it, especially as regards transitory or fluid phenomena. Thus Sapir (1911: 266) cites a Paiute verb with incorporated subject:

(1) pā   -γariɨ
     water   sitting

This corresponds conceptually to English 'lake.' But such forms are exceptional; in universal terms, we can predict that certain 'prototypical' percepts of thing-like entities will be coded in a grammatical form identifiable as N, while prototypical percepts of actions or events will be coded as grammatical Vs. In what follows, we accept this broad correlation as a starting point; but we refine it so as to show that the semantic congruence is actually rooted in predictable pragmatic (discourse) functions.

1.3.1. Semantics

We have pointed out that the major classes N and V have semantic correlates corresponding very approximately to perceived entities in the real world. For Ns, the entity is something like 'thing' or 'object'—or in a more general sense, a percept having what Givón (1979: 320–1) calls 'time-stability.' Vs, in contrast, are prototypically 'actions' or 'events'; they are used to symbolize percepts which lack time-stability. This perceptual duality is reflected in a universal TENDENCY to associate time-stable entities with the grammatical class of Ns, and non-time-stable entities with that of Vs. The correlation is so hard to apply in practice, however, that linguists striving for rigorous grammatical description have not usually resorted to it. Many Vs denote highly stable situations, e.g. 'to tower'; however, as has often been pointed out in the literature on categories, Ns may denote temporary situations ('fire,' 'fist') or entities which may not be perceived directly (abstractions such as 'justice').

The distinction made by Lyons (1977: 442–7) between different 'orders' of Ns goes some of the way toward resolving this inconsistency. Common, concrete Ns are 'first-order nouns'; they are readily re-identified, and can be referred to as individuals. 'Second- and third-order nouns' refer to states, events, and situations. This promising distinction is not pursued by Lyons in detail ('In what follows, the only nouns with which we shall be concerned are first-order nouns'; 447); however, he does point out the implicational relationship between first-order and second- or third-order Ns: no language which recognizes second- and third-order Ns will fail to recognize the first-order type. Thus a firm basis exists for considering first-order Ns as basic. This view agrees in general with Brown's observation (247–52) about the basicness of concrete Ns—and ultimately with our own view of prototypical categoriality. At the same time, Lyons' primarily semantic view of the basis for the distinction among the three orders seems to us mistaken. For this semantic basis, we would substitute the pragmatic basis of discourse function as the chief factor conditioning categoriality.

Especially damaging to the view that languages correlate the classes N and V with consistent semantic features has been the testimony of various students of Southeast Asian languages such as Javanese, or of Amerindian languages of the Pacific Northwest—purporting to show that, in some languages, semantic word classes have unrestricted morpho-syntactic behavior. The history of this debate is presented thoroughly by Jacobsen: in essence, it has been said that all major stems can occur freely with either nominal or verbal morphology, and that Ns themselves—even when 'topics'—must be analyzed as predicate forms. Jacobsen shows that, in the language group for which the most explicit arguments have been made (Nootkan), many stems in fact exist which are semantically Vs and which require NOMINALIZATION before they can be used in syntactic functions reserved for Ns. This nominalization process is not required for other stems, identifiable as basically Ns (Jacobsen, 103 ff.) Similarly, for Okanagan, another language from the same area, Hébert 1983 shows that a number of lexical categories can serve as predicates, but that only Ns can serve as arguments without further morphological modification.

The degree of freedom with which stems may be used with verbal and nominal morphology is, significantly, greatest in just those semantic areas which are obviously on the borderline between stable and unstable percepts, such as 'fire/burn.'

1.3.2. Acquisition

The tendency to associate a grammatical class conventionally called 'nouns' with physical 'things'—and a class called 'verbs' with visible, concrete 'actions'—is, as might be expected, very pronounced in young children acquiring speech. Brown shows (247–52) that the vocabulary of young children, when compared to that of mature adults, contains a considerably higher proportion of SUBORDINATE terms, i.e. concrete Ns and effective specific actions. Presented with new instances of such 'actions', children unhesitatingly assign them to the grammatical class of Vs; i.e., they use them as Vs in utterances. Likewise, new instances of concrete, tangible, contoured objects are almost invariably used as Ns. Later decisions as to the class membership of more ambiguous percepts are presumably made on conventional grounds; and it is well known that, even when the language learning process is complete, concepts remain whose category membership seems arbitrary; e.g. English has no V *to aggress.*

2. PROTOTYPICALITY IN GRAMMATICAL CATEGORIES

2.1. A property of human categorization

Since percepts which are thing-like and highly time-stable are almost certain to be classed as grammatical Ns, while percepts which involve participants in motion are almost certain to be classed as Vs, we might apply to the notion of categoriality the cognitive framework of PROTOTYPICALITY developed by Rosch and her associates (e.g. Rosch 1973, 1977a, b, 1978). This work presents the hypothesis that human categorization is not arbitrary, but proceeds from central to peripheral instances of categories. Central instances of a category are 'prototypical' for that category; and such instances appear to be more salient for speakers, according to a wide range of tests.

The notion of prototypicality is discussed by Lakoff 1977 in regard to both grammar (transitive sentences) and lexicon. Hopper and Thompson 1980 have shown that a crosslinguistic function of 'Transitivity' is of central importance in universal grammar, and at the same time is derived from the discourse salience of prototypically transitive clauses. Transitivity in this sense can be referred to as 'Cardinal Transitivity,' where the notion of cardinality is taken from the British school of phonetic theory. It is clear that the concept of prototypicality (the centrality vs. peripherality of instances which are assigned to the same category) plays an important role in the study of grammar. Theories of language which work with underlying, idealized structures necessarily ignore very real differences, both cross-linguistic and intra-linguistic, among the various degrees of centrality with which a single grammatical category may be instantiated. Even more important, perhaps, are the generalizations which can be made about the discourse functions assigned to central vs. peripheral instantiations of categories (as discussed in our 1980 paper), since these supply the possibility of a functional explanation for the discriminations made.

2.2. Function

The properties that prototypical Ns and Vs possess might be considered semantic, along the lines of the discussion above. In fact, Bates and MacWhinney (1982: 216) suggest that a prototypical V would then, perhaps, be one which denoted a concrete, kinetic, visible, effective ACTION—carried out by, and involving, participants. A prototypical N might be considered to be one which denoted a visible (tangible etc.) OBJECT. These semantic parameters would correspond to Brown's observations (247–9) about the primacy of such categories in child language acquisition, and to Rosch's assumption that prototypical instances of categories are acquired early. Furthermore, the easiest grammatical assignments to make of words to lexical categories are cross-linguistically of these kinds. Concrete, stable things are invariably assigned to the N class, and kinetic, effective actions to the V class.

However, although such semantic features are needed, they do not seem adequate for assigning a given form to its lexical class. Prototypicality in linguistic categories depends not only on independently verifiable semantic properties, but also—and perhaps more crucially—on linguistic function in the discourse. An apparently prototypical N like *fox* is not in fact prototypical in all instances of its use. It is this variability in N-like properties over discourse which suggests that any absolute, non-contextual division of the lexicon into 'noun stems' and 'verb stems' will have only a limited validity. Consider an utterance such as

(2) Foxes are cunning.

This contains an instance of the N stem *fox*, which has a syntactic function characteristic of Ns (topic), but falls short of denoting a concrete, perceptible entity in this use. A similar example is:

(3) We went fox-hunting in the Berkshires.

The prototype of the category is in fact achieved only when some individual fox is introduced as a participant in the discourse, as in:

(4) Early in the chase the hounds started up AN OLD RED FOX, and we hunted him all morning.

It seems that the semantic fact that the stem *fox* denotes a visible (etc.) entity is not the crucial one which makes *fox* a prototypical N; rather, the important fact is that IT MUST PLAY A CERTAIN ROLE IN THE DISCOURSE IN WHICH IT FIGURES. Whether this fact is designated to be a semantic or a 'pragmatic' one is a matter of terminology. We hope to present evidence here that the lexical semantic facts about Ns and Vs are secondary to their DISCOURSE ROLES; and that the semantic facts (perceptibility etc.) which are characteristic features of prototypical Ns and Vs are in fact derivative of (and perhaps even secondary to) their discourse roles. This morpho-syntactic evidence will show that the extent to which prototypical nounhood is achieved is a function of the degree to which the form in question serves to introduce a participant into the discourse.

The semantic features of prototypical Vs might similarly be considered to be visibility, movement (kinesis), and effectiveness, since these are the features which characterize the percepts assigned by children to the grammatical class of Vs, and are the ones which tend most universally to be so realized. But as with Ns, the semantic feature is not sufficient for pro-totypicality. To qualify as a prototypical V, a form must ASSERT THE OCCURRENCE OF AN EVENT OF THE DISCOURSE. Hence a V stem which has the appropriate semantic features for a prototypical V, e.g. *throw*, is less than prototypical in contexts like these:

(5) To throw a log that size takes a great deal of strength.

(6) We watched the log-throwing contest.

(7) The man throwing the log slipped and fell.

Prototypicality in a V is achieved only when an event of throwing is actually asserted:

(8) After the break, McTavish threw the log.

Again, the discourse role of the form seems to be the prime factor which conditions its appearance as a central vs. peripheral member of its category.

2.3. Contrast

A form which is prototypical of its category will tend to display all those characteristics which are representative of the category, and none which are representative of another. This means that prototypical instances of categories are maximally distinct from one another. This principle is discussed by Rosch (1978: 30):

To increase the distinctiveness and flexibility of categories, categories tend to become defined in terms of prototypes or prototypical instances that contain the attributes most representative of items inside and least representative of items outside the category.

This double characterization of prototypicality has important consequences for the theory of linguistic categoriality being developed here. It means that a prototypical N will be MAXIMALLY DISTINCT from a prototypical V.

Prototypical Ns, as we have seen, introduce a participant of the discourse. This definition will be refined and made more precise in §3, below. Prototypical Vs report an actual event of the discourse (again, this definition will be discussed in §4). We should therefore find that, in discourse environments where participants are introduced or events are reported, N and V will display the widest degree of morpho-syntactic contrast, i.e. the largest number of oppositions. Consider again clauses containing functionally prototypical instances of categories:

(9) Early in the chase the hounds started up an old red FOX, and we hunted him all morning.

(10) After the break, McTavish THREW the log.

Here a full range of attributes characteristic of Ns and Vs respectively will be manifested, either actually or potentially. In 9, *fox* may be singular or plural; it may take determiners, adjectives, and demonstratives; and it will be marked with an appropriate case morpheme if the language is a case-marking one. In 10, *threw* is free to appear in a variety of tenses, aspects, and modalities; and it will take agreement morphemes showing concord with subject or object, according to the language. But in discourse contexts which do not select prototypical instances of the categories, the possibility of contrast between Ns and Vs is greatly reduced:

(11) We went FOX-hunting in the Berkshires.

(12) To THROW a log that size takes a great deal of strength.

Thus, in 11, the form *fox* may not take N-like morphological trappings or modifiers; and in 12, the form *throw* cannot receive any verbal morphology. In general, these statements hold across languages. In non-prototypical environments, then, the CONTRAST between N and V tends to be neutralized (see Verhaar 1979 regarding grammatical and semantic neutralization).

In §2.2, we suggested that prototypicality in Ns and Vs is derivative of their respective discourse functions, and that semantic features such as kinesis (for Vs) and visibility (for Ns) should be viewed as secondary to these discourse functions. If prototypical Vs are 'kinetic' (i.e. involve movement and action), this is because of properties of prototypical events which Vs report, not because of intrinsic 'semantic' features of the Vs. Likewise, if prototypical Ns are in some sense thing-like, i.e. have properties such as tangibility and visibility, this is a fact about the nature of prototypical participants in a discourse, rather than a 'semantic' fact about a particular N. Categoriality, i.e. the property of being a prototypical instance of the grammatical category N or V, is thus imposed on linguistic forms by discourse. In discourse contexts where no participant is referred to or identified, or in which no discrete event is reported, the overt grammatical contrast between N and V is reduced or even canceled. Thus 11–12, show no overt morphological difference between the 'noun' *fox* and the 'verb' *throw*.

In contexts like these, no further grammatical specification of the two categories is possible: *fox* cannot pluralize or take modifiers or determiners, and *throw* may not show any trappings of tense, aspect, or person/number agreement. Although not all languages provide examples of such complete neutralization of categorical contrasts, we will demonstrate in this paper a very clear tendency across languages to correlate overt morpho-syntactic markings, characteristic of the categories N and V, with the degree to which the forms in question are performing their respective prototypical discourse functions.

In so demonstrating, we suggest a causal relationship at two levels. First, in an abstract sense, we align ourselves with much recent work (e.g. Givón 1979, 1981) which endeavors to show how morpho-syntactic phenomena can be explained in terms of general pragmatic principles of human communication. Thus, we are saying here that the linguistic categories V and N exist as functions of the need to report events and of the people and things involved in them. Second, on a more concrete level, we are also saying that the categories N and V in a given discourse in a given language will be identifiable AS THOSE CATEGORIES to the extent that they are performing their prototypical functions.

In emphasizing the relationship between categoriality and discourse function, we of course do not aim to deny idiosyncratic grammaticization and lexicalization. Our point is to call attention to the discourse basis for linguistic categories—partly as an antidote to the extreme form of structuralism which has so strongly influenced our field in recent decades, according to which discrete linguistic categories exist autonomously to be manipulated by language users.

In the two sections which follow, we will provide a wide range of cross-linguistic evidence for the categoriality hypothesis—first regarding Ns (§3), then Vs (§4).

3. NOUNS

From the discourse viewpoint, nouns function to introduce participants and 'props' and to deploy them. To the extent that a linguistic form is carrying out this prototypical function, it will be coded as N, and will manifest the full possible range of nominal trappings conventional in the language. Forms which fail in some way to refer to concrete, deployable entities will typically lack some of or all these trappings. In this section, we illustrate some of the recurrent phenomena associated in universal grammar with high vs. low categoriality of Ns.

Both Du Bois 1980 and Givón 1981 make the important point that the coding of participants in discourse depends very little, if at all, on the logic-based semantic notion of 'referentiality' as involving 'existence' in some 'world.' Rather, according to Du Bois, 'a noun phrase is REFERENTIAL when it is used to speak about an object as an object, with CONTINUOUS IDENTITY OVER TIME' (208, emphasis supplied). Further, Givón suggests that the coding of participants depends much more heavily on 'COMMUNICATIVE INTENT of the speaker uttering the discourse, specifically on whether a particular individual argument (NP) is going to be IMPORTANT enough in the SUBSEQUENT DISCOURSE, i.e. whether its SPECIFIC IDENTITY is important, or only its generic TYPE MEMBERSHIP' (85, emphasis in original).

We wish to show that it is precisely this factor which correlates with high vs. low categoriality for Ns. In presenting evidence for their claims, Du Bois and Givón use the term 'referential' for arguments whose referents have 'continuity of identity,' and are important in the subsequent discourse; 'non-referential' designates those which do not. Our data on the categoriality of arguments entirely support Du Bois and Givón; but we prefer the more mnemonic terms 'manipulable' and 'non-manipulable,' since the opposition 'referential/non-referential' has strong logical/semantic connotations for many linguists.

In the following sections we illustrate the low categorial status of NON-manipulable forms: the forms discussed in §3.1 also qualify as 'non-referential' in the semantic sense, but the non-manipulable forms discussed in §3.2 would be taken by most semanticists as 'referential.' In both cases, we will show that it is not semantic 'referentiality' that grammars signal, but rather manipulability in the discourse as perceived by the encoder.

3.1. Forms which do not refer

Perhaps the most widely represented and important type of decategorialization involves the loss of nominal trappings when a N is non-manipulable because it fails to refer to a concrete entity. In discourse, the combination of V plus non-referring object frequently functions to signal on-going, imperfective, or generic activities (Hopper and Thompson 1980: 256–8); in such activities, no specific entity, but instead the general or sortal class of such entities, is involved.

3.1.1. Incorporation of patient

In a number of languages, a non-referring N is bound to the stem of a V, forming a compound with the V as its head.[2] Often the N is truncated in some way, and it invariably loses the ability to take determiners and inflections. Steever (1979: 279) supports our claim that incorporated Ns are very low in categoriality with evidence that, in Tamil, they 'are not NPs at all'.

Fusion with the V stem may be manifested by such processes as vowel harmony (e.g. in Chukchee and Ponapean), and morphology showing that the verb/noun compound has formed a derived stem (Kosraean, Zuni, and Onondaga). Consider the following examples from Chukchee (Comrie 1973: 243–4):

(13) a. *Tumɣ-ə   nantəwat-ən kupre-n.*
      friends-ERG set-TRANS   net-ABS
      'The friends set the nets.'

   b. *Tumɣ-ət   kopra-ntəwat-ɣ'at.*
      friends-NOM net-set-INTR
      'The friends were setting nets.'

---

[2] For an extensive discussion of the semantic, pragmatic, and diachronic factors involved in noun incorporation cross-linguistically, cf. Mithun (1984).

Vowel harmony is shown by the change *u > o* in the Chukchee word for 'net,' whose high vowel must be lowered under the influence of the stem vowel of the V. Similarly in Ponapean (Sugita 1973: 401):

(14) a. *I pahn dok-o-mwomw.*
       I FUT spear-VWL-fish
       'I will spear fish.'
   b. *I pahn doakoa mwahmwa-o.*
       I FUT spear   fish-DET
       'I will spear the fish.'

Here the low vowels of the autonomous forms undergo a mutual change to *o* when incorporation takes place, and a linking vowel -*o*- joins the N root to the V. In both languages, the incorporated N has lost its determiners and case affixes.

The same point can be illustrated from the Micronesian language Kosraean (Lee 1975: 271):

(15) a. *El twem-lah   mitmit sahfiht sac.*
       he sharpen-ASP knife dull   ART
       'He sharpened the dull knife.'
   b. *El twetwe   mitmit-lac.*
       he sharpen.INTR knife-ASP
       'He has knife sharpened.'

In the last example, *mitmit* loses its determiner (*sac*) and is incorporated into the V, as is shown by its position in 15b—between the V and the perfective aspect marker *lah/lac*. Since the V meaning 'sharpen' has transitive (*twem*) and intransitive (*twetwe*) stems, the choice of the intransitive form in 15b shows with special clarity the fact that the incorporated N is no longer treated as autonomous participant.

Quite often, an incorporated N appears in a mutilated form—losing not only its determiners and inflections, but also part of its stem. Thus, in Zuni (Newman 1965: 73), some Ns have a 'short form':

(16)   *'i· –kih   'aš-ka.*
       RECIP-cerem.bro. make-PAST
       'They made each other ceremonial brothers.'

Incorporation is here accomplished by prefixation of the reciprocal morpheme to the noun–verb complex, and by the reduction of the N autonomous form of *kihe* 'ceremonial brother' to a truncated form. In the Iroquoian language Onondaga (Chafe 1970, Woodbury 1975), a parallel process of placing verbal affixes around the verb–noun complex is found. These examples are from Woodbury (p. 10):

(17) a. *wa'ha-hninu-'   ne'   o-ye'kw-a'.*
       TNS.he-buy-ASP   NOM   it-tobacco-NSFX
       'He bought the tobacco.'
   b. *wa'ha-ye'kw-a-hninu-'.*
       TNS.he-tobacco-VWL-buy-ASP
       'He bought tobacco.'

In this example, which is quite typical of all incorporation, *ye'kw* 'tobacco' loses its autonomous syntactic position in the clause, and drops the trappings characteristic of N categoriality: the nominal particle *ne'*, the nominal prefix *o*- (glossed as 'it'), and the nominal suffix -*a'*.

3.1.2. Incorporation of obliques

Oblique Ns which fail to refer show, in many languages, the same kinds of 'slippage' away from prototypical categoriality as do objects. The most common types are expressions of location/direction, e.g. Eng. *at school/to school*, and incorporated instrumentals, of which English expressions like *by train* form a restricted set. Often such obliques are formally indistinguishable from the usual type of object incorporation, as in Nahuatl (Sapir 1911: 260):

(18)   *ni-k-tle-watsa   in   nakatl.*
         I-OBJ-fire-roast DEF meat
         'I fire-roasted the meat.'

Here, besides being incorporated into the V stem, the full N form *tletl* 'fire' has been further reduced, i.e. de-categorialized, by truncation and vowel weakening. In English, the unspecified oblique—though it is not, strictly speaking, incorporated—is characteristically used of institutions and routinized activities; but when the N stands for a particular physical entity, it appears in its full prototypical form, i.e. with determiners and the possibility of modifiers:

(19)   a. We went to school early yesterday.
         b. We hid in the old abandoned school.

Body parts are especially susceptible of de-categorization in this generic locative/instrumental use. Parallels to Eng. *hand-carry* are numerous in other languages. In Mende, Ns which are linked or incorporated into another category undergo initial stem lenition; such lenition is found in unspecified instrumental forms involving body parts (Innes 1967: 45–7):

(20)   a. Autonomous form: *tokó* 'arm, hand'
         Mutated form: *lokó*
         mɛhê   mɛ́   a   loko 'to eat with the fingers'
         food   eat with hand
         b. Autonomous form: *kɔ́ɔ́* 'foot'
         Mutated form: *gɔ́ɔ́*
         lí   a   gɔ́ɔ́   má   wee 'to go on foot'
         go   by foot on   way

Similarly, in Zuni, an incorporated body part (like other incorporated Ns) loses its inflection for number, and shows no morphological indication of its instrumental function (Newman, 73):

(21)   *a·w-as   'a·w-allu-kka.*
         PL.ITR.SJ-hand PL.ITR.SJ-move.around(ITR)-PRET
         'They felt about with their hands.'

3.1.3. Noun compounding

The formation of compound Ns can be viewed as a process entirely parallel to the incorporation of an object N into a V stem (Sapir 1911: 255–6). Low categoriality is typically manifested through the loss of potential for case and number inflections, and sometimes through mutilation of the incorporated N root. In the Munda language Sora (Starosta 1979), many Ns have special compounding forms analogous to the reduced forms noted above in Zuni incorporation:

(22)   a. *bɔŋtɛl*   'buffalo'
         b. *ə-jɛlu-bɔŋ-ən* 'buffalo meat'
            VWL-meat-buffalo-DEF

In Southern Ute (Givón 1980b), a compounded N may not receive what in many Uto-Aztecan languages is referred to as the 'absolute' suffix *-ci*, whose function may in fact be regarded as a simple indicator of categoriality; thus:

(23) a. *nuu-ci*   'Ute person'
      Ute.person-ABS
   b. *nuu-gani* 'teepee'
      Ute.person-house

Just as with incorporation into Vs, the compounded N in such examples is non-referring; it can play no further discourse role unless it is re-introduced with full categorial status. It is insulated from reference to syntactic processes or anaphoric rules (cf. Mardirussian 1975).

One general strategy for embedding a N into a phrase is to convert it into an adjective. Typically, Ns which have been thus embedded into adjectival formatives show the usual symptoms of de-categorialization; e.g., they are insulated from pluralization, show no overt markers of case and gender, and may not themselves be modified by means of adjectives, demonstratives, or articles. Semantically, such adjectives usually refer only to the domain of the N, not to a specific referent. Thus the Eng. adjective *child-like* (and equivalent formations in other languages) can refer only to features characteristic of children in general—never to specific features of a particular child who is spoken of. Even when an adjective is formed from an individual name, that adjective (in English, at least, and in some other languages also) rarely denotes a characteristic of the individual alone, but instead refers to a characteristic transferred from that individual to others—or one recognized as having its source in that individual, but not being confined to her/him:

(24) a. the Chomskyan paradigm
   b. a Caesarian operation
   c. Cartesian linguistics

This 'de-individuation' is of course typical of de-categorialized Ns: it means that the embedded N is not manipulable as such in the discourse, and cannot be introduced into the discourse through this mention alone; nor can it be subsequently referred to anaphorically, unless it is first presented in its full form.

The point is nicely illustrated by Turkish, where a distinction is found between a genitive and a bare nominal-stem qualifier (Underhill 1976: 94):

(25) a. *çocuğ-un*   *kitab-ı*
      child-GEN   book-3sg.POSS
      'the child's book' (= book of some specific child)
   b. *çocuk*   *kitab-ı*
      child   book-3sg.POSS
      'a children's book'

As predicted by our hypothesis, the individuated possessor in 25a, to which subsequent mention can be made, has the genitive suffix; but the bare nominal in 25b refers to no discourse entity, but simply characterizes the type of book question.

It must also be pointed out that some languages (French etc.) differ from English in this respect; they freely allow modifiers to be formed from proper names and used as adjectives which are equivalent to a 'genitive case.' This is true in many IE languages (e.g. Slavic and Baltic). Thus in Czech, parallel to the genitive form *knihy* of *kniha* 'book,' we find the possessive adjective *Vlastin* 'Vlasta's' (Heim 1976: 163). Yet the morphological generalization stated above is widespread if not universal: Ns thus embedded show loss of otherwise typical morphological contrasts. The constraint against discourse manipulability of such N stems is also probably universal.

To a greater or lesser extent, the embedded N stem in such denominal adjectives may undergo the kind of 'mutilation' which we have described for incorporated Ns. It is not uncommon in English for the derived adjective stem to be suppletive to the corresponding N:

(26) a. brother: fraternal
     b. king: royal, regal

(For full discussion and many further examples, cf. Levi 1978.) Where the stem of the adjective is not suppletive, there is frequent phonological bonding (univerbation) which causes the stem to be more distant from the corresponding full N:

(27) a. angel: angelic [énjəl]: [ænjélɪk]
     b. Caesar: Caesarian [sízər]: [sɪzériən]

Or, in French

(28) a. *mer* 'sea': *marin* 'marine'
     b. *Descartes*: *cartésien*

This bonding again recalls the phenomenon of vowel harmony, and similar processes found when Ns are incorporated into other stems.

3.1.4. Predicate nominals

Nominals which are the predicates of Vs of being, or which complement transitive Vs in what might be called 'essive' or predicate nominal use—naming a class to which an entity belongs—often lose some of or all their categoriality. Such loss again correlates with an absence of intention to refer to an extant entity; the thing named is not used as a participant or prop in the discourse. In other words, there are no discourse contexts in which such a predicate nominal serves to introduce a participant into the discourse for further deployability. The predicate or essive nominal is typically lacking in the range of morphological oppositions available to Ns; but it may acquire those oppositions to the degree that it has discourse salience, and can be referred to and deployed in the discourse. Thus, in Mandarin, predicate nominals usually lack the classifiers associated with indefinite Ns:

(29)   *tā   shi gànbù*   'S/he is a cadre.'
        3sg. be cadre

The above might be said as a simple answer to the question 'What is s/he?' However, the classifier is used if the predicate nominal is continued in the discourse:

(30)   *tā   shi yī-ge   gànbù.*
        3sg. be one-CLF cadre

This can be translated as 'S/he is one of those cadres'; it suggests some further discussion of the role of cadres, e.g. an observation that s/he is expected to work harder or have different attitudes than others. In Japanese, predicate nominals lack case particles such as *wa*, *ga*, *o*:

(31)   *tai   wa   sakana da.*
        snapper TOP   fish   be

Such absence of determiners and cases is especially common when occupations are being attributed, as in French (32) and Indonesian (33):

(32)   *Il est professeur*   'He is a teacher.'

(33)   *Warjo tukang-besi*   'Warjo is a metal-worker.'
        W.   worker-metal

Essive complements are similar to predicate nominals, in that they generally name a class or sort of thing in apposition to the specific entity involved. In Malay texts, the complement is introduced in its bare form, without a complementizer meaning 'as,' and without determiners or classifiers:

(34)   *Di-beri-nya   hadiah kapada Tuan Farquhar.*
        PASS-give-he gift   to   Mr. F.
        'He gave [it] to Mr. Farquhar as a present.'

The pattern shown by examples like these is quite consistent: it is the thing given, not the fact of its being a gift, which is salient in the discourse; and it is the thing alone which will be talked about, manipulated, and referred to. The word *hadiah* in 34, then, mentions a quality or attribute, but does not introduce an entity; nor does it refer anaphorically to an entity of the discourse. It neither looks nor behaves like a prototypical N.

In Mokilese and Hungarian (optionally), and in French (obligatorily), predicate Ns occur without determiners:

(35)   Mokilese (Harrison 1976:74)
        Johnpadahkk-o doaktoa   'The teacher is a doctor.'
        teacher-DEF   doctor

(36)   Hungarian (Károly 1972:86)
        A   báty-ám   katona   'My brother is a soldier.'
        DEF brother-my soldier

(37)   French
        a. *Jean est   (*un) étudiant*   'John is a student.'
           John is   a.MASC student.MASC
        b. *Jeanne est   (*une) étudiante*   'Jeanne is a student.'
           Jeanne is   a.FEM student.FEM

Occasionally, the predicate nominal may appear as a V. This strategy may be seen from a morphological viewpoint as an incorporation of the nominal root into the verbal affix; like the well-known incorporation of N into V, discussed above, the 'verbalization' of the nominal predicate results in a de-categorialized form of the N, in which any reference to a specific, discourse-manipulable entity is excluded. An example of the construction is found in Bella Coola (Heather Hardy, p.c.):

(38)   *staltmx-aw*   *wa-ʔimlk*   'The man is a chief.'
        chief-3pl.INTR   PROX-man

3.1.5. Nominals in the scope of negation

Givón points out (1977, 1979: 93–103) that under the scope of negation, the opposition 'referential/non-referential' in non-anaphoric nouns is neutralized. Non-definite Ns in the scope of negation, of course, cannot refer to concrete entities, and can therefore be expected to show a corresponding lower degree of categoriality. In the Bantu language Bemba, a vowel prefix signaling 'referentiality' appears before the N class marker; as the following sentences illustrate, this 'referential' marker is lost in negative sentences when the N is in the scope of the negation:

(39) a. *u-mu-ana   a-a-somene   i-ci-tabo.*
        REF-CLF-child   SUBJ-PAST-read   REF-CLF-book
        'The child read the book.'

b. *u-mu-ana   t-a-a-somene   ci-tabo.*
REF-CLF-child NEG-SUBJ-PAST-read CLF-book
'The child didn't read any book.'

Entirely analogous facts are citable in other languages:

(40)   Modern Hebrew (Givón 1977:304)
        lo   kaniti   sefer (*-exad)   'I didn't buy a book.'
        NEG bought.I book one/a

(41)   Mandarin
        wǒ méi mǎi (*yī-běn) shū   'I didn't buy any book.'
        I   NEG buy one-CLF book

(42)   Hungarian (Givón 1979:98)
        Jancsi nem olvasott (*egy) könyvet
        John   NEG read   a   book   'John didn't read any books.'

3.2. Non-discourse-manipulable forms

So far, we have considered instances of Ns which do not refer to specific entities in the discourse, and which fail to manifest the trappings of nounhood. Now we will look at Ns which do refer to actual discourse entities, but whose referents are not important for the subsequent discourse. We will see that they show just the same types of neutralizations and lack of nominal oppositions as those which do not refer at all.

3.2.1. Anaphora

In §3.1, we discussed data indicating that Ns which do not refer show a lower degree of categoriality. Inability to refer implies an absence of SALIENCE in the discourse. Yet we have seen that the simple dichotomy 'referential/non-referential,' as usually discussed by philosophers and linguists, does not correspond well to the distinction generally found in the world's languages between 'manipulable' and 'non-manipulable.' Quite often an entity which has ostensive existence, in a strict sense, is treated grammatically as if it did not. The criterion which seems to be of the greatest LINGUISTIC significance is that of salience. Forms which are presented as playing a role in the discourse—which are manipulable or 'deployable' there—are universally able to adopt the full range of grammatical attributes of Ns: determiners, case, number, and gender affixes, as well as classifiers, modifiers, and morphemes signaling nounhood (such as the Uto-Aztecan absolute suffixes; cf. ex. 23). These Ns stand for autonomous, usually quite concrete and individuated entities; they can act as participants and props in the discourse, and can be referred to indirectly through anaphoric processes. A N which falls short of fulfilling this pragmatic function is often, as we have shown, 'less of' a N in the range of morphological oppositions which it can manifest, or in the degree of recognition which it receives in the overall morpho-syntax of its clause.

Let us consider a problem in Hungarian which illustrates our point. Bese et al. (1970) discuss such sentences as these:

(43) a. *A   fiú   újságot olvas.*
        DEF boy paper   read.SUBJ.CONJ
        'The boy is reading a newspaper.'
     b. *A   fiú   olvassa   az   újságot.*
        DEF boy read.OBJ.CONJ DEF paper
        'The boy is reading the newspaper.'

TABLE I

	Individuated		Non-Individuated
	Definite	Indefinite	
SVO order	+	+	−
Objective conj.	+	−	−

Transitive Vs in Hungarian are regarded as having 'subjective' and 'objective' conjugations. With 3rd person participants, this means that the V either contains (objective) or does not contain (subjective) a suffix referring to its object. In 43a, *olvas* is subjective; in 43b, *olvassa* is objective. In sentences like 43a, the number of the object—singular or plural—is irrelevant. In other words, *újságot* is categorial in the prototypical sense only in 43b, and it is here also that the N has a discourse role. But there is also a third type with an indefinite object:

(43) c. *A   fiú   olvas   egy   újságot.*
   DEF boy   read.SUBJ.CONJ   a   paper
   'The boy is reading a newspaper.'

Here the V is subjective, because the N is non-anaphoric (i.e. not recoverable from the discourse); but *újságot* still has a discourse role. It is individuated ('individual,' p. 118) but indefinite, i.e. without prior mention or inference. A threefold division is thus possible, as shown in Table 1.

The tendency to SVO word order—with the object N in an autonomous, non-incorporated slot—correlates with the presence of an article (definite or indefinite) and with the pragmatic function of discourse role. Conversely, the tendency to SOV word order—with the object N in the 'incorporated' position—correlates with the absence of an article (i.e. low categoriality) and with failure to relate the entity mentioned to the discourse (see also Hetzron 1971: 89–90).

At first sight, it might seem as if the distinction of zero, *az*, and *egy* could be accounted for in terms of semantic 'referentiality' at the sentence level; but the comment of Bese et al. about 43a–b strongly suggests that discourse factors are at work: in 43a, they claim, 'the object may be irrelevant for the communication' (118), and 'the reference to the context or to the communicative situation is irrelevant' (116). That the true criterion underlying the assignment of articles (i.e. conducive to high categoriality) is actually salience or PROMINENCE in the discourse is strongly suggested by some facts about the relationship of nominal morphology and discourse in other languages.

Givón 1981 discusses examples from Modern Hebrew and Bemba. Consider the following Hebrew data (p. 86):

(44) a. *az axarey   ha-avoda halaxti   la-sifriya   ve-yashavti   sham   ve-karati*
   so after   DEF-work went-1st to.the-library and-sat.1st there   and-read.1st
   sefer-exad ve-ze   haya sefer   metsuyan.
   book-one and-it was book   excellent
   'So after work I went to the library, and I sat there and read a book, and it was an excellent book.'

Here the phrase *sefer-exad* 'a book' refers to a specific book, and it figures in the discourse as a salient participant. This prominence is signaled by the appearance of the article *exad* 'one, a'. But in the following passage, *sefer* 'book' has no such role:

(44) b. *az axarey ha-avoda halaxti   la-sifriya   ve-lo   hay li   ma   la-asot,*
      so after   DEF-work went.1st to.the-library and-NEG was to.me what to-do
      az karati   sefer, ve-karati   shney itonim, ve-axar-kax   halaxti   ha-bayta.
      so read.1st book and-read.1st two   papers and-after-that went.1st to-home
      'So after work I went to the library and I had nothing to do, so I read a book
      and a couple of newspapers, and then went home.'

Although in 44b, *sefer* is, in the semantic sense, just as 'referential' as in 44a, it is PRESENTED as non-referential because it has no relevance to the discourse. It is, in Givón's terms, 'pragmatically non-referential.'

The same phenomenon occurs in Bemba: here 'non-referential' Ns, e.g. those in the scope of negation (cf. 39 above), lack the vowel prefix which characterizes 'referential' Ns. But this prefix is also lacking with Ns which are perfectly 'referential' PROVIDED that they lack relevance to the discourse, as in the following examples cited in full from Givón (1981: 87–8):

(45) a. *n-a-soma   ici-tabo.*
        I-PAST-read   REF-book
        'I read {a/the} book (and its identity mattered).'
     b. *n-a-soma   ci-tabo.*
        I-PAST-read   NREF-book
        'I did some book-reading (any old book would have done).'

What is clear is that the strictly logical criterion of 'referentiality' is immaterial to the choice of *i-* vs. Ø; instead, the principle around which many languages organize the marking of Ns is some notion of salience, prominence, or relevance in the discourse. In fact, we hypothesize that many of the instances in which grammars supposedly contain a special marker for 'definite' or 'referential' Ns actually involve this principle of 'pragmatic' or 'discourse' referentiality. For example, further discourse-based study may show that the well-known distinction in Spanish between non-referring objects with and without articles, which is so difficult to characterize semantically (but see Pease-Gorrissen 1980 for an informative discussion), is also characterizable in terms of discourse manipulability:

(46) a. *María siempre alimenta gaviotas*   } 'Mary always feeds seagulls.'
     b. *María siempre alimenta a las gaviotas* }

That is, 46a would be predicted to occur in discourse contexts in which *María* is being characterized (she is a seagull-feeder), and the *gaviotas* are not introduced as manipulable participants; but the discourse in which 46b would be expected would be one in which the *gaviotas* do figure as manipulable.

In Persian, to take another example, indefinite Ns receive the marker *ye* just in case they play a discourse role. The following examples, from G. Mardirussian (p.c.), illustrate this:

(47) a. *mixam   beræm birun, ye   sib   bexæræm o   beræm xune.*
        want.1st go.1st out   one apple buy.1st   and go.1st home
        'I want to go out, buy an apple, and go home.'
     b. *mixam   beræm birun, sib   bexæræm, ruzname bexæræm o   beræm xune.*
        want.1st go.1st out   apple buy.1st   paper   buy.1st   and go.1st home
        'I want to go out, buy an apple, buy a newspaper, and go home.'

Here 47a could be appropriately continued with some clause such as ...*boxoræm-eš* '...and eat it'—i.e. a clause in which the apple is a participant; in 47b, such a continuation would not be possible. It should be borne in mind, as with the Hebrew and Hungarian cases, that the discourse-manipulable N carries the nominal trappings which show it to be high in categorial status.

A somewhat more 'exotic' distribution of pragmatic/categorial morphemes is found in the West African language Bade (Chadic) in which three categorial levels in Ns can be distinguished (Schuh 1977: 113–16):

(a) Level 1 is characterized by so-called NUNATION: a suffix in -*n*, preceded by a stem-forming vowel, represents a residual gender distinction.
(b) Level 2 is that in which the N receives a nominal determining suffix in -*w*.
(c) Level 3 apparently consists of the simple stem form of the N.

These three levels are arranged in decreasing order of categoriality: Level 1 has both gender and a determiner-like suffix, Level 2 has only the determining suffix, and Level 3 only the bare stem of the N. The functional correlates of these levels are as follows:

Level 1, the highest in categoriality, functions to INTRODUCE NEW PARTICIPANTS into the discourse. An (unglossed) example of this is given by Schuh (1977: 129):

(48) ... *aci dauktiitu amangwan.*
               co-wife-NUN
'... he got her [his wife] a co-wife.'

Level 2, which is of intermediate categoriality, involves the 'prior reference marker.' This is a simple suffix -*w*, without the residual gender classification present in Level 1 forms. It functions to mark a N whose existence can be inferred from a context. It is thus an autonomous and individuated form, but is non-presentative; i.e., it is definite, but not necessarily anaphoric. However, it appears to compete in discourse with the Level 3 'definite' form.

Level 3, the lowest in morphological trappings characteristic of Ns in Bade, is called by Schuh the 'definite' form. It functions primarily to resume anaphorically a N which has received prior mention. Schuh cites the following as an example of the typical discourse use of the prior reference marker vs. the definite forms:

(49) *Kəntapo da ne ii ren* MIINA-*w da dari nama*, '*Mas! Mas! Mas!*' *No, daaci,*
    MIINI *da tli* ...
'Kentapo went to (the place of) the lion [PRM] and said, "Shoo! Shoo! Shoo!"
Well, then the lion [DEF] got up ...'

The distinction is evidently a subtle one. It seems that some notion of discourse salience would account for the occurrence of the three levels in many instances: the more autonomous the entity symbolized by the N, with respect to the discourse context, the more highly categorial it is in terms of its morphology. The most highly categorial is the form which refers immediately to an entity, by presenting it as a new participant in the discourse. In this context, the N is highest in manipulability, and its referent has the most autonomy. Next in degree of categoriality is the N standing for an entity which is known (i.e. definite) but has not necessarily been mentioned before. The lowest degree of categoriality is associated with anaphoric reference: reference is not to the entity itself, but to a preceding mention of it. (Further discussion of these points from the related language Hausa can be found in Jaggar 1983.)

Facts such as these strongly support our claim that the more a form serves to introduce a manipulable entity into the discourse, the more highly marked it needs to be. Once it has been introduced, it is no longer manipulable, and it may appear with much less linguistic marking.

In fact, information which refers either anaphorically to an item previously mentioned in the discourse, or to an object presupposed to be known, is often encoded in a form suggestive of low categoriality. Such Ns compete with pronouns, zero, and simple verbal 'agreement' morphemes; they are low in discourse prominence and autonomy. In that they have discourse reference, however, they may be higher in categoriality than Ns coded as non-manipulable. Several strategies for depriving 'old information' Ns of categoriality may be distinguished. A universal one is PRONOMINALIZATION, which can be viewed as the loss of semantic specificity, with retention of general discourse/grammatical information such as case, gender, number and deixis. A more extreme stage occurs when the pronoun is elided and an index is retained in the V; this morpheme may reflect subject, object, or indirect object Ns. Thus, in Hungarian (50) and Swahili (51), the objective conjugation of the V, without an explicit nominal object, may be used alone when the pronominal object is absent:

(50) *Peter olvassa*   'Peter reads it.'
     P.   read.OBJ.CONJ

(51) *a-li-m-piga*   'He beat him.'
     3sg.-PAST-3sg.OBJ-beat

Finally, the most extreme form of de-categorialization is ellipsis with no overt recoverability. Conventions may exist for recovering the reference of the elided element, but this is not necessarily so; recovery may instead be left to the purely pragmatic inference of the listener, as in Mandarin:

(52) *bu   xīhuan*   '(I) don't like (it).'
     NEG like

Ns which refer to known information occupy an intermediate position between (a) prototypically N-like forms referring to items being presented for the first time in a discourse, and (b) forms which are non-referring, and which stand for a class or sort of item rather than a specific instance. In terms of the categoriality hypothesis, then, known-information Ns may be classed with 'new' Ns, and be permitted the full range of nominal trappings; or they may constitute a class of 'definite' Ns, showing some restrictions in morphological oppositions (as in Bade, above); or they may take on the morphology of generic, non-specific Ns as in examples to be discussed below. Furthermore, in all languages, the semantic content of an anaphoric N may be lost (pronominalization), with only its discourse/grammatical residue retained. Schematically:

High Categoriality:	'Presentative' forms.
Intermediate Categoriality:	Anaphoric/Contextually-established forms.
Low Categoriality:	Pro-forms, Generic/Non-referring forms;
	Agreement morphemes;
	Zero anaphora.

The very lack of homogeneity of the 'low categoriality' class suggests that this is the 'unmarked' one. If so, it provides support for our contention that ZERO categoriality is in fact the MOST unmarked state for a form; categories like N and V emerge as distinct, then, only as required by the demands of discourse. We return to this point below.

We have been discussing the loss of categoriality in pronouns, agreement affixes, and zero anaphora. Anaphoric Ns in some languages retain the semantic stem, and undergo incorporation in exactly the same way as the 'sortal' predicates more often associated with incorporation phenomena; thus, in Nahuatl, the first-mention (presentative) form of the

N is an autonomous one, supported by the usual cross-referencing morphology (Merlan 1976: 85):

(53) *Ika tlaʔke ki-teteʔki panci.*
      with what it-cut.3sg. bread
      'What did he cut the bread with?'

A subsequent (anaphoric) mention of the same N is incorporated, as in the answer to the above:

(54) *Neʔ panci-teteʔki ika kočillo.*
      he bread-cut.3sg. with knife
      'He cut it with a knife.'

That this is no isolated phenomenon is shown in a discussion of incorporation in Paleo-Siberian languages by Ard 1979. Basing his analysis on Žukova 1954, Ard shows that, in Koryak, incorporated elements are anaphoric to elements presented earlier in the discourse. He recognizes the following three typical functions of incorporation:

(i)   The semantic feature 'sortal', i.e. a kind or sort of, accompanies the incorporated N (cf. Woodbury).
(ii) Incorporated elements are often typical or habitual objects (Sapir 1911).
(iii) Incorporated elements in some languages are anaphoric (cf. Merlan, Žukova).

Ard (16) notes that

The three functions of incorporation are different, but each is an elaboration of the basic aspect of the discourse function of incorporation—the incorporated element must be low in information value and emphasis.

Finally, anaphoric Ns in languages with classifier systems sometimes lack a classifier when the N is used anaphorically. In Malay narrative, a favorite use of the classifier is to introduce a new participant (presentative function):

(55) *Make ada-lah*   *ia   menaroh sa-orang perempuan China   makan*
     now happened-NARR   she employ one-CLF woman   Chinese eat
     gaji   menjahit pakaian-nya dan pakaian anak-anak-nya. Maka ka-pada
     wage sew   clothes-her and clothes children-her   and on
     suatu hari datang-lah   perempuan China   itu   ka-pada isteri Tuan Milne . . .
     one day came-NARR woman   Chinese that to   wife Mr. M.
     'Now it happened that she hired a [CLF] Chinese woman, paying her a wage to
     sew her clothes and her children's clothes. And one day this [NO CLF] Chinese
     woman came to Mrs. Milne . . .'   (Abdullah 1932: 106)

The 'new' (presentative) N is preceded by a classifier: *sa-orang perempuan China*; but the anaphoric N, marked with the 'previous mention' article *itu* 'that,' has no classifier. A similar phenomenon is found in the Australian language Kunjen (Sommer 1972: 79):

(56) *in   pigipig anbamand ewal ay, pigipig udal   arinimay.*
     CLF pig   bank.on saw Isg. pig   dog.AGT killed
     'I saw a pig on the bank, (one) which the dogs had killed.'

Here again, the 'new' N has a classifier; the 'old,' anaphoric N does not. Such anaphoric Ns without classifiers often translate into English with pronouns.

3.2.2. Body parts

Many languages present evidence for reduced categoriality when a N refers to an 'attached' body part. Typically, the attached part is treated as inalienably possessed, while a detached part is treated as alienably possessed, as in Aroma (Melanesian, cf. Lynch 1973: 78):

(57) a. *gage-ku*   'my leg (i.e. part of my body)'
        leg-my
     b. *ga-ku   gage*   'my leg (i.e. of chicken, pork) to eat'
        POSS-my   leg

The morphology of Ns referring to attached body parts points to reduced categoriality in a number of different ways. It is quite common for the body part to be incorporated into the verb, as in Tuscarora (Williams 1976: 216):

(58)   *waʔ-k-h-e-kvhs-ohare:-ʔ.*
        AOR-ISg.-OBJ-HUM-face-wash-PUNCT
        'I washed his face.'

It is also often the case that the body part is deprived of certain modifiers, e.g. possessive adjectives, demonstratives, and descriptive adjectives. In French (59), German (60), and some related languages, only the definite article normally occurs with body parts:

(59)   *Il   s'est   blessé la   main*   'He has injured his hand.'
        he himself.has wounded the hand

(60)   *Er hat sich   die Hand verletzt.*
        he has himself the hand injured

Possessive forms such as Fr. *sa* 'his' or Ger. *seine* would be out of place here. In Kosraean, body parts are normally incorporated into a possessor pronoun; when so incorporated, they may not take classifiers, determiners, or articles (cf. Lee, 62):

(61)   Citation form: *ne*   'leg'
        Incorporated forms: *niyacl* 'his leg'
                            niyom   'your leg'
                            niyuhk 'my leg'

When the body-part N is modified by an adjective, it may appear either in an 'impersonal' possessed form, as in 62a, or in its citation form with a classifier, as in 62b (Lee, 239):

(62) a. *niyac   unacnac kacl   Sepe ah   kihneta.*
        leg.IMPRS hairy   of.him S.   DET be.hurt
        'Sepe's hairy leg is hurt.'
     b. *lwac ne unacnac kacl   ah   kihneta.*
        CLF leg hairy   of.him DET be.hurt
        'His hairy leg is hurt.'

Lee's discussion of the difference between the citation form 62b and the impersonal form 62a suggests that no semantic distinction is perceivable. Yet one of the examples cited seems to indicate that the type of 62b is more appropriate for individuated body parts, viewed as distinct from their owners:

(63) a. *sifac   luhlahp kacl   Sohn arlac fiyacyac.*
        head.IMPRS big   of.him John very grey
        'John's big head is very grey-haired.'

b. *lwac sucf   lacyot kacl   Sohn arlac fiyacyac.*
   CLF head.CIT right of.him John very grey
   'The right side of John's head is grey-haired.'

In 63a, the head is individuated; but the statement still is interpreted as about John, rather than about his head. However, 63b is decidedly an assertion about a *head*, more exactly about the right side of a head. Whereas 63a can be paraphrased in English as something like 'John is grey-headed,' 63b can only be paraphrased with 'head' or 'side of head' as topic. Discourse salience and greater autonomy (individuation) again are correlated with higher categoriality: the N referring to the 'separated' body part is equipped with a wider array of the trappings characteristic of Ns, and is permitted to stand in its independent form.

A frequent strategy for depriving an attached body part of categorial status is to promote the owner to one of the major grammatical arguments of the clause (subject, object, or indirect object; see Fox 1981). In French, German, and some other languages, as mentioned above, the possessed part is thereby stripped of a possessive pronoun; it is thus viewed semantically as unpossessed, and without autonomous reference other than in relation to its possessor. In the Bantu language Haya, when a body part is affected, the grammatical trappings associated with affectedness refer exclusively to the possessor, not to the part itself (Hyman and Duranti 1982: 219, 222):

(64) a. *a-ka-hénd'   ómwáán' ómukôno.*
        3sg.-PAST-break child   arm
        'S/he broke the child's arm.'
    b. *n-ka-mu-hénd'   ómukôno.*
        1sg.- PAST -him-break arm
        'I broke his arm.'

Only the word for 'child' in 64a can be anaphorically indexed in the V, as in 64b. Furthermore, in 64a the word for 'child', and not the word for 'arm,' occupies the object slot; the order of the two Ns may not be reversed. In this case, although no special morphemes show a difference in categoriality between *ómwáán* and *ómukôno*, the absence of syntactic role for 'arm'—and, in particular, its failure to be recognized as a sentence participant by the V affixes—point to low categoriality.

The syntax of body-part Ns follows directly from their special discourse role. Note once again that the body part, which is low in categoriality, is, from a semantic point of view, just as 'referential' as its owner; to the extent that owner is claimed to 'exist,' so does the part. The explanation for the morpho-syntactic facts just presented lies, instead, in the fact that IN THE DISCOURSE body parts are not in general autonomous, discourse-salient entities. Since they are physically undifferentiated from their 'possessors,' body parts are treated in grammar and discourse as dependent, non-individuated entities. Typically they are not participants in the discourse as distinct from their 'owners.' As has been shown, the typical discourse role is reflected in a lower degree of categoriality; where a salient, individuated discourse role for body parts is nonetheless called for, the nominal trappings characteristic of a higher degree of categoriality tend to appear.

4. VERBS

We turn now to an examination of some of the data which suggest that Vs which do not report discourse events fail to show the range of oppositions characteristic of those which do. We will see that the functions which these non-prototypical Vs serve determine to a large extent the forms in which they occur.

A discourse event can be seen as an answer to the question 'What happened?' The examples below all demonstrate that when a V cannot be taken as answering this question, in the context where it occurs, it will tend not to manifest the morpho-syntactic trappings of prototypical Vs in that language.

4.1. Stativity

Stative Vs report not events, but states; they do not answer the question 'What happened?' We would predict, therefore, that the more stative the inherent meaning of a lexical item, the less likely it is to show the maximum number of oppositions associated with prototypical action Vs. Thus, in most languages which have stative Vs with meanings like 'know,' 'be aware,' 'love,' etc., certain aspectual distinctions are neutralized, particularly those opposing 'durative' and 'non-durative.'

4.1.1. Predicate adjectives

Many languages, of course, provide us with the best possible support for the above generalization: lexical items with property-naming stative meanings are not Vs at all, but belong to a class of 'adjectives.' In English, for example, adjectives show NONE of the oppositions found on prototypical Vs: they are not marked for subject number, nor do they occur with tense/aspect or modal morphology. Instead, they must occur with a lexically empty copula whose only function is to carry these oppositions.

Even in languages which mark some oppositions on predicate adjectives, these tend to be a highly reduced set as compared to the TIME-RELATED oppositions shown on prototypical Vs. In Chukchee,[3] for example, both Vs and adjectives show person 'agreement' with a 'central' participant, but adjectives do not show the range of tense/aspect oppositions typically found on Vs. Exx. 65a–d illustrate verbal sentences, while 65e–f are adjectival examples:

(65) a. ɣəm   tə-kətɣəntat-ɣʔek   'I ran.'
        I.ABS   ISG. SUBJ-run-PAST. Isg.INTR

     b. ətlon   kətɣəntat-ɣʔe   'He ran.'
        he.ABS   run-PAST. 3sg.INTR

     c. ɣəm   tə-kətɣəntat-ərkən   'I {run/am running}.'
        I.ABS   ISG. SUBJ-run- PROG

     d. ətlon   kətɣəntat-ərkən   'He {runs/is running}.'
        he.ABS   run-PROG

     e. ɣəm   n-erme-ygəm   'I {am/was} strong.'
        I.ABS   IMPF-strong-Isg.

     f. ətlon   n-erme-qin   'He {is/was} strong.'
        he.ABS   IMPF-strong-3sg.

Subject 'agreement,' which is found with both Vs and adjectives, is a much less time-oriented opposition than are tense, aspect, and mood, which are marked only on the V.

Further, Dixon 1977 has shown that, cross-linguistically, the properties most likely to be lexicalized as adjectives are the most durable and least event-like ones, e.g. size, width, length, color, gender, etc.; and that less durable properties are more likely to be lexicalized as Vs.

---

[3] We are grateful to Bernard Comrie for these data.

In Manam, an Austronesian language of New Guinea (Lichtenberk 1980), durable or more permanent properties are reported by forms which lack the person/mood marker, and are thus less verbal than those reporting more event-like properties:

(66) a. *ngau 'osi-'osi*   'I am single.' (i.e. permanently)
        1sg. single
   b. *ngau u-'osi*   'I am single.'(temporarily, newly, etc.)
        1sg. 1sg.REAL-single

An interesting argument in favor of the more verbal nature of active (as opposed to stative) Vs comes from Pamela Munro (p.c.). In the Muskogean language Chickasaw, Vs take three sets of 'subject agreement' affixes, e.g. I *–li*, II *sa-*, and III *am-* '1sg.' Affix sets II and III also mark possessors (inalienable and alienable, respectively) of Ns, which means that only the set I affixes are uniquely associated with Vs. It turns out that, in general, the set I affixes are reserved for active Vs, while sets II and III are used with stative Vs (cf. Munro and Gordon 1982, Payne 1982: 354, 356):

(67) a. *chokma-li*   'I act good.'
      good-I.1sg.
   b. *sa-chokma*   'I'm good.'
      II.1sg.-good
   c. *am-chokma*   'I feel good.'
      III.1sg.-good

4.1.2. Attribution

The more stative the inherent meaning of the lexical item, the more easily it can abandon its predicate role, and be incorporated into an NP as an attribute. Thus, in English, an adjective generally incorporates happily as an attribute:

(68) a. the black sheep

Stative (i.e. past) participles also function comfortably as attributes, but in so doing, of course, they relinquish the possibility of reporting an action; cf.

(68) b. the grazing sheep
   c. the stolen sheep

Active (i.e. present) participles, however, do not so easily become attributes, especially when their meanings are close to instantaneous actions:

(68) d. swinging cable
   e. ??snapping cable

The limited class of predicate adjectives in English which cannot serve as attributes, as pointed out by Bolinger (1967: 10) are, in general, those whose meanings describe fleeting or temporary states:[4]

(68) f. The dinner is ready.
   g. *the ready dinner
   h. My daughter is afraid.
   I. *my afraid daughter

Bolinger also discusses pairs in which the predicate adjective contrasts with the attributive adjective in having a more temporary, less durable meaning; some such contrasts have become

---

[4] Of course, some counter-examples exist; cf. *ill* vs. *sick*, or *afraid* vs. *fearful*.

lexicalized, but the distribution of meanings is always in the predicted direction:

(68) j. My friend is dizzy.
     k. my dizzy friend

In 68k, *dizzy* is interpreted as indicating a durable, slightly crazy quality; but in 68j it strongly suggests a current temporary state. Compare also

(68) l. The chairman is late.
     m. the late chairman

In Mandarin, there is no formal distinction between Vs and adjectives:

(69) a. *tā   hăo*   'S/he's good.'
         3sg. good
     b. *tā   păo*   'S/he runs.'
         3sg. run

Adjectival Vs, however, may function attributively either with or without the nominalizer-*de*:

(69) c. *hăo*   *rén*   'a good person'
         good   person
     d. *hăo-de*   *rén*   'a good person'
         good-NOM   person

But all other Vs may do so only if accompanied by -*de*:

(69) e. *păo-de   rén*   'a running person' *(*păo rén)*
         run-NOM   person

The difference between 69c–d is that *hăo* in 69c is more incorporated; the phrase is more like a name or label; in 69d, it is contrastive and restrictive. What is noteworthy is that the close relationship between *hăo* and *rén* 'person,' expressed iconically by the lack of the nominalizer, is not permitted with a 'true' event-reporting V. An exactly parallel situation exists in Indonesian, where the linker *yang* may not be omitted when the incorporated predicate is a true V.

Clauses describing the existence or the identity of some discourse participant are very poor exemplars of event-reporting discourse. Consequently, we would expect, as we will see below, that the Vs in such clauses will be impoverished members of the category 'verb.'

4.1.3. Existential clauses

Some language have no lexicalization for existence predicates. Thus, in most Australian languages, at least the existence of objects and physical characteristics in association with animate beings may be expressed with no V in the clause (Dixon 1976: 306), as in this example from Yidin[y]:

(70)   *yiŋu wuɣgun   njumbuldji.*
        this boy.NOM beard.having.NOM
        'This teen-age boy has a beard.'

Turkish is a language in which existential clauses have no V, but rather a special particle (Underhill, 102):

(71) a. *Oda-da   iskemle   var*
         room-LOC   chair   EXIST
         'There is a chair in the room.'

Underhill calls *var* a 'non-verbal' predicate. It may be inflected for person and number (as may adjectives), but it does not show tense/aspect oppositions as Vs do. Further evidence that this existential form is not very much of a V can be found in the fact that, unlike prototypical Turkish Vs, it may not be negated. Instead, a negative existential clause occurs with the suppletive negative existential particle *yok*:

(71) b. *Oda-da   iskemle yok.*
    room-LOC chair   NEG.EXIST
    'There are no chairs in the room.'

English is moving in the direction of having an invariant existential particle, *there's*, as in

(72)   There's a lot of people in there.

In Modern Hebrew, with the existential V *yeš*, no person distinctions are possible, and the gender/number marker is optional (Berman and Grosu 1976: 273):

(73)   *yeš   (nam) arbaa xatulim baxéder.*
    EXIST PL   four   cats   room.LOC
    'There are four cats in the room.'

With *nimca* 'be found,' while normative Hebrew prescribes the plural agreement suffix, colloquial Hebrew foregoes it (Andrew Fox, p.c.):

(74) a. *nimca-im šam   harbe sefer-im.*
    found-PL there many book-PL
    'There are many books there.' (normative)
   b. *nimca šam   harbe sefer-im.*
    found there many book-PL
    'There's many books there.' (colloquial)

In Mandarin, no aspect oppositions may be marked on the existential V:

(75) a. *yŏu   *{-le/-zhe/-guo}   mǎyǐ zài chōuti-li.*
    EXIST *{PERF/DUR/EXPER} ant   at   drawer-in
    'There are ants in the drawer.'

Further, as in Turkish, the existential form does not behave as prototypical Mandarin Vs do with respect to negation: this existential V takes a special negative particle *méi* rather than the *bu* which occurs with all other Vs:

(75) b. *{méi/*bu} yŏu   mǎyǐ zài chōuti-li.*
    NEG   EXIST ant   at   drawer-in
    'There aren't any ants in the drawer.'

Similarly, in Hausa, existence is expressed by the morpheme *àkwai:*

(76)   *àkwai yârā   à gidā.*
    EXIST children at home
    'There are children at home.'

Kraft and Kirk-Greene 1973 call such forms 'non-aspect verbals'; in fact, not only are they 'non-aspect' (i.e., they cannot be preceded by person/aspect markers), but they do not seem to resemble verbs in any respect.

4.1.4. Copula clauses

These clauses report events in discourse even less than do existential clauses, and are thus much more likely to be coded with no lexical item linking the subject and the predicate. Ngizim, a Chadic language, provides an example (Schuh 1972: 71):

(77) *ja maalam-cin*   'We are teachers.'
       we teacher-PL

Many Austronesian languages are similar. In Gilbertese, for example, not only does no V appear in equative sentences, but no 'aspectual' markers may appear either (Jacobs 1983):

(78) a. *Nakaa   te   tia-moti*   'Nakaa {is/was} a judge.'
        N.   ART   judge
     b. **Nakaa {na/a} te tia-moti.*
        IRR/REAL ART   judge

Many languages have a special copula particle, analogous to existential clauses. In Swahili, clauses with 1st/2nd person subjects have no copula morpheme at all, but 3rd person clauses show an invariant *ni* (Ashton 1944: 92):

(79) a. *Tu   wa-pishi.*
        we   SUBJ-cook
        'We are cooks.'
     b. *Hamisi ni   m-pishi.*
        H.   COP   SUBJ-cook
        'Hamisi is a cook.'
     c. *Hamisi na   Ali ni   wa-pishi.*
        H.   and A. COP SUBJ-cook
        'Hamisi and Ali are cooks.'

Unlike true verbs in Swahili, *ni* is marked neither for subject or object agreement nor for tense/aspect, nor can it be negated; like Turkish *var*, it alternates with a special negative copula particle.

In other languages, a copular V exists, but it is defective. The copula in Mandarin, though it can take the verbal negator *bu*, cannot be marked for aspect distinctions:

(80)   *wǒ shi *{le/-zhe/-guo}   Guǎngzhōu rén*   'I am Cantonese.'
        I   COP *{PERF/DUR/EXPER} Canton   person

Similarly, in Fante, the copula *yɛ* differs from other Vs in that it takes fewer tense/aspect markers, and in that it takes pronouns with low rather than high tone (Welmers 1973: 309–10):

(81)   *ɔ-yè kyéw*   'It's a hat.'
        it-COP hat

Thus far, we have been considering cases of Vs that are 'defective' by virtue of the fact that they have non-event lexical meanings. Below we consider other situations in which a V functions non-prototypically.

4.2. Irrealis

A V form can fail to carry out its prototypical verbal function by expressing not a report of an action, but a wish, desire, command, or projection into the future. Such forms, including those known as irrealis, future, subjunctive, optative, and hortative, typically show fewer oppositions than do prototypical forms, and are accordingly less V-like.

In many languages (Ultan 1972), 'future tense' forms are formed by a bare or defective V plus a modal which carries oppositions shunned by the V. Thus, in the Kru language Nyabo, the V 'go' is used as a modal to express future intention; the 'main' V occurs in its nominalized form, having relinquished its ability to register aspect to the auxiliary:

(82)   *ɔ mi   lé   mu-ɛ*
        he go.INCOMP there come-NOM
        'He will go there.' (Marchese 1979 [1986]: 182)

This point is also made in Plank [1984]: he argues that mood markers differ from Vs, and are thus more available for grammaticization, because they 'lack predicative autonomy, i.e. are incapable of forming predications when not accompanied by a lexical predicate.'

In clauses expressing wishes, desires, and injunctions, we similarly find neutralizations of oppositions. Thus imperatives in many languages, e.g. Wikchamni (Yokuts, California; Gamble 1978: 63–4), are signaled by the V stem alone:

(83)   a. *khame · na na 'hi'*   'I will dance.'
        b. *kham*   'Dance!'

The Portuguese (polite) imperative form consists simply of the stem plus the Subjunctive desinence; no oppositions of person, tense, or aspect may be expressed:

(84)   *Esper-e*   'Wait!'
        wait-IMPER

Similarly, in Ngizim, the imperative has its own auxiliary and tone contour, and no tense/aspect oppositions may be expressed (Schuh 1972: 23–4). The Papuan language Hua has a rich tense/aspect system; but imperative V forms are restricted to showing an opposition, by means of suffixes not found elsewhere, between a near and a remote future (Haiman 1980a: 162–3):

(85)   a. *hi-o*   'Give (pl.)!'
           give-IMPER.PL
        b. *hi-te*   'Give (pl.) later!'
           give-IMPER.FUT

That imperatives are lower in categoriality than prototypical Vs may at first sight seem anomalous. After all, imperatives are typically formed from action Vs, require volitional control of the addressee/agent, and are often perfective in languages which have morphological aspect in their Vs. Yet closer consideration suggests reasons for imperatives having fewer truly verbal features. Imperatives are pragmatically excluded from reportorial contexts, e.g. past tenses and narrative forms. They are restricted to future and irrealis actions, which are by their nature asserted to have no real existence at the time of the speech act. We have seen that the prototypical function of the V is to report an actual event; but it is in the very nature of imperatives to assume that the event named has not yet taken place—and indeed that there is considerable doubt that it will take place, unless the addressee/agent instigates it. The morpho-syntax of imperative clauses reflects this lack of the prototypical function of Vs: often there is no morphology at all, but only a bare stem of the V; transitive and intransitive Vs are treated alike with respect to ergative morphology (Dixon 1979: 112–14); and if the V shows any morphology, it is frequently of the irrealis type (optative or infinitive).

Optatives are defective in many languages. In English, for example, optative forms consist of simply the V stem, with no oppositions being expressible at all:

(86)   a. God save the Queen!
        b. Long live the King!

In a number of languages which have morphemes for subject person, e.g. Swahili, Latin, Lango, and Turkish, we find tense/aspect oppositions neutralized in the optative—though person oppositions, which are relevant for optative meanings, are retained:

(87) Swahili (Ashton, 31)
    a. *Ni-na-pik-a*   'I am cooking.'
       1sg.-PRES-cook-INDIC
    b. *Ni-li-pik-a*   'I cooked.'
       1sg.-PAST-cook-INDIC
    c. *Ni-pik-e*   'Let me cook.'
       1sg.-cook-SUBJUNC

(88) Turkish (Underhill)
    a. *Gid-iyor-um*   'I am going.'
       go-PROG-1SG.
    b. *Git-ti-m*   'I went.'
       go-PAST-1sg.
    c. *Gid-ey-im*   'Let me go!'
       go-OPT-1sg.

Imagined and hypothetical events are often expressed in what are known as conditional clauses; the Vs in these clauses form another subset of irrealis forms. They typically show a restricted range of tense/aspect choices, and are thereby less than ideal Vs. Thus in Godie, a Kru language of the Ivory Coast, tense/aspect oppositions are neutralized in conditionals. The expression of general truths requires the incompletive aspect in the consequent (Marchese 1976: 24–5):

(89) *wa kʉ ɔ dʉdɛ   nʌ   kɔ pʌ   kʌlı.*
      they if him make.fun.of NONFINAL he throw.INCOMP anger
      'If they make fun of him, he gets mad.'

Future and imaginative conditionals, by contrast, may not contain the incompletive aspect marker. Imaginative conditionals require a past-tense morpheme in the antecedent, the consequent, or both; and they must contain the future marker in the consequent:

(90) *ɔ kʉ a   monɨɨ ni nʌ   ɔ yi a   tobii pıʌ.*
      he if RECENT money see NONFINAL he FUT RECENT car buy
      'If he had some money, he'd buy a car.'

Thus Vs which function in discourse which predicts, orders, wishes, or imagines events, by neutralizing tense/aspect options, predictably manifest fewer signs of verbality than their event-reporting counterparts.

4.3. Verbs in negative clauses

Verbs in negative clauses are not prototypical event-reporting Vs, since negative clauses deny the affirmative state of affairs. Givón (1979: 121–2) points out that 'the number of tense-aspects in the affirmative paradigm is almost always larger but never smaller than in the negative.' He cites several languages which support his claim; thus, a distinction can be made in Bemba between 'tomorrow' (low tone *kà*) and 'after tomorrow' (high tone *ká*) in the future, but only in the affirmative:

(91) a. *n-kà-boomba.*
       1sg.-FUT$_1$-work
       'I will work tomorrow.'

   b. *n-ká-boomba.*
      1sg.-FUT$_2$-work
      'I will work after tomorrow.'

(92)   *nshi-kà-boomba.*
       1sg.NEG-FUT-work
       'I will not work, tomorrow and beyond.'

Ethiopian languages behave similarly. Robert Hetzron (p.c.) reports that Gurage has three distinct forms for the non-past: *yɨsabir* '*he breaks*,' definite future *yɨsäbɨrte* 'he will no doubt break,' and indefinite future *yɨsbɨrša* 'he might break.' But the three forms share only one negative, *esäbɨr* (Givón 1979: 124).

In languages with negative Vs, such Vs often fail to show the full range of oppositions available to affirmative finite ones. Thus Langdon (1970: 183) points out that, in Diegueño, the finite V is marked for aspect, tense, and person agreement with the subject and object, and for number agreement with the subject; but the negative V *-ma.w*, which acts as the main predicate of the sentence, may occur with only the morphological markings of tense and person agreement with the subject:

(93)   *m-ətəner-x*   *(m)ə-ma·w*   'You don't have it.'
       2nd-have-IRR 2-NEG

(94)   *ʔ-u·ya·w-x*   *ʔ-əma·w-x*   'I won't know.'
       1sg.-know-IRR 1sg.NEG-FUT

In Finnish, the negative V element is a defective V *e-*. It shows person and number agreement with the subject; but there are many verbal categories, including tense and mood, for which it may not be marked (Mulder 1979: 47–51):

(95) a. *Mene-n*   'I go.'
        go-1sg.
     b. *E-n*   *mene*   'I do not go.'
        NEG-1sg. go

(96) a. *(Me) to-i-mme*   *kirjan*   'We brought the books.'
        1pl. bring-PAST-1pl. books
     b. *(Me) e-mme*   *tuo-neet*   *kirjaa*   'We didn't bring the books.'
        1pl. NEG-1pl. bring-PART books

Thus negative Vs, which deny events and situations, often fail to qualify for full verbal status.

4.4. Serial verbs

A V form which 'shares the spotlight' with another is less like a V in reporting an event than one which reports the event by itself. Again, a single V in a series cannot convey what 'happened' in the discourse in which it occurs.

The Kwa languages of West Africa are well-known for their 'serial verb' constructions, in which there is no independent choice of tense or aspect for the two (or more) VPs in the construction. Different languages have different ways of implementing this generalization, as pointed out by Schachter 1974. In Akan, for example, tense/aspect marking on the first V is generally repeated on each subsequent V (Schachter, p.c.):

(97) a. *wo-didi nom.*   'They're eating and drinking.'
        3pl.-eat drink

    b. *wo-a-didi*   *a-nom.*   'They've eaten and drunk.'
       3pl.-PERF-eat PERF-drink
    c. **wo-a-didi*   *nom.*   'They've eaten and are drinking.'
       3pl.-PERF-eat drink

In Yoruba, however, only the first V generally carries overt tense/aspect (George 1975: 20):

(98) a. *Mo M̄-mú ìwé bọ̀.*   'I am bringing the book.'
     I   PROG-take book come
   b. **Mo M̄-mú ìwé wá.*
     I   PROG-take book came

A hallmark of these constructions, which distinguishes them from conjoined clause constructions, is that they are taken by speakers as representing parts of one event (cf. George 1975, Lord 1973, Foley and Olson 1983, Van Leynseele 1975). Thus, while both Vs may well be of the action type, as in (97–98a), neither functions in this context to report an event; each is doing only 'half the job'. We hypothesize that the impaired ability to show independent morphological tense/aspect oppositions follows directly from this non-functionality.

Vs with certain types of meanings—e.g. 'take,' 'hold,' 'give,' and 'use'—may lose so much categoriality in a serial construction that they are no longer clearly distinguishable from prepositions or case-markers, as illustrated by the following examples:

(99)   Yatye (Stahlke 1970:67)
       ìywe awá utsì ikù.   'The child shut the door.'
       child took door shut

(100)   Mandarin
       wǒ dǎ-diànhuà   gěi tā.   'I'll call him/her on the phone.'
       1sg. make-phone.call give 3sg.

(101)   Igbo (Hyman 1971:30)
       ó wèrè ḿmà bèé ánú.   'She cut the meat with a knife.'
       3sg. took knife cut meat

For extensive discussion of the verb-to-preposition shift in serial constructions, see Givón 1975, Li and Thompson 1974, Lord 1973, 1982, and Matisoff 1973, §4.3.

4.5. Compound verbs

A special case of two non-prototypical Vs reporting a single event is the compound V, found in such languages as Igbo, Mandarin, and Hindi. Compound Vs in these three languages are remarkably similar in both form and function (see Lord 1975 on Igbo; Chao 1968: 435ff. and Li and Thompson 1981, §3.2.3, on Mandarin; and Kachru 1979, Hook 1974 on Hindi). In general, the first V is an action form, while the second names the goal or result of the action:

(102)   Igbo (Lord 1975:23)
       tú-fù   'throw away'
       throw-be.lost

(103)   Mandarin
       lā-kāi   'pull open'
       pull-be.open

In such languages, these forms are best analysed as compounds—since, in a given clause, neither of the two verbs in the compound can function independently with respect to tense/aspect morphology or noun arguments, though each of the two verbs could occur as an independent predicate in some other clause. Thus, in Igbo, *tụ* 'throw' can occur alone in a clause such as this:[5]

(104) a. *ọ́   tụ̀-rụ̀   ákwụ́kwọ́.*
　　　　 he throw-PAST paper
　　　　 'He threw the paper.' (Lord 1975: 24)

But in the compound *tụ́-fụ̀* 'throw away', *tụ́* does not occur with the past-tense suffix:

(104) b. *ọ́   tụ̀-fu-rù   ákwụ́kwọ́.*
　　　　 he throw-be.lost-PAST paper
　　　　 'He threw away the paper.'
　　 c. **ọ́   tụ̀-ru-fù   ákwụ́kwọ́.*
　　　　 he throw-PAST-be.lost paper

Nor, being part of a compound, can it independently occur with N arguments. The same is true in Mandarin:

(105) a. *tā   lā-kāi-le   mén*   'S/he opened the door.'
　　　　 3.sg. pull-be.open-PERF door
　　 b. **tā   lā-le-kāi   mén*
　　　　 3.sg. pull-PERF-be.open door

The principle is precisely the same as with the serial Vs: since the two parts of the compound V are not functioning independently to report an event, neither is a GRAMMATICAL prototypical V. Note that the compound V taken as a unit is a perfectly viable prototypical V; our point is simply that neither of its parts is, since neither of them is doing prototypical verbal duty on its own.

4.6. Dependent clauses

So far, we have considered examples of situations in which Vs in independent clauses manifest a reduced number of oppositions because of their reduced capacity to report events. In connected discourse, speakers typically distinguish foregrounded reported events from other material which they intend to be taken as background. This background may include descriptive and evaluative material; but it may also include realis or irrealis events which are being presented as DISCOURSE-PRESUPPOSED, in the sense that they are not open to challenge (Givón 1981), and are subsidiary to the foregrounded reported events. Because these events are referred to only in the context of the foregrounded events to which they are viewed as ancillary, the clauses in which they occur are often marked as dependent. Several types of dependent clauses are particularly relevant to our hypothesis.

4.6.1. Verb functioning as noun

A very obvious situation in which a state of affairs is being presented as non-challengeable is that in which the V is functioning as a N, i.e. as an argument to another V. A V in this function is known as a 'nominalization,' whether or not it occurs with characteristic morphology. English nominalizations may be so marked, but in Mandarin they need not be:

(106)　We accepted her resignation.

---

[5] What we are glossing PAST is called 'factative' by Welmers (311): a tense/aspect form signaling 'past' for events, but 'present' or 'undefined time' for states.

(107)   *Tiàowǔ hěn méiyìsi*   'Dancing is very dull.'
         dance   very dull
         cf. *Tā   zài   tiàowǔ*   'S/he is dancing.'
         3SG. DUR   dance

Our hypothesis predicts that such Vs will signal relatively few of the oppositions associated with prototypical event-reporting forms. Data from a number of languages confirm this prediction. In English, for example, morphological tense distinctions are neutralized in nominalizations such as

(108)   the *mechanization* of the *weaving* of textiles

Even in languages in which some tense oppositions are marked on nominalizations, e.g. Turkish (Lewis 1967: 254), they do not show the full range of tense oppositions found on prototypical Vs.

In languages with a morphological aspect distinction, this is usually neutralized in nominalizations. Thus, in Russian, corresponding to the imperfective V *čitat'* and the perfective *pročitat'* 'to read', there is only one nominalization *čtenie* (B. Comrie, p.c.):

(109) a. *čtenie   takix   statej   daet mnogo radosti.*
         read.NOM such.GEN.PL article.GEN.PL gives much pleasure.GEN.SG
         'The reading of such articles gives much pleasure.'

Russian also provides an illustration of the loss of the voice distinction in nominalizations:

(109) b. *Vrag   razrušil   gorod.*
         enemy destroyed city
         'The enemy destroyed the city.'
      c. *Gorod byl razrušen   vrag-om.*
         city   be destroyed enemy-INST
         'The city was destroyed by the enemy.'
      d. *razrušenie   gorod-a*
         destruction city-GEN
         'the destruction of the city'

In Maori, where Vs are generally preceded by a tense/aspect particle, the nominalization replaces it with an article (Chung 1973: 642):

(110)   *te   reka-nga   o   te   kai*
         ART sweet-NOM POSS ART food
         'the food's being sweet'

A nominalization is apparently like a prototypical V in its ability to occur with arguments. However, two points are worth noting about the valency of a nominalization. First, in many languages, the grammatical association of a nominalization with its arguments is marked by morphology appropriate to NOUN PHRASES, rather than that found with event-reporting Vs. Thus, in English, arguments of a nominalization appear in the genitive case:

(111) a. Susan's arrival
      b. the rejection of my offer

Second, a nominalization may in principle take the full array of arguments which its inherent meaning allows; but in actual use, nominalizations tend to occur with at most one argument.

We counted the first 50 two-argument Vs used as nominalizations in Tannahill (1973: 42–93, 176–95), as exemplified below:

(111) c. the *introduction* of leavened bread
     d. the *gathering* of wild fruits

We found that only six of them, or 12 percent, actually appeared with both arguments:

(111) e. his *discussion* of breads.

Nominalizations, then, which are Vs functioning as Ns (though not very prototypical Ns, since they generally do not refer to manipulable entities), tend to exhibit the lack of potential for carrying verbal oppositions which we expect of non-event-reporting Vs. For further discussion, see Comrie 1976, Comrie and Thompson 1983.

We will have occasion to consider nominalizations in a number of contexts. In the next section, we look at one other function of a nominalized V: as incorporated material in an NP.

4.6.2. *Relative clauses*

We have seen that, when Vs function as arguments to other Vs, they are universally deficient. There is also a strong tendency for Vs which are incorporated into NPs (which linguists call 'relative clauses') to be nominalizations, or, at the very least, less than fully categorial Vs. In English, of course, the incorporated V appears in its nominalized form:

(112) a. the person standing in the corner
     b. their bread-baking techniques

Similarly, in Ancient Greek, the highly nominal 'participle,' which agrees with the head N in case and number, is found in this function (B. Fox 1983: 34):

(113)   *pólis*   *kállei*   *diapheroúsa*
       city.NOM.SG beauty excel.IMPF.PART.NOM.SG
       'a city excelling in beauty'

Luiseño relativization likewise uses a nominalization, a possessed 'non-finite' V form which is inflected for number and case (cf. Davis 1973, §5.2):

(114)   *čo·ʔun ná·ča·niš ʔu-lóʔxa*   *pilék ʔáxa·t.*
       all   food   your-make very delicious
       'All the food you prepare is very delicious.'

In Turkish, relative clauses are again incorporated nominalizations (called 'participles' by grammarians of Turkish), which can also function as arguments of Vs. Different nominalizations are used for subject and non-subject 'relative clauses':

(115)   *bekli-yen*   *misafir-ler*
       wait-PRES.PART guest-PL
       'the guests who are waiting'
       cf. *bekli-yen-ler*
       wait-PRES.PART-PL
       'the ones who are waiting' (Lewis, 158; S. West, p.c.)
(116)   *iste-diğ-im*   *kitap*
       want-NOM-1sg.POSS book
       'the book that I want'

cf. *kitap iste-diğ-im*
book want-NOM-1sg.POSS
'(the fact) that I want a book'   (Underhill, 288; K. Zimmer, p.c.)

We turn now to a different type of dependent clause, but one in which nominalizations are also often found.

4.6.3. Purpose clauses

These name unrealized states of affairs by way of providing motivation for some event; the purpose clause V, since it reports no event, is universally very low in categoriality. In most languages, the purpose V is an 'infinitive,' or otherwise marked as irrealis; it typically lacks tense/aspect and person morphology. Thus in Kinyarwanda, as in English, the purpose V is in its 'infinitive' form (Kimenyi 1980: 27):

(117)   *abaantu bi-iig-ir-a   ku-menya ubwéenge.*
         people   su-study-BEN-ASP INF-know knowledge
         'People study in order to learn.'

In Ngizim, the purpose clause V takes no tense/aspect and no independent subject, but only the irrealis ('subjunctive') marker *dà* (Schuh 1972: 380):

(118)   *vəru   gaaɗa dà ši   səma.*
         go.out.PFV PURP IRR drink beer
         'He went out to drink beer.'

In a number of languages, the purpose clause V is a nominalized form, complete with such nominal trappings as case-markers and possessive pronouns. Thus an allative case-marker ('to') may be attached to the nominalized V in the purpose clause:

(119)   Tamil (M. Dryer, p.c.).
         avan poo-R-atu-kku   kutu-tt-en.
         he   go-NONPAST-NOM-ALL give-PAST-1sg.
         'I'll give in order that he can go.'

(120)   Kanuri (Saharan; Hutchison 1976: 147)
         biska Monguno-ro lete-ro   tawange ciwoko
         yest. M.-ALL   go.NOM-ALL early.1sg. get.up.1sg.PAST
         'Yesterday I got up early to go to Monguno.'

A number of Australian languages behave analogously (see Dixon 1976, Topic C).
    Luiseño purpose clauses are possessed by their subjects (Davis, 299):

(121)   *yaʔáš ŋé·ŋi   ṣuŋá·l kí·š   pu-wá·qi-pi.*
         man   leave.REM woman house.ACC her-sweep-IRR.
         'The man left in order for the woman to sweep the house.'

In Wappo, the purpose suffix *-ema* is itself a nominalization suffix:

(122)   *isi celahaya čaphahaw-taʔ olol-ema.*
         1pl. things   put.away-PAST   dance-PURP
         'We put away things in order to dance.'

(123) a. *yok'-ema* 'chair'
         sit-PURP
      b. *lat-ema* 'a whip'
         whip-PURP

c. *kač-ema*   'a plow'
   plow-PURP

4.6.4. *The 'absolute' construction*

This, to borrow a term from the classical grammar tradition, is a convenient label for a sequence of two realis clauses, each reporting a distinct sub-event in a longer discourse: only one of them is presented as discourse-presupposed. We find that, as expected, the V in the discourse-presupposed clause is a much poorer example of a V than is the full-dress form in the 'main' clause.

In English, for example, the participial V form cannot mark tense, aspect, or 'agreement' (the auxiliary *having* serves to signal not tense, but anteriority):[6]

(124)   The Spaniards trudged forward, chasing one rumor after another.

(125)   Having put out the fire, we climbed into our sleeping bags.

In precisely the same way, in Ngizim, the participle contains a 'verbal noun' which cannot be marked for tense/aspect or person/number agreement:

(126)   *kalaktayi-gaa*   *ná*   *təfə-n-gaa*   *ii mənduwa.*
        return.VN.1sg.POSS 1sg.PERF enter-TOTAL-PRON to house
        'Having returned (lit. 'my returning'), I went right into the house.'
        (Schuh 1972:364)

In Luiseño, the participle shows no tense or aspect (Davis, 188):

(127)   *ʔó·nu-pil ney*   *wultúʔ-ya*   *ʔi·k.*   *nu-htíʔa-qala.*
        he-REM   1sg.ACC angry-REM there.DAT 1sg.POSS-go-PART
        'He got angry {because/when} I went there.' (lit. 'He got angry my going there.')

Many of the older IE languages show similar backgrounding use of participial constructions. Typically, the participle is inflected like a N, with endings showing case, gender, and number. It shows some characteristically verbal contrasts, but is defective in these by comparison with true Vs. In Latin, for example, the participle is marked according to the following convention: If the understood subject of the participle is co-referential with any N in the main clause, then the participle agrees with that N in case, number, and gender. In the following example (part of a famous line in the *Aeneid*), the present *ferentes* is masculine, plural, and accusative, to agree with *Danaos* in the main clause:

(128)   *...timeo*   *Danaos et*   *dona*   *ferentes.*
        I.fear   Greeks and   gifts   bearing
        'I fear the Greeks, even [those] bearing gifts.'

But if the main clause has no N for the subject of the participle to agree with, then both the subject of the participle and the participle itself appear in the ablative case. Since, for most Latin Vs, the preterit participle is passive, its subject is a passive subject. The following example, from Caesar, has two backgrounded clauses in the ablative absolute; in both clauses, the Ns and participles are in the ablative case:

(129)   *Caesar,*   *itineribus*   *iustis*   *confectis, nullo*   *die*
        C.   journeys.ABL whole.ABL   completed.ABL no.ABL   day.ABL
        intermisso,   *...Lilybaeum pervenit.*
        rested.ABL   L.   arrived

---

[6] On the relationship between form and discourse function in English participial clauses, see Thompson (1983).

'Caesar, whole-day journeys having-been-completed, no day having-been-rested, reached Lilybaeum.' (I.e. 'Caesar reached Lilybaeum having made full-day marches and having allowed no day for rest.') (*De Bello Africo*, 1)

In Ancient Greek (B. Fox 1983), the participle shows aspect, voice, and the usual N agreement morphemes; but as in Latin, it lacks 'conjugational' morphology, including tense, modality, and person oppositions. Fox illustrates the backgrounding function of these participles, as in the following:

(130) *spháksantes   dè   apotámnousi tèn kephalén*
      cut.throat.PERF.PART and   they-cut.off the head
      'And after cutting (its) throat, they cut off the head.' (Herodotus 2.390)

(131) *érkhetai   tòn huiòn ékhousa.*
      come.PRES.IMPF.3sg.   DEF son   have.IMPF.PART.NOM.SG
      'She comes bringing her son.' (Xenophon)

It is noteworthy that, in all these languages—and, indeed, in many languages with analogous constructions—the participle form itself has nominal characteristics: it can be used as a N, with appropriate determiners (including possessive pronouns), and even with case-markers. We will return to this point below.

4.6.5. The 'chaining' construction

This is a term for a sequence of realis clauses in which only the final one is presented as foregrounded. This can be distinguished from the 'absolute construction' simply by the fact that the number of preceding backgrounded clauses may be greater than one. Chaining constructions are particularly well exemplified in languages of South America and Papua New Guinea. As predicted by our hypothesis, at least certain Vs in medial clauses manifest fewer oppositions than those in final clauses.

In the Papuan language Barai, for instance, the 'medial' (i.e. non-final) V cannot be marked for independent tense, person, or number (Olson 1982):

(132) *no   ire   i-na   ame   ruor-ia   {-ke/-e}.*
      1pl. food eat-CONJ   child   wash-3pl. {FUT/PAST}
      'Having eaten food, we {will wash / washed} the children.'

(133) *agekasa   fu   ije   abe   dabe   usiae   m-uo-e.*
      agriculture 3sg. 3sg. take   carry   arrive   give-PL-PAST
      'The agriculture (officer) having taken, carried, arrived, he gave it to us.'

In another Papuan language, Chuave, only the final V is affixed for mood and tense. Medial Vs are, in general, not marked for mood and tense, but are suffixed either with a 'dependency' marker or a 'switch-reference' marker which signals person and number of the subject in the following clause (Thurman 1978: 12):

(134) *kan-i-k-a-i   kiapu guwai-nom   i   muruwo furuwai*
      see-1sg.-DEP-NONSIMULT-DEM   officer belongings-their this all   strew
           bei   de-Ø-im-ie.
           do   leave-NONFUT-3pl.-DECL
      'When I looked, they were strewing all the officers' belongings about.'

Note that the medial V is not only much less of a V than the final one, but in fact, as in the absolute participle, has the nominal property of occurring with a demonstrative suffix. Similarly, Haiman 1977, 1980a shows that extensive evidence exists for regarding all medial Vs in the related language Hua as NPs, including the fact that they may be followed by the 'connective particle' -*mo*, which occurs only with NPs. These 'adverbial' dependent clauses, then, providing non-challengeable background for a 'figure' clause, tend to be coded as only partially nominal by a number of languages.

However, Haiman (1980a, p.c.) points out that not all medial Vs show less categoriality than their final counterparts: in many Papuan languages, medial Vs which are 'coördinate' with the following V typically do not mark tense and mood independently, but ones which are 'subordinate' to the final V do mark these categories. This apparent paradox suggests that chained clauses are typically in a part-to-whole relationship to some higher discourse unit, e.g. paragraph or episode, all of which is in the scope of a single set of verbal tense and mood markers. Thus the V in a clause which is part of an event chain in the same episode may show less categoriality than Vs in subordinate clauses which break that chain; i.e. subordinate clauses, being irrelevant to the episode, must necessarily mark these tense and mood functions independently. The crucial point is that each chained clause does not alone report an event, but that the episode as a whole constitutes the reported event. (For further discussion of 'chaining' in Papua New Guinea, see Longacre 1972, Lawrence 1972, and Olson 1982, in addition to the references given just above.)

4.6.6. Bound clauses ('complements')

Givón 1980a shows a strong correlation between the degree to which the event described by a V is 'bound' by another V and the degree to which it is formally 'reduced.' A V is high in the 'binding scale' to the extent that its agent or experiencer exerts a strong influence over that of the complement clause (as in Eng. *force*), or is strongly purposive in accomplishing the event in the complement (as in Eng. *succeed*), or has a strong emotional commitment to the possibility of the realization of the complement event (cf. Eng. *want*).

Givón presents evidence from a range of languages to demonstrate that, in general, the higher a V is on the binding scale, the more its complement V (a) will tend not to be independent, but will be structurally integrated into the main clause; and (b) will fail to express independent tense/aspect/modality. That is, the HIGHER a V is on the binding scale, the LOWER the degree of categoriality of the complement V. Our hypothesis clearly predicts this generalization, since the greater the extent to which a complement V is bound, the less that V is performing the function for which Vs exist, namely to report an event.

Examples to support Givón's hypothesis abound. In English, for instance, *make* and *have*, at the top of the binding scale, take highly non-verbal bare infinitives; *order*, slightly lower, occurs with the slightly more V-like *to* infinitive; *insist*, lower still, is found with a 'subjunctive' *that* complement; and *think*, at the bottom, goes with a *that* clause, whose finite V is indistinguishable from a prototypical V.

To take another example, in Southern Ute, we can contrast a pair of roots such as *maku-* 'finish,' which strongly implies its complement, and *ʔasti-* 'want,' which implies its complement only to the extent that a certain amount of 'will' or 'desire' is directed toward the accomplishment of the event named in that complement. In 135a below, *wuuka* 'work' is actually incorporated into the V complex including *maku-*, and shows no verbal oppositions at all; but in 135b, *tuka-* 'eat' is somewhat more independent, and can at least be marked for its own modality (Givón 1980a: 361):

(135) a. *mamá-ci   wuuka-maku-kwa.*
         woman-ABS work-finish-PAST
         'The woman finished working.'
      b. *mamá-ci   tuka-vaa-ci   ʔasti-kya.*
         woman-ABS eat-MOD-NOM want-PAST
         'The woman wanted to eat.'

Note that *tuka-vaa-ci* 'eating', while indeed formally independent from *ʔasti*, is still not a prototypical V but a nominalization; this is, of course, because it expresses an irrealis event.

Givón points out (360) that the same 'want'/'finish' contrast can be seen in Palestinian Arabic, where the event which is implied by the V *halasa* 'he finished' is coded by a V in the form of a N. Its subject argument appears as a genitive pronominal suffix:

> (136) a. *halasa   shurl-u*   'He finished working.'
>   he.finished work-his

But *bidd* 'want' implies its complement much less strongly; hence the V in that complement is closer to being prototypical, in that it takes a pronominal prefix as if it appeared in an independent assertion:

> (136) b. *kana   bidd-u   yi-shrul*   'He wanted to work.'
>   was.it want-he he-work

But though *-shrul* is CLOSER to being a prototypical V, it is irrealis, and so fails to show the full range of tense/aspect distinctions found with such Vs.

Givón provides numerous examples, showing a finer gradation than we have presented here, of the correlation between the degree to which a complement is bound and the extent to which its V recedes from full-dress verbhood. As is clear from the three languages at which we have looked, languages differ as to how far a V must recede from the prototypical end of the scale before certain oppositions fail to be registered; however, the correlations are invariably in the predicted direction.

4.7. Summary

In a wide range of both independent and dependent clause types, then, we find cross-linguistic support for that part of our hypothesis relating to Vs: a V presents itself in discourse as fully capable of displaying all the oppositions available for event-coding only if it is reporting an actual event.

5. CATEGORY SHIFTS

Strong support for our categoriality hypothesis can be found by considering 'shifts' from the nominal to the verbal category, or vice versa.

Every language has roots whose semantic content makes them more likely to be realized as Ns than as Vs, and other roots for which the reverse is true. For ease of reference in this discussion, we can refer to these as 'nominal' and 'verbal' roots, respectively—recognizing, of course, that the distinction is often unclear, and may in fact be virtually absent in some languages. When we survey the languages of the world, we find that languages have a variety of derivational morphological processes for converting nominal roots into Vs, and verbal roots into nominal forms. Some of these processes contribute semantic content to the resultant form. For example, in Zulu (Kunene 1974: 107), the suffix *-i* adds the meaning 'one who—s' to a V stem:

> (137)   *-cul- > um-cul-i*   'singer'
>   sing   CLF-sing-AGT

Rukai, an Austronesian language of Taiwan, provides an example of derivation in the opposite direction (P. J. Li 1973:247): *i-*, prefixed to a place N, results in a V meaning 'to stay at':

(138)   *baLiw* > *i-baLiw*   'stay at home'
         home   stay-home

However, if we consider just those derivational processes which make no semantic contribution, but which simply serve to shift a root into the other category, then we discover a striking fact: languages often possess rather elaborate morphology whose sole function is to convert verbal roots into Ns, but no morphology whose sole function is to convert nominal roots into Vs.[7] For example, in English, a number of affixes can be found whose only purpose is to signal that a verbal root has been converted into a nominal form:

(139)   propose   proposal
         create   creation
         sell   selling
         excite   excitement

But to change a nominal root into a verbal form, it is sufficient simply to use it as a V, attaching standard verbal tense/aspect/mood and person morphology directly to it:

(140) a. We squirreled away $500 last year.
      b. She breakfasts with the mayor on Tuesdays.

Note that we are not denying that some English roots may be indeterminately nominal or verbal, e.g. *toast, dance, hike*. What we are pointing out is that English nicely exemplifies the apparently universal generalization that languages tend to have special nominalizing morphology, but no special PRODUCTIVE verbalizing morphology.

In fact, this asymmetry is characteristic even of those languages in which the distinction between inherently nominal and verbal roots would appear to be minimal, such as the Nootkan, Kwakiutlan, and Salishan languages discussed by Jacobsen. Thus Jacobsen concludes, as was pointed out in §1 above, that the distinction between nominal and verbal roots exists even in these languages, because 'there is a class of nouns which may occur in the role of subject or object, opposed to a class of verbs which may not so occur, but *only in nominalized form*' (Jacobsen, 106; emphasis supplied). For example, in the Salishan language Squamish, either nominal or verbal stems may be predicates—e.g. *puš* 'cat,' 'It is a cat'; *taqʷ* '(He) drink(s)'. However, only Ns may take the possessive affix; before a V can take a possessive affix, a N must be derived from it with *s-* (*puš-s* 'his cat,' but *s-taqʷ-s* 'his water'; Jacobsen, 98–9, discussing Kuipers 1967, 1968, 1969).

Languages, then, seem to be able to derive predicates productively from either nominal or verbal roots, while generally requiring nominalizing morphology to derive a N from a verbal root. Why should this be so? The answer, we suggest, lies in the difference between their functions in discourse, and can be stated as follows: a nominalization names an event taken as an entity;[8] however, a 'verbalization' does not name an 'entity taken as an event,' but simply names an event associated with some entity. In other words, a nominalization still names an event, albeit one which is being referred to rather than reported on in the discourse; it is, accordingly, still in part a V, and not a 'bona fide' N. However, a denominal V no longer

---

[7] Strictly speaking, the generalization should be stated as an implicational one, since some languages have neither purely nominalizing nor purely verbalizing strategies; Lakhota (Buechel 1939: 314) and Ancient Greek form nominalizations by simply adding the definite article to a clause. Thus, if a language has category-deriving morphology at all, what we find is that it has noun-deriving, but not verb-deriving processes.

[8] Thanks to Christian Matthiessen for helpful discussion of nominalizations.

names an entity at all, and thus has no nominal 'stains' to prevent its being a bona fide V. To put it another way, a nominalization qualifies as a METAPHOR in the sense of Lakoff and Johnson (1980: 3a): 'We use ontological metaphors to comprehend events, actions, activities and states. Events and actions are conceptualized metaphorically as objects.' The metaphorical process takes something abstract and treats it as if it were concrete precisely because human cognition can deal with concrete entities more easily than with abstractions; this process is thus unidirectional. This is why languages have nominalization processes, where an abstract event is treated as a concrete entity; this results in a form which is BOTH an event and an entity, and tends to be marked with signals of this fact. But there is no analogous 'verbalization' process, since we do not metaphorically treat concrete things as events.

We can illustrate from English:

(141) The preparation of the manuscript takes several weeks.

Hence we refer to the actual event of someone's preparing a manuscript, as background to the information that this event lasts for several weeks. The event has not ceased to be an event, but is treated grammatically as if it were an entity, so that it can be commented on as such. Cf. this example:

(142) The resulting mixture is shaped into balls.

Here the nominalization in fact refers to a concrete entity, but there still must have been an event of mixing.[9] But suppose that we say:

(143) We squirreled away $500 last year.

The V *squirrel away* reports an event, and has nothing to do with any squirrel. Its relationship with the N *squirrel* is in fact very loose, depending on an assumed property of this class of rodents (cf. Clark and Clark 1979, Aronoff 1980).

Note that, even in those languages where a major predicative use of nominal roots is as predicate nominals, there is still no entity involved in the predication—only reference to an abstract class. Consider this Nootka predicate:

(144) *qu·ʔas-ma*
man-INDIC
'He is a man.' (Swadesh 1939, cited in Jacobsen, 85)

Here no entity is referred to, but only the abstract class of men.

We find, then, that the function of nominalizations is to REFER TO EVENTS, but that there is no analogous function for 'verbalizations.' There is therefore no grammatical machinery for this non-existent function.

The categoriality hypothesis predicts this fact. A form referring to an event taken as an entity is functioning neither to report an event nor to refer to a manipulable entity; but it has elements of both. We would expect, then, that it would show morphology reflecting this ambivalence, and that is precisely what we find: like Vs, nominalizations may show aspect or mood and take arguments; like Ns, they may take possessive markers or determiners; being neither, they also require, in most languages, special morphology which is found neither on prototypical Ns or Vs—what we call 'nominalizing' morphology. A N 'used as' a V, however, is not in any sense referring to an entity; it is not a 'mermaid' type of form, but is simply a V.

---

[9] This is not to deny, of course, that there are etymological nominalizations—lexical Ns in their own right—which have broken their productive relationship with the Vs from which they are derived; thus a *commission* does not necessarily *commit* anything. Accordingly, most analysts would not describe such a form as a nominalization, even though its history is revealed by its form.

Hence, we predict, and find, that it shows precisely that morphology which is appropriate for its function as a V.

6. CONCLUSION

We have presented a wealth of evidence in favor of the categoriality hypothesis. By way of conclusion, we consider two implications of this hypothesis.

6.1. Iconicity

It is clear that the categoriality hypothesis is a statement of the DIAGRAMMATIC ICONICITY of grammars (in the Peircean sense; see Haiman 1980b): the less a linguistic element is required by the discourse either to report an event or introduce an entity for potential discourse manipulation, the less saliently it will be marked as a member of the category which languages universally designate to carry that function. This type of iconicity between language form and function is as strong an indication of the perceptual basis of the cognitive strategies underlying language systems as we can expect to find.

6.2. Discourse

Throughout this paper, we have for the most part presented the theory of categoriality in terms of the success or lack of success of a form in achieving full nounhood or verbhood. The ultimate existence of a distinction between N and V has been assumed. We should like to conclude, however, by suggesting that linguistic forms are in principle to be considered as LACKING CATEGORIALITY completely unless nounhood or verbhood is forced on them by their discourse functions. To the extent that forms can be said to have an a priori existence outside of discourse, they are characterizable as ACATEGORIAL; i.e., their categorical classification is irrelevant. Categoriality—the realization of a form as either a N or a V—is imposed on the form by discourse. Yet we have also seen that the noun/verb distinction is apparently universal: there seem to be no languages in which all stems are indifferently capable of receiving all morphology appropriate for both Ns and Vs. This suggests that the continua which in principle begin with acategoriality, and which end with fully implemented nounhood or fully implemented verbhood, are already partly traversed for most forms. In other words, most forms begin with a propensity or predisposition to become Ns or Vs; and often this momentum can be reversed by only special morphology. It nonetheless remains true that this predisposition is only a latent one, which will not be manifested unless there is pressure from the discourse for this to occur.

In other words, far from being 'given' aprioristically for us to build sentences out of, the categories of N and V actually manifest themselves only when the discourse requires it. Such a perspective may help remind us that questions of the relationship between language and the mind can be approached only by considering language in its natural functional context.

REFERENCES

Abdullah (1932). *Hikayat Abdullah*. Singapore: Malaya Publishing House.

Ard, J. (1979). 'A typological comparison of incorporation in Siberia and North America'. MS, University of Michigan.

Aronoff, M. (1980). 'Contextuals'. *Language* 56: 744–58.

Ashton, E. D. (1944). *Swahili Grammar*. London: Longman.

Bates, E., and B. MacWhinney (1982). 'Functionalist approaches to grammar'. In E. Wanner and L. Gleitman (eds.), *Language Acquisition: The State of the Art*. Cambridge: Cambridge University Press, 173–218.

Berman, R., and A. Grosu (1976). 'Aspects of the copula in Modern Hebrew'. In P. Cole (ed.), *Studies in Modern Hebrew Syntax and Semantics*. Amsterdam: North-Holland, 265–85.

Bese, L., et al. (1970). 'On the syntactic typology of the Uralic and Altaic languages'. In L. Dezsõ and P. Hajdu (eds.), *Theoretical Problems of Typology and the Northern Eurasian Languages*. Amsterdam: Gruner, 113–28.

Bolinger, D. L. (1967). 'Adjectives in English: attribution and predication'. *Lingua* 18: 1–34.

Brown, R. (1958). *Words and Things*. New York: Free Press.

Buechel, E., S. J. (1939). *A Grammar of Lakhota*. St Francis, SD: Rosebud Educational Society.

Chafe, W. (1970). 'A semantically based sketch of Onondaga'. *IJAL* 36: 2, pt. 2. Bloomington: Indiana University.

Chao, Y. R. (1968). *A Grammar of Spoken Chinese*. Berkeley: University of California Press.

Chung, S. (1973). 'The syntax of nominalizations in Polynesian'. *Oceanic Linguistics* 12: 641–86.

Clark, E. V., and H. H. Clark (1979). 'When nouns surface as verbs'. *Language* 55: 767–811.

Comrie, B. (1973). 'The ergative: variations on a theme'. *Lingua* 32: 239–53.

——(1976). 'The syntax of action nominals: a cross-linguistic study'. *Lingua* 40: 177–201.

——and S. A. Thompson (1983). 'Lexical nominalizations'. In T. Shopen (ed.) (1985), *Language Typology and Syntactic Description*, vol. iii. Cambridge: University Press.

Davis, J. (1973). 'A partial grammar of simplex and complex sentences in Luiseño'. Ph.D. dissertation, University of California, Los Angeles.

Dixon, R. M. W. (ed.) (1976). *Grammatical Categories in Australian Languages*. Canberra: Australian Institute of Aboriginal Studies.

——(1977). 'Where have all the adjectives gone?' *Studies in Language* 1: 19–80.

——(1979). 'Ergativity'. *Language* 55: 59–138.

Du Bois, J. W. (1980). 'Beyond definiteness: the trace of identity in discourse'. In W. Chafe (ed.), *The Pear Stories*. Norwood, NJ: Ablex, 203–74.

Foley, W., and M. Olson (1983). 'Clausehood and verb serialization'. In J. Nichols and Anthony Woodbury (eds.), *Grammar Inside and Outside the Clause*. Berkeley: University of California Press.

Fox, B. (1981). 'The syntax of body parts: towards a universal characterization'. *Studies in Language* 5: 323–42.

——(1983). 'The discourse function of the participle in Ancient Greek'. In F. Klein-Andreu (ed.), *Discourse Perspectives on Syntax*. New York: Academic Press.

Gamble, G. (1978). 'Wikchamni grammar'. Berkeley: University of California Press.

George, I. (1975). 'A grammar of Kwa-type verb serialization: Its nature and significance in current generative theory'. Ph.D. dissertation, University of California, Los Angeles.

Givón, T. (1975). 'Serial verbs and syntactic change: Niger-Congo'. In C. N. Li (ed.), *Word Order and Word Order Change*. Austin: University of Texas Press, 47–112.

——(1977). 'Definiteness and referentiality'. In J. Greenberg et al. (eds.), *Universals of Human Language*. Stanford, Calif.: Stanford University Press, 291–330.

——(1979). *On Understanding Grammar*. New York: Academic Press.

——(1980a). 'The binding hierarchy and the typology of complement'. *Studies in Language* 4: 333–77.

——(1980b). *Ute Reference grammar*. Ignacio, Colo.: Ute Press.

——(1981). 'Logic vs. pragmatics, with natural language as the referee'. *Journal of Pragmatics* 6: 81–133.

Haiman, J. (1977). 'Connective particles in Hua: an essay on the parts of speech'. *Oceanic Linguistics* 16(2): 53–107.

——(1980a). *Hua: A Papuan language of the Eastern Highlands of New Guinea*. Amsterdam: Benjamins.

——(1980b). 'The iconicity of grammar'. *Language* 56: 515–40.

——(ed.) (1983). *Studies in Iconicity*. Amsterdam: Benjamins.

Harrison, S. (1976). *Mokilese Reference Grammar*. Honolulu: University of Hawaii Press.

Hébert, Y. (1983). 'Noun and verb in a Salishan language'. *Kansas Working Papers in Linguistics* 8: 31–81.

Heim, M. (1976). *Contemporary Czech*. Ann Arbor: Dept. of Slavic, University of Michigan.

Hetzron, R. (1971). 'Presentative function and presentative movement'. *Studies in African Linguistics*, UCLA, Supplement 2: 79–105.

Hook, P. (1974). *The Compound Verb in Hindi*. Ann Arbor: University of Michigan.

Hopper, P. J., and S. A. Thompson (1980). 'Transitivity in grammar and discourse'. *Language* 56: 251–99.

—— —— (eds.) (1982). *Studies in Transitivity*. New York: Academic Press.

Hutchison, J. (1976). 'Aspects of Kanuri syntax'. Ph. D. dissertation, Indiana University, Bloomington.

Hyman, L. (1971). 'Consecutivization in Fe'Fe''. *Journal of African Languages* 10: 2.29–43.

——and A. Duranti (1982). 'On the object relation in Bantu'. In Hopper and Thompson (1982: 217–39).

Innes, G. (1967). *A Practical Introduction to Mende*. London: School of Oriental and African Studies.

Jacobs, R. (1983). 'Some syntactic processes in Gilbertese'. In B. Bender (ed.), *Studies in Micronesian Linguistics*. Canberra: Australian National University.

Jacobsen, W. H., Jr. (1979). *Noun and Verb in Nootkan*. Victoria: British Columbia Provincial Museum.

Jaggar, P. (1983). 'Some dimensions of topic–NP continuity in Hausa narrative discourse'. In T. Givón (ed.), *Topic Continuity in Discourse: A Quantitative Cross-Language Study*. Amsterdam: Benjamins.

Kachru, Y. (1979). 'Pragmatics and verb serialization in Hindi-Urdu'. *Studies in the Linguistic Sciences* 9: 2.157–69.

Károly, S. (1972). 'The grammatical system of Hungarian'. In L. Benkő and Samu Imre (eds.), *The Hungarian Language*, 85–144. The Hague: Mouton.

Kimenyi, A. (1980). *A Relational Grammar of Kinyarwanda*. Berkeley: University of California Press.

Kraft, C. H., and A. H. M. Kirk-Greene (1973). *Hausa*. London: Hodder and Stoughton.

Kuipers, A. H. (1967). *The Squamish Language: Grammar, Texts, Dictionary*. The Hague: Mouton.

——(1968). 'The categories verb–noun and transitive–intransitive in English and Squamish'. *Lingua* 21: 610–26.

——(1969). *The Squamish Language: Grammar, Texts, Dictionary*, part 2. The Hague: Mouton.

Kunene, E. (1974). 'Nominalization in Zulu'. In S. A. Thompson and C. Lord (eds.), *Approaches to the Lexicon*. Los Angeles: Dept. of Linguistics, UCLA, 107–28.

Lakoff, G. (1977). 'Linguistic gestalts'. In *Papers from the Thirteenth Regional Meeting of the Chicago Linguistic Society*, 236–87.

——and M. Johnson (1980). *Metaphors We Live By*. Chicago: University of Chicago Press.

Langdon, M. (1970). *A Grammar of Diegueño*. Berkeley: University of California Press.

Lawrence, M. (1972). 'Structure and function of Oksapmin verbs'. *Oceanic Linguistics* 11: 47–66.

Lee, K.-D. (1975). *Kusaiean Reference Grammar*. Honolulu: University of Hawaii Press.

Levi, J. (1978). *The Syntax and Semantics of Complex Nominals*. New York: Academic Press.

Lewis, G. L. (1967). *Turkish Grammar*. Oxford: Clarendon Press.

Li, C. N., and S. A. Thompson (1974). 'Co-verbs in Mandarin Chinese: verbs or prepositions?' *Journal of Chinese Linguistics* 2: 257–78.

—— ——(1981). *Mandarin Chinese: A Functional Reference Grammar*. Berkeley: University of California Press.

Li, P. J.-K. (1973). *Rukai Structure*. Taipei: Academia Sinica.

Lichtenberk, F. (1980). *A Grammar of Manam*. Honolulu: University Press of Hawaii.

Longacre, R. E. (1972). *Hierarchy and Universality of Discourse Constituents in New Guinea Languages*, ii: *Discussion*. Washington, DC: Georgetown University Press.

Lord, C. (1973). 'Serial verbs in transition'. *Studies in African Linguistics* 4: 269–97.

——(1975). 'Igbo verb compounds and the lexicon'. *Studies in African Linguistics* 6: 23–48.

——(1982). 'The development of object markers in serial verb languages'. In Hopper and Thompson (1982: 277–99).

Lynch, J. (1973). 'Verbal aspects of possession in Melanesian languages'. *Oceanic Linguistics* 12: 69–102.

Lyons, J. (1966). 'Towards a "notional" theory of the "parts of speech"'. *Journal of Linguistics* 2: 209–36.

——(1968). *Introduction to Theoretical Linguistics*. Cambridge: Cambridge University Press.

——(1977). *Semantics* (2 vols). Cambridge: Cambridge University Press.

Marchese, L. (1976). 'Subordination in Godie'. M.A. thesis, University of California, Los Angeles. (Published by Institut de Linguistique Appliqué, Société Internationale de Linguistique, Abidjan; *Publications conjointes*, vol. iv, 1978.)

——(1979) *Tense/Aspect and the Development of Auxiliaries in the Kru Languages*. Dallas: Summer Institute of Linguistics.

Mardirussian, G. (1975). 'Noun-incorporation in universal grammar'. In *Papers from the Eleventh Regional Meeting of the Chicago Linguistic Society*, 383–9.

Matisoff, J. (1973). *The Grammar of Lahu*. Berkeley: University of California Press.

Merlan, F. (1976). 'Noun incorporation and discourse reference in Modern Nahuatl'. *IJAL* 42: 177–91.

Mithun, M. (1984). 'The evolution of noun incorporation'. *Language* 60: 847–94.

Mulder, J. (1979). 'Universal grammar and diachronic syntax: the case of the Finnish negative'. M.A. thesis, University of California, Los Angeles.

Munro, P., and L. Gordon (1982). 'Syntactic relations in Western Muskogean: A typological perspective'. *Language* 58: 81–115.

Newman, S. (1965). *Zuni Grammar*. Albuquerque: University of New Mexico Press.

Olson, M. (1982). 'Barai clause junctures: towards a functional theory of interclausal relations'. Ph.D. dissertation, Australian National University.

Payne, D. (1982). 'Chickasaw agreement morphology: a functional explanation'. In Hopper and Thompson, (1982: 351–78).

Pease-Gorrissen, M. (1980). 'The use of the article in Spanish habitual and generic sentences'. *Lingua* 51: 311–36.

Plank, F. (1983). 'The moral of the modals story'. Not published in Haiman (1983), but see F. Plank, 'The modals story retold'. *Studies in Language* 8 (1984): 305–64.

Robins, R. H. (1952). 'Noun and verb in universal grammar'. *Language* 28: 289–98.

——(1979). *A Short History of Linguistics*, 2nd edn. Bloomington: Indiana University Press.

Rosch, E. H. (1973). 'Natural categories'. *Cognitive Psychology* 4: 328–50.

——(1977a). 'Classification of real-world objects: origins and representation in cognition'. In P. N. Johnson-Laird and P. C. Warren (eds.), *Thinking: Readings in Cognitive Science*. Cambridge: Cambridge University Press, 212–22.

——(1977b). 'Human categorization'. In N. Warren (ed.), *Studies in Cross-Cultural Psychology*. New York: Academic Press, 1–49.

——(1978). 'Principles of categorization'. In E. Rosch and B. Lloyd (eds.), *Cognition and Categorization*. Hillsdale, NJ: Erlbaum, 27–48.

Sapir, E. (1911). 'The problem of noun incorporation in American languages'. *American Anthropologist* n.s. 13: 250–82.

——(1921). *Language*. New York: Harcourt Brace.

Schachter, P. (1974). 'A non-transformational account of serial verbs'. *Studies in African Linguistics*, UCLA, Supplement 5: 253–70.

——(1983). 'Parts-of-speech systems'. In T. Shopen (ed.), *Language Typology and Syntactic Field Work*. Cambridge: Cambridge University Press.

Schuh, R. G. (1972). 'Aspects of Ngizim syntax'. Ph.D. dissertation, University of California, Los Angeles.

——(1977). Bade/Ngizim determiner system. *Afroasiatic Linguistics* 4: 101–74.

Sommer, B. (1972). *Kunjen Syntax*. Canberra: Australian Institute of Aboriginal Studies.

Stahlke, H. (1970). 'Serial verbs'. *Studies in African Linguistics* 1: 60–99.

Starosta, S. (1979). 'Sora combining forms and pseudo-compounding'. Paper presented at Symposium on Austro-Asiatic Languages, Helsingør, Denmark.

Steever, S. (1979). 'Noun incorporation in Tamil, or What's a noun like you doing in a verb like this?' In *Papers from the Fifteenth Regional Meeting of the Chicago Linguistic Society*, 279–90.

Sugita, H. (1973). 'Semitransitive verbs and object incorporation in Micronesian languages'. *Oceanic Linguistics* 12: 393–406.

Swadesh, M. (1939). 'Nootka internal syntax'. *IJAL* 9: 77–102.

Tannahill, R. (1973). *Food in History*. New York: Stein and Day.

Thompson, S. A. (1983). 'Grammar and discourse: the English detached participial clause'. In F. Klein-Andreu (ed.), *Discourse Perspectives on Syntax*. New York: Academic Press, 43–65.

Thurman, R. (1978). 'Interclausal relationships in Chuave'. M.A. thesis, University of California, Los Angeles.

Ultan, R. (1972). 'The nature of future tenses'. *Working Papers on Language Universals* (Stanford University) 8: 55–100.

Underhill, R. (1976). *Turkish Grammar*. Cambridge, Mass.: MIT Press.

Van Leynseele, H. (1975). 'Restrictions on serial verbs in Anyi'. *Journal of West African Languages* 10: 189–218.

Verhaar, J. W. M. (1979). 'Neutralization and hierarchy'. *Sophia Linguistica: Working Papers in Linguistics* 5: 1–16. Tokyo.

Welmers, W. E. (1973). *African Language Structures*. Berkeley: University of California Press.

Williams, M. M. (1976). *A Grammar of Tuscarora*. New York: Garland.

Woodbury, H. (1975). 'Onondaga noun incorporation: some notes on the interdependence of syntax and semantics'. *IJAL* 41: 10–20.

Žukova, A. N. (1954). 'Dva osnovnyx sposoba svjazi opredelenija s opredeljaemym v korjakskom jazyke'. *UZ Leningradskoja Pedag. Instituta* 101: 293–304.

17

Grammatical Categories

JOHN TAYLOR

The prototype model of categories was developed in the early 1970s as a response to empirical evidence concerning the way people categorize things in their environment. Important landmarks in this research were Labov's studies of the categorization of household receptacles, Berlin and Kay's findings on colour categories, and the work of Rosch and her associates, which refined and extended the insights of Berlin and Kay.

There were, from the outset, two orientations that prototype research could take. The direction of cognitive psychology (cf. Smith and Medin 1981) was to study the way concepts are structured and represented in the mind. Alternatively, research on categorization could be channelled into linguistics. Here the emphasis comes to be placed, not on concepts per se, but on the structure of the semantic pole of the linguistic sign, i.e. on the meanings of linguistic forms. The two orientations are closely intertwined. As we saw in the discussion of hedges (section 4.4 [not included here]), linguistic data and the psychologist's experimental findings mutually complement each other. Indeed, one of the main sources of evidence for conceptual structure is linguistic; conversely, any reasonable account of linguistic behaviour needs to make reference to the conceptual structures which linguistic forms conventionally symbolize.

Linguists, while keen to exploit the findings of the cognitive psychologists, were not likely to be content with data limited, in the main, to the names of natural kinds, like birds and fruit, and cultural artefacts, like vehicles and furniture. In the hands of linguists, the prototype model was rapidly extended so as to encompass concepts of increasing abstraction, not only notions like "murder" and "tell a lie", but also the meanings of grammatical formatives like prepositions and bound morphemes, and even the elusive nuances conveyed by intonation contours. And, of course, it was linguistic evidence (the all-pervasive presence of polysemy) that suggested that prototype categories can be co-ordinated in family resemblance structures.

Recent years have seen the extension of the prototype concept to ever more areas of linguistic research. Hudson (1980) has argued that many of the constructs of sociolinguistics—kinds of speech act (e.g. promise), types of interaction (e.g. business transaction), the parameters of power and solidarity, even the very concept of a speech community—can be usefully regarded as prototype categories, definable in the first instance in terms of clear cases. Another significant development has been the application of the prototype concept to the purely formal elements of linguistic description. Bybee and Moder (1983) claim that 'speakers of natural language form categorizations of linguistic objects in the same way that they form categorizations of natural and cultural objects', which suggests that 'the psychological principles which govern linguistic behavior are the same as those which govern other types of human behavior' (1983: 267). Bybee and Moder (see also Bybee and Slobin 1982) reached this conclusion from a study of certain morphological alternations in English. Amongst the strong

* John Taylor, 'Grammatical categories', ch. 10 of *Linguistic Categorization: Prototypes in Linguistic Theory*, (Oxford: Oxford University Press, 2nd edn., 1995). © 1989, 1995 John R. Taylor. Reprinted by permission.

TABLE I   Properties of English strong verbs having /æ/ – /ʌ/ or /ʌ/ – /ʌ/ in past tense and past participle. *Sing* and *cling*, which share a maximum number of properties typical of the verbs, have a more central status in the categories

	/ɪ/ *in present tense*	*Velar as final consonant*	*Nasal as final consonant*
sing	yes	yes	yes
cling	yes	yes	yes
hang	no	yes	yes
swim	yes	no	yes
stick	yes	yes	no
strike	no	yes	no

verbs in English are those which, like *sing*, show the vowel alternation /ɪ/ – /æ/ – /ʌ/ in the present tense, past tense, and past participle. Others, like *cling*, have the pattern /ɪ/ – /ʌ/ – /ʌ/. The two classes have been moderately productive over the centuries, having extended their membership to include verbs originally in other classes, such as *ring*, *fling*, *stick*, and *dig*. Also, verbs which have a vowel other than /ɪ/ in the present tense have been added, e.g. *hang*, *strike*, and, for some speakers, *sneak*, *shake*, and *drag*. These latter, on account of their non-conforming present tense forms, clearly count as more marginal members of the classes. In other respects, too, the classes exhibit a prototype structure (Table I). The majority of the verbs have as the final consonant of the stem a velar nasal (*sing*, *spring*, *cling*). Other verbs exhibit an only partial similarity to this characteristic of the central members. Some, for instance, have as their final consonant a non-velar nasal (*swim*, *win*, *spin*), others end in a non-nasal velar (*stick*, *dig*).

The extension of the prototype concept from word meanings to linguistic objects was perhaps inevitable, given the linguist's twofold interest in categories. Not only do linguistic forms symbolically stand for conceptual categories, linguistic forms themselves constitute categories. It is with the categorization of linguistic forms that we will be concerned in this chapter, in particular the categories WORD, AFFIX, and CLITIC, as well as the grammatical categories traditionally known as parts of speech. We shall see that there is a very remarkable parallelism between the structure of conceptual categories and the structure of linguistic categories. Just as there are central and marginal members of the conceptual category BIRD, so too a linguistic category like NOUN has representative and marginal members. And just as marginal instances of a conceptual category like CUP might overlap with marginal instances of neighbouring categories like BOWL or VASE—even though typical cups are quite distinct from typical bowls and typical vases—so too a category like WORD merges, at its boundaries, with categories like AFFIX and CLITIC. Facts like these provide further evidence against the view that prototype effects are merely an aspect of so-called performance, and thus outside the scope of a narrowly defined autonomous linguistics. Rather, prototype effects permeate the very structure of language itself.

WORDS, AFFIXES, AND CLITICS

In pre-generative days, the working out of criteria for the identification and classification of linguistic units was one of the primary concerns of linguistic enquiry. With the advent of the generative paradigm in the late 1950s and early 1960s, the exercise of 'grouping and classification' (Robins 1964: 180) appeared at best superfluous; the grammar itself would 'automatically, by its rules, characterize any relevant class' (Householder 1967: 103). Consequently, there has been very little discussion in generative circles of an issue which used to be thought fundamental, namely, how to define the word, the noun, the verb, etc. In this respect, the subject-matter of the present chapter harks back to earlier concerns, viewing them in the light of the prototype model which has been elaborated in preceding chapters.

As an illustration of what is involved in attributing prototype structure to a linguistic category, I will focus in this section on one of the most basic, and intuitively most salient (yet controversial) of all linguistic categories, the word.[1] It is notoriously difficult to give an adequate definition of WORD, such that one can unhesitatingly delimit the words in any given stretch of language. (Yet this has not prevented linguists from using the word as a theoretical construct.) No one, presumably, would question the word status of *mother* and *husband* in expressions like *This is Jane's mother, Meet Jane's husband.* Less clear is the number of words in the expressions *mother-in-law* and *ex-husband.* Problematic too is the number of words in contractions. How many words are there in the contracted form *there's* in *There's a man been shot*? Suppose we decide that the contraction consists of two words. What, then, is the identity of the second of the two words? (Note that **There is a man been shot* and **There has a man been shot* are both ungrammatical; cf. Lakoff 1987: 562 f.)

The existence of intuitively clear cases alongside a number of not-so-clear cases strongly suggests that we are dealing with a prototype category. We can give more substance to this intuition by restricting our attention, in the first instance, to the typical members of the category. We may begin by listing some of the attributes shared by those linguistic forms which we would unhesitatingly characterize as words:

(a) Words in the stream of speech can be optionally preceded and followed by pauses. In the limiting case, a word can stand alone as an independent utterance. As Bloomfield (1933: 178) put it, the word is 'the minimum free form'.

(b) In a stress language like English, each word is eligible for stress, both salience and tonic prominence.

(c) Words possess a fair degree of phonological invariance. Many phonological rules, for example, operate preferentially within the domain of the word, rather than over sequences of words. Thus we find instances of obligatory assimilation between component parts of words (*im*possible, *in*sensitive),[2] while between-word assimilations (e.g. the pronunciation of *good boy* as [gʊb bɒɪ]) are often optional, and dependent on speech style and speaking rate. Again, the stress pattern of a word is a fairly constant property of the word itself, and is determined in large part by the word's phonological and morphological structure (compare *réalist* and *realístic*). Only rarely is word stress affected by context (compare *He's only fourtéen* and *There are fóurteen people*).

(d) On the whole, words are rather unselective with regard to the kinds of item to which they may be adjacent. While we popularly think of adjectives as words which precede nouns, a moment's thought shows that an adjective can stand next to practically any part of speech.

---

[1] The term 'word' is ambiguous (Lyons 1977: 18 ff.). It can refer to a lexical item (in which case we would say that *run* and *running* are two forms of the same word), or to a segmentable portion of an utterance (in which case each occurrence of *run* and *running* in an utterance constitutes a separate word). Which sense is intended will hopefully be clear from the context.

[2] Assimilation is the process whereby one phoneme becomes 'more similar', with respect to some aspect of its articulation, to an adjacent phoneme. In *impossible*, the nasal of the negative prefix takes on the place of articulation (bilabial) of the following /p/, while in *insensitive*, the nasal has the alveolar articulation of the following /s/.

(e) Under appropriate conditions, words can be moved around in a sentence. The word sequences *X Y Z* and *Z X Y* might be equally acceptable (*I like John, John I like*). Again, under appropriate conditions, the second occurrence of a word in a sentence can be deleted: *She can sing but I can't sing* → *She can sing but I can't.*

We could go on listing further characteristics of words, but the above selection will suffice for our purposes. The five characteristics effectively distinguish words from units larger than the word (i.e. phrases, which consist of more than one word), and from component parts of words (i.e. stems and affixes). Consider for example the characteristics of affixes:[3]

(a) Affixes cannot occur independently of the stems to which they attach, neither can a pause, not even a hesitation pause, be inserted between an affix and its stem.
(b) Affixes are generally unstressable.
(c) Affixes are generally integrated into the phonological shape of the word of which they are a part. The phonological shape of the affix may be affected by the stem to which it is attached (e.g. by assimilation), or the phonological shape of the stem (e.g. with regard to stress placement) may be affected by the affix.
(d) Affixes are highly selective with regard to the kind of stem to which they attach. The third-person singular marker *-s* and the participial-forming *-ing*, for instance, can only attach to a verb stem.
(e) Affixes cannot be moved around independently of their stems, neither can the second occurrence of an affix be deleted; *singing and dancing* cannot be reduced to **singing and dance*, neither can *sings and dances* be replaced by **sings and dance*.

The various phonological and syntactic characteristics of words as opposed to affixes are analogous to the attributes on whose basis we decide membership of a conceptual category. In many instances, the attributes are correlated, and the word-affix distinction appears clear-cut. But just as there are entities which exhibit only some of the attributes typical of a conceptual category, with the consequence that these entities are accorded a more marginal status within the category, so sometimes an application of the tests for word and affix status can give ambiguous results. Consider the definite article *the:*

(a) Although the definite article alone cannot constitute a well-formed utterance, it may be separated from what follows by a hesitation pause.
(b) The definite article, although generally unstressed, can sometimes bear sentence stress.
(c) There is a degree of phonological integration between the article and an adjacent item, in that the phonetic form of the article is affected by the following sound: *the* [ðə] *man*, but *the* [ði] *earth*.
(d) *The* can stand in front of practically any part of speech: adjective (*the old man*), adverb (*the incredibly old man*), verb (*the—dare I say old—man*), preposition (*the in my opinion old man*), and so on.
(e) The definite article cannot be moved around by itself; if it moves, it moves along with the noun phrase of which it is a component. Often, a second occurrence of the article can be deleted (*the men and the women* → *the men and women*), but sometimes it cannot (*the old man and the sea* → **the old man and sea*).

---

[3] It is usual to distinguish between derivational, or word-forming affixes, and inflexional affixes. However, as Carstairs (1987: 4f.) notes, the distinction may be more of a continuum than a matter of discreteness. (Is the adverb-forming *-ly* derivational or inflexional?) Derivational affixes are used to create new words, while inflexional affixes change the form of a word according to its syntactic role in a sentence. Examples of the former include the verb-forming *-ize* in *characterize* (> *character*) and the negative-forming *un-* of *untidy*. Examples of inflexional affixes include the number agreement *-s* of *says* and the participial-forming *-ing* of *saying*.

What then is the status of *the*? Is it an affix? No, because it possesses a certain degree of autonomy: it can be preceded and followed by a pause, it can bear stress, and it is fairly unselective with regard to adjacent elements. Is it then a word? No, because it does not possess the full autonomy of a word: it cannot stand alone in an utterance, it cannot be moved independently of its host, and it is not always subject to deletion under identity. Probably, on the whole, *the is* more of a word than an affix—a fact reflected by our writing system. The main motivation for this decision is the freedom of *the* to stand adjacent to practically any part of speech. The importance of this criterion derives from the fact that the five tests for wordhood all point to the word as a syntactically and phonologically autonomous entity, intermediate in status between the minimally meaningful unit of language, the morpheme, and the complex units of phrase and sentence. Thus the concatenation of words is subject to syntactic constraints; at the same time the word is the domain for the operation of a number of phonological and morphophonological processes. The hierarchical structure of sentences is in turn consistent with a modular, or compartmentalized conception of grammar. One component of a grammar is responsible for word formation, through, for example, the combination of stems and derivational affixes. Words, in their appropriate phonological form, are listed in the lexicon. Another component is the syntax, which assembles words from the lexicon into well-formed syntactic units, while a further component puts words into their correct inflexional form. Within this kind of framework, it is clearly preferable to assemble noun phrases in the syntax, than to attach the article to all kinds of items in the word-formation or inflexional components. Hence the definite article, in spite of some affix-like properties, is best considered a word.

The distinction between words and affixes is complicated by the existence of another unit of linguistic structure, the clitic. In some respects, clitics are rather like words, in other respects they are like affixes. In addition, certain characteristics suggest that clitics form a category of their own. There are no really good examples of clitic in English, so I will illustrate from Zulu. Zulu has the morpheme *ke*, which attaches indifferently to practically any part of speech— noun, verb, adverb, etc.—generally at the end of whatever happens to be the first constituent of a clause. Its meaning corresponds roughly to English *and...then*. More precisely, it seems that *ke* underlines the given status of the sentence topic. Since only one element in any clause can be topicalized, it follows that *ke* can occur only once in a clause. Let us apply the word/affix tests to *ke*.

(a) *Ke* can never stand alone, neither can it be separated from its host by a pause.

(b) Zulu does not have sentence stress, so this test does not apply.

(c) There is obligatory phonological integration with the host. The penultimate syllable of a Zulu word is lengthened. For the purpose of the lengthening rule, *ke is* regarded as an integral part of the word, i.e. the addition of *ke* causes lengthening to shift one syllable to the right. The following examples illustrate the process (the colon represents vowel length, the hyphen indicates a morpheme boundary):

(1) (a) Ng-uba:ni igama lakho?
      It's-what name your
      "What's your name?"

 (b) Ng-ubani:-ke igama lakho?
      It's-what-then name your
      "And what's *your* name then?"

(d) Up to now, *ke* looks like an ordinary affix. One thing that distinguishes *ke* from affixes is the fact already noted, that *ke* can attach to practically anything, even to a word like *yebo* "yes" (*Yeboke* "OK, then"). Affixes, it will be recalled, are very highly constrained with regard to the stems to which they attach. Furthermore, there are often a number of arbitrary gaps in the distribution of affixes. While the past tense forming affix *-ed* only attaches to verb stems, not every verb stem can take the *-ed* suffix. There are no such restrictions on the occurrence of *ke*.

(e) Like affixes, *ke* cannot be moved around. Deletion of a second occurrence is not applicable, since *ke* can only occur once in a given sentence.

It is largely because of their freedom to attach to practically any part of speech that clitics are recognized as a special linguistic unit. Consistent with their special status, it has been proposed that clitics get inserted into a sentence by a special post-syntactic component of the grammar, distinct from both the word formation and the syntactic components (Zwicky 1985). This view is also supported by the fact that semantically clitics are usually different from affixes. Affixes change the semantic content and/or the syntactic function of a word. Clitics, on the other hand, do not affect word meaning or word function, but generally have to do with text structure or speaker attitude.

In spite of the general validity of the distinction, we again, not surprisingly, find borderline cases. Some putative clitics seem more like words, while others are not too different from affixes. Zulu has another morpheme, *nje*, which, like *ke*, attaches freely to different parts of speech; semantically it functions as a downtoner, with the meaning "only", "just". Unlike *ke*, however, *nje is* not phonologically integrated with its host, i.e. it does not affect the location of syllable lengthening; it can also stand as a one word utterance, with the meaning "so-so", "not bad". *Nje*, then, is a fairly word-like clitic. Or consider the possessive *'s* in English. If *'s* only attached to nouns denoting a possessor, it would constitute a fairly run-of-the-mill affix. But *'s* is not so tightly restricted, cf. *A friend of mine's house, Who the heck's book is this?* Consequently, *'s* could be regarded as a fairly affix-like clitic (or clitic-like affix). On the other hand the definite article, because of its freedom to attach to practically anything, might be categorized as a clitic-like word.

Table 2 displays the characteristics of words, affixes, and clitics. The table provides compelling evidence for graded membership of the categories in question. There are good, representative examples of words (*mother*), of affixes (*-ed*), and of clitics (Zulu *ke*); there are not such good examples (*the*), and there are borderline cases (*nje* and *'s*). That the categories have graded membership is not a new insight. It was clearly recognized by Robins in a passage

TABLE 2   Properties of words, affixes, and clitics

	Can stand alone	Can be separated by pauses	Can be stressed	Phonological autonomy	Selectivity of adjacent item	Subject to movement and deletion
mother	yes	yes	yes	high	low	yes
nje (Zulu)	sometimes	sometimes	n/a	high	very low	no
the	no	sometimes	sometimes	low	fairly low	sometimes (deletion)
-ed	no	no	no	low	very high	no
possessive *'s*	no	no	no	low	fairly high	no
-ke (Zulu)	no	no	n/a	low	very low	no

which uncannily anticipates the terminology of the prototype theorists:

> Words…are the products of several different though related criteria. Thus they comprise nuclear members of the category, to which all the criteria apply, more peripheral or marginal ones to which only some apply, and very marginal or doubtful cases in which the criteria may conflict and different conclusions may be reached by the different weighting of the conflicting criteria. (Robins 1964: 194–5)

Even so, most linguists, past and present, have operated on the assumption that what counts as a word or an affix *is* a matter of either-or. Indeed, the modular conception of grammar, outlined in an earlier paragraph, presupposes this approach. To permit degrees of membership in linguistic categories makes it necessary to revise, perhaps even to give up, the modular conception of grammar. The absence of a clear boundary between affixes and words (and between words and phrases) means of necessity that the grammar of the word (morphology) must merge into the grammar of the sentence (syntax). Both Lakoff (1987) and Langacker (1987) have argued that the lexicon and the syntax are not so much discrete components of grammar, but rather the ends of a continuum. For Hudson (1984), too, there is no natural division between the way a phrase is composed of words, and the way a word is composed of morphemes.

GRAMMATICAL CATEGORIES[4]

I now turn to a discussion of word classes—the traditional parts of speech—and of syntactic categories like NOUN PHRASE. A useful starting-point is the definition of *noun* in *Collins English Dictionary*.

(2) *Noun*: a word or group of words that refers to a person, place or thing or any syntactically similar word.

This definition consists of two parts. Firstly there is a semantic definition (nouns are defined in terms of what they mean) followed by a syntactic definition (nouns are defined in terms of their similar syntactic behaviour).

The inadequacy of an exclusively semantic definition of parts of speech has been recognized at least since the earliest days of structuralism. Thus Robins (1964: 228 f.) warns us that 'extra-linguistic' criteria, like meaning, must play no role in the assignment of words to word classes. Although one might quibble at Robins's view of meaning as something extra-linguistic, the strict exclusion of semantic criteria would at first sight appear a *sine qua non* for the definition of parts of speech. *Teacher* and *table* are both pretty good instances of words that refer to persons and things. But what about *doorway* and *sky*? Arguably, these are also 'things', but things of a rather intangible nature. We need to relax further our notion of thing as a discrete concrete entity in order to be able to say that a period of time like year, a colour like red, a property like height, or a state of mind like happiness, are things. Nouns like *swim* (as in *have a swim*) and *arrival*, on the other hand, would appear to refer not to things at all, but rather to activities and events. Thus, on purely semantic grounds, we would have to recognize a gradience of nounhood. *Teacher* and *table* are good examples of nouns, *doorway* and *sky* are less good examples, *year*, *red*, *height*, and *happiness* are rather marginal examples, while *swim* and *arrival* would not appear to be candidates at all. Semantic definitions of other parts of speech turn out to be equally unsatisfactory. Collins defines *adjective* as 'a word imputing a characteristic to a noun or pronoun'. Apart from the fact that it is not nouns as such to which

---

[4] I use the term 'grammatical category' to cover both lexical categories (i.e. parts of speech) and syntactic categories (i.e. NOUN PHRASE, SENTENCE, and other syntactic constructions).

characteristics are imputed, but rather their referents, this definition would exclude from the class of adjectives the word *late* in the expression *my late husband* ('being late' is not a characteristic of 'my husband'), as well as e.g. *former* and *each* in *my former wife* and *each day*.

An alternative to a purely semantic approach is given in the second half of the Collins definition of *noun*. Words are assigned to classes on the basis of common syntactic properties. As Gleason put it, word classes must be characterized by 'maximum homogeneity within the class' (1965: 130). The aim is to set up classes in such a way as to maximize the correlation of syntactic properties over the members of the class, and to minimize the correlation of properties over members of different classes. 'Syntactic properties', as used here, is a cover term which includes at least three kinds of phenomena:

(a) Phonological. In some cases, a grammatical category may be regularly associated with a distinctive phonological structure. In English, compound nouns (*bláckboard*, *phýsics teacher*) are characterized by initial stress, in contrast to adjective-plus-noun combinations (*black bóard*, *American téacher*), which have final stress.

(b) Morphological. It frequently happens that words of a given class, and only words of that class, can take on the morphological trappings of the class. Thus, in English, only verbs can be marked for tense; only nouns can appear in singular and plural form; only adjectives and adverbs admit of degrees of comparison. The ability to be inflected for, e.g. tense, can thus serve as a heuristic test for verb status.

(c) Distributional. Typically, certain slots in a syntactic construction are reserved for words of a particular form class. A characteristic of adjectives, for example, is their possibility of occurring in the second place in the noun phrase construction DET ADJ N.

Before proceeding, we might note that the kinds of criteria listed above do not always yield unambiguous evidence for category membership. Consider again the adjective category. An adjective like *cheap* exhibits a number of typically adjectival properties. It may be used both attributively and predicatively (*the cheap book*, *the book is cheap*); it can be graded (*very*, *extremely cheap*) and admits both comparative and superlative forms (*cheaper*, *cheapest*); the modified noun may be replaced by pronominal *one* (*an expensive book and a cheap one*). Not all adjectives share all of these properties. Some can be used only in attributive position (*my former husband*, **my husband is former*), others only in predicative position (*the child is asleep*, *the asleep child). Others cannot be graded, and do not have comparative forms (*each*, *first*). Consider, as a particularly problematic example, the status of *apple* in *apple pie*. At first glance, *apple* looks like a noun, and *apple pie* an N N compound, analogous to *physics teacher*. Yet some speakers accept the predicative construction (*This pie is apple*, cf. **This teacher is physics*), some even accept comparative and pronominal expressions (*This pie is more apple than that one*, *I wanted a meat pie, not an apple one*). Also, some speakers employ the stress pattern of an ADJ N phrase, not that of an N N compound, i.e. they say *apple píe* rather than *ápple pie*. Is *apple*, then, a noun or an adjective?

With the advent of the generative paradigm, a fourth kind of syntactic property has come to the fore; this concerns the ability of a string of words to undergo a transformation. Transformational rules (e.g. rules of movement and deletion) do not operate blindly on any random string of items; each rule requires as input an ordered string of constituents of the appropriate syntactic class. For instance, the rule of yes-no question formation converts a string of the form NP AUX VP into AUX NP VP, i.e. the rule inverts the subject NP and the auxiliary. The possibility of a rule applying to a given string of words (more precisely, to the phrase marker underlying the string) can thus provide evidence for the grammatical categories present in the input, i.e. yes-no question formation may be used as a test both for NP status, and for auxiliary-verb status.

Now, the transformational paradigm absolutely requires that membership in grammatical classes is a clear-cut matter. To see why this is so, let us briefly consider some of the properties of Chomsky's Extended Standard Theory (see e.g. Chomsky 1976). The EST model envisages a grammar consisting of a number of autonomous modules. One module is the so-called 'base component', responsible for generating 'initial phrase markers' (the 'deep structures' of earlier versions of the theory). Initial phrase markers are generated in two stages. Firstly, the 'categorial component' of the base generates, by means of rewrite rules of the kind S → NP AUX VP, NP → DET N, an 'abstract phrase marker', i.e. a string of category symbols with an associated structural description. The other module of the base, the 'lexical insertion component', slots items from the lexicon into the abstract phrase marker. Any item in the lexicon marked with an appropriate feature, e.g. [N], is a candidate for insertion into the N-slot of the abstract phrase marker. The output of the base is thus a string of items with an associated structural description. This initial phrase marker serves as input to the other components of the grammar, e.g. the transformational and phonological components.

Botha (1968: 67 f.) has pointed out that generative grammar offers an exclusively extensional characterization of word classes—which items count as members of a class is ultimately a matter of exhaustive listing. Nouns are simply those items in the lexicon which bear the feature specification [N], and which, in virtue of this feature specification, are candidates for insertion under the N-nodes generated by the categorial component. The further properties of nouns—their morphological characteristics, their distinctive distribution, their accessibility to transformational rules—are derivative, in that they fall out from the operation of the base component, and the manner in which its output is handled in the other components of the grammar. Further, the generative model presupposes a limited number of (putatively universal) categories, like NOUN, VERB, DETERMINER, as well as, of course, subcategories of these categories, e.g. COUNT NOUN and MASS NOUN as subcategories of NOUN (but these subcategories are subject to the same kind of extensional definition as the superordinate categories), the items in the lexicon being associated with the corresponding syntactic features, like [N], [V], [DET], and so on. These features are the syntactic counterparts of the classical phonological and semantic features discussed in Chapter 2 [not included]. The features, that is, are construed as binary, primitive, universal, and (presumably) innate, and they necessarily establish either-or membership in the respective categories. As already mentioned, it is in virtue of their feature specification that lexical items can get inserted into the abstract phrase marker; the meaning of the lexical item is irrelevant in this respect. Similarly, transformational rules operate on underlying phrase markers, independently of the semantics of the lexical items which fill the category slots. As a consequence, not only are grammatical categories clear-cut entities, the category GRAMMATICAL SENTENCE has clear-cut boundaries too. A grammatical sentence is whatever string happens to be generated as output of the transformational component. Even a language has clear-cut boundaries, comprising all and only the grammatical sentences generated by the grammar. Sentences not generated by the grammar are, by definition, ungrammatical, and therefore not part of the language.

The far-reaching implications of the generative conception of grammatical categories—in particular the exclusion of semantic criteria from grammaticality, the postulation of a clear dividing line between the grammatical sentences of a language and non-grammatical sentences, and the related notion of a language as a well-defined set of grammatical sentences—have been queried by a number of scholars (e.g. Hockett 1968, Matthews 1979, Sampson 1980a). Here, I want to restrict my attention to the assumption that it is all-or-nothing membership in a grammatical category that determines syntactic behaviour. In fact, it has been known since the earliest days of generative grammar that category membership, as specified by a phrase marker, does not always guarantee the applicability of a transformational rule. The matter was investigated by George Lakoff in his 1965 dissertation (Lakoff 1970). Lakoff assembled numerous instances of rules which fail to apply to input strings, even though the inputs met the structural description of the rule. The phenomenon is particularly frequent with regard to the 'minor' rules of word derivation. Thus not all transitive verbs undergo agentive nominalization:

(3) (a) John is one who imports rugs →
        John is an importer of rugs
    (b) John was one who knew that fact →
        *John was the knower of that fact

and not all verbs undergo able-substitution:

(4) (a) His handwriting can be read →
        His handwriting is readable
    (b) The lighthouse can be spotted →
        *The lighthouse is spottable

'Major' rules are also implicated. For instance, not all transitive sentences of the form NP V NP undergo passivization:

(5) (a) John kicked the ball →
        The ball was kicked by John
    (b) John owes two dollars →
        *Two dollars are owed by John

Such irregularities can be (and were) taken care of by the flagging of individual items in the lexicon; a verb, for example, could be marked [−PASSIVE], so as to block the application of the passive transformation. Alternatively—but given the extensional characterization of word classes, the alternative amounts to the same thing—word classes may be subcategorized such that one subcategory undergoes the rule in question, while the other does not. Even so, these solutions ignore the possibility that some items might be better candidates for a transformation than others, i.e. the putative subcategories might themselves have fuzzy boundaries. Consider passivization. Some transitive verbs (like *kick*) readily passivize, others (like *resemble*) do not passivize at all. With *owe*, the situation is not so clear. Lakoff's *Two dollars are owed by John* does seem odd. But what about *Millions of dollars are currently owed by third-world governments*?

The fuzziness of grammatical categories shows up very clearly in a series of papers by Ross (e.g. Ross 1972, 1973), which extended the approach taken by Lakoff in his dissertation. Ross showed that in many cases members of a category can be graded with respect to their ability to undergo a range of transformations. The transformations themselves can also be graded—some apply more or less across the board to all input strings of the appropriate structure, while others are much choosier in this regard. Consider, for example, the category NOUN PHRASE (Ross 1973). Only some NPs—preferentially those which designate humans—can undergo the rule of double raising,[5] as illustrated in (6):

(6) (a) It is likely to be shown that John has cheated →
        John is likely to be shown to have cheated
    (b) It is likely to be shown that no headway has been made →
        *No headway is likely to be shown to have been made

[5] Raising is a rule which moves a constituent from a 'lower' embedded sentence into a 'higher' sentence. Double raising involves two such movements.

Double raising is a fairly choosy rule, and *headway* (part of the idiom *make headway*) is not very accessible to it. Question tag formation, on the other hand, applies more or less across the board to any subject NP. Even here, though, there are some dubious cases:

(7) (a) Some headway has been made →
        Some headway has been made, hasn't it?
    (b) Little heed was paid to her →
        ?*Little heed was paid to her, was it?[6]

Not even one of the most robust properties of NPs—the fact that, in subject position, an NP determines the number of the auxiliary verb—shows up in all instances. By most of the criteria for subject NP status, such as inversion with the auxiliary in yes-no questions (8)(b), raising (8)(c), accusative-gerund complementation (8)(d), *there* in (8)(a) must be considered a subject NP. Yet it fails to determine the number of the verb in (8)(e):

(8) (a) There's a man at the door
    (b) Is there a man at the door?
    (c) There seems to be a man at the door
    (d) I was surprised at there being a man at the door
    (e) There are (*is) two men at the door[7]

Contrary to one of the major assumptions of the generative paradigm, it seems, then, syntactic rules *are* sensitive to the lexical content of a phrase marker. Furthermore, lexical items can be graded, according to how readily they undergo specific transformations. Neither Ross nor Lakoff employed the terminology of prototype theory, which was being developed independently by cognitive psychologists like Rosch. Yet when we read (Ross 1973: 98) of 'copperclad, brass-bottomed NPs', and of some noun phrases being 'more noun-phrasy' than others, we readily recognize the commonality with a prototype approach. Some NPs share a maximum number of typical noun phrase attributes; they constitute more central members of the category. Others—the more marginal members—display only a few of the attributes typical of the category.

The gradience of grammatical categories—like the gradience of the category WORD—is not in itself a new discovery. The notion that word classes have central members, which satisfy a maximum number of criteria of the respective class, and more peripheral, borderline members, was fully articulated in Crystal (1967) [included in this volume]. With the almost total hegemony of the generative paradigm in the late 1960s and the 1970s, the insights of non-generative linguists on this topic tended to be ignored, or forgotten. The last few years, however, have seen a rediscovery of category gradience. Symptomatic is the importance assigned to degree of category membership in the recent *Comprehensive Grammar of the English Language* (Quirk et al. 1985), as compared with the earlier, 1972 grammar (Quirk et al. 1972). Interesting, too, is McCawley's recent comparison of parts of speech with the categories of biological natural kinds:

Parts of speech are much more like biological species than has generally been recognized. Within any part of speech, or any biological species, there is considerable diversity. Parts of speech can be distinguished from one another, just as biological species can be distinguished from one another, in terms of characteristics that are typical for the members of that part of speech (or species), even though none of

---

[6] The acceptability judgements in (6) and (7) are Ross's.
[7] The case of subject *there is* actually more complicated. Plural verb agreement appears in the raised construction, e.g. *There seem (*seems) to be two men at the door*, suggesting that *there* copies, without overt morphological marking, the number of the following noun phrase (*a man, two men*) (cf. Lakoff 1987: 548). Even so, a noun phrase with no inherent number is a pretty untypical exemplar of the category!

those properties need be instantiated by all members of the parts of speech (or species). (McCawley 1986: 12)

This view is not quite so innovative as McCawley would have us believe; Botha (1968: 56) had mentioned (and, as a committed generativist, dismissed), the idea that word classes might exhibit the same kind of structure as biological natural kinds.

THE SEMANTIC BASIS OF GRAMMATICAL CATEGORIES

In the discussion so far I have endeavoured to adhere to the structuralist maxim of the irrelevance of semantic criteria for word class definitions, and considered grammatical categories solely in terms of their syntactic properties. Even this approach, as we have seen, strongly points to the prototype structure of the categories. I would now like to reappraise the semantic basis for category definition. Cognitive linguists reject the notion of a syntactic level of linguistic organization, autonomous of semantics. The aim, as Lakoff (1987: 491) puts it, is to 'show how aspects of form follow from aspects of meaning'. Langacker is even more explicit: 'Cognitive grammar makes specific claims about . . . the notional basis of fundamental grammatical categories' (1987: 183), including the claim that 'all members of a given [grammatical] class share fundamental semantic properties' (1987: 189).

Clearly any attempt at a semantic definition of grammatical categories like NOUN and VERB will have to be more sophisticated than the traditional dictionary definitions cited earlier. If nouns and verbs do share semantic properties, these are obviously going to be of a highly abstract nature. Langacker discusses the issue at considerable length (1987: chs. 5–7). His proposal is that NOUN be defined as a linguistic unit which profiles a 'thing', where 'thing' is defined as a 'region in some domain' (1987: 189). Similarly, verbs are defined as linguistic units which profile a 'temporal relation', while adjectives, adverbs, and prepositions profile an 'atemporal relation'. Langacker's definition of NOUN readily incorporates the traditional notion of a noun as the name of a person or a concrete object. Persons and objects are bounded regions in the domain of three-dimensional space, while mass concrete nouns, like *water*, profile *un*bounded regions in three-dimensional space. But the definition does not give any priority to the spatial domain. *Red* shares the common property in that it profiles a region in the domain of colour, a year is a bounded region in the domain of time, C-sharp is a region in the domain of pitch, and so on. Langacker then goes on to characterize 'region' in terms of the 'interconnectedness' of entities within a domain. In this way, nouns which refer to groups of discrete entities, like *archipelago*, *constellation*, and *team*, are brought under the schematic definition. Interconnectedness is inversely related to the 'cognitive distance' between entities within a domain, which is in turn a function of cognitive scanning over time. This understanding of interconnectedness makes it possible to account for the status of deverbal nouns like *arrival*. *Arrival* profiles, not a temporal relation per se, but a collectivity of temporally adjacent relations. The profile of a deverbal noun like *jumping*, on the other hand, is analogous, in the temporal domain, to that of a concrete mass noun like *water*. Jumping, as well as other abstracts like love and envy, is construed as a relatively homogeneous and unbounded 'substance', which is instantiated whenever some specific instance of the process or quality occurs.

An alternative to searching for what is common to all members of a grammatical class is to capitalize on traditional definitions, and to incorporate these into a prototype account. It may be noted that the manner in which Langacker takes his reader through his definition of NOUN itself suggests the plausibility of a prototype account. Thus we may say, following tradition, that a noun designates, in the first instance, a discrete, concrete, three-dimensional entity (i.e.

a bounded region in three-dimensional space). By a projection of the thing-schema on to non-spatial domains, linguistic units which profile regions in the other domains, e.g. colour, time, pitch, etc., get included in the noun category. Then, with a more sophisticated definition of region, we account for the noun-status of *archipelago*, *team*, *arrival*, and so on. Finally, we establish a metaphorical link between concrete substances and abstract qualities; Langacker himself needs to appeal to such analogies in order to account for the noun status of abstracts like *love* and *envy*.

A prototype view of a category is not necessarily incompatible with an account which attempts to capture what is common to all the category members. It would seem, though, that there are good reasons for assigning a certain primacy to the prototype account of NOUN. A prototype view of NOUN entails that some nouns are better examples of the category, while others have a more marginal status. Significantly, the closeness of an item to the (semantically characterized) prototype tends to correlate, in many instances, with its closeness to the prototype defined on purely syntactic criteria. This correlation emerges very clearly from Ross's paper on NPs (1973). As we saw, NPs can be hierarchically ordered according to their accessibility to various transformational rules. The most accessible (i.e. the most 'noun-phrasy') are those NPs which refer to conscious, volitionally acting, animate creatures, primarily human beings. Somewhat lower on Ross's hierarchy are NPs which refer to concrete inanimates, followed by those which refer to events and abstracts. Even lower are 'meteorological *it*' (*It's muggy*) and 'subject *there*' (*There's a man at the door*). The relevance of the semantic prototype will be obvious. Interestingly, the syntactic criteria even suggest that our earlier characterization of the noun prototype may have been too broad. It seems that the best examples of the category refer, not to any concrete three-dimensional object, but, more specifically, to human beings.

The correlation of syntactic and semantic criteria for nounhood shows up in many places. For an illustration we may take the possessive genitive construction, as represented by the formula NP's N. Consider the kinds of noun which can serve as the head of the 'possessor' NP. A noun like *teacher* is readily available: *the teacher's house*, *the teacher's work*, *the teacher's arrival*, and so on. Nouns which are semantically more distant from the prototype are less satisfactory; *the table's surface* and *the building's age* are still (perhaps) OK, but *the sky's colour* and *the doorway's height* are more dubious. Some of the non-prototypical nouns behave rather erratically. *In a year's time* and *the year's work* are standard expressions. One would normally prefer *by the end of the year* to *by the year's end*, although the latter expression is sometimes encountered in journalistic texts. Yet analogous expressions like *before the year's middle* and *since the year's start* are impossible. Equally bad are possessive expressions with nouns like *arrival* and *swim*: *my arrival's time*, *the swim's place*. In brief, not any noun can be inserted with equal facility into the possessive construction. Some occur freely, some hardly at all, while with some insertion is dubious or sporadic. And the ease with which nouns can designate a 'possessor' appears to correlate with closeness to the *semantically* defined prototype.[8]

A prototype approach to word classes has been adopted (implicitly) by Givón (1979). Givón argues that the essential difference between nouns and verbs resides in the 'time-stability' of their referents. Time-stability constitutes a continuum. At one pole are those

---

[8] A similar state of affairs holds with other uses of the 's morpheme. Optionally, the 's morpheme may be used in a gerundial expression following a preposition: *without the teacher('s) knowing*, *in spite of the teacher('s) being aware*, etc. As nouns diverge from the prototype, the possibility of using the 's morpheme declines much more rapidly than with the possessive construction: *without the table's being moved*, *in spite of the year's having started*, *as a result of his arrival's having been delayed*. The 's morpheme, then, only seems to attach to nouns of the very highest degree of (a semantically defined) nouniness, i.e. nouns which refer to human beings.

entities with the highest time-stability, i.e. entities which do not change their identity over time. These are (typically) referred to by nouns. Prototypical verbs, on the other hand, refer to entities which lack time-stability, i.e. events and rapid changes in state (1979: 14). A further corollary is that the referents of nouns are characterized in terms of their existence in space; the typical noun-referent is an identifiable, enduring thing. Verb-referents, on the other hand, typically have existence only at a certain point in time; the typical verb-referent is thus an identifiable event (1979: 320 f.).

Developing Givón's approach, Hopper and Thompson (1985) have pointed out that the status of a word within its respective grammatical category is by no means a fixed property of the word in question. The semantically relevant properties—in the case of nouns, the extent to which the noun refers to an identifiable, enduring thing, with verbs, whether the verb refers to a specific dynamic event—can vary according to context. Consider the following sentences (based on Hopper and Thompson 1985):

(9) (a) We trapped a bear in the forest
    (b) Bear-trapping used to be a popular sport

In (a), both *trap* and *bear* are being used as prototypical members of their respective classes. Consistent with this function, both verb and noun can take on the whole range of typically verbal and nominal trappings. The verb is marked for tense (past rather than present), aspect (simple rather than progressive), polarity (affirmative rather than negative), mood (indicative rather than imperative), and voice (active rather than passive). Similarly, the noun can take on the various trappings typical of its class. It can appear as singular or plural, it can be preceded by a determiner, it can be modified by adjectives and relative clauses. The (b) sentence is very different. *Bear* in this sentence does not refer to a discrete identifiable object, neither does *trap* refer to a single identifiable event. Symptomatic of this loss of semantic categoriality is the fact that neither word can be inflected or modified. The potential oppositions between singular and plural, affirmative and negative, past and present, active and passive, and so on, are to all intents and purposes neutralized.

The phenomenon is quite general. As Hopper and Thompson (1985) document with data from a range of languages, when a noun which can potentially refer to a discrete entity does not in fact do so, it tends to lose the morphological and distributional attributes of the noun class. In the (a) sentences below, *fire*, *buffalo*, and *president* function, both syntactically and semantically, as highly representative examples of the noun class. The (b) sentences, in contrast, exemplify the partial decategorialization of the nouns. In (10)(b) the noun has been incorporated into a complex verb (*to make fire*), in (11)(b) the noun is modifying another noun, while in (12)(b) the noun does not refer to a specific individual, but designates a role in a social institution. In all three cases, the nouns cannot be inflected for number, neither can they be modified by adjectives.

(10) (a) We made a big fire
     (b) We made (*big) fire
(11) (a) We ate the meat from a slaughtered buffalo
     (b) We ate (*slaughtered) buffalo meat
(12) (a) Meet the new president of the society
     (b) He was elected (*the new) president

The decategorialization of nouns is paralleled by the case of verbs which, in certain contexts, lose the morphological trappings typical of their class. Givón (1984) makes an important distinction between 'realis' and 'irrealis' verb forms. The former—restricted in the main to affirmative, declarative main clauses in the present or a past tense—report on some state of affairs that actually exists, or existed. Irrealis forms, on the other hand, refer to some non-existing, or not-yet-existing, state of affairs. Irrealis forms include futures and negatives, and are typically found in counterfactual clauses and clauses expressing a wish, desire, or command. Very often, irrealis forms exhibit a neutralization of oppositions characteristic of realis. In English, tense contrasts are neutralized in the imperative; the demise of the past subjunctive in modern spoken French and Italian has left only one tense form in the irrealis subjunctive mood; in Zulu, the realis contrast between the recent past tense and the remote past tense gives place in the negative to a single past tense form (Taylor 1987).

The decategorialization of verbs is especially striking in subordinate clauses. It is here that verbs, in English, may appear as infinitives or gerunds. As such, the verbs lose many of their morphological and distributional characteristics, such as agreement with a third-person singular subject, and the ability to be preceded by auxiliaries. Givón (1980) has noted that the occurrence of these non-finite verb forms correlates strikingly with the extent to which the subordinate clause describes a state of affairs which is dependent on the wishes, intentions, or influence of the subject of the main clause. In (a) below, Peter's departure is an autonomous event, independent of John's act of reporting. The subordinate verb can realize any of the contrasts typically associated with categorial verbs. In the remaining sentences, Peter's departure is to a greater or lesser extent dependent on the wishes or action reported in the main clause.

(13) (a) John said that Peter would leave/had left/might leave, etc.
    (b) John enabled Peter to leave
    (c) John persuaded Peter to leave
    (d) John forced Peter to leave
    (e) John insisted on Peter leaving

To the question whether semantic criteria are relevant to grammatical categorization, the answer must be affirmative. Semantic criteria surely play a role in any intensional definition of word classes, so noticeably lacking in generative treatments of the subject. This is not to claim that all the members of a grammatical category necessarily share a common semantic content. (But neither do all the members of a grammatical category necessarily share the same syntactic properties.) Even less would one want to put forward semantic criteria as the sole basis for deciding category membership. Grammatical categories have a prototype structure, with central members sharing a range of both syntactic and semantic attributes. Failure of an item to exhibit some of these attributes does not of itself preclude membership.

REFERENCES

Bailey, C.-J. N., and R. W. Shuy (eds.) (1973). *New Ways of Analysing Variation in English*. Washington, DC: Georgetown University Press.

Bloomfield, L. (1933). *Language*. London: Allen & Unwin.

Botha, R. P. (1968). *The Function of the Lexicon in Transformational Generative Grammar*. The Hague: Mouton.

Bybee, J. L., and C. L. Moder (1983). 'Morphological classes as natural categories'. *Language* 59: 251–70.

——and D. I. Slobin (1982). 'Rules and schemas in the development and use of the English past tense'. *Language* 58: 265–89.

Carstairs, A. (1987). *Allomorphy in Inflexion*. London: Croom Helm.

Chomsky, N. (1976). *Reflections on Language*. London: Fontana.

Crystal, D. (1967). 'English'. *Lingua* 17: 24–56.

Givón, T. (1979). *On Understanding Grammar*. New York: Academic Press.

——(1980). 'The binding hierarchy and the typology of complements'. *Studies in Language* 4: 333–77.

——(1984). *Syntax: A Functional-Typological Introduction*, vol. i. Amsterdam: Benjamins.

Gleason, H. A. (1965). *Linguistics and English Grammar*. New York: Holt, Rinehart & Winston.

Haiman, J. (ed.) (1985). *Iconicity in Syntax*. Amsterdam: Benjamins.

Hockett, C. F. (1968). *The State of the Art*. The Hague: Mouton.

Hopper, P. J., and S. A. Thompson (1985). 'The iconicity of the universal categories "noun" and "verb" '. In Haiman (1985: 151–83).

Householder, F. W. (1967). 'Ancient Greek'. *Lingua* 17: 103–28.

Hudson, R. (1980). *Sociolinguistics*. Cambridge: Cambridge University Press.

——(1984). *Word Grammar*. Oxford: Blackwell.

Lakoff, G. (1970). *Irregularity in Syntax*. New York: Holt, Rinehart & Winston.

——(1987). *Women, Fire, and Dangerous Things: What Categories Reveal About the Mind*. Chicago: University of Chicago Press.

Langacker, R. W. (1987). *Foundations of Cognitive Grammar*, vol. i: *Theoretical Prerequisites*. Stanford, Calif.: Stanford University Press.

Lörscher, W., and R. Schulze (eds.) (1987). *Perspectives on Language in Performance. Studies in Linguistics, Literary Criticism, and Language Teaching and Learning. To Honour Werner Hüllen on the Occasion of His Sixtieth Birthday*. Tübingen: Narr.

Lyons, J. (1977). *Semantics* (2 vols). Cambridge: Cambridge University Press.

McCawley, J. D. (1986). 'What linguists might contribute to dictionary making if they could get their act together'. In P. C. Bjarkman and V. Raskin (eds.), *The Real-World Linguist: Linguistic Applications in the 1980s*, 3–18. Norwood: Ablex.

Matthews, P. H. (1979). *Generative Grammar and Linguistic Competence*. London: Allen & Unwin.

Quirk, R., S. Greenbaum, G. Leech and J. Svartvik (1972). *A Grammar of Contemporary English*. London: Longman.

———————(1985). *A Comprehensive Grammar of the English Language*. London: Longman.

Robins, R. H. (1964). *General Linguistics: An Introductory Survey*. London: Longman.

Ross, J. R. (1972). 'Endstation Hauptwort: the category squish'. In *Papers from the Eighth Regional Meeting of the Chicago Linguistic Society*, 316–28.

——(1973). 'A fake NP squish'. In Bailey and Shuy (1973: 96–140).

Sampson, G. (1980). *Making Sense*. Oxford: Oxford University Press.

Smith, E. E., and D. L. Medin (1981). *Categories and Concepts*. Cambridge, Mass.: Harvard University Press.

Taylor, J. (1987). 'Tense and metaphorisations of time in Zulu'. In Lörscher and Schulze (1987: 214–29).

Zwicky, A. M. (1985). 'Clitics and particles'. *Language* 61: 283–305.

PART IV
Gradience in Grammar

18

Gradience

DWIGHT BOLINGER

THE ALL-OR-NONE

One thing more than all else together has set the compass for contemporary linguistics: the discovery that a continuous stream of speech can be divided into systematically recurring segments that succeed one another in time. Segmental analysis has swept the field so triumphantly that for a number of years nothing else has seemed of much importance in language. All that matters, it appeared, could be formalized in statements of presence or non-presence, or of *A* versus *B*, and if anything of obvious significance did not readily fit this scheme, the lack was in us as observers, not in it as a datum.

The theoretical tenets that follow from the success of segmentation are simple ones and have been stated many times, most forthrightly, perhaps, in the following by Martin Joos: "Ordinary mathematical techniques fall mostly into two classes, the continuous (e.g. the infinitesimal calculus) and the discrete or discontinuous (e.g. finite group theory). Now it will turn out that the mathematics called 'linguistics' belongs in the second class. It does not even make any compromise with continuity, as does statistics, or infinite-group theory. Linguistics is a quantum mechanics in the most extreme sense. All continuity, all possibilities of infinitesimal gradation, are shoved outside of linguistics in one direction or the other."[1] He has in mind principally phonetics, which we might say is shoved down, and semantics, which is shoved up.

Hockett puts it more succinctly: "In general . . ., if we find continuous-scale contrasts in the vicinity of what we are sure is language, we exclude them from language."[2] Likewise Roman Jakobson: "Grammar, a real *ars obligatoria*, imposes upon the speaker its yes-or-no decisions."[3]

What with vigorous leadership and willing followership, the doctrine of discontinuity has found its fullest acceptance among American scholars. But not all of them have from the very first kept the pledge of total abstinence. When Stanley Newman described his "rhetorical accent" in English, he did it along lines of continuity, not discreteness. This accent, he says, "is characterized primarily by quantitative features. In *He lives in a la.rge house*, the word *large* . . . may be stretched to an abnormal length . . . The rhetorical accent is subject to gradations . . . [with] overtones of awe, amazement, admiration, and many other subtle and elusive shadings in attitude."[4]

* Dwight L. Bolinger, 'The all-or-none', ch. 1 of *Generality, Gradience, and the All-or-None* (The Hague: Mouton, 1961). © 1961 Mouton de Gruyter. Reprinted by permission.

[1] 'Description of Language Design', *Journal of the Acoustical Society of America*, 22 (1950): 701–8.
[2] *A Manual of Phonology* (Baltimore, 1955), p. 17.
[3] *American Anthropologist*, 61 (1959): 5, 2.141.
[4] 'On the stress system of English', *Word* 2 (1946): 171–87.

Later, the very success of linguistic analysis came to put a strain on the theory of discontinuity as outsiders were attracted to it and asked themselves what significance it might have for them. For communications engineers it was made to order. Others, among them the psychologists, have asked questions that are hard to answer. One that is pertinent came recently from Howard Maclay and Charles Osgood, who suggest that the rejection of continuity may have been due to identifying it with a particular kind of continuity that is not really typical. The continuity that phonemics rescued us from was that of continuous variations in phonetic quality, the features that a spectrogram makes visible in the shape of formants and transitions. But these, they point out, are a special set. They are the ones that "are systematically related to language structure, since ... [they] may be translated into discrete phonemic categories by means of linguistic discovery methods. Hesitations"—these being the phenomena that interest the authors—"are not pre-linguistic in this sense; they function as auxiliary events which help to identify and circumscribe linguistic units, rather than as part of the raw data for which a structural statement must account." They are in "non-random relation to linguistic forms". So Maclay and Osgood ask "whether a structural statement" should not "account for statistically relevant hesitations as it now does for continuously varying phonetic qualities", and in this way bring more emphasis on statistics in a field that up to now "has preferred to rely on [an] ... 'either-or' approach".[5]

Other recent declarations in favor of continuity are to be found in the fields of lexicon,[6] transformational analysis,[7] and dialectology.[8] These do not challenge the traditional recourse to discontinuity in phonemic analysis, but look to ways of handling other kinds of linguistic data that pour in on us in increasing volume as investigators leave the comparatively jagged terrain of recurrent partials and explore the smoother slopes that lie above. Where the basic units are concerned, most would still agree with R. B. Lees when he chides the "delusive notion that linguistics must surrender its traditional 'all-or-none' view of occurrence for a 'probabilistic view in which we are concerned with the likelihood that one class will occur rather than another'".[9]

From the standpoint of what has become traditional in American linguistics, the question is not whether there are such things as continuous phenomena in parts of human behavior that lie close to linguistics—many would grant that there are—but whether such

[5] 'Hesitation phenomena in spontaneous English speech', *Word* 15 (1959): 19–44, esp. 39. For the phonetic continuum and devices to extricate us from it, see W. Haas, 'Relevance in phonetic analysis', *Word* 15 (1959): 1–18.

[6] "One must reckon, then, with a continuum of subtly graded possibilities of matching [of degree of fusion in binomials such as *free and easy, to and fro, dead or alive,* etc.]." Yakov Malkiel, 'Studies in irreversible binomials', *Lingua* 8 (1959): 113–60. "Between these two extremes of literalness and symbolism there stretches a continuum of finely graded possibilities." *Ibid.* 138.

Floyd Lounsbury moves in from the direction of anthropology. Writing on kinship usage—"A semantic analysis of Pawnee kinship usage", *Language* 32 (1956): 158–94—he concludes his article with these remarks: "In some areas of lexicon, semantic structure may be so complex that it is impossible or unprofitable to approach it ... with Aristotelian class logic and the 'same or different' pragmatic test as the principal tools. It may become necessary to abandon the Aristotelian dichotomy of *A* vs. *not-A* ... Continuous scales may be introduced in place of these sharp dichotomies ... and tests other than the simple 'same or different' may have to be devised."

[7] Zellig Harris, in 'Co-occurrence and transformation', *Language* 33 (1957): 283–340, is concerned (292–3) about how to test "for identity of co-occurrence ranges", how information may be elicited from informants about whether co-occurrence ranges are identical or not. "This is a very different type of experimental condition ... The results involve a new measure: degree or type of acceptability (natural, uncomfortable, nonce-form); for example, if we are testing co-occurrents of ( )*ish*, an informant may be uncertain about *grandfatherish*, consider *deepish* uncomfortable, and *countryside-ish* a nonce-form, and reject *uncle-ish* or *wise-ish* outright."

[8] G. R. Cochrane distinguishes gradations in strength of correspondence between one dialect and another in *Word* 15 (1959): 78.

[9] *Language* 35 (1959): 301.

phenomena should be regarded as the object of linguistic study. It comes down more to a scheme of priorities than to a denial of possible ultimate importance: a higher value, for the present, is placed on phenomena that lend themselves to an all-or-none analysis. Later, when we get around to them, we may interest ourselves in peripheral matters and be better equipped to deal with them as a result of our earlier self-discipline—and there is always the hoped-for possibility that what looked to be continuous from a distance is actually discontinuous.

One can argue that there are as many faults as there are virtues in such an approach—that while taking in too much results in imprecision, taking in too little results in provincialism and loss of perspective: the field should be smaller because we want it to be exact, or it should be larger because without a theory of the whole it becomes circular. I do not intend to argue along these lines. What I want to consider is whether there are continuous phenomena permeating the very core of micro-micro-linguistics, whether microlinguists have played with them without realizing the nature of the stuff, fitting round pegs into square holes.

I believe that they have, that in practice microlinguistics has not been able to get along without continuous phenomena, so it has taken a small bite out of them, chewed some discontinuity into it, and let the rest go. Take the following from Pike's treatment of English stress: "There is a further phonemic degree of stress...limited to superimposed usage. Phonetically it is EXTRA STRONG, and has the meaning of EMPHASIS, or exclamation...There are an infinite variety of degrees of exclamatory stress. Rather than forming separate contrasting elements, with separate meanings, however, they are in GRADATION. Socially, the general amount of stress may have some significance, but once intensity reaches (at an indefinable boundary) the exclamatory stage, all degrees of it are within the same meaningful superimposed phoneme."[10] Leaving aside the question of whether a phoneme can have "meaning" (and this may not represent the author's current view anyway), the trouble here is that if you find that ANY degree of stress contrasting one morpheme with another has some relevance to the notion of 'emphasis', you have nowhere to go. The bottom of stress has been sliced off; you have a phonemic stress-versus-nonstress on the one hand, and a non-phonemic stress-versus-stress on the other. In order to capture just what was needed for microlinguistics and no more, an artificial dichotomy has been introduced into what may well be a continuum, something that cannot safely be cut in two until its range has been explored, cannot be assumed to be discontinuous at one extreme merely because that suits the convenience of a discontinuous analysis.

What I want to do is to show a few of the unexpected ways in which the continuum calls the tune and the discontinuum is forced to dance. I shall draw examples from three areas: generality, length, and intonation. I take these because they reflect more than just imperfections in the observer or insufficiencies in his data. They are not continuous in the sense that they are indeterminate, of that order of things concerning which Pike says that "indeterminacy is an essential part of language."[11] Rather, their non-switching character, their continuity, has a function in communication. From them I believe that we can draw the moral that when one stops talking about switches and begins to talk about potentiometers, one does not necessarily cease talking about electrical systems.

---

[10] *The Intonation of American English* (Ann Arbor, 1945), p. 85.
[11] *Texas Quarterly* 2 (1959): 49.

GENERALITY AND AMBIGUITY

A continuum can be of two kinds: undifferentiated, in which the phenomena that fill the continuous space are homogeneous, and differentiated, in which the phenomena themselves are not homogeneous but have some function of RATE which is—for example, at one extreme the density is 1, at the opposite extreme 10, and at a point 55 percent of the way from 0 to 10 it is $5\frac{1}{2}$. An example of an undifferentiated continuum is a confined gas theoretically free of gravitation, or is the semantic space of the word *apple*, which covers Macintosh and Jonathan equally and where the concepts "more" and "less" do not apply. An example of a differentiated continuum is the earth's atmosphere, or a gradual increase in loudness such that at one point it is possible to say that there is twice as much or three times as much as at some other point. If in addition twice as much loudness is correlated with, say, twice as much excitement, we can then refer also to a semantic differentiated continuum.

We look first at an undifferentiated continuum, one that by definition does not involve degrees along a scale but merely some indefinite point between two or more other points.

I take as my prime example the one given by Joos, *They put their glasses on their noses.* English, he says, categorizes verbs into past versus present, and the tyranny of the categories is such that "the listener will react to exactly one of the categories" in a given dimension, "not...to more than one, or to none, whether the utterance is ambiguous or not". With the verb *put* in the example, the reader has already made up his mind in favor of past or in favor of present, in spite of the fact that there was nothing to tell him which was intended.

There is no question that we have here an all-or-none choice between two meanings of *put*, or perhaps we should say "between the two words *put*" (as much two words as *eat* and *ate* are two words). But is the tyranny that it illustrates actually typical of categories so much as it is of something much broader, namely the arbitrariness of designation by ANY lexeme or syntagmeme? The form *put* is ambiguous by virtue of the two categories to which it is assigned, but so is the form *light* by virtue of the two conceptual categories to which it is assigned: *The picture is too light* (*to need all that postage*), *The picture is too light* (*with that developing process*)—here, exactly as with *put*, we automatically select one or the other meaning (or, if you prefer, one or the other of the two words).[1]

As with the overtly paradigmatic *put* and the unparadigmatic *light*, so with covert categories, partially grammaticized forms that lie between the two extremes. When Adlai Stevenson wrote "moral and social solidarity in the family of man is still to be found",[2] did he mean 'findable' or 'unfound'? When we find in *Language* the sentence "The secondary stress, once primary, was lost...,"[3] do we interpret 'formerly primary' or 'as soon as it became primary'? English makes no overt categorization of passive infinitives into classes of 'possibility' versus 'futurity', and the function word *once* is ambiguous. There is no essential difference between these cases and those of *put* and *light*; in all of them we have to choose; there is no tertium quid.

The problem then boils down to this: why necessarily *A* or *B*, and not something halfway between? The answer seems obvious: anything between would be ridiculous; it could not give rise to communication except communication about the utterance itself, that is, a pun. Some

---

* Dwight L. Bolinger, 'Generality and ambiguity', ch. 2 of *Generality, Gradience, and the All-or-None* (The Hague: Mouton, 1961). © 1961 Mouton de Gruyter. Reprinted by permission.

[1] It does not really matter whether we speak of the same word with different meanings, or view the form as two homonyms—the same arbitrary selection is present in *It's too rough* meaning 'It's too hard' or 'It's not smooth enough'.

[2] *Progressive*, March 1959, p. 9.

[3] 28.143 (1952).

puns can be continua of a sort, which I mention only in passing because we are not concerned with this kind of continuum—for example, *Chopinhauer, the great philosopher-musician.* We do not ordinarily get puns with linguistic categories not because there is a different principle of choice between *put-put* and *light-light* but because the categories lack the ludicrousness that makes for a good pun.

With this broader base, in which the tyranny of the categories is only one of countless tyrannies including all the homonyms and metaphorical extensions in the lexicon, we are in a better position to assess the nature of the tyranny. Linguistic categories are special in just one particular: if there is such a thing as a middle ground, it would be less likely to be found among paradigmatic homonyms than almost anywhere else. The ambiguity of *put-put* tends to be of the extreme kind, like that of *light-light* with a sharp cleavage between, not like that of *dreaming* in *He's dreaming* (asleep? daydreaming? imagining things?), where the cleavage is blurred. The categories chop up and draw rather sharp lines on the semantic side. Where verbs are concerned, our culture conceptualizes a time frame in which there are divisions without a middle ground. Whenever the choices are between alternatives that our culture sharply distinguishes, we must take one or the other. That is the nature of reality rather than the nature of language. There is no logical middle ground between an orange and a regret, and if some historical accident resulted in the same morph being used for both, they would still have to be discriminated just as sharply as they are with the two morphs that we now have.

This leaves us with an interesting question. Suppose the ambiguity does not compel us to embrace alternatives that are poles apart. Might there then be a continuum? Is it sometimes unnecessary to "resolve an ambiguity"? Can one find an undifferentiated continuum perhaps even among paradigmatic homonyms?

There will be a continuum if there is a "generality" in the sense given by Y. R. Chao: "A symbol is general when it is applicable to any one of a number of things whose differences are not denied or necessarily overlooked, but regarded as irrelevant in the context in which the symbol is used. Thus, the Chinese word *ren* is more general than the English word *man* or *woman* and is used when there is no point in distinguishing between the two. Again, *colored* is more general than *brown* or *red* and there are many occasions when the general idea of *colored* is the intention of the communication." Generality is to be distinguished from ambiguity, the latter exemplified in the sentence *Ta ideal mei sheng-chih*: "with *sheng-chih* taken as (1) 'grows anger—becomes angry' the sentence means 'He did not at all become angry', while with *sheng-chih* taken as (2) 'growing atmosphere—lively appearance' it means 'He is not at all forward-looking'; and there is little occasion for grouping becoming angry and forward-looking under any general conception of *sheng-chih*..."[4] In *He took a friend* we generalize *friend* to include old and young, male and female, free and slave. Whoever he took had to be one of these, say a free young male, but there is no "tyranny of categories"; the choices are simply ignored. But if one hears "Are they friends?" expecting the reply "Yes, they are quite friendly" and instead hears "No, they are Baptists", one is forced to a *put-put* kind of switching. This is an ambiguity.

A better example of generality is perhaps the word *rain* because of the evenness of its semantic continuity: it can embrace anything from a drizzle to a cloudburst. (It is the existence of these latter narrower generalities—along with categories of modification—that enables us to talk about the larger generality.)

The Voegelins make the same distinction between ambiguity and generality in terms of "discontinuous referent ranges" and "continuous referent ranges". An example of the one is a single Hopi morpheme meaning both 'sun' and 'clock'. An example of the other is a single

---

[4] 'Ambiguity in Chinese', in *Studia Serica Bernhard Karlgren Dedicata* (Copenhagen, 1959), p. 1.

Hopi morpheme "with a continuous range from 'thinking' to 'worrying'".[5] Malkiel cites the Spanish verb *despechar*, whose participle *despechado* could be used in any one of three meanings or in "any free combination of these meanings".[6]

Our main problem, however, is not to find generalities in the lexicon at large, where they are pervasive, but in the categories, where they are scarce. I take first the most difficult case of all, Joos's *put-put* example itself.

There is a type of question, clearly formalized in English, in which the auxiliary verb is omitted (potentially also the subject), and the minimum requirement is an infinitive, a participle, or a complement of *be*.[7] They are related to expanded forms which we can give as their "meanings". Thus *See them yet*? may mean 'Do you see them yet?' or 'Did you see them yet?' and *Seen them yet*? (retaining the same subject) means 'Have you seen them yet?' If we line these up, (1) 'Do you see them yet?' (2) 'Did you see them yet?' and (3) 'Have you seen them yet?' we find that (1) is incongruous with both (2) and (3), but that (2) and (3) are semantically rather compatible. Yet (1) and (2), which are semantically incongruous, are formally identical, whereas (2) and (3), which are compatible, are formally different. Project this situation onto the verb *put*, which has not two forms in the kinds of questions indicated as *see* has (*do see*, *did see*, *have seen*), but only one (*do put*, *did put*, *have put*). We can now arrange a collision between two compatible items (*did put*, *have put*), and not merely, as Joos did, between two incompatible ones (*do put*, *did put*). If I say *Put them away yet*? I will force you to an either-or choice between the two incongruous meanings 'Do you put them away yet?' ('Has it become your habit?') and 'Did you put them away yet?'; but I do not force you to an either-or choice between the two compatible meanings 'Did you put them away yet?' and 'Have you put them away yet?', in spite of the formal difference, elsewhere in the structure, between *see* and *seen*, *do* and *done*, *go* and *gone*, etc. And if you were to ask me "Which did you mean, 'did you put' or 'have you put'?", I could not make a sensible answer.

What I am saying is that there is a generality in this type of question at the point where preterit and present perfect overlap: the speaker simply makes no distinction between the two. Is there evidence for this, other than one's intuitive feeling? While the burden of proof does not fall on me to prove a negative—rather it is up to one who maintains that there is a difference to prove that one exists—I believe that one can find some evidence in the answer received. As a test, I devised the following sequence: "Well, my assignment's almost done. You finish yours?"—"No, I...n't." This was submitted in written form to 53 persons who were instructed to fill the blank with whatever "according to your quick first impression belongs there". The results showed *have* 21, *did* 23, one undecided between *have* and *did*, and eight scattered among *shan't*, *couldn't*, *won't*, *wouldn't*, and *ain't*. The choice of *have* or *did* seems to be random, and this despite the fact that *have* cannot be in concord with the infinitive *finish* but calls for the past participle. All the more reason, then, to suppose that the same randomness can apply to *put*, where whichever is chosen, *have* or *did*, is in apparent concord.

---

[5] *Hopi domains*. Memoir 14 of the *International Journal of American Linguistics* (Baltimore, 1957), p. 5.

[6] 'Studies in Hispano-Latin homonymics', *Language* 28 (1952): 299–338. This suggests a term that may be ambiguous and general at the same time. An imaginative speaker or writer may deliberately choose an ambiguous term in order to plant his audience somewhere in the middle. But such an example is not the best for proving our case, as it may contain a weakness in logic: we cannot be sure whether the combination involves a freedom of the listener to choose one or another, even to hop at will in a series of successive choices, or is homogenized for him in advance. It is the mixture of the kaleidoscope versus the mixture of the cake recipe. With the kaleidoscope we never rest in the middle but only cross it on the way from one alternative to another, and it can be claimed then that the middle is an illusion.

[7] See Bolinger, *Interrogative Structures of American English*, No. 28 of the Publications of the American Dialect Society (University of Alabama, 1957), p. 38.

It can be argued that the appearance of *did* or *have* in the answer automatically categorizes the word in the question, and the choice is therefore once again all-or-none. But this will not hold up. First, it does not account for the *finish...have* type, which is too common to put down as a lapse. Second, the same thing occurs with the more obvious lexical generalities and has no categorizing effect. If the answer to the question *Did you see my friend?* is to contain a pronoun, it must be *him* or *her*: *Yes, I saw him (her)*. But the categorical choice in the pronoun does not categorize *friend* as masculine or feminine; *friend* is indifferent to gender.[8]

I take as my second example a covert category, that of active-passive reciprocal relationships evidenced in morpheme pairs like *buy-sell* (*John sold the house to James, James was sold the house by John, James bought the house from John*), *give-take, inflict-suffer, teach-learn*. Straddling both sides of these pairs, and usually demanding an either-or choice, is the verb *rent*. In *I've been busy renting a house* we must take either 'obtaining a house' or 'providing a house', not a generality covering both. But what about *a rented house*? We do not have to choose. Whatever contrast there was before has been suspended; the only relevant contrast now is between *rented*, 'occupied by tenants' (who rent the house ∼ to whom the house is rented) and *bought*, 'occupied by owners'.

Thus far we have looked for continuity only where there is morphemic identity. A more promising area might be that of blends, since here we find formal evidence of overlapping semantic fields. In a way, a generality such as *put* under the circumstances described is a blend, since it is a merger of two things which in other parts of the structure are distinguished—unlike *friend* or *rain*, where no such merger has occurred.

Blends are the opposite of homonyms. Studies of homonyms indicate that they can be tolerated under the same conditions that we found compelled us to make an either-or choice in the present and preterit of *put*, namely, when the ranges are sharply distinguished.[9] The formal identity of two words is not a hindrance when even the slightest external clue gives us the information we need. With blends, however, there is a merger of form that follows from sharing a semantic range. When someone unconsciously refers to a person as a *milksap*, he seems to have got himself in between *sap* and *milksop*. A hotel manager confided that catering had been a terrible *bugabear* since the war. I'll labor the obvious and identify the middle ground as between *bugbear* and *bugaboo*. Hoping to get good term papers from a class, I advised the students to be sure to hand in a *crack-up report*. A little back-tracking located my position somewhere between *bang-up report* on the one hand and *crack* or *crackerjack report* on the other. (The fact that *crack, bang*, and *report* are all synonyms in another area of course facilitated this.) Blends of semantically allied forms are probably more frequent than we realize. In one forty-minute speech (appropriately, it was delivered by

---

[8] A possible instance of generality imposing itself on one part of the paradigm that is differentiated in other parts is afforded by case syncretism in Russian. Cf. review of Jakobson's paper in *American contributions to the Fourth International Congress of Slavicists*, in *Language* 35 (1959): 661. A more doubtful one, since there is no semantic continuum, is implied in the segmentation of Spanish verbs proposed by Sol Saporta, *Language* 35 (1959): 614. He defines the type *am-e-n* as containing in its ending two morphs and two morphemes, /-e-/ and /-n/, each with one semantic component, 'tense' and 'third person plural' respectively. The segmentation of *am-o*, however, has /-o/ as "one morph and one morpheme, but with two semantic components, 'tense' and 'first person singular'". This means that whereas tense and person-number are categorized separately in one form, they are combined in another. No either-or choice is imposed; both are delivered in one package.

There is perhaps a partial syncretism of singular and plural in English, and here I would judge that there is a true generality since the merged semantic ranges are singular and plural both as 'indefinite'. In answer to the question "What about the Marbro firm?" one never hears *It hasn't asked me to work for it*, but may readily hear *They haven't asked me to work for them*, which might seem to categorize *Marbro firm* as a plural; yet if the noun is restored in the answer, the verb is in the singular, though *them* is retained: *The Marbro firm hasn't asked me to work for them*.

[9] Cf. Edna Rees Williams, *The Conflict of Homonyms in English* (New Haven, 1944), p. 4.

a professor of chemistry [10]) I identified three: *you have at your avail = you have available + you have at your command; at base = basically + at bottom; a whole-scale embracing (of mechanism) = full-scale + wholesale.* These escape our notice because they are so natural that we do not realize when they occur—it is usually the more outlandish blends that get themselves recorded. By the same token the inconspicuous ones are likely to gain some currency: *squawk, dumbfound,* and *luncheon* are instanced by Mencken. Add *soonever = as soon as + whenever, he like to (died laughing) = he was like to (die laughing) + he almost (died laughing),* and of course *most everywhere (everybody* etc.*) = most places + almost everywhere.* [11]

I believe that the less clearly marked the form class, the larger and fuzzier the units that compose it, and the more complex the structure that they enter into, the greater the likelihood of unconscious and undetected blends. [12] Here we have what might be termed syntactic blends, of which I shall give a few examples.

English has a form class of nouns, marked at its core by singularity-plurality and at its periphery in various distributional ways. When a speaker says *She found it easy cooking with gas,* the hearer confronts an either-or choice: either *cooking* is a noun and the utterance means 'She found cooking with gas easy', or it is an adjective and the utterance means 'She, cooking with gas, found whatever she was doing to be easy'. The *-ing* form is automatically classed one way or the other. But when one motorist cuts ahead of another and the victim angrily mutters *That dirty dog—turning in front of me like that,* there is no way to tell which class the *-ing* belongs to; and it doesn't matter, for the message is the same either way. The haziness of the *-ing* is manifested in the structure in the uncertainty one finds in the type *I don't like his going so fast* ∼ *I don't like him going so fast.* (In my own speech I prefer a possessive pronoun where one person is involved—*I don't like your going so fast*—but an objective pronoun if more than one are involved—*I don't like you and him going so fast.*) The whole thing is loosely thrown together and the classes are straddled. Householder points out a similar indefiniteness with the *-ing* in *while buying roses.* [13]

The moment a complex string is uttered for the first time, it begins to lead to a certain extent an existence of its own—its components are never afterward totally "free" in their relationship to the whole. The extreme case is of course the idiom, and we can refer to the gradient of idiomatic stereotyping as "idiomization" and the process as "to idiomize"—the analog, in the idiom grammar, of "grammaticization" in the transform grammar. Viewed as an independent syntagmeme, the idiom's relationships with other strings cease to be entirely analyzable in terms of their respective components, and—more and more in proportion as other speakers take it up and repeat it—begin to resemble phonesthetic relationships: we say that *A* "reminds one of" *B* rather than that *A* "is derived from or is analyzable into" *B*. As totalities, *A* and *B* have each their semantic field, which overlap in the same way as the fields of *bugbear* and *bugaboo* overlap. This means that in tracing the relationships it may be necessary to go in more than one direction, adding to the uncertainties of a transformational analysis because it

---

[10] Prof. Robert Maybury of the University of Redlands (Calif.), 26 March 1960.

[11] This whole line of reasoning can be disparaged on the grounds that the semantic field lies outside language proper anyway and might well induce a temporary upset in the system, just as a sneeze in the middle of a word may do strange things to the phones in it, but that is something for the pathologist, not the linguist. Specifically, we can imagine a psychological state in which a speaker has been vacillating between *bugbear* and *bugaboo* and vocalizes a moment too soon, while he is still straddling the choice. But the spontaneity and unconsciousness of many blends make it hard to regard them as ordinary lapses (e.g. spoonerisms, in which elements of the chain are transposed—blends are vertical to the chain, so to speak, being drawn from choices made prior to it). It is hard to imagine any such vacillation with its hybrid result not calling attention to itself.

[12] The factor of size and fuzziness complicated by lack of practice on the part of the speaker is evident in case syncretism in English: *for him and I* against *for me, The victory belongs to him* against *The victory belongs to he who wins it.*

[13] *Language* 35 (1959): 517.

envisages something partially in the idiom grammar and not purely and simply in the transform grammar. Take the sentence *I'll see you in hell first*. What are the kernel sentences here? On the one hand, *I see you* and *You are in hell*. On the other hand, *I see you* and *I send you to hell*—in this case *I'll see you in hell* is like *I'll see you to the door* or *I'll see you through the lines* or *I'll see you down the road a piece*. I do not believe that the latter is the meaning the phrase originally had, but it has always been present to my mind as much as the other meaning when I have heard it. We do not have to decide; the constructions overlap because the conceptual ranges overlap—the ranges here being a prediction ('You will be in hell') and a threat ('I'll help you get there'), between which humanity historically fails to discriminate.

If we argue that *put* present and *put* preterit pose an either-or choice because of the existence, elsewhere in the structure, of *do* and *did* and *eat* and *ate*, then it is not too far-fetched to accept the other side of the coin and reason that *full-scale* and *wholesale* did not for one speaker pose an either-or choice because there was too much overlapping of semantic ranges.[14]

---

[14] For the most convincing evidence of the blending of form corresponding to a blending of semantic ranges, the reader should consult the writings of Yakov Malkiel.

19

Degrees of Grammaticalness

NOAM CHOMSKY

Since the point has been widely misunderstood, I would like to emphasize that I am using the terms 'grammatical' and 'degree of grammaticalness' in a technical sense (which is, however, not unrelated to the ordinary one). In particular, when a sentence is referred to as semi-grammatical or as deviating from some grammatical regularity, there is no implication that this sentence is being "censored" (Jakobson, 'Boas' view of grammatical meaning,' *The Anthropology of Franz Boas, American Anthropologist* (1959), p. 144) or ruled out, or that its use is being forbidden. Nor, so far as I can see, are there any "ontological" considerations involved (Chomsky, *Logical Structure of Linguistic Theory* (mimeographed, 1955 [1975]), p. 377; Jakobson 1959, p. 144), except insofar as these are reflected in grammatical categories and subcategories. Use of a sentence that is in some way semi-grammatical is no more to be censured than use of a transform that is remote from the kernel. In both cases, what we are attempting to do is to develop a more refined analysis of sentence structure that will be able to support more sophisticated study of the use and interpretation of utterances. There are circumstances in which the use of grammatically deviant sentences is very much in place. Consider, e.g., such phrases as Dylan Thomas' "a grief ago,"[1] or Veblen's ironic "perform leisure." In such cases, and innumerable others, a striking effect is achieved precisely by means of a departure from a grammatical regularity.

Given a grammatically deviant utterance, we attempt to impose an interpretation on it, exploiting whatever features of grammatical structure it preserves and whatever analogies we can construct with perfectly well-formed utterances. We do not, in this way, impose an interpretation on a perfectly grammatical utterance (it is precisely for this reason that a well-chosen deviant utterance may be richer and more effective. Linguists, when presented with examples of semi-grammatical, deviant utterances, often respond by contriving possible interpretations in constructed contexts, concluding that the examples do not illustrate departure from grammatical regularities. This line of argument completely misses the point. It blurs an important distinction between a class of utterances that need no analogic or imposed interpretation, and others that can receive an interpretation by virtue of their relations to properly selected members of this class. Thus, e.g., when Jakobson observes (Jakobson, 1959, p. 144) that "golf plays John" can be a perfectly perspicuous utterance, he is quite correct. But when he concludes that it is therefore as fully in accord with the grammatical rules of English as "John plays golf," he is insisting on much too narrow an interpretation of the notion "grammatical rule"—an interpretation that makes it impossible to mark the fundamental distinction between the two phrases. The former is a perspicuous utterance precisely because of the series of steps that we must take in interpreting it—a series of steps that is initiated by

---

* Noam Chomsky, 'Some methodological remarks on generative grammar', *Word* 17 (1961): 219–39, section 5 on 'degrees of grammaticalness'. © 1961 Noam Chomsky. Reprinted by kind permission of the author.

[1] One of the examples analyzed in Ziff's interesting study of the problem of deviation from grammaticalness, 'On Understanding "Understanding"' (mimeographed, 1960).

the recognition that this phrase deviates from a certain grammatical rule of English, in this case, a selectional rule that determines the grammatical categories of the subject and object of the verb "play." No such steps are necessary in the case of the nondeviant (and uninteresting) "John plays golf."

I am not, of course, suggesting that every difficult, interesting or figurative expression is semi-grammatical (or conversely). The important question, as always, is to what extent significant aspects of the use and understanding of utterances can be illuminated by refining and generalizing the notions of grammar. In the cases just mentioned, and many others, I think that they can. If this is true, it would be arbitrary and pointless to insist that the theory of grammatical structure be restricted to the study of such relatively superficial matters as agreement, inflectionally marked categories, and so on.[2]

In short, it seems to me no more justifiable to ignore the distinctions of subcategory that give the series "John plays golf," "golf plays John," "John plays and," than to ignore the rather similar distinctions between seeing a man in the flesh, in an abstract painting, and in an inkblot. The fact that we can impose an interpretation in the second case and sometimes even the third, using whatever cues are present, does not obliterate the distinction between these three strata.

Examples such as these provide a motive for the study of degrees of grammaticalness. Thus [...] we can try to account for the observation that such phrases as (1) are not as extreme in their violation of grammatical rules as (2), though they do not conform to the rules of the language as strictly as (3):

(1) a grief ago; perform leisure; golf plays John; colorless green ideas sleep furiously; misery loves company; John frightens sincerity; what did you do to the book, understand it?

(2) a the ago; perform compel; golf plays aggressive; furiously sleep ideas green colorless; abundant loves company; John sincerity frightens; what did you do to the book, justice it?

(3) a year ago; perform the task; John plays golf; revolutionary new ideas appear infrequently; John loves company; sincerity frightens John; what did you do to the book, bite it?

Here too, we can find innumerable relatively clear cases, and we can attempt to express these distinctions in a generative grammar (and, more importantly, we can try to find some basis for them through the study of generative grammar).

The question then arises: by what mechanism can a grammar assign to an arbitrary phone sequence a structural description that indicates its degree of grammaticalness, the degree of its deviation from grammatical regularities, and the manner of its deviation? This is a natural question to ask within the framework of §2 [not included].

Suppose that we have a grammar that generates an infinite set of utterances with structural descriptions. Let us call the units in terms of which these utterances are represented by the neutral term *formatives* (following a suggestion of Bolinger's). Suppose, in addition, that we

---

[2] Notice that if we do, arbitrarily, limit the study of grammar in this way, we cannot even account for the difference between (6) and (9), on the one hand, and (7) and (8), on the other, since this difference can be expressed only in terms of categories that are established in terms of syntactic considerations that go well beyond inflection. But if we distinguish (6) from (9) by rules involving such syntactic categories as Adjective, Noun, etc., we can just as well distinguish "John plays golf" from "golf plays John" by rules involving such syntactic subcategories as Animate Noun etc. These are simply a refinement of familiar categories. I do not see any fundamental difference between them. No general procedure has ever been offered for isolating such categories as Noun, Adjective, etc., that would not equally well apply to such subcategories as are necessary to make finer distinctions. I return to this below.

have an m-level hierarchy of categories of formatives with the following structure. On level one we have a single category denoted C_1^1, the category of all formatives. On level two, we have categories labelled $C_1^2, \ldots, C_{n_2}^2$. On level three we have categories $C_1^3, \ldots, C_{n_3}^3$, where $n_3 > n_2$, and so on, until we reach the mth level with categories $C_1^m, \ldots, C_{n_m}^m$ ($1 < n_2 < \ldots < n_m$). On each level, the categories are exhaustive in the sense that each formative belongs to at least one; perhaps more (in the case of grammatical homonymy). We might also require that each level be a refinement of the preceding one, i.e. a classification into subcategories of the categories of the preceding level.

Let us assume, furthermore, that the mth level categories are the smallest categories that appear in the rules of the generative grammar. That is, the members of C_1^m are mutually substitutable in the set of generated utterances. Many of them may contain just a single formative.

For concreteness, think of the formatives as English words.[3] Suppose we have a three-level hierarchy. Then C_1^1 is the class of all words. Let $C_1^2 =$ Nouns, $C_2^2 =$ Verbs, $C_3^2 =$ Adjectives, $C_4^2 =$ everything else. Let $C_1^3, \ldots, C_j^3$ be subcategories of Verbs (pure transitives, those with inanimate objects, etc.); subcategories of Nouns, and so on. Every sequence of words can now be represented by the sequence of first level, second level, third level categories to which these words belong. Thus "misery loves company" is represented $C_1^1 C_1^1 C_1^1$ on level one, $C_1^2 C_2^2 C_1^2$ (i.e., NVN) on level two, $N_{abstr} V_k N_{abstr}$ on level three (where these are the appropriate C_i^3's). One of the selectional rules of the generative grammars (i.e., in the transformational model of [SS], one of the context-restricted constituent structure rules) will specify that V_k occurs only with animate subjects. Thus "misery loves company" will not be generated by the grammar, though "John loves company" will. However, "misery loves company" has a level two representation in common with a generated utterance, namely, NVN. We therefore call it semi-grammatical, on level two. "Abundant loves company," on the other hand, has only a level one representation in common with a generated utterance, and is therefore labelled completely ungrammatical.

Without going into details, it is obvious how, in a similar way, a degree of grammaticalness can be assigned to any sequence of formatives when the generative grammar is supplemented by a hierarchy of categories. The degree of grammaticalness is a measure of the remoteness of an utterance from the generated set of perfectly well-formed sentences, and the common representing category sequence will indicate in what respects the utterance in question is deviant.[4] The more narrowly the mth level categories circumscribe the generated language (i.e., the more detailed the specification of selectional restrictions) the more elaborate will be the stratification of utterances into degrees of grammaticalness. No utterances are "lost" as we refine a grammatical description by noting more detailed restrictions on occurrence in natural sentences. By adding a refinement to the hierarchy of categories, we simply subdivide the same utterances into more degrees of grammaticalness, thus increasing the power of the grammar to mark distinctions among utterances.[5]

---

[3] This is merely an illustrative example.

[4] We can represent only one "dimension" of deviation from grammaticalness in this way. There are others. Cf., e.g., Chomsky (1957) *Syntactic Structures*, The Hague, §5, footnote 2. In obvious ways, we could give a more refined stratification of utterances by considering their parts, but I will not go into this.

[5] What is the natural point where continued refinement of the category hierarchy should come to an end? This is not obvious. As the grammatical rules become more detailed, we may find that grammar is converging with what has been called logical grammar. That is, we seem to be studying small overlapping categories of formatives, where each category can be characterized by what we can now (given the grammar) recognize as a semantic feature of some sort. If this turns out to be true in some interesting sense when the problem is studied more seriously, so much the better. This will show that the study of principles of sentence formation does lead to increasingly deeper insights into the use and understanding of utterances, as it is continually refined.

Thus a generative grammar supplemented with a hierarchy of categories can assign a degree of grammaticalness to each sequence of formatives. If we could show how a hierarchy of categories can be derived from a generative grammar, then the latter alone would assign degree of grammaticalness. There are, in fact, several ways in which this might be possible.

Notice, first, that a transformational grammar will have such symbols as Noun, Adjective, ... (in addition to much narrower subcategories) at intermediate levels of representation, even if it is designed to generate only a narrow class of highly grammatical sentences, since these larger categories will simplify the descriptions of the domains of transformational rules. Thus we can expect to find a hierarchy of categories embedded within the constituent structure rules of the transformational grammar. This might be the appropriate hierarchy, or a step towards its construction.[6]

We might approach the question of projecting a hierarchy of categories from a set of utterances in a different way, by defining "optimal k-category analysis," for arbitrary k. Suppose, for simplicity, that we have a corpus of sentences all of the same length. Let $C_1, \ldots, C_k$ be (perhaps overlapping) categories that give an exhaustive classification of the formatives appearing in the corpus. Each sentence is now represented by at least one category sequence. Each such category sequence, in turn, is the representation of many sequences of formatives, in particular, of many that may not be in the original corpus. Thus a choice of k categories extends the corpus to a set of sentences that are not distinguishable, in terms of these categories, from sentences of the corpus. It is natural to define the optimal k-category analysis as that which extends the corpus the least, i.e., which best reflects substitutability relations within the corpus. Given, for each k, the optimal k-category analysis, we might select the optimal k-category analysis as a level of the hierarchy if it offers a considerable improvement over the optimal $k - 1$-category analysis, but is not much worse than the optimal $k + 1$-category analysis (this could be made precise, in various ways). It is easy to see that there are circumstances under which the optimal k-category analysis might contain overlapping classes (homonyms).[7] It is also easy to drop the restriction that all sentences be of the same length, and that the corpus be finite. Such suggestions as these, when made precise,[8] offer an alternative way in which the generative grammar itself may impose degrees of grammaticalness on utterances that are not directly generated, through the intermediary of the category hierarchy projected from the set of generated sentences.

This suggestion is schematic and no doubt very much oversimplified. Nevertheless, such an approach as this to the problem of defining syntactic categories has many suggestive features, and offers some important advantages over the alternatives (e.g., substitution procedures)[9]

---

[6] This possibility was suggested by some remarks of R. B. Lees.

[7] In general, it is to be expected that overlapping of categories will lead to an extension of the set of generated sentences, since categories will now be larger. Therefore, in general an analysis with disjoint categories will be preferred, by the evaluation procedure suggested above, over an analysis with an equal number of overlapping categories. Suppose, however, that the overlap includes true homonyms—suppose, e.g., that the categories N and V are allowed to overlap in such elements as /riyd/ (*read, reed*), etc. We now have two ways of representing the sentences *read the book* (namely, VTN or NTN), *the reed looks tall* (TNVA or TVVA), and so on, instead of just one (e.g., VTN and TVVA, if /riyd/ is assigned to V). We can select, in each case, the representation which is required, on independent grounds, by other sentences, i.e., VTN and TNVA, in this example. In this way we can reduce the number of generated sentences by allowing categories to overlap. Overlapping of categories will be permitted, then, when the gain that can be achieved in this way more than compensates for the loss resulting from the fact that categories are larger. We might inquire then whether homonyms can be defined as elements that are in the overlaps in the optimal set of categories on some level. Some evidence in favor of this assumption is presented in Chomsky's *Logical Structure of Linguistic Theory* (mimeographed, 1955 [1975]).

[8] This approach to degrees of grammaticalness was described in more detail in Chomsky's *Logical Structure of Linguistic Theory* (mimeographed, 1955 [1975]). It was presented, with some supporting empirical evidence, in a Linguistic Institute lecture in Chicago in 1954, and again in the discussions of the IVth Texas conference, 1959.

that have been described in the literature (cf. Chomsky, *Logical Structure of Linguistic Theory* (mimeographed, 1955 [1975]) for a detailed discussion—in particular, it allows for the possibility of setting up a hierarchy of categories and subcategories and for a principled and general solution to the problem of recognizing homonyms). I mention it here to indicate one way in which the further investigation of deviation from grammaticalness might be systematically pursued.

[9] It is often proposed that categories be defined in terms of particular sets of inflectional morphemes, but unless some general method is given for selecting the relevant sets (none has ever been proposed, to my knowledge), such definitions are completely ad hoc, and simply avoid the problem of discovering the basis for categorization.

20

Descriptive Statement and Serial Relationship

RANDOLPH QUIRK

I

When the aims and methods of the Survey of English Usage were preliminarily drafted, analysis was envisaged as focussing upon 'the plotting of variables'.[1] The purpose of the present paper[2] is to consider what types of variable need to be distinguished and what kinds of relevance the variables have for descriptive statement.

If we take the italicized pair of nominal groups in the sentence

> They disapproved of *his running after Mary* and even *his liking for Mary*

the numerous characteristics in terms of which these sequences can be compared and contrasted fall into three interlocking sets of features (Fig. 1).

Set *a* comprises what is textually 'observable' (given the observer's knowledge of the language), the items stable at any level—or with any kind—of abstraction we choose: *deictic + head + post-modifier*, or *poss. pron.* $+ N_{ab} + prep. + N_{con}$, or *poss. pron.* $+ N(ing) + prep. + Name$.

Set *b* comprises the covert features which the analyst's tests reveal. They will include the fact that *him* can replace *his* in the first nominal group within certain (stylistic) limits that permit no such replacement in the second; that *running* (but not *liking*) may be preceded by an adverb such as *eagerly*; that neither N(ing) can be made plural. It should be noted that the latter, negative comparison is only justifiable within the wider framework of knowing that number is a relevant category for the head of a nominal group and even for a N(ing) as head (*his winnings*). It is thus a 'real' covert feature, though negative, that has been attributed to *running* and *liking* here, whereas to compare similarly *after* and *for* in sharing the property of having no plural would be to set up an 'unreal' and inadmissible covert feature.[3]

$$\begin{array}{l} \text{overt} \quad \left. \begin{array}{l} a \text{ manifested} \end{array} \right\} \\ \qquad\qquad \left\{ \begin{array}{l} b \text{ potential} \\ c \text{ transformational features} \end{array} \right. \end{array}$$ constituent features

overt — *a* manifested ⎫
⎬ constituent features
covert — { *b* potential ⎭
{ *c* transformational features

FIG. 1

* Randolph Quirk, 'Descriptive statement and serial relationship', *Language* (Journal of the Linguistic Society of America) 41(2) (1965): 205–17. © 1984 The Linguistic Society of America. Reprinted by permission.

[1] R. Quirk, 'Towards a description of English usage', *TPS* (1960): 51.

[2] I am grateful to several colleagues, notably H. T. Carvell, D. Davy, J. Godfrey, S. Greenbaum, J. Mulholland, and J. Svartvik, for help and criticism.

[3] The arguments for and against taking negative correspondences into consideration are conveniently summarised in R. R. Sokal and P. H. A. Sneath, *Principles of Numerical Taxonomy* 128–31 (San Francisco, 1963), modifying Sneath's earlier views as expressed in 'Some thoughts on bacterial classification', *Journal of General*

(continues)

Set *c* comprises the features relating to the degree of similarity with which the two sequences are related to other structures in the language by regular 'process' or 'transformation'. Thus, each nominal group has a comparably statable correspondence to a finite-verb clause, such that the possessive pronoun corresponds to the subject and the N(ing) to the verb; but in the first case the preposition remains while in the second it does not: *he runs after Mary*, but not **he likes for Mary*.

2

Taking account of sets *b* and *c* means, it should be noted, that the corpus-based technique of the Survey entails proceeding beyond the corpus from the very outset and that some of the objections to corpus studies (for example, that they can provide rules only for the generation of an identical corpus) are unsoundly based. On the other hand, the ability to assemble sets *b* and *c* is still too often taken for granted, and the very real problems involved[4] have only recently begun to receive serious attention and the overdue recognition that they are far from being merely scholastic pseudo-procedures of discovery. In the present paper, the convention of assuming perfected techniques is followed, but work is in progress (by Quirk and Svartvik) on a study in informant-reaction elicitation and assessment.

It might be argued, of course, that assembly of set *a* itself made unacknowledged use of the analyst's intuition—at any rate in silently assigning 'well-formed' status to a given sequence (*his running after Mary*) and 'anacoluthal' status to another (*the most ∂ the the great he's daft*). Leaving aside the question of our ability to segment the latter into 'words' at all, it should be noted that there would be no difficulty in principle in solemnly registering such a sequence as a nominal group in terms of all its constituent features; its irregularity would automatically become clear in the course of the ordinary taxonomic process. Our practice therefore of choosing to anticipate such a classification on the basis of our knowledge of the language involves no principle of theoretical importance.

3

The sets of characteristics thus catalogued may be said to have three broad uses. First, and basically, they are markers of DEFINITION: even in a totally unordered presentation, they serve to distinguish one sequence from another.[5] Thus, if *a*, *b*, and *c* are instances of one structure, and *x*, *y*, *z* are instances of another, and they are characterised according to their having (+) or not having (−) sets of features 1–8 and I–VIII respectively, this first task of definition can be achieved by a simple display as in Table 1. The uses of such information are of course limited: we demonstrate that *a* is different from *b* and *b* from *c* (though the differences are very slight and could easily be overlooked without such a careful analysis), and that *x*, *y*, and *z* are very different from each other.

Microbiology 17 (1957): 194, and 'The application of computers to taxonomy', ibid. 202; see also A. Ellegård, 'Statistical measurement of linguistic relationship', *Language* 35 (1959): 136 ff. The question of applying taxonomic procedures in linguistic analysis is examined in J. Svartvik and H. T. Carvell, 'Linguistic classification and numerical taxonomy' (mimeograph, 1964).

---

[4] Briefly discussed in Quirk, 'Substitutions and syntactic research', *Archivum linguisticum* 10 (1958): 37–42; cf. also *TPS* 1960 59 f.

[5] Cf, M. A. K. Halliday on 'microclasses' in 'Class in relation to the axes of chain and choice in language', *Linguistics* 2 (1963): 11.

4

But from the information we can derive analyses of much greater interest. This second use of the data is a rearrangement of the sequences and of the parameters registering characteristics to establish with precision the DEGREES OF IDENTITY between the sequences—the property which M. A. K. Halliday assigns to his scale of DELICACY.[6] Thus it is important to be able to reckon a, b, c as identical to a specific extent and to state in precisely which respects this identity holds; it is equally important to state that the identity which caused x, y, and z to be regarded as 'one' structure is manifested in only one characteristic, while y and z have a different identity in two respects, an identity which is 'lower in degree' ('further down' the delicacy scale) only of course as regards the comparison with x. The most striking delicacy distinctions would be shown as in Table 2.

To take a simple instance in English grammar, we may consider three important degrees of identity obtaining in the sequences *She watched the man*, *She listened to the man*, *She stood near the man*, as shown in Table 3. It is perhaps easiest to supply some of the characteristics which formed the parameters leading to the lowest degree of identity (γ) that needs to be distinguished here; γ_1 acknowledges the unique absence of a preposition; γ_2 acknowledges the inadmissibility of the shortened form *She listened to* beside the admissibility of both *She watched* and *She stood near*; γ_3 further acknowledges the difference between *to* and *near* which allows the latter to be preceded by *very*. The point on the scale of delicacy at which the identification labeled β_1 becomes relevant reflects the readiness of the passive transformation in *The man was watched* and *The man was listened to*, but not in *The man was stood near*. The

TABLE 1

	1	2	3	4	5	6	7	8			I	II	III	IV	V	VI	VII	VIII
a	+	+	−	+	+	+	+	+		x	−	−	+	−	+	+	−	+
b	+	+	+	+	+	+	+	+		y	+	+	+	+	−	−	+	−
c	+	+	−	+	+	−	+	+		z	−	+	+	+	+	−	−	−

TABLE 2

	1 2 4 5 7 8	3	6			III II IV		I...
a		−	+	x				−
b	+	+	+	y	+	+		+
c		−	−	z				−

TABLE 3

			γ_1	She watched the man
α	β_1	γ_2	She listened to the man
	β_2	γ_3	She stood near the man

[6] 'Categories of the theory of grammar', *Word* 17 (1961): 272.

basis for the maximum degree of identity, labeled α, is perhaps less obvious, but it is important to recognise in English clause structure an abstraction SVX, embracing SVC and SVA, where 'X' can be informally read as 'postverbal piece'. It is not perhaps sufficiently realised that model intransitive clauses of the type *Birds sing* are significantly rare, and that only about one in thirty of the clauses occurring in spoken or written text have this minimal SV form. We need in fact to recognise the broad but apparently basic degree of identity that is manifested not only as α in the three sentences above but also in others such as *He arrived late, The dress suited the girl, The man was seen by a porter,* and *The man was seen in the road.*[7]

5

The third use of the assembled characteristics is, like the investigation of delicacy, derived from the first. The complementary facet of dismissing irrelevant differences for a given descriptive purpose is the scrutiny of common features demonstrating a connexion between structures which otherwise too readily suffer the fate endemic in classificatory linguistics of being unrevealingly separated in distinct pigeonholes. Such scrutiny leads to the establishment of GRADIENCE, as this term has been used by D. L. Bolinger.[8] Thus, whereas earlier it was shown that the degree of delicacy at which *a, b,* and *c* were identical could be displayed as in Table 2, we now turn our attention to the two remaining parameters 3 and 6 and by a reordering show in Table 4 the gradience between *a, b,* and *c*.

6

The relevance of gradience in description can be conveniently demonstrated by the structure of the English verbal group. If we consider the range of 'finites' that can operate at X in the sequence *He X (to) come every day* with seven parameters accounting for the differences as regards X in the variant sequences

1 He X_1 and X_2 (to) come every day
2 He *X* to come every day
3 Did he *X* to come every day?
4 He would *X* to come every day
5 He *X* that

TABLE 4

	6	3
b	+	+
a	+	−
c	−	−

[7] Awareness of an SV degree of identity distinct from SVX is apparently what permits special stylistic effect in such an utterance as *My father drank—so my mother ate.* An experiment in establishing degrees of identity by investigating speakers' implicit awareness of 'sames' is reported in R. Quirk and D. Crystal, 'On scales of contrast in connected English speech' (mimeograph, 1963), to appear in the J. R. Firth memorial volume [1966].
[8] See especially his *Generality, Gradience, and the All-or-None* (The Hague, 1961).

6 He *X* us to come every day

7 He *X* that we should come every day

we can set up a matrix (Table 5) which will simultaneously display delicacy by means of the vertical dimension and gradience by means of the diagonal.

It is obvious that the features attributed to *used* in this matrix refer to the item [juˇst] and not to [juˇzd]. Less obviously, perhaps, those attributed to *is* and *has* would not apply to these items as head of verbal group or as aspectual auxiliaries; the distinctions are further illustrated by

$$\left\{ \begin{array}{l} \text{I am a soldier} \\ \text{I am enjoying the book} \\ \text{I am to go} \end{array} \right.$$: I have been a soldier
: I have been enjoying the book
: *I have been to go

$$\left\{ \begin{array}{l} \text{I have to go} \\ \text{I have a pen} \\ \text{I have enjoyed the book} \end{array} \right.$$: I am having to go
: *I am having a pen
: *I am having enjoyed the book

Nor can the matrix be held invalidated by the existence of *He had us come* (cf. parameter 6), *He helped me (to) come*, *He need not come*, *He dare not come*, and several other examples merely because it does not accommodate them. Rather we would claim that the usages not accommodated lead to the further important point that two-dimensional matrices are ultimately inadequate for the description of delicacy and gradience; only with a polydimensional model is a full statement conceivable.[9]

The appearance of question marks along the diagonal (indicating free variation or doubtful usage) is of course itself indicative of the gradience; it is because of the gradience, in fact, that we may expect hesitation over the use of *do* with *used to* and *ought to* and may find in speech 'mistaken' constructions of the form *He doesn't want that anyone should*... Recognition of the gradience and of the first degree of delicacy (represented by parameter 1) alike helps us to understand the quasi-modality expressed by a wide range of finites operating at X (as in *He'd like to come, He's obliged to come*) and to understand too the inevitably wide discrepancies that exist in the definition and treatment (according to descriptive standpoint and purpose) of so complex a unit as the English verbal group.[10]

TABLE 5

	1	2	3	4	5	6	7
intends	+	+	+	+	+	+	+
wants	+	+	+	+	+	+	–
seems	+	+	+	+	?	–	–
has	+	+	+	+	–	–	–
used	+	+	?	–	–	–	–
is	+	+	–	–	–	–	–
may	+	–	–	–	–	–	–

[9] Cf. K. L. Pike, 'Dimensions of grammatical constructions', *Language* 38 (1962): 221–44, and R. E. Longacre, *Grammar Discovery Procedures* esp. 59 and 139 f. (The Hague, 1964).

[10] For example, cf the recent accounts in W. F. Twaddell, *The English verb auxiliaries* (Providence, 1960); B. M. H. Strang, *Modern English Structure*, esp. ch. 8 (London, 1962); W. Diver, 'The chronological system of the English verb', *Word* 19 (1963): 141–81; M. Joos, *The English verb: Form and meanings* (Madison, 1964); and F. R. Palmer, *A linguistic study of the English verb* (London, 1965).

7

One further illustration of the interrelated concepts of delicacy and gradience may be given from recent work on the prosodic features of English, especially as it provides a convenient occasion to note an alternative technique for establishing variable contrasts. By studying the degrees of accuracy with which informants repeated a tape-recorded utterance, it could be concluded[11] that, with the tone unit as that maximally identified, identities of tonicity (nucleus location), onset-location, nuclear exponent, and pitch-range followed in that order.

So much for the 'vertical' distinctions, as it were, of delicacy. But the experiment also suggested that this scale maintained its neatness only when the nuclear exponent was a simple 'fall' or 'rise'. When the nucleus was 'fall-rise', 'rise-fall', or 'fall-plus-rise', two phenomena were observed. First, these nuclei could be replaced more readily by (a) other nuclei or (b) other prosodic features (stress, pitch-booster, or pitch-range) or (c) combinations of (a) and (b); this phenomenon is ascribable to the gradience between prosodic features and also indicates, within the nuclei, a distinct delicacy scale on which 'fall' and 'rise' have primacy. Second, the complex nuclei appeared to change places in relative importance with pitch-range, the latter having a higher identification (=replication) score; this seemed to indicate the operation of a subsystem, or—in terms of matrix display as expressed above—the necessity for a polydimensional model. While, however, a range of subsystems may be more readily accepted among the 'variations infinitésimales' of intonation, the point that must be stressed here is that this is not because with prosodic features 'on quitte le domain proprement linguistique des unités discrètes';[12] rather, it is precisely the discreteness of other linguistic units that is called in question by the analogous instances of gradience.

8

The illustrations of gradience so far have been closely tied to illustrations of delicacy; that is, attention has been drawn to instances in which the starting point was gross identity. If, however, we now return to consider the properties of the sequences x, y, and z (Tables 1 and 2), we find that rearrangement to demonstrate gradience produces a different type of display (Table 6) from the others that have been presented. This is probably, in fact, the commonest type of gradient phenomenon and the one whose investigation should occupy the linguist's attention most centrally. An item a_n in any set of structures whose similarity we are studying must be analysed in such a way as to demonstrate (1) all the features it shares with a_{n-1} in the set, (2) the features which make it unique, and (3) the features shared with the item a_{n+1}. The

TABLE 6

	6	8	5	3	2	4	I	7
x	+	+	+	+	−	−	−	−
z	−	−	+	+	+	+	−	−
y	−	−	−	+	+	+	+	+

---

[11] Quirk and Crystal, op. cit.
[12] A. Martinet, 'Réflexions sur la phrase', *Language and Society* 117 (Copenhagen, 1961).

kind of overlapping gradience plotted for x, y, and z constitutes what we have come to call 'serial relationship', and z would be said to be serially related to x on the one hand and to y on the other.[13]

TABLE 7

	1	2	3	4	5	6	7	8
pretend	+	+	+	?	−	−	−	−
feel	?	+	+	+	+	?	−	−
say	+	+	+	−	+	−	−	−
know	−	+	+	+	+	−	−	−
find	−	+	+	?	+	+	?	+
think	+	+	+	+	+	+	+	+
declare	−	+	+	+	+	+	+	+
regard	−	−	?	?	?	+	?	?
like	−	−	+	+	−	?	−	−
persuade	−	−	−	+	+	−	−	−
make	−	−	−	−	+	+	+	+
call	−	−	−	−	−	+	+	+
elect	−	−	−	−	−	−	−	+

9

As an analogue to z in English grammar, we may take the structure $S + BE + said\ to\ be + C$ (as in *He was said to be foolish*), where *said* is probably the commonest member of a subclass of past participles of which *alleged* is another member. This has worried linguists because, unlike *He was considered to be foolish*, it has no corresponding active form like *(They) considered him to be foolish* of which it could be regarded as a straightforward transform.[14] If we examine the *say* subclass in relation to other subclasses of verbs taking 'factive' or parafactive complements, it seems useful to take account of at least eight parameters relating to our ability to use the verbs in the structures here given in partially abstract form and in the order which appears to be serially relevant:

1 They V so.
2 They V that he is Adj.
3 It is Ved that he is Adj.
4 They V him to be Adj.
5 He is Ved to be Adj.
6 They V him Adj.
7 He is Ved Adj.
8 They V him N. (where *N* and *him* are coreferential)

---

[13] A similar approach is outlined by H. Hiż, who speaks of sentence affiliation and of sentences entering 'a set of related sequences at the same sequence' or of being 'congrammatical' by virtue of other sets of related sequences: 'Congrammaticality, batteries of transformations and grammatical categories', *Proceedings of symposia in applied mathematics* 12: 47 (Providence, 1961). Computer programs for mechanically sorting and clumping distinctive features so as to show the kind and extent of interrelationship between grammatical structures are discussed by Svartvik and Carvell, op. cit.

[14] Cf R. B. Lees, *The grammar of English nominalizations* 63 (Bloomington, 1961).

It may be of interest to go well beyond the points in the series most relevant for the properties of *say* by citing thirteen subclasses of verbs, taking as their representatives the items listed in the left-hand column of Table 7.

10

In the theory of serial relationship, we go beyond noting the gradient between structures with *say*, *find*, *think*, etc., and make the claim that vertical agreement in the matrix is actually generative by reason of the total configuration of gradience. That is to say, given that it should be found convenient to set up a general rule in the language deriving passives from actives, it is reasonable of course to take horizontal agreement in respect of parameters 4 and 5 as equivalent to deriving the property of 5 from the property of 4. But while property 4 may be a usual, it is not a necessary condition for property 5. The subclass represented by *like* (other members are *want*, *love*, *need*) shows that the mere existence of the active does not entail the existence of the passive transform (**He is liked/wanted/loved/needed to be careful*). More interestingly, as we see from the description of *say* and *make* in the matrix (cf. also *find*), the existence of the passive does not entail the existence of the corresponding active (**They say/ make/?find him to be careful*). In these instances, the configuration of gradience suggests the possibility of 'vertical' derivation; because *say* has a common distribution with *feel* and *know* in such expressions as *They feel/say/know that he is careful, It is felt/said/known that he is careful* (parameters 2 and 3), and because *feel* and *know* have a further property in such expressions as *He is felt/known to be careful* (parameter 5, 'regularly' accountable through the postulated relation with parameter 4), there is developed directly from this the possibility of using the *say*-subclass in this structure without necessitating the prior—or indeed subsequent—acquisition of property 4. It is no doubt relevant to this postulation (and relevant also to estimating the value of observation-based description) both that we find instances of the structure type *He is Ved to be Adj* occurring considerably more frequently in the corpus than instances of the type *They V him to be Adj*, and also that there are roughly twice as many verbs for which we would register a plus in column 5 as there are verbs positive to parameter 4.

11

Similarly, with regard to *make*, we would claim that the matrix of Table 7 justifies our postulation that its positiveness to parameter 5 (*He is made to be quiet*) is to be explained in part by the corresponding property in *persuade*, a verb class which in turn has this property by virtue of the potentiality for the active structure represented by parameter 4. In this case, the extension to *make* of a structure possible with *persuade* is also conditioned by the grammatical identity (and of course lexicological similarity) of these verbs in respect of structures like *He was made/persuaded to do it*. This and other features not demonstrated in Table 7 would be relevant (in a polydimensional display, having an intersection as it were with this matrix somewhere below the center) for a full account of the serial relationships involving verbs (*like*, *persuade*, *help*, *tempt*, *oblige*, etc.) whose objects can be the subjects of verbs other than *be*.

One further verb in the matrix may be briefly mentioned. The uncertain properties of *regard* (readily attested in everyday examples of speech and writing as well as in the vociferous complaints of purists) provide a good illustration of the usefulness of plotting serial relationship, not least in that it provides 'an insight into the dynamic synchrony of language' which, as has recently been insisted, 'must replace the traditional pattern of arbitrarily restricted *static* descriptions'.[15] Despite the continuing membership of *regard* in a subclass of particle-associated verbs (*regard* N *as*, *describe* N *as*, *look upon* N *as*, *take* N *for*, etc.), there are constantly operating tendencies to give it the properties of such verbs as *think* (cf *OED* s.v. *regard*, v., 6); it is significant that *consider* shares more firmly than *regard* the properties of *think* and of the particle-associated verbs.[16] This 'is simply an expression of the fact that relationship is an infinitely variable quantity', that 'there are many cross-relationships between very diverse families', and that, above all, 'similarity is multi-dimensional'.[17]

I 2

Serial relationship is clearly of great importance in linguistic structure and capable of much more precise formulation than we find in the insightful but generally vague accounts of 'analogy' to which the phenomena concerned have usually been relegated. It is certainly an area of linguistics which has attracted welcome attention in recent years. One thinks of C. F. Hockett's interesting postulation of a grammatical theory that 'makes provision for the building of a grammatical form by "blending" ',[18] and of his 'Grammar for the hearer', a concept which, by its handling of sequential choices, offers an explanatory model readily associable with serial relationship.[19] Above all, perhaps, there are the closely analogous ideas on syntactic blending which are developed by Bolinger.[20] This is not to say, of course, that the concept of blending in syntax is anything new; it was advanced for explanatory purposes in Jespersen's *Modern English Grammar* (cf. 3.2.67). It is rather that such a concept has been generally unattractive in the ambience of rigid discreteness that has characterised most theoretical linguistics since Bloomfield, whether the discreteness be that of phonemic and IC segmentation or that born of the more recent interest taken by transformative-generative linguists in unidirectional transformations and unique derivations. One may in fact question the need to regard such divergent theories as mutually exclusive and hesitate to agree that the choice lies simply between TG's 'short list of long rules' and PS's 'long list of short rules'.[21] There is surely every reason to suppose that the production of sentences proceeds by a complex interplay involving 'transformation' and what Miller calls 'a sentence-frame manufacturing device'; we might represent the interplay as in Table 8. Though the arrow and the implied priority of the left column ('abcd' as compared with 'dbca') suggest a unidirectional process, it may turn out to be more valid to speak of a certain kind of transformational CORRESPONDENCE between the upper parts of the left and right columns. Indeed for Mitchell (op.cit.), 'a transformational relationship is regarded as mutual between transforms and not as unidirectional.'

[15] R. Jakobson, 'Linguistics and communication theory', *Proceedings of symposia in applied mathematics* 12: 248 (Providence, 1961).

[16] Note that *It's too hot to eat* has been taken as demonstrating 'the existence of overlapping series with *eat* a member of more than one such series' by T. F. Mitchell, 'Some English phrasal types' (mimeograph, 1964), to appear in the J. R. Firth memorial volume [1966].

[17] Sneath, 'Some thoughts on bacterial classification', loc. cit: 187, 196.

[18] 'Linguistic elements and their relations', *Language* 37 (1961): 52.

[19] *Proceedings of symposia in applied mathematics* 12: 220-36 (Providence, 1961).

[20] 'Syntactic blends and other matters', *Language* 37 (1961): 366-81.

[21] G. A. Miller, 'Some psychological studies of grammar', *American Psychologist* 17 (1962): 756.

TABLE 8

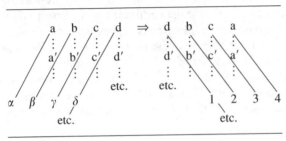

I 3

The 'diverging paths' metaphor of Table 8 may be elucidated as follows. By *abcd, a'b'c'd'* we understand manifestations of a given English structure; let us illustrate them with *The man gave the boy a book* and *The girl showed the inspector a ticket*. These may be regarded as having paradigmatic interdependence, being produced congruently in the structure frame. By *dbca* we understand the transformed correspondent of *abcd*: *A book was given the boy by the man*. Clearly, however, with *d'b'c'a'* (*A ticket was shown the inspector by the girl*) we have the choice of regarding it as transformationally derived from *a'b'c'd'* or as paradigmatically produced from the pattern established on the right by the transformation and manifested by *dbca*. The point has little importance until we come to consider well-attested examples like the following (one of them explicitly acknowledged as nondeviant for its user, an American linguist):

A lexicon is provided the learner by the institute.
An informant was provided us by the government.
The facts were presented us by the Public Relations Officer.
The load on the left is compensated by a long extension on the right.

These clearly belong somewhere on the right-hand side of Table 8, but they cannot be ascribed to the transformational process since sentences like *The institute provided the learner a lexicon* have only a doubtful existence. In these cases, therefore, we find welcome the alternative choice of accounting for their production paradigmatically, and, to symbolise their non-derivation from the pattern on the left or from a different order of elements, they may be represented as '1234'.[22]

It is unrealistic to dismiss sentences of the type 1234 as rare and minor deviations. In the first place, structures which find a place on 'diverging paths' in this way are neither few in number nor rare in frequency of occurrence. Secondly, to take a diachronic standpoint, every new development in language begins as a 'deviant' form, and our linguistic theory must face the task of providing for the essential regularity of such irregularities. Nor, of course, as we recall our allusion to Roman Jakobson's concept of 'dynamic synchrony', is this a matter of concern only from the standpoint of accommodating diachronic statement.

I 4

With reference to the left side of Table 8, we may understand by the $\alpha\beta\gamma\delta$ string one of several sentence types which can be exemplified by *The dinner cost the man a pound*. Just as 1234 has

---

[22] For a full consideration of the problems presented by the English passive, see Svartvik's book, *On voice in the English verb* (The Hague, 1965).

no transformational correspondence with the left, so $\alpha\beta\gamma\delta$ has no transformational correspondence on the right; but this should not oblige us to regard $\alpha\beta\gamma\delta$ as a wholly different pattern having no relation to *abcd*. Not only are the structures identical at the degree of abstraction SVC_1C_2; the identity is maintained when we state the exponents of C_1 and C_2 to be nouns (contrast *He thought the man silly* which also has a relevant abstraction SVC_1C_2), and when we proceed to describe them as animate and inanimate respectively, *The dinner cost a pound the man* being as ungrammatical as *The man gave a book the boy*. Still more delicately, C_1 is deletable but not C_2 (*He gave the boy, *It cost the man*); there are analogous interrogative potentialities; and so on.

That the diagram's metaphor is artificially simple and that once again the need for a polydimensional concept must be stressed can be illustrated from the penultimate point. In respect of C_1-deletion, $\alpha\beta\gamma\delta$ is more like *abcd* than the type represented by *He taught the boy algebra* (*He taught the boy*; *He taught algebra*) while nevertheless this is more like *abcd* than $\alpha\beta\gamma\delta$ in respect of its voice potentiality (*The boy was taught algebra*).

15

Confronted, then, with structures in which we have a range of similarity such as that between the realization of *abcd* and $\alpha\beta\gamma\delta$ or between *dbca* and 1234, we seek to specify the serial relationship operating through them. Confronted by variant forms like *He is regarded as insane* and *He is regarded insane*, we seek to specify the conditioning factors underlying the existence of such a choice. The same is true when we find a correspondence between *The news surprised/thrilled/pleased them* and *They were surprised/thrilled/pleased by/at/with the news* on the one hand, and on the other hand between the latter and *They were sad/happy/angry at/with the news* (manifested not least by our ability to insert *very* after *were*).[23] The currency of *different from/to/than* is accountable with reference to (a) the endorsement of the *from* selection by the existence of *differ from*; (b) the conditioning of the *to* selection by the pattern similarities of *opposite to*, *similar to*, and, more remotely, by the correlation of *from/to* in expressions like *changed/increased/converted from...to...*; (c) the conditioning of the *than* selection by congruence with the *as* Adj *as/ more* Adj *than* correlation through the *same/ different* polarity (*same as x and different than y*).

Similar considerations would apply to explaining the discreteness of *Too many cooks come from Ireland* and *Having too many cooks spoils the broth* as compared with the blend in *Too many cooks* SPOIL *the broth* (compare *Are ninety-year-old men wise?* and a recent newspaper headline *Are ninety-m.p.h. cars wise?*). And of course they apply to the explanation of 'anacolutha'; two neighboring examples from the Survey material may be cited. *What I'm fascinated is to know that they are such bad shots* (5b.16.10) obviously involves a blending of *What fascinates me is to know...*, *I'm fascinated to know...*, and *What I'm fascinated by is...* The other is more interestingly complex:

...position to :sày [/whether it would be :chèaper [or /whether it would be nòt#]#]#
(5b.16.51)

There are three 'well-formed' possibilities for ending this sentence according as (a) the structure is to be complete with realized complement, (b) the verbal group is realized but not the complement, (c) only the first element of the verbal group is realised:

(a)...or whether it would be dèarer

---

[23] Cf. N. Chomsky, *Third Texas conference on problems of linguistic analysis* 172 (Austin, 1962).

(b) ... or whether it wòuldn't be

(c) ... or whether it would nòt

In the event, the prosodic pattern of (a) is realized with the grammatical pattern of (b), but we should postulate the existence of (c) as a conditioning factor.

16

Finally, let us consider briefly in the light of what has been said some of the problems inherent in the adjective structures illuminatingly discussed by Lees.[24] Our first reaction may be to find it plausible to derive *He is splendid to wait* by 'a generalized grammatical transformation' from the two kernels *He is splendid* and *He waits* (219). But reflection raises doubts on three grounds:

(a) This postulation perhaps creates more problems than it solves, for example in the complexity of restrictions required to prevent us from deriving *He is hot to sit from *He is hot* and *He sits*, or **He is angry to walk* from *He is angry* and *He walks*.

(b) The postulation to some extent reverses the required direction of derivation, in that we may intuitively prefer to see the relation between *He is splendid to wait* and *He is splendid* as one in which the latter is a contracted version of the former.

(c) The postulation enforces too sharp a break between

1 He is splendid to wait

2 He is splendid to see

3 He is easy to please

the last two of which cannot have such a derivation), and too close a relation between 1 and

4 He is eager to help

5 He must be angry to go

(for which three structures three derivations are possible and in part demanded).

Taking the primary abstraction at which 1–5 are 'sames' as SVC, we shall find that antecedent in the serial relationship toward 1, 2, and 3 there must be the propensity of S to be animate and C a congruent adjective, thus giving sequences basic to 4 and 5 such as *John is eager*, *John is angry*. To this is added by a subordinating process an intransitive structure (*John helps*, *John goes*) via $S_1 V_{be} Adj \, conj \, S_2 V_i$ where S_1 and S_2 may be coreferential and of which a condensation for the sequence with coreferential S_1 and S_2 is $SV_{be} Adj \, to \, V$ (that is, 4 and 5).

17

A series also beginning with the primary SVC develops the propensity for having a factive S and congruent adjective as C, producing sequences like *The situation is splendid* (but not **The situation is eager*: hence objection (c) in §16). A subordinating process then allows a connexion with other structures (including those of the type *John waits*, *Mary sees John*, *Mary pleases John*) such that these can operate as S. It should be noted that what we have established here is a pattern, not a number of fully realised sentences which must be held to underlie other

---

[24] 'A multiply ambiguous adjectival construction in English', *Language* 36 (1960): 207–21.

sentences which are indirectly related to the pattern. That is, the description so far allows us to produce *That John waits is splendid*, but it is crucial to the theory of serial relationship that we are not forced to produce **That Mary pleases John is easy*. From the 'clause as S' pattern, condensation processes as postulated in §16 operate to produce patterns which may be manifested as *John's waiting is splendid*, *For John to wait is splendid*, *To wait is splendid*, and it is at this point that the series is extended by the production of *For Mary to please John is easy*.

Further stages, for which it is unnecessary to hypothesize details, include the patterns producing *It is easy for Mary to please John* and the contractions *It is easy to please John*, *It is easy*, the latter significantly endorsed by the factive SVC sequence determined earlier in the series. Only now need we envisage the bringing together of 123 with 4 and 5 by a serial interaction which neutralizes contrasts that remain in less contracted structures:

John is eager to help + It is easy to please John
   → John is easy to please

Similar neutralizations, of course, have to be set up for the superficial but highly relevant degrees of identity developed in pairs like

To consider a possible objection, it might be thought unwise that we...
To consider a possible objection, we must first understand exactly what the objection is.

Nor is a series-influenced transfer of elements postulated ad hoc merely to spirit away a specific problem. Analogous processes are needed to account for *John can't seem to work* beside *John seems to be unable to work* and *It seems that John is unable to work*. Similarly, there are well-known neutralizations involving transferred aspect and modality, as in *I should have liked to go there*, *I should like to have gone there*, and *I should have liked to have gone there*; negation, as in *I wouldn't be surprised if it didn't rain*; and number, as in *All the members present raised their arms*.

18

For all these phenomena, the problem is to envisage a complex interaction between patterns and manifestations of patterns so that the logic of our statement does not force us to specify stages that we do not need in our description or utterances for which there can be no observational evidence. We need a descriptive apparatus that will liberally and economically enable us to account for the 'dynamic synchrony' of the creative linguistic process, and to this end we should recognize serial relationship, gradience, neutralization, and blending as central.

21

On the Analysis of Linguistic Vagueness

JIŘÍ V. NEUSTUPNÝ

INTRODUCTION

If the development of applied and mathematical linguistics led recently to some decrease of interest in that property of language phenomena which we call vagueness, then the further road of linguistics will most likely lead to emphasizing its importance and to its recognition as a methodological principle of the first rank without which truly realistic linguistics cannot advance. A mere recording of the individual conspicuous cases of vagueness in a language is, in the present stage, insufficient: the main task of today's linguistics is to determine the full extent of vagueness, to analyse and to explain it and to make possible the combination of its thorough consideration with the stream of the world linguistic tradition.[1]

The phenomenon which is understood under the term vagueness is referred to in linguistics by a number of various terms as "complexity and indeterminacy" (Kruševskij), "potentiality" (Mathesius), "border-line cases" (Bloomfield), "Klarheit der Differenziation" (Skalička), "asymmetry" (Skalička), "des nuances plutôt que des oppositions" and "oppositions phonologiques de stabilité différente" (Malmberg), "open systems" (Milewski), "complexity" (Skalička), "continuities", "differences of degree" (Wells), "degrees of relevance" (Jensen), "generality and gradience" (Bolinger), "vagueness of linguistic structure", "asymmetry" (Neustupný), "Zentrum, Peripherie, Übergang" (Daneš), "peripheral elements" (Vachek), and the like.[2] It seems that problems of neutralisation, functional load[3] and, perhaps, also a

* J. V. Neustupný, 'On the analysis of linguistic vagueness', *Travaux linguistiques de Prague* 2 (1966): 39–51. © 1966 J. V. Neustupný. Reprinted by kind permission of the author. Some minor corrections have been made by the editors.

This article is based on a lecture delivered on March 26, 1964 in the Linguistic Association in Prague.

[1] e.g., such questions should be considered as to whether vagueness is a feature of all linguistic phenomena or only of some (in such a case, of which), how to transform vague elements into non-vague ones, how vagueness in language originated and why it persists (W. Quine, *Word and Object* (New York-London 1960), p. 125: "Vagueness is a natural consequence of the basic mechanism of word learning"). It can be deduced from the following paragraphs that attention has frequently been drawn to vagueness in linguistics, but also that it has been equally frequently overlooked. Only a few linguists take vagueness really seriously and are successful in solving the problems of its analysis (see for instance V. Skalička in *Zur ungarischen Grammatik* (Praha 1935), 'Asymetrický dualismus jazykových jednotek' [The Asymmetric Dualism of Language Units], *NŘ* 19 (1935): 296–303, 'Komplexnost jazykových jednotek' [The Complexity of Language Units], *AUC-Philologica* 3(1) (1957), 15–25, and other works dedicated to particular questions). Consistent consideration of vagueness does not in the least mean a break with the results hitherto achieved by linguistics. Such apprehension would be uncalled for. We should fall into opposite extreme if we assumed that vagueness of linguistic oppositions means the disappearance of units and the rule of absolute continuity. Reality is composed of firm knots and only among them do we find single transitional cases. Hence the results of linguistics which do not take transitions into account, are mostly rather incomplete and insufficiently precise than incorrect.

[2] N. Kruševskij, *Očerk nauki o jazyke* (Kazaò, 1883); V. Mathesius, 'O potenciálnosti jevů jazykových', *Věstntk Královské české společnosti nauk, třída filosoficko-historicko-jazykozpytná* (1911), ii. 1–24 (the English version in

(continues)

number of other questions of classical linguistic science are closely related to vagueness. By using the term vagueness, we believe it possible to bring all the above terms, and perhaps some others too, to a common denominator without eliminating their differences—and to put them on a firm theoretical foundation.

LOGICAL THEORIES OF VAGUENESS

Many objections have been raised against vagueness in the name of logic. It would seem at first glance that the *principium exclusi tertii* excludes "border-line cases" and all indeterminateness. The combination of two morphemes means either one or two words: *tertium non datur*. In the textbooks of logic we learn that "many terms of everyday life are inaccurately defined terms. For the purpose of normal communication even such inaccurately defined terms can serve us well enough. But in a precise scientific deliberation, it is necessary to work with terms exactly defined; hence "science often replaces inaccurate terms of current speech with exact scientific terms".[4] This naturally means that linguistic terms, too, must conform to this requirement. At the same time, criticism of this kind does not count with the possibility of inaccuracy of terms resulting not from an inaccurate, but from a precise reflection of the object.

Contemporary logic now has at its disposal the means with which it can deal with vague elements in such a way that chaos is eliminated and they can be built into consistent axiomatic systems. From the available logical literature on vagueness, we can mention important studies by M. Black, T. Kubiński, and W. Quine.[5] It is of interest that these works were mostly based on linguistic materials and were using other materials only secondarily.

Logical theories on vagueness agree that vagueness must be primarily differentiated from generality and ambiguity. While by vagueness of the word "chair" is meant the fact that there exist objects the terming of which as "chair" is uncertain or dubious, the generality of the word "chair" shows the possibility of using it to indicate a great number of different objects, and the ambiguity of the English "put", for example, lies in the fact that it designates the present tense, past tense, or the past participle. It is only just to admit that though generality and ambiguity are not identical with vagueness, they provide very favourable conditions for it: if the same word is used for a large number of objects, then there is an increased possibility that a number of uncertain cases will also occur among them: ambiguity also, the members of which are

---

PSRL, 1–32); L. Bloomfield, *Language* (New York, 1933); V. Skalička, *Zur ungarischen Grammatik*...(1935); V. Skalička, *Asymetrický dualismus*...(1935); B. Malmberg, 'Observation sur le système vocalique du français', *Acta linguistica* 2 (1940–1): 232–46; B. Malmberg, 'A propos du système phonologique de l'italien', *Acta linguistica* 3 (1942–3): 34–43; T. Milewski, 'Derywacja fonologiczna', *Biuletyn Polskiego Towarzystwa Językoznawczego* (Bulletin de la Société Polonaise de Linguistique) 9 (1949): 43–57; V. Skalička, *Komplexnost*...(1957); R. Wells, 'Is a structural treatment of meaning possible?', *Reports for the Eighth International Congress of Linguists* (1957): 197–209; M. K. Jensen, *Tonemicity* (Bergen-Oslo, 1961); D. L. Bolinger, *Generality, Gradience, and the All-or-None* ('s-Gravenhage, 1961); J. V. Neustupný, 'The asymmetry of phonological oppositions', *Bulletin of the Phonetic Society of Japan* [Onsei gakkai kaihō] 106 (1961): 1–6; F. Daneš, Zusammenfassung des Diskussionsbeitrages, *Zeichen und System der Sprache*, ii (Berlin, 1962), 62; J. Vachek, 'On peripheral phonemes of Modern English', *BSE* 4 (1964): 7–109.

---

[3] Cf. Vachek, op. cit.; also Jensen, *Tonemicity*, 35–6.

[4] O. Weinberger, *Logika* (Praha, 1959), 122.

[5] M. Black, *Language and Philosophy* (Ithaca, NY, 1949); T. Kubiński, 'Nazwy nieostre', *Studia Logica* 7 (1958): 116–79; T. Kubiński, 'Systemy pozornie sprzeczne', *Zeszyty naukowe Uniwersytetu Wrocławskiego, Seria B, Matematyka, Fizyka, Astronomia* (1959), 53–61; T. Kubiński, 'An attempt to bring logic nearer to colloquial language', *Studia Logica* 10 (1960), 61–75; W. Quine, *Word and Object*...(1960).

semantically close, offers an increased possibility of the occurrence of objects, the classification of which under some of its members might be doubtful. Bolinger gives an example in which it is difficult to specify whether the word "turning"[6] in a given sentence represents a substantive or an adjective and it would be possible to provide quite a number of similar examples from any language.

Black[7] quotes Peirce's definition of vagueness: "A proposition is vague when there are possible states of things concerning which it is intrinsically uncertain whether, had they been contemplated by the speaker, he would have regarded them as excluded or allowed by the proposition. By intrinsically uncertain we mean not uncertain in consequence of any ignorance of the interpreter, but because the speaker's habits of language were indeterminate". Black further exemplifies vagueness in the word "chair" and names for colours: in the latter, it is especially clear that because of the perfect continuity of the spectrum it is not possible in a designation of its sections by degrees to find the exact point where, for instance, red changes into orange, orange into yellow, etc. In the following parts of his study, Black introduces the term "fringe": That is a sphere of "uncertainty and doubts" on the use of the vague word.[8] He then demonstrates that fringe is not in accord with the usual conception of negation and in further analysis he evades it and works out a method of measuring the degree of vagueness by means of a so-called consistency profile: for vague words such as "chair" it is presumed that in a number of judgements, whether the elements of a series of objects are chairs or not, some of the objects will be called chairs more often and some of them less often; it is in fact the statistical determination of consistency in calling particular objects "chairs" during the course of judgements repeated several times, which is the basis for Black's measuring of vagueness.

For a logical interpretation of vagueness, Kubiński uses a different method.[9] As the usual conception of negation does not admit the existence of fringe, he replaces it by another conception from which it follows that if x is y, then it is not non-y, but from which it does not follow that if x is not non-y, then it is y, because x might lie on the fringe. In the systems formulated by Kubiński, the law of the excluded middle is then not valid, though they are consistent logical systems.

Kubiński's third study[10] is probably the most important for us. The author introduces in it as primitive terms of his system, in addition to a new functor of negation, a functor ε which has an intuitive content "is undoubtedly" (e. g. εxy we read "x is undoubtedly y") and a very important functor η, with which it is possible to express the relation between x, y, z, of the type "x is rather y than z". There are defined functors ν in the same system describing the relation "x is rather y than non-y" and functor ω expressing the relation of equidistance "x is y and z in the same degree". This means that we have at our disposal an apparatus for describing the following frequent situations in problems of language units, for instance word:

(a) M is one word; M are two words (functor ε)
(b) M is not undoubtedly a single word, but it is nearer to an evaluation as one word than as two words (functor η)
(c) M is just on the boundary between one and two words (functor ω).

Elements for which ωxyz valid (i.e. x is in the same degree y and z) we shall call in our study boundary elements and their class BOUNDARY. Elements for which ηxyz (i.e. x is rather y than z) is valid we shall call peripheral and their class PERIPHERY. Elements for which neither εxy or εxz is valid, are situated on the MARGIN and hence we may call them marginal, while elements

---

[6] He quotes the sentence "That dirty dog—turning in front of me like that!" (Bolinger, *Generality* ..., 21). It is just such cases that Bolinger terms generality, hence in disagreement with the above quoted terminology.
[7] Black, *Language and Philosophy*, 30.   [8] Ibid. 34.   [9] Kubiński, 'Nazwy nieostre', 120–1.
[10] Kubiński, 'An attempt'.

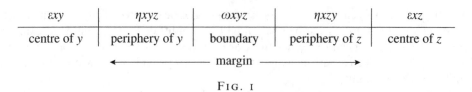

εxy	ηxyz	ωxyz	ηxzy	εxz
centre of *y*	periphery of *y*	boundary	periphery of *z*	centre of *z*

←———————— margin ————————→

FIG. I

for which εxy or εxz are valid will be called central and their class CENTRE.[11] From the given definitions it follows that the margin covers the whole boundary and periphery of elements *y* as well as of elements *z*. This situation can be graphically demonstrated as in Fig. I.

The terms with which Kubiński's study provides us are certainly more differentiated than a mere demarkation of centre and margin or analysis by the use of the consistency function (Black). The terms periphery and boundary are undoubtedly more important for linguistics without a doubt than an unanalysed term margin. In fact, mostly we come across peripheral elements; boundary (equidistant) elements are probably very rare and are not so important in language (and in other spheres of reality too) as peripheral elements. We are convinced that by using the terms VAGUENESS, MARGIN, BOUNDARY, PERIPHERY, and CENTRE we come much closer in linguistics to the requirements of a dialectical way of thinking. "Hard and fast lines", "forcibly fixed boundary lines and differences in classes" are no longer prescribed to us as logical necessities. Thus linguistics can reach a state in which it will be able to describe language just as it is, with all irregularities and complexities.

On the other hand, of course, it is not possible to say that contemporary logical theories of vagueness have satisfied us completely. For instance, Kubiński's systems presume an exact division of the centre, periphery and boundary. One of the problems which will certainly merit attention in the future is adoption of the possibility of gradual transition from the centre to the periphery and from the periphery to the boundary.

SOME TYPES OF VAGUENESS

Another disadvantage of logical theories is the fact that they take only one type of vagueness, which we shall call DISCOURSE VAGUENESS, into account: they are usually concerned with cases of a single symbol (word) describing a series of similar objects. When investigating the discourse vagueness, the process of classing definite objects (thus non-language elements) with a certain word (language element)[12] serves as material. This process takes place in discourse, can be many times repeated (by the same or different speakers of the language) and then statistically evaluated by using Black's method of consistency function. Discourse vagueness, however, is not the only, and also not the most important, type of vagueness. In linguistics we

---

[11] I accept now Daneš's ('Zusammenfassung') and Vachek's ('On peripheral phonemes of Modern English') terms periphery and centre as more suitable than asymmetry, pole, and the like, which I used earlier. Daneš's term "transition" for boundary is a less happy choice, because peripheral elements also are "transitional".

[12] There exist two types of discourse vagueness:
(a) Vagueness of content units. Some objects are classed with a word, for instance, "chair", more consistently and others less consistently and thus we arrive at the distinction between central and marginal elements. Interesting notes on this problem can be found in Bolinger's *Generality*, ch. 2, even though it seems that we still have to wait for a systematic elaboration of this question. As Quine demonstrated (*Word and Object*, 126), vagueness is not necessarily a matter of general terms; we find marginal utilizations with singular terms also. For instance, with "Mount Rainier", hesitation may arise as to where the mountain of this name actually begins. In such a case, we divide the whole region of the mountain range into smaller parts, each one of which we then attach separately to the term "Mount Rainier".

want to apply this term mainly to cases of linguistic units such as phoneme, morpheme, word and the like. The matter in question in such cases is usually the problem of classing a definite (linguistic) unit of lower order with definite more general (linguistic) units of a higher order. We can consider such classing only on the basis of knowledge of all units of the lower order, their linguistic properties (including vagueness) and, of course, neighbouring elements of the system. As classing in this case is a state, the property of *la langue*, and not a process, we obtain results only once and it is impossible to evaluate them statistically. Let us call this type SYSTEMIC VAGUENESS.[13]

Non-terminologically, vagueness is often spoken of in a very broad sense. However, should we consider vagueness in the sense of the terms defined in 'Logical theories of vagueness (above), we have to consider simultaneously two circumstances:

(a) the vagueness of which linguistic unit is under consideration and
(b) to which other linguistic unit the marginal elements of vague units approximate. It may be a certain concrete unit (e.g. marginal elements of the glottal stop may approach /h/), or zero (for instance, the glottal stop with marginal elements in which the articulation diminishes and is close to annihilation). The first of these cases might be called AP-PROXIMATION VAGUENESS and the second ANNIHILATION VAGUENESS. The given types of vagueness are definitely not unique. Detailed consideration of all the terms quoted in the introduction above which point to vagueness but are not identical with it, offer here a good basis for further study.

AN ANALYSIS OF LINGUISTIC VAGUENESS

As we have observed above, the mere registration of vagueness, unaccompanied by its ana-lysis, cannot be satisfactory. Analysis with the aid of Black's consistency profile—though of great help when applied to discourse vagueness—is of no use in cases of systemic vagueness.

(b) Vagueness of expression units. Some sounds are classed with a certain phonological unit in a greater number of "identifications" than others. The assumption that each phonetic unit may be, in case of normal, careful pronunciation and under normal conditions of listening, classed with a definite phonological unit (i.e. phoneme, prosodeme, etc.) without any hesitation, proves to be false. For instance, we have analysed statistically the classing of a large number of phonetic manifestations with a certain variant of the Japanese free accent (the so-called final variant). A result of 0% or 100% was not obtained in a single one of the phonetic manifestations, which means that all manifestations were marginal in the sense defined in §2, and hence the final variant of the Japanese free accent is a very vague unit. In this respect, our results are not the first. From his Dutch dialects Ebeling presents a vague opposition /v/ : /f/—some manifestations can clearly be identified as /v/, others as /f/, but most manifestations lie between these two extremes (Linguistic Units, 's-Gravenhage, 1960, pp. 46, 48–9). Discourse vagueness of the Norwegian accent is analysed statistically by Jensen, *Tonemicity*. It is interesting that numerous reviewers did not pay appropriate attention to the conclusions of the author which are of paramount importance for the theory of language. Jensen was in fact the first to prove statistically the discourse vagueness of phonological units.

---

[13] More attention is generally being paid to systemic vagueness than to discourse vagueness. However, equally often it is disclaimed in practice. Bloomfield, e.g., in his *Language*, says for instance on p. 181: "None or these criteria can be strictly applied: many forms lie on the border line between bound forms and words, or between words and phrases", but on pp. 178–9 of the same work, he categorically asserts that "the man I saw yesterday's" is simply one long word.—In addition to his previous works, Skalička analyses the systemic vagueness of grammatical units e.g. in his study *Komplexnost jazykových jednotek*; the author of the present study has presented a few notes on vagueness in syntax (review of E. H. Jorden, 'The syntax of modern colloquial Japanese', *Zeitschrift für Phonetik und allgemeine Sprachwissenschaft* 13 (1960: 83–9) and an attempt to analyse phonological vagueness ('The Asymmetry'). But vagueness applies also to such oppositions as of *la langue* and *la parole* (cf. already Skalička, 'The need for a linguistics of *la parole*', *Recueil linguistique de Bratislava* 1 (1948): 21–36). Vachek's essay 'On peripheral phonemes in Modern English' is a very interesting contribution to this problem. I tried to further develop the analysis of the vagueness of *la langue* in an essay on foreign phonological elements in Japanese, to appear in the volume *Jazykovaja situacija v stranach Azii i Afriki* (Moscow, 1966).

The analysis which we propose in the following paragraphs can, on the contrary, be used in both types of vagueness.[14]

Classes of linguistic units

The first step in an analysis of vagueness is a determination that linguistic phenomena are classes composed of elements which themselves may again be classes. Such a determination, naturally, is not at all a new discovery and we come across it in linguistics very frequently, sometimes under various terms. A few examples of classes: a language in the sense of "language of a certain nation" is regularly a class, the elements of which are geographical, social and functional dialects; each such dialect is usually a class of group or individual dialects, etc.; the phoneme in general is a class the elements of which are classes of vowels and consonants; a certain phoneme is a class of its variants, and so on.

For an analysis of vagueness, we obviously have to presume classes different from those normally used in logic and in which it is valid that "it is possible to make a basic determination on each individual as to whether it belongs or does not belong to the class under consideration."[15] We must reckon with classes which have not only the elements appropriate to them "undoubtedly" but also with such elements which belong to a given class "rather" than to any other, or which lie on the boundary between two classes: simply, classes which are an application of Kubiński's principle to the theory of classes and which should be called OPEN CLASSES.[16]

Complexity of linguistic units

Another important term for the analysis of linguistic vagueness is that of complexity. By complexity we understand the fact that each class is regularly characterized by a greater number of features simultaneously and not by a single feature.[17] In Japanese, for instance, a word is characterized by the following features:

(a) it is composed of a small group of semantemes which may be followed by several formemes,
(b) Certain variants of phonemes do not occur at its beginning (ŋ, dz, dʒ),

---

[14] This analysis is based on previous works by V. Skalička. In principle it was formulated earlier in our essay in 1961 ('The Asymmetry').

[15] K. Berka in *Modernt logika*, ed. O. Zich (Prague, 1958), 94.

[16] Cf. Milewski's "systemy otwarte" (*Derywacja fonologiczna*). Milewski, however, has in mind only language as a whole, and not individual linguistic classes.—Openness of the classes represents but a different formulation of their vagueness.

[17] Complexity, conceived in this way, differs from the complexity as defined by V. Skalička (*Komplexnost*) for whom it is a fact identical with what we call vagueness. In the sphere of linguistic analysis, the problem of complexity is projected as a problem of the "plurality of criteria". Considerations of this subject are very important for the theory of complexity, though they are often not sufficiently consistent. Although several criteria are often admitted, they are usually not independent but complement each other in such a manner that where one criterion is insufficient, only then does the other (or others) come to assert itself. The criteria of the word mentioned by Bloch ('Studies in colloquial Japanese II', *Language* 22 (1946)) are in such a relation, and a similar relation exists also among Trubetzkoy's criteria of monophonemicity (Grundzüge der Phonologie, Praha, 1939). Sometimes hierarchy among criteria is conceived in such a way that some criteria are considered merely as auxiliary (C. E. Bazell, 'The choice of criteria in structural linguistics', *Linguistics Today* (1954): 15). Such a standpoint means, however, that although we should recognize the plurality of criteria in linguistic analysis, this does not lead to complexity in linguistic description. Various use of criteria in the course of analysis does not, in fact, come out anywhere in the resulting description, which is contrary to the rule that each step in analysis should correspond to data in the description of the language.

(c) It has at the most one bound and one free accent,

(d) it is not interrupted by a pause,

(e) it can form an utterance on its own, etc.

Complexity thus understood is closely connected with the problem of redundant features which manifests itself first of all in phonology. The principle of complexity is naturally strongly opposed to the exclusion of redundant features from phonology.[18] It is indisputable that not everything in an act of speech is the manifestation of *la langue*. But, in our opinion, such a narrow limitation of *la langue* which excludes redundancy from language, does not give a true picture of the correct structure of reality. For a correct description of a language we need both: a recording of the main outlines of the structure with the aid of non-redundant features, and, of course, a recording of details in structure which must necessarily also include redundant features.

But I believe one cannot emphasize enough the fact that the principle of complexity does not exclude the hierarchy existing among features. It is quite clear that not all features are of the same importance for a class. Nevertheless, it is impossible to solve this situation by omitting some of the features completely. Such a procedure does not result in building up a hierarchy but, on the contrary, in its annihilation.

The problem of the hierarchy of features is of course very complicated in practice and it is not easy to find criteria according to which it would be possible to determine it simply. It is, however, clear, for instance, that features characterizing all the elements of a certain class and no other are very important. If, let us say, a consonant is obligatorily voiced in all positional variants of the phoneme, while it is tense only in some variants and not in others, then, for the given phoneme, the presence of voice is more important than tenseness. This, nevertheless, in no way diminishes the need for a perfect description of tenseness within the same linguistic discipline which describes the presence of voice and other features of the given consonant.

Asymmetry of features

For an explanation of vagueness, the statement of its complexity is obviously not sufficient. We can imagine complex classes exactly separated one from the other, without any marginal elements between them. The cause of vagueness lies in the fact that not all elements of a class can be characterized by all the features of the class, and that some features may be characterized by the features of other classes. This property we shall call ASYMMETRY of features.[19] The elements which are less characterized or are characterized by features of the opposite class, but still belong to the given class, are evidently the elements which we called peripheral. The elements which are so negligibly characterized that it is not clear whether they belong to

---

[18] In the Cercle Linguistique de Prague, too, voices were raised against a strict division of features into phonological and extra-phonological. Cf. de Groot's note on the definition of Variation extraphonologique concomitante in *TCLP* 4, (1931): 319, and his article in the same volume of *Travaux*. For new opinions on this question we quote only C. F. Hockett: "Of course it is easy to miss some relatively subsidiary secondary features and this obviously impairs our description of the phonological system of a language less than it would to miss some clearly primary feature. But we should not intentionally overlook them" (*A Manual of Phonology* (Baltimore, 1955), 175).

[19] Here we make use of V. Skalička's terminology (*Asymetrický dualismus*). Contrary to our own article from 1961 we apply the term "asymmetric" only to features. Less characterized elements we call here—in agreement with Daneš and Vachek—peripheral, and a class with peripheral elements we call a vague class.

		CLASS A							CLASS B		
elements:		e_1	e_2	e_3	e_4	f_1	f_2	g_1	g_2	g_3	g_4
features:	a_1	+	+	+	+	+	+	+			
	a_2	+	+	+	+		+		+		
	a_3	+	+		+						
	:										
	b_1			+			+	+	+	+	+
	b_2		+			+			+	+	+
	:										
		centre A	periphery A		boundary		periphery B	centre B			

FIG. 2

the given or to the opposite class, are no doubt those which we called boundary elements. This situation can be demonstrated something like this.

The marginal character of elements is doubtlessly influenced not only by the asymmetry of the features in the given class but also by the asymmetry of features in the opposite class, the elements characterized by the features of the opposite class being also peripheral within their own class. We shall call the above table the Table of Asymmetry. Such a table is certainly nothing new or surprising in linguistics. But if we try to elaborate it in concrete cases, and it should accompany an analysis of every linguistic class, we recognize that the matter is not so simple. It must be considered which class is concerned, what are its elements, what are the features of the class, what sort of hierarchy obtains among the features, with which other classes it has common marginal elements, what are the features of these classes etc.

In conclusion, we may say the following, concerning our analysis of vagueness: linguistic units are classes which are (1) complex, i.e. their elements are characterized by a greater number of features, (2) their features are asymmetric, i.e. all elements of the class are not necessarily characterized by the features of the class and, vice versa, some elements can be characterized by the features of other classes. The elements less characterized by the features of another class are marginal elements which cause the vagueness of the given class. These marginal elements can be further analysed into boundary and peripheral elements.

THE IMPORTANCE OF THE THEORY OF VAGUENESS

It is obvious that the theory of vagueness is still in its initial stage. In addition, the mode of analysis we have proposed and tested experimentally in several cases elsewhere,[20] is certainly also not the last word. Even so, it may mean a step forward which need not be quite devoid of value for linguistics. Vachek's study[21] has already revealed that a concept related to vagueness

---

[20] On the Japanese prosodic system (work concluded in 1963, and partly published as 'Nihongo no akusento wa kootei akusento ka' in *Onsei gakkai kaihoo* 121 (1966): 1–7, and ' "Haná" to "hana" ' in *Wa hatashite chigau ku* (1966), translated as 'Variability of the Japanese Accent' in J.V. Neustupný, *Poststructural Approaches to Language*. Tokyo: University of Tokyo Press, 1978, pp. 58–73), and on the foreign phonemic system of Japanese (published originally in the 1967 volume *Jazykovaja situacija v stranach Azii i Afriki*, and translated as 'The phonology of loanwords in Japanese' in J.V. Neustupný, *Poststructural Approaches to Language*. Tokyo: University of Tokyo Press, 1978, pp. 74–97
[21] J. Vachek, 'On peripheral phonemes of Modern English'.

can explain some linguistic changes such as the gradual transition of some or all elements on to the periphery of a given class, then on to the boundary, and finally, on to the periphery or into the centre of the opposite class. This complete process can be traced, thanks to the theory of vagueness, in all its stages by means of linguistic description.

The second perspective is concerned with the application of mathematical procedures in linguistics. We are afraid that as long as so-called mathematical linguistics will not be able to take into consideration the vagueness of linguistic units,[22] it will hardly be possible to speak of even relatively final results. (In some types of applied linguistics, the neglect of vagueness will probably remain a programmatic necessity. In such cases, it would of course be unwise to demand consistent consideration for vagueness.)

The third perspective is concerned with broader problems than those of linguistics. It is quite clear that vagueness is not limited to language only and that an analysis of linguistic vagueness can substantially support studies of vagueness in non-linguistic spheres of reality.

CLARITY AND VAGUENESS

We should like to add a note on one of the terms introduced in §1 which points to vagueness but is not identical with it. This term we call, with V. Skalička[23], clarity. While in considering vagueness we are interested in the elements of which there can be doubt as to the class to which they belong, in the case of clarity we are interested in the degree of differentiation between two terms of opposition, the strength of the opposition, the clarity of the very existence of a definite unit in the language system.

As an example we may introduce two dialects, between which there are several sub-dialects about which there can be hesitation as to which of the said two dialects they belong. Hence, the opposition of these two dialects is vague. Apart from this, however, we can speak about the clarity of this opposition, which is evidently the greater (a) the more features there are which distinguish the two dialects (such features are separate phenomena of phonology, grammar, vocabulary etc. of both dialects), and (b) the smaller is the vagueness of the opposition[24].

---

[22] So far we have no knowledge of any attempt to use open classes. From the point of view of the theory of vagueness, J. I. Levin's article 'Ob opisanii sistemy lingvističeskich ob'jectov obladajuščeich obščimi sredstvami', *VJa* 4 (1964): 112–19 is very interesting. But Levin, too, counts only with closed classes.

[23] Skalička, 'Zur ungarischen Grammatik'.

[24] Very lucid is Skalička's formulation: "Die grammatischen Differenziationen sind in den einzelnen Sprachen verschieden. Ihre Klarheit hängt von der Anzahl der Merkmale und dem Masse der Konsequenz dieser Merkmale in einer Differenziation ab." (Zur ungarischen Grammatik ... 1935, pp. 36–7).

22

Nouniness

JOHN ROBERT ROSS

I. INTRODUCTION

In this paper, I will extend the theory of non-discrete grammar which underlies Ross (1972a). In that paper, I was concerned with demonstrating that the traditional view of the categories *verb*, *adjective*, and *noun*, under which these three are distinct and unrelated, is incorrect. Instead, I argued, these categories are (possibly cardinal) points in a linear *squish*, or quasi-continuous hierarchy, such as that shown in (1.1).

(1.1)   *Verb* > Present participle > *Adjective* > Preposition > Adjectival Noun (e.g. *fun*)
         > *Noun*

As this notation suggests, adjectives are "between" verbs and nouns with respect to a number of syntactic processes. A number of these are shown in Ross (op. cit.) to apply "most" to verbs, "less" to adjectives, and "least" to nouns.

The present paper is concerned with demonstrating the existence of a similar squish—that in (1.2), the *Nouniness Squish*.

(1.2)   *that* > *for to* > Q > *Acc Ing* > *Poss Ing* > Action Nominal > Derived Nominal
         > Noun

The entries in (1.2) are abbreviations for types of complements, as explained and exemplified in (1.3).

(1.3) a. *that* = *that*-clauses (*that Max gave the letters to Frieda*)
    b. *for to* = *for* NP *to* V X (*for Max to have given the letters to Frieda*)
    c. Q = embedded questions (*how willingly Max gave the letters to Frieda*)
    d. *Acc Ing* = $\left[\begin{matrix} \text{NP} \\ +\text{Acc} \end{matrix} \right]$ V + *ing* X (*Max giving the letters to Frieda*)
    e. *Poss Ing* = NP's V + *ing* X (*Max's giving the letters to Frieda*)
    f. Action Nominal $\left(\left\{ \begin{matrix} Max's \\ the \end{matrix} \right\} giving \ of \ the \ letters \ to \ Frieda \right)$
    g. Derived Nominal $\left(\left\{ \begin{matrix} Max's \\ the \end{matrix} \right\} gift \ of \ the \ letters \ to \ Frieda \right)$
    h. Noun (*spatula*)

To show that these complement types are hierarchically grouped, I will cite a number of syntactic phenomena which "work their way into" (1.2) and (1.3), as it were. That is, some of these phenomena will apply to (1.3a), but not to (1.3b–h); some to (1.3a–b), but not to (1.3c–h); some to (1.3a–c), but not to (1.3d–h), etc. My claim is simply this: there exists no syntactic phenomenon which applies to, say, (1.3a), (1.3d), and (1.3g), but not to the other elements of (1.3).

* John Robert Ross, 'Nouniness', in Osamu Fujimura (ed.), *Three Dimensions of Linguistic Research* (Tokyo: TEC Company Ltd., 1973), 137–257. © 1973 John Robert Ross. Reprinted by kind permission of the author. Some minor corrections have been made by the editors.

2. THE EVIDENCE

2.1. *It* S

Let us begin with the rule, however it is formulated, which either inserts *it*, or, viewed from an opposite perspective, fails to delete an underlying *it*, before the complements of certain verbs. This process can result in the appearance in surface structure of an *it* before *that*, *for to*, and possibly before Q but not before any other elements of (1.2). Cf. (2.1).

(2.1) *It Deletion*

a. I $\left\{ \begin{array}{l} \text{regret} \\ \text{resent} \\ \text{(dis)like} \\ \text{hate} \\ \quad\text{etc.} \end{array} \right\}$ it $\left\{ \begin{array}{l} \text{that you left} \\ \text{for you to leave} \\ \text{(?)how long you stayed} \\ \text{* you(r) staying so long} \\ \text{* the giving of money to UNESCO} \end{array} \right\}$

b. *I $\left\{ \begin{array}{l} \text{doubt} \\ \text{said} \\ \text{believe} \\ \quad\text{etc.} \end{array} \right\}$ it that he was dumb.

As the contrast in verb classes in whose complements this type of *it* appears indicates (cf. the verbs of (2.1a) vs. those of (2.1b)), this construction exists only for factive complements, a correlation which suggests to me that the source for this *it* is the noun *fact*, and that the rule that the Kiparskies refer to as *Fact Deletion*[1] should be viewed as passing through a stage of pronominalization on the way to the total obliteration of the noun which they argue to be the head of all factive complements. That is, though it is not immediately relevant to nouniness, I would suggest the two rules shown in (2.2)

(2.2) a. *Fact* → *It*
    b. *It Deletion*

What is relevant to nouniness is the environment for (2.2b). As (2.1a) shows, *It Deletion*, though generally optional with *that* and *for to*,[2] becomes almost obligatory before Q and totally obligatory before any elements of (1.2) that are below Q, i.e., before nounier complements than Q.

2.2. Preposition deletion

The next process which dances variably to the tune of nouniness is the rule of *Preposition Deletion*, which was first proposed, to my knowledge, in Rosenbaum (1967). Its operation can be seen in (2.3).

---

[1] Cf. Kiparsky and Kiparsky (1970), and also Ross (MS a), for discussions of and motivation for this rule.

[2] In many idiolects, a subset of factive verbs prohibits the deletion of *it* before *that*-clauses. For me, this is true of the verbs *love*, *like*, *dislike*, and *hate*.

In addition, Douglas Ross has pointed out to me that in his idiolect, no forms like those in (2.1a) are allowed. *It Deletion* thus appears to be a fairly capriciously applied rule. As far as I know, the differences in rule valency that this rule exhibits in various idiolects are not traceable back to any other properties of these idiolects.

(2.3) *Preposition Deletion*

$$
\text{I was surprised}
\left\{
\begin{array}{l}
(*\text{at}) \text{ that you had hives} \\
(*\text{at}) \text{ to find myself underwater} \\
(\text{at}) \text{ how far I could throw the ball} \\
*(\text{at}) \text{ Jim ('s) retching}
\end{array}
\right\}.
$$

The underlying *at* which is lexically associated with *surprised* **must** delete before *that* and *for to*, can optionally (for many speakers) be retained before Q and must not delete before any complements of greater nouniness.

2.3. Extraposition

The next rule that interacts with (1.2) was also discussed in Rosenbaum (op. cit.), where it was referred to as *Extraposition*. It produces such sentences as those in (2.4) by doubling complement clauses of sufficiently low nouniness at the end of their matrix sentences, leaving behind the pronoun *it*.

(2.4) *Extraposition*

$$
\text{It was a shame}
\left\{
\begin{array}{l}
\text{a. that your hens couldn't sleep} \\
\text{b. for Max to have to pay rent} \\
\text{c. how long you had to fight off the hyenas} \\
\text{d.} \left\{ \begin{array}{l} ?\text{Max} \\ ?*\text{Max's} \end{array} \right\} \text{getting arrested} \\
\text{e.} *\text{Joan's unwillingness to sign}
\end{array}
\right\}.
$$

This rule is optional for *that*, *for to*, and Q complements, and is generally impossible for complements of higher nouniness. However, as Edward Klima has called to my attention, there are certain predicates, such as *be a shame*, which do weakly allow the extraposition of *Acc Ing* complements, and even more weakly, the extraposition of *Poss Ing* complements. No predicate I know of allows any complements of greater nouniness to extrapose, however.

2.4. The Island-Internal Sentential NP Constraint

The fourth syntactic phenomenon which interacts with the squish in (1.2) has to do with the output condition whose violation produces such unfortunate question sentences as those in (2.5).

(2.5)

$$
\text{Was}
\left\{
\begin{array}{l}
*\text{that the boss had warts rumoured?} \\
?*\text{that your arm was asleep noticed?} \\
??\text{for him to enter nude unexpected?} \\
?\text{why he had come obvious?} \\
?\text{him entering nude a shock?} \\
\text{Jack's applauding appreciated?}
\end{array}
\right\}
$$

The corresponding affirmative sentences are all grammatical, as the reader can verify, which suggests that the graded deviances of (2.5) are produced by violations of the following output condition:

(2.6)   *The Island-Internal Sentential NP Constraint (I^2SNPC)*
Star any surface structure island[3] of the form
X [S]$_{NP}$ Y, where X, Y $\neq \emptyset$,
the degree of violation depending on the nouniness of the internal complement.

It is necessary to restrict the X and Y in (2.6) to portions of the tree in the same island as the complement, because otherwise, this condition would throw out such sentences as those in (2.7).

(2.7)   a. I know *that he's a merman,* || but I still have a crush on him.
   b. Although occultism *is* rampant, || *for you to show up there with that stake in your heart* will cause raised eyebrows.
   c. That Boris will be delayed, || and *that Bela can't make it at all,* || is regrettable, my dear, but we shall just have to start the transmogrification without them.

The *that*-clauses in (2.7a) and the *for-to* clause in (2.7b) end and begin, respectively, their islands, as I have suggested by drawing parallel vertical lines for the relevant island-boundaries in these sentences. And since coordinated nodes form islands, the second conjunct of the subject of (2.7c) is an island of its own, and thus cannot be starred by the I^2SNPC.

It appears impossible to replace (2.6) by a parallel condition which would reject only *clause-internal* sentential complements. To see this, consider (2.8), which, while its underlined sentential NP is not internal to the first clause above it (i.e., the bracketed object of *believe*), still seems to be afflicted by the sort of disease which (2.6) cures.

(2.8)   ??Homer and Jethro believe [*for us to boo now* would make enemies]$_S$.

This sentential NP, though not *clause*-internal (it is the left-most element of the clause it is in), is *island*-internal, which is what has led me to formulate (2.6) in the way I have.

To return to (2.6), the very words in which it is phrased show its dependence upon the squish of (1.2). For it is obvious that such violations as those in (2.5), which (2.6) or any theoretical structure cognate to it must explain, are not of an on-off, discrete nature. Rather, the nounier the island-internal clause is, the mellower the resulting string is.[4]

---

[3] For discussion of this term, cf. Ross (1967: ch. 6).

[4] The failure to account for the gradations in the deviances of such sentences as (2.5) is, to my mind, the most significant fault of the early version of the I^2SNPC which was informally proposed in Ross (1967) (cf. §3.1.1.3.).

And it must be regarded as an equally serious problem for any reanalysis such as that of Emonds (1970). Emonds suggests, in essence, that such structures as (2.4a–c) are more nearly basic, and that a rule whose effect is roughly the reverse of *Extraposition* produces such sentences as those in (i).

(i) $\left\{ \begin{array}{l} \text{That your hens couldn't sleep} \\ \text{For Max to have to pay rent} \\ \text{How long you had to fight off the hyenas} \end{array} \right\}$ is a shame.

Emonds attempts to block such sentences as (2.8) by claiming that this reverse rule (let us call it *Intraposition* here) is a "root transformation," in his terminology (i.e., one which operates, roughly speaking, only in highest clauses). Evidently, however, if the deviances of such sentences as those in (2.5) *do* vary in approximately the way that I have indicated, the degree of "rootiness" of *Intraposition* would have to vary with complementizer choice, paralleling that in (1.2). While I think that it is correct to recharacterize Emonds' important notion of root transformation in non-discrete terms (cf. Ross MS b for details), I must emphasize that even such a recharacterization could not repair the discreteness-linked difficulties in Emonds' analysis. The reason is that whatever process produces cleft sentences, like (2.12) in the text, it is clearly not a "root transformation," in Emonds' sense, nor does it have the slightest degree of rootiness, to re-view the problem non-discretely. And yet such sentences as (2.12) exhibit the same graded unacceptabilities as (2.5). Clearly, then, what is he matter with (2.5) and (2.8) cannot be that a root transformation has applied elsewhere than in a root S, for such an account would leave the parallel rottenness of (2.12) unexplained.

Even disregarding the matter of the squishiness of the violations produced by the I^2SNPC, there are a number of other independent problematical characteristics of Emonds' *Intraposition* analysis, as Higgins has pointed out

One final wrinkle of the I²SNPC should be noted here. This is the fact that some structural environments are more "tolerant" of embedded headless nominal complements than others. I have thus far been able to isolate the four differing configurations shown in (2.9).

(2.9) (a) $\begin{bmatrix} V \\ +Tns \end{bmatrix}$ — < (b) $\begin{bmatrix} V \\ -Tns \end{bmatrix}$ — < (c) *that* — < (d) clefted

To see that the four environments of (2.9) are in fact arranged according to the gravity of the violations they occasion with the I²SNPC, compare the sentences in (2.5), which correspond to (2.9a), with those in (2.10), (2.11), and (2.12), which correspond to (2.9b), (2.9c), and (2.9d), respectively.

(2.10)
a.
$\left\{ \begin{array}{l} ?*\text{Explain [that your license has expired] to the judge,lady} \\ ?? \text{ I will arrange [for the bomb to go off at noon] with the anarchist leaderhip} \\ ? \text{ Explain [how well you can drive without a license] to the DA, lady} \\ \text{Explain [the speedometer ('s) being stuck at 135] to him,too} \end{array} \right\}$

b. I consider $\left\{ \begin{array}{l} ?*\text{that he will leave likely} \\ ?? \text{for him to leave likely} \\ ? \text{ how long he went without a bath disgusting} \\ \left\{ \begin{array}{l} ? \text{ him} \\ \text{his} \end{array} \right\} \text{leaving likely} \end{array} \right\}$.

(2.11)
I think that $\left\{ \begin{array}{l} ?? \text{ that we stayed on} \\ ? \text{ for us to stay on} \\ \text{how long we slept} \\ \left\{ \begin{array}{l} \text{us} \\ \text{our} \end{array} \right\} \text{staying on} \end{array} \right\}$ was deplorable.

(2.12)
It was $\left\{ \begin{array}{l} \text{that you had been a spy that I} \left\{ \begin{array}{l} *\text{thought} \\ ? \text{ forgot} \end{array} \right\}^5 \\ ? \text{ for the } Red \text{ Sox to win that we were hoping for} \\ \text{which faction he } was \text{ supporting that was hard to determine} \\ \left\{ \begin{array}{l} \text{them} \\ \text{their} \end{array} \right\} \text{being so all-fired snooty that I objected to} \end{array} \right\}$.

I have neither any explanation for the hierarchical arrangement of the environments of (2.9) nor anything more to say about it than that no account of I²SNPC phenomena which does not provide such an explanation can be considered viable.

(cf. Higgins 1973). One particularly weak point is that the *Intraposition*-analysis forces Emonds to postulate, in order to account for bisentential verbs like *entail* and *prove*, the theoretical device of "doubly-filled nodes," which is a device of such theoretical power as to remove the explanatory power of Emonds' notion of structure-preserving rules. For example, if the S node which ends Emonds' deep structure for bisentential clauses containing verbs like *entail* and *prove* can be "doubly filled," why can't the NP node after *like*? But if this NP node *can* be "doubly-filled" in deep structure (Emonds bars such "doubly-filled" nodes from surface structure), then what would block (ii), in which one of the double fillers has been topicalized?

(ii) *Football games I like the opera.

Such arguments as these suggest to me that *Intraposition* must be rejected in favor of the earlier postulated *Extraposition*, supplemented by the I²SNPC.

---

[5] I believe it to be the case that factive *that*-clauses differ systematically from non-factive *that*-clauses, in a number of environments other than this one. I have not investigated this problem in detail, however.

2.5. Plural agreement

The next set of facts which interacts with (1.2) has to do with the question as to when conjoined NPs trigger plural agreement (cf. (2.13)).

(2.13) a.
$$\left\{ \begin{array}{l} *\text{That he lost and that you won} \\ *\text{For him to lose and for you to win} \\ ?*\text{Him winning and you losing} \\ ??\text{His winning and your losing} \end{array} \right\} \text{are wonderful.}$$

     b. Jack's winning of the bingo tournament, and your losing of the hopscotch marathon, were unexpected joys.

     c. Senator Phogbottom's nomination and the ensuing rebellion in Belgrade were unforeseen by our computer.

The basic generalization is clear: the nounier a complement type is, the more plural will be any NP which results from conjoining two or more tokens of this type. Though more could be said on this topic (for instance, the question as to what happens with mixed-type conjunctions could be investigated), the basic facts seem to provide clear support for the squish of (1.2).

2.6. Extraposition from NP

The next sets of facts that provide evidence for the correctness of (1.2) are of a fundamentally different kind than the facts on which § 2.1–2.5 were based. Those sections all had to do with processes which were *external* to the complement types in question. That is, I showed how the applicability of the rules that form $it + S$ constructions, that delete prepositions and that extrapose complement clauses varies with the nouniness of the complement clause in the environment, with nounier complements undergoing fewer operations than more sentential ones. And I showed that only nouny complements are immune to the stigma of the I^2SNPC or can trigger plural agreement.

What I will discuss in the twelve sections to follow is a number of respects in which nounier complements are more restricted in their *internal* structure than more sentential ones. This is above all true with respect to the subjects of these complements. The generalization that holds is this: the nounier a complement is, the fewer are the types of constituents that can figure as its subject.[6]

A first example is provided by the rule I refer to in Ross (1967) as *Extraposition from NP*, a rule which optionally moves noun complements and relative clauses to clause-final position, under complicated conditions which need not concern us here. That this rule can operate freely from the subject NPs of *that*-clauses, *for to*-clauses and embedded questions is apparent from a comparison of the sentences in (2.14) and (2.15).

(2.14) a. That a man [who was wearing size 29 Keds]$_S$ was in this closet is too obvious, Watson, to need belaboring.

     b. For a criminal [who had no knowledge of the Koran]$_S$ to have slipped through our cordon is too fantastic a notion to bear scrutiny.

     c. How many numbers people [who have had no previous experience]$_S$ will have to do is not sure.

---

[6] I should mention at the outset that much of my thinking about nouniness, but especially with respect to restrictions on the internal structure of nouny clauses, was stimulated by Edwin Williams' important paper, 'Small clauses in English' (1971).

(2.15) a. That a man was in this closet [who was wearing size 29 Keds]$_S$ is too obvious, Watson, to need belabouring.

b. For a criminal to have slipped through our cordon [who had no knowledge of the Koran]$_S$ is too fantastic a notion to bear scrutiny.

c. How many numbers people will have to do [who had no previous experience]$_S$ is not sure.

Clearly, then, there are no restrictions in principle on the application of the rule of *Extraposition from NP* from the subjects of complements of low nouninss, like these three. The situation is different, however, with regard to complements of greater nouniness. For me, the facts are as shown in (2.16).

(2.16) *Extraposition from NP*

a. $\left\{ \begin{array}{l} \text{A man} \\ ? *\text{A man's} \end{array} \right\}$ trying to register who was wearing no under-garments was most upsetting, most.

b. *A student's careless combining of the ingredients who doesn't know about sodium and water could ruin the punch.

c. *An old friend's visit to Rio who I hadn't seen for years cheered me considerably.

d. *An old friend's hat who I hadn't seen for years hung on the book.

Thus I find a sharp decrease in acceptability here as soon as any extraposition is attempted from possessivized subjects of complements.[7] It is quite possible that this is a consequence of the Left Branch Condition (cf. Ross (1967), § 4.4 for a definition of this condition), but since my present purposes do not require me to evaluate this possibility, I will not go into it further here. What *is* clear is that the contrast between (2.15) and (2.16) is in line with, and provides further support for, the squish in (1.2).[8]

2.7. Fake NPs

In this subsection, I will examine a number of idiomatic and expletive subject NPs, in an attempt to show that they are hierarchically arranged, as in (2.17).

---

[7] The ungrammaticality of the second sentence of (2.16a) was first noticed by Williams (1971), who drew from this ungrammaticality the conclusion that *Poss Ing* complements differ structurally from *that* and *for-to* complements in being "smaller" than these , by virtue of not containing a sentence-final slot for extraposed clauses (Williams does not use the term "slot," and ties in his observation to Emonds' notion of structure-preserving rules, but the basic idea is highly similar to the more familiar concept of "slot," so I have used this term here.)

I do not think, however, that Williams' conclusion is justified. Extraposed clauses *can* appear in *Poss Ing* complements, and even in complements of greater nouniness, as shown in (i), (ii), and (iv) below.

(i) Harry's sending all those tubas to her which we hadn't checked out was a disaster.
(ii) Your patient repeating of all the lessons to me which I had missed through oversleeping certainly made me respect your self-control.
(iii) *A man's attempt to visit this plant who hadn't been fingerprinted led to a security crackdown.
(iv) The attempt of a man to visit this plant who hadn't been fingerprinted led to a security crackdown.

The contrast here between *(iii) and (iv), which are presumably transformationally related, suggests strongly that what is not allowed is the extraposition of clauses from possessivized subjects, not the absence of a slot for extraposed clauses in nouny complements.

[8] Again, here, as elsewhere, I unfortunately have no explanation for the fact that the judgments concerning *Extraposition from NP* are almost binary, where this is not the case with other nouniness-linked phenomena.

(2.17)
$$ tack > \left\{ \begin{array}{c} it\ weather/\_\_\ be \\ headway \end{array} \right\} > \left\{ \begin{array}{c} it\ sentential \\ there \end{array} \right\} > \left\{ \begin{array}{c} it\ weather/\_\_V \\ tabs \end{array} \right\} $$

The inequality signs in (2.17) are to be interpreted as meaning the following: if, for any two elements, A and B, of (2.17), A > B, then wherever B is possible, A is possible, but not conversely. I base (2.17) on the judgments below.[9]

(2.18) *Take a tack*
   This tack('s) being taken on pollution disgusts me.

(2.19) *Weather* **it** *with copular predicates and* **make headway**

   a. $\left\{ \begin{array}{c} \text{It} \\ ?\ \text{Its} \end{array} \right\}$ being muggy yesterday kept the Colts out of the cellar.

   b. $\left\{ \begin{array}{c} \text{Significant headway} \\ ?\ \text{Significant headway's} \end{array} \right\}$ being made on this by March is unlikely.

(2.20) *Sentential* **it** *and* **there**

   a. $\left\{ \begin{array}{c} \text{It} \\ *\text{Its} \end{array} \right\}$ being possible that the Rams will sweep is staggering.

   b. $\left\{ \begin{array}{c} \text{There} \\ *\text{There's} \end{array} \right\}$ being no beer was a nightmare.

(2.21) *Weather* **it** *with verbs and* **keep tabs on**

   a. $\left\{ \begin{array}{c} \text{It} \left\{ \begin{array}{c} ??\ \text{raining} \\ ?\ \text{having rained} \end{array} \right\} \\ *\text{Its} \left\{ \begin{array}{c} \text{raining} \\ \text{having rained} \end{array} \right\} \end{array} \right\}$ threw me off-stride.

   b. $\left\{ \begin{array}{c} ?\text{Close tabs} \\ *\text{Close tabs's} \end{array} \right\}$ being kept on my domestics is an affront.

I refer to the subjects of these sentences as "fake NPs" because it is possible to demonstrate in other areas, as well as in the subjects of nouny complements, that they do not exhibit the full range of syntactic behavior which can be observed with non-idiomatic, non-expletive NPs.[10]

   The generalization that I would like to suggest about such facts (in my dialect) as those in (2.18)–(2.21) is that while some idioms, like *take a tack on*, which are relatively compositional,

---

[9] I must point out here that it has become clear to me as a result of presenting this material in a number of lectures, that dialectal variation in this area is particularly rampant. In particular, there are dialects which violate the squish in (1.2)—dialects in which *its raining* is better than *it raining*. At present, I have not been able to detect any clear groupings among dialects with respect to these facts—the situation just seems chaotic. Robert Greenberg has suggested that the judgments of many informants may be being colored by the inveighing of prescriptive grammarians against the whole *Acc Ing* construction, especially when it appears in subject position. The perceived dialectal chaos would, then, have one component of significant linguistic restrictions (of some at present unguessable sort) and another—very strong—component of Miss Fidditchitis.

I am both attracted to and repelled by this mode of explanation. What attracts me is my intuition that it is right (cf. Morgan 1972 for some illuminating discussion of a (probably) similar case). What repels me is the capaciousness of the escape hatch that it opens here, unless we can develop some kind of litmus for Miss Fidditchitis, so that it can be agreed upon in advance as to the conditions under which it is justifiable to bring in Miss Fidditch to extricate the beleaguered grammarian from a chaotic situation.

At any rate, I have elected to present here the (= my) facts about the interaction of fake NPs and complements containing *ing*-forms in the belief that when the correct balance of grammar and Fidditch has been established here, an interaction with the nouniness squish will be demonstrable.

[10] This matter is discussed at length in Ross (1973).

and non-idiomatic,[11] can appear freely in passive form in *Ing*-complements, other fake NPs are more restricted. The best of the remaining fakes are the *it* of copular weather predicates like *be muggy, be foggy, be fair*, etc. and the noun (?) *headway* in the idiom *make headway*. Following these, for me, are the *it* of *Extraposition* and the expletive *there*: while the presence of the possessive morpheme merely weakens the sentences in (2.19), it degrammaticalizes those in (2.20). And for the final two fakes, weather *it* with true verbs like *drizzle, hail, sleet*, etc., and the noun (?) *tabs*, it seems to be difficult to construct sentences which contain complements with the verbs of these items appearing in an *ing*-form.[12]

Thus for my dialect, the facts of fake NPs bear out the squish of (1.2). Any fake NP that can occur possessivized can also occur as the subject of an *Acc Ing* complement, but the converse is not true.

2.8. Possessivizability of complements

A related restriction is apparent from the fact that only highly nouny complements can possessivize. To see this, contrast the sentences of (2.22) with those of (2.23)–(2.24).[13]

(2.22) a. That the odor is unpleasant is understandable.
        b. The odor's being unpleasant is understandable.

(2.23) a. ??That that you have to go to Kuhkaff is unpleasant is understandable.
        b. ?That for you to have to visit Mildred is unpleasant is understandable.
        c. ?That how long you have to stay there is unpleasant is understandable.
        d. That you having to sleep with the goat is unpleasant is understandable.
        e. That your having to comb your bed-mate is unpleasant is understandable.
        f. That your feelings towards Mildred are unpleasant is understandable.

(2.24) a. **That you have to go to Kuhkaff's being unpleasant is understandable.
        b. **For you to have to visit Mildred's being unpleasant is understandable.
        c. *How long you have to stay there's being unpleasant is understandable.
        d. *You having to sleep with the goat's being unpleasant is understandable.
        e. ?*Your having to comb your bed-mate's being unpleasant is understandable.

---

[11] That idiomaticity is a squishy property, and not a discrete one, has been perceived by many previous researchers. For a challenging and significant attempt to cope, within the framework of a discrete transformational grammar, with the fact that some idioms are more frozen than others, cf. Fraser (1970).

Parenthetically, it does not seem correct to me to claim, as Paul Ziff has suggested to me (personal communication), that *take a tack on* is not idiomatic at all. While it is true that the noun *tack*, especially with regard to its use in sailing, can appear in a far greater number of contexts than can the noun *tabs*, it is still the case that *tack*, in its metaphorical meaning, is far more restricted than near synonyms like *approach* and *slant*.

(i) This $\left\{ \begin{array}{l} \text{??tack on} \\ \text{approach to} \end{array} \right\}$ the problem of security is important.

(ii) This $\left\{ \begin{array}{l} \text{?tack on} \\ \text{approach to} \end{array} \right\}$ unemployment is familiar from the WPA.

(iii) I fear this $\left\{ \begin{array}{l} \text{?tack} \\ \text{slant} \end{array} \right\}$ on boldness.

(iv) This $\left\{ \begin{array}{l} \text{? * tack on} \\ \text{approach to} \end{array} \right\}$ the problem of opacity has been successful in the past.

Thus I would argue, at present, that *tack*, in the meaning of 'approach,' *is* in fact "idiomatically connected" to *take*, even though the collocation is low on the idiomaticity squish.

[12] The noun (?) *advantage* of the idiom *take advantage of* is similar to *tabs* in its restrictedness, but I have not been able to decide whether it is loose enough to go in with the items in (2.20) or whether it should be put in (2.21).

[13] The awkwardness of the earlier sentences in (2.23), which have been included here only to make the parallel to (2.24) complete, is of course a result of the I²SNPC.

    e′. ??Having to comb your bed-mate's being unpleasant is understandable.

    f. ??Your combing of your bed-mate's being unpleasant is understandable.

    g. Your feelings toward Mildred's being unpleasant is understandable.

Except for the contrast between (2.24e) and (2.24e′), which suggests that subjectless complements are nounier than ones with subjects, these facts seem self-explanatory. They are exactly what would be predicted from (1.2).

A further comment is in order, however: it is easy to show that the requirement that only highly nouny phrases can be possessivized is itself a squishy restriction, for there are some environments which weight this restriction more heavily than others. In particular, the environment sub-squish in (2.25) is easily demonstrable.

(2.25) $[NP \_\_ Ving\ X] \gg [NP \_\_ N]_{NP}$

(2.25) merely asserts that possessives with plain nouns are far more restricted than possessives which are the subjects of *ing*-complements. To see this, merely substitute *unpleasantness* for *being unpleasant* in (2.22b) and (2.24). (2.22b) remains grammatical, but all of the sentences in (2.24) take a giant step outward: only (2.24g) retains any vestiges of Englishness. This refinement thus indicates the need for replacing the judgments of (2.24) by a matrix in which they would be a column.

There is a final, more general, point that can be made now. The facts considered so far in this section, and the facts presented in §2.8, show that possessivizability requires a high degree of nouniness. (2.24) demonstrate the necessity for subjects of *Poss Ing* complements to be highly nouny. And (2.23) (and (2.11)) showed the necessity for subjects of *that*-clauses not to be too sentential. But what of the subjects of, say, *for to*-complements? Compare (2.24) and (2.26).

(2.26) a. *For that you have to go to Kuhkaff to be unpleasant is understandable.

    b. **For for you to have to visit Mildred to be unpleasant is understandable.[14]

    c. *For how long you have to stay there to be unpleasant is understandable.

    d. ?*For you having to sleep with the goat to be unpleasant is understandable.

    e. ?For your having to comb your bed-mate to be unpleasant is understandable.

    e′. For having to comb your bed-mate to be unpleasant is understandable.

    f. For your feelings toward Mildred to be unpleasant is understandable.

Apparently, then, (2.23) > (2.26) > (2.24). This suggests the following generalization.

(2.27)   The nounier a complement is, the nounier its subject must be.

Why there should be such a linkage as that specified in (2.27), and why it should not also obtain for objects, are at present mysteries for which I cannot suggest answers.

2.9. Quantifiability of complement subjects

A further restriction on complement subjects (unless it is somehow reducible to (2.27)) is that only fairly sentential complements can have subjects incorporating quantifiers. The relevant facts are shown in (2.28).

(2.28) a. That many people are willing to leave is surprising.

    b. For many people to be willing to leave is surprising.

---

[14] Possibly the extra dollop of badness of this sentence is caused by the double *for*. I have no other explanation for it.

c. For how long many people are willing to leave is surprising.
d. ?Many people being willing to leave is surprising.
e. ??Many people's being willing to leave is surprising.
f. *Many people's tickling of *Felis Leo* was ill-advised.
g. *Many people's willingness to leave is surprising.

2.10. Quantifier postposing

A further restriction involving subjects and the nouniness squish has to do with a rule that I will refer to as *Quantifier Postposing*. This rule converts such sentences as (2.29a) into (2.29b) or (2.29c).

(2.29) a.
$$
\left\{ \begin{array}{l} \text{All} \left(\left\{ \begin{array}{l} \text{three} \\ \text{nine} \\ \text{729} \end{array} \right\} \right) \\ \text{Both} \\ \text{Each} \\ \text{Several} \\ \text{Some} \\ \text{Five} \end{array} \right\} \text{of} \left\{ \begin{array}{l} \text{them} \\ \text{us} \\ \text{the children} \end{array} \right\} \text{hate Spam.}
$$

b.
$$
\left\{ \begin{array}{l} \text{They} \\ \text{We} \end{array} \right\} \left\{ \begin{array}{l} \text{all} \left(\left\{ \begin{array}{l} \text{three} \\ \text{?nine} \\ \text{*729} \end{array} \right\} \right) \\ \text{both} \\ \text{each} \\ \text{*several} \\ \text{*some} \\ \text{*five} \end{array} \right\} \text{hate Spam.}
$$

c.
$$
\text{The children} \left\{ \begin{array}{l} \text{all} \left(* \left\{ \begin{array}{l} \text{three} \\ \text{nine} \\ \text{729} \end{array} \right\} \right) \\ \text{both} \\ \text{each} \\ \text{*several} \\ \text{*some} \\ \text{*five} \end{array} \right\} \text{hate Spam.}
$$

As is apparent, this rule only affects universal quantifiers, among which, *all* can be followed by a small number, but only if the quantified NP is pronominal. Thus *Quantifier Postposing* applies in subject position more freely from pronouns than from full NPs, a fact which shows up even more clearly in object position, where no postposing is possible at all, except from pronouns. Cf. (2.30):

(2.30)

$$\text{I inspected} \left\{ \begin{array}{l} \text{them} \\ \text{us} \\ \text{*the children} \end{array} \right\} \left\{ \begin{array}{l} \text{all} \\ \text{both} \end{array} \right\}$$

This fact, that this rule is more restricted in object position than in subject position, is argued in Ross (MS b) to constitute evidence for a general notion of primacy, defined roughly in (2.31).

(2.31)   Node A of a tree *has primacy over* node B of a tree if A is an element of a sentence that dominates B, or when A and B are clause-mates, if A is to the left of B.

I argue further that primacy figures in a far-reaching constraint, roughly that stated in (2.32).

(2.32)   *The Primacy Constraint*
If a rule applies to node B, or in environment B, it must also apply to node A, or in environment A, for all nodes A that have primacy over B.

In other words, while (2.32) would admit the possibility of a process applying only in subject position, it would rule out any process applying only in object position. And while processes may be less restricted in subject position than in object position, (2.32) predicts that the opposite will never be the case.

The primacy constraint is obviously related to the important NP accessibility hierarchy developed in Keenan and Comrie (1972), though their emphasis differs slightly from that of Ross (op. cit.): their concern is the construction of a more finely graded primacy relation than that described in (2.31). The notion they arrive at is justified by examination of relative clause strategies in a wide range of languages, while (2.32) seeks to cover a broader set of rules. The two approaches should not, of course, be viewed as being in conflict. I hope that when my own research has progressed far enough, it will be possible for me to argue that the Keenan–Comrie notion of accessibility can be extended to constrain the application of all rules, as has been done with subject-object primacy in (2.32).

To return to the main concerns of the present paper, *Quantifier Postposing* interacts with nouniness in the following way: the rule is only applicable to the subjects of complements of a low nouniness. Cf. (2.33):

(2.33) a. That they both were re-elected is disgusting.
b. For them both to be renominated would drive me to despair.
c. Why they both must be cackling at the prospect of being able to sit on us for another term is revealed in this report.
d. ?Them both trying to muzzle the press is a frightening omen.
e. ?*Their both having succeeded to such a large extent bespeaks worse to come.
f. *Their both rattling of sabers in foreign policy is an old, old song.
g. *Their both love of demonstrators is legion.

The contrast between (2.29) and (2.30) above shows *Quantifier Postposing* to be subject to the Primacy Constraint, and (2.33) shows it to be limited by nouniness.[15] If such parallels crop up in a significant number of other cases, it will be necessary to modify the definition of primacy in (2.31) to incorporate nouniness as a part of it.

---

[15] There is another process, similar to *Quantifier Postposing*, which also dances to the tune of nouniness. This process converts (i) into (ii) (and later (iii)?):

(i) $\left\{ \begin{array}{l} \text{Both} \\ \text{All} \\ \text{Each} \\ \text{None} \end{array} \right\}$ of them will be drinking from it.

2.11. PP subjects

Another area in which the nouniness of a complement interacts with a restriction pertaining to subjects has to do with certain cases of the output of the rule of *Copula Switch*, the rule which permutes subject and object NPs around the main verb *be* in such pseudo-cleft sentences as those in (2.34).

(2.34) a. What I found was a poisoned grapenut.
b. What I realized was that we were being duped.
c. What I attempted was to mollify the enraged ducks.
d. Where we slept was under the bathtub.
e. What I have never been is taciturn.

The rule of *Copula Switch* converts these to the corresponding sentences of (2.35).

(2.35) a. A poisoned grapenut was what I found.
b. That we were being duped was what I realized.
c. To mollify the enraged ducks was what I attempted.
d. Under the bathtub was where we slept.
e. Taciturn is what I have never been.

What is of immediate interest for my present purposes is such sentences as (2.35d), which have prepositional phrase subjects. As the sentences in (2.36) suggest, these subjects must be regarded as being NPs (in part), because they can undergo such processes as *Verb-Subject Inversion*, *Raising*, *Passive*, and *Tag Formation*.

(ii) They $\left\{ \begin{array}{l} \text{?both} \\ \text{all} \\ \text{??each} \\ \text{?none} \end{array} \right\}$ of them will be drinking from it.

(iii) They will $\left\{ \begin{array}{l} \text{both} \\ \text{all} \\ \text{?each} \\ \text{none} \end{array} \right\}$ of them be drinking from it.

This process might appear to provide problems for the hypothesis that there is a nouniness squish, for consider (iv):

(iv) a. That they all of them solved it is wonderful.
b. *For them all of them to solve it would be a miracle.
c. How they all of them solved it is not known.
d. *Them all of them solving it was great.
e. ??Their all of them solving it was fabulous.
f. *Their all of them rapid solving of it is encouraging.
g. **Their all of them final solution to it is ingenious.

If this process is interacting with a squish, however, why are (ivb) and (ivd) worse than the next-nounier sentences? One answer, pointed out to me by George Williams, is that this process, however it is to be formulated, prefers to work from nominative NPs and will not work from oblique NPs. Cf. *(v).

(v) *I drove them all of them crazy.

The process is not overjoyed when it applies to possessive NPs, but if I am right in my feeling that (ive) > (ivf) > (ivg), it would appear that nouniness plays a role in its operation.

Incidentally, it may be the case that the non-standard oblique case which shows up with coordinated pronouns is enough to weaken the output of this rule, if I am right in hearing (vib) as being slightly defective.

(vi) a. He and I have both of us worked on this.
b. ?Him and me have both of us worked on this.

(2.36) a. Was under the bathtub where we slept?

b. They believe under the bathtub to be where we slept.

c Under the bathtub is believed to be where we slept.

d. Under the bathtub is where we slept, isn't it?

These facts thus tend to support the familiar conclusion that PPs, though obviously different from NPs in many ways, should at some deep level be considered to be merely a kind of NP.[16]

However, it is easy to show that they are somewhat "fake," in the sense of Ross (1973): when the structure underlying copula-switched pseudo-clefts like (2.35d) appear in nounier complements, the fakeness of their subject NP produces deviances of progressively greater seriousness.

(2.37) a. That under the bathtub is where you slept is staggering.

b. ?For under the bathtub to be where you sleep would crimp our social life.

c. ?Why under the bathtub was where he slept has baffled modern Napoleonology for decades.

d. ?*Under the bathtub being where you sleep will upset the negotiations.

e. *Under the bathtub's being where you slept must have been a real down.[17]

---

[16] I am indebted to Tony Kroch and Howard Lasnik for calling to my attention the existence of such interesting and unstudied sentence as (i).

(i)   Under the bathtub $\left\{\begin{array}{l}\text{is a nice place}\\\text{is comfortable}\\\text{?pleased Milty}\\\text{??stinks}\end{array}\right\}$.

Their point was that while it might be possible to proceed sentences like (2.36) and (i) to the conclusion that locative and directional PPs are NPs, the broader claim that *all* PPs are NPs could not be supported by such sentences, which can only be constructed for locatives and directionals.

While I find their objections well-taken in the present case, there is additional evidence for the broader identification of PP and NP from the fact that pied piping affects NPs and PPs equally, from the fact that almost all superficially non-prepositional NPs show up in other syntactic contexts with prepositions associated with them, and from the fact that prepositional phrases are almost always islands (i.e., in only a few languages is it possible for prepositions to be stranded: in most languages, only sentences corresponding to (ii) below can be found.)

(ii)   Of what does your Greas-o Shortening consist ?

(iii) What does your Greas-o Shortening consist of ?

The fact that most languages do not permit the objects of prepositions to move away, stranding the preposition, as in (iii), can be shown to derive from a general principle to the effect that such immediately self-dominating constituents as NP_a in (iv) below generally form islands. But this explanation is only available if prepositional phrases are self-dominating nodes, as in (iv).

(iv)

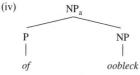

If instead, some more traditional structure for PP, like (v), is postulated, another explanation for the general unstrandability of prepositions must be sought.

(v)

[17] No nounier complements than *Poss Ing* can be checked, because pseudo-cleft sentences will not appear in nounier environments (a fact which itself argues for a hierarchically structured list of complement types). However, it is easy to show the inadmissibility of PP subjects in nounier environments, using the Kroch–Lasnik constructions mentioned in note 16. Cf. the ungrammaticality of (i).

Thus the distribution of complements with PP subjects again supports the implicational hierarchy proposed in (1.2).

2.12. AP subjects

Mutatis mutandis, the behavior of AP subjects of such copula-switched pseudo-cleft sentences as (2.35e) above is exactly the same, with the exception that they seem to be systematically worse than the corresponding copula-switched pseudo-clefts with prepositional phrase subjects. Compare (2.37) and (2.38).

(2.38) a. ?That taciturn is what you think I am is incredible.
   b. ?*For taciturn to be what I strive to be would be wasted effort.
   c. ??Why loquacious is what they have always been puzzles me.[18]
   d. *Taciturn being what I want to be but am not makes for grey days.
   e. **Taciturn's being what Sam is has earned him a reputation as a hard-nose poker player.

In fact, of course, the other two copula-switched sentences of (2.35) that have abstract subjects, namely (2.35b) and (2.35c), are also restricted when these structures appear as complements themselves, as was pointed out in part in connection with (2.27) above. A summary of how the complements in (1.2) interact with the constraint in (2.27) is provided by the chart in (2.39).

(2.39)

Fillers / Frames	N Der. Nom. Act. Nom.	Poss Ing	Acc Ing	PP	for NP to V X	that S	AP
that __V X	OK	OK	OK	OK	?	??	?
for__to V X	OK	OK	OK	?	|*|	|*|	?*
wh-X __V Y	OK	OK	OK	?	?	?	??
__Ving X	OK	OK	?	|?*|	??	??	*
__'s Ving X	OK	?	??	*	*	**	**

In general, (2.39) is almost entirely "well-behaved," in the sense of Ross (1973). That is, in each row, the transition from grammaticality to ungrammaticality, as the row is scanned from left to right, is monotonic. For a matrix to be well-behaved, the vertical transition from grammaticality to ungrammaticality must also be monotonic. The flies in the ointment here are, for example, the fourth cell of the fourth row from the top, which is *horizontally*

(i)   *Under the bathtub's niceness exceeds over the stove's.
That we do not have to do here merely with a restriction on possessives can be seen from *(ii).
(ii)   *The niceness (of) under the bathtub exceeds the niceness (of) over the stove.

---

[18] If the squish in (1.2) were the only thing influencing the grammaticality of such AP-subject pseudo-cleft sentences, we would predict that (2.38c) should be no better than (2.38b). That it does seem to be slightly better suggests that some other factor may be influencing things here. I have nothing to propose at present.

ill-behaved, being more ungrammatical, for unknown reasons, than the cells to its left and right. I indicate such horizontal ill-behavior by including two vertical lines in this cell. The same notation is used to point up the horizontal ill-behavior of the fifth and sixth cells of the second row, which are, in addition, also *vertically ill-behaved*, as is indicated by the parallel horizontal lines enclosing them and the only other such cell, the seventh cell of the third row. As they stand, such ill-behaved cells constitute counter-evidence to the claim that the complement types we have been investigating do form a squish, and unless other factors can be isolated which can be used to dispose of such ointment-flies, we will be driven to the conclusion that even more radical departures from present linguistic theory than that which well-behaved matrices necessitate must be admitted. For the time being, however, let us assume that (2.39) represents the interaction of a well-behaved matrix—a squish—with some additional factors. This matrix is evidently in line with what (1.2) predicts.

2.13. Fake NPs in object position

Fairly nouny complements seem to exclude fake NP objects, with the degree of deviance being proportional to the fakeness of the object. Thus compare (2.40) and (2.41) with (2.42).

(2.40) a. That he took this tack repeatedly cost him my vote.
       b. For them to make headway rapidly would be encouraging.
       c. How long we will keep tabs on him accurately has not been decided yet.

(2.41) a. His taking this tack repeatedly cost him my vote.
       b. Their making headway rapidly is encouraging.
       c. Our keeping tabs on him accurately may prove invaluable.

(2.42) a. ??His repeated taking of this tack cost him my vote.
       b. *Their rapid making of headway is encouraging.
       c. **Our accurate keeping of tabs on him may prove invaluable.

Again, results in this direction are to be expected, given (1.2), though why there should be such a sudden jump here between (2.41) and (2.42) remains to be explained.

2.14. Promotion

I will assume that a rule that I will, following a suggestion of Paul Postal's, refer to as *Promotion*, converts such sentences as those in (2.43) to the corresponding ones in (2.44).

(2.43) a. Jim's disregarding the consequences shocked me.
       b. Jim's disregarding of the consequences shocked me.
       c. Jim's disregard for the consequences shocked me.

(2.44)

a. Jim shocked me $\left\{ \begin{array}{l} \left\{ \begin{array}{l} \text{by} \\ *\text{with} \end{array} \right\} — \text{disregarding the consequences} \\ \left\{ \begin{array}{l} ?\text{by} \\ ?*\text{with} \end{array} \right\} \text{his disregarding the consequences} \end{array} \right\}$.

b. Jim shocked me $\left\{ \begin{array}{l} ??\text{by } *(\text{his}) \\ ?\text{with his} \end{array} \right\}$ disregarding of the consequences.

c. Jim shocked me $\left\{ \begin{array}{l} ? *\text{by } *(\text{his}) \\ \text{with his} \end{array} \right\}$ disregard for the consequences.

This rule copies the subject of the complement into the subject of the matrix verb, while postposing the complement and adjoining a preposition to it. The rule works for all predicates of the class of *shock, surprise, amaze, please, disgust*—the verbs which form adjectives in *-ing*—and for all of these, *by* is the preposition that is inserted if the complement is a *Poss Ing* construction. The preposition *with* cannot, for many speakers, be inserted under *Promotion* unless the complement is nounier than *Poss Ing*. With action nominals, both prepositions are somewhat acceptable, though the construction itself seems difficult then.[19] With derived nominals, *all* dialects, to the best of my knowledge, show a marked preference for *with*. Furthermore, as is clear from (2.44), while *by* favors the deletion of the pronominal copy of the promoted NP, *with* is only possible if this copy is retained.

The facts of (2.44), no matter whether I am correct in assuming that it derives from (2.43) or not, argue strongly that there is a hierarchy of nouniness. What goes with the sentence end of the hierarchy are the preposition *by* and deletion of the pronominal copy, while *with* and pronoun retention go with the nouny end. Many other logically thinkable assignments of grammaticality valences to the sentences in (2.44) would not be compatible with such a hierarchical account. The fact that the observed data are compatible with such an account thus supports the postulation of a hierarchy.

2.15. Negation

The general law here is stated in (2.45).

(2.45)   Nouniness is incompatible with (unincorporated) negation.

The facts that originally drew my attention to this generalization were cited by Howard Lasnik in another connection (cf. Lasnik 1972). He noted such contrasts as those in (2.46).

(2.46) a. That not everyone passed the exam upset Ted.
   b. ?For not everyone to pass the exam would upset Ted.
   c. ?*Not everyone's passing the exam upset Ted.

If we extend (2.46) to (2.47), by adding in the other complement types, we find grammaticalities which are in accord with (2.45).

(2.47) a. That not everyone will refuse our offer is expected.
   b. ?For not everyone to refuse our offer is expected.
   c. ?Under what circumstances not everyone will refuse our offer is the subject of a heated debate.
   d. ??Not everyone refusing our offer was expected.
   e. ?*Not everyone's refusing our offer was expected.
   f. **Not everyone's refusing of our offer was a surprise.
   g. **Not everyone's refusal of our offer was a surprise.[20]

---

[19] I should emphasize that this reluctance on the part of *Promotion* to apply to action nominals is counterevidence to the claim that action nominals are part of the squish in (1.2).

[20] Some speakers may accept (2.47f) and (2.47g), with a meaning like that suggested in (i), where it is *be a surprise* that is being negated,

(i) It is not the case that $\left\{ \begin{array}{l} \text{everone's} \left\{ \begin{array}{l} \text{refusing} \\ \text{refusal of} \end{array} \right\} \text{our offer was a surprise} \\ \text{it was a surprise that everyone refused our offer} \end{array} \right\}$.

but this reading is irrelevant for our present purposes. What is being asserted is that (2.47f) and (2.47g) do not have any readings (for me, at least) on which they are synonymous with (2.47a).

Actually, the situation with regard to negation is more complex than has been indicated so far, with factors other than nouniness playing a role. For reasons unclear to me, some negative items are more offensive to nouny complements than others. The hierarchy that seems correct for my speech is shown in (2.48).

(2.48)   Post-verbal *seldom* > Post-verbal *never* >
Pre-verbal *not* > Pre-verbal *never* >
no in subject > *few* in subject > *not* in subject

When this hierarchy intersects with the nouniness hierarchy, the sub-squish shown in (2.49) results.

(2.49)

	Post-verbal *seldom*	Post-verbal *never*	Pre-verbal *not*	Pre-verbal *never*	*no* in subject	*few* in subject	*not* in subject
That S	OK	OK	OK	OK	OK	OK	OK
for NP *to* V X	OK	OK	OK	OK	OK	?	?
Q	OK	OK	OK	OK	OK	$\overline{\text{OK}}$	?
Acc Ing	OK	!?!	OK	OK	??	??	??
Poss Ing	?	!??!	?	??	!*!	?*	?*
Act. Nom.	??	?*	*	*	**	**	**
Der. Nom.	?*	*	**	**	**	**	**
	(2.50)	(2.51)	(2.52)	(2.53)	(2.54)	(2.55)	(2.47)

The evidence for setting up this matrix is drawn from the sentences in (2.50)–(2.55) below, and from (2.47), with each column of the matrix corresponding to the sentences indicated by the number at the bottom of that column.[21]

(2.50) a. [That he prepares dinner seldom] is good for her health.
    b. [For him to prepare dinner seldom] is good for her health.
    c. [Why he prepares dinner seldom] is well-known.
    d. [Him preparing dinner seldom] is good for her health.

---

[21] The brackets around the subject clauses of (2.50) and (2.51) are meant to indicate that the adverbs *seldom* and *never* are to be taken as modifiers of the embedded predicate, not as modifiers of the matrix predicate, where they would not produce the desired kind of ungrammaticality.

e. [His preparing dinner $\left\{ \begin{array}{l} \text{often} \\ \text{?seldom} \end{array} \right\}$[22]] is good for her health.

f. [His preparing of dinner $\left\{ \begin{array}{l} \text{?often} \\ \text{??seldom} \end{array} \right\}$[23]] is good for her health.

g. [His preparation of dinner $\left\{ \begin{array}{l} \text{??often} \\ \text{?*seldom} \end{array} \right\}$[23]] is good for her health.

(2.51) a. [That he prepares dinner never[24]] is good for her health.
b. [For him to prepare dinner never] is good for her health.
c. [Why he prepares dinner never] is well-known.
d. ?[Him preparing dinner never] is good for her health.
e. ??[His preparing dinner never] is good for her health.
f. ?*[His preparing of dinner never] is good for her health.
g. *[His preparation of dinner never] is good for her health.

(2.52) a. That he does not prepare dinner is good for her health.
b. For him not to prepare dinner is good for her health.
c. Why he does not prepare dinner is good for her health.
d. Him not preparing dinner is good for her health.
e. ?His not preparing dinner is good for her health.
f. *His not preparing of dinner is good for her health.
g. **His not preparation of dinner is good for her health.[25]

(2.53) a. That he never prepares dinner is good for her health.
b. For him never to prepare dinner is good for her health.
c. Why he never prepares dinner is well-known.
d. Him never preparing dinner is good for her health.
e. ??His never preparing dinner is good for her health.
f. *His never preparing of dinner is good for her health.
g. **His never preparation of dinner is good for her health.

(2.54) a. That no children prepare dinner is good for her health.
b. For no children to prepare dinner is good for her health.
c. Why no children prepare dinner is well-known.
d. ??No children preparing dinner is good for her health.
e. *No children's preparing dinner is good for her health.
f. **No children's preparing of dinner is good for her health.[26]
g. **No children's preparation of dinner is good for her health.[26]

---

[22] The slight, but I think clear, difference in grammaticality between (2.50e) with *often* and the same string with *seldom* is a clear proof that negativity is at least part of the cause of the deviance of the strings in (2.50e), (2.50f), and (2.50g).

[23] The fact that even *often* produces awkwardness in sentences like (2.47f) and (2.47g) is due to the fact that post-verbal adverbs of all types are frowned on in nouny environments. What is preferred is for these adverbs to be adjectivalized and to be moved to pre-verbal (actually, prenominal) position. This need is particularly urgent for adverbs in *-ly* (*his decision rapidly >> his rapid decision*), slightly less so for adverbs which are homophonous with their adjectival forms (like *hard* and *fast*: ? ?*his decision fast > his fast decision*), and may even be slightly less than that for forms like *often*, which are unambiguously adverbial, and are thus excluded prenominally (*?his absence often << *his often absence*).

Cf. Ross (1972a) for further illustrations of the squishy connection between nouniness and pre-predicate position.

[24] Sentence-final position is difficult for *never* in the best of cases. The sentences all seem to be extremely emphatic. Possibly it is this emphatic flavor that is behind the systematic downshift from (2.50) to (2.51).

[25] The fact that *non-preparation* in place of *not preparation* in (2.52g) improves this sentence markedly is the reason for restricting (2.45) with the parenthesized modifier that appears there. But this leaves us with the mystery of why such negative-incorporated forms as *never*, *no*, and *few* still produce violations.

[26] Some speakers may find (2.54f) and (2.54g) acceptable, but presumably, only when it is the predicate *good* that is being negated, parallel to the grammatical but irrelevant readings mentioned in note 20.

(2.55) a. That few children prepare dinner is good for her health.
 b. ?For few children to prepare dinner is good for her health.
 c. ?*Why few children prepare dinner is well-known.
 d. ??Few children preparing dinner is good for her health.
 e. *Few children's preparing dinner is good for her health.
 f. **Few children's preparing of dinner is good for her health.
 g. **Few children's preparation of dinner is good for her health.

Not only are the three horizontally and the one vertically ill-behaved cells of (2.49) unexplained at present, it is also a total mystery as to why the items in (2.48) should be ordered in the way they are. I can discern no intuitive basis for *not* causing more "trouble" for equally nouny complements when it appears in subjects than when it appears pre-verbally, etc., etc.

Nevertheless, the fact that such a squishoid matrix as (2.49) should be constructible at all is extremely telling evidence for the correctness of the claim that the complement types of (1.2) are hierarchically arranged.

2.16. NP Shift

This rule, called "Complex NP Shift" in Ross (1967), moves post-verbal heavy NPs to the end of clauses that otherwise would have to limp along with a fat constituent in their midst. Thus it converts (2.56a) into (2.56b).

(2.56) a. The Patent Office found [a proposal to power jumbo jets by giant rubber bands, instead of by pollution-producing oil by-products,]$_{NP}$ intriguing.
 b. The Patent Office found intriguing [a proposal to power jumbo jets by giant rubber bands, instead of by pollution-producing oil by-products]$_{NP}$.

Interestingly, however, this rule seems to balk at shifting headless complements, unless they are fairly nouny. Thus, though several of the sentences in (2.57) are rendered inoperative because they violate the I²SNPC, *NP Shift* is not allowed to fix them up by postposing the offending internal complement, as the corresponding sentences in (2.58) attest.

(2.57) a. *I found that Ron had lied to us like that disgraceful.
 b. ?*I found for Ron to lie to us like that disgraceful.
 c. ?*I found who Ron had lied to when disgraceful.
 d. ?I found Ron lying to us like that disgraceful.
 e. I found Ron's lying to us like that disgraceful.
 f. I found Ron's adroit suppressing of the data disgraceful.
 g. I found Ron's lies to us disgraceful.

(2.58) a. *I found disgraceful that Ron had lied to us like that.
 b. *I found disgraceful for Ron to lie to us like that.
 c. ?*I found disgraceful who Ron had lied to when.
 d. ??I found disgraceful Ron lying to us like that.
 e. ?I found disgraceful Ron's lying to us like that.
 f. I found disgraceful Ron's adroit suppressing of the data.
 g. ?I found disgraceful Ron's lies to us.[27]

The facts seem fairly straightforward here: the less nouny a complement is, the worse will be the result when this complement is postposed by the rule of *NP Shift*. The only further point

---

[27] This sentence may strike some as weak, but presumably only because the shiftee, *Ron's lies to us*, is not "heavy" enough. If supplemental modifiers adorn this phrase, (2–58g) becomes fine, for me.

that seems worthy of note here is that if some such restriction as this is the correct one to impose on *NP Shift*, then some operation other than this rule must be responsible for the clause-final position of the bracketed complements in such sentences as those in (2.59).

(2.59) a. I explained to Jason [that I had no intention of leaving].
b. I would urge strongly [for there to be a new trial].
c. He enquired of us [where we had left his batteries].
d. We took into consideration Mildred ??('s) having been heavily sedated at the time.[28]

It is possible that all that is necessary is to state the restriction on *NP Shift* that the ungrammaticalities in (2.58) show to be necessary in such a way as to mention the material that the prospective shiftee is to cross over, with its passage not being restricted by non-nouniness if it is only to cross over a prepositional phrase, adverb, or idiom chunk (namely, *into consideration*), as in (2.59), while being prohibited from crossing over such predicates as *disgraceful*.

On the other hand, it may be that the output of the crossing of an element of the first type (say a prepositional phrase) is structurally distinct from the output of a crossing of a predicate. Thus note that (2.60a), where the shiftee has crossed a prepositional phrase, allows a piece of the bracketed moved constituent to be questioned more easily than is possible in (2.60b), where the bracketed shiftee has crossed an adjective. Compare (2.61a) and (2.61b).

(2.60) a. He found for them [a previously unpublished photo of that Surf God].
b. He found objectionable [a previously unpublished photo of that Surf God].

(2.61) a. ?Which Surf God did he find for them a previously unpublished photo of ?
b. ?*Which Surf God did he find objectionable a previously unpublished photo of?

To my ear, the two sentences in (2.60) also seem to be different in intonation—the *b*-sentence requires a far bigger pause than is necessary in the *a*-sentence.

However, since these facts, though interesting, do not seem to bear directly on the way *NP Shift* interacts with nouniness, I will leave them for future research.

2.17. Determiners

An exceedingly interesting set of sentences, from the point of view of the theory of English complementation, is the one exemplified by (2.62).

(2.62) "In my work in both France and Italy much looking, *much simple being there* preceded any photography."[29]

What kind of complement can the italicized phrase in (2.62) be? The word *much* is elsewhere a (prenominal) quantifier, and *simple* is an adjective. This would indicate that what follows is a noun. But though *being* can be a count noun, as in (2.63),

(2.63) The beings on that remote planet appear to be able to survive without Wonder-bread.

---

[28] For some reason, sentences seem considerably weirder when their sentence-final complements are *Acc Ing* clauses than when they are *Poss Ing* clauses. I have no explanation for this fact, but must call attention to it, because my theory would lead me to predict that such restrictions on only one element of the ordering in (1.2) should not exist. Thus, the badness of the *Acc Ing* version of (2.59d) should be seen as a counterexample to the claim that the elements of (1.2) form a squish.

[29] My italics. This sentence is due to Paul Strand, from *US Camera*, 1955, as quoted in *The New Yorker Magazine*, March 17, 1973.

it can be shown that *being there* in (2.62) functions as the "VP" of an *Acc Ing* (or *Poss Ing*) complement. To see this, note that such *ing*-phrases can have various transformational rules apply to them which, as is correctly observed in Chomsky (1970), cannot be applied in action nominals. Thus, compare the grammatical sentences of (2.64), which have the same kind of construction as (2.62), with the ungrammatical, transformed, versions of the action nominals in (2.65).

(2.64) a. This looking $\left\{ \begin{array}{l} \text{up addresses} \\ \text{addresses up} \end{array} \right\}$ has got to stop.

b. No giving $\left\{ \begin{array}{l} \text{lumpy cigarettes to freshmen} \\ \text{freshmen lumpy cigarettes} \end{array} \right\}$ will be tolerated.

c. Some simple showing $\left\{ \begin{array}{l} \text{that it is necessary to wash them} \\ \text{it to be necessary to wash them} \end{array} \right\}$ may be requested.

(2.65) a. Bill's looking $\left\{ \begin{array}{l} \text{up of addresses} \\ *\text{of addresses up} \end{array} \right\}$ was efficient.

b. Your generous giving $\left\{ \begin{array}{l} \text{of lumpy cigarettes to freshmen} \\ *\text{freshmen of lumpy cigarettes} \end{array} \right\}$ has been approved of.

c. Sam's quick showing $\left\{ \begin{array}{l} \text{that it is necessary to wash them} \\ *\text{of it to be necessary to wash them} \end{array} \right\}$ was masterful.

The stars in (2.65) show that the rules of *Particle Movement, Dative,* and *Raising* must not be applied in action nominalizations. But they may be in constructions of the type shown in (2.62) and (2.64).

A final type of evidence which would seem to render implausible any analysis which treated the *ing*-forms in such sentences as some kind of lexical noun is provided by such sentences as those in (2.66), which show that it is possible for such *ing*-forms to be based on auxiliaries.

(2.66) a. That having been followed for years must have been nerve-wracking.
b. This being seduced continually is kind of fun.
c. That having had to pay early must have crimped your vacation plans.

The only conclusion that one can draw here, as far as I can see, is that it is possible for *Poss Ing* complements (or possibly even for *Acc Ing* ones—which kind cannot be decided, as far as I know) to co-occur with certain determiners, like *this/that, much, no,* etc. Whatever this type of *ing*-complement derives from ultimately, there are arguments that they must have subjects in underlying structure, as is suggested by the reflexives in (2.67) and standard transformational arguments about *Equi*.

(2.67) a. This having to defend himself seems to be bugging Melvin.
b. That wanting to throw herself into the shredder must have been difficult for Gloria.

Moreover, it is even possible to cite examples which show that what follows these determiners is a clause which actually manifests a subject, albeit in a postposed position. Cf. the sentences in (2.68).

(2.68) a. ?This coming home late of Janet's has got to stop.

b. No more telling lies on the part of $\left\{ \begin{array}{l} \text{officials} \\ ?\text{Mayor Fresca} \\ *\text{you (and Ted)} \end{array} \right\}$ [30] will be condoned.

---

[30] I do not understand why only some of the subjects in (2.68b) are grammatical. Possibly there is some restriction pertaining to genericity that must be imposed. I have not looked into this problem in sufficient detail.

Though this is not the time to delve deeply into the syntax of this fascinating construction, the relevance that it has for the study of the nouniness of the complement types in (1.2) should have become apparent. For, though it has been claimed that there is a sharp, binary distinction between derived nominals and the other complement types in (1.2), in that only the former type "has the internal structure of a noun phrase"[31]—i.e., determiners—in fact, we find some determiners occurring with types which exhibit such non-nouny behavior as taking auxiliaries and making aspectual differences (cf. (2.67)), and modifying clearly derived "VPs". In other words, the ability to take determiners seems not to be a binary, yes-no, matter, but rather one of degree.

In my speech, there is a hierarchy of "noun-requiringness" of determiners, with those on the left end of the hierarchy occurring in a wider range of contexts than those on the right.

$$
\begin{matrix} (2.69) \\ \text{NP's} \end{matrix} \overset{?}{>} \left\{ \begin{matrix} this \\ that \end{matrix} \right\} > \left\{ \begin{matrix} no \\ some \\ much \\ little \end{matrix} \right\} > \left\{ \begin{matrix} the \\ prior \\ occasional \\ frequent \end{matrix} \right\} > \left\{ \begin{matrix} careful \\ reluctant \\ etc. \end{matrix} \right\} > \left\{ \begin{matrix} good \\ bad \end{matrix} \right\} \overset{?}{>} \left\{ \begin{matrix} other \\ mere \end{matrix} \right\}
$$

When intersected with the nouniness hierarchy of (1.2), (2.69) produces the subsquish shown in (2.70).

(2.70)

	NPs	*this* *that*	*no* *some* *much* *little*	*the* *prior* *occasional* *frequent*	*careful* *reluctant* *etc.*	*good* *bad*	*other* *mere*
that S	*	*	*	*	*	*	*
for NP *to* V X	*	*	*	*	*	*	*
Q	*	*	*	*	*	*	*
$\left\{ \begin{matrix} Acc \\ Poss \end{matrix} \right\}$ *Ing* with Aux	OK	OK(?)	?	*	*	*	*
$\left\{ \begin{matrix} Acc \\ Poss \end{matrix} \right\}$ *Ing* w/o Aux	OK	OK	OK	?	?*	*	*
Action Nominal	OK	OK	OK	OK	OK	OK	?*̲
Derived Nominal	OK	OK	OK	OK	OK	OK	OK(?)
N	OK	OK	OK	OK	OK	OK	OK

    (2.71)   (2.72)   (2.73)   (2.74)   (2.75)   (2.76)   (2.77)

As was the case in (2.49), the facts corresponding to each column of (2.70) are given in the example sentences corresponding to the number at the bottom of the column.[32]

---

[31] Cf. Chomsky (1970: 188–90).
[32] I have not distinguished between *Acc Ing* and *Poss Ing* complements in (2.70) because, as noted above, I can see no way to do so.

(*continues*)

(2.71) a. *Ed's (that he) refused her offer angered me.[33]
   b. *Ed's (for him) to refuse her offer angered me.
   c. *Ed's (when he) refused her offer angered me.
   d. Ed's having refused her offer angered me.
   e. Ed's refusing her offer angered me.
   f. Ed's refusing of her offer angered me.
   g. Ed's refusal of her offer angered me.
   h. Ed's garbage angered me.

(2.72) a. *That (that Ed) refused her offer angered me.[34]
   b. *That (for Ed) to refuse her offer angered me.
   c. *That (when Ed) refused her offer angered me.
   d. ?? That having refused her offer angered me.[35]
   e. That refusing of her offer angered me.
   f. That refusal of her offer angered me.
   g. That garbage angered me.

(2.73) a. *Some (that Ed) refused her offer angered me.
   b. *Little (for Ed) to refuse her offer angered me.
   c. *No (when Ed) refused her offer angered me.
   d. i. No being arrested will be tolerated.[36]
    ii. ?? Some being arrested is expected.
    iii. *? Little having preregistered has been reported.

Instead, I have distinguished between *ing*-clauses whose main verb is an auxiliary and those whose main verb is a true verb, for these two types seem to differ systematically with respect to determiner choice, with the latter being nounier than the former.

---

[33] The first three rows of (2.70) are so bad that writing them seems almost academic. With or without the parenthesized material, I doubt whether any speaker can be found who could use *a-*, *b*, or *c*-versions of (2.71)–(2.77). But, for the record, here they are.

[34] Of course, with properly placed pauses—after *this* and *offer*—the string of words in (2.72a) is grammatical. Needless to say, . . .

[35] I do not know why this sentence is worse than those in (2.66). In general, the differences between the first two columns of (2.70) are small, if indeed any exist. This is why I have placed a question mark above the first inequality sign in (2.69), and a question mark in parentheses in the second box from the left of row four of (2.70). Basically, my intuitions are as follows: sometimes, under conditions which I cannot dope out, *this/that* preceding an *ing*-phrase will produce a worse NP than would a sequence of NPs followed by the same *ing*-phrase. The reverse, however, never obtains: NP's + *ing*-phrase is never worse than *this/that* + *ing*-phrase.

The cases where I have been able to find differences all involve auxiliaries or other stative present participles as *ing*-forms. Cf. (ii)–(vi).

(ii) $\left\{ \begin{array}{l} \text{Ed's} \quad > \\ \text{??That} \end{array} \right\}$ seeming to like pizza angered me.

(iii) Her soup's containing arsenic was suspicious.
(iv) ?*That containing arsenic (*of her soup (*'s)) was suspicious.
(v) The children's looking as if they've been fed is a nice surprise.
(vi) ?This looking as if they've been fed is a nice surprise.

Since it does not seem that much hangs on being able to distinguish NPs and *this/that* in (2.69), I will leave the matter here.

[36] The sentences in (2.73d), all of which contain an *ing*-ed auxiliary, are a mixed lot. Sometimes, as in (2.73di), it appears to be possible to follow members of the class *no/some/much/little* by such an *ing*-form, but in general, they are weaker than they would be if *this/that* preceded the same *ing*-form, as such minimal pairs as ?? (2.72d) and *(2.73dv) attest. Note also that bad though the *this/that*-versions of (ii), (iv) and (vi) of note 35 are, they are far worse with one member of the set *no/some/much/little*. Clearly, matters are much more complex here than can be handled in a paper of such limited scope as this one, but since all the inequalities I now know of [i.e., inequalities like ?? (2.72d) > *(2.73dv)] seem to point in the same direction, I have tentatively concluded that *this/that* should be separated from the set in column 3 of (2.70).

iv. ?? Much having been wined and dined was acknowledged by the Congressmen.

v. *No having refused her offer (on the part of the Roman generals) was recorded.

e. i. No looking at feelthy rugs will be allowed.

ii. ? Much giving gum to strangers was reported.

iii. ?*Much giving strangers gum was reported.

f. Some refusing of her offers was expected.

g. No refusal of her offer is contemplated.[37]

h. Some garbage angered me.

(2.74) a. *The (that Ed) refused her offer angered me.

b. *Prior (for Ed) to refuse her offer angered me.

c. *Occasional (when Ed) refused her offer angered me.

d. i. *Frequent being followed angered me.

ii. *Prior having replied is frowned on.

iii. ? The having been fired on was predictable.[38]

e. i. The looking at feelthy rugs was anticipated.

ii. ? Occasional looking at feelthy rugs was reported.

iii. ?? Frequent giving false data out is to be expected.

iv. ?* Occasional giving gum to strangers was reported.

v. *Occasional giving strangers gum was reported.

f. Ed's/the occasional/prior/frequent refusing of her offers was to be expected.

g. Occasional/Prior/Frequent refusals of her offers have been reported.

h. The garbage angered me.[39]

(2.75) a. *Careful (that Ed) refused her offer angered me.

b. *Reluctant (for Ed) to refuse her offer angered me.

c. *Clever (when Ed) refused her offer angered me.

d. *(Ed's/That/The) careful having looked at the evidence angered me.

e. i. ?* (Ed's/That/The) thoughtless looking at the evidence angered me.

ii. *(Ed's/That/The) sneaky looking the answer up angered me.

f. Ed's/That/The reluctant refusal of her offer angered me.

g. Ed's/That/The greedy refusal of her offer angered me.

h. The careful doctor angered me.

(2.76) a. *Good (that Ed) refused her offer angered me.

b. *Bad (for Ed) to refuse her offer angered me.

c. *Bad (when Ed) refused her offer angered me.

---

[37] Note that *much* and *little* are excluded before nominalizations like *refusal* for an interesting, but irrelevant, reason. Namely, it is typically the case that nominalizations of non-stative predicates like *refuse* are count nouns (*many hops/examinations/changes/commands*, etc., etc.), while nominalizations of stative predicates are mass nouns (*much knowledge/hatred/cleverness/expressivity/agreement*, etc., etc.). This striking parallel between non-stative/count and stative/mass remains to be explained. Since *much* and *little* only modify mass nouns, *much/little refusal* is ungrammatical.

[38] Sentences like this strike me as being far superior to other sentences of the type of (2.74d), so possibly I am wrong in placing *the* in the fourth column of (2.70). I have not collected enough data to warrant drawing any firm conclusions, so I will leave the matter open.

[39] Such phrases as *occasional/prior/frequent garbage* are, of course, nonsense, for selectional reasons. I would say that these adjectives only modify derived nominals, treating such nouns as *blizzard* (cf. *the occasional blizzards*), *mistake* (cf. *frequent mistakes*), *notice* (cf. *prior notice*) etc. as deriving from underlying predicates which have associated with their lexical representations an output condition to the effect that they must be nouns in surface structure. Whether or not such an analysis is tenable, it is clear that the ill-formedness of *occasional garbage* need not concern us further.

    d. *Ed's bad having been had has finally been noticed.[40]

    e. ?*The good paying attention to us both continued.

    f i.   *Ed's bad refusing of her offer angered me.

       ii. *Ed's good demonstrating of undecidability angered us.

      iii. *Ed's bad solving of the enigma angered me.

    g. i.   ?? Ed's bad refusal of her offer angered me.[41]

       ii. Ed's good demonstration of undecidability angered me.

      iii. Ed's bad solution to the enigma angered me.

    h. The bad garbage angered me.

(2.77) a. *The mere (that Ed) refused her offer angered me.

    b. *Another (for Ed) to refuse her offer angered me.

    c. *A mere (when Ed) refused her offer angered me.

    d. *(Ed's/That/The) other being followed home angered me.

    e. i.   *The mere looking at classified documents is forbidden.

       ii. *Other giving gum to strangers is most strictly forbidden.

    f. i.   ?? The mere collecting of specimens got Mike jailed.

       ii. *The other solving of the enigma will occur shortly after 2 a.m.

    g. i.   ?A mere attempt at reconciliation would be viewed with suspicion.

       ii. ?*Bill's mere belief that everything would work out all right in the end drew upon him the scorn of the villagers.

      iii. ? Their mere presence might cause a riot.

      iv. *His mere operation of this vehicle while blasted is grounds for incarceration.

       v. Another attempt at reconciliation would be viewed with suspicion.

      vi. *Bill's other belief that everything would work out all right in the end drew upon him the scorn of the villagers.

      vii. ? *Their other presence in the jam cupboard resulted in a spanking.

     viii. ?Sam's other marriage to a Venusean took only 3 months.

      ix. Selma's other suggestion about what to do with the rolling pin met with a frosty silence.

    h. i.   A mere boy could solve it.

       ii. The other garbage angered me.

A word about (2.77): sentences like those in (2.77g), a mixed bag, admittedly, are the basis for my feeling that *mere* and *other* may require even nounier head nouns to modify than *good/bad*. I know of no systematically excluded class of non-derived nouns which are bad when preceded by *mere* and *other*,[42] but it does seem that many derived nominals do not co-occur with these two modifiers. However, since some do (e.g., (2.77g.v) and (2.77g.ix)), it may well be that it is not nouniness at all that is sorting the sheep from the goats here, and that there is in fact no demonstrable difference between derived and non-derived nouns with respect to the determiners that they co-occur with. If this is so, (2.70) will become one column narrower, and one row shorter, but will otherwise remain unchanged. Pending further study, I have

---

[40] Some of these, inexplicably, sound far better than they have any right to. Cf. (i)–(ii).

  (i) ? That bad being idolized will have to stop soon.

  (ii) ? This good having been notified that we're getting a tax refund makes me glow with pride.

Unsurprisingly, I have no explanations to offer here.

[41] I do not know what other facts about *refuse* differentiate it from *demonstrate* and *solve*. The important thing to note, for the purposes of (2.70), is that while some derived nominals are modifiable by *good/bad*, no action nominals appear to be so modifiable.

[42] Except that *mere* + mass noun (e.g., ?? *mere wine*) is generally pretty weird.

question-marked the last ' > ' of (2.69) and the corresponding cell of (2.70)—the seventh from the left of the seventh row from the top.

What is to be concluded from the data in (2.71)–(2.77)? Briefly, it would appear that the predicate *has the internal structure of an NP* cannot be treated as if it were a binary predicate, with phrases either having such a structure or not having it. Rather, with respect to the determiners they co-occur with, the elements of (1.2) would appear to approach true nouns [i.e., the nouniest elements] gradually. Thus action nominals have a determiner structure which is *more* similar to that of a noun phrase headed by a non-derived noun than is the determiner structure of such *ing*-phrases as those in (2.62), (2.64), and (2.66)–(2.68). And that of derived nominals is *more* similar than that of action nominals. But the subsquish in (2.70) does not give any indication that there is any row between the fourth and the eighth at which one could justify such a statement as "Complements above this row do not have the internal structure of an NP, while complements below do." To be sure, there is a clear break between the third and fourth rows—*no* determiners at all occur with the complement type of the first three rows. But as I showed, with respect to other syntactic properties—such as the possibility of marking aspectual differences, and the ability of derived structures to occur, the rows above row three share much with those below. I thus conclude that the facts of determinerizability support the hypothesis that there is a gradual progression—a squish—from *Acc/Poss + Ing* to N.[43]

2.18. Accessibility and chopping

In the last twelve subsections of §2, I have cited a variety of ways in which complements become more restricted in their internal structure as they become nounier. In the first five sections of §2, I had discussed a number of respects in which the complement types of (1.2) affected their neighbors in the clause (i.e., expletive *it*, prepositions, agreeing verbs, etc.) differentially. And now, in the concluding subsections, I will discuss some respects in which the nouniness of a complement type interacts with processes involving variables, in the sense of Ross (1967)—processes which link elements which asymmetrically command the complement type with elements which the complement type commands.

I have called the phenomena discussed in §§ 2.1–2.5 "external" phenomena, and those in §§ 2.6–2.17 "internal" phenomena. Let us refer to this last type of phenomena as *accessibility*

---

[43] I might note in passing that as far as another test for "internal structure of an NP"—namely pluralizability— goes, there seems to be a squish here too. Non-derived Ns pluralize fine (cf. (i)),

  (i) a. The cat is on the mat.
     b. The cats are on the mat.

and so do derived nominals (cf. (ii)),

  (ii) a. The attempt to self-destruct was made on Friday.
      b. The attempts to self-destruct were made on Friday.

but plurals are difficult, if possible at all, with action nominals, as (iii)–(v) show.

  (iii) a. His marshalling of my data takes him all day.
       b. ?? His marshallings of my data take him all day.

  (iv) a. Their weakening of a previous claim was to be expected.
      b. ? Their weakenings of previous claims were to be expected.

  (v) a. His discussing of the problems was helpful.
     b. *His discussings of the problems were helpful.

This particular index of nouniness draws a firm line above action nominals—plurals with *Poss Ing* are a bad dream.

  (vi) **His havings gone off his diet so many times will not surprise you.

phenomena. The reasons for using the same term as in Keenan and Comrie (op.cit.) should become clear as we proceed.

The general principle which we shall see several instances of is stated in (2.78).

(2.78)   The nounier a complement is, the less accessible are the nodes it dominates to the nodes which command the complement.

As a first particular case of (2.78), let us examine the interaction of nouniness and chopping rules,[44] rules which extract some constituent from under the domination of another constituent and reattach it elsewhere in the tree. One such rule is *Question Formation*, which chops a question word from its underlying location and moves it (leftwards) towards the question-taking predicate that binds it.[45] As we would infer from (2.78), this type of chopping should become harder and harder as the complement type whose constituent is being chopped gets nounier and nounier. Cf. (2.79).

(2.79) a. I wonder who he resented (it) that I went steady with.
         b. I wonder who he would resent (it) for me to go steady with.
         c. *I wonder who he resented how long I went steady with.[46]
         d. ?I wonder who he resented me going out with.
         e. ??I wonder who he resented my going out with.
         f. ?*I wonder who he resented my careless examining of.
         g. ?*I wonder who he resented my careless examination of.[47]
         h. ?*I wonder who he resented the daughter of.[48]

In general, *pace* note 47, the dwindling Englishness of the sentences in (2.79) supports (2.78).

---

[44] Cf. Ross (1967: ch. 6) for more discussion of this term.

[45] For an excellent discussion of this rule from the standpoint of universal grammar, cf. Bach (1971).

[46] (2.79c) is worse than (2.78) would lead us to expect, but this is for an irrelevant reason—namely, in the embedded question which is the complement of *resent* in (2.79c), the questioned phrase has passed over the clause *he went out with who*. It is a general fact about such "crossed over" clauses that their constituents cannot be chopped. Thus when *Topicalization*, a chopping rule, fronts the NP *Marjorie* to clause-initial position in the complement object of *said* in converting (i) to (ii), the direct object becomes unchoppable, as *(iii) shows.

  (i) They said that we should give these books to Marjorie.
  (ii) They said that Marjorie we should give these books to.
  (iii) *It is these books that they said that Marjorie we should give to.

I would attribute the badness of *(2.79c) to the same factors that make *(iii) unfit for duty, which means that the former sentence does not constitute counterevidence to the claim that the sentences in (2.79) are a column of the nouniness squish.

For further discussion, cf. Ross (MS c).

[47] There is a large and poorly understood class of counterexamples, known in the trade as *picture*-nouns (cf. Ross 1967 and Postal 1971 for discussion), to the generalization that nouny complements prohibit chopping.
Thus beside *(2.79g) and *(2.79h), we find such grammatical sentences as (i) and (ii),

  (i) I wonder who you read a description of.
  (ii) I wonder who he is a friend of.

where *description* and *friend* are the *picture*-nouns, derived and (superficially) non-derived, respectively, in question.

Unless some *deus ex pictura* should materialize in future studies of this class of nouns, the generalization implicit in (2.79) cannot be maintained.

[48] Many speakers I have asked find (2.79h) fine, thus presumably treating *daughter* as a *picture*-noun, to name the problem which such a grammaticality presents. For me, however, it is very weak.

2.19. Sloppiness

The next accessibility phenomenon concerns what I have referred to as "sloppy identity" (cf. Ross (1967), Chapter 5). Basically, the problem is that of characterizing when the reading of (2.80) corresponding to (2.81b) is possible.

(2.80) Ed$_i$ said$_E$ that he$_i$ was sincere, and Mort$_j$ said$_M$ so too.

(2.81) a. Ed$_i$ said$_E$ that he$_i$ was sincere, and Mort$_j$ said$_M$ that he$_i$ (=Ed$_i$) was sincere too.
       b. Ed$_i$ said$_E$ that he$_i$ was sincere, and Mort$_j$ said$_M$ that he$_j$ (= Mort$_j$) was sincere too.

Under the assumption that (2.80) can be derived from either of the sentences in (2.81) by a rule of **So** *Pronominalization*,[49] we see that while (2.81a) could be converted into (2.80) by merely inserting *so* for the object clause of *said*$_M$ in (2.81a), which clause is morpheme-for-morpheme identical to and coreferential with the object clause of *said*$_E$,' to convert (2.81b) to (2.80) by **So** *Pronominalization*, obviously a different sort of identity will be required, for the objects of *said*$_E$ and *said*$_M$ in (2.81b), though morphemically identical, are not identical when it comes to the references of their subject pronouns. This new type of identity I referred to as *sloppy* identity.

Of relevance for the present investigation of nouniness is the fact that sloppy readings are harder to obtain as the complements being deleted get nounier and nounier. Cf. (2.82), in which the grammaticality judgments correspond only to the reading of this sentence under which Mort's resentment is directed at my examination of Mort.

(2.82) a. Ed resents (it) that I examined him, and Mort does too.[50]
       b. Ed resents (it) for me to examine him, and Mort does too.
       c. Ed resents (it) how often I examined him, and Mort does too.
       d. ? Ed resents me having examined him, and Mort does too.
       e. ? Ed resents my having examined him, and Mort does too.
       f. ?? Ed resents my careful examining of him, and Mort does too.
       g. ?? Ed resents my careful examination of him, and Mort does too.

Thus it would seem that nouniness is one of the many factors that bear on the question of when sloppy readings exist.[51]

2.20. Pied piping

In Ross (1967), I used this term to describe the phenomenon shown in (2.83).

(2.83) a. Bill, who I sent you a picture of, is cranky.
       b. Bill, of whom I sent you a picture, is cranky.
       c. Bill, a picture of whom I sent you, is cranky.

When sentence (2.84) is embedded as an appositive clause modifying *Bill*,

(2.84) I sent you a picture of Bill.

the Rule of *Relative Clause Formation* has several ways of applying. It can front only the relative pronoun *who*, which corresponds to *Bill* in (2.84)—the NP identical to the modified NP.

---

[49] Cf. Ross (1972b) for examples of this rule's operation.

[50] For arguments that the anaphoric second conjunct of the sentences in (2.82) is produced by a transformational deletion, cf. Ross (1969).

[51] Some others will be discussed in Ross (MS d).

Or it can front, in addition, the preposition *of*, producing (2.83b). Or it can even front a larger NP which contains *whom*, as in (2.83c). When material other than the relative pronoun is fronted, I will say that such material undergoes *pied piping*—it "travels along" with the fronted *who*.

The basic rule for *pied piping* that was arrived at in Ross (1967) is that stated approximately in (2.85).

(2.85)   If one NP (NP_m) is moved by a rule, any NP (NP_d) which dominates it can move with it, as long as there is no node S_i such that NP_d dominates S_i and S_i dominates NP_m.

In other words, when moving some NP_m, any higher NP_d can pied pipe, unless there is an intervening S_i. This restriction is necessary, because otherwise the *that*-clause of (2.86), which many syntactic tests show to be an NP, could pied pipe when (2.86) is an appositive clause modifying *Eloise*, as in (2.87). If only the relative pronoun is fronted, the grammatical (2.87a) results. But if the *that*-clause pied pipes, the hash in (2.87b) ensues.

(2.86)   They liked it [$_{NPd}$ that we loved [$_{NPm}$ Eloise]].

(2.87)   a. Eloise, who they liked it that we loved, is an accomplished washboardiste.
          b. *Eloise, [$_{NPd}$ that we loved [$_{NPm}$ whom]] they liked (it), is an accomplished washboardiste.

What makes the phenomenon of pied piping relevant in the present context is the fact that it can be shown that the condition mentioning S_i in (2.85) must be squishified. That is, the correct restriction should read something like (2.88).

(2.88)   If NP_m is moved by a transformation, NP_d may pied pipe with it. If a complement node intervenes, the more sentential (i.e., the less nouny) it is, the less well-formed the resultant pied-piped construction will be.

The need to replace (2.85) by (2.88) becomes apparent from the sentences in (2.89), all of which have pied piped a larger complement in addition to the relative pronoun.

(2.89)   a. *Eloise, [for us to love [whom]] they liked, is an accomplished washboardiste.
          b. *Eloise, [us loving [whom]] they liked, is an accomplished washboardiste.
          c. *Eloise, [our loving [whom]] they liked, is an accomplished washboardiste.
          d. ?*Eloise, [our loving of [whom]] they liked, is an accomplished washboardiste.
          e. ?Eloise, [our love for [whom]] they liked, is an accomplished washboardiste.[52]
          f. Eloise, [a part of [whom]] they liked, is an accomplished washboardiste.

Many additional factors interact in the syntax of such pied pipings, which makes the view of the phenomenon which (2.89) provides somewhat inaccurate. Without going into the detail that these problems merit, let me single out two such factors for mention.

First, if the complement to be pied piped has no subject, things are significantly improved. Thus compare the *a*- and *b*-versions of (2.90)–(2.92) below.

(2.90)   a. *Eloise, [for us to renominate [whom]] will be expensive, is a consummate tri-angularian.
          b. ??Eloise, [to renominate [whom]] will be expensive, is a consummate triangularian.

---

[52] (2.89e) is worse than most sentences in which derived nouns pied pipe. In general, I have not been able to discover any systematic differences between pied piping (obviously) derived nouns and (apparently) non-derived ones. The difference which appears between (2.89e) and (2.89f) seems to be idiosyncratic.

(2.91) a. ??Eloise, [our renominating [whom]] may prove counterproductive, can sing in several keys simultaneously.

b. ?Eloise, [renominating [whom]] may prove counterproductive, can sing in several keys simultaneously.

(2.92) a. ?Eloise, [his renominating of [whom]] was greeted by storms of boos, is peerless on the suaronophone.

b. Eloise, [the renominating of [whom]] was greeted by storms of boos, is peerless on the suaronophone.

Secondly, if the complement is in subject position, the sentences are better than if it is necessary to lug it to the front via pied piping. Thus compare the *a*- and *b*-versions of (2.93)–(2.94) below.

(2.93) a. ??Eloise, [to invite [whom]] had been attempted by the Board, wanted to wear sneakers.

b. *Eloise, [to invite [whom]] the Board had attempted, wanted to wear sneakers.

(2.94) a. ?Eloise, [inviting [whom]] has profited us immensely, was a smash hit with the Under-77 Set.

b. *Eloise, [inviting [whom]] we have profited from immensely, was a smash hit with the Under-77 Set.

I will leave a more thorough scrutiny of these constructions to future researchers, but it should have already become clear, from the increases in grammaticality that can be perceived from (2.87b) to (2.89f), from (2.90) to (2.92), and from (2.93) to (2.94), that a squishified version of the pied piping constraint, one like (2.89), is what the facts indicate to be necessary.

2.21. Pied wiping

Jorge Hankamer has proposed[53] this name for the deletion rule that obliterates under identity the complements of certain types of verbs when they appear in various types of comparative structures. This rule is what effects the optional conversion of (2.95a) to (2.95b).

(2.95) a. Mandrake$_i$ was wilier than Lothar $\begin{Bmatrix} \text{thought} \\ \text{suspected} \\ \text{knew} \\ \text{realized} \end{Bmatrix}$ [that he$_i$ was].

b. Mandrake was wilier than Lothar $\begin{Bmatrix} \text{thought} \\ \text{suspected} \\ \text{knew} \\ \text{realized} \end{Bmatrix}$

The verbs in curly brackets in (2.95) all take *that*-clauses, and we see from the conversion of (2.96a) to (2.96b) that infinitival complements can also be pied wiped, for *want* only takes *for to* complements.

(2.96) a. Ted woke up earlier than I had wanted [him to wake up].

b. Ted woke up earlier than I had wanted.

However, as far as I have been able to ascertain, nounier complements than *for to* cannot be pied wiped. Thus if *contemplate* and *think about*, which take *Acc/Poss Ing*-complements, lose them via *Pied Wiping*, weak sentences are derived.

---

[53] In a paper with the same title as this section, which was presented at the third annual meeting of the North East Linguistic Society, at the University of Massachusetts, Amherst, Massachusetts, October, 1972.

(2.97) a. He woke up earlier than he had contemplated [waking up].
      b. ??He woke up earlier than he had contemplated.

(2.98) a. He woke up earlier than he had thought about [waking up].
      b. ?*He woke up earlier than he had thought about.

And if *Pied Wiping* applies to the complement of *achieve*, which, as (2.99) shows, takes a complement at least as nouny as an action nominal,

(2.99)
$$\text{Milt achieved} \begin{Bmatrix} \text{*to convert} \\ \text{*converting} \\ \text{??the converting of} \\ \text{the conversion of} \end{Bmatrix} \text{7000 rebels.}$$

we get a solidly ungrammatical sentence, *(2.100b).

(2.100) a. Milt converted more rebels than I thought that he would achieve [the conversion of].
       b. *Milt converted more rebels than I thought that he would achieve.

Thus *Pied Wiping* must be constrained by a condition specifying that the prospective wipee not be overly nouny.

2.22. Control for VP deletion

The rule of *VP Deletion*, some effects of whose operation we saw in the second clauses of (2.82) above, prefers a sentency complement as a controller for its operation—i.e., as the chunk of structure under identity with which a "VP"[54] elsewhere in the text can be deleted.[55] This is obvious from inspection of the sentences in (2.101), in which the dash marks the remote location of the deleted node.

(2.101) a. That he inspected more latrines than the other generals would ___ is fascinating.
      b. For him to have inspected more latrines than the other generals would ___ is fascinating.
      c. How resolutely he inspected more latrines than the other generals would ___ is fascinating.
      d. Him having inspected more latrines than the other generals would ___ is fascinating.
      e. His having inspected more latrines than the other generals would ___ is fascinating.
      f. ??His inspecting of more latrines than the other generals would ___ is fascinating.
      g. ?*His inspection of more latrines than the other generals would ___ is fascinating.

Thus it would appear that nominalizing a clause makes the verb and objects of this clause unfit as a controller for the rule of *VP Deletion*, the more so the nounier the result is.

Note that if we restore the verb *inspect* in all the blanks in (2.101), thus producing sentences which, presumably, have been formed by whatever rule makes this type of comparatives, we produce another set of sentences, (2.101a′)–(2.101g′), whose grammaticality also dwindles,

---

[54] Some of the reasons for my belief that there is no such category as VP are contained in McCawley (1970).
[55] The term "controller" was first used in this sense in Postal (1970), in connection with the rule of *Equi*.

but, to my ear at least, less rapidly than in the original sentences in (2.101). In particular, (2.101f′) and (2.101g′) have, for me, the following grammaticalities.

(2.101) f.′ ?His inspecting of more latrines than the other generals would inspect is fascinating.

        f.′ ??His inspecting of more latrines than the other generals would inspect is fascinating

Thus it appears that the '??' and '?*' valences of (2.101f) and (2.101g) are in actuality the products of nouniness-linked constraints on two rules. The first, *Comparative Formation*, which forms the sentences in (2.101a′)–(2.101g′) [in conjunction with other rules, of course], lowers the grammaticality of (2.101f′) and (2.101g′) to '?' and '??', respectively, as shown above. The second, *VP Deletion*, applying to the output of the first, weakens these valences another notch apiece, producing the values observed for (2.101f) and (2.101g).

Thus, apparently the sentences in (2.101) provide two pieces of evidence for a squish of nouniness.[56]

2.23. Control for *do it* and *do so*

The source which I regard as correct for the anaphoric elements *do it* and *do so* which appear in (2.102)

(2.102)   After Casey started massaging his gums, all the managers started $\left\{ \begin{array}{c} \text{doing it} \\ \text{doing so} \end{array} \right\}$.

I have discussed in Ross (1972b). Whether or not the proposed source is correct, however, the rules which link such pro-forms to their controllers must have the same kind of nouniness-related condition as was shown in §2.22 to limit *VP Deletion*. This follows immediately from the graceful glide into ungrammaticality which the following sentences exhibit.

(2.103) a. That Fimley successfully deceived the IRS seems to please him, but I would hate to try to do it/so.

       b. For Fimley to successfully deceive the IRS seems to please him, but I would hate to try to do it/so.

       c. ?How long Fimley successfully deceived the IRS seems to please him, but I would hate to try to do it/so.[57]

       d. Fimley having successfully deceived the IRS seems to please him, but I would hate to try to do it/so.

---

[56] Note, incidentally, that the argument of §2.22 is unchanged by the fact that there are many environments in which using an action nominal or a derived nominal produces such salad as one finds in (i) and (ii).

(i) *His inspecting of the latrines was thorough, but I just can't ____.

(ii) *The uprising followed his inspection of the latrines when his officers were unable to ____.

These ungrammaticalities are simply due to other limiting conditions on *VP Deletion*, which preclude nouny controllers even more severely than is the case for the comparative constructions of (104).

Nor would the argument be affected by data from speakers who reject totally such sentences as (2.101f, g) and (2.101 f′, g′), (and possibly other sentences of (2.101) and (2.101′) as well), nor by data from speakers who find all sentences good. The claim is only that the following inequalities should hold:

(iii) (2.101f) ≥ (2.101g)

(iv) (2.101f′) ≥ (2.101g′).

No claim is made with respect to whether the sentences of (2.101) should be better or worse than those of (2.101′).

[57] The sentences in (2.103c) are more awkward than expected, but this seems not to be attributable to the use of *do it* or *do so*, because the sentence is not improved if *deceive the IRS* appears in their place.

e. Fimley's having successfully deceived the IRS seems to please him, but I would hate to try to do it/so.
f. ? Fimley's successful deceiving of the IRS seems to please him, but I would hate to try to do it/so.
g. ?? Fimley's successful deception of the IRS seems to please him, but I would hate to try to do it/so.

The parallels between (2.101), (2.101′), and (2.103) are strong, and it will probably be possible sometime to state a generalization covering the interaction of all types of anaphoric linkage and nouniness. But since my concern here is merely to demonstrate a number of processes in which accessibility is a function of nouniness, I have not undertaken this broader task.

2.24. The Sentential Subject Constraint

In Ross (1967), on the basis of such contrasts as that between (2.104) and (2.105), I proposed the constraint roughly stated in (2.106).

(2.104) a. They figure that the bomb damaged the hoods of these cars.
    a′. Of which cars do they figure that the bomb damaged the hoods?
    b. They figure that [the hoods of these cars] were damaged by the bomb.
    c. Of which cars do they figure that the hoods were damaged by the bomb?

(2.105) a. They think that the drivers resented having to send money to these hoodlums.
    a! To which hoodlums do they think that the drivers resented having to send money?
    b. They think that [having to send money to these hoodlums] was resented by the drivers.
    b! *To which hoodlums do they think that having to send money was resented by the drivers?

(2.106)   No elements can be chopped out of a clause which is the subject of a sentence.

Note that it would be incorrect to say that no part of a subject can be chopped, for in converting (2.104b) to (2.104b′), we see that the prepositional phrase *of which cars* can emerge from the bracketed subject phrase. But when the subject is clausal, as it is in (2.105b), no part of this bracketed subject may be chopped: (2.105b′) is bad.

In fact, however, (2.106) must be squishified, as in (2.107).

(2.107)   *The Sentential Subject Constraint*
    If a part of a subject is chopped out of it by any rule, the grammaticality of the result will vary directly with the nouniness of the subject.

That is, what I did not realize in Ross (1967) is that there are intermediate stages between the fully grammatical (2.104b′) and the fully ungrammatical (2.105b′). They are shown in (2.108b), (2.109b), and (2.110b).

(2.108) a. They think that [the collection of these kinds of facts] was premature.
    b. ? Of which kinds of facts do they think that the collection was premature?

(2.109) a. They think that [the collecting of these kinds of facts] was superfluous.
    b. ?? Of which kinds of facts do they think that the collecting was superfluous?

(2.110) a. They think that [Ted's collecting of these kinds of facts] was amateurish.
   b. ?*Of which kinds of facts do they think that Ted's collecting was amateurish?

My judgments on sentences like (2.109b) are not as sharp as are those on such sentences as (2.108b) and (2.110b), of which the former is clearly preferable to the latter, with the latter being slightly better than (2.105b'). I believe there to be a slight preference for chopping out of action nominals without subjects, like (2.109a), over action nominals with subjects, like (2.110a). If so, this difference would parallel the facts about pied piping noted in (2.90)–(2.92) above.

2.25. Summary

This concludes my presentation of the evidence for the existence of a squish of nouniness which orders various types of complements as shown in (1.2). Above, for the purposes of exposition, I have broken down this evidence into three groups: external behavior of the complements (§§2.1–2.5), internal limitations (§§2.6–2.17), and accessibility phenomena (§§2.18–2.24). Of course, the data in each of these subsections should be taken as a column in the large matrix which represents the nouniness squish. I have given this squish in (2.111), rearranging these columns to yield the maximally well-behaved matrix. The parenthesized numbers at the top of each column are the numbers of the examples in the text which contain the information on which the column is based, and the bracketed numbers under each column refer to the appropriate subsections of §§2.[58]

For typographical reasons, I have split up the nouniness squish into two parts, which should be thought of as being joined together. 2.111a, shows "sentence-based" phenomena, 2.111b, "noun-based" phenomena.

I have called the syntactic processes that head the columns in (2.111a) *sentence-based* for the reason that they all work in the most sentential (= least nouny) of the complements-—tensed *that*-clauses. The constructions toward the left of (2.111a) are extremely "choosy," applying only with complements of extremely high sententiality. But as we proceed rightwards in (2.111a), the processes become less choosy, and are willing to work not only with highly sentential complements, but even with complements that have little in their outward form that suggests a sentential nature.

By contrast, the processes in (2.111b) I refer to as *noun-based*: all, except *Promotion*, which can be seen to be something of a maverick anyway, work with pure nouns, with the less choosy processes (this time, they are on the left of the matrix) working even with things that have superficial features that are incompatible with pure nouns–features like aspect.

Mentally placing (2.111a) and (2.111b) together, the former on the left, and the latter on the right, we find the *sentence-choosy* processes on the left, and the *noun-choosy* ones on the right, with the less discriminating ones in the middle.

To give some examples of what I mean by choosiness, we can see that *Extraposition*, in column (ix), is choosier than *VP Deletion*, in column (xxi)—fewer types of complements can extrapose than can serve as controllers for *VP Deletion*. And *tabs*, in column (viii), is a choosier idiom chunk than is *headway*, in column (xix)—the former won't be the subject of *Poss Ing* complements, while the latter will.

---

[58] In some cases, as with such complex data as those presented in (2.73)–(2.75) above, I have entered an average value in a particular cell of (2.111), for otherwise the data could not be presented in matrix form.

Note also that since (2.111) conflates the distinction made in (2.70) between those *ing*-complements whose main verb is an auxiliary and those whose main verb is a true verb, (2.111) will present a less detailed picture of the interaction of determiners and nouniness than (2.70) in this respect too.

(2.111)

The Nouniness Squish[59]

a. *Sentence-based phenomena*

	(i)	(ii)	(iii)	(iv)	(v)	(vi)	(vii)	(viii)	(ix)	(x)	(xi)	(xii)	(xiii)	(xiv)	(xv)	(xvi)	(xvii)	(xviii)	(xix)	(xx)	(xxi)	(xxii)	(xxiii)
	AP in subject position (2.38)	PP in subject position (2.37)	*not* + Q in subject (2.47)	*It* + complement (2.1)	*Preposition Deletion* (2.3)	*Pied Wiping* (2.97)–(2.100)	*no and few* in subject (2.54)–(2.55)[61]	*tabs* and weather *it* with V (2.21)	(2.4)+(2.33) *Extraposition + Q Postposing*	*Subject Quantifiability* (2.28)	*Post-verbal never* (2.51)	*Chopping* (2.79)	*Sloppiness* (2.82)	*Sentential it and there* (2.20)	*Extraposition from NP* (2.14)–(2.16)	*Pre-verbal never* (2.53)	*Pre-verbal not* (2.52)	*Copular weather it* (2.19)	*headway* (2.19)	*Post-verbal seldom* (2.50)	*Control for VP Deletion* (2.10)	*Fake NPs in object* (2.42)	*Control for do it/do so* (2.103)
that S	?	OK	OK	OK	OBL	OK	OK	OK	OK	OK	OK	OK	OK	OK	OK	OK	OK	OK	OK	OK	OK	OK	OK
for to	?*	?	?	OK	OBL	OK	OK	OK	OK	OK	OK	OK	OK	OK	OK	OK	OK	OK	OK	OK	OK	OK	OK
Q	??	?	?	OPT	⊠	OK	OK	OK	OK	OK	|*62|	OK	OK	OK	OK	OK	OK	OK	OK	OK	OK	OK	|?|
Acc Ing	*	!?*!	!??!	*	DNA	?*	??	?	?	?	?	?	?	OK	OK	OK	OK	OK	OK	OK	OK	OK	OK
Poss Ing	**	*	!?*!	*	DNA	!?*!	*	*	?*	??	??	??	?	|*|	!?*!	!??!	?	?	?	?	OK	OK	OK
Act. Nom.	⊠	⊠	**	*	DNA	*	|**|	⊠	*	*	?*	?*	??	⊠	|*|	|*|	|*|	⊠	??	??	??	?	
Der. Nom.	⊠	⊠	**	*	DNA	*	|**|	⊠	*	*	*	|?*|	|??|	*63	*	|**|	|**|	*64	⊠	?*	?*	??	

← 3 dots
← 5 dots
← 13 dots
← 16 dots
← 15 dots
← 6 dots

[12] [11] [15] [1] [2] [21] [15] [7] [3,10] [9] [15] [18] [19] [7] [6] [15] [15] [7] [7] [15] [22] [13] [23]

DNA – does not apply   OPT – optional   OBL – obligatory

⊠ the cell in question cannot be checked for gramaticality[60]

Also, the restriction specifying what types of complement can be possessivized (cf. column (xxxiii)) is choosier than the one specifying what types can undergo *NP Shift* (cf. column (xxv))—what can be possessivized can be *NP-shifted*, but not conversely. And *good/bad* are choosier determiners than are the demonstratives *this* and *that*.

[59] The notational device of enclosing horizontally ill-behaved cells in parallel vertical lines, and vertically ill-behaved cells in horizontal lines, is the same as in (2.39) above. This matrix seems remarkably well-behaved, vertically, and highly well-behaved horizontally too.

[60] Thus the lower left-hand corner of (2.111a) contains ⊠, because AP subjects only occur in pseudo-cleft sentences, and there is no nominalization of *be* which could be used to check whether AP subjects are possible in derived nominals. Nor is there an action nominal of this stative predicate, which accounts for various occurrences of ⊠ in the sixth line of (2.111a).

[61] For simplicity, I have chosen to ignore the difference between (2.54b) and the vertically ill-behaved (2.55b) and have conflated these two sets of data into one column in (2.111a).

[62] Cf. note 46 above for discussion of the ill-behavior of this cell.

[63] Examples of this cell, which were not given in (2.20) above, are as follows: while *there* can be the subject of verbal forms of *exist* (cf. (i)), it cannot be the subject of the nominalization *existence*. Cf. *(ii).

(i) There exist counterexamples.

(ii) *There's existence of counterexamples render shaky your argument.

Similarly, though non-sentential *it* can be a subject of derived nominals (cf. (iii)), the expletive *it* of *Extraposition* cannot be. Cf. *(iv).

(iii) Its weight makes me sick.

(iv) *Its possibility that I may be wrong makes me sick.

[64] As an example of this cell, which was omitted in (2.19) above, consider the fact that there is no derived nominal form of (i): *(ii) is bad.

(i) That it is muggy outside means that we shan't wish to prolong our stroll, Fawnsworth.

(ii) *Its mugginess outside means that we shan't wish to prolong our stroll, Fawnsworth.

b. *Noun-based phenomena*

(2.111)	(xxiv) (2.5) I²-SNPC	(xxv) (2.59) NP Shift	(xxvi) (2.71) NP's as Det.	(xxvii) (2.66)–(2.68), (2.72) this/that as Det.	(xxviii) (2.44) Promotion with by	(xxix) (2.44) Promotion with with	(xxx) (2.73) no/some/etc. as Det.	(xxxi) (2.74) the/prior etc. as Det.	(xxxii) (2.13) Plural agreement	(xxxiii) (2.24) Possessivizability	(xxxiv) (2.75) careful/etc. as Det.	(xxxv) (2.77) other/mere as Det.	(xxxvi) (2.76) good/bad as Det.	(xxxvii) (2.89)+ (2.108)–(2.110) Pied Piping + SSC	
that S	*	*	*	*	DNA	DNA	*	*	*	**	*	*	*	*	←1 dot+3 dots from (2.111a)=4 dots
for to	?*	*	*	*	DNA	DNA	*	*	*	**	*	*	*	*	←3 dots+5 dots from (2.111a)=3 dots
Q	?	?*	*	*	DNA	DNA	*	*	*	*	*	*	*	*	←5 dots+13 dots from (2.111a)=18 dots
Acc Ing	?	!??!	╳	OK?	DNA	DNA	??	?*	?*	*	*	*	*	*	←4 dots+16 dots from (2.111a)=20 dots
Poss Ing	OK	!?!	OK	OK?	!OK!	!?*!	??	?*	!??!	?*	*	*	*	*	←9 dots+15 dots from (2.111a)=24 dots
Act. Nom.	OK	OK	OK	OK	!??!	!?!	OK	OK	?	??	!OK!	??	!*!	?*	←5 dots+6 dots from (2.111a)=11 dots
Der. Nom.	OK	OK	OK	OK	!?*!	OK	OK	OK	OK	OK	OK	!?!	OK	?	←2 dots =2 dots
N	OK	OK	OK	OK	DNA	DNA	OK	OK	OK	OK	OK	OK	OK	OK	

3. THEORETICAL IMPLICATIONS

3.1 Squishy categories

When one asks the question as to what kind of formal theory could be developed that would approach adequacy in describing such a complex array of facts as those summarized in (2.111), the answer that would first suggest itself to me is that what is needed here is not a new type of rules that will operate upon two types of constituents (or perhaps some larger number, as suggested in Williams (1971)) in such a way as to project some underlyingly discrete system into the superficially fuzzy, smeary, quasi-continuous matrix we find ourselves confronted with, but that possibly a more radical departure from the previous transformational literature may be called for. I cannot of course demonstrate logically that the continuous system I will propose below must be correct, and that no discrete system can be made to work. I doubt, however, that a discrete system capable of accounting for such arrays as (2.111) would be seen as a minor adjustment to, or logical extension of, the kind of descriptive apparatus now currently in use in transformational grammar.

With this preamble, let me propose that what is necessary is a relaxation of the claim that sequences of elements either are or are not members of some constituent class, like NP, V, S, etc. Rather, I suggest, we must allow *membership to a degree*. Thus in particular, I propose that the previously used node S, sentence, be replaced by a feature $[\alpha \text{ S}]$, where α ranges over the real numbers in $[0, 1]$.[65] Each of the complement types in (1.2) would be given a basic value

---

[65] It seems too obvious to me to need much discussion that at present, I am in no position to answer any questions such as whether the real numbers are necessary or whether we can get by with the rational numbers, or with some kind of topological partial ordering that I am not mathematician enough to know how to talk about. I use the real numbers merely for purposes of illustration.

of α, and rules, filters, and other types of semantactic processes, would be given upper and lower threshhold values of α between which they operate (cf. §3.3 below).

Let us first try to specify what the central values for the elements of (1.2) should be. If we set the extremes as in (3.1), what values can we assign to the intermediate elements?

(3.1) *that* S [1.0 S]
    for to
    Q
    Acc Ing
    Poss Ing
    Act. Nom.
    Der. Nom.
    N. [0.0 S]

Can we assume that, since there are seven elements to cover the interval from 0.0 to 1.0, each element is equally far away from its neighbors, i.e., are the elements about 0.1428...units apart? Or must we instead recognize some kind of "bunching," with some elements of (3.1) being close to one neighbor and farther away from the other one?

I suspect that the latter situation obtains, though I am not at present able to specify exactly what the bunching function is. An indication that such a function may exist is given by the dots in (2.111).

I have placed a dot on every line between two cells in (2.111) where the upper cell differs from the one below in its indication of grammaticality.[66] Thus in column (i), there is a dot between the highest and the next highest cells, because the former contains '?' and the latter '?*'. However, there is no dot between the top two cells of column (iv), for instance, because each contains 'OK': dots appear only between any two cells which differ in grammaticality.[67] If we then count up the dots on each line, we have an index of the difference between the types of complements immediately above and immediately below the line in question.[68]

The sums of dots for each line are given to the right of (2.111b). If the number of dots per line is a fair first approximation to the desired bunching function, then, since there are dots in all, and since

$$\frac{1.00}{87} \cong 0.0115$$

we could multiply the number of dots per line by 0.0115 and arrive by simple arithmetic at the bunching function in (3.2).

(3.2) *that* S   -   [1.0 S]
     for to   - $[(1.0-4 \times 0.0115)\ S] = [0.954\ S] \cong [0.95\ S]$
     Q   - $[(1.0-12 \times 0.0115)\ S] = [0.862\ S] \cong [0.86\ S]$
     Acc Ing   - $[(1.0-30 \times 0.0115)\ S] = [0.655\ S] \cong [0.66\ S]$
     Poss Ing   - $[(1.0-50 \times 0.0115)\ S] = [0.425\ S] \cong [0.43\ S]$
     Act. Nom.   - $[(1.0-74 \times 0.0115)\ S] = [0.149\ S] \cong [0.15\ S]$
     Der. Nom.   - $[(1.0-85 \times 0.0115)\ S] = [0.023\ S] \cong [0.02\ S]$
     N   -   [0.0 S]

---

[66] Except that I have not dotted columns (xxviii) and (xxix), in line with a feeling I have that the representation of the facts of *Promotion* in the form of two columns in a matrix is a distortion. Note also the disproportionately high incidence of ill-behaved cells in these two columns.

[67] Or, in the case of column (v), which differs with respect to the valence (i.e., obligatory, optional, does not apply) of the rule in question.

[68] Incidentally, the reason that (2.111a) is one row less high than (2–111b) is that adding a row for N to (2–111a) would produce almost exclusively cells marked '⊠' and would yield no dots.

A further refinement would be to investigate the "grammaticality distance" between vertically contiguous cells. That is, if we assume that the six grammaticality prefixes which fill the cells of $(2.111)^{69}$, which are presented in (3.3),

(3.3) OK/?/??/?*/*/**

divide a continuum from flawless grammaticality to splendid ungrammaticality into six equal "steps" of grammaticality loss, then we might decide to weight the dot on line 1 in column (i) less heavily than the dot on line 3 in column (iv), since the first marks a two-step loss, while the second marks a three-step loss.

I have not undertaken the conversion of dots to steps in detail, but my impression is that a revision of (3.2) in terms of steps would yield a bunching function with even more clustering at the extremes, and even greater spreading in the middle, especially around line 4.

3.2. Dialect and idiolect

But by now, many readers may have asked themselves the question "How firm are the data in (2.111)? Can they support such arithmetical manipulation, or isn't this all just symbol-mongering?"

As is so often the case, the readers are right on target with these questions. I have asked many speakers of English many of the questions I have asked myself in order to try to find out which of the 6^{273} possible assignments of the 6 values in (3.3) to a matrix with the 273 cells of (2.111) is "the" correct one. I have not, however, constructed questionnaires, nor collected tapes of actual speech, to try to get "hard" data about the extent to which (2.111) is in accord with the intuitions of the rest of the English-speaking community.

Why not?

The answer is a complex one. First of all, the questioning that I have done, which, while not conducted formally, has been quite extensive, leads me to expect that while some judgments at the extremes may be relatively invariant among speakers, those in the middle are so mixed as to fingerprint each individual speaker of a language differently. When questions of any subtlety are tested against speakers' intuitions, my experience has been that no two speakers will answer a set of even ten questions in the same way.

If this is true, then what is a dialect? How do we know when two speakers speak the same dialect, if no two English-speakers will output the same variant of (2.111)? The usual answer, within transformational grammar, at least, has been (3.4):

(3.4) To speak the same dialect (or language) as someone else is to have the same intuitions about some set of sentences as (s)he has.

My contention is that under this reconstruction of the notion "dialect," there are no dialects. No one, in particular, would agree with anyone else on a variant of a matrix like (2.111).

However, it is a fact, as clear as any linguistic fact I know, that there are dialects, and that speakers have intuitions about when they speak the same dialect as some other speaker. Therefore, we must abandon (3.4), and replace it with something a good deal more abstract.

Just what a viable reconstruction of the notion "dialect" might be, however, is a thorny question—one that I have not had any success in resolving. While extended speculation, given my present inability to offer any characterization that does not collapse quickly, would be fruitless, it is worthwhile to point out the defects of one theory that might seem a strong candidate.

Under this theory, a dialect would still be equated with a set of sentences, but speakers would be rated as being "generous" or "stingy," to varying degrees. The most generous

---

[69] Again, except for column (v).

speakers would accept all the sentences, and each degree of stinginess would shrink the set, where if speaker A is [α Stingy], and speaker B [β Stingy], α, β ∈ [0, 1], and α < β, then any sentence B accepts, A will accept. That is, diagrammatically, if B is stingier than A, B's set of sentences is a subset of A's, as in (3.5).

(3.5)

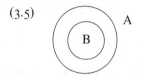

The crucial flaw in this theory is that speakers may be stingy in one respect, and generous in others. That is, one speaker may accept many different kinds of passives, but may accept sentences with backward pronominalization only under very stringent conditions. And another may exhibit the reverse of this mix. I have looked for implicational relationships among various areas of stinginess or generosity, but so far, I have found none. It would appear to be the case that each speaker has a generosity profile, as in (3.6).

(3.6)

	Speaker A	Speaker B
Passives:	[α_1 Stingy]	[β_1 Stingy]
Particle Movement over heavy NPs:	[α_2 Stingy]	[β_2 Stingy]
Sloppiness:	[α_3 Stingy]	[β_3 Stingy]
Backwards Pronominalization:	[α_4 Stingy]	[β_4 Stingy]
Gapping:	[α_5 Stingy]	[β_5 Stingy]

and that the elusive notion of dialect does not emerge as a simple function of the profiles $(\alpha_1, \alpha_2, \alpha_3 \ldots \alpha_n)$, $(\beta_1, \beta_2, \beta_3 \ldots \beta_n)$, …

The next question is, "If there is no viable notion of dialect, then what are linguists to study while they wait for one to emerge?"

The answer that I would like to propose is that they should study idiolects, in as detailed a way as possible. That is, they should try to delve as deeply as possible into the structure of each speaker's intuitions. For instance, the matrix in (2.111), though ill-behaved in a number of ways, clearly bears a strong resemblance to the ideal of a squish. And even though the corresponding matrices for other speakers might differ from (2.111) in having a smaller number of columns (fairly likely), a smaller number of rows (less likely), the columns in a different order (still less likely), or the rows in a different order (least likely), we could still make the claim:

(3.7) Every speaker has some squish of nouniness.

Maybe there are speakers whose data are incompatible with (3.7)—discrete speakers. These would, in (2.111a), have only OKs above line 3, say, and only *s below.

And there may be speakers whose data are unsquishable in an even more radical way, speakers with data in such a checkerboard arrangement as that shown in (3.8):

(3.8)

	Rule 1	Rule 2	Rule 3	Rule 4
That S	OK	*	OK	*
Q	*	OK	*	OK
Acc Ing	OK	*	OK	*
Der. Nom.	*	OK	*	OK

At present, the questioning of other speakers that I have carried out has uncovered neither checkerboard speakers nor discrete ones, in the area of nouniness. I would hope that a claim at least as strong as (3.7) could be maintained, but at present, such a claim would be premature.

The point is, however, that such a squishoid as (2.111) is a *possible system*, because, barring the possibility of deception, either conscious or subconscious, at least one speaker has such a system. And it is a system with enough articulation, enough "texture," as it were, to be worthy of study in its own right, even if very few of its properties are shared by whatever turns out to correspond to it in the system of the dialect of English that I speak, when a workable definition of dialect becomes available.

An analogy to psychology may prove fruitful here. In psychology, the establishment of general laws, which hold across a wide number of subjects, such as George Miller's celebrated Magic Number 7 ± 2 (cf. Miller 1956), is an important goal of research. But no less important is the detailed study of a particular subject, such as the prodigious mnemonist reported on by Luria (1969). Both types of study can tell us about the structure of mind, and the organization of memory, in this particular case.

In transformational grammar, we have tended to concentrate on the former type of study, to the exclusion of the latter type. What I have been trying to suggest, in this section, is that it is time to right the balance, especially in view of the difficulties, at present unresolvable, as far as I know, in finding a viable characterization of the notion of dialect.[70]

3.3. Ranges of applicability

Let us now turn our attention to another area which is suggested by the structure of (2.111)—the issue of threshold values for syntactic processes. Assuming that we have found some satisfactory values of α to assign to the elements of (1.2), what can we say of the *range of applicability* of any rule? The first claim, itself quite strong, is that all rules must be specified for *continuous segments of the interval [0,1]*. That is, we would like to be able to maintain the formal claim stated in (3.9).

(3.9) Any rule involving nouniness is assigned two threshhold values,
L(lower bound) and U (upper bound), such that
$$0 \leq L < U \leq 1$$
where R will not operate on a complement of nouniness α if (a) or
(b) (below) holds, but will operate on any α such that (c) holds.
b. $0 \leq \alpha < L$
c. $U < \alpha \leq 1$
d. $L \leq \alpha \leq U$

Assuming for the moment that (3.9) is essentially correct, can we go beyond it to maintain (3.10)?

(3.10) For any rule conforming to (3.9), either $L = 0$ or $U = 1$, or both.

In other words, must the range of applicability of every rule contain at least one extreme?

The only counterexample to (3.10) in (2.111) is our old friend *Promotion*. I know of two other possible counterexamples, however: *Tough-Movement*[71] and *Raising*.

The first rule, which converts (3.11a) to (3.11b),

(3.11) a. It is tough to imagine a spotless ocelot.
    b. A spotless ocelot is tough to imagine.

is clearly sentence-based: the conversion of (3.12a) to (3.12b) becomes more difficult as the complement in (3.12a) gets nounier.[72]

(3.12) a. It is tough $\left\{\begin{array}{l}\text{for me to imagine gravel pizza}\\ \text{for me to imagine}\left\{\begin{array}{l}\text{him}\\ \text{his}\end{array}\right\}\text{liking gravel pizza}\\ \text{for me to imagine Bill's}\left\{\begin{array}{l}\text{ingesting}\\ \text{ingestion}\end{array}\right\}\text{of gravel pizza}\end{array}\right\}$.

    b. Gravel pizza is tough $\left\{\begin{array}{l}\text{for me to imagine}\\ \text{for me to imagine}\left\{\begin{array}{l}\text{him}\\ \text{?his}\end{array}\right\}\text{liking}\\ \text{*for me to imagine Bill's}\left\{\begin{array}{l}\text{ingesting}\\ \text{ingestion}\end{array}\right\}\text{of}\end{array}\right\}$.

However, as has often been remarked, *Tough Movement* will not operate out of *that*-clauses—cf. *(3.13b).

(3.13) a. It is tough for me to prove that she thought of gravel pizza.
    b. *Gravel pizza is tough for me to prove that she thought of.

The rule of *Raising*, which is discussed extensively in Postal (1974), removes the subjects of infinitival and gerundive complements and makes them constituents of the matrix clause. Thus (3.14a) and (3.15a) become (3.14b) and (3.15b), respectively.

(3.14) a. For Biff to whiff is likely.
    b. Biff is likely to whiff.

(3.15) a. Jed's being hassled by Ernie continued.
    b. Jed continued being hassled by Ernie.

The rule does not work for derived nominals—cf. *(3.16b).[73]

(3.16) a. The city's destruction by the invaders continued.
    b. *The city continued (its) destruction by the invaders.

Nor, apparently, is there any evidence that it works directly upon *that*-clauses—that is, that the correct source for (3.14b) is not (3.14a), as I have assumed, but rather (3.17).

(3.17)   That Biff will whiff is likely.

If evidence could be found to support deriving some sentences which involve *Raising* from remote structures containing *that*-clauses, this rule would cease to be a counterexample to (3.10), which would leave only *Promotion* and *Tough-Movement* to account for. Since I know

---

[72] Again, except for *picture*-nouns.
[73] Such sentences as (i) are demonstrably produced by *Equi*, not by *Raising*

    (i) Jack continued the investigation of Jeffrey.

In passing, there is an intriguing possibility, which I have not investigated in detail, that *Promotion* may be some alloform of *Raising*.

of no way around them at present, however, I mention (3.10) only as an interesting possibility, and cannot advance it as a valid restriction.

I will close these brief remarks on the subject of ranges of applicability by calling attention to one final problem—that of specifying the *rate of decay*.

Compare column (iv) of (2.111), where the judgments go from 'OK' to '*' in the space of two cells; column (x), where the same transition takes three cells; column (ii), where it takes four cells; column (iii), where a slightly longer transition takes five cells; and column (xiii), where the fading of grammaticality is so gradual that absolute ungrammaticality is not even attained in the column.

The implications of such a comparison are, I think, quite clear: instead of the absolute thresholds L and U specified in (3.9), it will be necessary to provide each rule with some *decay function*, noting both the level of nouniness at which decay sets in and also the slope of the function.

Hosts of questions about the formal nature of such functions immediately suggest themselves: Are they linear, or of a higher order? How high? Logarithmic? What kinds of decay functions are to be excluded? What are the connections between the formal operation which a rule carries out (deletion, permutation, etc.) and its decay function? etc., etc.

Important though such questions undoubtedly are, at present, the only data we have to bring to bear on them are too insufficient to even attempt answers.

3.4. Squishy command and squishy primacy

An important consequence of the hypothesis that there is a feature of sententiality is that the traditional definition of command,[74] which is given in (3.18a), must be changed along the lines suggested in (3.18b) below.

(3.18) a. A *commands* B $=_{df.}$ all the S nodes that dominate A dominate B. If all the S nodes that dominate B also dominate A, A and B are *clause-mates*. But if there is some node S_i which dominates A but not B, then A *asymmetrically commands* B.

   b. A α-*commands* B $=_{df.}$ all the S nodes that dominate A dominate B, and in addition, there is a node K, with the feature $[\alpha \text{ S}]$, which dominates B but does not dominate A. And if A α-commands B, for some fixed α, then B will be said to $(1-\alpha)$-command A.

Thus in (3.19a), where *Mary*, is dominated by a *that*-clause, which has the value [1.0 S], and where this clause does not dominate *John*, as is indicated in the diagram, the α-command facts are as stated in (3.19b).

(3.19) a.

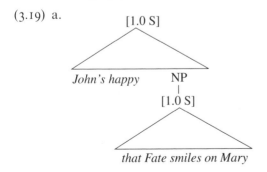

b. *John* (1.0)-commands *Mary*;
   Mary (0.0)-commands *John*.

However, in (3.20a), where the *Acc Ing* complement has been assigned, for the purposes of discussion, the value [0.66 S] (as suggested in the first-order approximation to a bunching function that is given in (3.2) above), the α-command facts are as stated in (3.20b).

(3.20) a.

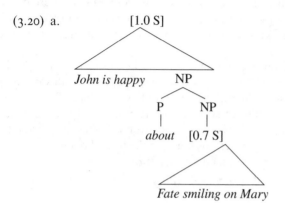

$$[1.0\ S]$$

John is happy   NP

P   NP

about   [0.7 S]

Fate smiling on Mary

b. *John* (0.66)-commands *Mary*;
   Mary (0.34)-commands *John*.

It is an important piece of evidence for features like [α S] that there are semantactic phenomena whose description requires, as far as I can see, a predicate like the squishy command of (3.18b). I will discuss three in the sections immediately below.

3.4.1. *Pronominalization and topicalization*

That pronominalization linkages must be stated on the output of *Topicalization* is apparent from the contrast in (3.21) below.

(3.21) a. *He$_i$ never realized that Ed$_i$ was under surveillance.[75]
       b. That Ed$_i$ was under surveillance he$_i$ never realized.

As (3.21) shows, forward pronominalization becomes possible out of a topicalized constituent. However, this is not always the case. Thus note that forward pronominalization in (3–22b) is still impossible, despite the fact that the antecedent NP has undergone *Topicalization*.

(3.22) a. *He$_i$ didn't realize that Mary doted on Ed$_i$.
       b. *Ed$_i$ he$_i$ didn't realize that Mary doted on.

Why the contrast between (3.21b) and (3.22b)? The correct generalization, which I am grateful to George Lakoff for pointing out to me, would seem to be along the lines of the one stated in (3.23).

(3.23)   If, in an input tree S$_k$, NP$_1$ commands[76] and precedes NP$_2$, and if, after *Topicalization* in S$_{k+1}$, NP$_2$ precedes NP$_1$ but the command relationship is unchanged, then NP$_2$ can be the antecedent for a pronoun at NP$_1$.

---

[75] Identical subscripts denote presupposed coreference (cf. Postal (1971) for discussion). Thus (3.21a) is only ungrammatical if *he* is taken to be anaphoric to *Ed*.

[76] For this generalization, and what immediately follows, let us use the unquantified notion of command that is given in (3.18a).

Thus the command relationships between (3.21a) and (3.21b) are unchanged: he_i commands Ed_i in both trees. However, in (3.22), the command relationships change: in (3.22a), he_i commands Ed_i, but in (3.22b), the reverse is the case.

What is important for the notion of squishy command is that (3.21b) and (3.22b) are just the endpoints of a gradient of acceptability. Consider the sentences in (3.24).

(3.24) a. *Ed_i's pony he_i realizes that Mary dotes on.

     b. ?*Your love for Ed_i he_i realizes that Mary never talks about.

     c. ??The photographing of Ed_i he_i didn't resent.

     d. ?Our razzing Ed_i he_i didn't resent.

     e. ?Us razzing Ed_i he_i didn't resent.

     f. Why they didn't invite Ed_i over he_i never learned.

     g. For us to tickle Ed_i with a feather he_i would really love.

Intuitively, it seems quite clear what is going on here. The series (3.22b), (3.24a), (3.24b), ..., (3.24g), (3.21b) could be added to (2.111) as another column, probably between columns (xii) and (xiii). Formally, however, some problems of detail remain before this intuition can be captured in such a way that the desired results emerge.

Informally, we seem to have here a case where the two primacy relations discussed in Langacker (1969), *precedence* and *command*, are working against one another. In a case like (3.22b), the fronted NP, NP_2, bears both primacy relations—precedence and command—to NP_1, its old commander. But in (3.21b), it bears only the relationship of precedence, while still remaining commanded. In the intermediate cases, NP_2 comes more and more to bear the relationship of command to NP_1, as we proceed from (3.24g) to (3.24a).

While I am not sure that the following sketch of a formal model will ultimately be satisfactory, as a first step let me propose that Langacker's two primacy relations are related by subtraction. Thus the definition of primacy given in (2.31) above should be replaced by the squishified definition given in (3.25).

(3.25)   *Squishy Primacy*[77]

        In establishing the primacy of one node over another, command is twice[78] as important as precedence.[79] Thus if two nodes, A and B, are clause-mates, and A precedes B, then $A \xrightarrow{0.33} B$ [read: 'A has (0.33)-primacy over B']. If B precedes A, then $B \xrightarrow{0.33} A$, or $A \xrightarrow{-0.33} B$.

---

[77] Note that the restriction in (2.31) to the effect that A and B must be clause-mates, for precedence to be relevant to primacy, has been dispensed with here.

[78] "Twice," in (3.25), should of course be taken only as an approximate coefficient, used here for the purposes of illustration only.

[79] There are several reasons for assuming that the precede-component of primacy has less weight than the command-component. One example of this has to do with the scope of quantifiers. Basically, if in shallow structure there are two quantifiers, Q_1 and Q_2, such that Q_1 has primacy over Q_2, then semantically, Q_2 is taken to be within the scope of Q_1. Thus in (i), *every* has primacy over *two*, by virtue of preceding it, and the preferred reading of (i) is that given in (ii).

    (i) Every visitor liked two buildings.

    (ii) For each visitor, there were two buildings that he or she liked.

      Similarly, in (iii), since *every* (1.0)-commands *two*, the former has primacy over the latter, and (iv) is, accordingly, the preferred reading.

    (iii) Every visitor thought that two buildings were attractive.

    (iv) For each visitor, there were two buildings that he thought were attractive.

      But what if the law linking primacy and semantic scope is violated? That is, supposing we try to hear (i) as having reading (ii'), and to hear (iii) as having reading (iv').

    (ii') There were two buildings that every visitor liked.

    (iv') There were two buildings that every visitor thought were attractive.

      For most speakers, (i) can have reading (ii') more easily than (iii) can have reading (iv'). Thus the precede-component of primacy would appear to have less weight than the command-component.
For other examples of a similar sort, cf. Ross (MS a).

If A is a member of a higher clause, and A (1.0)-commands B, then ceteris paribus, A $\xrightarrow{0.67}$ B, or B $\xrightarrow{-0.67}$ A.

That is, if A precedes and (1.0)-commands B, A $\xrightarrow{(0.33)+(0.67)=1.0}$ B.

If, however, B precedes A, but A (1.0)-commands B, then the 0.33 coefficient of primacy that B has over A by virtue of the precede-component (PC) will be subtracted from the 0.67 coefficient that A has over B by virtue of the command-component (CC): thus A $\xrightarrow{(-0.33)+(0.67)=(0.34)}$ B.

If the complement node that intervenes between A and B does not have the value [1.0 S], as above, but has rather some lesser value of α, $0 \leq \alpha < 1$, then A will α-command B, and the command-component of primacy will be less than its maximum value, 0.67. Its value will be given by multiplying 0.67 by α.

Symbolically, where P(A, B) is the amount of primacy A has over B, and PC(A, B) is the precede-component of this amount, and CC(A, B) is the command-component of it,

P(A, B) = PC(A, B) + CC(A, B),

where if A α-commands B, then

CC(A, B) = $\alpha \times 0.67$

To give some illustrations of the operation of the equation in (3.25), let us derive the values of the squishy primacy of Ed_i and he_i for (3.21b), (3.24g)–(3.24a), and (3.22b). The computations are given in (3.26), where the values of α are taken from the approximation to the bunching function that was given above in (3.2).

(3.26) a. In (3.21b), *he* (1.0)-commands *Ed*, so *Ed*, 0-commands *he*.
Thus P(*Ed, he*) = (0.33 + (0.00)(0.67) = 0.33.
Therefore, *Ed* $\xrightarrow{0.33}$ *he*.

b. In (3.24g), *he* (0.95)-commands *Ed*, so *Ed* (0.05)-commands *he*.
Thus P(*Ed, he*) = 0.33 + (0.05)(0.67) = 0.36
Therefore, *Ed* $\xrightarrow{0.36}$ *he*.

c. In (3.24f), *he* (0.86)-commands *Ed*, so *Ed* (0.14)-commands *he*.
Thus P(*Ed, he*) = 0.33 + (0.14)(0.67) = 0.42
Therefore, *Ed* $\xrightarrow{0.42}$ *he*.

d. In (3.24e), *he* (0.66)-commands *Ed*, so *Ed* (0.34)-commands *he*.
Thus P(*Ed, he*) = 0.33 + (0.34)(0.67) = 0.56
Therefore, *Ed* $\xrightarrow{0.56}$ *he*.

e. In (3.24d), *he* (0.43)-commands *Ed*, so *Ed* (0.57)-commands *he*.
Thus P(*Ed, he*) = 0.33 + (0.57)(0.67) = 0.71
Therefore, *Ed* $\xrightarrow{0.71}$ *he*.

f. In (3.24c), *he* (0.15)-commands *Ed*, so *Ed* (0.85)-commands *he*.
Thus P(*Ed, he*) = 0.33 + (0.85)(0.67) = 0.90
Therefore, *Ed* $\xrightarrow{0.90}$ *he*.

g. In (3.24b), *he* (0.02)-commands *Ed*, so *Ed* (0.98)-commands *he*.
Thus P(*Ed, he*) = 0.33 + (0.98)(0.67) = 0.99
Therefore, *Ed* $\xrightarrow{0.99}$ *he*.

h. In (3.24a) and (3.22b), *he* 0-commands *Ed*, so *Ed* (1.0)-commands *he*.
Thus P(*Ed, he*) = 0.33 + (1.0)(0.67) = 1.0
Therefore, *Ed* $\xrightarrow{1.0}$ *he*.

If we now compare the values of P(*Ed, he*) computed in (3.26) with the grammaticalities of the sentences in question, we arrive at the correspondence in (3.27).

(3.27) a. Gram (3.21b) = OK, $P(Ed, he) = 0.33$
    b. Gram (3.24g) = OK, $P(Ed, he) = 0.36$
    c. Gram (3.24f) = OK, $P(Ed, he) = 0.42$
    d. Gram (3.24e) = ?, $P(Ed, he) = 0.56$
    e. Gram (3.24d) = ?, $P(Ed, he) = 0.71$
    f. Gram (3.24c) = ? ?, $P(Ed, he) = 0.90$
    g. Gram (3.24b) = ?*, $P(Ed, he) = 0.99$
    h. $\left\{ \begin{array}{l} \text{Gram}(3.24a) \\ \text{gram}(3.24b) \end{array} \right\} = {}^*$, $P(Ed, he) = 1.00$

As we proceed from (3.24f) to (3.24a) or (3.22b), we see a fairly smooth transition from 'OK' to '*' with the exception that the transition has a slow start and an accelerated finish.[80] This means one of two things: either decay functions in general, and this one in particular, cannot be restricted to being linear functions, or the bunching function of (3.2) is wrong, and when replaced by an improved version, would produce a more linear succession of increments of $P(Ed, he)$ from (3.27d) to (3.27h).

In the absence of more data, it would be fruitless to attempt to make a choice between these alternatives, but it should be clear, I think, that we must replace Lakoff's generalization, (3.23), with something squishy along the lines of (3.28).

(3.28)   If NP_1 precedes NP_2 before *Topicalization* and NP_2 precedes NP_1 after it, then the grammaticality of an output structure in which NP_2 is the antecedent for a pronoun at NP_1 will vary inversely with the degree to which NP_2 has primacy over NP_1.

While there are many flaws in the above sketch of squishy primacy,[81] it seems likely that some such generalization about the facts I have been discussing as that contained in (3.28) will prove to be necessary. If this is so, squishy command and squishy primacy will also be necessary.

3.4.2. Backwards 'any'

For a second phenomenon whose description suggests the necessity of squishy command, consider the paradigm in (3.29) and (3.30).

(3.29) a. What I (never) said was that he had brains.
    b. What I *(never) said was that he had any brains.

(3.30) a. That he had brains was what I never said.
    b. *That he had any brains was what I never said.

The *(never)* of (3.29b) shows that the quantifier *any* is dependent on the presence of a negative trigger like *never*—without *never*, the sentence is out.[82] And as (3.30a) shows, such pseudo-cleft sentences as those in (3.29a) can generally undergo *Copula Switch*, the rule that interchanges subject and predicate of pseudo-cleft sentences.

---

[80] That is, if we view grammaticality as a function of squishy primacy, in the mid range of primacy, fairly large variations have no effect on grammaticality, while for high primacy values, a small increment (from 0.99 to 1.00) causes a one-step loss of grammaticality.

[81] One is the fact that in $Ed \xrightarrow{0.33} Ann$ (i), and $Ed \xrightarrow{0.34} Ann$ in (ii).

(i) Ed watched Ann.
(ii) That Ed watched upset Ann.

Intuitively, however, we feel that *Ed* has more primacy over *Ann* in (i) than in (ii). I have as yet found no way to resolve this difficulty.

[82] The same is true of a wide range of other so-called "negative polarity items"—items such as *ever*, *at all*, *budge*, *whatsoever*, *a red cent*, etc. I will resolutely gloss over mountainous problems pertaining to the study of this type of negative triggering, for an insightful discussion of many of which cf. Horn (1972).

What then is the matter with (3.30b)? It cannot be that *any* cannot appear before its trigger, for (3.31) is good with *never*.

(3.31) That he had any brains was *(never) claimed.

That whatever rules out (3.30b) cannot be limited to pseudo-cleft sentences can be seen by inspection of the *d*-sentences in (3.32)–(3.34).

(3.32) a. It will be easy to keep writing descriptions of { some / *any } body down.[83]

   b. Descriptions of { some / *any } body will be easy to keep writing down.

   c. It will be easy to keep from writing descriptions of { some / any } body down.

   d. Descriptions of { some / *any } body will be easy to keep from writing down.[84]

(3.33) a. They realized too late that he had { some / *any } brains.

   b. That he had { some / *any } brains, they realized too late.

   c. They never realized that he had { some / any } brains.

   d. That he had { some / ?*any } brains they never realized.

(3.34) a. I realized too late that he has { some / *any } brains.

   b. That he has { some / *any } brains, I realized it too late.

   c. I never realized that he had { some / any } brains.

   d. That he has { some / *any } brains, I never realized it.

For me, these *d*-sentences with *any* are all—except for (3.33d), which is slightly better—as bad as (3.30b), which almost all speakers reject. However, many speakers I have checked with find the *d*-sentences far superior to (3.30b), though some find some *d*-sentences worse than others, with individual variations that have so far baffled me. The restriction I will state below will thus only be valid for speakers who share my negative feelings about not only (3.30b), but also the *d*-sentences of (3.32)–(3.34).

For me, the restriction is one of command. While the *any* in (3.31) is commanded by its trigger *never*, this is not the case for the triggers in (3.30d) [*never*], in (3.32d) [(*keep*) *from*], in (3.33d) [*never*], and in (3.34d) [*never*]. This is apparent in (3.30b)—both subject and object of *was* are obviously clausal. In (3.32d), we know that *keep from* does not command *any* because of the many arguments (some given in §2 above) that *to*-phrases are highly sentential. To return briefly to one, observe that *Extraposition* can convert (3.35a) to (3.35b).

(3.35) a. To have to pay a 257% sales tax might arouse the public.

   b. It might arouse the public to have to pay a 257% sales tax.

---

[83] This string is good with *anybody*, with the meaning of *just anybody*, but only if *any* is heavily stressed. If *down* is stressed, which is the intonation I intend, the sentence cannot contain *any*.

[84] The same injunction against stressing *any* as was given in note 83 applies here. For a satisfying star in (3.32d), stress *down*.

But we have seen, in § 2.3 above, that only highly sentential complements extrapose. Hence we know that the *keep from* in (3.32d) does not command its *any*.

As for (3.33d) and (3.34d), which are produced by the rules of *Topicalization* and *Left Dislocation*, respectively, if we make the assumption that the constituents which are fronted by these two rules are Chomsky-adjoined to the sentence, as in (3.36a), and not sister-adjoined, as in (3.36b), then the trigger *never* will not command any elements in the fronted clause.

(3.36) a.

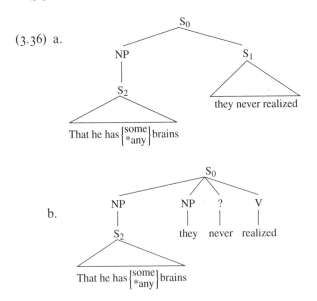

b.

That (3.36a) is in fact the correct derived constituent structure for both rules is argued for by the fact that parenthetical inserts are generally inserted only into "niches" between the major constituents of the highest clause(s). Thus note that *said Ed* can follow *never* in (3.33c), but not in (3.33d). The preferred niche in (3.33d) and (3.34d) is right after the fronted constituent, which accords well with (3.36a), but would remain unexplained if structures like (3.36b) were postulated.[85]

If we assume such output structures as (3.36a) for *Topicalization* and *Left Dislocation*, the relevant generalization about *any* is stated in (3.37):

(3.37) Negative polarity items (like *any*) can only precede their triggers if their triggers command them at the end of the first covering cycle.

The necessity of making (3.37) a cycle-final filter rather than an output condition was pointed out by Paul Postal.[86] He observed that while the structure in (3.38), to which *Raising* has not applied, would meet the condition specified in (3.37),

(3.38)   It seems that [him having any brains]$_S$ is [un]likely.

where the trigger is boxed, if the structure underlying (3.38) had undergone the cyclic rule of *Raising*, producing (3.39),

(3.39)   Him having any brains seems [to be [un]likely]$_S$.

---

[85] For more discussion of the interesting rule of *Niching*, which effects, the insertion of parentheticals, cf. Ross (MS e).
[86] In a lecture at the Second Scandinavian Summer School of Linguistics, at Säby Säteri, Sweden, in August 1970.

the condition in (3.37) would no longer be met. This is so because of the fact that *to*-phrases are highly sentential, as is shown by (3.35b).

I note in passing the fact that (3.37) provides support for the theory of global grammar,[87] which provides for static filters, of which (3.37) is an instance, at at least four levels: semantics, cycle-final, shallow structure,[88] and surface structure.

The relevance of (3.37) for squishy command can be seen from the sentences in (3.40), which worsen gradually as the degree to which the boxed triggers command the *any*s lessens.

(3.40) a. That he'll win anything is ⟨un⟩likely.
　　　 b. For him to win anything is ⟨un⟩likely.
　　　 c. How he won anything is ⟨un⟩known.
　　　 d. Him winning anything is ⟨un⟩likely.
　　　 e. ?His winning anything is ⟨un⟩likely.
　　　 f. ?*His repairing of any broken toys would ⟨not⟩ take long.[89]
　　　 g. ??The discovery of any results of significance is ⟨un⟩likely.
　　　 h. ?*Pictures of anybody were not on the table.[90]
　　　 i. *Anybody does⟨n't⟩ resemble Tom.

Thus, we must squishify (3.37). (3.41) is the result.

(3.41)　　If a negative trigger α-commands a preceding polarity item at the end of the first covering cycle, the grammaticality of the sentence will vary directly with the value of α.

3.4.3. Predicate crossing

In Lakoff (1969), justification is given for a global rule linking the superficial precede and command relationships of any two quantifiers with their semantic scope (cf. note 79 above). A rough statement of this rule is given in (3.42).

(3.42)　　For any two quantifiers, Q_1 and Q_2, if Q_1 is semantically higher than Q_2, then in shallow structure, Q_2 can precede Q_1 only if Q_2 does not command Q_1.

Thus (3.43a) has the (preferred) reading suggested by (3.43b); but (3.43c), the passive of (3.43a), has the reading suggested by (3.43d), in which the semantic dominance of the quantifiers is reversed.

(3.43) a. Every legislator fondled many waitresses.
　　　 b. For each legislator, there were many waitresses that he fondled.
　　　 c. Many waitresses were fondled by every legislator.
　　　 d. There were many waitresses who every legislator fondled.

However, when (3.44a) is passivized to (3.44b), we find no such scope shift—both sentences are paraphrased by (3.44c), not by (3.44d).

(3.44) a. Every legislator expects that many waitresses will pad the bill.
　　　 b. That many waitresses will pad the bill is expected by every legislator.
　　　 c. For each legislator, there are many waitresses who he expects will pad the bill.
　　　 d. There are many waitresses who every legislator expects will pad the bill.

---

[87] Cf. Lakoff (1970) for discussion of some other global processes.

[88] In case anybody ever succeeds in locating this elusive level.

[89] This sentence can be improved, for me, by making the action nominal subjectless:

(i) ??The repairing of any broken toys would ⟨not⟩ take long.

[90] In note 47 above, I called attention to the fact that *picture*-nouns behaved differently from other nominalizations in a number of ways. This is one of them.

The difference in the scope of *many* and *every* between (3.43c) and (3.44b), despite the fact that *many* precedes *every* in each case, is correctly predicted by (3.42). However, the sentences in (3.45) show that (3.42), too, must be squishified: a semantically higher reading for *many* becomes increasingly possible as we proceed from (3.45a) to (3.45h). The grammaticality prefixes in this example should be understood as indicating the viability of this reading in the string in question.

(3.45) a. *That Ann photographed many people angered every guest.
      b. *For Ann to photograph many people angered every guest.
      c. *How Ann photographed many people angered every guest.
      d. ?*Ann photographing many people angered every guest.
      e. *Ann's photographing many people angered every guest.
      f. ??Ann's photographing of many people angered every guest.
      g. ?Ann's photographs of many people angered every guest.[91]
      h. Photographs of many people angered every guest.[91]

I have no idea why (3.45e) is vertically ill-behaved, but despite this aberrance, it seems clear that squishy command is at work here. The squishification of (3.42) is on view in (3.46).

(3.46)   For any two quantifiers, Q_1 and Q_2, if Q_1 is semantically higher than Q_2, then if Q_2 precedes Q_1 in the shallow structure of some sentence, with Q_1 α-commanding Q_2, the grammaticality of the sentence will vary directly with α.

3.3.4. Summary

To recapitulate, since the generalizations about backwards *any*'s and about predicate crossing, as stated in (3.41) and (3.46) respectively, make crucial use of the notion of squishy command, and since the notion of squishy primacy on which (3.28) depends in turn depends on squishy command, the hypothesis of §3.1, namely, that there exist such squishy categories as [αS], is strongly supported, since without [α S], there could be no such definitions as (3.18b) and (3.25).

3.5. Meta-remarks on nominalization

Although there have been many other analyses of the elements of (1.2), both within transformational grammar and in other theoretical frameworks, I will comment in this paper only on the implications of the non-discrete theory advanced above for the discrete theory proposed in a recent paper by Chomsky (1970), because this paper has had a wide readership, and has given rise to much discussion.

3.5.1. Arguments for lexicalism

Chomsky (op. cit.) develops three arguments for what he calls a lexicalist theory of derived nominals. The previous, transformationalist, theory of the source of such derived nominals as the subject of (3.47a) was that they arose from such paraphrases as the subject of (3.47b) by a transformation called *Nominalization*.

(3.47) a. John's refusal to go made his teacher impatient.
      b. That John refused to go made his teacher impatient.

---

[91] For some reason I do not understand, the wide reading of these strings would become impossible, for me, if *photographs* were not plural.

Chomsky compares *Poss Ing* complements with derived nominals, noting three major differences:

(3.48) a. *The Derived Structures Argument (DSA)*
   There are *Poss Ing* structures which correspond to sentences that have undergone transformations, but there are no derived nominals which correspond to such derived structures.

   b. *The Semantic Kinkiness Argument (SKA)*
   While the relationship between *Poss Ing* complements and synonymous NPs containing finite clauses is (generally) fairly regular and one-to-one,[92] that between derived nominals and synonymous NPs with finite clauses is often much less regular, and is usually one-to-many.

   c. *The Internal Structure Argument (ISA)*
   While derived nominals have the internal structure of NPs (i. e., they pluralize and take determiners), *Poss Ing* complements do not.

Chomsky cites such facts as those presented in (3.49)–(3.51) [his (6)–(8)] as evidence for the DSA.

(3.49) a. John is easy (difficult) to please.
   b. John is certain (likely) to win the prize.
   c. John amused (interested) the children with his stories.

(3.50) a. John's being easy (difficult) to please.
   b. John's being certain (likely) to win the prize.
   c. John's amusing (interesting) the children with his stories.

(3.51) a. *John's easiness (difficulty) to please.
   b. *John's certainty (likelihood) to win the prize.
   c. *John's amusement (interest) of the children with his stories.

The three sentences of (3.49) have been produced by **Tough** *Movement, Raising,* and *Promotion,* respectively, and Chomsky is correct in noting that while we find that these processes can operate within the source of the *Poss Ing* complements of (3.50), we do not find them operating within the source of the derived nominals in (3.51).

In support of the SKA, Chomsky cites a number of nouns—those listed in (3.52)

(3.52)   laughter, marriage, construction, actions, doubt, activities, revolution, belief, conversion, trial, permutation, residence, qualifications, specifications.

—as examples of a much larger list that could be given of forms whose relationship to NPs containing in non-nominalized form the predicates upon which they are morphologically based is extremely complex. Some examples are suggested in (3.53).

(3.53) a. his residence (here):
$$\begin{cases} \text{the place at which he resides here} \\ \text{the fact that he resides here} \\ \text{the time at which he resided here} \\ \quad \text{etc.} \end{cases}$$

---

[92] Usually, *Poss Ing* complements correspond to NPs of the form *the fact that S*. There are contexts where this correspondence fails, as in (i)–(iii) below:

(i) His returning the money to us is unlikely.
(ii) His sewing us up shouldn't take a minute.
(iii) John's bargaining with Archie dragged on.

but they need not concern us here.

b. the permutation of X and Y: $\left\{ \begin{array}{l} \text{the time at which X and Y were permuted.} \\ \text{the result of permuting X and Y} \\ \text{the way that X and Y were permuted} \\ \qquad \text{etc.} \end{array} \right\}$

c. their doubt: $\left\{ \begin{array}{l} \text{the fact that they doubt} \\ \text{the extent to which they doubt} \\ \qquad \text{etc.} \end{array} \right\}$

In support of the ISA, Chomsky cites such contrasts as those in (3.54).

(3.54) a. the $\left\{ \begin{array}{l} \text{proof of} \\ \text{*proving} \end{array} \right\}$ the theorem

b. John's unmotivated $\left\{ \begin{array}{l} \text{criticism of} \\ \text{*criticizing} \end{array} \right\}$ the book.

To account for these facts, Chomsky advances a new theory of derived nominals: that they do not come from sentences. That is, Chomsky rejects any transformational analysis that would convert a clause to a nominal structure. Rather, he proposes that the base component of the grammar be enriched, in ways that need not concern us here, so that such derived nominals as the subject of (3.47a) would be directly generated in the base. This direct generation, Chomsky alleges, allows him to explain the ungrammaticality of *(3.51), for the rules involved in the formation of (3.49) only apply to sentences, and derived nominals are never sentences. Furthermore, with direct generation, such semantic kinkinesses as are evident in the (partial) paraphrases of (3.53) are no longer an issue. There is no need to look for synonymous NPs containing finite clauses to serve as sources for NPs with such semantically troublesome head nouns as those in (3.52)—in most essential respects, their surface structures are their sources. And finally, it will follow that the determiners, possibilities of pluralization, etc. of derived nominals are those of nouns like *boy*, for both types of nouns are generated in the same phrase structure configurations.

3.5.2. Rejoinders

In this section, I will attempt to show that while Chomsky has performed an important service in stressing the above three arguments, which definitely do pose difficulties for a transformationalist solution to the problem of nominalization, the alternative theory of lexicalism that he proposes does not provide the solution to these difficulties that he imagines it to. I will take up the arguments of (3.48) in order.

3.5.2.1 The derived structures argument. Chomsky opens the DSA with the following statement:

(3.55)   Consider first the matter of productivity. As noted above, the transformation that gives gerundive nominalizations [= *Poss Ing* complements—JRR] applies quite freely. (Chomsky 1970: 188)

I have presented many kinds of evidence in §2 above showing that the "quite freely" of this quote must be taken rather loosely. And this is true even if we restrict our attention to the internal phenomena of §§2.6–2.15. What is more important, however, is the fact that the many ways in which *Poss Ing* complements diverge from *that*-clauses are not different in *kind* from the way that derived nominals diverge from *Poss Ing* complements (or from *that*-clauses, for that matter) but only in *degree*. Though these divergences in behavior are important to note, Chomsky is incorrect in his belief that they are discrete.

404   *Fuzzy Grammar: A Reader*

Let us now turn to the method by which Chomsky proposes to deal with the claim of the DSA: that no derived structures nominalize. What about the fact that we find, in apparent correspondence to (3.56a), the passive of (3.56b); and not only the nominalization in (3.57a), but also the one in (3.57b)?

(3.56) a. The enemy destroyed the city.
        b. The city was destroyed by the enemy.
(3.57) a. The enemy's destruction of the city.
        b. The city's destruction by the enemy.

Chomsky argues (op. cit.: 202f.) that rather than NPs like (3.57b) being the nominalizations of passives, they are

(3.58)   ... in effect, passives of base-generated derived nominals, by independently motivated transformations. (ibid.: 205)

That is, Chomsky's base rules generate (3.57a). To this, his rule of *Agent-Postposing* will apply, yielding (3.59):

(3.59)   the destruction of the city by the enemy

Finally, another rule of *NP Preposing* will prepose and possessivize the NP *the city* in (3.59), yielding (3.57b).

Chomsky views his rule of *Agent-Postposing* as a generalization of the rule that forms *by*-phrases in passive sentences, like (3.55b). The concept of "independent motivation" is highly obscure in Chomsky's original article: he says of this generalization only the following:

(3.60)   Agent-postposing will then apply, as in the passive, giving *the destruction of the city by the enemy*. To provide this result we need only generalize the operation so that its domain may be a noun phrase as well as a sentence, a modification of the theory of transformations that is implicit in the lexicalist hypothesis... (ibid.: 204)

The problem here lies in the words "need only." Because obviously, by the same token, the operation of **Tough**-*Movement*, and the operation of *Raising*, and the operation of *Promotion*, "need only" be generalized so that their domains may be NPs as well as sentences, and the ungrammatical phrases in *(3.51) will result.

To put it in a slightly different way, if a lexicalist theory of nominalization is to succeed in *explaining* the ungrammaticality of *(3.51), it must show why these latter three rules *cannot* be generalized to NPs.

To give another example which makes the same point, under the assumption that a transformational I will call *PP Shift* converts (3.61a) to (3.61b), and that a transformation of *Dative* converts (3.62a) to (3.62b),

(3.61) a. We talked with Gretchen about hockey.
        b. We talked about hockey with Gretchen.
(3.62) a. We gave a bull moose to Mark.
        b. We gave Mark a bull moose.

Why is it that the operation of the former rule "need only" be generalized to NPs (cf. (3.63)), while the latter may not be generalized (cf. *(3.64b))?

(3.63) a. Our talk with Gretchen about hockey
        b. Our talk about hockey with Gretchen

(3.64) a. Our gift of a bull moose to Mark
       b. *Our gift Mark (of) a bull moose.[93]

That is, if one "need only" generalize when the facts show this to be necessary, how could there ever be any counterexamples to the DSA?[94]

Although Chomsky does not indicate how he would avoid this problem of circularity in Chomsky (1970), the original paper on lexicalism, in a later paper (Chomsky 1972), he indicates more clearly what he has in mind.

(3.65)   Secondly, the patterns in question must exist independently for noun phrases, quite apart from these nominalizations [i.e., *John's certainty that Bill will leave, John's eagerness to please, the gift of the book to Mary, the belief that John was killed* and *John's surprise at Bill's antics*—JRR], as we see from such expressions as *the story of Bill's exploits, the message from John to Bill about money, a war of aggression against England, the secretary-general of the UN, his advantage over his rivals, his habit of interrupting, the prospects for peace, prolegomena to any future metaphysics, my candidate for a trip to the moon, a nation of shopkeepers,* and many others. (Chomsky 1972: 91)

That is, apparently, what constitutes, for Chomsky, the "independent motivation" mentioned in the quote in (3.58) is the existence of some derived nominal *which is not visibly derived morphologically from some existing predicate*. Then since there are no verbs like **to story, *to message* (*to war*, of course, does exist—presumably it (and *prospect* (?)) are in the above list by accident) **to secretary-general, *to advantage, *to habit*, etc., etc., the processes which apply in such morphologically complex NPs as *certainty, eagerness, gift*, etc. in (3.65) have independent motivation . Thus Chomsky is claiming that any rule which applies within such morphologically simple abstract nouns as those cited in (3.65) will apply also in morphologically motivated nominalizations. That is, the independent motivation for the *Agent Postposing* that converts (3.57a) into (3.59) is the existence of such NPs as those in (3.66).

(3.66)   the story about Hawaii by Major Minor.

If I am correct in interpreting Chomsky in this way, the DSA reduces to a claim that is of far less interest than it might be taken to have—the claim in (3.67):

(3.67)   The rules which apply within NPs whose head noun is morphologically complex will not differ from those that apply within NPs whose head noun is morphologically simple.

To see why this claim is not the answer to the weakness in the transformationalist analysis of nominalizations that Chomsky correctly identified, let me take up one more case in some detail. It concerns the behavior of the adjective *ready*, which occurs in structures exhibiting two types of deletion. The first type, which converts (3.68a) to (3.68b), is called *Equi*,

(3.68) a. Thom is ready for₁ [for₂ Thom to operate on Sue].[95]
       b. Thom is ready to operate on Sue.

and the second, which converts (3–69a) to (3–69b), is called *Object Deletion*.

---

[93] It is immaterial that such NPs as (i) exist,
     (i) our gift to Mark of a bull moose
for this could be produced by applying *PP Shift* to (3.164). The crucial difference between *PP Shift* and *Dative* is that the latter deletes a preposition. It is precisely this feature that renders its output unnominalizable.
[94] I am grateful to George Lakoff for pointing out this weakness in the DSA to me.
[95] The *for₂* of (3.168a) goes as a consequence of *Equi*, and the *for₁* vanishes by the rule of *Preposition Deletion* that was discussed in §2.2 above.

(3.69) a. Thom is ready for [for Sue to operate on Thom].
b. Thom is ready for Sue to operate on.

When we examine the behavior of the derived nominal *readiness*, we find that *Equi*-ed structures are compatible with it, but not ones that have undergone *Object Deletion* (cf. the contrast in (3.70)).

(3.70) a. Thom's readiness to operate on Sue
b. *Thom's readiness for Sue to operate on

What reason does the theory of lexicalism provide for (3.70)? This theory can only say that *Equi* is, on the basis of such *Equi*-ed structures as those in (3.71), whose head noun is morphologically simple, "independently motivated for NPs,"

(3.71) a. Thom's habit of operating on Sue
b. Mike's effort to make 8 No Trump
c. Nan's yen to spin on the sun

while, because there are no NPs like those in *(3.72), which would motivate generalizing *Object Deletion* to NPs, this rule is limited to sentences.

(3.72) a. *Sue's tibah of Thom's operating on
b. *8 No Trump's troffe for Mike to make
c. *The sun's yen for Nan to spin on

But now the real inadequacy of lexicalism's answer is apparent. For why shouldn't (3.72) be grammatical, instead of (3.71)? Or why not both? And why, though (3.73) shows it is true that *PP Shift* has "independent motivation" in NPs,

(3.73) a. The message from Aix to Ghent
b. The message from Ghent to Aix

should we not find *(3.74b) which would allow us to conclude that *Dative* is also independently motivated for NPs?

(3.74) a. the letter of hope to Mary
b. *the letter Mary (of) hope

The problem for all syntacticians is to explain ungrammaticalities like *(3.51), and contrasts like those we have just seen between *Equi* and *Object Deletion*, or between *PP Shift* and *Dative*. I cannot see that the mystery that surrounds these facts under a transformationalist analysis of nominalizations is dispelled at all by lexicalism.[96] I thus regard the DSA as being without force in choosing between these two theories.

---

[96] Though it would go beyond the scope of the present, rather hasty, treatment of the derived-structures problem to explore this in detail, I suspect that the concept of nouniness may prove helpful in clearing up some of these mysteries. Note the contrast between *(i), which shows that *Object Deletion* cannot operate into a highly sentential complement when within an NP; ??(ii), where the rule operates into a slightly less sentential complement, and which is improved in grammaticality; and ?(iii), which is almost perfect, and which has had *Object Deletion* apply into a derived nominal.

   (i)   *The stocks are risky—their readiness for us to re-evaluate is obvious.
   (ii) ??The stocks are risky—their readiness for our re-evaluating is obvious.
   (iii) ?The stocks are risky—their readiness for our re-evaluation is obvious.

   What these facts suggest is that there may be processes which require for their operation what we might refer to as an assimilation of nouniness. Another possible candidate for such a process is described in §3.5.3 below.

3.5.2.2 The semantic kinkiness argument. It is difficult to see how the SKA could justify choosing a lexicalist analysis of nominalization over a transformationalist one. Note first that there can be no argument based on simplicity. To be sure, the transformationalist will seek to explain such synonymies as those in (3.53) by postulating some rules to convert structures like those to the right of the colons in (3.53) into the derived nominals to the left of the colons. The lexicalist will start each of these classes of structures from different syntactic deep structures, but will have to account for their synonymy by various semantic rules. We clearly have a trading relationship here—while the transformationalist will have to formulate kinky, non-productive syntactic rules, the lexicalist will have to postulate cognates to these rules in his semantics.

There is one comment Chomsky makes in this connection which deserves some discussion.

(3.75) Consider, for example, such nominals as [the same list appears as (3.52) above— JRR], and so on, with their individual ranges of meaning and varied semantic relations to the base forms. There are a few subregularities that have frequently been noted, but the range of variation and its rather accidental character are typical of lexical structure. (Chomsky 1970: 189)

There is a strong implication here to the effect that syntactic processes are general and exceptionless—that they are not "accidental," while lexical processes have the opposite characteristics. This implication may not have been intended, but if it was, it is hard to ascertain on what basis it could be defended. Transformations seem to be conditioned sometimes by semantic factors,[97] sometimes by phonological ones,[98] sometimes by lexical ones,[99] sometimes by perceptual ones,[100] and sometimes by any number of mixes of the above

---

[97] Thus, as Ed Klima pointed out in class lectures at MIT, it is often only possible to passivize an NP in a prepositional phrase that is loosely bound to the verb if there is a presupposition that the NP in question can be affected by the action of the verb. Thus compare (i) and (ii).

(i) This bed has been $\left\{ \begin{array}{l} \text{slept} \\ \text{fought} \\ \text{?hidden} \\ \text{??eaten} \end{array} \right\}$ in.

(ii) ??This bed has been $\left\{ \begin{array}{l} \text{breathed} \\ \text{thought} \\ \text{dreamt} \end{array} \right\}$ in.

Many similar examples of other semantic-syntactic interdependence could be cited.

[98] Thus, as Naomi Baron has called to my attention, the more polysyllabic a verb is, the less likely it is to undergo *Dative*. Cf. the sentences in (i)–(iii).

(i) I brought / ?? transported Ted an oboe.
(ii) I gave / ?*donated / *contributed the IRS all my savings.
(iii) I'm going to fry / ?parboil / ?*tempura my parents a banana.

[99] Cf. (i).

(i) Fred is $\left\{ \begin{array}{l} \text{likely} \\ \text{*probable} \end{array} \right\}$ to have a nice time.

[100] Thus the usual rule which converts (i) to (ii)

(i) the friend of the girl

(ii) the girl's friend

will not work on (iii),

(iii) the friend of the husband of my daughter

presumably because the "wrong" bracketing of the output, which is shown in parentheses in (iv), is so predominant perceptually over the "right" bracketing, which is shown with square brackets.

(iv) [The daughter of (my husband]'s friend)

factors, or by yet Other Ones.[101] Possibly linguists use the term "lexical" to describe those processes whose causal relationships are the least discernible, but in my opinion, all areas of language are shot through with the partial parallels and half-generalities that are the normative grammarian's undoing and the punster's delight.

Although the problems connected with the area of nominalization are complex beyond belief, far more so than can even be hinted at in such a cursory sketch as the present treatment,[102] I would like to make a brief digression at this point to propose a derivational route for nominalizations which has not been suggested before in the literature that I am familiar with, and which shows a lot of promise, in my opinion, as a way of overcoming several of the objections that Chomsky raises to previous transformationalist analyses.

A foreshadowing of the derivation I will argue for is suggested in a footnote by Chomsky himself:

(3.76)   The artificiality [of assigning a range of meanings to a base form, stipulating that with certain semantic features the form must nominalize and with others it cannot—JRR] might be reduced by deriving nominals from underlying nouns with some kind of sentential element included, where the meaning can be expressed in this way: for example, *John's intelligence* from *the fact that John is intelligent* (in *John's intelligence is undeniable*) and from the *extent to which John is intelligent* (in *John's intelligence exceeds his foresight.* (ibid.: note 11)

What I would propose is that Chomsky's suggested source be adopted, but with a slightly different path to nominalized forms than Chomsky envisions. Succinctly, the scheme is that shown in (3.77).

---

[101] Thus why should *as (of) yet*, a negative polarity item, as shown in (i),

(i) They have *(not) found a solution as (of) yet.

be the only polarity item, to the best of my knowledge, which can be permuted to precede *and asymmetrically command* its trigger? Cf. (ii).

(ii) As yet, I know that they feel that you think that they have *(not) found a solution.

   Or to take some other examples, in case it should be thought that the facts about *as (of) yet* are just a repetition of such government facts as were given in note 99, why is it that That *Deletion* should be sensitive to the application of a fronting rule in the clause that the *that* introduces? Cf. (iii)–(vi).

(iii) He realizes (that) we should invite nobody who is fluent in Bavarian.

(iv) He realizes *(that) nobody should we invite who is fluent in Bavarian.

(v) He thinks (that) all the combustibles should be placed in the metal cannisters.

(vi) He thinks *(that) in the metal cannisters should be placed all the combustibles.

   And—coals to Newcastle—why should there be a connection between the nature of a matrix verb and the subcategorization of an adjective in its complement, just in case *Raising* and **To Be** *Deletion* have applied? Cf. (vii)–(ix), which were pointed out to me by Paul Postal.

(vii) Tom$_i$ $\left\{ \begin{matrix} \text{says} \\ \text{finds} \\ \text{knows} \end{matrix} \right\}$ that it is interesting (to $\left\{ \begin{matrix} \text{him}_i \\ \text{her}_j \end{matrix} \right\}$) that there are so few rickshaws in Urbana.

(viii) Tom$_i$ $\left\{ \begin{matrix} \text{knows} \\ \text{finds} \end{matrix} \right\}$ it to be interesting (to $\left\{ \begin{matrix} \text{him}_i \\ \text{her}_j \end{matrix} \right\}$) that there are so few rickshaws in Urbana.

(ix) Tom$_i$ finds it interesting (*to $\left\{ \begin{matrix} \text{him(self)}_i \\ \text{her}_j \end{matrix} \right\}$) that there are so few rickshaws in Urbana.

   Note that to call such facts as those in (i)–(ix) above "irregularities," "paradoxes," "mysteries," etc., is not to abandon attempts to deduce them, ultimately, from general laws, but to make a contingent statement about the current state of linguistic knowledge to the effect that no such deductions are now available.

[102] Some more accurate indications of the size of the problem can be gleaned from a study of Lees (1960), the most extensive treatment of nominalization within the literature of transformational grammar that I know of, and from the bibliography there.

(3.77) a. *Remote structure*: every nominalization starts out as an abstract head noun which is modified by a sentence.[103]

b. *Nominalization*: the modifying sentence (whose value of the feature [αS] was 1.0 in remote structure) assumes a lesser value, in effect becoming a gerundive or derived nominal modifier of the abstract head noun.

c. *Beheading*: the head noun is deleted.

That is, I would propose such derivations as those which proceed from the remote structures in (3.78) through the corresponding structures in (3.79) to emerge finally as the derived nominals which are the subjects of (3.80).

(3.78) a. The fact that Fred is sallow (is beyond question).

b. The extent to which Fred is sallow (exceeds Tom's).

c. The time at which Jim departed (preceded the detonation of the podium).

d. The $\left\{ \begin{array}{l} \text{manner} \\ \text{way} \end{array} \right\}$. $\left\{ \begin{array}{l} \text{in which} \\ \text{that} \end{array} \right\}$ Fermat solved it (was intricate).

e. The path along which they marched to L.A. (went through the woods).

f. The frequency with which he visited us (doubled).

g. The interval during which he was imprisoned (was interminable).

h. The question $\left\{ \begin{array}{l} \text{of} \\ \text{as to} \end{array} \right\}$ whether the statement is $\left\{ \begin{array}{l} \text{true} \\ \text{false} \end{array} \right\}$ (is indeterminate).

(3.79) a. The fact of $\left\{ \begin{array}{l} \text{Fred('s) being sallow} \\ \text{Fred's sallowness} \end{array} \right\}$ (is beyond question).

b. The extent of Fred's sallowness (exceeds Tom's).

c. The time of Jim's departure (preceded the detonation of the podium).

d. *The $\left\{ \begin{array}{l} \text{manner} \\ \text{way} \end{array} \right\}$ of $\left\{ \begin{array}{l} \text{Fermat ('s) solving it} \\ \text{Fermat's solution to it} \end{array} \right\}$ (was intricate).

e. The path of their march to L.A. (went through the woods).

f. The frequency of his $\left\{ \begin{array}{l} \text{?? visiting us} \\ \text{visits to us} \end{array} \right\}$ (doubled).

g. The duration of Fred's imprisonment (was interminable).

h. The question $\left\{ \begin{array}{l} \text{of} \\ \text{as to} \end{array} \right\}$ the statement's $\left\{ \begin{array}{l} \text{truth} \\ \text{falsity} \end{array} \right\}$ (is indeterminate).

(3.80) a. $\left\{ \begin{array}{l} \text{Fred('s) being sallow} \\ \text{Fred's sallowness} \end{array} \right\}$ (is beyond question).

b. Fred's sallowness (exceeds Tom's).

c. Jim's departure (preceded the detonation of the podium).

d. Fermat's solution to it (was intricate).

e. Their march to L.A. (went through the woods).

f. His visits to us (doubled).

g. Fred's imprisonment (was interminable).

h. The statement's $\left\{ \begin{array}{l} \text{truth} \\ \text{*falsity} \end{array} \right\}$ (is indeterminate).

---

[103] I would like to be able to maintain the claim that the modifying clause is always a relative clause, but I cannot take the time here to investigate the possibility that this is true even for clauses that modify the noun *fact*. If such clauses do turn out to be arguably de-relatival, I would expect that the shared NP will be a modality NP, the one which has *wh-* attached to it in *whether*-clauses. (Note that in other cases, it is fairly clear that what *wh-* attaches to can be taken to be an NP in remote structure.)

Assuming for the moment that this path of derivation is basically correct, many questions of detail remain to be answered. Some of them are mentioned briefly below.

Question 1. Why is *(3.79d) bad? Apparently, just this type of nominal requires the operation of the rule which, with mixed success, can apply to extract the subject of the nominalized modifiers of (3.79) and substitute it for the determiner of the abstract head noun. Cf. (3.81):

(3.81) a. *Fred's fact of $\left\{ \begin{array}{l} \text{being sallow} \\ \text{sallowness} \end{array} \right\}$ (is beyond question).

   b. Fred's extent of $\left\{ \begin{array}{l} \text{*being sallow} \\ \text{sallowness} \end{array} \right\}$ $\left\{ \begin{array}{l} \text{*exceeds Tom's} \\ \text{?is unknown}^{104} \end{array} \right\}$.

   c. Jim's time of $\left\{ \begin{array}{l} \text{departing} \\ \text{departure} \end{array} \right\}$ (preceded the detonation of the podium).

   d. Fermat's $\left\{ \begin{array}{l} \text{manner} \\ \text{way} \end{array} \right\}$ of $\left\{ \begin{array}{l} \text{solving it} \\ \text{*solution to it} \end{array} \right\}$ (was intricate).

   e. ?*Their path of $\left\{ \begin{array}{l} \text{marching} \\ \text{march} \end{array} \right\}$ (went through the woods).

   f. His frequency of $\left\{ \begin{array}{l} \text{visiting us} \\ \text{*visits to us} \end{array} \right\}$ $\left(\left\{ \begin{array}{l} \text{?doubled} \\ \text{is unknown}^{105} \end{array} \right\} \right)$.

   g. *Fred's duration of imprisonment (was interminable).

   h. **The statement's question $\left\{ \begin{array}{l} \text{of} \\ \text{as to} \end{array} \right\}$ $\left\{ \begin{array}{l} \text{truth} \\ \text{falsity} \end{array} \right\}$ (is indeterminate).

If we agree to call this rule *Possessive Fronting*, there are a number of unsolved problems about *its* formulation which are posed by the unsightly littering by stars and other blemishes that dot the landscape in (3.81).

Question 2. Why, given the acceptability of the sentences in (3.82) and (3.83), are the sentences of (3.84) unacceptable?

(3.82) a. The path along which they traveled went through the woods.
   b. The path along which the blimp descended was a parabola.

(3.83) a. The path of their travels went through the woods.
   b. The path of the blimp's descent was a parabola.

(3.84) a. *Their travels went through the woods.
   b. *The blimp's descent was a parabola.

Similarly, why can *question* only undergo *Beheading* with *truth*, and not with *falsity* in (3.8oh)? In short, what factors, in detail, govern the applicability of the rule of *Beheading*?

Question 3. *Frequency* is itself morphologically complex. Thus *the frequency of X* should presumably be derived from *the extent to which X is frequent*. But this provides the wrong meaning for *frequency* when it is the subject of such verbs as *double*. Then what is the source of *frequency* in this sense?

---

[104] Note—horreurs!—that this rule must be made sensitive to various kinds of upper context. Apparently, such derived nominals as that of (3.81b) can only exist in contexts which admit of such embedded questions as *how sincere Fred was.*

[105] Remarks similar to those in note 104 are also applicable here.

Question 4. What type of operation can produce *the duration* from *the interval during which*? Is this in fact the correct source for *duration*?

A much more serious question is the following:

Question 5. The proposal of (3.77) is that all derived nominals arise from modified head nouns. But many derived nominals seem to have no such paraphrase. Some examples appear in (3.85).[106]

(3.85) a. Fritz's trial will begin at one a.m. on Sunday.
      b. The revolution in consciousness stemmed from the Court's decision on umbrellas.
      c. The accompaniment of a kazooist is a prerequisite for employment.
      d. John's beliefs are intense.[107]

Clearly, until such questions as these have been answered, the theory of nominalizations outlined in (3.77) cannot be considered a complete theory. Nonetheless, it has a number of desirable points, which make it a much more attractive candidate for future exploration than previously proposed transformationalist analyses.

Point 1. Any theory of nominalizations must specify what kinds of nominal groups like the subjects in (3.79) are possible. That is, why are the subjects of (3.79) selectionally well-formed, by and large, while the nominal groups of (3.86) are not?

(3.86) a. *Frend's $\left\{ \begin{array}{l} \text{manner} \\ \text{way} \end{array} \right\}$ of being sallow

      b. *The extent of $\left\{ \begin{array}{l} \text{Jim's departure} \\ \text{their march to L.A.} \end{array} \right\}$

      c. *The path of $\left\{ \begin{array}{l} \text{Fred's sallowness} \\ \text{Fermat's solution to it} \end{array} \right\}$

---

[106] Some of Chomsky's examples from (3.52) appear to merely require head nouns which are rarely deleted. Cf. (i)–(ii) below.

(i)   (The sound of) Smedley's demented laughter filled the command module.

     [similarly for *cough, retching, gasp*, etc.]

(ii) $\left\{ \begin{array}{l} \text{Fred and Jan's marriage} \\ \text{Fred and Jan's state of} \left\{ \begin{array}{l} \text{??being married} \\ \text{marriage} \end{array} \right\} \end{array} \right\}$ is happy.

     [similarly for *inebriation, doubt, shock, disrepair*, etc.]

And for Chomsky's example in (iii), I propose the source shown in (iv).

(iii) John's beliefs are mutually inconsistent. (ibid.: footnote 11)
(iv) The set of John's beliefs is mutually inconsistent.

That *set* is a noun which must be able to be beheaded can be seen from examples of the following kind, which are due to Susumu Kuno.

(v) This policy covers graduate students, which does not include students' wives.

The fact that *include* generally selects subjects that are sets and the fact that there is singular agreement in the appositive clause of (vi), suggest a source like (vi) for (v).

(vi) This policy covers the set of graduate students, which set does not include (the set of (?)) students' wives.

     As for the derived nominal *belief* in (iv), I would suggest the source shown in (vii), which parallels the other object-deleted nominals shown in (viii).

(vii) what John believes ⇒ John's beliefs

     John's hopes/desires/needs/fears/plans, etc.

     [Cf. also *what remains* ⇒ *the remainder*]

[107] This example is taken from Chomsky (op. cit.: footnote 11).

The *Beheading* analysis of (3.77) traces the contract between (3.79) and (3.86) to the well-formedness of the modifying clauses of (3.78), which also must be generated, independently of the problems of nominalization, and to the ill-formedness of the clauses in (3.87).

(3.87) a. *The $\left\{\begin{array}{l}\text{manner} \\ \text{way}^{108}\end{array}\right\}$ $\left\{\begin{array}{l}\text{in which} \\ \text{that}\end{array}\right\}$ Fred is sallow

     b. *The extent to which $\left\{\begin{array}{l}\text{Jim departed} \\ \text{they marched to L.A.}\end{array}\right\}$

     c. *The path along which $\left\{\begin{array}{l}\text{Fred was sallow} \\ \text{Fermat solved it}\end{array}\right\}$

Where there are differences, as in (3.88)–(3.91), it appears always to be the case that the less nouny versions is better than the more nouny version.

(3.88) a. The fact that he visited us
     b. ? The fact of his visit to us

(3.89) a. The extent to which Fermat solved it
     b. *The extent of Fermat's solution to it

(3.90) a. The interval during which Fred was sallow
     b. ?The duration of Fred's sallowness

(3.91) a. The path along which the marble rolled
     b. ??The path of the marble's roll

I am not sure exactly how to explain these deviations, which definitely constitute a problem for the rule of *Nominalization* mentioned in (3.77b). I will leave this problem for future research.

Point 2. The rule of *Beheading* has abundant motivation, independently of the way nominalizations are analysed.[109] Thus note that in the sentences in (3.92), the forms of *I* all derive from the fuller NP *my car*, where *car* is the head noun that is undergoing *Beheading*.

(3.92) a. I'm parked on Elm Street.[110]
     b. Some nut hit me in the right rear fender.
     c. I'm idling a little fast.
     d. Can you put me up on the rack for a minute?

---

[108] Some speakers may accept (3.87a) with *way*, but only if *way* has the reading of *respect* or *regard*, not if it means *manner*, which is the sense on which I have starred it.

[109] It is the subject of an important study by Ann Borkin (1971), where fascinating questions like the following are discussed. Since *Dylan Thomas's poetry* ⇒ *Dylan Thomas*, via *Beheading* (cf. (i)),

(i) I like to read Dylan Thomas.

why do we not find (ii)?

(ii) ?*Dylan Thomas likes to read himself.

Apparently, different rules treat differently NPs which are underlyingly distinct but come to be identical because of *Beheading*. The badness of ?*(ii) shows that *Reflexivization* uses a pretty choosy definition of identity, and the fact that (iii) is so much better than (ii) shows that *Equi* is fairly devil-may-care.

(iii) Dylan Thomas likes $\left\{\begin{array}{l}\text{Dylan Thomas} \\ \text{?_____}\end{array}\right\}$ to be read on talk shows.

Borkin shows conclusively, I think, that it is impossible to maintain the strong position on identity taken by Ross (1967, ch. 3, footnote 19), which is used in Chomsky (1970: footnote 11) as a basis for an argument against the analysis of the quotation in (3.76) above. While it is still too early to be able to say with any confidence what theory of identity will emerge as a viable one, we must, I think, abandon the position that was taken in Ross (1967) to the effect that the only available notion of identity is underlying identity.

[110] These sentences are due to Jorge Hankamer.

Also, as Roger Higgins has pointed out to me, (3.93a) must derive from (3.93b) via beheading of the head noun *water*.

(3.93) a. The kettle is boiling.
 b. The water in the kettle is boiling.

And Postal (1974) cites a number of additional cases of this rule, a few of which appear in (3.94).

(3.94) a. IBM (stock) split 2-for-1.
 b. (The people in) Boston must be nervous about 1976.
 c. (The price of) lettuce dropped to $1.19.

Therefore, though the phenomenon of beheading, which I suspect will prove to be fantastically pervasive in natural languages, must still be the object of much detailed research in the future, it seems clear to me that it exists, and that part of the analysis in (3.77) is a free ride.

Point 3. Where a nominal group is of doubtful acceptability, the beheaded version of that group will be of equal (or greater) doubtfulness, *on the reading that the fuller group paraphrases*. Thus note that just as (3.88b) is weak—to be sure, for reasons I do not understand—so is (3.95), in which the derived nominal *his visit to us* must have a factive interpretation.

(3.95) ?His visit to us is beyond question.

Very often, however, the beheaded version, in the sense of the fuller version, will be significantly worse than this fuller version. Thus compare (3.96a–c) with (3.89b), (3.90b), and (3.91b), respectively.

(3.96) a. **Fermat's solution to it exceeded Pascal's.
 b. ?*Fred's sallowness was interminable.
 c. *The marble's roll went through the woods.

I do not know the reasons for this slump in grammaticality, but it feels very much like that commented on in connection with (3.88)–(3.91) above.

To return to the SKA of (3.48), which was the reason for contrasting lexicalism and the *Beheading* analysis of (3.77), it seems to me that there is no evidence from semantic kinkiness which would unambiguously support either of these proposals. The problems of distinguishing the good nominal groups of (3.79) from the bad ones of (3.87) are shared by both analyses, and for each of the questions above for the *Beheading* analysis (Questions 1–5), there is a cognate question in lexicalism, though sometimes these cognate questions become questions of semantics. On balance, then, the SKA cannot be used to reject a transformationalist account of nominalization in favor of a lexicalist account.

3.5.2.3 The internal structure argument. Given the discussion in §2.17 above, very little further need be said about this argument. The elements of (1.2) "have the internal structure of NPs" to greater or lesser degrees, not all or none. In particular, such "mixed" examples as (2.62), (2.64), and (2.66), which are nouny by virtue of their determiners, but sentency by virtue of having aspectual elements or having undergone transformations, would seem to pose serious problems for any discrete theory of complements.[111]

---

[111] There is one possible approach to such mixed examples which might allow the retention of a discrete analysis. Namely, one might look for arguments for deriving such sentences as (i) from something like (ii), and (iii) from (iv).

 (i) This calling people up at night has to stop. *(continues)*

In connection with the ISA, Wasow and Roeper discuss the difference in interpretation between (3.97a) and (3.97b) (cf. Wasow and Roeper 1971).

(3.97) a. I abhor singing.
b. I abhor singing operas.

They point out that in (3.97b), the subject can only be *I*, while in (3.97a), it can be anyone, and suggest that this difference in interpretation follows from a lexicalist analysis of these two complement types. The first sentence they treat as an instantiation of the phrase structure generated by the two rules of (3.98),

(3.98) a. NP → Specifier N

b. Specifier → $\begin{Bmatrix} \text{Article} \\ \text{NP} \end{Bmatrix}$

an instantiation in which the article has a null realization. That is, along the general lines of lexicalism, the complement in (3.97a), which I have referred to above as an action nominal, would not be analyzed as having derived from a sentence, while the complement of (3.97b) would derive from a *Poss Ing* complement via *Equi* or its equivalent.

The explanation that they propose is that the difference in interpretation follows from the fact that sentences must always have subjects in deep structure, and can only appear without them in surface structure by virtue of a deletion which removes them. For lexicalism, what corresponds to the subject of derived nominals is the NP of (3.98b), and since this NP is not an obligatory component of derived nominals (of which, for them, action nominals are a sub-type), all derived nominals can have an unspecified subject interpretation whenever they appear with an article as a Specifier instead of an NP.

The central hypothesis of this paper is their principle (A) (1971: 5), which I reproduce in (3.99).

(3.99)   Those gerunds without obligatory control are just those gerunds with the internal structure of NPs.

That is, as is made clear elsewhere in their paper, Wasow and Roeper claim that gerunds with the internal structure of NPs are action nominals, which derive from the rules of (3.98),

---

(ii)   This $\begin{Bmatrix} \text{?state of affairs of} \\ \text{tradition of} \\ \text{practice of} \end{Bmatrix}$ calling people up at night has got to stop.

(iii)   More looking at cases is necessary.
(iv)   More instances of looking at cases are necessary.

Under such an analysis, a rule akin to *Beheading* would be used to delete the head nouns of (ii) and (iv), if it could be established that they had to have been there.

One fact which might support such an analysis, under which, in effect, the determiners which precede the *-ing*-forms have nothing to do with them in underlying structure, but are rather remnants of NPs whose heads were such nouns as *practice, state, instance*, etc., is the dubious existence of such sentences as (v)–(vii).

(v)   ?This nobody being at home is a drag.
(vi)   ??That everybody talking all at once really makes me sick.
(vii)   ?*The him thinking that he had all the answers really got to us, after a while.

If it is possible for NPs to intervene between the determiner and the *-ing*-form, then it would seem that we may be dealing with an *Acc Ing* complement in apposition to something. And this something might be a garden-variety NP whose head has been deleted.

If such sources as (ii) and (iv) can be justified, one mystery will remain: why is it that the determiners should form the fairly neat squish that was shown above in (2.70)? That is, assuming that it is right to analyze such determiners as *this* in (i) as deriving from the determiner on a deleted noun, why is it that only certain of these determiners allow the noun to delete? And that a subset of those determiners should be the class that appears before action nominals?

always must have an unspecified subject interpretation—these are, in their terms, gerunds "without obligatory control."

However, there are clear counterexamples to (A): verbs which take action nominals, and which delete the subjects of these complements only by *Equi*. Consider the sentences in (3.100).

(3.100) a. The tedious recataloguing of the manuscripts all by myself took me all day.
      b. Hans took up the painstaking reshelving of books about himself just after he moved.
      c. I'm going to have to begin with a thorough reassessing of my own contracts.

In the face of (3.100), I do not see how Wasow and Roeper's principle (A) can be maintained, and without it, the discrete, lexicalist analysis of the complements of (3.97) is also without support.[112]

Nonetheless, Wasow and Roeper's observations about (3.97) are correct, and require explanation. I suspect that the explanation may be part of the more general phenomenon of argumentlessness, which was discussed in Ross (1972a). If we compare verbs, adjectives and nouns with respect to the question of whether various objects are required, we find many pairs like those in (3.101).

(3.101) a. That $\left\{ \begin{array}{l} \text{benefited * (me)} \\ \text{was beneficial (to me)} \end{array} \right\}$.

      b. That $\left\{ \begin{array}{l} \text{surprised * (me)} \\ \text{was surprising (to me)} \end{array} \right\}$.

      c. That $\left\{ \begin{array}{l} \text{appealed * (to me)} \\ \text{was beneficial (to me)} \end{array} \right\}$.

Similarly, when we compare verbs and related nouns, we often find that the former category requires objects where the latter does not. Cf. (3.102).

(3.102) a. I $\left\{ \begin{array}{l} \text{strongly prefer *(chess to checkers)} \\ \text{have a strong preference (for chess over checkers)} \end{array} \right\}$.

      b. Bill tried to swim, but she wouldn't attempt *(it).
      c. Bill tried to swim, but the attempt (at it) failed.

Thus, as words become nounier, fewer and fewer of their complements are required. This may be the same phenomenon as the fact that Wasow and Roeper call attention to—the fact that while less nouny complements, like *Poss Ing* complements, can only lose their subjects by deletion under identity, complements of at least the nouniness of action nominals can lose theirs by a free deletion rule. I will not pursue this matter further here, however.

To conclude, then, this review of Chomsky's third argument, it would seem that it cannot be used as evidence to support lexicalism over transformationalism any more than the first two arguments of (3.48) can.

3.5.3. *The adverb squish*

There is one more matter raised in Chomsky (1970) which can be discussed fruitfully in connection with the general issue of nouniness. This is the contrast between (3.103a) and (3.103b) (Chomsky's (15) and (16)).

---

[112] If Wasow and Roeper are correct in their claim that principle (A) follows from lexicalist assumptions, then (3.100) would have to be taken as being incompatible with lexicalism, not as merely not supporting it.

    However, I do not see how lexicalism would exclude in principle a language which allowed the unspecified subjects of sentences to delete freely, but manifested no such deletions in NPs. Therefore, (3.100) should be taken merely as counterevidence to principle (A).

(3.103) a. his criticizing the book before he read it (because of its failure to go deeply into the matter, etc.)
   b. *his criticism of the book before he read it (because of its failure to go deeply into the matter, etc.)

Chomsky's claim is that (3.103b) is out because "true verb phrase adjuncts such as *before*-clauses and *because*-clauses will not appear as noun complements in base noun phrases" (Chomsky 1970: 193).[113]

In fact, however, when we examine other types of adverbs as modifiers of derived nominals, we find that there are a range of intermediate grammaticalities for such constructions. Cf. (3.104).

(3.104) a. *His criticism of the book, the train having left
   b. *His criticism of the book, since he was hungry
   c. ?*His criticism of the book before he read it[114]
   d. ?His criticism of the book before reading it
   e. ?His criticism of the book before its publication
   f. His criticism of the book before 1945

And when we examine the results of modifying the other types of complements in (1.2) by adverbs of the sort shown in (3.104), we find the squish shown in (3.105).

(3.105) *The Adverb Squish*

Adverbial Modifier \ Modifiee	Nominative absolute: (*his money*) (*being*) *gone*)	*unless, since, (al)though*	*before, after, because, when, if, while*	P conj + V*ing* O: *instead of, upon, while, when, in*	P + Der. Nom.: *dur-ing, before, after, upon, since, due to*	P + NP
that S	?	OK	OK	OK	OK	OK
for NP *to* V	?	?	OK	OK	OK	OK
Q	?	?	OK	OK	OK	OK
Acc Ing	??	?	OK	OK	OK	OK
Poss Ing	??	?	OK	OK	OK	OK
Act. Nom.	?*	??	?	?	?	OK
Der. Nom.	*	*	??	?	?	OK
N(*weather*)[115]	*	*	?		OK	OK

(3.106)   (3.107)   (3.108)   (3.109)   (3.110)   (3.111)

---

[113] In a footnote to the sentences in (3.103), Chomsky observes that NPs like *his criticism of the book for its failure* ... are grammatical, commenting "Presumably, *for*-phrases of this sort are part of the complements for verbs and nouns." Since Chomsky gives no other criterion for what is a verb-phrase adjunct and what is a noun-phrase adjunct than such ungrammaticalities as (3.103b), his treatment here suffers from circularity.

[114] The prefix on this example represents my assessment of its grammaticality. I do not find it as far out as Chomsky does.

[115] I have included in (3.105) a row for such superficially underived nouns as *weather, climate, storm, fog*, etc. which can appear with some adverbs—cf. (i).

(i)   the weather in March, the storm after supper, the fog after midnight

The judgements on which this matrix is based can be found in (3.106)–(3.111) below, where the numbers at the bottom of each column of (3.105) correspond to the examples which give the grammaticalities in the column in question.

(3.106) a. ?I realize that Mary's money ??(being) gone, Caesar will have to pay.
b. ?For Caesar to have to pay, Mary's money ?*(being) gone, is likely.
c. ?I don't know [where Joe will live, the storm having flattened his house].
d. ??Him living in a hotel, apartments being hard to find, is a possibility.
e. ?His having to get up at 6:45, Jennifer sleeping another hour, was a cause of some resentment.
f. ?*His skillful shelling of the walnuts, the Shellomatic being broken, was a wonder to behold.
g. *His refusal of help, the memories still being too fresh, is understandable.
h. *[The fog, the rain having stopped,] drifted in.[116]

(3.107) a. I realize that he doesn't like me, since he thinks 2.13%/day is usurious.
b. ?For him to order lobster, although it's bad for him, would surprise me.
c. ?Where he's staying, since it's 10:30 already, is a riddle.
d. ?Him ordering lobster, though none was safe to eat, was daring.
e. ?His wolfing it down, though I warned him not to, may lead to an ache in his tum-tum.
f. ??His immediate calling of the doctor, unless you think a bicarb would be better, is imperative.
g. *His drive to the hospital, though he was in pain, was incredible.
h. *[A late storm, though it's humid,] would be welcome.

(3.108) a. That he burned the contract before he read it was improper.
b. For him to burn the contract before he read it was improper.
c. How long he kept the ashes after he did it is unknown.
d. Him being willing to pay Xerox costs when we get back is encouraging.
e. His having been arrested while he was strolling in the park is frightening.
f. ?His singing of sea chanteys while he was lighting the pipes was uncalled for.
g. ??His destruction of the fortune cookie before he read the fortune is to be regretted.[117]
h. ?[The storm after you left] was terrifying.

(3.109) a. That he sat down instead of running is unfortunate.
b. For him to sit down while the rhino was charging was ill-considered.
c. How long he was unconscious before coming to hasn't been determined.
d. Him muttering like that when being sewed up is understandable,
e. Your not talking about the accident while visiting him was tactful.
f. ?His lawyer's handling of the civil suit while remaining a member of the Rhin. Lover's Association was masterful.

---

[116] Note that this sentence is fine if the absolute construction is taken to modify the whole sentence, but it is impossible as a modifier of *fog*. The same remarks apply in all cases pertaining to (3.105).

[117] This sentence, for me, is far superior to Chomsky's in (3.103b), especially when *criticism* has the reading not of an event, but of something that has been written. I suspect that this difference is a systematic one, but I do not agree with Chomsky (op.cit.: 194) that this shows that some of the sentences underlying the squish in (3.105) are directly generated, while others are only derivatively generated. What it would indicate to me is that (3.105) should be refined, with two rows appearing in place of the derived nominal row of (3.105).

g. ?His destruction of the fortune cookie before reading the fortune is to be regretted.

h. [118]

(3.110) a. That she wrote it during Bill's interrogation is a proof of her serenity.

b. For them to arrest you upon the king's arrival would cause a scandal.

c. I don't know how they snuck out after the attack.

d. Ted buying popcorn during Sarah's coronation disturbed the Duchess.

e. Fred's having written all he knew after his internment opened my eyes.

f. ?Famoso's accurate rendering of the stirring "O Caterwaulia!" after his inauguration won him the hearts and souls of the Caterwaulians.

g. ?Dirty Dick's betrayal of his comrades before their examination of the manuscripts touched off a wave of riots in Canterbury.

h. The weather during the performance was seasonally rotten.

(3.111) a. That he left after 6 a.m. is too bad.

b. For him to leave before Ted was predictable.

c. Why he stayed until breakfast is a mystery.

d. Sandy getting sick at night was a coincidence.

e. Arthur's having found a tarantula during the Late Show was a coincidence.

f. Myla's discovering of a poisoned orange in the morning was a coincidence.

g. Biff's obvious insanity over the holidays must have had a natural cause.

h. The weather after 6 p.m. was even rottener.

In this particular squish, it would appear that the feature $[\alpha \text{ S}]$ is a factor not only vertically, as in other cases discussed above, but also horizontally. While I cannot explain why the first three columns of (3.105) are ordered as they are, it would seem that as we proceed from left to right in the last four columns, the modifiers become progressively less sentential. The generalization here seems to be along the lines of that in (3.112).[119]

(3.112)   If a complement C, of sententiality α, is modified by an adverbial A, of sententiality β, $\alpha \geq \beta$.

In other words, complements must be at least as sentential as their modifiers.

Why the inequality sign should point the way it does in (3.112), instead of the other way, is of course a mystery, as is the reason for there being any connection whatsoever between the sententialities of complement and modifier, instead of, say, between that of the subject of the complement and that of the object, or between that of the subject and that of the adverbial modifier, or any number of other conceivable linkages.

3.5.4. Summary

To summarize the above observations on lexicalism, it does not appear that this approach to nominalizations provides an explanation for the factual observations which Chomsky uses as a point of departure for this theory, where these observations are accurate. In particular, since the predicate "has the internal structure of an NP" seems to be quantifiable, and not discrete, it is at present unclear how a discrete theory like lexicalism can be modified to give a squishy

---

[118] The cell in (3.105) corresponding to this sentence is (☒) because the relevant examples, which would be strings such as (i),

(i) **[The fog while being humid] cleared.

are bad for other reasons.

[119] My thinking in this area has been greatly influenced by Edwin Williams.

output. Furthermore, lexicalism seems to provide no explanation for why *Equi* and *PP Shift* do work inside derived nominals, while *Object Deletion* and *Dative* do not. In addition, lexicalism gives the incorrect impression that there is a discrete difference between derived nominals and all other kinds of complements, whereas in fact these differences form an integral part of the overlapping structure of differences which is visible in (2.111). And finally, given the fact that there is nothing to be gained by trying to remove from the syntax all processes that are partially productive, or kinky in other ways, only to deposit these processes in the semantics, there seems to be no reason to prefer a lexicalist treatment of nominalization to a transformationalist one.

4. CONCLUSION

Where do we go from here? And where have we come from? To take up the second of these questions first, and to answer it for myself, the facts I have gathered in §2 all arose from my fascination with offhand remarks of Zellig Harris in classes at the University of Pennsylvania in 1962 to the effect that some nominalized versions of a sentence were more noun-like than others. As the facts which bore out Harris' observation began to come to my attention over the years,[120] I struggled to incorporate them within the discrete framework of traditional generative grammar, but with dwindling success, as the complexity of the facts and of their interactions increased.

Finally, I came to the conclusion, possibly a wrong-headed one, that any discrete treatment of data like those in §2 above, or those in Ross (1972a) or Ross (1973), would impose a distortion upon these data. I began to think within a non-discrete framework.

To return to the first of the two questions above, my answer is that the great benefit which linguistic theory has derived and continues to derive from the rigor that Chomsky's formal, algorithmic, theory of generative grammar introduced to syntax must somehow be preserved, even if syntax changes to become a calculus of quasi-continuously varying parameters, like the [αS] proposed above.

One of the major strengths of Chomsky's conception of a language as a set of structures, and of a grammar as a recursive device that enumerated this set, was that it became as important to study what the grammar did not generate—the starred structures—as to study what it did generate. To be sure, previous syntacticians would use expressions like "one does not say" or "there are no attested occurrences of expressions like," and so on, but in Chomsky's conception, the focus changed. What we might now call "shooting for the stars" has become so prevalent that I would guess that a sizeable majority of the examples cited in transformational studies are ungrammatical sentences, not grammatical ones.

This star-shooting went hand in hand with a focus upon the *goodness of fit* between theory and data. One was led more directly to compare the stars that the grammar assigned with those that speakers assigned. If the grammar assigned stars to strings which speakers did not star, the grammar *undergenerated*; if the grammar assigned too few stars, it *overgenerated*.

To me, it seems appropriate to re-emphasize now the point that this concern with goodness of fit that characterizes generative grammar is a valuable and hard-won methodological advance, one that must not be lost sight of in the effort to accommodate squishy facts. That is,

[120] Many of the observations that I have made in this paper have also been made independently by other scholars. One striking example is to be found in Kuno (1972), where a number of processes, overlapping only in part with those in §2, are shown to parallel each other by virtue of the nouniness of the complements involved (cf. Kuno (op. cit.), exs. (1.45)–(1.50). Another example is Williams (1971), in which a number of the processes that §2 treats non-discretely are analyzed in terms of a discrete framework.

we must not allow ourselves to obscure the fact that some proposed squishy analysis fits the data badly by using fuzziness as a rug to sweep the bad fit under. In a way, I regard the ill-behaved cells in the matrices I have proposed above as one of the most important parts of the theory I have outlined. Vague and half-formed though it is, in its present form, if it is at least exact enough to produce clearly visible cases of bad fits, the concern for overgeneration and undergeneration of analyses has not been lost.

As time goes on, it will hopefully be possible to arrive at better approximations to the bunching function of (3.2), to propose exact constraints on the decay functions discussed in §3.3, to improve the equation for squishy primacy in (3.25), to convert the inequality in (3.112) to a function, and so on. All of these theoretical tightenings will represent moves towards greater rigor; and will doubtlessly generate more and more instances of ill-behavior.[121]

What kind of a theory of non-discrete grammar will emerge is at present entirely unclear to me. The nouniness squish is the first case I have encountered of what Quirk calls "a serial relationship"—the kind of structure shown in (4.1a) (cf. Quirk 1965). All the other phenomena I have investigated seemed more or less compatible with the simpler type of structure shown in (4.1b).

(4.1)   (a) *Serial relationship*

OK	*	*	*	*	OK	OK	OK	OK
OK	OK	*	*	*	*	OK	OK	OK
OK	OK	OK	*	*	*	OK	OK	OK
OK	OK	OK	OK	*	*	*	*	OK

(b) *Simple squish*

OK	*	*	*	*
OK	OK	*	*	*
OK	OK	OK	*	*
OK	*	OK	OK	*

What I do not know at present is whether other conditioning factors can be found which determine a phenomenon will produce a serial relationship or a simple squish.

I hope that when the outlines of a theory of non-discrete grammar have become clearer than they now are, this theory will prove to be a useful tool in studying such recalcitrant areas as (degrees of) idiomaticity and metaphor, and the types of constructions that Bolinger calls *blends*. Whether this hope will be realized, however, lies in a squishy future.

ACKNOWLEDGEMENTS

My conscious investigations of squishy phenomena began in 1971 while I was associated with the Language Research Foundation. They were supported by a grant from the National Science Foundation (Grant Number GS-3202). Subsequently, this work was supported in

---

[121] In Lakoff (1973), a number of formal proposals are made, with an eye to characterizing more precisely the type of fuzzy calculus that seems to be necessary in semantax and logic.

part by a grant from the National Institute of Mental Health (Grant Number 5 PO1 MH 13390–07). I wish to express my appreciation for the support from both of these sources.

My thoughts on nouniness have been shaped and sharpened and pruned of a lot of dead wood and blind alleys, by a number of audiences who have heard me lecture on this topic—the first being at Queens College, of the State University of New York, on March 13, 1972. I wish to thank them, and also the classes to which I have presented versions of a theory of non-discrete grammar—classes at MIT, at the Linguistic Institute at the University of North Carolina, at Brown University, and at the State University of New York at Buffalo.

I am afraid that I am bound to forget some of the many colleagues and friends who have blasted me with counterexamples, and cheered me with pro-examples. I apologize for forgetting, but be thanked anyway. But to the following, whose names I do remember, many thanks:

Don Albury, Lloyd Anderson, Noam Chomsky, Bruce Fraser, Ken Hale, Edward Klima, Susumu Kuno, George Lakoff, Barbara Hall Partee, David Perlmutter, Paul Postal, Robert Sacks, Carlota Smith, Edwin Williams, and Arnold Zwicky.

A special kind of thanks goes to Dwight Bolinger, who has been saying the kind of things I say in this paper for a lot longer than I have been able to hear them.

And to Osamu Fujimura, who has shown previously unknown types of patience and forbearance while waiting for this paper to emerge, and to Jim McCawley, ditto, doomo arigatoo gozaimasu.

And finally, to my wife Elke-Edda, whose exasperation with my obtuseness and whose own proposals have given the thoughts in §3.2 a lot of their present shape, and who has helped me to grow in many other ways, I say thanks, you mistbeuh.

REFERENCES

Bach, E. (1971). 'Questions'. *Linguistic Inquiry* 2(2): 153–6.

Borkin, A. (1971). 'Coreference and beheaded NPs'. Paper presented at the 46th Annual Meeting of the Linguistic Society of America, St Louis, Missouri.

Chomsky, N. (1970). 'Remarks on nominalization'. In R. A. Jacobs and P. S. Rosenbaum (eds.), *Readings in English Transformational Grammar*. Waltham, Mass.: Ginn, 184–221.

——(1972). 'Some empirical issues in the theory of transformational grammar'. In P. S. Peters (ed.), *The Goals of Linguistic Theory*. Englewood Cliffs, NJ: Prentice-Hall, 63–131.

Elliott, D., S. Legum, and S. A. Thompson (1969). 'Syntactic variation as linguistic data'. In R. Binnick, A. Davison, G. Green, J. Morgan et al. (eds.), *Papers from the Fifth Regional Meeting of the Chicago Linguistic Society*, 52–9.

Emonds, J. E. (1970). 'Root and structure-preserving transformations'. Ph.D. dissertation, Massachusetts Institute of Technology.

Fraser, J. B. (1970). 'Idioms within a transformational grammar'. *Foundations of Language* 6(1): 22–42.

Higgins, R. (1973). 'On J. Emonds' analysis of Extraposition'. In J. Kimball (ed.), *Syntax and Semantics*, vol. ii. New York: Seminar Press.

Horn, L. R. (1972). 'On the semantic properties of logical operators in English'. Ph.D. dissertation, University of California, Los Angeles.

Keenan, E., and B. Comrie (1972). 'NP accessibility and universal grammar'. Unpublished paper, King's College (Cambridge) Research Centre.

Kiparsky, P., and C. Kiparsky (1970). 'Fact'. In M. Bierwisch and K.-E. Heidolph, *Progress in Linguistics*. The Hague: Mouton.

Lakoff, G. (1969). 'On derivational constraints'. In R. Binnick, A. Davison, G. Green, J. Morgan et al. (eds.), *Papers from the Fifth Regional Meeting of the Chicago Linguistic Society*, 117–39.

——(1970). 'Global rules'. *Language* 46: 627–39.

Lakoff, G. (1973). 'Fuzzy grammar and the performance/competence terminology game'. In C. Corum et al. (eds.), *Papers from the Ninth Regional Meeting of the Chicago Linguistic Society*.

Langacker, R. (1969). 'Pronominalization and the chain of command'. In D. Reibel and S. Schane (eds.), *Modern Studies in English*. Englewood Cliffs, NJ: Prentice-Hall, 160–86.

Lasnik, H. (1972). 'Analyses of negation in English'. Ph.D. dissertation, Massachusetts Institute of Technology.

Lees, R. (1960). *The Grammar of English Nominalizations*. Bloomington, Indiana: Indiana University Research Center in Anthropology, Folklore, and Linguistics.

Luria, A. R. (1969). *The Mind of a Mnemonist*. New York: Avon Books.

McCawley, J. D. (1970). 'English as a VSO language'. *Language* 46: 286–99.

Miller, G. (1956). 'The magical number seven, plus or minus two'. *Psychological Review* 63: 81–97.

Morgan, J. (1972). 'Verb agreement as a rule of English'. In P. M. Peranteau, J. N. Levi, and G. C. Phares (eds.), *Papers from the Eighth Regional Meeting of the Chicago Linguistic Society*, 278–86.

Postal, P. M. (1970). 'On coreferential complement subject deletion'. *Linguistic Inquiry* 1(4): 439–500.

——(1971). *Crossover Phenomena: A Study in the Grammar of Coreference*. New York: Holt, Rinehart, & Winston.

——(1974). *On Raising*. Cambridge, Mass.: MIT Press.

Quirk, R. (1965). 'Descriptive statement and serial relationship'. *Language* 41: 205–17.

Reps, P. (n.d.) *Zen Flesh, Zen Bones*. Garden City, NY: Anchor Books.

Rosenbaum, P. S. (1971). *The Grammar of English Predicate Complement Constructions*. Cambridge, Mass.: MIT Press.

Ross, J. R. (1967). 'Constraints on variables in syntax'. Ph.D. dissertation, Massachusetts Institute of Technology.

——(1969). 'Guess who?' In R. Binnick, A. Davison, G. Green, J. Morgan et al. (eds.), *Papers from the Fifth Regional Meeting of the Chicago Linguistic Society*, 252–86.

——(1972a). 'Endstation Hauptwort: the category squish'. In P. M. Peranteau, J. N. Levi, and G. C. Phares (eds.), *Papers from the Eighth Regional Meeting of the Chicago Linguistic Society*, 316–28.

——(1972b). 'Act'. In D. Davidson and G. Harman (eds.), *Semantics of Natural Languages*. Dordrecht: Reidel, 70–126.

——(1973). 'A fake NP squish'. In C.-J. N. Bailey and R. Shuy (eds.), *New Ways of Analyzing Variation in English*. Washington, DC: Georgetown University Press.

——(MS a). 'Primacy'.

——(MS b). 'Treetops'.

——(MS c). 'Variable strength'.

——(MS d). 'Sloppier and sloppier: a hierarchy of linguistically possible open sentences'.

——(MS e). 'Niching'.

Wasow, T., and T. Roeper (1971). 'On the subject of gerunds'. Unpublished paper, Massachusetts Institute of Technology.

Williams, E. (1971). 'Small clauses in English'. Unpublished paper, Massachusetts Institute of Technology.

23

The Coordination–Subordination Gradient

RANDOLPH QUIRK, SIDNEY GREENBAUM, GEOFFREY LEECH, AND JAN SVARTVIK

Syntactic Features of Coordinators

13.6

In 13.3 we showed how the same semantic linking function could be performed not only by coordinators, but by subordinators and conjuncts:

He tried hard, *but* he failed.
He tried hard, *although* he failed.
He tried hard, *yet* he failed.

Since all three of these word classes can in a general sense be termed LINKERS, it is important to understand the syntactic basis of the distinctions between them, and at the same time to appreciate that these distinctions are gradient rather than clear-cut.

We shall therefore examine six features which apply to the central coordinators, *and* and *or*. For each feature, we note whether it is applicable not only to *and* and *or*, but also to items which resemble them. At this stage we restrict ourselves mainly to central coordinators as CLAUSE LINKERS.

(a) CLAUSE COORDINATORS ARE RESTRICTED TO CLAUSE-INITIAL POSITION

13.7

And, or, and *but* are restricted to initial position in the clause:

John plays the guitar, *and* his sister plays the piano.
*John plays the guitar; his sister *and* plays the piano.

This is generally true of both coordinators and subordinators, but it is not true of most conjuncts:

John plays the guitar; his sister, *moreover*, plays the piano.

---

* From Randolph Quirk, Sidney Greenbaum, Geoffrey Leech, and Jan Svartvik, *A Comprehensive Grammar of the English Language* (London and New York: Longman, 1985), sections 13.6–13.19, pp. 921–8. © 1985 Longman Group Limited. Reprinted by permission of Pearson Education Limited.

Note [a] There are two or three *subordinators* which are exceptional in that they can occur noninitially:
Though he is poor, he is happy.   Poor *though* he is, he is happy.
[b] In colloquial Australian English *but* can occur in noninitial position; this indicates that in this variety, it resembles conjuncts.

(b) COORDINATED CLAUSES ARE SEQUENTIALLY FIXED

13.8

Clauses beginning with *and*, *or*, and *but* are sequentially fixed in relation to the previous clause, and therefore cannot be transposed without producing unacceptable sentences, or at least changing the relationship between the clauses:

They are living in England, *or* they are spending a vacation there.
*Or they are spending a vacation there, they are living in England.

This is true for coordinators and conjuncts, but not for most subordinators. Contrast the unacceptability of [1a], containing the conjunct *nevertheless*, with the acceptability of [1b], containing the subordinator *although*:

*Nevertheless John gave it away, Mary wanted it.   [1a]
Although Mary wanted it, John gave it away.   [1b]

In this respect, however, the subordinators *for* and *so that* resemble coordinators. Contrast:

*For he was unhappy, he asked to be transferred.
Because he was unhappy, he asked to be transferred.

and the resultative *so that* in [2] with the purposive *so that* in [3]:

*So that we arrived home late, the rush hour traffic delayed us.   [2]
So that he could buy a car, he sold his stamp collection.   [3]

13.9

Related to the fixed position of the coordinate clause is the fact that when clauses are linked by the coordinators *and*, *or*, and *but* (also by *for* and *so that*), a pronoun in the first clause cannot normally have cataphoric reference to a noun phrase in the second clause. For example, *she* in [1a] and [1b] does not corefer to *my mother*:

She felt ill, and *my mother* said nothing.   [1a]
She felt ill, but *my mother* said nothing.   [1b]

On the other hand, a pronoun can (but need not) have cataphoric reference when it occurs in an initial subordinate clause:

Although she felt ill, *my mother* said nothing.   [1c]

But the most common position for a subordinate clause is final, in which case a coreferring pronoun will be anaphoric:

My mother said nothing, although *she* felt ill.   [1d]

Again, as with cataphoric reference, the antecedent must be in the superordinate clause:

She said nothing, although *my mother* felt ill.   [2]

In [2], *She* cannot cataphorically refer to *my mother*.

Note
> There are both apparent and real exceptions to the rule that a pronoun cannot have cataphoric reference to an element in a following coordinate clause. Consider:
>
> > No one who met *her* on social occasions could imagine a harsh word passing *her* lips—but *Liz Pettigrew* was notorious for speaking her mind on matters of business. [3]
>
> The two occurrences of *her* in the first clause appear to corefer cataphorically to *Liz Pettigrew*; but this sentence would normally occur in a context in which Liz was already being discussed. These pronouns could then be explained as anaphorically coreferring to part of an earlier sentence. Exceptionally, however, a sentence such as [3] could occur without preceding anaphoric reference—e.g. at the beginning of a novel.

(c) COORDINATORS ARE NOT PRECEDED BY A CONJUNCTION

13.10

And and *or* do not allow another conjunction to precede them. This is also true for *but*, *for*, and *so that* (of which the latter two will be treated as subordinators; cf. 13.18f). On the other hand, subordinators as well as conjuncts can usually be preceded by conjunctions:

He was unhappy about it, *and yet* he did as he was told.

In [1] and [2] two subordinate clauses are linked by *and*, which precedes the second subordinator *because* and the second subordinator *so that* (with purposive meaning):

He asked to be transferred, *because* he was unhappy *and because* he saw no prospect of promotion.   [1]
She saved money *so that* she could buy a house, *and so that* her pension would be supplemented by a reasonable income after retirement.   [2]

In contrast, the conjunctions *but*, *for*, and resultative *so that* cannot be preceded by *and* in this way:

*He was unhappy about it, *and but* he did what he was told.
*He asked to be transferred, *for* he was unhappy *and for* he saw no possibility of promotion.
*We paid her immediately, *so (that)* she left contented *and so (that)* everyone was satisfied.

Note   A subordinate clause cannot normally be coordinated with a superordinate clause; but this is what appears to happen in the following case:

> She wouldn't do it—and (*all*) *because I didn't ask her in person.*

The explanation of this example, however, is that the coordinated construction in italics is an elliptical appended clause, the *because* clause being subordinated to this appended clause, rather than to the initial clause *She wouldn't do it.*

13.11

In initial position, some conjunct adverbs resemble coordinators in that they commonly occur with asyndetic coordination, and therefore provide a link similar to coordination:

I told her to go home, *yet* she refused to move. [cf: *but* she refused ...]

The rain fell, *so* we all went home. [cf: *and* we all . . .]
Tom doesn't drink, *neither* does he use bad language.
The car turned suddenly, *then* screeched to a halt.

The ease with which the coordinator is omitted in these cases suggests that not only the possibility of adding a coordinator, but the probability of its being omitted should be considered a factor in comparing the behaviour of linkers. One way of explaining the unexpected likelihood of asyndeton in such cases is to postulate an optional merger of the coordinator *and* with the adverb; e.g.: *and* + *yet* merge into *yet*; *and* + *so* merge as *so*. This is a more convincing analysis where, as in all the examples except *then* above, the adverb is immobile in initial position. Other adverbs which behave similarly are *nor* (cf. 13–18), *otherwise*, *neither*, *only* (as a conjunct), and *hence*.

(d) COORDINATORS CAN LINK CLAUSE CONSTITUENTS

13.12

And and *or* may link constituents smaller than a clause; for example, they may link predicates, thus in effect allowing ellipsis of a second or subsequent subject.

[I may see you tomorrow] *or* [I may phone later in the day].
I [may see you tomorrow] or ₐ [may phone later in the day].

Less frequently, this feature also applies to *but*:

The Polish athletes [have succeeded today], *but* ₐ [may not repeat their success tomorrow].

However, it does not apply to *for* and *so that*:

*He [did not want it], *for* ₐ [was obstinate].
*He [did not spend very much], *so that* ₐ [could afford a trip abroad].

Nor does it apply to other conjunctions or to most conjuncts. But this construction seems to be acceptable with the conjunct *yet* and (to a lesser extent, at least in informal spoken English) with the conjunct *so* and the time adverb *then* (meaning 'after that'):

They didn't like it, *yet* (they) said nothing.
They were tired, *so* (they) left early.
They went home, *then* (they) went straight to bed.

13.13

A subordinator, on the other hand, does not allow ellipsis of the subject even when its clause is linked by a coordinator:

*She didn't say anything about it *because* he was new and *because* looked unwell.   [1]

If the second subordinator of [1] is omitted, ellipsis is possible:

She didn't say anything about it *because* he was new and (he) looked unwell.   [1a]

This is allowed, being a regular case of coordination of predicates, whereas that of [1] is an ungrammatical type of ellipsis. For the same reason, ellipsis is possible preceding or following a conjunct (such as *nevertheless*) if the elided subject is itself preceded by a coordinator (Fig. 1).

$$\text{He went to bed early, but } \left\{ \begin{array}{l} \triangle\textit{nevertheless} \\ \textit{nevertheless}_\triangle \end{array} \right\} \text{ felt tired.}$$

FIG. I

(e) COORDINATORS CAN LINK SUBORDINATE CLAUSES

13.14

As well as linking two main clauses, as we saw in 13.10 [1] above, *and* and *or* can link subordinate clauses:

He asked to be transferred, *because* he was unhappy, (*because*) he saw no prospect of
  promotion, *and* (*because*) conditions were far better at the other office.   [1]
I wonder *whether* you should go and see her *or whether* it is better to write to her.   [2]

Usually, as in [1], the second and any subsequent subordinators may be omitted. Such linking is not possible for conjuncts or for the other conjunctions except *but*. *But*, however, is restricted to linking a maximum of two clauses (cf. 13.16):

She said *that* John would take them by car *but* (*that*) they might be late.   [3]

Even so, *but* can link only certain types of subordinate clauses:

(a) *That*-clauses as in [3] above; only with *that*-clauses can the second subordinator, the one
  following *but*, be omitted.
(b) Temporal adverbial clauses:

  I spoke to him *after* the conference was over, *but before* he started work.

(c) Clauses introduced by the same conjunctions, such as *in order that, so that*, and *because*,
  or by the same *wh*-words. In such cases the first part of the sentence has to be negative,
  so that it contrasts with the positive meaning of the part which follows *but*:

  She didn't see who MĔT the ambassador, *but* who took him awÀY.
  He didn't save in order to go to school, *but* in order to buy a car.

13.15

But cannot link most other subordinate clauses, because such clauses normally lie outside the scope of negation, and so cannot contrast with the negative implication of the first conjoin:

?They won't help you *if* you pay them, *but if* you promise to help them in return.
*They didn't stay *although* they were happy, *but although* they were bored.

An example with *if*-clauses, such as the one above, is marginally acceptable in a context which enables it to be interpreted as a reformulation of what someone has said or implied. Moreover, if the negation is outside the verb phrase, *but* can more easily link adjunct and subjunct clauses, including such *if*-clauses as:

It might have turned out all right, *not if* he had been more forceful *but if* he had been more
  tactful.

(f) COORDINATORS CAN LINK MORE THAN TWO CLAUSES

13.16

And and *or* can link more than two clauses, and the construction may then be called one of MULTIPLE COORDINATION. All but the final instance of these two conjunctions can be omitted. Thus:

> The battery may be disconnected, the connection may be loose, *or* the bulb may
> be faulty.   [1]

is interpreted as:

> The battery may be disconnected, *or* the connection may be loose, *or* the bulb may
> be faulty.   [2]

In this respect, *and* and *or* differ from subordinators and conjuncts. They differ even from *but*, since *but* semantically speaking can only link two conjoins at the same level. While it is possible (though unusual) to construct a sentence such as:

> John played football, Mary played tennis, *but* Alice stayed at home.   [3]

such a sentence is interpreted as if the first two clauses had been linked by *and*:

> John played football, *and* Mary played tennis, *but* Alice stayed at home.   [4]

An indefinite number of clauses can be linked by *and* or *or*. But there is another way in which more than two elements can be combined by coordination: one set of coordinate clauses may become the conjoin of a higher-level coordinate construction. This is indeed what happens in [4], where the coordination by *but* is at a higher level than the coordination by *and*. The constituent structure can be conveniently shown by bracketing: [[A] *and* [B]] *but* [C]. When two different coordinators occur, like this, in the same complex construction, structural ambiguities are liable to arise. The ambiguity can be demonstrated by different bracketings. For example, in the following sentences, [A], [B], and [C] represent three clauses:

> [A] I'll pay for the meal *and* [B] you pay for the taxi, *or* [C] perhaps I'll pay for both. [5]

The relationship between the clauses can be represented as follows:

> [[A] *and* [B]] *or* [C].

On the other hand, the sentence:

> [A] His parents live in New York *and* [B] he writes to them from time to time
> *or* [C] (he) phones them.   [6]

can be represented by a bracketing in which [B] and [C] make up a single conjoin of *and*:

> [A] *and* [[B] *or* [C]].

The contrast between [5] and [6] can be also represented by tree diagrams (Fig. 2).

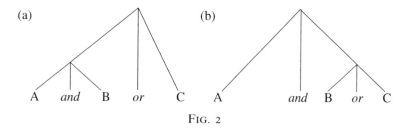

FIG. 2

Note   Punctuation is often used to make clear which is the major constituent structure boundary in mixed multiple coordinate constructions such as [5] and [6]. Thus, the potential ambiguity of the above two constructions can be eliminated by placing a comma before the main coordinator:

[[A] *and* [B]], *or* [C]; [A], *and* [[B] *or* [C]]].

A similar distinction can be made prosodically, by placing a tone-unit boundary before the major coordinator, and using additional forms of prosodic emphasis if required.

POLYSYNDETIC COORDINATION

13.17

When a construction with *and* or *or* has more than two conjoins, the ellipsis of all but the last coordinator is customary. Hence 13.16 [1] above, rather than [2], illustrates the usual pattern. In this way, the insertion of the coordinator between two conjoins signals that the last conjoin is about to be added. But where a coordinator occurs between each pair of conjoins, e.g. in [A] *and* [B] *and* [C], the construction is traditionally termed POLYSYNDETON:

The wind roared, *and* the lightning flashed, *and* the sky was suddenly as dark as night.   [7]

Polysyndetic coordination thus contrasts both with asyndetic coordination and with ordinary syndetic coordination. Since it transgresses the principle 'reduce where possible', poly-syndeton tends to be reserved for stylistically marked effects; for example, in [7] above it is used to emphasize a dramatic sequence of events and in 13.16 [2] it suggests (in contrast to [1] that the last of three possibilities may not be complete).

COORDINATION–SUBORDINATION GRADIENT

13.18

Fig. 3 displays the gradient from the central coordinators *and* and *or* to subordinators like *if* and *because*, with *but*, *for*, and *so that* on the gradient. The conjuncts *yet, so*, and *nor* are added to the Table, because, as we have seen, they in some respects resemble coordinators. The six features of *and* and *or* noted in 13.7–17 have provided six criteria used in constructing the matrix. If an item satisfies a criterion, this is indicated by a '+' in the relevant cell. If it fails to satisfy the criterion, '−' is entered. The combination '±' takes care of cases, explained in the previous discussion, where the item satisfies the criterion only under certain conditions. The six criteria to be applied to each item are:

(a) It is immobile in front of its clause.
(b) A clause beginning with it is sequentially fixed in relation to the previous clause, and hence cannot be moved to a position in front of that clause.

		(a)	(b)	(c)	(d)	(e)	(f)
coordinators	*and, or*	+	+	+	+	+	+
	but	+	+	+	+	±	+
conjuncts	*yet, so, nor*	+	+	×	+	−	−
	however, therefore	−	+	−	−	−	−
subordinators	*for, so that*	+	+	+	−	−	−
	if, because	+	±	+	−	−	−

FIG. 3   Coordination–conjunct-subordination gradient.

(c) It does not allow a conjunction to precede it.
(d) It links not only clauses, but predicates and other clause constituents.
(e) It can link subordinate clauses.
(f) It can link more than two clauses, and when it does so all but the final instance of the
    linking item can be omitted.

The cross '×' in column (c) records the fact, already noted in 13.11, that words like *yet*, *so*, and
nor, although they allow a preceding coordinator, also allow the omission of the coordinator
more readily than other conjuncts. In other words, they favour asyndeton, and to that extent
resemble coordinators with respect to column (c) as much as they resemble conjuncts.

Note   [a] When *because* introduces a disjunct clause, it resembles *for* and *so that*, in that the clause which it introduces
cannot be moved to initial position in the sentence:

> She PÁID for the book, *because* I SÁW her. ≠ *Because* I saw her, she paid for the book.

This explains the '±' in column (b).

[b] For many speakers, especially in AmE, *nor* cannot be preceded by a coordinator. In BrE, the combination
but nor is somewhat more acceptable than *and nor*.

13.19

Although Fig. 3 demonstrates the absence of a clear divide between coordinators and other
linking items, we can justify the traditional inclusion of *but* among the coordinators and the
exclusion of *for* and *so that* or *yet* and *so* by pointing to two facts which distinguish *but* from
these words: (i) it behaves like a coordinator with respect to subject ellipsis (see criterion (d)
above), and (ii) it resembles coordinators in its ability to link two clauses subordinate to the
same main clause (criterion (e)). The latter potentiality, in particular, reflects its status as a
coordinator, in that it links constituents at the same level. By the same criteria, *for* and *so that*
are shown to be subordinators rather than coordinators; and yet they are more coordinator-
like than the more typical subordinators *if* and *because*. Similarly, *yet*, *so*, *neither*, and *nor* are
best treated as conjuncts which are nevertheless more coordinator-like than more typical
conjuncts such as *however* and *therefore*. These words which share some of the distinguishing
features of coordinators may be called SEMI-COORDINATORS.

24

The Nature of Graded Judgments

CARSON T. SCHÜTZE

IS GRAMMATICALITY DICHOTOMOUS?

The following passage, from R. Lakoff (1977), probably reflects the beliefs of most newcomers to linguistics regarding the possible grammatical status of sentences: "It was tempting to believe that linguistic markers, like other animals, came in pairs, and it was therefore natural to assume that grammaticality was an either-or question.... This seemed to us the way things ought to be in a well-ordered universe, and we were still capable of believing, with our endearing childlike faith, that the linguistic universe was well-ordered" (p. 73). Despite Lakoff's apparent disillusionment, many linguists have wanted to maintain the principle that grammaticality is a dichotomous notion: "In general, then, if we find continuous-scale contrasts in the vicinity of what we are sure is language, we exclude them from language" (Hockett 1955, p. 17); "What with vigorous leadership and willing followership, the doctrine of discontinuity has found its fullest acceptance among American scholars" (Bolinger 1961, p. 2). On the other hand, it is clear that *judgments* of grammaticality come in more degrees, and in many cases these represent genuine multivalued phenomena (see below). Even in as early a work as *The Logical Structure of Linguistic Theory*, Chomsky asserts that "there is little doubt that speakers can fairly consistently order new utterances, never previously heard, with respect to their degree of 'belongingness' to the language" (p. 132). How are we to reconcile scalar judgments with an underlying dichotomy? Is it that the grammar assigns degrees of status to strings after all, and judgments simply reflect these? Or is it the judgment process itself that maps two-valued grammaticality to scalar acceptability by factoring in behavioral variables? Both views have been argued for in the literature, along with a third, intermediate position. Let us consider them in turn, before surveying the experimental literature to see to what extent each gains empirical support.

The best-known proponents of the view that grammaticality occurs on a continuum are Ross, Lakoff, and their followers in the late 1960s and early 1970s. Ross (e.g., 1972) used the term *squish* to refer to a continuum of grammaticality in connection with a particular construction (see Hindle and Sag 1975 for more on squishes). G. Lakoff (1973) summarizes the conclusions of this line of research as follows:

(i) Rules of grammar do not simply apply or fail to apply; rather they apply to a degree.

(ii) Grammatical elements are not simply members or nonmembers of grammatical categories; rather they are members to a degree.

(iii) Grammatical constructions are not simply islands or non-islands; rather they may be islands to a degree.

* Carson T. Schütze, 'The nature of graded judgments', section 3.3 of *The Empirical Base of Linguistics: Grammaticality Judgments and Linguistic Methodology* (Chicago and London: The University of Chicago Press, 1996), 62–81. © 1996 The University of Chicago. Reprinted by permission.

(iv) Grammatical constructions are not simply environments or non-environments for rules; rather they may be environments to a degree.

(v) Grammatical phenomena form hierarchies which are largely constant from speaker to speaker, and in many cases, from language to language.

(vi) Different speakers (and different languages) will have different acceptability thresholds along these hierarchies. (p. 271)

Lakoff continues, "We are saying that fuzzy grammar has a mental reality. The judgments that people make, which are matters of degree, are functions, perhaps algebraic functions, of unconscious mental judgments, which are also matters of degree" (p. 286). (See Levelt et al. (1977) for a somewhat different application of fuzzy grammar.) While I cannot review in detail the evidence that led to these conclusions, the key point is that the features of sentences that lead to graded judgments when varied do *not* have perceptually related causes, such as the taxing of short-term memory capacity, but rather are based on linguistic concepts such as clause, nominal, adverb, etc.

Let us take as an example some slightly later work by Watt (1975), who investigated whether grammaticality occurs in degrees. His domain of investigation was strained anaphora, as illustrated by the following set of related sentences:

(1) a. All those who follow Nixon say they approve of his annexing Mackenzie Territory as the fifty-fifth State.

  b. All followers of Nixon say they approve of his annexing Baffin Island as the fifty-sixth State.

  c. All Nixon-followers say they approve of his annexing The Bahamas as the fifty-seventh State.

  d. All Nixonites say they approve of his annexing British Honduras as the fifty-seventh State.

From a very detailed study of contrasts in sentences involving strained anaphora, Watt concludes that there are gradations among grammatical sentences that are *not* due to known performance factors, such as memory limits. Rather, these gradations can be accounted for in terms of factors that are already part of the grammar itself, such as linear order, contrastive stress, and specificity of reference. Watt argues that to try to account for such gradations by extragrammatical means would require needless duplication of the grammar in another part of the mind. This is the complement of Bever's argument, presented in section 2.2 [not included in this volume]. Bever attempts to avoid duplicating *within* the grammar features that are already required *outside* of it.

Despite their seemingly complementary lines of argumentation, it is clear that Bever and Watt disagree strongly in the conclusions that they draw. Bever (1975) is unequivocal in his position:

To give up the notion that a grammar defines a set of well-formed utterances is to give up a great deal. This is not to say that it is impossible in principle that grammars are squishy. Rather the possibility of studying precise properties of grammar and exact rules becomes much more difficult, as Ross himself points out. Thus, if we can maintain the concept of discrete grammaticality, we will be in a better position to pursue an understanding of grammatical universals. (p. 601)

Bever argues that, if at all possible, judgment continua should be derived from independently motivated theories of speech perception and production, while the grammar should be left discretely intact. He and Carroll lay out two alternative positions, then proceed to knock them down:

First, we may with Ross assume that non-discrete data directly imply non-discrete theories of grammar. This is not satisfactory: Non-discrete grammar offers no account of why the continua are the way they are. The correspondences between such grammatical analyses and the predictions of our behavioral account would have to be viewed as mere coincidence. And moreover, no distinction at all could be drawn between the squishy intuitions we have been concerned with here and the ineluctable intuitions upon which linguistic theory relies. A second option is to treat *all* acceptability phenomena as behavioral and non-structural (Clark and Haviland, 1974). This alternative also is inadequate: It cannot explain the categorical (un)acceptability of examples at either end of a continuum.

The third alternative is that examples with intermediate acceptability rest on an internal confusion by the informant between the application of a linguistic process to a category (e.g., "S") and to the typical behavioral reflex of that category (e.g., "perceptual clause"). This explanation explains a variety of acceptability facts as well as predicting hitherto unnoticed ones. However, it is important to specify what the general conditions are that will lead to an acceptability squish. . . .

An underlying theme of our proposal is that *all* grammatical properties are categorical and that all apparent departures from this have a general explanation in an interactionist framework—a totally discrete system of grammar interacting with behavioral processes. (Bever and Carroll 1981, pp. 232–3)

(An argument for the third alternative is presented in the study by Gerken and Bever discussed in section 1.3 [not included in this volume].) Thus, the claim that the grammar is discrete does not preclude the existence of graded phenomena like those studied by Watt, it merely asserts that part of their explanation must be extragrammatical; see Katz and Bever 1976 for a more detailed general argument.

Bever and Carroll's dismissals of positions other than their own are not entirely convincing. First, I do not see how one could ask for more of an account of "why the continua are the way they are" than Ross et al. provide, unless one already presupposes that the continua do not come from the grammar—language just *is* the way it is. Second, Clark and Haviland do not wish to exclude structural accounts of acceptability phenomena; rather, they argue that structural sources cannot be disentangled from the effects of processing. They claim that grammatical knowledge is not separable from comprehension and production processes, and that traditional grammatical constraints can be alternatively formulated as constraints on the comprehension process, but the latter can still contribute to structurally based judgments. There is no reason why they cannot get categorical judgments from their model. Furthermore, it is an open empirical question whether there really are large classes of sentences at either end of the scale within which people do not find any acceptability differences.

The discrete, dichotomous view of grammar has been defended from a somewhat different angle by Carr (1990):

It is as well to respond briefly to a frequently voiced but unworrying objection concerning grammaticality judgements as evidence. It is at times pointed out that there are cases of "asterisk fade", where intuitive responses supply us with a gradient scale of well-formed to ill-formed expressions. The objection is that the evidence here contains grey areas and that the ill-formed vs. well-formed distinction upon which [autonomous linguistics] rests is thus undermined.

A moment's reflection shows that, far from undermining the distinction, asterisk fade *presupposes* it: one cannot coherently speak of a cline from well-formed to ill-formed without a clear conception of what these are. Furthermore, once we have erected a set of theoretical proposals to deal with the ill-formed and well-formed cases, the theory itself will allow us to decide on the status of asterisk-faded expressions, as Chomsky has long since observed. (p. 57; emphasis in original)

I argue against Carr's second point in sections 2.2 and 2.3 [not included in this volume]; his first argument also does not stand up to scrutiny. One can certainly speak coherently of a continuum, e.g., from rich to poor, without there being any non-arbitrary dividing line between the two. To my mind, the most compelling reason to believe in grammars embodying small numbers of discrete choices comes from learnability. Given the standard poverty-of-the-stimulus argument, arriving at settings of continuous-valued parameters would seem to be impossibly hard for children.

Although Chomsky already assumed in *LSLT* that there were degrees of ungrammaticality, he went further in *Aspects* (pp. 148–53), proposing that the grammar predicts at least three levels or kinds of deviance, corresponding to the violation of selectional restrictions, subcategorization, and lexical category requirements. It is important to recognize that Chomsky's theory assumes the existence of absolute grammaticality. Sentences that violate no constraints of the grammar are assumed to be uniformly grammatical. If a sentence is less than absolutely grammatical, it must violate some constraint(s) of the grammar, and these con-straints come in varying degrees of importance. Thus there are no degrees of grammaticality, but there are degrees of ungrammaticality. (See Levelt 1974, vol. 3, and below for some alternative proposals.) In terms of string sets, then, we have a primary dichotomy of good versus bad, with no distinctions among the good sentences but graded distinctions among the bad. It is reasonable to ask whether there is any psychological evidence that this theoretical distinction reflects cognitive reality. Even though acceptability is affected by factors other than grammaticality, one might expect the good/bad dichotomy to show through them, if the other factors are relatively independent of grammaticality and ungrammaticality. I am not aware of any clear evidence of this sort. Ross (1979, reported in section 4.2 [not included in this volume]) does make a distinction between good, marginal, and bad sentences (on the basis of questionnaire data) and found that judgments on the first class showed the least inter-speaker and intraspeaker variation, but his study was so methodologically naive that this result cannot be taken as anything more than suggestive until further experimentation is done. Quirk and Svartvik (1966) make a similar distinction. Watt (1975) claims that his findings argue against Chomsky's proposal because his sentences are all generated by the grammar of English, and yet they show differences of goodness. Furthermore, there is no evidence that these differences are of some other kind than the differences we find among ungrammatical sentences. Chomsky's proposal also suffers from a major theoretical problem—namely, there is no algorithm for determining which grammatical sentence to compare an ungrammatical sentence to, in order to compute its degree of ungrammaticality (Fillmore 1972). (See Watt 1975 for a review of Chomsky's later proposals, which I do not discuss here.)

More likely than Chomsky's proposal is a scenario in which grammaticality rating works in much the same way as conceptual classification ratings of the sort elicited by Rosch (1975) under the rubric of prototype theory. Just as we can ask, "How good an example of a bird is a robin/ostrich/butterfly/chair?" we can ask, "How good an example of a grammatical sentence is *X*?" for any string *X*. The responses will likely spread along a continuum with no indication of a clear-cut break of the sort discussed above, provided they are not biased by a lopsided rating scale. Kess and Hoppe (1983, p. 47) concur: "Apparently shared linguistic abilities operate on the same type of a graded continuum scale that cognitive abilities of a more general sort do." (See section 6.2 [not included in this volume] for an attempt to formalize judgment gradience along these lines.) We must be cautious in extrapolating from such a result (if it is found) to the nature of grammar, however. Prototypicality effects do not necessarily imply the absence of an underlying discrete system. As G. Lakoff (1987) reminds us, Rosch herself never suggested that graded classification effects reflect degrees of category membership or repres-entation in terms of prototypical features or exemplars. In fact, empirical demonstrations to the contrary have been made.

Armstrong, Gleitman, and Gleitman (1983) applied Rosch's original experimental paradigms to uncontroversially discrete concepts such as *even number* and *female*. Subjects were instructed to rate the extent to which exemplars represented the meaning of the category, and were timed on their responses to true/false categorial questions. They found that the discrete concepts presented the same pattern of results as Rosch's original taxonomic materials. Specifically, the goodness of various exemplars was rated quite uniformly across subjects, and reaction times for deciding membership in a category were longer for the worse exemplars, again with as much cross-subject consistency as for the taxonomic concepts that Rosch studied. Despite being able to grade exemplars consistently on a continuum, the subjects demonstrably knew that membership in categories such as *even number* was an either/ or proposition. Which behavior reflects subjects' true cognitive representations of these concepts? Armstrong, Gleitman, and Gleitman do not see these results as contradictory, because their experiment involved two different tasks, judging exemplariness and deciding membership. They discuss various possible theoretical explanations of their results, assuming that the real concepts are discrete and suggesting possible origins of the gradations, e.g., that they might stem from a quick, heuristic identification procedure. Lakoff argues against this last idea, and proposes that prototype effects reflect a mismatch between potentially discrete conceptual knowledge and the real world. For example, in the real world not all unmarried men are eligible to be married, and hence cannot be rated as bachelors to the full extent. However, there are still concepts for which there appears to be no discrete decision criterion, e.g., whether someone is rich, and these also exhibit prototypicality effects. Thus, it appears that graded structure in prototype tasks tells us nothing about the nature of the underlying mental representations. Is the same true of graded structure in grammaticality judgments and its bearing on mental grammars?

Barsalou (1987) suggests that graded structure might be a universal property of categories, and that the properties of an exemplar that determine its goodness as an instance of some category can vary depending on the situation. These properties might include, but are not limited to, similarity to the central tendency; similarity to the ideals of the category frequency of occurrence; and context. Barsalou summarizes his conclusion as follows:

The graded structures within categories do not remain stable across situations. Instead a category's graded structure can shift substantially with changes in context. This suggests that graded structures do not reflect invariant properties of categories but instead are highly dependent on constraints inherent in specific situations. (p. 107)

As I argue, particularly in chapter 5 [not included in this volume], Barsalou's view jibes well with the findings on grammaticality. Judgments are not invariant, and any of a large number of factors can come into play in making a judgment. Barsalou also looked at intra- and intersubject reliability across a wide variety of conceptual types. When people order exemplars by typicality, the average between-subject correlation is about .45. For the same subject judging the same stimuli on two occasions one month apart, it is roughly .75. In both cases it is the moderate exemplars (neither very good instances nor very good non-instances) that are the most unstable. These results also jibe with Ross's findings. Barsalou goes on to argue that there simply are no invariant representations of categories in the human cognitive system. Invariant representations are merely analytic fictions created by psychologists; perhaps linguists should be added to the list of culprits. Nonetheless, he suggests that the task of judging typicality might not make use of the same representations as judging set membership; the former might use probable properties, while the latter might use discriminative ones.

It might be the case that the nature of the particular tasks used by prototype theorists (and linguists) inherently induces graded behavior, independent of the nature of the underlying knowledge. If this is so, the status of that underlying knowledge as discrete or continuous must be demonstrated by other means. But how could we ever know whether a grammar, if it exists independent of performance mechanisms, classifies sentences dichotomously? If performance mechanisms induce graded structure by themselves, and if (as I argue) they can never be circumvented because competence is not directly accessible, then it might not be possible to investigate empirically how a grammar itself classifies sentences.[1] There are many possible combinations of mental structures that could yield graded acceptability judgments. For instance, Fillmore, Kempler, and Wang (1979) argue that judgment ratings might reflect the interaction of discretely varying elementary components that only have the appearance of continua.[2] Carroll (1979) follows Bever in suggesting that graded acceptability can result from a discrete grammar plus performance rules of some sort. In either case, neither grades of grammaticality nor grades of ungrammaticality would be part of the grammar. It could be that while fully grammatical sentences can be judged as such without much reference to their meaningfulness, interpretability becomes an important factor in judging some ungrammatical sentences. That is, the closer we can come to figuring out what an ungrammatical sentence is supposed to mean, the more likely we are to judge it to be acceptable. (See Fowler 1970 for essentially this argument; he insists that "an ungrammatical sentence is an ungrammatical sentence is an ungrammatical sentence," regardless of how it might be interpretable on the basis of extragrammatical information. Others, such as Katz (1964), have claimed that there is an identifiable class of semigrammatical sentences, by which is meant ungrammatical utterances that are comprehensible.) Questions about the nature of the concept *grammatical sentence* might eventually be answerable, but for now I leave them open and move on to a related question that likely *is* answerable—can we obtain useful judgments of degree of acceptability from subjects?

EXPERIMENTS ON CHOMSKY'S THREE LEVELS OF DEVIANCE

An enormous amount of research on degrees of (un)grammaticality was generated by Chomsky's identification of three levels or kinds of deviance. (See Schnitser 1973 for comparison of Chomsky's ideas with other contemporary ideas about degrees of badness.) The discussion in *Aspects* spurred a flurry of experiments designed to test Chomsky's idea by obtaining judgment ratings. In retrospect, these experiments seem somewhat misguided. Chomsky himself never claimed that degrees of *grammaticality* would correspond to degrees of *acceptability*; in fact, he explicitly states that the two do *not* coincide (see section 2.2 [not included in this volume]).[3] Predictably, the ensuing results have often been contradictory.[4] Nevertheless, we can learn quite a bit about the nature of scalar judgment from these

---

[1] Wayne Cowart (personal communication) suggests that part of the problem here could lie at the level of implementation: although our brains may be trying to realize a discrete system, their hardware is analog, which makes the implementation imperfect.

[2] Technically there cannot be a true continuum of grammaticality values of sentences, because continua involve an uncountably infinite number of values, and most linguists believe that there is only a countably infinite number of sentences. When linguists speak of grammaticality being a continuum, they typically mean that it is a discrete scale with more than two possible values.

[3] It is ironic, then, that current work in syntactic theory regularly makes heavy use of relative degrees of badness.

[4] There has been much selective interpretation of acceptability as bearing on grammaticality in this area. If the results go the right way, they are taken as evidence; if not, they are dismissed as performance artifacts.

experiments. I present here a selective review; see Moore 1972 and works cited therein for further references.

Downey and Hakes (1968) studied the effects of Chomsky's three levels of deviance on acceptability ratings, paraphrasing, and free recall. Subjects rated sentences on a scale from 0 ("completely acceptable") to 3 ("completely unacceptable"). Subjects were given two examples of how a sentence could be unacceptable, but Downey and Hakes do not provide details of these examples. The order among subjects' mean acceptability ratings was as predicted, although the difference between subcategorization and phrase structure violations was not significant. However, the recall scores showed a reversal of this pattern, with sentences containing selectional violations being harder to remember correctly than those with subcategorization errors.[5] Stolz (1969) performed a replication of this study, adding finer distinctions from Chomsky's hierarchy of selectional features, e.g., that the difference between mass nouns and count nouns is greater than that between human nouns and nonhuman nouns, although problems with materials made the possible effect of this difference inconclusive. Stolz also used a 4-point response scale, and told subjects that their responses should be based on *any* kind of deviance, including anomalous meanings as well as form. His results showed that sentence types were rated in the following order from least to most acceptable: random strings; sentences with subcategorization violations; sentences with selectional violations; analytic grammatical sentences; and contingently true grammatical sentences.[6]

Moore (1972) set out to test a hypothesis somewhat more general than Chomsky's proposal, which applies only to verbal features. He asked whether there is an acceptability hierarchy created by Chomsky's three types of violation, regardless of where in a sentence they occur. He also sought corroboration for such a hierarchy from sources other than judgments, in particular, subjects' reaction times in making those judgments. Moore's prediction was that a severely ungrammatical sentence should be processed faster than a marginally ungrammatical one, because more thorough processing would be required to detect a subtler error. His first experiment used a paradigm that was adopted in many subsequent studies. Subjects were shown a written sentence with a blank line where a missing word would go (e.g., *Sincerity may__the boy*). They were then shown a word that could fill the blank on a separate screen and were asked to decide as quickly as possible whether the sentence would be "appropriately completed" by that word.[7] The incomplete sentences were designed so that there was no way of assessing their grammaticality until the missing word was seen. The sentences in (2), (3), and (4) below illustrate stimulus sentences with blank lines in verb, subject, and object position, respectively (shown by the underline under the subsequently presented target word). In each set, the first sentence contains a lexical category violation. Example (2b) violates strict subcategorization, while (3b) and (4b) violate selectional restrictions between the verb and the noun phrase. Example (2c) violates a selectional

---

[5] Results from the paraphrase task were not quantitatively analyzable; the authors merely discuss what strategies they believe the subjects used.

[6] An analytic sentence is true simply by virtue of the meanings of its words, whereas a contingently true sentence makes a true claim about something in the world.

[7] Moore apparently wanted to ensure that subjects took selectional restrictions into account in making their decisions. He says, "The [experimenter] explained to [the subject] that terms such as 'appropriate' and 'acceptable' were deliberately being used, instead of 'grammatical,' because of the fact that the inappropriate sentences were inappropriate for varying reasons, some more syntactic than semantic. Inasmuch as 'ungrammatical' is frequency employed as being synonymous with 'syntactically deviant,' such instructions attempted to preclude any such dichotomy being set up by [the subject]." Since his subjects were not linguistics students, however, being presented with this terminology may only have confused them.

restriction of the verb, while (3c) and (4c) violate selectional restrictions between the noun and its modifying adjective.[8]

(2) a. Smart voters <u>uncle</u> honest politicians.
  b. Noisy dogs <u>growl</u> night animals.
  c. Catchy slogans <u>believe</u> unwary citizens.

(3) a. Modern <u>wanders</u> improve factory efficiency.
  b. Sensible <u>ideas</u> distrust public officials.
  c. Nosey <u>ditches</u> annoy suburb dwellers.

(4) a. Large factories utilize efficient <u>hesitates</u>.
  b. Big corporations appoint many <u>machines</u>.
  c. Factory foremen appreciate eager <u>tools</u>. (Moore 1972, p. 553)

The main effect of level of violation seemed to support Chomsky's theory: reaction times increased from (a) to (b) to (c) sentences. Interestingly, the mean reaction time for filler sentences that were grammatical was between those for (a) and (b) sentences. However, there were several mitigating interactions. In particular, there was no difference between reaction times for sentences like (2b) and (2c), while sentences like (3c) and (4c) did show longer decision time than their (b) counterparts (but Chomsky's theory might not have predicted the latter difference). Moore takes this as evidence that the process of checking grammaticality occurs in two passes. First, the major relations between subject, verb, and object are checked, and then relationships within the NP constituents are examined. Under this view, both verbal subcategorization and selectional restrictions are examined in the first pass and have no differential status, as reflected in the reaction time data. Several results support the importance of the verb in determining requirements for the rest of the sentence. For instance, although (2c) and (3b) constitute exactly the same type of violation, (2c) took significantly longer to reject. A large problem with this paradigm, of course, is that the sentences differ in many ways not relevant to the violations under study.

A second experiment examined whether grammaticality ratings of the same sets of sentences on a 20-point scale would conform to Chomsky's hierarchy. A new group of subjects was told that a sentence was "acceptable" if it "could occur in normal, everyday usage."[9] Subjects were asked to rate acceptable sentences with a score of 1, whereas scores of 2 to 20 represented increasing unacceptability.[10] Once again, the main effect of level of violation was as predicted. Mean ratings for (a), (b), and (c) sentences were 13.5, 11.0, and 9.2, respectively, but the latter two ratings did not differ significantly for sentences with blank lines in verb position, contradicting several previous studies.[11] Moore and Biederman (1979) attempted to distinguish various possible serial and parallel models that could account for subject-verb-object relations being checked faster than noun-adjective ones, using the same blank-line paradigm that was used in Moore's first experiment, but with sentences that contained *two*

---

[8] Moore did not consider strict subcategorization to be a property of nouns, and therefore could not make all violations in the (b)-level sentences of the same type. He seems to assume that Chomsky's theory predicts that all selectional restriction violations are equally ungrammatical, so (5b) and (5c) should be equivalent, and (6b) and (6c) should be equivalent. However, since I am not particularly concerned with the theoretical implications of Moore's study, I do not address this issue here.

[9] Moore does not explain why the definition of acceptability was changed from that of the first experiment.

[10] One positive feature of Moore's instructions was that they explicitly encouraged subjects to look over a few of the (practice) sentences to get an idea of the range within which they were working. Subjects were told to make use of the full range of the rating scale.

[11] Moore suggests that other studies failed to control for the location of the violation, and hence would not have seen the crucial interaction.

kinds of violation, e.g., *Old houses quarrel valuable relics*, where both subject-verb selection and verbal subcategorization are violated. If both kinds of violation are searched for in parallel, one would expect an average judgment speed gain on such sentences as compared to the judgment time required to search for either of the two violations by itself (assuming the search for ungrammaticality is self-terminating), but no such significant gain was found. On the other hand, no significant increase in judgment time was found, suggesting that the search does terminate when one violation is encountered. Moore and Biederman take this as support for a serial model, where subject-verb-object relations are checked before internal NP relations. A follow-up rating task with no time constraint showed that double violations did decrease the grammaticality of sentences as compared to single violations, so that this rating process, unlike the speeded determination of grammaticality, does not terminate on encountering the first violation.[12]

The most recent study dealing with Chomsky's three levels of deviance was performed by Nagata (1990). His subjects used a 7-point scale to rate three types of violation: lexical category violations; selectional restriction violations between verbs and their objects; and selectional restriction violations between nouns and their modifying adjectives. Nagata found significant differences of rating in the predicted order; his results thus support Chomsky's distinctions.

OTHER EXPERIMENTS

Chomsky's three levels of violation are not the only theoretical constructs that have spawned experimental work on levels of grammaticality. Around the time of Chomsky's proposal, some researchers were taking different approaches to the study of degrees of grammaticality. Coleman (1965) looked at four kinds of stimuli, ranging from random strings to strings where each word correctly matched a valid phrase structure rule in lexical category. His intermediate levels were less sensible; they involved choosing words from the correct *phrasal* category, e.g., approximating a noun phrase by choosing any two words that could appear in a noun phrase. Example (5) shows example sentences from each of Coleman's four levels.

(5) a. Think apron the wits for about.
    b. One the could to a her.
    c. The grass seldom were struck Lindy.
    d. The dust could always be Disneyland.

Coleman found that subjects' rank-orderings were significantly monotonically correlated with degree of grammaticality defined in this way. Moreover, other measures besides judgment correlated with this scale. For example, the more grammatical strings were easier to memorize and to perform a cloze test on correctly. Like many cases to be reviewed in this subsection, these results seem neither particularly surprising nor particularly informative.

Around the same time, Marks (1968) looked at those most mystical of linguistic beasts, multiply self-embedded sentences. He instructed subjects to judge their grammatical structure, not their length, complexity, difficulty of comprehension, or frequency of usage. For sentences with up to five self-embeddings, his results showed a power-law correlation between degree of embedding and subjects' ratings. That is, unacceptability grew as a function of the number of embeddings to a constant exponent. Another study by Marks (1965, 1967) was inspired by

---

[12] This experiment used a 100-point rating scale, but the authors do not say why they felt that such a wide range of possible ratings was necessary.

Chomsky's informal statement that some ungrammatical sentences obviously have more structure than others. Marks's hypothesis was that, in forming judgments of ungrammatical sentences, people consider the serial position of a violation within a sentence as well as the sentence's status as described by the grammar. Since sentences are processed from left to right, earlier errors should interfere more with processing, because early words prepare the processor for later ones and set up expectations and restrictions. Marks constructed stimulus materials by taking simplex sentences and sentences with infinitival clauses and reversing the order of two adjacent words in various positions, producing a paradigm like the one in (6):

(6) a. The boy hit the ball.
    b. Boy the hit the ball.
    c. The boy hit ball the.
    d. The hit boy the ball.
    e. The boy the hit ball.

Sentences were presented in groups with random order and subjects were asked to rank them from the best English to the worst English. As predicted, noun-determiner inversion was judged less acceptable if it occurred earlier in the sentence. Moreover, sentences like (6d) were judged to be worse than those such as (6e), although Marks points out that the two types of inversion found in these sentences are not the same, and serial position might not be the important factor here. But at least in the former case, it is hard to see how any traditional grammar would distinguish the grammaticality of the sentences, since such grammars treat all noun phrases as equivalent. Serial position of anomaly thus constitutes a reasonable candidate for an extragrammatical factor that contributes to acceptability.

Scott performed a series of similar experiments (Scott 1969; Scott and Mills 1973), except that he used a single basic sentence order (subject-verb-object-qualifier) and rearranged whole constituents rather than words. His subjects rated each permutation as "acceptably grammatical" or "not grammatical."[13] The percentage of subjects who accepted various permutations ranged from 100% to 0%. Scott takes the results to show that there are at least five degrees of grammaticality among these sentences, but this number seems to be arbitrary. We should also keep in mind that, unlike Marks's subjects, Scott's were only giving good/bad judgments, so the gradations appeared only in the pooled results and do not bear on the judgments of individual subjects. Scott tries to account for the numbers of acceptances on the basis of how many constituents were moved and in how many places the canonical constituent order was split. This index does not yield a perfect correlation with judged grammaticality, so Scott and Mills looked for other factors that might have determined the outcome—in particular, meaningfulness.[14] This factor was found to have no significant effect, but a useful outcome of the experiment was that when the permutations were not presented all together with their canonical form, grammaticality was rated much lower, suggesting that people accept a sentence more often if they can see that it is a rearrangement of a grammatical sentence.

In yet another study of the effect of word order on grammaticality judgments, Danks and Glucksberg (1971) considered violations of adjective ordering constraints (e.g., *Swiss red big tables* versus *big red Swiss tables*) using a ranking test with the six possible permutations of

---

[13] Subjects were offered a third choice, namely, "grammatical but with a different meaning from the unpermuted sentence"; we shall not be concerned with this possibility here.

[14] Scott and Mills cite various psychological sources for their definition of *meaningfulness* as "the association value of a single written verbal unit," for which they use frequency of occurrence as a metric. This does not correspond to what other authors have meant by the meaningfulness of a sentence.

three prenominal adjectives. The results showed that the position of the adjective that was most closely related to an intrinsic property of the noun was the primary determinant of acceptability: the closer it was to the noun, the higher the sentence was ranked.

More recently, Crain and Fodor (1985, 1987) looked at the effects of different kinds of ungrammaticality on a sentence matching task, where the subject must decide whether two simultaneously displayed sentences are identical. The basic finding was that number agreement and quantifier placement errors (shown in (7) and (8), respectively) increase matching times, while Subjacency and (certain) Empty Category Principle violations (shown in (9) and (10)) do not.

(7) *Mary were writing a letter to her husband.

(8) *Lesley's parents are chemical engineers both.

(9) *Who do the police believe the claim that John shot?

(10) *Who did the duchess sell Turner's portrait of?

While previous work had attributed this difference to different levels of ungrammaticality, Crain and Fodor argue that it was due instead to the correctability of the error: the first two types of error are easy to correct automatically, while for the other two there is no obvious correction that can convert them directly into grammatical sentences. Their claim is that if a correction is made, it must be *undone* in order to perform the matching task, since the subject must decide whether the sentences are literally identical. In cases like (9) and (10) no correction is possible, hence the bad sentence can be compared directly. Forster and Stevenson (1987) question this interpretation, suggesting that the correlation with correctability is epiphenomenal and cannot be the cause of the observed time differences. Both sets of authors acknowledge that other factors are at work as well, but the possibility that the correctability of a sentence could be a factor in relative ratings of acceptability should not be dismissed; whether it bears any relation to theories of degree of grammaticality is a matter of debate.

RATINGS, RANKINGS, AND CONSISTENCY

It is a fundamental assumption throughout this book that empirical facts are useful (and interesting) if they are systematic, because they must tell us something about the minds of the subjects who produce them. It remains a matter of analytical interpretation to decide *what* these facts tell us. Thus, we must determine whether graded judgments are systematic, and the results mentioned throughout this section strongly suggest that they are. The next thing one might wish to determine is just how many meaningful distinctions of levels of acceptability (relative or absolute) can be made. This would provide a basis for establishing a procedure for eliciting such distinctions.[15] Chaudron (1983) cites several psychometric studies showing that rating scales generally increase in reliability with increasing numbers of levels up to 20.[16] Presumably this can be shown by giving subjects different sizes of scale on which to rate the same stimuli: if you have too few levels, people collapse true distinctions arbitrarily, whereas if you have too many, people create spurious distinctions arbitrarily. Thus, the "true" number of distinctions will show the greatest consistency within (and perhaps also between) subjects.

---

[15] But see Cowart (1995) for the claim that the choice of response scale might not make much difference to patterns of relative acceptability.

[16] Snow (1975) points out the apparently contradictory finding that psychologists who measure attitudes have shown that subjects find scales with more than seven points hard to use.

It follows that studies that choose inappropriate numbers of levels add spurious variation to their results, possibly concealing the effects they are supposed to uncover. As far as I am aware, a psychometric investigation along these lines has never been done with specific regard to grammaticality judgments.

Even if we can find the optimal size of rating scale, there will still be problems with this measure of grammaticality judgments. One major problem is how to quantify inter- and intrasubject consistency, which is an important part of much work in this field. If we use a 20-point scale, should we require two subjects to give exactly the same rating of a sentence in order to consider them consistent? Would plus or minus one position be sufficient? What if two subjects show exactly the same distances between ratings of multiple sentences, but their absolute ratings are offset by some constant? Can we merely say that one is biased toward more conservative or more liberal judgments, and consider their responses to be fully consistent? Depending on the size of the offset constant, that might not seem appropriate, but neither would a conclusion of total inconsistency. If we standardize means and standard deviations, can we be sure we are not throwing away real differences?[17] Similar problems arise if some subjects simply fail to use the whole range of the scale, which can easily happen unintentionally if subjects have no idea what range of sentence types they will see. (For this reason alone, practice trials with representative anchor sentences are a good idea.) If we are attempting to compare consistency of subjects between studies that use different rating scales, the consistency measure will have to be scaled accordingly. Such problems have prompted many researchers to consider whether, instead of asking for absolute ratings of sentences, we should instead require subjects simply to rank order them from most to least acceptable. This approach does have certain advantages. For one thing, psychometric research indicates that people are much more reliable on comparative, as opposed to independent, ratings (Mohan 1977). Rank orders also solve the problem of different baselines on a rating scale, and there are nonparametric statistical tests for assessing the consistency or correlation between sets of rank orders. Relative judgments are not without problems, however. One problem is efficiency (Maclay and Sleator 1960): the amount of information one can extract from a given number of relative judgments is much less than the amount one can extract from absolute ratings. While exhaustive pair-wise comparisons are not necessary to arrive at an ordering of a set of sentences, there is surely a limit to how many sentences subjects can handle in one group; intergroup orders must then somehow be elicited.

A further problem with the interpretation of relative judgments is that pair-wise differential acceptability might not be transitive. That is, a subject who judges sentence A better than sentence B, and also judges sentence B better than sentence C when considering them two at a time, does not necessarily judge sentence A better than sentence C when they are examined side by side.[18] Hindle and Sag (1975) cite an instance of this situation with regard to the sentences in (11) that contain *anymore*, although they only present group data.

(11) a. They've scared us out of eating fish anymore.
    b. It's dangerous to eat fish anymore.
    c. All we eat anymore is fish.

---

[17] In doing so, we would be implicitly adopting the theoretical position that any such differences simply are not part of what we are studying. For instance, the fact that Speaker A could be consistently more conservative in grammaticality judgments than Speaker B does not tell us anything about their grammars. I do not think we are in a position to say this with any degree of certainty. See Cowart (1995) for more on the use of standard scores.

[18] A hybrid solution that solves this and some other problems is to *elicit* absolute ratings but *convert* them to rankings. Under this solution, circularity can never arise.

Twenty-two such sentences were presented to 36 subjects, who were asked to compare them and then give each a grammaticality rating on a 5-point scale.[19] It was determined for each subject which of a given pair of sentences he or she had rated more grammatical, or whether the pair had been rated equally grammatical, and subjects' ratings were tallied on this basis. Hindle and Sag found that while more subjects preferred (11a) over (11b) than vice versa, and more preferred (11b) over (11c), more preferred (11c) over (11a).[20] They conclude that their comparison data are spurious, because they involve an apples-and-oranges comparison: the sentences are too structurally diverse and hence their acceptability might be affected by different determining factors. Danks and Glucksberg (1970) encountered similar circular triads on an individual level, and take them as a measure of a subject's inconsistency. While a detailed examination of this issue would take us too deeply into psychometric theory, my purpose is merely to point out that such methodological problems will have to be dealt with if a paradigm involving relative judgments is followed. (See Gardner 1974 for a discussion of nontransitive paradoxes in various domains, and the argument that these *can* be rational if the pairwise comparisons involve different criteria. This could easily happen in the case of relative grammaticality judgments; see Watt (1975) for this view. Einhorn (1982) notes similar phenomena under the name of "intransitive choices" and shows how they can easily occur in everyday situations.)

It is also an open question what to make of discrepancies between absolute ratings and rank-orderings given by the same subjects, as have been found by Snow and Meijer (1977) and others. Even if we can establish that the discrepancies are due to context or contrast effects from neighboring sentences, this does not determine which kind of judgment is closer to the truth. Greenbaum and Quirk (1970) also examined the question of intra- and intersubject consistency, and this rating-ranking contrast in particular, using tests of evaluation versus performance. Their evaluation test involved a rating on a 3-point scale: "perfectly natural and normal," "wholly unnatural and abnormal," or "somewhere between." Their performance test involved the presentation of multiple variants of a sentence together, and required subjects to rank them as well as to rate each sentence individually (my summary is necessarily imprecise, since these researchers describe in great detail numerous experiments with minor variations). Greenbaum and Quirk typically used groups of 20–30 subjects and found that cross-group consistency was quite high, with very few significant differences on judgments (and other kinds of metalinguistic tasks). Also, their design allowed for several sentences to be judged a second time. Most sentences showed 90–95 percent consistency (measured as the number of subjects giving the same judgment both times a sentence was presented), but consistency for some sentences was as low as 54 percent. A very few sentences were both rated and ranked. The two measures generally correlated with each other, but sometimes sentences that were rated equally grammatical were ranked differently, even though tied rankings were allowed. This might mean that the 3-point scale was too limiting, not allowing enough room for the distinctions subjects wanted to make.

Yet another study comparing rating and ranking was conducted by Mohan (1977). Ratings were on a scale of 1 ("completely well-formed") to 10 ("completely ill-formed") that was anchored by an example sentence for each of the extremes (probably a very good idea). There were 11 sentences to be ranked; procedure was a within-subjects variable, the two tasks being separated by a 2-week interval. Unfortunately, the instructions seem a bit too usage-oriented: "Consider each of the sentences and decide if it would be possible that you would say this in

---

[19] These data are not quite equivalent to ranked comparisons, since a maximum of five distinctions could be made.
[20] The differences in ratings were quite small, with many subjects rating the pairs as equally grammatical, which is not surprising given the small size of the rating scale compared to the number of sentences.

conversation." The study was actually concerned in part with establishing whether individual speakers can do ordinal scaling of sentences, or whether such scaling only emerges by pooling multiple speakers' dichotomous judgments, where speakers might have different thresholds of acceptability and no differentiations within the good and bad sentence groups. Nonparametric statistical analysis showed that the cross-speaker agreement in rankings was much higher than would be expected under the latter interpretation. Mohan also found some evidence for a yea-saying factor, a tendency to favor acquiescence, i.e., accepting some sentences regardless of their grammatical status, by correlating the number accepted by each individual on two unrelated sets of sentences; there was a small but significant positive correlation. As for rating versus ranking, correlating the number of acceptances under the two procedures again gave a highly significant result,[21] although the correlation itself was modest (.57).

REFERENCES

Armstrong, S. L., L. Gleitman, and H. Gleitman (1983). 'What some concepts might not be'. *Cognition* 13: 263–308.
Barsalou, L. W. (1987). 'The instability of graded structure: implications for the nature of concepts'. In Neisser (1987: 101–40).
Bever, T. G. (1975). 'Functional explanations require independently motivated functional theories'. In R. E. Grossman, L. J. San, and T. J. Vance (eds.), *Papers from the Parasession on Functionalism*. Chicago: Chicago Linguistic Society, 580–609.
——and J. M. Carroll (1981). 'On some continuous properties in language'. In T. Myers, J. Laver, and J. Anderson (eds.), *The Cognitive Representation of Speech*. Amsterdam: North-Holland, 225–33.
Bolinger, D. L. (1961). *Generality, Gradience, and the All-or-None*. The Hague: Mouton.
Carr, P. (1990). *Linguistic Realities: An Autonomist Metatheory for the Generative Enterprise*. Cambridge: Cambridge University Press.
Carroll, J. M. (1979). 'Complex compounds: phrasal embedding in lexical structures'. *Linguistics* 17: 863–77.
Chaudron, C. (1983). 'Research on metalinguistic judgments: a review of theory, methods and results'. *Language Learning* 33(3): 343–77.
Chomsky, N. (1965). *Aspects of the Theory of Syntax*. Cambridge, Mass: MIT Press.
——1975 [1955–6]. *The Logical Structure of Linguistic Theory*. New York: Plenum. Repr. Chicago: University of Chicago Press.
Clark, H. H., and S. E. Haviland (1974). 'Psychological processes as linguistic explanation'. In Cohen (1974: 91–124).
Cohen, D. (ed.) (1974). *Explaining Linguistic Phenomena*. Washington, DC: Hemisphere.
Coleman, E. B. (1965). 'Responses to a scale of grammaticalness'. *Journal of Verbal Learning and Verbal Behavior* 4(6): 521–7.
Cowart, W. (1995). 'The stability of introspective judgments of sentence acceptability'. MS, University of Southern Maine.
Crain, S., and J. D. Fodor (1985). 'Rules and constraints in sentence processing'. In S. Berman, J.-W. Choe, and J. McDonough (eds.), *Proceedings of NELS* 15. Amherst, Mass.: Graduate Student Linguistic Association, University of Massachusetts at Amherst, 87–104.
————(1987). 'Sentence matching and overgeneration'. *Cognition* 26(2): 123–69.
Danks, J. H., and S. Glucksberg (1970). 'Psychological scaling of linguistic properties'. *Language and Speech* 13(2): 118–38.

---

[21] Sentences rated 1–5 were treated as acceptances; subjects drew a threshold line in their rank orderings, which allowed the comparison.

——————(1971). 'Psychological scaling of adjective orders'. *Journal of Verbal Learning and Verbal Behavior* 10(1): 63–7.

Downey, R. G., and D. T. Hakes (1968). 'Some psychological effects of violating linguistic rules'. *Journal of Verbal Learning and Verbal Behavior* 7(1): 158–61.

Einhorn, H. J. (1982). 'Learning from experience and suboptimal rules in decision making'. In D. Kahneman, P. Slovic, and A. Tversky (eds.), *Judgement under Uncertainty: Heuristics and Biases*. Cambridge: Cambridge University Press, 268–83.

Fillmore, C. J. (1972). 'On generativity'. In Peters (1972: 1–19).

——— D. Kempler, and W. S.-Y. Wang (eds.) (1979). *Individual Differences in Language Ability and Language Behavior*. New York: Academic Press.

Forster, K. I., and B. J. Stevenson (1987). 'Sentence matching and well-formedness'. *Cognition* 26(2): 171–86.

Fowler, R. (1970). 'Against idealization: some speculations on the theory of linguistic performance'. *Linguistics* 63: 19–50.

Gardner, M. (1974). 'On the paradoxical situations that arise from nontransitive relations'. *Scientific American* 231(4): 120–5.

Gerken, L., and T. G. Bever (1986). 'Linguistic intuitions are the result of interactions between perceptual processes and linguistic universals'. *Cognitive Science* 10: 457–76.

Greenbaum, S. (ed.) (1977). *Acceptability in Language*. The Hague: Mouton.

——— and R. Quirk (1970). *Elicitation Experiments in English: Linguistic Studies in Use and Attitude*. Coral Gables, Fla.: University of Miami Press.

Hindle, D., and I. Sag (1975). 'Some more on *anymore*'. In R. W. Fasold and R. W. Shuy (eds.), *Analyzing Variation in Language: Papers from the Second Colloquium on New Ways of Analyzing Variation*. Washington, DC: Georgetown University Press, 89–110.

Hockett, C. F. (1955). *A Manual of Phonology*. Baltimore: Waverly Press.

Katz, J. J. (1964). 'Semi-sentences'. In J. A. Fodor and J. J. Katz (eds.), *The Structure of Language: Readings in the Philosophy of Language*. Englewood Cliffs, NJ: Prentice-Hall, 400–16.

——— and T. G. Bever (1976). 'The fall and rise of empiricism'. In D. T. Langendoen, J. J. Katz, and T. G. Bever (eds.), *An Integrated Theory of Linguistic Ability*. New York: Crowell, 11–64.

Kess, J. F., and R. A. Hoppe (1983). 'Individual differences and metalinguistic abilities'. *Canadian Journal of Linguistics* 28(1): 47–53.

Lakoff, G. (1973). 'Fuzzy grammar and the performance/competence terminology game'. In C. Corum, T. C. Smith-Stark, and A. Weiser (eds.), *Papers from the Ninth Regional Meeting of the Chicago Linguistic Society*, 271–91.

——— (1987). 'Cognitive models and prototype theory'. In Neisser (1987: 63–100).

Lakoff, R. (1977). 'You say what you are: acceptability and gender-related language'. In Greenbaum (1977: 73–86).

Levelt, W. J. M. (1974). *Formal Grammars in Linguistics and Psycholinguistics* (in 3 vols). The Hague: Mouton.

——— J. A. W. M. van Gent, A. F. J. Haans, and A. J. A. Meijers (1977). 'Grammaticality, paraphrase, and imagery'. In Greenbaum (1977: 87–101).

Maclay, H., and M. D. Sleator (1960). 'Responses to language: judgments of grammaticalness'. *International Journal of American Linguistics* 26(4): 275–82.

Marks, L. E. (1965). 'Psychological investigations of semi-grammaticalness in English'. Ph.D. dissertation, Harvard University.

——— (1967). 'Judgments of grammaticalness of some English sentences and semi-sentences'. *American Journal of Psychology* 80(2): 196–204.

——— (1968). 'Scaling of grammaticalness of self-embedded English sentences'. *Journal of Verbal Learning and Verbal Behavior* 7(5): 965–7.

Mohan, B. A. (1977). 'Acceptability testing and fuzzy grammar'. In Greenbaum (1977: 133–48).

Moore, T. E. (1972). 'Speeded recognition of ungrammaticality'. *Journal of Verbal Learning and Verbal Behavior* 11: 550–60.

Moore, T. E., and I. Biederman (1979). 'Speeded recognition of ungrammaticality: double violations'. *Cognition* 7(3): 285–99.

Nagata, H. (1990). 'Speaker's sensitivity to rule violations in sentences'. *Psychologia* 33(3): 179–84.

Neisser, U. (ed.) (1987). *Concepts and Conceptual Development: Ecological and Intellectual Factors in Categorization.* Cambridge: Cambridge University Press.

Peters, S. (ed.) (1972). *Goals of Linguistic theory.* Englewood Cliffs, NJ: Prentice-Hall.

Quirk, R., and J. Svartvik (1966). *Investigating Linguistic Acceptability.* The Hague: Mouton.

Rosch, E. (1975). 'Cognitive representations of semantic categories'. *Journal of Experimental Psychology: General* 104: 192–233.

Ross, J. R. (1972). 'Endstation Hauptwort: the category squish'. In P. M. Peranteau, J. N. Levi, and G. C. Phares (eds.), *Papers from the Eighth Regional Meeting of the Chicago Linguistic Society,* 316–38.

——(1979). 'Where's English?' In Fillmore et al. (1979: 127–63).

Schnitser, M. L. (1973). 'In search of an unproblematical notion of grammaticality'. *Le Langage et l'Homme* 21: 27–38.

Scott, R. I. (1969). 'A permutational test of grammaticality'. *Lingua* 24(1): 11–18.

——and J. A. Mills (1973). 'Validating the permutational test of grammaticality'. *Language and Speech* 16(2): 110–22.

Snow, C. E. (1975). 'Linguists as behavioral scientists: towards a methodology for testing linguistic intuitions'. In A. Kraak (ed.), *Linguistics in the Netherlands 1972–1973.* Assen: Van Gorcum, 271–5.

——and G. Meijer (1977). 'On the secondary nature of syntactic intuitions'. In Greenbaum (1977: 163–77).

Stolz, W. S. (1969). 'Some experiments with queer sentences'. *Language and Speech* 12: 203–19.

Watt, W. C. (1975). 'The indiscreteness with which impenetrables are penetrated'. *Lingua* 37: 95–128.

PART V
Criticisms and Responses

25

Description of Language Design

MARTIN JOOS

Physicists describe speech with continuous mathematics, such as Fourier analysis or the autocorrelation functions. Linguists describe language instead, using a discontinuous or discrete mathematics called 'linguistics'. The nature of this odd calculus is outlined and justified here. It treats speech communication as having a telegraphic structure. (Non-linguists normally fail to orient themselves in this field because they treat speech as analogous to telephony.) The telegraph-code structure of language is examined from top to bottom, and at each of its several levels of complexity (compared to the two levels of Morse code) its structure is shown to be defined by possibilities and impossibilities of combination among the units of that level. Above the highest level we find, instead of such absolute restrictions, conditional probabilities of occurrence: this is the semantic field, outside linguistics, where sociologists can work. Below the lowest level we find, instead of such absolute restrictions, conditional probabilities of phonetic quality: this is the phonetic field, outside linguistics, where physicists can work. Thus linguistics is peculiar among mathematical systems in that it abuts upon reality in two places instead of one. This statement is equivalent to defining a language as a symbolic system; that is, as a code.

The word 'design' may be interpreted in at least two senses without violating engineering usage. First, there is the work of the engineer who is designing something, for example a telephone system. Second, there is the finished something, such as that same telephone system, considered now as something to be analysed and described. Our description of it, then, can also be called its 'design'. It is in this last sense that the word 'design' has to be understood when we are talking about the design of language and how it is analysed for description.

Engineers never have occasion to analyse a gadget the way linguists do a language. The nearest thing to it might be this sort of episode: A supplier had been asked to furnish a band-pass filter, single T section, with rather modest cut-off requirements. Instead of the expected classical constant-k filter—two series arms, one parallel arm, total three coils, and three capacitors—he furnished a filter with three coils and four capacitors connected in an unexpected way. The writer was asked to analyse the design and report whether it was worth adopting for future routine construction of band-pass filters. It turned out that the odd design had two advantages: one of the coils could be a large stock-size coil used without trimming, and the design gave any desired impedance-transformation without a transformer. But—and here is the crucial point—it did not seem possible to arrive at these conclusions without taking into consideration the designer's intentions; and the experience seemed to show that a 'why' question has an answer only when intention is in the picture—when the presence of intention is given, so to speak, as a boundary-condition.

* Martin Joos, 'Description of language design', *Journal of the Acoustical Society of America* 22 (1950): 701–08. © The Acoustical Society of America. Reprinted by permission. The version used here appeared in Martin Joos (ed.), *Readings in Linguistics: the development of descriptive linguistics in America 1925-56* (Chicago and London: The University of Chicago Press, Fourth edn., 1966), 349–56. With thanks to The American Council of Learned Societies.

Linguists have described numerous languages, and have observed language design-changes through the centuries. But although quite a body of 'how' knowledge concerning these matters has been built up, we have so far nothing but a number of unconfirmable guesses concerning the 'why'. Hence most of us are now pretty sure about one thing: there is nothing conscious, nothing deliberate, about language-design. (Naturally we don't mean to study Basic English or Esperanto until we have first built up the theory of natural language-design.) Accordingly we do not present the design of any language as the result of intentions—we do not answer 'why' questions about the design of a language.

Having thus limited our problem, we proceed with greater confidence to look for answers to the 'how' questions of language-design. In other words, we try to describe precisely; we do not try to explain. Anything in our description that sounds like explanation is simply loose talk-deliberately loose, perhaps, for the sake of persuasion by analogy—and is not to be considered part of current linguistic theory.

We can allow other people—telephone engineers or sociologists, for example—to speak artistically, imprecisely, about language. But as linguists we lay upon ourselves the condition that we must speak precisely about language or not at all. We can do that, of course, only under two conditions, of which the first has already been hinted at. First, we must limit our field, leaving outside it certain things to be treated precisely by engineers or by sociologists, while we speak of them more or less artistically. Second, within our field we must adopt a technique of precise treatment, which is by definition a mathematics. We must make our 'linguistics' a kind of mathematics, within which inconsistency is by definition impossible. True, miscalculations may occur through inadvertence. And different workers describing the same language may arrive at conflicting statements because they have started out from different sets of axioms. But in principle every possible statement of ours must be either true or false—nothing half-way.

Have linguists succeeded in setting up such a mathematical style for describing language designs? Well, not quite; but our science is still young. In its mathematical phase it is just a quarter of a century old, for we date it from Bloomfield's 'A set of postulates for the science of language' (in the journal *Language*, 1926 (26)). And even physics has not yet entirely resolved the conflict between quantum theory and the wave theory of light. But of all the sciences and near-sciences which deal with human behavior, linguistics is the only one which is in a fair way to becoming completely mathematical, and the other social scientists are already beginning to imitate the strict methods of the linguists.

Presenting only 'how' statements without regard to 'why', we of course have no assurance that we are 'right' in any sense that would satisfy a theologian. And we feel that our descriptive statements fit actual speech-behavior, but we have no right to claim that they are 'correct' in the sense that they fit the neural events in the brains of the speaker and listener. Such arrogant modesty is not peculiar to linguists; it is simply the normal attitude of mathematicians confronting the real world. The mathematical description for reality has been most illuminatingly called a 'map'. Now when one holds a map (in the ordinary sense) in one's hands, one may say, "I feel that this is a map of the countryside around me here," but there is no way to prove logically that it is not instead a map of a piece of Australia or perhaps of some imaginary Treasure Island. Undeterred by the impossibility of logical justification, explorers use maps, scientists use mathematics, and linguists use the descriptive technique called 'linguistics'. All three have the same attitude toward the map. One proceeds across the terrain and simultaneously traces a line across the map; one notes discrepancies between one's reading of the map and the sense impressions from the real world, until the discrepancies seem to form a pattern themselves; then one corrects the map and starts all over again. All this is intuitive behavior, and logically unjustifiable.

Nor does it need justification. The place for logic is inside the map, not between the map and the real world.

Ordinary mathematical techniques fall mostly into two classes, the continuous (e.g. the infinitesimal calculus) and the discrete or discontinuous (e.g. finite group theory). Now it will turn out that the mathematics called 'linguistics' belongs in the second class. It does not even make any compromise with continuity as statistics does, or infinite-group theory. Linguistics is a quantum mechanics in the most extreme sense. All continuity, all possibilities of infinitesimal gradation, are shoved outside of linguistics in one direction or the other. There are in fact two such directions, in which we can and resolutely do expel continuity: semantics and phonetics.

Every language has 'meaningful' molecules called 'morphemes', sub-assemblies which roughly correspond to subdivisions of the real world outside language. The word *nose*, for example, consists of one such morpheme; the word *noses* consists of two, the second having as its real-world correspondent the conventional category of numerousness, one of our customary subdivisions or categorizations of the real world. Now consider these facts. The English word *nose* may refer to a part (how much?) of an airplane. With a lipstick draw a loop on your own face to enclose your nose and nothing else; another person will say that you have enclosed either too much or too little. Say in English: "The councillors all put their glasses on their noses" and then get the sentence translated into German; for English *noses* you will get the singular noun-form *Nase*, not the plural *Nasen*. The German knows that numerous councillors have equally numerous noses, and he has a word for 'noses', but in this sentence he uses his word for 'nose' instead. In linguistic terminology we simply say that the form *Nase* belongs to the category which we have called 'singular'. We chose that name the way the physicist chose the name 'work', because in German the category most often refers to lack of numerousness in the things referred to; but this is not a logical reason, it is only a motivation out of convenience. High-school Physics teachers often have good reason to regret the choice of the term 'work' for force times distance, and in expounding linguistic theory we often have the same reason for regretting the choice of terms 'singular' and 'plural'. The trained listener, the listening linguist in this case, is not deceived; he knows that in calling *Nase* 'singular' we have not said whether one nose or more than one nose was involved.

We keep on and say a few thousand things like this, but as long as we are talking about German or English we never place a noun-form in a third category side by side with 'singular' and 'plural', say a category which is neither singular nor plural, or is both, or is ambiguous as to number. The listening linguist, noting the absence of this other kind of statement, sooner or later decides that in German or in English every noun-form is either singular or else plural—tertium non datur. This may be called the tyranny of linguistic categories. It is found in every language. It is not a question of 'correctness' in the popular sense of the word, for every kind of speech, elegant or sub-standard, has its own categorical tyrannies. For example, in the writer's dialect the form *whom* can't follow a pause: it is permissible to say "To whom did you give it?" or "Who did you give it to?" but not "Whom did you give it to?" In situations where the normal language-design is not quite adequate, such as in the composition of a paper like this, we get amusing difficulties, such as finding it necessary to say either 'one nose or more than one nose was involved' or else 'one nose or several noses were involved.' The difficulty is just as severe if we say 'one sheep or more-than-one/several sheep was/were involved.' That is, it is the category that tyrannizes over us, not the form, and not the meaning either; and even a word like *sheep* must be, each time that it is used, either singular or else plural. We might like to replace *was/were* with a verb-form which was, like the Irishman's trousers, singular at the top and plural at the bottom, but we haven't got any such category in English. In fact, in every known language there is a limit to the kinds and numbers of its categories, a limit which may seem very low compared to the elaborations which philosophers and poets indulge in. Then when an unusual message is to be transmitted, the categories are never split or supplemented, but are instead used in unusual combinations. The listener's total reaction may or may not be as expected, but his detail reactions are predictable at least to this extent: For every form-class represented in the utterance ('noun' is one form-class, 'verb' is another) there are a certain number of dimensions of categorization (in the English noun there are two: possessive-vs.-common, and singular-vs.-plural); and now, for every dimension thus introduced into the utterance, the listener will react to exactly one of the categories in that dimension—he will not react to more than one, or to none, whether the utterance is ambiguous or not. The reader can check this fact easily. Without looking back to the sentence about the councillors, let him ask himself whether it referred to present time or to past time. He will find that he has made up his mind one way or the other; and yet, on checking the wording, he will find that he was not told. The English categorization, past-vs.-present, forced him to decide, even though the decision had to be made at random. Each language does this within the range of its own categories, *which will not be the same range as in our language.* In Chinese, for example, the translation lacks both the past-vs.-present dimension and the singular-vs.-plural dimension; these 'meanings' can be indicated on occasion, but when they are not, the Chinese listener leaves the question open—he says he is not even aware that it is a question.

The linguistic categories, then, are absolutes which admit of no compromise. They correspond roughly to favorite categorizations in the real world, and it is widely held that every community subdivides the phenomena in the real world according to the categories of its language, rather than the reverse. But the correspondence between the discrete categories of the language and the continuous phenomena of the real world is not and cannot be precise. Our reaction, as linguists, to this situation, is very simple: all phenomena, whether popularly regarded as linguistic (such as the tone of anger in an utterance) or not, which we find we cannot describe precisely with a finite number of absolute categories, we classify as non-linguistic elements of the real world and expel them from linguistic science. Let sociologists and others do what they like with such things—we may wish them luck in their efforts to describe them precisely in their own terminology, but no matter whether they describe them with discrete categories or not, for us they remain vague, protean, fluctuating phenomena—in a word, they represent that 'continuity' which we refuse to tolerate in our own science.

Have we ever had any choice? Could we have chosen to use a continuous rather than a discrete mathematics for describing language-design? Our experience with the analysis of a few hundred of the world's several thousand languages makes us very sure that we must answer negatively. We can, with some effort, begin to imagine a quasi-language used on some other planet by creatures unlike ourselves, in which a quasi-word [kul] (identical with the way I have just now pronounced English *cool*) signifies a temperature of +10° centigrade, and another one, [kold], signifies −10°, while any intermediate temperature worth mentioning is precisely signified by an intermediate pronunciation, with a vowel between [u] and [o] at just the right proportionate distance from them both (phonetically a reasonable thing to say: [o] and [u] are phonetically neighbors, and continuous gradation of quality from one towards the other is a commonplace) and just the right strength of [d] (from zero strength, or lack of [d], at one end of that segment of temperature scale, up to that full strength which I used just now at the other end of it) to measure and signify just the temperature meant. But neither this sort of thing, nor indeed any other gradation or continuity *in either form or meaning*, has ever been found *in any language* on this planet. True, the sounds (and thus all the forms) occurring in the use of the language are variable by continuous gradation, and so are not only temperatures but all things and phenomena spoken of. But *in the design* of the language we never find a trace of those facts! Messages are communicated in the language, both in speech and in writing, as if the forms (words, etc.) were invariants and as if the referents (things, etc.) were also invariants: that is, the only way the forms and meanings of a language are ever used is the way an accountant uses 'dollars' or 'shillings'—not the way a numismatist or even an economist uses them.

The accountant banishes two kinds of continuity from his debits-and-credits mathematics: the continuous variation in 'state' of a coin that interests a numismatist, and the continuous variation in 'real value' that interests an economist. Linguists do the same in describing language: from their linguistic calculus they banish the continuous variation in phonetic 'state' of the utterance, and the continuous variation in semantic 'real value' thereof. Now is this the right way to discuss language? Is it somehow adequate to the way languages work? Or is it instead a falsification, a Procrustean mistreatment? Let us consider the phonological half of it first.

Here we have 'phonemics' inside of linguistic science; and 'phonetics', which is not so very different from and may even be considered a division of the physicist's 'acoustics', in the realm of overt speech-behavior, which is not the realm of linguistics but belongs to the real world outside of linguistics. When a physicist analyses speech he finds a continuum of articulatory activity, of sound, and of events in the ear—at least until, working both ways from the sound, he comes to the all-or-none discharging of single nerve-fibers—and for describing any or all of this he uses a continuous mathematics, such as Fourier analysis or the auto-correlation function. On the other hand, linguists have found it appropriate always to describe every language so far studied as having, and every act of speech as corresponding to, combinations of an astonishingly small number of smallest signalling units called 'phonemes' which recur identically insofar as they can be said to occur at all. Thus the word *hotel* can't be spoken the same way twice, from the physicist's viewpoint, no matter whether the same person or different persons should utter it; and yet from the linguist's viewpoint it always has in the middle a phoneme /t/ which is identically the same every time. And it is not considered the same through neglect of unimportant variations in reality; rather, it is identical by definition, simply because it is a linguistic atom, a category, and these are either identically the same or absolutely different.

Here, then, linguistics insists upon being atomistic. Is this the right and only thing for a linguist to do? Telephone engineers have been known to protest at this point and say something like this: "When you were discussing linguistic discreteness and nonlinguistic continuity in the semantic field you had me where you wanted me, for how should an engineer know anything about semantics? But now you are talking about sound, and here I am perfectly at home; I have even made extensive and precise observations upon normal speakers and listeners: for instance, I have gathered statistics about the variations in vowel qualities. Your mathematically identical phonemes are a delusion; what you've got are statistical norms, clusterings around averages which you take as norms and then arbitrarily make into absolutes. We are both talking about phonetics; and when you admit that I can prove continuity, you can't claim to prove discreteness.

"Let us agree to neglect the least important features of speech sound, so that at any moment we can describe it sufficiently well with n measurements, a point in n-dimensional continuous space, n being not only finite but a fairly small number, say six. Now the quality of the sound becomes a point which moves continuously in this 6-space, sometimes faster and sometimes slower, so that it spends more or less time in different regions, or visits a certain region more or less often. In the long run, then, we get a probability-density for the presence of the moving point anywhere in the 6-space. This probability-density varies continuously all over the space. Now wherever you can find a local maximum of probability-density, a place where the probability-density does not increase for short distances in any direction away from the place in question, I will let you call that place a 'phoneme'; and I expect, just as you do, that there will be not only a finite but a fairly small number of such points, say less than a hundred. Thus you see that there is no need to use a discrete mathematics to get a finite number of phonemes out of the phonetic continuum."

We could answer that our name for that would be, not 'phoneme', but 'allophone', and allophones belong to phonetics while phonemes belong to linguistics. But that would be evading the issue. The engineer's argument is a formidable one, and deserves to be met squarely. According to our view concerning the relationship between any mathematical map and the real phenomena to which it corresponds, it is not possible to argue logically in this field; therefore we have to argue by means of analogy. Fortunately a suitable analogy lies ready to hand.

Let us consider telegraphy, using Morse or Baudot coding. The units are the mark and the space; it doesn't matter whether the 'space' is an electrical impulse of opposite polarity to the 'mark', or an electrically neutral period. A Morse dash could be considered as three integrally sequent marks, and a letter-space as three spaces; then the units differ in only one dimension. Or the dash and the letter-space maybe considered as independent signals; then there are four signals, differing from each other in two dimensions, namely electrical intensity (or polarity) and duration. Thus there are at least two ways of describing the Morse code, both discrete and both correct, each by its own axioms. They differ in their grammar, though. The first way requires the grammatical rule that each occurrence of mark after space (or of space after mark) is always followed by exactly two more of the same or else by one or three of the other. The second way requires the rule that either mark is followed by a space, and either space by a mark. This sort of interrelation between a set of axioms and a set of grammatical rules is a commonplace in linguistics. But now let us continue with telegraphy.

A Morse S is mark-space-mark-space-mark. A Baudot Y is mark-space-mark-space-mark—shall we say "also"? That depends; we can settle it later. At the far end of a long line, the marks and spaces are slurred together into a continuous smooth fluctuation so that on first inspection it may be far from easy to tell what the original signals must have been. Then a regenerative repeater is used to square up the marks and spaces so that they can be read or will operate an ordinary teletypewriter. But if the line is very long, not much noise will be needed to cause occasional errors in the repeater's operation. A regenerative repeater for Baudot signals will in general not handle Morse signals, nor vice versa. (We begin to see why we had better not say "also" as proposed at the beginning of this paragraph.)

Now let us find a telephone engineer who knows nothing about telegraphy, and give him the output of a long telegraph line. What does he do with it? He does Fourier analysis and auto-correlation and perhaps something else—at any rate, at first he works on it with continuous mathematics, for the material is obviously continuous. But as long as he does that, he can make no sense out of it. In desperation he next differentiates the output voltage, so that he has two data for every instant, the voltage and its first time-derivative. Now for each five milliseconds he averages each of these, and plots the two averages as a single point on a sheet of graph-paper. When he has put a few thousand points on his paper, he sees a continuous variation of point-density, with a number of local maxima—perhaps a few dozen of them. To each maximum he assigns a label, a letter or a number, arbitrarily. Now he interprets his original data, his voltage and derivative data, in terms of these labels: every time the line-output and its derivative come close to one of those maximum-density points, he will write down the label of that point, so that finally he has replaced the original data by a string of those labels. Now he can turn this result over to a cryptanalyst, who will be able to read the original plain-language text out of it—not quite completely on first reading, but probably he will be able to reconstruct a good text if he knows the language well.

Ridiculous? Not at all. This is exactly what our telephone engineer wanted to do with phonetics and phonemics.

Now we also know what that same telephone engineer will do after we tell him of the existence of telegraph codes employing molecular signals made up of atomic units, each unit being identically one or another of a very small number of atoms. He will not use Fourier analysis or any other continuous mathematics at first. Rather, he will start out by looking for wave-trains that look nearly alike, their slight differences being explicable, as he can easily see, either as the effects of noise or as the effects of context. He will see many occurrences of a three-peaked wave-train, no two occurrences precisely alike. But when the first peak is rather low, then there will be a long hollow before it; when there is no hollow, the first peak is as high as the second or a bit higher. This is a context-effect. Once most of the context-effects have been spotted, the remaining variations will be ascribed to noise. In this fashion he will learn to identify the three-peaked wave for Morse S or Baudot Y, and also all the other common molecular signals.

Next he will set up the hypothesis that there are just n atomic signalling units, and that not only the inter-molecular context-effects but also the intramolecular smoothings can be accounted for by low-pass filtering. Here he can use continuous mathematics for a while, and the result will be that this hypothesis works best if n equals two. Now it won't take him long to reconstruct the entire telegraphic code; quite easily if it is Baudot, not so easily or swiftly if it is Morse, but in either case with absolute certainty.

Finally he will describe the design of the telegraphic code, and he will describe it in terms of absolutely identical square-wave signalling atoms, even though he has never observed anything that could be called absolute identity, and even though he knows that square waves are impossible. And when he has thus finished his job, he will be able to convince his colleagues, the other telephone engineers who knew nothing about telegraphy, that this is the right way to do it. Convince them by logic? Not a chance. Nothing but the superior elegance of his results will speak for the rightness of his method, but that will be enough.

Linguists find themselves so successful in describing languages in this fashion that they have elevated their descriptive technique to the rank of a theory about the nature of language. They say, in effect, that the design of any language is essentially telegraphic—that the language has the structure of a telegraph-code, using molecular signals made up of invariant atoms, and differing e.g. from the Morse code principally in two ways: the codes called 'languages' have numerous layers of complexity instead of only two, and in each layer there are severe limitations upon the combinations permitted. This much, we find, all languages have in common. But the particular code is different from one language or dialect to another, as the Baudot and Morse codes differ. Those two telegraphic codes share, on the phenomenal level, this molecular signal among others: mark-space-mark-space-mark. Now suppose we find this signal in the output of one telegraph line, and find it again in the output of another telegraph line; are they the same or are they not the same? That depends. If they are both Morse or both Baudot, then they are identically the same signal, no matter whether or not they are distorted by different noises or different line characteristics, or are sent at different speeds, or by a well-adjusted or a badly-adjusted transmitter. If one is Morse and the other is Baudot, then they are not in the least the same signal, even when their oscillograms come out the same within the limits of instrumental error.

This is obvious to any telegraph engineer. But in the linguistic field it did not seem obvious or even credible to a certain engineer who said to the writer: "Surely you can tell when two men pronounce the word *father* alike!" The answer had to be: "On the data you have given me, the question has no meaning. First I have to find out whether they rhyme *father* with *bother*. If they both do, or neither does, then I must find out whether both of them or neither of them pronounces *cot* the same as he pronounces *caught*. Then I have a few more questions, of the same sort, with which I explore their contrasts for some distance around the word *father* in all directions. If I always get the same answer from both of them, then I say, 'Yes, they pronounce *father* alike,' meaning 'identically the same,' even if they sound quite different when they say the word. But if, during this exploration, I find a discrepancy between their systems of phonemic contrasts before I have gone very far from the word *father* itself, then I shall have to say, 'No, they pronounce it differently,' meaning 'their pronunciations are incommensurable,' even if they sound so much alike that no difference can be heard." This statement was met with amazed incredulity, and a request to state honestly whether anybody else held similar views. It is to be feared that the answer to this request was not accepted at face value. The trouble was, of course, that no bridge had been built between the engineer's knowledge of telegraphy and the language experience of linguists.

Now let us go on with the design of language. We have dealt with the phonemes individually, and shown that the most important thing about them is that they are either absolutely the same or absolutely different. And yet, in another sense it is to be expected that two of them can be partly the same and partly different. This can be possible in this way. If it is possible to put phoneme /A/ into three categories x, y, and z (as the word *noses* simultaneously belongs to the three categories 'noun', 'common rather than possessive', and 'plural'), and to put phoneme /B/ into three categories v, w and z (as the word *were* belongs to the three categories 'verb', 'past', and 'plural'), then /A/ and /B/ can be said to be similar, but of course only in the sense that they are partly identical: similarity can't be gradual, but only quantized, as in this instance, where /A/ and /B/ are identical to the extent of z and otherwise absolutely different, hence are called 'similar'. This is another way of stating the discrete nature of the descriptive method called 'linguistics': similarity is described as fractional identity. We naturally use quantized identity, wherever we can find it, to describe what we find in a language; and what has been described in that fashion has been rigorously described.

The Morse code uses two signalling units, 'mark' and 'space', differing in one dimension; or it can be considered as using four units, 'dot', 'dash', 'space', and 'letter-space' different in two dimensions, namely electrical intensity (or polarity) and duration. On the other hand, every known language uses more than a dozen (and less than a hundred) phonemes, different from each other in at least four, more probably at least five, dimensions. Spanish, for example, seems to have at least nine dimensions in its phonemic system (which some phonologists will reckon as fewer by the trick of identifying some dimension found in one area of the phonology with a dimension found only in another area) and English is known to have more than Spanish.

These are so many that a complete catalog would be confusing, but a sample may be helpful. One of the Spanish dimensions is 'vowel-vs.-consonant'. Among the five Spanish vowels, two more dimensions are clearly evident. In one dimension, the five are categorized as 'high, mid, low'; in the other, as 'front, central, back'. /i/ and /u/ are high; /e/ and /o/ are mid; /a/ is low. /i/ and /e/ are front; /u/ and /o/ are back; /a/ is neither, so it is called central. The six category-names were borrowed from phonetics into phonemics, just as the word 'work' was borrowed by physics, and as we borrowed 'plural' from other fields of discussion, where it was a synonym for 'numerous': in linguistics it is not! In phonetics, 'high, mid, low, front, central, back' refer to tongue-position in the mouth; in phonemics, of course, we have to strip away those denotations of the words, which have now become distracting connotations. Instead, the phonemic categories get whatever denotations may be useful in the further description of the language. The *phonetic* term 'labial' means 'articulated with a lip or lips'. The *phonemic* term 'labial' means different things for describing different languages. In describing the Oneida language it would be a meaningless term. In describing English, it means 'forbidden after /aw/'

(where /aw/ means what we spell *ou* in such words as *council*)—that is, after /aw/ without any sort of break (such as the /+/ break in *cowboy*) we never have any of the phonemes /p, b, f, v, m, k, g/ and perhaps certain others; now the first five of these are said to be forbidden after /aw/ because they are labials, and other reasons are found for the others that never occur after /aw/. Thus the term 'labial' is not *used* in phonemics (though it might still be spoken or written casually) unless to make statements about what occurs, or, because it has not yet been found to occur, is taken to be impossible. Such statements are the characteristic statements of descriptive linguistics; and among them, the statements of non-occurrence are, oddly, of the greatest importance, as will appear again below.

A telegraphic 'mark' does not signal anything by itself. In principle, it takes an assembly of marks and spaces to make up a signal. Then the one-dot Morse E is a sort of accident, what mathematicians call a 'trivial' or 'degenerate' case; it is a molecule of only one atom, like a helium molecule.

The same is true of phonemes. Linguistic signalling is done, not with phonemes, but with morphemes, like either morpheme of the word *noses*. It is only when the coding has been built up at least to the morpheme level that it is permissible to talk of 'meaning'. The morphemes, when viewed from the phonemic level, are assemblies; viewed from levels of higher complexity, the morphemes appear as unanalysable units; viewed from the outside, the morphemes are sub-assemblies in engineering terminology. They combine into larger sub-assemblies, and these again and again into more and more massive ones, until a complete utterance has been built up, through a number of stages of assembly. In the English sentence about the councillors, at least seven stages of assembly can be found, at least seven layers of complexity in the coding of a fairly simple message. We shall discuss them only summarily.

If we start with the complete utterance and break it down by stages until we arrive at the phonemes, a pattern of analysis emerges which has interesting peculiarities. As a whole it belongs to the category 'sentence'; nothing less than all of it is classified thus; this classification is plainly marked by details of rhythm and intonation which the spelling does not indicate but which are essential structural details of English. Parts of it belong to different classes, as we shall see in detail; and the classes found early in the analysis are partly the same and partly not the same classes as those found later.

First analysis: cut it into *the councillors* and *all put their glasses on their noses*. The first part is a 'noun-phrase' because it fits into the sentence in the same way as a plain 'noun' might, such as the word *councillors*; its further analysis will of course agree with this, for example it contains the word *the* and a 'noun', and such combinations generally make up noun-phrases. It is an 'actor-expression', we might say "by default" (as so often in English) because of the absence of any other candidate for the job, while the rest of the sentence, the 'action-expression', can use one and will cause anything to be so classified which is not marked as having a different value: this one is rather marked as probably being an 'actor-expression' by the fact that it is a 'noun-phrase' and stands first (a position which signifies 'actor' in this language and certain others, not including German!), and its classification as an 'actor-expression' is not forbidden by any such mark as the *s* of *man's*. Hence it is 'common' rather than 'possessive', although it is not marked as such, as the words *man* and *men* are: the apostrophe of *councillor's* or of *councillors'* belongs to the spelling, not to the language. Therefore the final *s* here marks it as belonging to the 'plural' category; this is at least not forbidden by the form *put*, while *puts* would refuse to fit it; therefore, when we later analyse the 'action-expression' we shall classify *put* as 'plural' whereupon it will be seen that *put* is not marked as either 'present' or 'past', while *puts* would have been marked as 'present'. It is marked as 'definite' by the presence of *the* in it; being 'definite', it will fit a 'plural' 'action-expression' containing the word *all* used as it is here, which at least some 'indefinite' 'actor-expressions' will not fit, for instance *some councillors*. In summary, this *the councillors* is a 'common definite plural noun-phrase' functioning as an 'actor-expression'; it will not do simply to call it a 'common definite plural noun-phrase actor-expression' because then 'common' would be made redundant by 'actor-expression'. On the other hand, 'actor-expression' is not made redundant by 'common', for 'common rather than possessive' will fit other categories besides 'actor-expression', as in *I met the councillors*. It is precisely such asymmetries, found everywhere in language, which makes our analysis possible and keeps our arguments from being circular. The reader may check through this paragraph for other asymmetries and see how they were taken advantage of.

Second analysis: cut *the councillors* into *the* and *councillors*. The reader can set up the discussion himself on the model of the preceding paragraph.

Third analysis: cut *councillors* into *councillor* and *s*. Now *councillor* looks like a word, but in this sentence it is not a word; we can call it a 'stem' here; to it is added the 'morpheme' *s*. Discussion of this would use up our space unprofitably.

Fourth analysis: cut *councillor* into *council* and *or*. Either one of these is a morpheme. The first of them looks like the one-morpheme word *council*, but here it isn't; a 'morpheme' is all we can call it. It belongs to that category of morphemes which is defined by the fact that each of them will combine with the morpheme *or*; and it belongs to other categories similarly defined by possibilities of combination: for example, it will combine with certain *s* morphemes, to make the possessive singular *council's* or the plural *councils* or *councils'*. It will be noted that these criteria of classification are essentially of the same sort as those used in our first analysis, but now the categories are different.

Fifth analysis: we may or may not choose to break *council* into two syllables, but it appears that we can never get any profit out of doing so in our language, so we cut it at once into seven phonemes—by an odd accident, the same as the number of letters in the spelling—by a single act of analysis.

Now we have arrived at the phoneme level, and no further analysis is called for by the kind of procedure we have been following. We can classify the phonemes into different categories of vowels and consonants, as was indicated above for Spanish and English. Then we could, if we chose, treat these intersecting categories as component parts, and this work, known as componential analysis or analysis into distinctive features, is done by some linguists. But although this procedure helps in settling arguments about the adequate phonemic analysis of a language, it doesn't often shed any light on the higher organization of the language. Hence we may as well stop here and say that we have reached the lowest level of analysis when we have split *council* into seven phonemes. Here it was called the fifth analysis; to get to the bottom of the second half of the same sentence would have required going to a seventh analysis. This is the reason why we prefer to start numbering from the bottom, and to speak rather of successive syntheses, from phonemes up to the complete utterance, reaching different heights in different parts of it.

Within an English morpheme some sequences of phonemes are forbidden. For example, what is commonly spelled *ou* (as in *council*) is never followed immediately by any of /p, b, f, v, m/. We have seen that analogous restrictions apply at every level of analysis up to the complete utterance. Above the level of the phonemic system, these restrictions define for us the 'grammar' of the language, and all without reference to what is popularly thought of as the 'meaning', namely the popular categorizations of continuous reality such as 'nose' or 'numerous', just as we find it expedient to define the phonemic system independently of the phonetician's categorizations of continuous speech (although borrowing some of his terms). Typically, the elements of a grammar are stated as possibilities and impossibilities of occurrence, especially the latter, for example the English elementary grammatical fact that *this* is not followed by *men* without at least a comma between: *this men* is not English, but *This, men, is what I want* is. (Statements of what *can* occur are more difficult.) And these possibilities and impossibilities are all a posteriori: they are based on observation only, not on logic, and thus not on meaning.

Could we perhaps do something further with 'meaning' inside linguistics? Yes, but only on condition that we distinguish sharply between the inside and the outside. Let the sociologists keep the outside or practical meaning; then we can undertake to describe the pure linguistic meaning. We can do it thus:

Among permissible combinations of morphemes, some are commoner than others. Thus there are conditional probabilities of occurrence of each morpheme in context with others. The conditional probability of a forbidden occurrence is of course *zero* and drops out of the picture. If we ever found a conditional probability of *one*, we should decide that we had made a miscalculation, and that what we thought was composed of two morphemes was really unanalysably one morpheme (perhaps a discontinuous one).

Now the linguist's 'meaning' of a morpheme is by definition the set of conditional probabilities of its occurrence in context with all other morphemes—of course without inquiry into the outside, practical, or sociologist's meaning of any of them. Of course we have no zero probabilities in the set, and in practice we should neglect all very small probabilities. So far we have done almost nothing with pure linguistic 'meaning' as so defined, for the obvious reason that its mathematics is of the continuous sort, which we are not accustomed to handling—continuous by statistical derivation from discreteness, but still unmanageable under our working habits. Still, a beginning has been made on a structural semantics by one linguist. He replaces all small conditional probabilities by *zero*, and all large ones by *one*, so as to get a discrete mathematics again, in which he can work with synonymy that is absolute by definition. (He makes no such claims for his procedure, incidentally: he calls it 'discourse analysis' and applies it to single texts.) This work is very recent, and is the most exciting thing that has happened in linguistics for quite a few years; in spite of its theoretical flaw as a semantic analysis, it has produced some very elegant and illuminating results.

We can close with a general characterization of linguistics and language. Most well-known mathematical maps are connected with the real world by a single intuitive bridge; linguistics is connected with reality by two of them, so that a language makes a correspondence between a real noise and a real thing or the like (between an utterance and its referents). This defines language as symbolic. Overt acts of speech alter reality in that changes in listener's behavior correspond to them. This defines speech as communication. The technique is organized, patterned, as disclosed by linguistic science. This defines language as systematic. Altogether, then, we have defined a language as a symbolic communication system, or in one word, as a 'code'.

26

'Prototypes Save'

ANNA WIERZBICKA

INTRODUCTION

Prototypes are 'in'. After years of self-doubt and inferiority complexes, it may seem that semantics has found the key to unlock—at last—the mysteries of meaning. This key resides in the concept of prototype.[1]

The role that the concept of prototype plays in current semantics is analogous to that which the concept of Gricean maxims has played in generative grammar. A well-placed witness, James McCawley (1981: 215), identified this role with the excellent slogan: 'Grice saves'. In grammar, if there is a conflict between postulated rules and the actual usage, Grice rescues the grammarian: the usage can now be accounted for in terms of Gricean maxims. (Cf. Bach and Harnish 1982; for a critical discussion, see Green 1983; Wierzbicka 1986b, c, 1987b.)

Similarly in semantics. For example, the actual usage of individual words is too messy, too unpredictable, to be accounted for by definitions. But fortunately, semanticists don't have to worry about it any longer: they can now deploy the notion of 'prototype'. And just as the failure of grammatical rules to work can now be proclaimed as evidence of progress in linguistics (because we have discovered the all-explaining role of Gricean maxims in language), the failure of semantic formulae to work can also be proclaimed as evidence of progress in semantics. 'Semantic formulae *should not* "work"'; that's one thing that 'prototypes' have taught us.

In what follows, I will discuss two sets of examples. The first set will illustrate the tendency to abuse the concept of prototype (the 'prototypes save' attitude); the second set of examples will illustrate the usefulness of this concept when it is used as a specific analytical tool and not as a universal thought-saving device.

THE 'PROTOTYPES SAVE' APPROACH

The meaning of *boat*

Discussing the meaning of the English word *boat*, Verschueren (1985: 48) says the following:

In trying to determine the meaning of the word BOAT, one could come up with a definition such as a 'man-made object that can be used for travelling on water'. A defender of the checklist approach, coming across a boat with a hole in it and deciding that he/she still wants to call it a BOAT (though it cannot be

---

* Anna Wierzbicka, ' "Prototypes save": on the uses and abuses of the notion of "prototype" in linguistics and related fields', in Savas L. Tsohatzidis (ed.), *Meanings and Prototypes: Studies in Linguistic Categorization* (London: Routledge, 1990), 347–67. © 1990 Anna Wierzbicka.

[1] I would like to thank Dwight Bolinger and David Wilkins for their helpful comments on an earlier draft of this paper.

used for travelling on water anymore), would have to revise his/her definition: 'a man-made object that can normally be used for travelling on water, but in which there can also be a hole'. Further, he/she would have to determine how big the hole can be before the object in question is not a BOAT anymore, but simply a WRECK. The impracticality of the checklist approach is such that not even its proponents would want to be guilty of the absurdities mentioned. A defender of the alternative theory could simply stick to his/her definition and describe a boat with a hole in terms of deviations from the prototypical boat.

The reasoning in this passage goes like this: 'The formula we have proposed ("boat" is a man-made object that can be used for travelling on water) doesn't work; one might think that this formula should be rejected, therefore, and that a better one should be sought; fortunately, this is not the case—we can accept the leaking formula as it is, and blame the leaking on the "nature of meaning"; this will dispense us from the need to do any further work on the concept "boat"; the first formula which comes to mind is good enough, no matter how it leaks, because we can always appeal to the notion of prototype.'

But instead of appealing to prototypes, couldn't we simply rephrase the formula just a little? Couldn't we say, in the first place, that boats are a kind of thing *made* for 'travelling on water' rather than *able* to 'travel on water'? It is quite true that a boat with a very big hole can't 'travel on water', but why phrase the definition in terms of *ability* rather than *intended function* anyway?

The meaning of *bachelor*

Extolling 'fuzziness' and 'prototypes' in language, Lakoff (1986: 43–4) writes:

Fuzziness may also arise from nongraded concepts—concepts defined by models that have no scales built into them. Fillmore (1982) gives as an example the time-honoured case of *bachelor*. He observes that *bachelor* is defined relative to an idealized model of the world, one in which there is a social institution of marriage, marriage is monogamous, and between people of opposite sexes...

This idealized model fits the classical theory of categories. Within the model, *bachelor* is a very clearly defined Aristotelian category. But this idealized cognitive model, or ICM, does not fit the world as we know it very well. When this model is placed within the context of the rest of our knowledge, fuzziness arises—not because of what is in the model but because of discrepancies between the background assumptions of the model and the rest of our knowledge. Here are some cases where the background conditions fail, and as a result it is difficult to give clear, unequivocal answers:

Is Tarzan a bachelor?

Is the Pope a bachelor?...

The answers to such questions are not clear-cut, and the reason is that the idealized model with respect to which *bachelor* is defined may not fit well with the rest of our knowledge. The source of fuzziness here is not within the model, but in the interaction of the model with other models characterizing other aspects of our knowledge.

Fuzziness of the above sort leads to prototype effects—cases of better and worse examples of bachelors.

Thus the perennial *bachelor* turns up again in a new role. Thirty years ago, the most fashionable semantic theory of the time—Katz and Fodor's (1963) 'new semantic theory'— made its triumphant entry into linguistics perched precariously on this same example; today, the theory of prototypes finds the *bachelor* example equally serviceable. But if the formula 'bachelor—an unmarried (adult) male person' doesn't work, couldn't we perhaps revise it slightly, to make it work—couldn't we, to wit, replace it with the following definition: 'bachelor—an unmarried man thought of as someone who could marry'?

What cases such as this make clear is that discussions of 'necessary and sufficient features' typically focus on physical features, and ignore mental ones. Yet natural language concepts often constitute amalgams of both kinds of components. For 'bachelor', being thought of as someone who can marry is as necessary as being male and unmarried.

The meaning of *congratulate*

According to Verschueren (1985: 47), 'a typical congratulation is an expression of the speaker's being pleased about the hearer's success in doing or obtaining something important. The first aspect (i.e. the speaker's pleasure, A. W.) of this prototypical meaning is completely absent from many formal acts of congratulating. The second aspect (i.e. the hearer's success) is being tampered with in the following headline from the *International Herald Tribune*: "Begin congratulates Sadat on *their* Nobel [Prize]." '

I would like to take issue with the assertion that the expression of pleasure 'is completely absent from many formal acts of congratulating'. Apparently, the *expression* of pleasure (i.e., *saying* that one is pleased) is being confused here with the *experience* of pleasure (i.e. with *being* pleased). Of course in many acts of congratulating, the *experience* of pleasure is absent; but if one doesn't *say* (or otherwise *convey*) that one is pleased, there is no act of congratulating. Surely, an expression of pleasure is part of the invariant of the concept 'congratulate', not just part of its prototype?

The meaning of *bird*

In a number of recent (and not so recent) articles, George Lakoff has been accusing other linguists of dealing in various 'convenient fictions', and castigating them for failing to recognize that semantic categories are 'fuzzy'—a point which he believes has been established in Eleanor (Heider) Rosch's work. For example, he writes (Lakoff 1972: 458–9):

Eleanor Rosch Heider [1973b] took up the question of whether people perceive category membership as a clear-cut issue or a matter of degree. For example, do people think of members of a given species as being simply birds or nonbirds, or do people consider them birds to a certain degree? Heider's results consistently showed the latter. She asked subjects to rank birds as to the degree of their birdiness, that is, the degree to which they matched the ideal of a bird. If category membership were simply a yes-or-no matter, one would have expected the subjects either to balk at the task or to produce random results. Instead, a fairly well-defined hierarchy of 'birdiness' emerged.

(1) Birdiness hierarchy
   robins
   eagles
   chickens, ducks, geese
   penguins, pelicans
   bats

Robins are typical of birds. Eagles, being predators, are less typical. Chickens, ducks, and geese somewhat less still. Bats hardly at all. And cows not at all.

It is hard to see, however, how this reasoning can be reconciled with native speakers' firm intuition that whereas a bat is definitely *not* a bird at all, an ostrich *is* a bird—a 'funny' bird, an atypical bird, but a bird. This would seem to support a conclusion opposite to Lakoff's: bats, which have no feathers and no beaks and don't lay eggs, are disqualified, because feathers, beaks and eggs are thought of as *necessary* (rather than merely prototypical) components of the concept 'bird'[2] (cf. Wierzbicka 1985: 180); for further discussion of 'bird' see below.

Of course, if informants are specifically instructed to *range* a set of given species terms on a 'scale of birdiness', and if the set they are given includes both bats and cows, one can understand why they might decide to place bats above cows, but does this really establish that bats are thought of as having any degree of 'birdiness', and that it is impossible to draw a line between words for birds and words for things other than birds?

The meaning of *lie*

According to Coleman and Kay (1981), whether or not an utterance is a lie is a matter of degree, and there is no set of necessary and sufficient components characterizing the concept 'lie'. This conclusion, which has since been accepted and endorsed in countless linguistic articles and books, is based partly on so-called social lies and white lies and partly on cases of deception by evasion. For example, insincere utterances such as 'What a lovely dress!' or 'How nice to see you!' or 'Drop in any time!' are claimed to be partial lies, rather than either lies or non-lies. Similarly, false reassurances given to terminally ill patients are regarded as partial lies, rather than either lies or non-lies. Finally, answers which are literally true but which are intended to mislead or deceive the addressee (e.g., 'Where are you going?' 'We're out of paprika.') are also categorized as partial lies.

It is very interesting to see that many informants are prepared to classify 'social lies', charitable lies and evasions as 'partial lies' or the like. However, semanticists are not obliged to take informants' judgements at face value. Coleman and Kay's methodology—like Rosch's—tends to produce results expected and desired by the researchers. Since the informants were given a seven-point scale from 1 ('very sure not-lie') to 7 ('very sure lie'), they acted as expected and arranged all the instances offered them somewhere along the scale. In any case, Coleman and Kay's aim ('we intend to challenge the very notion of the discrete semantic feature') can hardly be said to have been achieved. The word *lie* can be given a perfectly valid definition in terms of 'discrete semantic features' (cf. Wierzbicka 1985a: 341–2):

X lied to Y. =
X said something to Y
X knew it was not true
X said it because X wanted Y to think it was true
[people would say: if someone does this, it is bad]

Of course there are similarities between lies and insincere or evasive utterances, as there are similarities between birds and bats, and informants are aware of that. But this does not demonstrate that the notion of the discrete semantic feature is not valid.

The fact that informants' responses are often graded is interesting, but as Armstrong *et al.* (1983: 284) put it, it is probably 'a fact about something other than the structure of concepts'—particularly in view of the fact that graded responses are also triggered by evidently discrete concepts such as 'odd numbers' (some odd numbers being rated by informants as odder than others, e.g. 3 being rated as odder than 501; Armstrong *et al.* 1983).

---

[2] When I speak of the concept 'bird' I mean the concept encoded in the English word *bird*. Other languages may of course have no word for 'bird', having lexically encoded slightly different concepts. For example, the closest counterpart of *bird* in the Australian language Nunggubuyu does include bats, as well as grasshoppers (Heath 1978: 41). The closest equivalent of *bird* in the Australian language Warlpiri excludes bats, but it also excludes emus (Hale *et al.*, forthcoming). The prototype may well be the same in all these languages, but the boundaries are drawn differently. An adequate semantic analysis should reflect this.

It might be added that Sweetser (1987: 62) goes even further than Coleman and Kay in the direction of 'prototypical reduction', and claims that 'a lie is simply a false statement'. She realizes, of course, that the use of *lie* cannot be fully predicted from this simple definition, but, she claims 'we all know from bitter experience how readily the complexities of meaning elude the reductionist formal analysis' (1987: 63)—that is, how difficult it is to define anything in a way which would make the right predictions. Luckily, she thinks, the prototype theory can save us from the trouble of even trying to do so. In the case of *lie*, it is enough to define it as a 'false statement'; the lack of fit between the definition and the use can then be explained in terms of our cultural models of relevant areas of experience.

This explanation clearly collapses, however, when one realizes that a language may have two, or more, words designating 'false statements', and that they may be used differently. For example, Russian has two words corresponding to lying: *vrat'* and *lgat'*, whose uses overlap rather than coincide. If students of Russian are told that both these words mean 'false statement' and that any further guidelines concerning their use should be deduced from the Russian 'cultural model', how will they know how to differentiate the uses of *vrat'* and *lgat'*? On the other hand, carefully phrased definitions *can* guide the students in their use, and in their interpretation, of these words.

Cultural models are important indeed, but they are not 'another important factor', in addition to meaning. Cultural models are reflected in the meanings of words. The model encoded in the meaning of *vrat'* is somewhat different from that encoded in the meaning of *lgat'*; and both of these models are somewhat different from that encoded in the meaning of *lie*.[3] It may be difficult to articulate these meanings adequately (that is, in a way which would ensure full predictive power), but it is not impossible to do so. (For a large body of predictive definitions of speech act verbs see Wierzbicka 1987a.)

The meaning of *mother*

According to George Lakoff (1986: 37), the concept of 'mother' cannot be given an invariant definition, because it is an 'experiential cluster' and because no definition 'will cover the full range of cases'. The range of cases coming under this concept is, according to Lakoff, very wide, and cannot be reduced to any common core (such as, for instance, 'a woman who has given birth to a child'), because the word *mother* refers not only to 'biological mothers' but also to adoptive mothers, 'donor mothers' (who provide eggs but not wombs), 'surrogate mothers' (who provide wombs but not eggs), and so on.

Lakoff's argument is so idiosyncratic that if one is not to be suspected of misrepresenting it, it is best to quote it verbatim:

This phenomenon is beyond the scope of the classical theory. The concept *mother* is not clearly defined, once and for all, in terms of common necessary and sufficient conditions. There need be no necessary and sufficient conditions for motherhood shared by normal biological mothers, donor mothers (who donate an egg), surrogate mothers (who bear the child, but may not have donated the egg), adoptive mothers, unwed mothers who give their children up for adoption, and stepmothers. They are all mothers by virtue

---

[3] De Jonge (1982: 155) defines *vran'e* (a noun corresponding to *vrat'*) as 'creative lying designed to make the liar appear interesting and important', and he calls it 'a particular Russian habit' (*vrat'* being indeed the most basic Russian word corresponding to *lie*). Bogusławski (1983: 110) notes, however, that one can also say *termometr vret* 'the thermometer is "lying"' or *časy vrut* 'the watch is "lying"', meaning that the instruments in question are unreliable or inaccurate. I think De Jonge is right in implying that the concept of *vrat'* embodies an important cultural model, and it is a challenging task to construct an adequate definition of this concept; but it certainly won't do to say that *vrat'* means simply 'to make a false statement', as it won't do for the English concept of 'lying'.

of their relation to the ideal case, where the base models converge. That ideal case is one of the many kinds of cases that give rise to prototype effects. (Lakoff 1986: 39; see also Lakoff 1987: 83)

It is interesting to note that Lakoff's ideas on these matters have been warmly endorsed by the anthropologist Roger Keesing (1985), in whose view they open completely new perspectives for the anthropological study of kinship.

From a semantic point of view, however, Lakoff's claims carry little conviction. The crucial point which Lakoff overlooks is that foster mothers, adoptive mothers, 'genetic mothers', 'surrogate mothers' and so on are not 'mothers' on a par with 'biological mothers' (cf. Bogusławski 1970). Without a modifier, the word *mother* ('X is Y's mother') refers clearly to birth-givers, not to the donors of eggs, providers of wombs, caretakers, or fathers' spouses.

Lakoff points out that the expression *real mother* may refer to a caretaker as well as to a birth-giver ('She raised me and I called her mother, but she is not my real mother'; 'She gave birth to me, but she was never a real mother to me'), but he fails to notice the syntactic—and hence the semantic—difference between *my real mother* (either birthgiver or caretaker) and *a real mother to me* (caretaker only). Furthermore, he fails to notice that the test with *real* is not semantically reliable. For example, sentences such as 'he is a real man' or 'she is a real woman' may refer to the speaker's views or prejudices about men and women which have no basis in the semantics of the words *man* and *woman*. He fails to appreciate the implications of the fact that the expression *biological mother* would be used only in a contrastive context, and that normally (without a contrastive context) one would not say, 'she is his biological mother', whereas expressions such as *foster mother*, *adoptive mother* or *surrogate mother* are not restricted to contrastive contexts.

To treat 'biological mothers' as being on a par with 'surrogate mothers' or 'foster mothers' is a little like saying that there are two kinds of horses: biological horses and rocking horses (or that there are two diverging 'models of horsehood': a biological model and an artifact model); and that we cannot define *horse* as 'a kind of animal...' because a rocking horse is not a kind of animal at all.

I am not saying that the meaning of the word *mother* can be wholly reduced to that of 'birth-giver'; arguably, a social and psychological component is also present:

X is Y's mother. =
(a) before Y was a person Y was inside X and was like a part of X
(b) because of this one would think that X would think this:
  'I want to do good things for Y
  I don't want bad things to happen to Y'

But the social and psychological component (b) has to be formulated in terms of expectations, not in terms of actual events; by contrast, the biological component (a) has to be formulated as actual (cf. Wierzbicka 1980: 46–9).

The meaning of *furniture*

In a paper entitled 'Cognitive representations of semantic categories', Rosch (1975b: 193) wrote:

When we hear a category word in a natural language such as *furniture* or *bird* and understand its meaning, what sort of cognitive representation do we generate? A list of features necessary and sufficient for an item to belong to the category? A concrete image which represents the category? A list of category members? An ability to use the category term with no attendant mental representation at all? Or some other, less easily specified, form of representation?

This passage contains an implicit assumption that *bird* and *furniture* are the same sort of 'category words'. Following Rosch, countless psychologists and, more surprisingly, linguists, adopted this assumption as self-evidently correct. There are, however, clear grammatical indications (as well as semantic evidence) to show that the two words embody completely different kinds of concepts. *Bird* is a taxonomic concept, standing for a particular 'kind of creature'. But *furniture* is not a taxonomic concept at all: it is a *collective* concept (cf. Wierzbicka 1984 and 1985a; Zubin and Köpke 1985), which stands for a heterogeneous collection of things of different kinds. One can't talk of 'three furnitures' as one can of 'three birds', and one can't imagine or draw an unspecified piece of furniture, as one can draw an unspecified bird. For *birds*, one can draw a line between birds and not-birds (bats being clearly in the latter category). For *furniture*, one *cannot* draw a line between kinds of things which are included in this supercategory and things which are not—because by virtue of its meaning, the word *furniture* doesn't aim at identifying any particular kind of thing. The concept 'furniture' may indeed be said to be 'fuzzy'—like those encoded in all the other collective nouns designating heterogeneous collections of things (*kitchenware*, *crockery*, *clothing*, and so on). But it is hard to see how the study of such collective nouns (mistaken for words of the same kind as countables such as *bird*) may constitute anything like 'a refutation of the psychological reality of an Aristotelian view of categories' in general (Rosch 1975b: 225).

People may argue whether or not a radio is 'furniture' (cf. Abelson 1981: 725), but not whether or not a pelican is a bird (cf. Armstrong *et al.* 1983: 268).

The meaning of *toy*

According to George Lakoff (1972), (who bases his claims on Rosch's investigations), *ball* and *doll* are among the 'central members' of the category 'toy', just as *robin* and *sparrow* are among the 'central members' of the category *bird*. *Swing* and *skates* are among the 'peripheral members' of the category 'toy', just as *chicken* and *duck* are among the 'peripheral members' of the category *bird*. Consequently, just as one cannot say whether chickens, ducks (and bats) are birds or not-birds, one cannot say whether swings and skates are toys or not-toys. All one can say is that they are toys to a certain degree (less than balls or dolls).

But the analogy between *bird* and *toy* is just as spurious as that between *bird* and *furniture*. While *bird* is a taxonomic concept, which stands for a particular *kind* of thing, *toy* is no more a taxonomic concept than *furniture* is. It is a purely functional concept, which stands for things of *any kind* made for children to play with. One cannot draw an unspecified toy, just as one cannot draw an unspecified piece of furniture. The category 'toy' is 'fuzzy'—because, by virtue of its semantic structure (entirely different from the semantic structure of 'bird') it does not aim at identifying any particular *kind* of thing. Words such as *sparrow*, *chicken* and *ostrich* can be shown to contain in their meaning the component 'bird' (cf. Wierzbicka 1985a), and it is quite legitimate to start their definitions with the phrase *a kind of bird*. But words such as *ball* or *doll* do not contain in their meaning the component 'toy'. They may be seen as 'central members' of the category 'toy', but this is quite irrelevant from the point of view of their semantic structure. It would be completely unjustified to open the definitions of the words *ball* and *doll* with the phrase *a kind of toy*. There are many balls used in various sports (rugby, soccer, cricket, etc.) which are not thought of as 'toys' at all; and there are many dolls (e.g. china dolls kept on the mantelpiece) which are not thought of as toys. Whatever we discover about the structure of purely functional concepts such as 'toy' (or 'vehicle', or 'weapon', or 'tool'), it cannot be transferred to taxonomic supercategories such as 'bird', 'flower' or 'tree'. The semantic relation between *sparrow* and *bird* is entirely different from that between *ball* and *toy*.

The meaning of *game*

The concept of 'game' was no doubt the most influential example of the alleged 'fuzziness' of human concepts which has been offered in the literature. It was brought up by Ludwig Wittgenstein, in a famous passage of his *Philosophical Investigations*. Wittgenstein didn't appeal to the concept of prototype, but he appealed to—and indeed introduced—the related concept of 'family resemblance' between concepts. The underlying assumption was the same: concepts cannot be given clear definitions in terms of discrete semantic components; it is impossible to capture the semantic invariant of a concept such as, for example, 'game'—because all that different instances share is a vague 'family resemblance', not a specifiable set of features.

Wittgenstein's idea of 'family resemblance' has played a colossal role in the development of 'prototype semantics', and the popularity of this school of thought is no doubt due substantially to his intellectual charisma.

In the present writer's view, Wittgenstein's writings contain some of the deepest and the most insightful observations on semantic matters to be found anywhere. But despite my gratitude to Wittgenstein I think the time has come to re-examine his doctrine of 'family resemblances', which has acquired the status of unchallengeable dogma in much of the current literature on meaning (cf., for example, Jackendoff 1983; Baker and Hacker 1980; Fehr and Russell 1984). Wittgenstein (1953: 31–2) wrote:

Consider for example the proceedings that we call 'games'. I mean board-games, card-games, Olympic games, and so on. What is common to them all? Don't say: 'There *must* be something common, or they would not be called "games"—but *look and see* whether there is anything common to all. For if you look at them you will not see something that is common to *all*, but similarities, relationships, and a whole series of them at that. To repeat: don't think, but look! Look for example at board-games, with their multifarious relationships. Now pass to card-games; here you find many correspondences with the first group, but many common features drop out, and others appear. When we pass next to ball-games, much that is common is retained, but much is lost. Are they all 'amusing'? Compare chess with noughts and crosses. Or is there always winning and losing, or competition between players? Think of patience. In ball games there is winning and losing; but when a child throws his ball at the wall and catches it again, this feature has disappeared. Look at the parts played by skill and luck; and at the difference between skill in chess and skill in tennis. Think now of games like ring-a-ring-a-roses; here is the element of amusement, but how many other characteristic features have disappeared! And we can go through the many, many other groups of games in the same way; can see how similarities crop up and disappear.

And the result of this examination is: we see a complicated network of similarities overlapping and criss-crossing: sometimes overall similarities, sometimes similarities of detail.

I can think of no better expression to characterize these similarities than 'family resemblances'; for the various resemblances between members of a family: build, features, colour of eyes, gait, temperament, etc. etc. overlap and criss-cross in the same way. And I shall say: 'games' form a family.

Passages like these have a hypnotic force, and it is not surprising that they have exercised a great influence on countless philosophers, psychologists, and linguists. But are Wittgenstein's claims really *true*? Is it indeed impossible to say what all games have in common, i.e. impossible to capture the *invariant* of the concept 'game'?

The only valid form of challenge in a case like this is to try to *do* the 'impossible', to try to define the concept of 'game'. I would suggest that the following components are essential to this concept: (1) human action (animals can play, but they don't play games); (2) duration (a game can't be momentary); (3) aim: pleasure; (4) 'suspension of reality' (the participants imagine that they are in a world apart from the real world); (5) well-defined goals (the participants know what they are trying to achieve); (6) well-defined rules (the participants know what they can do and what they cannot do); (7) the course of events is unpredictable (nobody can know what exactly is going to happen). Accordingly, I propose the following definition: *games*

(1) things that people do
(2) when they do something for some time,
(3) for pleasure,
(4) imagining that they are in a world
(5) where they want to cause some things to happen,
(6) where they know what they can do and what they cannot do
(7) and where no one knows all that will happen

I believe that this definition[4] applies satisfactorily to board-games, card-games, ball-games, and countless other kinds of activities called 'games'. It does not apply to a situation when a child idly throws his ball at the wall and catches it again, but in English this activity would not be called a game. In German, the word *Spiel* has a wider range of use, corresponding roughly to the English *playing*. But this very fact contradicts Wittgenstein's (1953: 33) claim that 'we do not know the boundaries because none have been drawn...' Boundaries do exist, and they have been drawn differently in different languages, and native speakers subconsciously know them and respect them. One feature which separates the concept of 'game' lexically encoded in English from the concept of 'Spiel' lexically encoded in German, is the idea of rules: of knowing beforehand what one can do and what one cannot do. Another difference has to do with the idea of a well-defined goal, which may or may not be attained. If features like these are not identified and clearly stated, cross-linguistic lexical research cannot succeed. It is not surprising that linguists who have become intoxicated with 'family resemblances' do not engage in such research.

USEFULNESS OF THE CONCEPT OF 'PROTOTYPE' IN SEMANTICS

So far, the discussion has been focused primarily on what I see as the abuses and misuses of the concept of 'prototype'. It is time to turn to the more positive aspects of the idea of 'prototype'. 'Prototype' doesn't save, but it can help if it is treated with caution and with care, and, above all, if it is combined with verbal definitions, instead of being treated as an excuse for not ever defining anything.

Lexicographic practice suggests that the concept of 'prototype' can be utilized in a number of different ways. Limitations of space here permit only a bird's eye survey of a number of different illustrative examples.

The meaning of colour terms

As I have argued in Wierzbicka (1980a), the meaning of words such as *red* or *blue* can be defined along the following lines:

red—colour thought of as the colour of blood
blue—colour thought of as the colour of the sky

---

[4] The definition of *games* proposed here is not meant to cover cases of metaphorical extension, ironic or humourous use, and the like, as, for example, in the case of the phrase 'the games people play', or in the case of 'games' played by mathematicians, generative grammarians, or other scholars who enjoy solving difficult problems for their own sake. Here as elsewhere in semantics, playful extensions have to be distinguished from the basic meaning (which explains both the 'normal' use of the word and any extensions from that use).

Since this analysis was first proposed, a number of critics have questioned the use of the phrase *thought of as* in these definitions, and one critic (Goddard, 1989) has proposed the addition of the concept 'like' to my proposed list of universal semantic primitives. Taking this into account, one could perhaps rephrase the explications of colour terms along the following lines:

X is red—the colour of X is like the colour of blood
X is blue—the colour of X is like the colour of the sky

The details remain controversial (cf. Wilkins, forthcoming, and Wierzbicka 1985a: 77–80), but there is a wide range of evidence to suggest that, in principle, the use of 'prototypes' such as blood or sky in the explications of colour terms is well justified.

Jackendoff (1983: 113), among others, has tried to use colour terms as evidence that natural language concepts cannot be exhaustively defined into primitives. He wrote: 'once the marker *color* is removed from the reading of "red", what is left to decompose further? How can one make sense of redness minus coloration?' I hope that the formulae adduced above provide an answer to these questions (cf. also Wierzbicka 1990).

The meaning of words for emotions

In a sense, one cannot convey to a blind person what the word *red* stands for (cf. Locke 1947: 239); or to someone who has never experienced envy what the word *envy* stands for. None the less, it IS possible to define *envy* in terms of a prototypical situation, along the following lines (cf. Wierzbicka 1972, 1980a, and 1986d):

X feels envy. =
X feels like someone who thinks this:
    something good has happened to that other person
    it hasn't happened to me
    I want things like that to happen to me

Definitions of this kind demonstrate, I think, the spuriousness of the dilemma of whether emotions are better thought of as prototypes or as 'classically definable' (cf. Ortony *et al.* 1987: 344). It has often been argued that emotion concepts cannot be defined because nobody has managed to define them (cf. e.g. Fehr and Russell 1984). But, as pointed out by Ortony *et al.* (1987: 344), 'the observation that philosophers and psychologists have so far failed to specify adequate definitions of emotion(s) does not establish that the goal is impossible'. Whether or not definitions of the kind proposed above for *envy* constitute a 'classical' account is a matter for discussion. They do establish, however, that emotions ARE definable; and that they are definable in terms of a prototypical situation, and a prototypical reaction to it. Without definitions of this kind, it would be impossible to account for the relationships between concepts such as 'envy', 'jealousy', 'hatred', 'contempt', 'pity', 'admiration', and so on. It would also be impossible to compare, and to interpret, emotion concepts cross-linguistically (cf. Wierzbicka 1986d). If the study of emotion concepts encoded in different languages is ever to get off the ground, it is crucial to understand that there is no conflict between prototypes and definitions.

The meaning of *cup*

According to Hersh and Caramazza (1976:274), 'Labov (1973) has shown that attempts to give well-defined characterizations in terms of traditional componential analysis of the semantic structure of a common concept such as "cup" are inadequate.' Strictly speaking, however, Labov has only shown that definitions of *cup* offered by conventional dictionaries, such as Webster's Third, are inadequate. This is hardly surprising, but does it really establish that no 'well-defined characterizations . . . of a common concept such as "cup"' are possible? Questions of this kind are best answered by simply doing what allegedly cannot be done. For 'cup', and for a host of related concepts, I believe I have done it in Wierzbicka (1985a). The definitions provided in that work distinguish between characteristic components which are not part of the invariant, and components which are absolutely necessary.

For example, a Chinese cup, small, thin, dainty, handleless and saucerless, can still be recognized as a cup—as long as it is clearly adequate for drinking hot tea from, in a formal setting (at a table), being able to raise it to the mouth with one hand. This means that while a saucer and a handle are definitely included in the prototype of a cup (an 'ideal' cup MUST have a handle, and a saucer) they are not included in what might be called the essential part of the concept. On the other hand, the components 'made to drink hot liquids from' and 'small enough for people to be able to raise them easily to the mouth with one hand' have to be included in it. (Wierzbicka 1985: 59)

In that sense, these definitions cannot be criticized 'for treating all components as contributing equally to the definition of a term' (Hersh and Caramazza 1976: 274). At the same time, they do contradict the assertion that 'no subset of these components can conclusively be said to be necessary and sufficient to define a term' (ibid.); and they demonstrate that the opposite is true.

The meaning of *uncle*

According to Chomsky (1972: 85), it is obvious that expressions such as (33–5) below (his numbers) 'must have the same semantic representation'.

(33) John's uncle
(34) the person who is the brother of John's mother or father or the husband of the sister of John's mother or father
(35) the person who is the son of one of John's grandparents or the husband of a daughter of one of John's grandparents, but is not his father.

In my view, the meaning (and the 'semantic representation') of (35) is vastly different from that of (34). What is more relevant in the present context is that (34) is not semantically equivalent to (33) either, and that it would be wrong to regard (34) as an explication of (33). (34) treats the mother's or father's brother in the same way as a mother's or father's sister's husband, and therefore it distorts the meaning of (33). If a mother's (or a mother's mother's) sister's husband is categorized as 'uncle' at all it is done by analogy with the focal, proto-typical uncle. A definition which would exclude marginal uncles completely (such as 'X's uncle = a brother of X's mother or father') would be empirically inadequate, but a disjunction which makes no difference between focal and marginal members, is also inadequate. In my view, a satisfactory definition should account for both the invariant and the prototype. For *uncle*, the invariant consists in a certain type of human relationship; and the quality of this relationship is conveyed by the reference to the prototype. I propose the following:

X is Y's uncle. =
if someone is the brother of my mother or father
I can say of him: this is my uncle
Y can think of X like I would think of this person

The meaning of *bird*

As I have argued earlier, bats, *pace* Rosch and Lakoff, are no more birds than cows are, but ostriches and emus—which do not fly—*are* birds. Does this mean that flying is not an essential part of the concept 'bird'?

In my view, flying *is* an essential part of this concept, and the full definition of *bird*, which I have proposed in Wierzbicka (1985: 180), does mention flying (or the ability to move in the air), alongside components referring to feathers, beaks, eggs, and nests. But the definition of *bird* (like all the other definitions of 'natural kinds') is phrased in such a way that it doesn't imply that all the essential features of the concept 'bird' are realized in all creatures categorized as birds. The definition opens with the following frame:

> imagining creatures of this kind people would say these things about them . . .

Accordingly, properties such as flying, feathers, and so on are presented as essential parts of the stereotype, not as necessary features of every bird. In addition, however, the full explication of *bird* includes the following proviso: 'some creatures of this kind cannot move in the air, but wanting to imagine a creature of this kind people would imagine a creature able to move in the air'.

The meaning of *tomato, cabbage,* and *apples*

It has often been claimed that the names of biological species and other 'natural kinds' cannot be fully defined.[5] In Wierzbicka (1972) and (1980) I advocated this theory myself. Since then, however, I have found—through extensive lexicographic research—that this is a fallacy, and that *tigers* or *lemons* are no more indefinable than other concrete concepts (such as *cups* or *mugs*) or than abstract concepts (such as *freedom, love,* or *promise*).[6]

But to define either natural kinds or cultural kinds, we do need the concept of prototype. For example, for *cups* we have to predict both the fact that a prototypical cup has a handle and the fact that some cups (e.g. Chinese tea cups or Turkish coffee cups) don't have handles. Similarly, in the case of *tomatoes* we have to account both for the fact that prototypical tomatoes are red and for the fact that there are also yellow tomatoes, which are also called *tomatoes*, or at least *yellow tomatoes*. For *cabbage*, we have to predict both the fact that *cabbage* without modifier is greenish (except in elliptical sentences), and the fact that there is also the so-called *red cabbage*. For *apples*, we have to predict the fact that they can be red, green or yellow; but also the fact that wanting to imagine (or paint) 'good apples', people are more likely to imagine them red than either yellow or green.

To account for facts of this kind, it is justified, I think, to have recourse to analytical devices similar to that which has been used to account for flightless birds. For example, in the definition of *cabbage* I have included the following components.

> the leaflike parts are greenish or whitish-greenish
> in some things of this kind the leaflike parts are reddish
> wanting to imagine things of this kind people would imagine them as greenish

---

[5] See Putnam (1975a), Kripke (1972). For an excellent discussion, see Dupré (1981).
[6] For a definition of *love*, see Wierzbicka (1986a); of *freedom* (forthcoming); of *promise* (1987a). For definitions of *cup, mug,* and many other similar concepts, see Wierzbicka (1985).

The meaning of *climb*

The verb *climb* has recently had a spectacular career as a key example of a word which—allegedly—cannot be defined in terms of any necessary and sufficient components and which can only be analysed in terms of a prototype. For example, Verschueren (1985: 46) wrote:

To show that a similar analysis is feasible for verbs, I adopt an example given by Fillmore (1978); the verb TO CLIMB typically describes an *ascending* motion in a *clambering* fashion. I quote: 'A monkey climbing up a flagpole satisfies both of these conditions. The monkey climbing down the flagpole satisfies the clambering component only, but is nevertheless engaged in an action that can be properly called climbing. A snail climbing up the flagpole satisfies the ascending condition and can still be said to be climbing. But the snail is not privileged to *climb down* the flagpole, since that activity would involve neither clambering nor ascending.'

However, this analysis fails to explain why a sentence such as 'the monkey climbed the flagpole' cannot be interpreted as meaning that the monkey climbed *down* the flagpole. If the direction upward was part of the prototype but not part of the invariant, how could we be so sure that the monkey who 'climbed the flagpole' was climbing upwards?

Difficulties of this kind have prompted Jackendoff (1985) to devote to the verb *climb* a whole study, and to use it as evidence for his own version of prototype semantics, developed in Jackendoff (1983). In essence, however, Jackendoff's analysis is not very different from Fillmore's: he, too, posits for *climb* components such as 'upward' and 'clambering fashion', and he, too, claims that either of these components can be 'suppressed', though they cannot both be suppressed at the same time. For example, in the sentence 'the train climbed the mountain' the clambering manner' component is suppressed, and the component 'upwards' is present, whereas in the sentence 'Bill climbed down the ladder' it is the other way around. The semantic formulae proposed for these sentences are shown in Fig. 1 (1985: 288–9):

But this analysis is deficient, too, because it fails to predict, for example, that if a train went quickly up a hill it couldn't be described as 'climbing'. There is a difference in meaning between the (a) and (b) variants in the following pairs of sentences:

(a) The train climbed the mountain.
(b) The train shot up the mountain.

(a) The temperature climbed to 102 degrees.
(b) The temperature shot to 102 degrees.

Despite his rich arsenal of descriptive devices, including multiple brackets and 'preferential features', Jackendoff's analysis cannot account for facts of this kind.

The train climbed the mountain. =

$$\left[_{Event} \text{GO (TRAIN,} \left[_{Path} \begin{matrix} \text{TO TOP OF } \left[_{Thing} \text{MOUNTAIN}\right] \\ \text{VIA} \left[_{Place} \text{ON} \left[_{Thing} \text{MOUNTAIN}\right]\right] \\ \text{UPWARD} \end{matrix} \right])\right]$$

Bill climbed down the ladder. =

$$\left[_{Event} \begin{matrix} \text{GO(BILL, } \left[_{Path} \text{DOWN THE LADDER}\right]) \\ \left[_{Manner} \text{CLAMBERING}\right] \end{matrix} \right]$$

FIG. 1

In my view, all that is really needed to account for such facts is a more careful, and more imaginative, phrasing of the necessary and sufficient components of the concept 'climb'. Tentatively, I would propose the following:

X climbed ... =
X moved like people move in places where they have to use their arms and legs to move
upwards

For temperature, the similarity in question can hardly be interpreted as referring to anything other than slowness. For trains, it can be interpreted as referring to slowness and apparent difficulty. For people, too, it can be interpreted as referring to slowness and apparent difficulty; but it can also be interpreted as referring to a quick and apparently effortless movement upwards in places where normally people would have to use their arms and legs to move upwards at all (cf. 'Watching him climb the cliff quickly and effortlessly I was filled with pride and admiration').

Thus, a prototype is indeed relevant to the concept 'climb'. But this prototype is not 'suppressed' in less typical uses of the verb. It is part of the semantic invariant itself.

CONCLUSION

There was a time when almost any problem in linguistic analysis could be 'solved' by appealing to the distinction between 'competence' and 'performance'. These days, this particular solution to linguistic problems is usually viewed with suspicion. But the desire to find simple solutions to a range of linguistic problems has survived. 'Grice saves' and a facile resort to prototypes are two characteristic examples.

Posner (1985: 58) wrote recently: 'As impressed as I am with the insights obtained from Rosch's work, it is rather hard for me to get very excited about the great Aristotle versus Rosch debate.' Rosch's work indeed contains interesting insights, but they have not so far contributed much to semantic description. In too many cases, these new ideas have been treated as an excuse for intellectual laziness and sloppiness. In my view, the notion of prototype has to prove its usefulness through semantic description, not through semantic theorizing (cf. Wierzbicka 1985). But if it is treated as a magical key to open all doors without effort, the chances are that it will cause more harm than good.

Concepts encoded in natural language are, in a sense, vague (cf. Black 1937), but this does not mean that their semantic description should be vague, too. The challenge consists in portraying the vagueness inherent in natural language with precision. I agree entirely with Hersh and Caramazza (1976: 273) when they say that 'natural language concepts are inherently vague'. But I cannot agree with them when they go on to say that 'the meaning of a term could be specified as a *fuzzy set of meaning components*' [original emphasis]. Natural language concepts are characterized by referential indeterminacy in the sense that while 'there are things of which the description "tree" is clearly true and things of which the description "tree" is clearly false, ... there are a host of borderline cases' (Putnam 1975: 133). This doesn't mean, however, that the meaning of the word *tree* can only be specified as a fuzzy set of meaning components. I have tried to demonstrate this point conclusively by providing precise, non-fuzzy definitions of *tree*, and numerous similar concepts in Wierzbicka (1985). I have also attempted to show that even the 'fuzziest' concepts of all—'hedges' such as *approximately*, *around*, *almost*, *at least*, or *roughly*—can be given precise, non-fuzzy definitions, composed of fully specified discrete components (see Wierzbicka 1986e).

If people argue whether or not a radio is 'furniture', we don't have to account for this by saying that *radio* possesses the meaning component 'furniture' to a certain degree, less than *table* or *desk*. There are sufficient (linguistic) reasons for not including the feature 'furniture' in the meaning of either *radio* or *table* at all, as there are sufficient reasons for not including features such as 'kitchenware', 'tableware' or 'crockery' in the meaning of *cup*. It is not a matter of degree whether concepts such as *pelican, oak* or *rose* contain in their meaning components such as 'bird', 'tree', and 'flower'; they simply do contain them. Nor is it a matter of degree whether concepts such as *table, radio, refrigerator,* or *cup* contain in their meaning components such as 'furniture', 'kitchenware', 'tool', 'device', or 'implement'; they simply don't. (For justification of this claim, and for detailed semantic analyses, see Wierzbicka 1985.)

Vagueness may reside in the semantic components themselves. Components such as 'like the colour of blood' (in 'red') are indeed vague, and this vagueness is mirrored in the referential indeterminacy of the corresponding words. Components such as 'thought of as someone who can marry' are perhaps not vague but are 'subjective', not 'objective'; they refer not to the 'reality out there', but to the speakers' ways of conceptualizing reality. But neither vagueness nor subjectivity of semantic components should be confused with any 'presence to a degree'. It is not the Aristotelian notion of necessary and sufficient features which causes trouble in semantic analysis; it is the tacit behaviourist assumption that the necessary and sufficient features should correspond to measurable, objectively ascertainable aspects of external reality.

One can excuse the numerous psychologists and philosophers who have eagerly embraced the prototype theory on the assumption that most concepts have resisted all attempts to define them. (Hasn't Wittgenstein 'established' that the concept 'game' cannot be defined?)

Psychologists and philosophers are often under the impression that 'enormous efforts have gone into the attempt to identify a featural substrate' (Armstrong *et al.* 1983: 299). But this is an illusion. In fact, very little effort by professional semanticists has gone into that so far. Armstrong and her colleagues support their assertion with a reference to Katz and Fodor (1963) and Katz (1972). But, with all due respect to these writers, they are, essentially, semantic theorists, not practitioners of semantic description. It is a misunderstanding to credit theorists such as these with 'enormous efforts to identify' the semantic components of any everyday concepts.

As Armstrong *et al.* (1983: 268) point out, 'the only good answer [to the question "why do so many doubt the validity of the definitional view?", A.W.] is that the definitional theory is difficult to work out in the required detail. No one has succeeded in finding the supposed simplest categories (the features).'

But how many *bona fide* semanticists have tried to do that? It is true that not only numerous philosophers and psychologists, but also 'generations of lexicographers' (Armstrong *et al.* 1983: 301) have failed to produce successful componential definitions of everyday concepts. But lexicography has always lacked a theoretical basis. Theoretical semantics has flourished in an empirical vacuum, and lexicographers have grappled with their 'practical' tasks without any theoretical framework (cf. Wierzbicka 1985a). Given this lack of help from semantic theory, it is the lexicographers' achievements, not their failures, which are truly remarkable.

The era of serious lexicographic research, based on rigorous theoretical foundations, is just beginning (cf. Mel'čuk and Žolkovskij 1984; Wierzbicka 1986f). The success of this research will depend partly on its ability to absorb and to develop insights from the psychological and philosophical inquiry into the role of prototypes in human thinking. Above all, however, it will depend on the sustained efforts to establish the basic stock of human concepts—universal semantic primitives—out of which thoughts and complex concepts are constructed (cf. Osherson and Smith 1981: 55; cf. also Wierzbicka 1972, 1980, 1985, and 1989, forthcoming).

The natural conviction that 'the primitive conceptual repertoire *cannot* be as rich as the available repertoire of categories; hence that many concepts *must* be analysable' (Fodor *et al.* 1980: 52) has been questioned on the grounds that 'the definitions and analyses haven't been forthcoming' (ibid.). In works such as Wierzbicka (1985, 1987a), however, the definitions and analyses *have* been proposed, on a reasonably large scale. I contend that the escape from definitions was premature. We do not need prototypes to save us.

REFERENCES

Abelson, R. (1981). 'Psychological status of the script concept'. *American Psychologist* 36: 715–29.

Armstrong, S. L., L. Gleitman, and H. Gleitman (1983). 'What some concepts might not be'. *Cognition* 13: 263–308.

Bach, K., and R. Harnish (1982). *Linguistic Communication and Speech Acts.* Cambridge, Mass.: MIT Press.

Baker, G. P., and P. M. S. Hacker (1980). *Wittgenstein: Understanding and Meaning.* Oxford: Blackwell.

Black, M. (1937). 'Vagueness'. *Philosophy of Science* 4: 427–55.

Bogusławski, A. (1970). 'On semantic primitives and meaningfulness'. In A. J. Greimas, R. Jakobson, and M. R. Mayenova (eds.), *Sign, Language, Culture.* The Hague: Mouton.

——(1983). *Ilustrowany Słownik Rosyjsko-polski i Polsko-rosyjki.* Warsaw: Wiedza Powszechna.

Chomsky, N. (1972). *Studies on Semantics in Generative Grammar.* The Hague: Mouton.

Coleman, L., and P. Kay (1981). 'Prototype semantics: the English word "lie" '. *Language* 57: 26–44.

De Jonge, A. (1982). *The Life and Times of Grigorij Rasputin.* Glasgow: Fontana.

Dupré, J. (1981). 'Natural kinds and biological taxa'. *Philosophical Review* 90: 66–90.

Fehr, B., and J. Russell (1984). 'Concepts of emotion viewed from a prototype perspective'. *Journal of Experimental Psychology: General* 113: 464–86.

Fillmore, C. J. (1978). 'On the organization of semantic information in the lexicon'. In D. Farkas, W. Jakobsen, and K. Todrys (eds.), *Papers from the Parasession on the Lexicon.* Chicago: Chicago Linguistic Society.

——(1982). 'Frame semantics'. In Linguistic Society of Korea (ed.), *Linguistics in the Morning Calm.* Seoul: Hanshin.

Fodor, J. A., M. F. Garrett, E. C. Walker, and C. H. Parkes (1980). 'Against definitions'. *Cognition* 8: 263–367.

Goddard, C. (1989). 'Issues in natural semantic metalanguage'. *Quaderni di Semantica* 10: 51–64.

Green, G. (1983). 'Review of Bach and Harnish'. *Language* 59: 627–35.

Hale, K., M. Langhren, and D. Nash (forthcoming). *A Warlpiri Dictionary Project.* Cambridge, Mass.: MIT Center for Cognitive Science.

Heath, J. (1978). 'Linguistic approaches to Nunggubuyu ethnology'. In L. R. Hiatt (ed.), *Australian Aboriginal Concepts.* Canberra: Australian Institute of Aboriginal Studies.

Hersh, H., and A. Caramazza (1976). 'A fuzzy set approach to modifiers and vagueness in natural language'. *Journal of Experimental Psychology: General* 105: 254–76.

Jackendoff, R. (1983). *Semantics and Cognition.* Cambridge, Mass.: MIT Press.

——(1985). 'Multiple subcategorization: the case of "climb"'. *Natural Language and Linguistic Theory* 3: 271–95.

Katz, J. J. (1972). *Semantic Theory.* New York: Harper & Row.

——and J. A. Fodor (1963). 'The structure of a semantic theory'. *Language* 39: 170–210.

Keesing, R. (1985). 'Schneider on kinship: the view from prototype category theory'. Paper presented at a session of the American Ethnological Society Meeting, Washington, DC, 5 Dec.

Kripke, S. (1972). 'Naming and necessity'. In D. Davidson and G. Harman (eds.), *Semantics of Natural Language*. Dordrecht: Reidel.

Labov, W. (1973). 'The boundaries of words and their meanings'. In C.-J. Bailey and R. Shuy (eds.), *New Ways of Analysing Variation in English*. Washington, DC: Georgetown University Press.

Lakoff, G. (1972). 'Hedges: a study in meaning criteria and the logic of fuzzy concepts'. In *Papers from the Eighth Regional Meeting of the Chicago Linguistic Society*, 183–228.

——(1986). 'Classifiers as a reflection of mind'. In C. Craig (ed.), *Noun Classes and Categorization*. Amsterdam: Benjamins.

——(1987). *Women, Fire, and Dangerous Things: What Categories Reveal About the Mind*. Chicago: University of Chicago Press.

Locke, J. (1947). *An Essay Concerning Human Understanding*, ed. A. S. Pringle-Pattison. Oxford: Clarendon Press.

McCawley, J. D. (1981). *Everything that Linguists Have Always Wanted to Know about Logic—But Were Ashamed to Ask*. Chicago: University of Chicago Press.

Mel'čuk, I., and A. Žolkovskij (1984). *Tolkovo-kombinatornyi slovar' sovremennogo russ kogo jazyka* [Explanatory combinatorial dictionary of Modern Russian]. Vienna: Wiener slaw istischer Almanach, Sanderband 14.

Ortony, A., G. Clove, and M. Foss (1987). 'The referential structure of the affective lexicon'. *Cognitive Science* 11: 341–64.

Osherson, D. N., and E. E. Smith (1981). 'On the adequacy of prototype theory as a theory of concepts'. *Cognition* 9: 35–58.

Posner, M. (1986). 'Empirical studies of prototypes'. In C. Craig (ed.), *Noun Classes and Categorization*. Amsterdam: Benjamins.

Putnam, H. (1975). 'The meaning of "meaning"'. In K. Gunderson (ed.), *Language, Mind and Knowledge*. Minneapolis: University of Minnesota Press.

Rosch, E. [Heider, E.] (1971). '"Focal" color areas and the development of color names'. *Developmental Psychology* 4: 447–55.

——(1973). 'On the internal structure of perceptual and semantic categories'. In T. E. Moore (ed.), *Cognitive Development and the Acquisition of Language*. New York: Academic Press.

——(1975). 'Cognitive representations of semantic categories'. *Journal of Experimental Psychology: General* 104: 192–233.

Sweetser, E. (1987). 'The definition of "lie": an examination of folk models underlying a semantic prototype'. In D. Holland and N. Quinn (eds.), *Cultural Models in Language and Thought*. Cambridge: Cambridge University Press.

Verschueren, J. (1985). *What People Say They Do with Words*. Norwood, NJ: Ablex.

Wierzbicka, A. (1972). *Semantic Primitives*. Frankfurt: Athenäum-Verlag.

——(1980). *Lingua Mentalis*. New York: Academic Press.

——(1984). 'Apples are not a kind of fruit: the semantics of human categorization'. *American Ethnologist* 11: 313–28.

——(1985). *Lexicography and Conceptual Analysis*. Ann Arbor, Mich: Karoma.

——(1986a). 'Metaphors linguists live by: Lakoff and Johnson contra Aristotle'. *Papers in Linguistics* 19: 287–313.

——(1986b). 'Italian reduplication: cross-cultural pragmatics and illocutionary semantics'. *Linguistics* 24: 287–315.

——(1986c). 'A semantic metalanguage for the description and comparison of illocutionary meanings'. *Journal of Pragmatics* 10: 67–107.

——(1986d). 'Human emotions: universal or culture-specific?' *American Anthropologist* 88: 584–94.

——(1986e). 'Precision in vagueness: the semantics of English approximatives'. *Journal of Pragmatics* 10: 597–613.

——(1986f). Review of Mel'čuk and Žolkovskij. *Language* 62 (1984): 684–7.

——(1987a). *English Speech Act Verbs: A Semantic Dictionary*. New York: Academic Press.

——(1987b). 'Boys will be boys: radical semantics vs. radical pragmatics'. *Language* 63: 95–114.

——(1989). 'Semantic primitives and lexical universals'. *Quaderni di Semantica* 10(1): 103–21.

Wierzbicka, A. (forthcoming). 'Freedom—Liberté—Svoboda: universal human ideals or language-specific lexical items?' In D. Wilkins (ed.), *Conceptual Primitives and Semantic Analysis: A Cross-Linguistic Perspective*. Berlin: Mouton de Gruyter.

Wilkins, D. (forthcoming). *Towards a Theory of Semantic Change*. New York: State University of New York Press.

Wittgenstein, L. (1953). *Philosophical Investigations*. Oxford: Blackwell.

Zubin, D., and K.-M. Köpcke (1986). 'Gender and folk taxonomy'. In C. Craig (ed.), *Noun Classes and Categorization*. Amsterdam: Benjamins.

27

Fuzziness and Categorization

DENIS BOUCHARD

If syntactic form maps onto a general Conceptual Structure, we expect aspects of syntax to reflect characteristics of elements in that general CS. Jackendoff (among many others) presents an argument to that effect: in grammatical categorization, he argues, we find fuzziness of the same type as that found in conceptual categorization. Words, contrary to common-sense intuition, do not have definite and precise meanings which can be exhaustively decomposed into necessary and sufficient conditions. Jackendoff (1983) discusses several examples to illustrate his point. Here are a few.

(a) COLOR: what exhaustive decomposition of RED can one give? Once the feature COLOR is stated, what is left to decompose further and how can one make sense of redness minus coloration?[1]

(b) BIRD: This is the old problem of accounting for the fact that a robin is a better example of a BIRD than an ostrich or a penguin.

(c) VASE, CUP, and BOWL: a famous example ever since it was discussed in Labov (1973), who showed that at certain height-width ratios, the choice of label is highly sensitive to context, but it is not at others. "Such a graded response pattern shows that the boundaries of 'vase,' 'cup,' and 'bowl' are not precisely defined, as they should be if the [TYPES] were necessary and sufficient conditions" (Jackendoff 1983, 85–6).

(d) GAME: Wittgenstein's (1953) discussion of this word convinced many of the inadequacy of necessary and sufficient conditions in characterizing a word.

(e) KILL: Although Jackendoff (1990, 150–1) shows that Fodor's celebrated (1970) argument against decomposing KILL as CAUSE TO BECOME NOT ALIVE is not so strong after all, the problem of the exact decomposition of the verb and of finding the "real" primitives still exists and is revealed in small descriptive inadequacies: "A rock's being not alive does not qualify it as dead. One can die slowly or horribly, but it is odd to talk of becoming dead slowly or horribly" (Jackendoff 1983, 113). This difficulty in pinning down the primitives is supposed to show, once again, the inadequacy of necessary and sufficient conditions.

(f) PERCEPTUAL WORDS: "Since among the possible words must be those for perceptual concepts, the theory of word meanings must be at least expressive enough to encompass the kinds of conditions such concepts require" (Jackendoff 1983, 128). He then argues that human beings make use of a whole system of grouping well-formedness rules and preference

* Denis Bouchard, 'Fuzziness and categorization', section 1.5.1 of *The Semantics of Syntax: A Minimalist Approach to Grammar* (Chicago and London: The University of Chicago Press, 1995). © 1995 The University of Chicago. Reprinted by permission. With thanks to the author for supplying an electronic version of this chapter.

[1] See Lakoff's (1987: 332–3) discussion the Kay–Kempton color experiment. As far as I can tell, the experiment does not show that fuzziness is an inherent part of grammar: it only shows that having a name for something can help in deciding difficult cases of conceptualization.

rules in deciding whether a particular collection of pitch-events in a musical stream is identified as a #group# and concludes that these rules must therefore be contained in the sense of the word (musical) *group*. "The complexity of this system thus sets a lower bound on the potential complexity of word meanings" (Jackendoff 1983, 135).

(g) MOVEMENT VERBS: walk, run, lope, jog, sprint, scurry; . . . These verbs also form a class of fuzzy and graded words.

Jackendoff concludes from such examples that fuzziness is widespread in language: "The moral is that fuzziness must not be treated as a defect in language; nor is a theory of language defective that countenances it. Rather . . . fuzziness is an inescapable characteristic of *the concepts that language expresses* [my emphasis]. To attempt to define it out of semantics is only evasion" (1983, 11).

But do these examples really show anything about how some aspects of syntax reflect characteristics of elements in general Conceptual Structure? Does fuzziness affect the linguistic behavior of any word? For example, can it be shown that some words are better examples of the categories Noun or Verb and that this has grammatically testable effects on the sentence? The examples do not show any such effects. Rather, as the words I emphasized in the quotation from Jackendoff indicate, it is not some grammatically relevant properties of words that are graded, but rather the concepts that are expressed. This gradience plays no role in the Grammar, as Jackendoff himself recognizes in his discussion of movement verbs:

The differences among these verbs are not of particular grammatical import. . . . In this respect they resemble the color words, which also are grammatically homogeneous and can be really distinguished only by ostension. This suggests that these verbs share a set of necessary conditions having to do with travelling in physical space. . . . However, each will have its own centrality condition of manner, containing a central visual and/or motor pattern that specifies a characteristic gait and speed (1983, 149).

Clearly, these differences are not relevant for any grammatical process. Similarly, how we decide whether some entity is red, and whether we have difficulty in doing so, is irrelevant for the Grammatical behavior of the NP referring to the entity or of the adjective *red*. Such gradience effects *should* be defined out of Grammar Semantics and put in Situational Semantics, the web on which language is built. Therefore, my position is close to the one taken by Fodor (1975, 62), who showed that, for certain objects, it is difficult to determine whether or not they are a "chair." He proposes to attribute the fuzziness of "chair" to the concept rather than to the actual word. Jackendoff criticizes this position because "it leaves unaddressed how to characterize the fuzziness of the concept, *the issue that should be of concern*" (1983, 124; my emphasis). I disagree on the last point: fuzziness is of interest, but since it has no effects relevant to the behavior of grammatical entities such as words, it is *not* of concern to the linguist, but rather to the psychologist.

Claims have been made about cognitive categorization actually affecting Grammar. For example, Lakoff (1987, chapter 3) reviews several arguments to the effect that there are prototype effects in linguistic categories. Consider the most famous one, that *syntactic categories exhibit prototype effects*, which is based on Ross's argument (1981). He argues that nouns should be classified hierarchically, as in (1).

(1) toe > breath > way > time (where "x > y" indicates that *x* is "nounier" than *y*).

Ross gives three syntactic environments in which only the nounier nouns follow the rule:

(2) *Modification by a passive participle:*
 a. A *stubbed toe* can be very painful.
 b. **Held breath is usually fetid when released.
 c. **A lost way has been the cause of many a missed appointment.
 d. **Taken time might tend to irritate your boss.

(3) *Gapping:*
 a. I stubbed my toe, and she hers.
 b. I held my breath, and she hers.
 c. *I lost my way, and she hers.
 d. *I took my time, and she hers.

(4) *Pluralization:*
 a. Betty and Sue stubbed their toes.
 a′. *Betty and Sue stubbed their toe.
 b. Betty and Sue held their breaths.
 b′. Betty and Sue held their breath.
 c. *Betty and Sue lost their ways.
 c′. Betty and Sue lost their way.
 d. *Betty and Sue took their times.
 d′. Betty and Sue took their time.

Lakoff adds a fourth test to differentiate *way* and *time.*

(5) *Pronominalization:*
 a. I stubbed my toe, but didn't hurt *it.*
 b. Sam held his breath for a few seconds and then released *it.*
 c. Harry lost his way, but found *it* again.
 d. *Harry took his time, but wasted *it.*

Notice that all these tests depend on the referentiality of the noun phrase in some way or other. Thus, both (3) and (5) involve pronominalization of the object NP; the contrast between the two seems to have to do with the fact that the subject is the same on both sides of the coordination in (5), but not in (3). Compare (5c) with (6).

(6) *Harry lost his way, but she found *it* again.

On the other hand, it seems that it is not the pronominalization of *his time* that is problematic in (5d), but rather the oddness of the situation described by the sentence. Compare it to (7).

(7) Instead of giving his time to a good cause, Harry wasted it.

Pluralization in (4) raises the problem of distributive effects and of factors like the count/mass distinction; again, aspects of referentiality. Even passivization as in (2) involves referentiality: in his study on idioms, Ruwet (1991) notes that a passive subject must have a certain referential autonomy (see Higgins 1979, Keenan 1975). One example of this is discussed by Giry-Schneider (1978), who shows that some syntactic idioms in French with no determiner in the active must have a determiner and a modifying element, such as an adjective, in the passive.[2]

---

[2] See also Simatos (1986) for an in depth study of the nonreferentiality of idiomatic expressions.

(8) a. Glaucon a pris part/une part importante à cette discussion.
      Glaucon took (an important) part in this discussion
   b. Une part importante/*part a été prise par Glaucon à cette discussion.
      (An important) part was taken by Glaucon in this discussion

Interestingly, if the NPs in (2) are made more referentially autonomous by similar modification, the examples are much better:

(9) a. Improperly held breath is many a swimmer's biggest problem.
   b. Way lost because of negligence has been the cause of many a missed appointment.
   c. Time taken on the job might tend to irritate your boss.

To summarize, the fuzziness effects we have seen do not arise from grammatical categorization, but rather from the conceptual entities to which grammatical elements are linked. For
example, the grammatical category N is not fuzzy in any sense: *toe* is not a better example of
a N than *time*; it is a better example of a THING. I fully agree with Jackendoff's claim that
"fuzziness is an inescapable characteristic of *the concepts that language expresses*." But contrary to his claim, I think that fuzziness is not present in Grammar in any way, as the
discussion of the examples above indicates. Rather, fuzziness is in the web, the background
knowledge on which language is woven, and therefore it has no effect on the form and
functioning of language.

Of course, much more could be said on the topic of fuzziness. Let me briefly discuss four
more cases. (Thanks to John Goldsmith, personal communication, for bringing these to my
attention.) First, modal verbs are a well-known example of words that have a fuzzy status, as
far as rules applying to verbs are concerned. But in fact, assuming that these are rules applying
to *verbs*, per se, biases the discussion. Such an assumption has no status in most current theories
in any event, since movement is typically triggered by morphophonological or semantic
properties, such as the need for some element to bear a Tense affix or to be bound by a Tense
operator, as in the analyses of Pollock (1989) or Chomsky (1991). Until we know precisely what
forces an element to appear in a given position or with a certain inflection, we cannot decide
whether, for example, it is a requirement based on categorial or semantic reasons.

A second example has to do with serial verb constructions in West African languages, which
are built by stringing together things that look like VPs with other VPs or PPs. The problem is
that the governing element sometimes oscillates between the behavior of a verb, a preposition,
or something else. But why call the construction "serial VERB" in the first place? If it is
a misnomer, if the proper notion is instead something like "argument-taking element," then
the categorial problem is unfounded.

A third case of what looks like fuzziness can be built on extraction facts: bounding nodes
often leak, and extraction out of relative clauses or coordinate structures is often fine, under
the appropriate semantic and lexical conditions. But this is an argument for fuzziness of
categorization only if bounding nodes are the right account of extraction facts. There is
a plausible analysis along the lines of Erteschik-Shir (1973), based on the notion of
Dominance, in which the fuzziness of bounding nodes is not an issue because the notion of
bounding node is irrelevant.

As a final example, consider the category of the word *faim* 'hunger' in French. It appears to
be a noun, since it has a fixed gender (it is feminine) rather than the two possible genders we
would expect if it were an adjective. However, sometimes it appears to behave like an
adjective, in that it can be modified by the degree adverb *très*, as in *J'ai très faim* 'I am very
hungry' (literally, I have very hunger). Thus, its category appears to be fuzzy. In order to
understand what is going on, we must first observe that *très* is only possible with *faim* when

the latter does not have a DET. Thus, whereas *J'ai une faim de loup* 'I have a hunger of a wolf = I am as hungry as a wolf' is fine, **J'ai une très faim de loup* 'I have a very hunger of a wolf' is totally impossible. One possibility is that a degree adverb like *très* is possible with an N, but not a DP. A closer look at the phenomenon may reveal that referential autonomy is at work here, too, just like in the Ross (1981) examples discussed above. Thus, it may be that one of the conditions of whether *très* can be an N modifier is the weak referential autonomy of the noun. This predicts that any predicative N could be modified by *très*, all things being equal, and indeed this seems to be the case; for example, *Celui-là, je te dis qu'il est très avocat* 'That one, I tell you, he's really lawyer.'[3] If the distribution of *très* is based on the category of the element being modified, *J'ai très faim* is indeed odd; but if the distribution of *très* is not based on the category, but on semantic aspects of the modified element—such as its referential autonomy—the problem of category fuzziness disappears.

The foregoing discussion suggests that words do have definite and precise meanings that can be exhaustively decomposed into necessary and sufficient conditions, once the effects of the background have been removed. This is why verbs used to describe movements are often used to describe other situations, such as Extension, Time, Identification, etc., again and again across languages: they are not movement verbs, per se, but their semantic representations are such that they are predisposed for many uses, including movement.

In short, my position is that the speaker "knows" when and where a word or sentence can apply: fuzziness arises when the speaker has some difficulty in determining whether such a situation is present. Therefore, fuzziness is not in the realm of Grammar.

There are two objections to such a view: it is too abstract, and having fuzziness in general conceptualization, but not in language, which is a subpart of general conceptualization, is incongruous. Consider first the abstractness problem: "The classical theory of categories does not do very well on the treatment of polysemy. In order to have a single lexical item, the classical theory must treat all of the related senses as having some abstract meaning in common—usually so abstract that it cannot distinguish among the cases and so devoid of real meaning that it is not recognizable as what people think of as the meaning of a word. And where there are a large number of related senses that don't all share a property, then the classical theory is forced to treat such cases as homonymy, the same way it treats the case of the two words *bank*. Moreover, the classical theory has no adequate means of characterizing a situation where one or more senses are 'central' or 'most representative'" (Lakoff 1987, 416; see also Jackendoff 1983, 112 ff, who has similar qualms about categorization and necessary and sufficient conditions). Although some aspects of this objection do indeed hold against a classical theory of categorization, they do not hold against the position advocated here. First, although very abstract, the representations that will be proposed can distinguish among the cases because, contrary to the classical theory, the present approach crucially assumes that language is not used in a vacuum. For example, although the meaning of French *venir* that I will give in Part II [not included] is very abstract, it can account for what is common to the three uses in (10) because the nature of the arguments gives us sufficient information to determine the kind of situation to which the whole utterance can correspond.

---

[3] It is more complicated than I suggested in the text. Not all nouns which are not referentially autonomous can be modified by *très*. While *faim* is not referentially autonomous (for example, it cannot passivize **Faim a été eue par Jean* 'Hunger has been had by Jean'), we saw in (8) that *part* is not referentially autonomous, yet it cannot take a degree adverb *Glaucon a pris (*très) part à cette discussion* 'Glaucon has taken very part to that discussion'. There are certainly other factors involved.

(10) a. Jean vient de Paris. (movement)
        Jean is coming from Paris
     b. Jean vient de Paris. (origin)
        Jean comes from Paris (He is a Parisian)
     c. Cette route vient de Québec. (extension)
        This road comes from Québec

The second point raised by Lakoff is an odd one: why should the "real meaning" of a word correspond to what people think of as the meaning of that word? Folk theories should no more be a criterion in semantics than they are in syntax or any other aspect of linguistics. The problem with lexical meanings is that, in general, there is such an immediacy to the situation in which the word is used that we tend to attribute these situational properties to the word itself, as if they were part of its semantic representation, instead of abstracting away from them.

As for the "large number of related senses that don't all share a property," this may apparently be true when all the background factors are taken into account and blur our view, but once we abstract away from such factors, shared properties do emerge, as we will see in the case studies in subsequent chapters. Finally, the fact that one or more senses are "central" or "most representative" can be captured in the present approach, but this is done by cognitive principles that form the background for language. As argued above, they have no effect in the Grammar and so must be removed from it.

The second possible objection takes the following form: "Considering that categorization enters fundamentally into every aspect of language, it would be very strange to assume that the mind *in general* [my emphasis] used one kind of categorization and that language used an entirely different one" (Lakoff 1987, 182). But how general is the use of fuzzy categorization compared to classical categorization? Both Lakoff and Jackendoff provided numerous examples where fuzzy categorization is indeed found in dealing with the "external" or "projected" world. Does this leave classical categorization completely out? Not at all, for either Lakoff or Jackendoff. Millenniums spent studying categorization based on necessary and sufficient conditions are not swept aside by these authors: "I should make it clear that I will not be claiming that classical categories are never relevant to cognition. . . . The point is that not all categories—either of mind or of nature—are classical, and therefore we cannot assume, a priori, as objectivist metaphysics does, that all nature is structured by classical categories" (Lakoff 1987, 160). More crucially for our point, both authors make use of classical categorization in their linguistic analyses. Thus, Jackendoff (1983, 115) subscribes to the following passage from Putnam (1975, 133) ". . . words in natural language are not generally 'yes-no': there are things of which the description 'tree' is clearly true and things of which the description 'tree' is clearly false, to be sure, but there are a host of borderline cases." But this really hinges only on whether one can decide if a given THING is actually a tree or not; it is of no consequence to the syntactic behavior of *tree*. Thus, this kind of fuzziness never affects how that N should project in a structure, or whether it occupies the position [$_S$NP . . .] ('subject of S'), or how it will agree with the verb or a pronoun, or whether it is governed. Notions like "subject of", "governed by", "c-commands x", and so forth are all "yes-no." In some case, it might be hard to determine whether a relation holds because of the complexity of the construction, but either it holds or it does not; there is nothing indeterminate about it.

Thus, both classical and fuzzy categorization are needed. Therefore, what kind of categorization is relevant for the form and functioning of grammar is an empirical question. In looking at studies on Grammar, including those of the two authors cited above, the overwhelming evidence is that fuzzy categorization is involved only in the processes dealing with perception or beliefs about the "external world" and that it is not intrinsically involved in the functioning of Grammar. Externalizing processes such as perception and belief must "reach out", whereas grammatical processes are strictly internal.[4] If fuzziness is a property of externalizing processes only, grammatical processes could very well be strictly classical. It is very important to bear in mind the distinction between the form of the sentence, that is, *how* it expresses something, and *what* it expresses. Only the former is relevant to Grammar.

I therefore conclude that there is nothing strange in the possibility that language uses only classical categorization and that preliminary observations point in this direction.

REFERENCES

Bouchard, D. (1984). *On the Content of Empty Categories*. Dordrecht: Foris.

Chomsky, N. (1991). 'Some notes on economy of derivation and representation'. In R. Freidin (ed.), *Principles and Parameters in Comparative Grammar*. Cambridge, Mass.: MIT Press.

Erteschik-Shir, N. (1973). 'On the nature of island constraints'. Ph.D. dissertation, Massachusetts Institute of Technology.

Fodor, J. (1970). 'Three reasons for not deriving "kill" from "cause to die" '. *Linguistic Inquiry* 1: 429–38.

——(1975). *The Language of Thought*. Cambridge, Mass.: Harvard University Press.

Giry-Schneider, J. (1978). *Les nominalisations en français: l'opérateur 'faire' dans le lexique*. Paris: Droz.

Higgins, F. R. (1979). *The Pseudo-Cleft Construction in English*. New York: Garland.

Jackendoff, R. (1983). *Semantics and Cognition*. Cambridge, Mass.: MIT Press.

——(1990). *Semantic Structures*. Cambridge, Mass.: MIT Press.

Keenan, E. (1975). 'Some universals of passive in relational grammar'. In R. E. Grossman, L. J. Sam, and T. J. Vance (eds.), *Papers from the Eleventh Regional Meeting of the Chicago Linguistic Society*, 340–52.

Labov, W. (1973). 'The boundaries of words and their meanings'. In J. Fishman (ed.), *New Ways of Analyzing Variation in English*. Washington, DC: Georgetown University Press, 340–73.

Lakoff, G. (1987). *Women, Fire, and Dangerous Things*. Chicago: University of Chicago Press.

Pollock, J.-Y. (1989). 'Verb movement, universal grammar, and the structure of IP'. *Linguistic Inquiry* 20: 365–424.

Putnam, H. (1975). *Mind, Language, and Reality: Philosophical Papers*, vol. ii. Cambridge: Cambridge University Press.

Ross, J. R. (1981). 'Nominal decay'. MS, Dept. of Linguistics, Massachusetts Institute of Technology.

Ruwet, N. (1991). *Syntax and Human Experience*. Chicago: University of Chicago Press.

Simatos, I. (1986). 'Eléments pour une théorie des expressions idiornatiques'. Ph.D. dissertation, Université de Paris VII.

Tasmovski-De Rijk, L., and P. Verluyten (1981). 'Pragmatically controlled anaphora and linguistic form'. *Linguistic Inquiry* 12: 153–4.

Wittgenstein, L. (1953). *Philosophical Investigations*. New York: Macmillan.

---

[4] The grammatical system itself is not required to have a relation with reality. In fact, if it projects at all, it seems to project to a diffferent world, where objects have gender, for example. See Tasmovski-De Rijk and Verluyten (1981) and Bouchard (1984).

28

The Discrete Nature of Syntactic Categories: Against a Prototype-based Account

FREDERICK J. NEWMEYER

I. PROTOTYPES, FUZZY CATEGORIES, AND GRAMMATICAL THEORY

I.I. Introduction

There are many diverse approaches to generative grammar, but what all current models share is an *algebraic* approach to the explanation of grammatical phenomena.[1] That is, a derivation consists of the manipulation of discrete formal objects drawn from a universal vocabulary. Foremost among these objects are the syntactic categories: NP, V, S, and so on. The inventory of categories has changed over the years and differs from model to model. Likewise, their distribution has been constrained by proposals such as X-bar theory, feature subcategorization schemes, and the current (albeit controversial) distinction between lexical and functional categories. Nevertheless, what has remained constant, for the past two decades at least, is the idea that among the primitives of grammatical theory are discrete categories whose members have equal status as far as grammatical processes are concerned. That is, the theory does not regard one lexical item as being 'more of a noun' than another, or restrict some process to apply only to the 'best sorts' of NP.[2]

This classical notion of categories has been challenged in recent years by many working within the frameworks of functional and cognitive linguistics (see especially Comrie, 1989; Croft, 1991; Cruse, 1992; Dixon, 1997; Heine, 1993; Hopper and Thompson, 1984, 1985;

*Frederick J. Newmeyer, 'The discrete nature of syntactic categories: against a prototype-based account'. In Robert D. Borsley (ed.), *The Nature and Function of Syntactic Categories* (*Syntax and Semantics*, vol. 32; New York: Academic Press, 2000), 221–50. © 2000 Elsevier Science (USA). Reprinted by permission. With thanks to the author for supplying an electronic version of this chapter.

[1] An earlier version of this paper was presented at Universidade Federal de Minas Gerais, Universidade de Campinas, Universidade Federal do Rio de Janeiro, the University of California at San Diego, and the University of Washington, as well as at two conferences: The International Conference on Syntactic Categories (University of Wales) and the Fifth International Pragmatics Conference (National Autonomous University of Mexico). It has benefited, I feel, from discussion with Paul K. Andersen, Leonard Babby, Robert Borsley, Ronnie Cann, William Croft, John Goldsmith, Jeanette Gundel, Ray Jackendoff, Jurgen Klausenburger, Rob Malouf, Pascual Masullo, Edith Moravcsik, Elizabeth Riddle, Margaret Winters, and Arnold Zwicky. I have no illusions, however, that any of these individuals would be entirely happy about the final product. For deeper discussion of many of the issues treated here, see Newmeyer (1998).

[2] In most generative approaches, categories have an internal feature structure, which allows some pairs of categories to share more features than others and individual categories to be unspecified for particular features. Head-driven Phrase Structure Grammar (HPSG) goes further, employing default-inheritance mechanisms in the lexicon. These lead, in a sense, to some members of a category being "better" members of that category than others (see, for example, the HPSG treatment of auxiliaries in Warner (1993a, b). A similar point can be made for the "preference rules" of Jackendoff and Lerdahl (1981) and Jackendoff (1983). Nevertheless, in these (still algebraic) accounts, the distance of an element from the default setting is not itself directly encoded in the statement of grammatical processes.

Langacker, 1987, 1991; Taylor, 1989; Thompson, 1988). In one alternative view, categories have a *prototype* structure, which entails the following two claims for linguistic theory:

(1) Categorial Prototypicality:
   a. Grammatical categories have 'best case' members and members that systematically depart from the 'best case.'
   b. The optimal grammatical description of morphosyntactic processes involves reference to degree of categorial deviation from the 'best case.'

Representatives of both functional linguistics and cognitive linguistics have taken categorial prototypicality as fundamental to grammatical analysis, as the following quotes from Hopper and Thompson (leading advocates of the former) and Langacker (a developer of the latter) attest (I have added emphasis in both passages):

It is clear that *the concept of prototypicality* (the centrality vs. peripherality of instances which are assigned to the same category) *has an important role to play in the study of grammar*. Theories of language which work with underlying, idealized structures necessarily ignore very real differences, both cross-linguistic and intra-linguistic, among the various degrees of centrality with which one and the same grammatical category may be instantiated. (Hopper and Thompson, 1985: 155)

How then will the theory achieve restrictiveness? Not by means of explicit prohibitions or categorical statements about what every language must have, but rather *through a positive characterization of prototypicality and the factors that determine it*....The theory will thus incorporate substantive descriptions of the various kinds of linguistic structures with the status of prototypes. (Langacker, 1991: 513–14)

These approaches attribute prototype structure to (virtually) all of the constructs of grammar, not just the syntactic categories (see, for example, the treatment of the notion 'subject' along these lines in Bates and MacWhinney, 1982; Langendonck, 1986; Silverstein, 1976; and Van Oosten, 1986). However, this paper will focus solely on the syntactic categories.

Another position that challenges the classical approach to grammatical categories is that they have nondistinct boundaries:

(2) Fuzzy Categories: The boundaries between categories are nondistinct.

My impression is that the great majority of functionalists accept categorial prototypicality, and a sizeable percentage accept fuzzy categories. Comrie (1989) and Taylor (1989), for example, are typical in that respect. However, Langacker (1991), while accepting an internal prototype structure for categories, rejects the idea that the boundaries between them are nondistinct, arguing that syntactic categories can be defined by necessary and sufficient semantic conditions. Wierzbicka (1990) accepts this latter conception, but rejects prototypes. She writes:

In too many cases, these new ideas [about semantic prototypes] have been treated as an excuse for intellectual laziness and sloppiness. In my view, the notion of prototype has to prove its usefulness through semantic description, not through semantic theorizing. (p. 365)

And Heine (1993), on the basis of studies of grammaticalization, was led to accept fuzzy categories, but to reject categorial prototypicality. In his view, the internal structure of categories is based on the concept of "degree of family resemblance" rather than "degree of prototypicality."

The specific goal of this paper is to defend the classical theory of categories. First, it will provide evidence against categorial prototypicality by rebutting (1b), namely the idea that descriptively adequate grammars need to make reference to the degree of prototypicality of the categories taking part in grammatical processes. To the extent that it is successful, it will thereby provide evidence against (1a) as well. Since grammatical behavior gives us the best clue as to the nature of grammatical structure, any refutation of (1b) ipso facto presents a strong challenge to (1a).

To be sure, it is possible to hold (1a), but to reject (1b). Such a view would entail the existence of judgments that categories have "best-case" and "less-than-best-case" members, without the degree of "best-casedness" actually entering into grammatical description. Does anybody hold such a position? It is not clear. George Lakoff seems to leave such a possibility open. He writes that "prototype effects . . . are superficial phenomena which may have many sources" (1987: 56) and stresses at length that the existence of such effects for a particular phenomenon should not be taken as prima facie evidence that the mind represents that phenomenon in a prototype structure (see in particular his discussion of prototype effects for even and odd numbers in chapter 9). On the other hand, his discussion of strictly grammatical phenomena suggests that he does attribute to grammatical categories a graded structure with inherent degrees of membership, and the degree of membership is relevant to syntactic description (see his discussion of "nouniness" on pages 63–4, discussed in section 3.4.3 below).

In any event, in this paper I will be concerned only with theories advocating the conjunction of claims (1a) and (1b). That is, I will attend only to approaches in which descriptively adequate grammars are said to make reference (in whatever way) to graded categorial structure.

Limitations of space force me to ignore a number of topics that are relevant to a full evaluation of all facets of prototype theory. In particular, I will not address the question of whether nonlinguistic cognitive categories have a prototype structure. Much has appeared in the psychological literature on this topic, and a wide variety of opinions exist (see, for example, Armstrong, Gleitman, and Gleitman, 1983; Dryer, 1997; Fodor and Lepore, 1996; Kamp and Partee, 1995; Keil, 1989; Lakoff, 1987; Mervis and Rosch, 1981; Rosch and Lloyd, 1978; and Smith and Osherson, 1988). However, the evidence for or against a prototype structure for grammatical categories can, I feel, be evaluated without having to take into account what has been written about the structure of semantic, perceptual, and other cognitive categories.

The question of whether grammatical categories have a prototype structure is, to a degree, independent of whether they can be defined notionally, that is, whether they can be defined by necessary and sufficient semantic conditions. The arguments put forward to support notional definitions of categories will be addressed and challenged in Newmeyer (1998).

Second, I will argue against fuzzy categories. Nothing is to be gained, either in terms of descriptive or explanatory success, in positing categorial continua.

The remainder of section 1 provides historical background to a prototype-based approach to syntactic categories. Section 2 discusses how prototype theory has been applied in this regard and discusses the major consequences that have been claimed to follow from categories having a prototype structure. Section 3 takes on the evidence that has been adduced for (1b) on the basis of the claim that prototypical members of a category manifest more morphosyntactic complexity than nonprototypical members. I argue that the best account of the facts makes no reference, either overtly or covertly, to categorial prototypicality. Section 4 argues against fuzzy categories and is followed by a short conclusion (section 5).

1.2. Squishes and their legacy

Prototype theory was first proposed in Rosch (1971/1973) to account for the cognitive representation of concepts and was immediately applied to that purpose in linguistic semantics (see Lakoff, 1972/1973).[3] This work was accompanied by proposals for treating *syntactic* categories in nondiscrete terms, particularly in the work of J. R. Ross (see especially Ross, 1973a, 1973b, 1975). Ross attempted to motivate a number of "squishes," that is, continua both within and between categories, among which were the "Fake NP Squish," illustrated in (3), and the "Nouniness Squish," illustrated in (5). Consider first the Fake NP Squish:

(3) The Fake NP Squish (Ross, 1973a):
    a. Animates
    b. Events
    c. Abstracts
    d. Expletive *it*
    e. Expletive *there*
    f. Opaque idiom chunks.

Progressing downward from (3a) to (3f) in the squish, each type of noun phrase was claimed to manifest a lower degree of noun phrase status than the type above it. Ross's measure of categorial goodness was the number of processes generally characteristic of the category that the NP type was able to undergo. Consider the possibility of reapplication of the rule of Raising. The "best" sort of NPs, animates,[4] easily allow it (4a), "lesser" NPs, events, allow it only with difficulty (4b), while "poor" NPs, idiom chunks, do not allow it at all (4c):

(4) a. John is likely to be shown to have cheated.
    b. ?The performance is likely to be shown to have begun late.
    c. *No headway is likely to have been shown to have been made.

Ross proposed the 'Nouniness Squish' to illustrate a continuum *between* categories. Progressing from the left end to the right end, the degree of sententiality seems to decrease and that of noun phrase-like behavior to increase:

(5) The "Nouniness Squish" (Ross, 1973b:141):
    that clauses > *for to* clauses > embedded questions > Acc-*ing* complements >
    Poss-*ing* complements > action nominals > derived nominals > underived nominals

Ross put forward the strong claim that syntactic processes apply to discrete segments of the squish. For example, preposition deletion must apply before *that* and *for-to* complements (6a), may optionally apply before embedded questions (6b), and may not apply before more "nouny" elements (6c):

(6) a. I was surprised (*at) that you had measles.
    b. I was surprised (at) how far you could throw the ball.
    c. I was surprised *(at) Jim's victory.

Given the apparent fact that different processes apply to *different* (albeit contiguous) segments of the squish, Ross was led to reject the idea of rigid boundaries separating syntactic categories.

---

[3] For more recent work on prototype theory and meaning representation, see Coleman and Kay (1981); Lakoff (1987); Geeraerts (1993); and many of the papers in Rudzka-Ostyn (1988) and Tsohatzidis (1990). For a general discussion of prototypes, specifically within the framework of cognitive linguistics, see Winters (1990).

[4] Ross's work did not employ the vocabulary of the then nascent prototype theory. However, as observed in Taylor (1989: 189), his reference to "copperclad, brass-bottomed NPs" (p. 98) to refer to those at the top of the squish leaves no doubt that he regarded them as the most "prototypical" in some fundamental sense.

In other words, Ross's approach involved hypothesizing both categorial prototypicality and fuzzy categories. By the end of the 1970s, however, very few syntactic analyses were still being proposed that involved squishes. Ross's particular approach to categorial continua was problematic in a number of ways. For one thing, it did not seek to provide a more general explanation for why categories should have the structure that he attributed to them. Second, his formalization of the position occupied by an element in the squish, the assignment of a rating between 0 and 1, struck many linguists as arbitrary and unmotivated. No reasonable set of criteria, for example, was ever proposed to determine if an abstract NP merited a rating of, say, .5 or .6 on the noun phrase scale. Third, Ross dealt with sentences in isolation, abstracted away from their extralinguistic context. Since at that time those linguists who were the most disillusioned with generative grammar were the most likely to take a more "socio-linguistic" approach to grammar, Ross's silence on the discourse properties of the sentences he dealt with seemed to them to be only a slight departure from business as usual. And finally, some doubts were raised about the robustness of the data upon which the squishes were based. Gazdar and Klein (1978) demonstrated that one of them (the "Clausematiness Squish" of Ross, 1975) did not exhibit statistically significant scalar properties that would not show up in an arbitrary matrix.

But while Ross's particular approach was abandoned, the central core of his ideas about grammatical categories has lived on. In particular, many linguists continued to accept the idea that they have a prototype structure and/or have fuzzy boundaries. The 1980s saw the development of alternatives to generative grammar that have attempted to incorporate such ideas about categorial structure into grammatical theory. It is to these approaches that we now turn, beginning with an examination of prototypes within functional linguistics.

2. PROTOTYPE THEORY AND SYNTACTIC CATEGORIES

Among linguists who take a prototype approach to syntactic categories there is considerable disagreement as to how to define the prototypical semantic and pragmatic correlates of each category. Just to take the category "adjective," for example, we find proposals to characterize its prototypical members in terms of a set of concepts such as "dimension," "physical property," "color," and so on (Dixon, 1977); their "time-stability" (Givón, 1984); their role in description, as opposed to classification (Wierzbicka, 1986); and their discourse functions (which overlap with those of verbs and nouns respectively) of predicating a property of an existing discourse referent and introducing a new discourse referent (Thompson, 1988).

This lack of consensus presents a bit of a dilemma for anyone who, like this author, would wish to evaluate the success of prototype theory for syntax without undertaking an exhaustive critique of all positions that have been put forward as claiming success in this matter. My solution will be to adopt for purposes of discussion what I feel is the best motivated, most elaborate, and most clearly explicated proposal for categorial prototypicality, namely that presented in Croft (1991). His proposals for the prototypical semantic and pragmatic properties of noun, adjective, and verb are summarized in Table 1.

In other words, the prototypical noun has the pragmatic function of reference, it refers to an object with a valency of 0 (i.e., it is nonrelational), and it is stative, persistent, and non-gradable. The prototypical verb has the pragmatic function of predication, it refers to an action, it has a valency of 1 or greater, and is a transitory, nongradable process. The links between semantic class and pragmatic function are, of course, nonaccidental (see Croft, 1991: 123), though I will not explore that matter here.

TABLE I   Prototypical Correlations of Syntactic Categories

		Syntactic category	
	Noun	*Adjective*	*Verb*
Semantic class	Object	Property	Action
Valency	0	1	≥ 1
Stativity	state	state	process
Persistence	persistent	persistent	transitory
Gradability	nongradable	gradable	nongradable
Pragmatic function	Reference	Modification	Predication

(from Croft, 1991: 55, 65)

Table I characterizes the most prototypical members of each category, but not their internal degrees of prototypicality. Most prototype theorists agree that definite human nouns are the most prototypical, with nonhuman animates less prototypical, followed by inanimates, abstract nouns, and dummy nouns such as *it* and *there*.

As far as adjectives are concerned, Dixon (1977) finds that words for age, dimension, value, and color are likely to belong to the adjective class, however small it is, suggesting that adjectives with these properties make up the prototypical core of that category. Words for human propensities and physical properties are often encoded as nouns and verbs respectively, suggesting that their status as prototypical adjectives is lower than members of the first group.

Finally, Croft notes that it is difficult to set up an elaborated prototypicality scale for verbs. However, there seems to be no disagreement on the point that causative agentive active verbs carrying out the pragmatic function of predication are the most prototypical, while nonactive verbs, including "pure" statives and psychological predicates are less so.

It is important to stress that the approach of Croft (and of most other contemporary functional and cognitive linguists) differs in fundamental ways from that developed by Ross in the 1970s.[5] Most importantly, it adds the typological dimension that was missing in Ross's squishes. Prototypes are not determined, as for Ross, by the behavior of particular categories with respect to one or more grammatical rules in a particular language. Rather, the prototypes for the syntactic categories are privileged points in cognitive space, their privileged position being determined by typological grammatical patterns. Hence, no direct conclusion can be drawn from the hypothesized universal (cognitive) properties of some prototypical syntactic category about how that category will behave with respect to some particular grammatical process in some particular language. Indeed, it is consistent with Croft's approach that there may be languages in which the category Noun, say, shows no prototype effects at all. Another difference has to do with the structure of categories themselves. Ross assumes that all nonprototypical members of a category can be arranged on a one-dimensional scale leading away from the prototype, that is, hierarchically. Croft, on the other hand, assumes a radial categorial structure (Lakoff, 1987). In such an approach, two nonprototypical members of a category need not be ranked with respect to each other in terms of degree of prototypicality.

Croft's theory thus makes weaker claims than Ross's. One might even wonder how the notion "prototypicality" surfaces at all in grammatical description. Croft explains:

These [markedness, hierarchy, and prototype] patterns are universal, and are therefore part of the grammatical description of any language. Language-specific facts involve the degree to which

---

[5] I am indebted to William Croft (personal communication) for clarifying the differences between his approach and Ross's.

typological universals are conventionalized in a particular language; e.g. what cut-off point in the animacy hierarchy is used to structurally and behaviorally mark direct objects. (Croft, 1990:154)

In other words, grammatical processes in individual languages are sensitive to the degree of deviation of the elements participating in them from the typologically established prototype.

3. PROTOTYPICALITY AND PARADIGMATIC COMPLEXITY

The most frequently alluded to morphosyntactic manifestation of prototypicality is that it correlates with what might be called "paradigmatic complexity." That is, more prototypical elements are claimed to have a greater number of distinct forms in an inflectional paradigm than less prototypical elements or to occur in a larger range of construction types than less prototypical elements. In this section, I will challenge the idea that any correlation other than the most rough sort holds between paradigmatic complexity and prototypicality. My conclusion will serve to undermine the grammatical evidence for the idea that categories are nondiscrete.

In section 3.1, I review the evidence that has been adduced for the correlation between categorial prototypicality and paradigmatic complexity. Section 3.2 outlines the various positions that could be—and have been—taken to instantiate this correlation in a grammatical description. Section 3.3 shows that for three well-studied phenomena, the postulated correlation is not robust, while section 3.4 presents alternative explanations for phenomena that have been claimed to support a strict correlation and hence nondiscrete categories.

3.1. Paradigmatic complexity and prototypes

Croft (1991: 79–87) defends the idea that the prototypical member of a category manifests more distinct forms in an inflectional paradigm than the nonprototypical and occurs in a broader range of construction types. As he notes (p. 79), each major syntactic category is associated with a range of inflectional categories, though of course languages differ as to which they instantiate:

Nouns: number (countability), case, gender, size (augmentative, diminutive), shape (classifiers), definiteness (determination), alienability;
Adjectives: comparative, superlative, equative, intensive ("very Adj"), approximative ("more or less Adj" or "Adj-ish"), agreement with head;
Verbs: tense, aspect, mood, and modality, agreement with subject and object(s), transitivity.

Croft argues that there is systematicity to the possibility of a particular category's bearing a particular inflection. Specifically, if a nonprototypical member of that category in a particular language allows that inflection, then a prototypical member will as well. Crosslinguistically, participles and infinitives, two nonpredicating types of verbal elements, are severely restricted in their tense, aspect, and modality possibilities. (Nonprototypical) stative verbs have fewer inflectional possibilities than (prototypical) active verbs (e.g. they often cannot occur in the progressive). Predicate Ns and (to a lesser extent) predicate As are often restricted morphosyntactically. Predicate Ns in many languages do not take determiners; predicate As do not take the full range of adjectival suffixes, and so on. The same can be said for mass nouns, incorporated nouns, and so on—that is, nouns that do not attribute reference to an object.

Furthermore, nonprototypical members of a syntactic category seem to have a more restricted syntactic distribution than prototypical members. As Ross (1987: 309) remarks: 'One way of recognizing prototypical elements is by the fact that they combine more freely and productively than do elements which are far removed from the prototypes.' This point is amply illustrated by the Fake NP Squish (3). Animate nouns are more prototypical than event nouns, which are more prototypical than abstract nouns, which are more prototypical than idiom chunks. As degree of prototypicality declines, so does freedom of syntactic distribution. The same appears to hold true of verbs. In some languages, for example, only action verbs may occur in the passive construction.

3.2. Paradigmatic complexity and claims about grammar–prototype interactions

The idea that inflectional and structural elaboration declines with decreasing categorial prototypicality has been interpreted in several different ways. Four positions can be identified that express this idea. In order of decreasing strength, they are "Direct Mapping Prototypicality," "Strong Cut-off Point Prototypicality," "Weak Cut-off Point Prototypicality," and "Correlation-Only Prototypicality." I will now discuss them in turn.

According to Direct Mapping Prototypicality, morphosyntactic processes make direct reference to the degree of prototypicality of the elements partaking of those processes. In other words, part of our knowledge of our language is a Prototypicality Hierarchy and a grammar-internal mapping from that hierarchy to morphosyntax. Ross's squishes are examples of Direct Mapping Prototypicality. As I interpret his approach, the correlation in English between the position of a noun on the Prototypicality Hierarchy and its ability to allow the reapplication of Raising (see 4a–c) is to be expressed directly in the grammar of English.

In Strong Cut-off Point Prototypicality, the effects of prototype structure are encoded in the grammar of each language, but there is no language-particular linking between gradations in prototypicality and gradations in morphosyntactic behavior. To repeat Croft's characterization of this position:

These [markedness, hierarchy, and prototype] patterns are universal, and are therefore part of the grammatical description of any language. Language-specific facts involve the degree to which typological universals are conventionalized in a particular language; e.g., what cut-off point in the animacy hierarchy is used to structurally and behaviorally mark direct objects. (Croft, 1990: 154)

One can think of Strong Cut-off Point Prototypicality as a constraint on possible grammars. For example, it would prohibit (i.e., predict impossible) a language in other respects like English, but in which the reapplication of Raising would be *more* possible with nonprototypical NPs than with prototypical ones.

Weak Cut-off Point Prototypicality allows a certain number of arbitrary exceptions to prototype-governed grammatical behavior. Thus it would admit the possibility that the reapplication of Raising could apply to a less prototypical NP than to a more prototypical one, though such cases would be rather exceptional. I interpret the analyses of Hungarian definite objects in Moravcsik (1983) and English *there*-constructions in Lakoff (1987) as manifesting Weak Cut-off Point Prototypicality. The central, prototypical, cases manifest the phenomenon in question, and there is a nonrandom, yet at the same time unpredictable, linking between the central cases and the noncentral ones.

Correlation-only Prototypicality is the weakest position of all. It simply states that there is some nonrandom relationship between morphosyntactic behavior and degree of prototypicality.

3.3. On the Robustness of the Data Supporting Cut-off Point Prototypicality

In this section, I will demonstrate that for three well-studied phenomena, Cut-off Point prototypicality, in both its strong and weak versions, is disconfirmed. At best, the data support Correlation-only Prototypicality.

3.3.1. The English progressive

English is quite poor in "choosy" inflections, but it does permit one test of the correlation between prototypicality and paradigmatic complexity. This is the marker of progressive aspect, *-ing*. Certainly it is true, as (7a–b) illustrates, that there is a *general* correlation of categorial prototypicality and the ability to allow progressive aspect (note that both verbs are predicating):

(7) a. Mary was throwing the ball.
    b. *Mary was containing 10 billion DNA molecules.

However, we find the progressive with surely nonprototypical temporary state and psychological predicate verbs (8a–b), but disallowed with presumably more prototypical achievement verbs (9):

(8) a. The portrait is hanging on the wall of the bedroom.
    b. I'm enjoying my sabbatical year.

(9)   *I'm noticing a diesel fuel truck passing by my window.

Furthermore, we have "planned event progressives," where the possibility of progressive morphology is clearly unrelated to the prototypicality of the verb (cf. grammatical 10a and ungrammatical 10b):

(10) a. Tomorrow, the Mariners are playing the Yankees.
     b. *Tomorrow, the Mariners are playing well.

In short, the English progressive falsifies directly the idea that there is a cut-off point on the scale of prototypicality for verbs and that verbs on one side of the cut-off point allow that inflection, while those on the other side forbid it. Furthermore, the exceptions (i.e., the verbs of lesser prototypicality that allow the progressive) do not appear to be simple arbitrary exceptions. Therefore, the facts do not support Weak Cut-off Point Prototypicality either.

One could, of course, attempt to by-pass this conclusion simply by exempting English progressive inflection from exhibiting prototype effects in any profound way. One might, for example, appeal to some semantic or pragmatic principles that account for when one finds or does not find progressive morphology. Indeed, I have no doubt that such is the correct way to proceed (for discussion, see Goldsmith and Woisetschlaeger, 1982; Kearns, 1991; Smith, 1991; Žegarac, 1993; and Swart, 1998). But the point is that degree of verbal prototypicality fails utterly to account for when one finds progressive morphology in English. Therefore the facts lend no support to Croft's claim that the prototypical member of a category manifests more distinct forms in an inflectional paradigm than the nonprototypical member.[6]

---

[6] Along the same lines, Robert Borsley informs me (personal communication) that Welsh and Polish copulas provide evidence against the idea that prototypical members of a category necessarily have more inflected forms than nonprototypical members. One assumes that the copula is a nonprototypical verb, but in Welsh it has five (or six) tenses compared with three (or four) for a standard verb, and in Polish it has three tenses, compared with two for a standard verb. On the other hand, one might take the position expressed in Croft (1991) that copulas are categorially auxiliaries, rather than verbs.

3.3.2. Adjectives

Dixon (1977: 22–3) cites two languages which distinguish a certain subset of adjectives morphologically. Rotuman (Churchward, 1940) has an open-ended adjective class, but only the (translations of) the following 12 have distinct singular and plural forms: *big*; *long*; *broad*; *whole, complete*; *black*; *small*; *short*; *narrow, thin*; *old*; *white*; *red*; *female*. Acooli (Crazzolara, 1955) has a closed class of about 40 adjectives, 7 of which have distinct singular and plural forms: *great, big, old (of persons)*; *big, large (of volume)*; *long, high, distant (of place and time)*; *good, kind, nice, beautiful*; *small, little*; *short*; *bad, bad tasting, ugly*. The remaining adjectives translate as *new*; *old*; *black*; *white*; *red*; *deep*; *shallow*; *broad*; *narrow*; *hard*; *soft*; *heavy*; *light*; *wet*; *unripe*; *coarse*; *warm*; *cold*; *sour*; *wise*.

These two languages, then, refute Strong Cut-off Point Prototypicality. While 11 of the 12 Rotuman adjectives fall into the prototypical adjective classes of age, dimension, value, and color (*female* would appear to be the exception), any number of adjectives in these classes do not have distinct singular and plural forms. Since there is an open-ended number of adjectives in the language, and there is no reason to think that *old* is more prototypical than *new* or *young*, or *female* more prototypical than *male*, there is no cut-off point separating the prototypical from the nonprototypical. And in Acooli there are even *more* putatively prototypical adjectives in the class with only one form for number than in the class with two forms.

Weak Cut-off Point Prototypicality does not fare much better. It is true that no nonprototypical adjectives (except for the word for *female* in Rotuman) have two number possibilities. But in this language the exceptions turn out to be the norm: 12 forms out of an open-ended number and 7 out of 40 do not provide very convincing support for what is put forward as a universal statement about prototypicality.

Weak Cut-off Point Prototypicality is in even more serious trouble for Turkish. Croft (1991: 128), citing work by Lewis (1967), mentions that only a subset of Turkish adjectives allow reduplication for intensification. These include "basic color terms, 'quick,' 'new,' and 'long,' as well as less prototypical adjectives."[7]

3.3.3. English verbal alternations

As we have noted, Strong Cut-off Point Prototypicality predicts that there should be no grammatical processes applying *only* to nonprototypical forms. Levin (1993) has provided us with the means to test this hypothesis with respect to English verbal alternations. Depending on how one counts, she describes from several dozen to almost one hundred such alternations. Significantly, many of these are restricted to nonprototypical stative and psychological predicates. The following are some of the alternations that illustrate this point:

Various subject alternations:

(11) a. The world saw the beginning of a new era in 1492.
    b. 1492 saw the beginning of a new era.

(12) a. We sleep five people in each room.
    b. Each room sleeps five people.

(13) a. The middle class will benefit from the new tax laws.
    b. The new tax laws will benefit the middle class.

There-Insertion:

(14) a. A ship appeared on the horizon.
    b. There appeared a ship on the horizon.

---

[7] And it should be pointed out that Dixon says that words in the semantic field of "speed" (e.g., *quick*) tend to lag behind the four most prototypical classes in their lexicalization as adjectives.

Locative inversion:

(15) a. A flowering plant is on the window sill.
     b. On the window sill is a flowering plant.

3.4. Some explanations for prototypicality effects

We have seen several examples that seem to falsify cut-off point prototypicality. And yet, there are undeniable *correlations* between prototypicality and the possibility of morpho-syntactic elaboration. In general, actives do progressivize more easily than statives; it would seem that in general certain adjective classes allow more structural elaboration than others; and undeniably there are more verbal alternations in English involving active verbs (or an active and its corresponding stative) than statives alone.

Any theory of language should be able to explain why this correlation exists. This section will examine a number of English syntactic processes that manifest such correlations and have thereby been invoked to suggest that categories are nondiscrete. For each case, I will argue that the facts fall out from a theory with discrete categories and independently needed principles.

3.4.1. Measure verbs and passive

An old problem is the fact that English measure verbs (*cost*, *weigh*, *measure*, etc.) do not passivize:

(16) a. The book cost a lot of money.
     b. John weighed 180 pounds.

(17) a. *A lot of money was cost by the book.
     b. *180 pounds was weighed by John.

The earliest work in generative grammar attempted to handle this fact by means of arbitrarily marking the verbs of this class not to undergo the rule (Lakoff, 1970). But there has always been the feeling that it is not an accident that such verbs are exceptional—there is something seemingly less "verb-like" about them than, say, an active transitive verb like *hit* or *squeeze*. Translated into prototype theory, one might suggest that measure verbs are "on the other side of the cut-off point" for passivization in English. And, in fact, such an analysis has been proposed recently in Ross (1995) (though Ross refers to "defectiveness" rather than to "lack of prototypicality").

I will now argue that these facts can be explained without recourse to prototypes.[8] I believe that it was in Bresnan (1978) that attention was first called to the distinction between the following two sentences (see also Bach, 1980):

(18) a. The boys make good cakes.
     b. The boys make good cooks.

Notice that the NP following the verb in (18a) passivizes, while that following the verb in (18b) does not:

(19) a. Good cakes are made by the boys.
     b. *Good cooks are made by the boys.

---

[8] I would like to thank Pascual Masullo and Ray Jackendoff (personal communication) for discussing with me the alternatives to the prototype-based analysis.

Bresnan noted that the argument structures of the two sentences differ. *Good cakes* in (18a) is a direct object patient, while *good cooks* in (18b) is a predicate nominative. Given her theory that only direct objects can be "promoted" to subject position in passivization, the ungrammaticality of (19b) follows automatically.

Turning to (16a–b), we find that, in crucial respects, the semantic relationship between subject, verb, and post-verbal NP parallels that of (18a–b). "A lot of money" and "180 pounds" are predicate attributes of "the book" and "John" respectively. In a relationally based framework such as Bresnan's, the deviance of (17a–b) has the same explanation as that of (19b). In a principles-and-parameters approach, a parallel treatment is available. Since "a lot of money" and "180 pounds" are predicates rather than arguments, there is no motivation for the NP to move, thereby accounting for the deviance of the passives.[9] Crucially, there is no need for the grammar of English to refer to the degree of prototypicality either of the verb or of the NP that follows it.

3.4.2. There *as a nonprototypical NP*

Recall Ross's Fake NP Squish, repeated below:

(3) The Fake NP Squish:
   a. Animates
   b. Events
   c. Abstracts
   d. Expletive *it*
   e. Expletive *there*
   f. Opaque idiom chunks.

Expletive *there* occupies a position very low on the squish. In other words, it seems to manifest low NP-like behavior. First, let us review why one would want to call it a NP at all. The reason is that it meets several central tests for NP status. It raises over the verb *seem* and others of its class (20a); it occurs as a passive subject (20b); it inverts over auxiliaries (20c); and it can be coindexed with tags (20d):

(20) a. There seems to be a problem.
    b. There was believed to be a problem.
    c. Is there a problem?
    d. There is a problem, isn't there?

The null hypothesis, then, is that *there* is an NP, with nothing more needing to be said.

Now let us review the data that led Ross to conclude that rules applying to NPs have to be sensitive to their categorial prototypicality. He gives the following ways that *there* behaves like less than a full NP (the asterisks and question marks preceding each sentence are Ross's assignments): It doesn't undergo the rule of "promotion" (21a–b); it doesn't allow raising to reapply (22a–b); it doesn't occur in the "*think of...as X*" construction (23a–b) or the "*what's...doing X*" construction (24a–b); it doesn't allow "*being*-deletion" (25a–b); it doesn't occur in dislocation constructions (26a–b); it doesn't undergo *tough*-movement (27a–b),

---

[9] Adger (1992; 1994) offers a treatment of measure verbs roughly along these lines. In his analysis, measure phrases, being "quasi-arguments" (i.e., not full arguments), do not raise to the specifier of Agreement, thereby explaining the impossibility of passivization. Indeed, thematic role-based analyses, going back at least to Jackendoff (1972), are quite parallel. For Jackendoff, measure phrases are "locations." They are unable to displace the underlying "theme" subjects of verbs such as *cost* or *weigh*, since "location" is higher on the thematic hierarchy than "theme." Calling them "locations," it seems to me, is simply another way of saying that they are not true arguments.

topicalization (28a–b), "swooping" (29a–b), "equi" (30a–b), or conjunction reduction (31a–b). In each case an example of a more prototypical NP is illustrated that manifests the process:

Promotion:
(21) a. Harpo's being willing to return surprised me. / Harpo surprised me by being willing to return.
    b. There being heat in the furnace surprised me. / *There surprised me by being heat in the furnace.

Double raising:
(22) a. John is likely _ to be shown _ to have cheated.
    b. ?*There is likely _ to be shown _ to be no way out of this shoe.

Think of . . . as NP:
(23) a. I thought of Freud as being wiggy.
    b. *I thought of there as being too much homework.

What's . . . doing X?:
(24) a. What's he doing in jail?
    b. *What's there doing being no mistrial?

Being deletion:
(25) a. Hinswood (being) in the tub is a funny thought.
    b. There *(being) no more Schlitz is a funny thought.

Left dislocation:
(26) a. Those guys, they're smuggling my armadillo to Helen.
    b. *There, there are three armadillos in the road.

Tough movement:
(27) a. John will be difficult to prove to be likely to win.
    b. *There will be difficult to prove likely to be enough to eat.

Topicalization:
(28) a. John, I don't consider very intelligent.
    b. *There, I don't consider to be enough booze in the eggnog.

Swooping:
(29) a. I gave Sandra my zwieback, and she didn't want any. / I gave Sandra, and she didn't want any, my zwieback.
    b. I find there to be no grounds for contempt proceedings, and there may have been previously. / *I find there, which may have been previously, to be no grounds for contempt proceedings.

Equi:
(30) a. After he laughed politely, Oliver wiped his mustache. / After laughing politely, Oliver wiped his mustache.
    b. After there is a confrontation, there's always some good old-time head busting. / *After being a confrontation, there's always some good old-time head-busting.

Conjunction reduction:
(31) a. Manny wept and Sheila wept. / Manny and Sheila wept.
    b. There were diplodocuses, there are platypuses, and there may well also be diplatocodypuses. / *There were diplodocuses, are platypuses, and may well also be diplatocodypuses.

I wish to argue that all of these distinctions follow from the lexical semantics of *there* and the pragmatics of its use. What does expletive *there* mean? The tradition in generative grammar has been to call *there* a meaningless element, or else to identify it as an existential quantifier with no intrinsic sense. Cognitive linguists, on the other hand, following earlier work by Dwight Bolinger (1977), have posited lexical meaning for it. To Lakoff (1987), for example, expletive *there* designates conceptual space itself, rather than a location in it. To Langacker (1991: 352), *there* designates an abstract setting construed as hosting some relationship. In fact, we achieve the same results no matter which option we choose. Meaningless elements / abstract settings / conceptual spaces are not able to intrude into one's consciousness, thus explaining (21b) and (23b). (24b) is bad because abstract settings, and so on, cannot themselves "act"; rather they are the setting for action. Furthermore, such elements are not modifiable (29–30) nor able to occur as discourse topics (26–28). (25b) is ungenerable, given the uncontroversial requirement that *there* occur with a verb of existence. In my opinion and that of my consultants, (22b) and (31b) are fully acceptable.

In short, the apparent lack of prototypical NP behavior of expletive *there* is a direct consequence of its meaning and the pragmatics of its use. Nothing is gained by requiring that the rules that affect it pay attention to its degree of prototypicality. Syntax need no more be sensitive to prototypicality to explain the examples of (21–31) than we need a special syntactic principle to rule out (32):

(32)   The square circle elapsed the dragon.

As a general point, the possibility of syntactic elaboration correlates with the diversity of pragmatic possibilities. Concrete nouns make, in general, better topics, better focuses, better new referents, better established referents, and so on than do abstract nouns. We can talk about actions in a wider variety of discourse contexts and for a greater variety of reasons than states. The syntactic accommodation to this fact is a greater variety of sentence types in which objects and actions occur than abstract nouns and states. There is no reason to appeal to the prototypicality of the noun or the verb.

3.4.3. English idiom chunks

Notice that in the Fake NP Squish, idiom chunks occupy an even lower position than expletive *there*. Lakoff (1987: 63–4), in his presentation of cognitive linguistics, endorsed the idea that their behavior is a direct consequence of their low prototypicality and even went so far as to claim that idiom chunk NPs can be ranked in prototypicality *with respect to each other*. Drawing on unpublished work by Ross (1981), he ranked 4 of them as follows, with *one's toe* the highest in prototypicality, and *one's time* the lowest:

(33) a. to stub one's toe
     b. to hold one's breath
     c. to lose one's way
     d. to take one's time.

Lakoff (for the most part citing Ross's examples), argued that each idiom was more restricted in its syntactic behavior than the next higher in the hierarchy. For example, only *to stub one's toe* can be converted into a past participle-noun sequence:

(34) a. A *stubbed toe* can be very painful.
     b. **Held breath* is usually fetid when released.
     c. **A lost way* has been the cause of many a missed appointment.
     d. **Taken time* might tend to irritate your boss.

To stub one's toe and *to hold one's breath* allow gapping in their conjuncts:

(35) a. I stubbed my toe, and she hers.
     b. I held my breath, and she hers.
     c. *I lost my way, and she hers.
     d. *I took my time, and she hers.

Pluralization possibilities distinguish *to stub one's toe* from *to hold one's breath* and both of these from *to lose one's way* and *to take one's time*. When *to stub one's toe* has a conjoined subject, pluralization is obligatory; for *to hold one's breath* it is optional; and for the latter two it is impossible:

(36) a. Betty and Sue stubbed their toes.
     b. *Betty and Sue stubbed their toe.
     c. Betty and Sue held their breaths.
     d. Betty and Sue held their breath.
     e. *Betty and Sue lost their ways.
     f. Betty and Sue lost their way.
     g. *Betty and Sue took their times.
     h. Betty and Sue took their time.

Finally, Lakoff judges all but *to take one's time* to allow pronominalization:

(37) a. I stubbed my toe, but didn't hurt *it*.
     b. Sam held his breath for a few seconds, and then released *it*.
     c. Harry lost his way, but found *it* again.
     d. *Harry took his time, but wasted *it*.

Lakoff concludes:

In each of these cases, the nounier nouns follow the general rule . . . while the less nouny nouns do not follow the rule. As the sentences indicate, there is a hierarchy of nouniness among the examples given. Rules differ as to how nouny a noun they require. (Lakoff, 1987: 64)

In all cases but one, however, I have found an independent explanation for the range of judgments on these sentences. Beginning with the participle test, we find that (for whatever reason) *held* and *taken* never occur as participial modifiers, even in their literal senses:

(38) a. *Held cats often try to jump out of your arms.
     b. *The taken jewels were never returned.

I confess to not being able to explain (34c), since *lost* does occur in this position in a literal sense:

(39)   A lost child is a pathetic sight.

Turning to Gapping, sentences (40a–d) show that the facts cited by Lakoff have nothing to do with the idioms themselves:[10]

(40) a. I lost my way, and she her way.
     b. I took my time, and she her time.
     c. ?I ate my ice cream and she hers.
     d. In the race to get to the airport, Mary and John lost their way, but we didn't lose ours (and so we won).

[10] I am indebted to Ronnie Cann for pointing this out to me.

(40a–b) illustrates that the idioms *lose one's way* and *take one's time* do indeed allow gapping in their conjuncts. The correct generalization appears to lie in discourse factors. Gapping apparently requires a contrastive focus reading of the gapped constituent. Hence (40c) seems as bad as (35c–d), while (40d) is fine.

In the examples involving plurals, what seems to be involved is the ability to individuate. We can do that easily with toes and less easily, but still possibly, with breaths. But we cannot individuate ways and times. So, nonplural (41a) is impossible—legs demand individuation—while plural (41b) is impossible as well, for the opposite reason. Rice in its collective sense is not individuated:

(41) a. *Betty and Sue broke their leg.
  b. *My bowl is full of rices.

Finally, (42a) and (42b) illustrate that *time* in *take one's time* is not resistant to pronominalization. (42a) is much improved over (37d) and (42b) is impeccable:

(42) a. Harry took his time, and wasted it.
  b. Harry took his time, which doesn't mean that he didn't find a way to waste it.

Again, there is no reason whatever to stipulate that grammatical processes have to be sensitive to the degree of prototypicality of the NP. Independently needed principles—none of which themselves crucially incorporate prototypicality—explain the range of acceptability.

3.4.4. *Event structure and inflectional possibilities*

Let us further explore why there is in general a correlation between degree of prototypicality and inflectional possibilities. Since Vendler (1967) it has been customary to divide the aspectual properties of verbs (and the propositions of which they are predicates) into four event types, generally referred to as "states," "processes," "achievements," and "accomplishments." States (*know, resemble*) are not inherently bounded, have no natural goal or outcome, are not evaluated with respect to any other event, and are homogeneous. Processes (*walk, run*) are durative events with no inherent bound. Achievements (*die, find, arrive*) are momentary events of transition, while Accomplishments (*build, destroy*) are durative events with a natural goal or outcome. There have been a number of proposals for the representation of event structure (Dowty, 1979; Grimshaw, 1990; Pustejovsky, 1995). The proposals of Pustejovsky (1991) are shown in Figs 1 and 2.

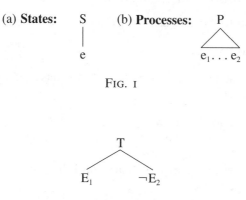

FIG. 1

FIG. 2

c. **Achievements** and **Accomplishments** have the same schematic structure (both are called "transitions"), though the former are nonagentive and the latter agentive:

Two observations are in order. The first is that there is a general increase in the complexity of event structure from states to accomplishments. The second is that this increase in complexity corresponds roughly to the degree of prototypicality for verbs. From these observations, we may derive the reason for the correlation between prototypicality and inflectional possibilities to hold for verbs as a general tendency. There is clearly a mapping between the event structure of a proposition and those aspects of morphosyntactic structure in which tense, aspect, modality, and so on are encoded. In standard varieties of principles-and-parameters syntax, again, this is the "functional structure" representation of the sentence. Now, the more complex the event structure of a proposition, the more aspectual possibilities that it allows. Hence, the more complex (in terms of number of projections) the functional structure can be. And, of course, it follows that the possibilities for inflection will be greater. In other words, we have derived a general correlation between degree of prototypicality and potential richness of verbal inflection without any reference to prototypicality per se.

It should be pointed out that this approach demands that functional projections exist only where they are motivated (i.e., that there can be no empty projections). Otherwise, there would be no difference in functional structure between states and accomplishments. In other words, it presupposes the principle of Minimal Projection, proposed and defended in Grimshaw (1993). According to this principle, a projection must be functionally interpreted, that is, it must make a contribution to the functional representation of the extended projection of which it is part.[11]

The correlation between semantic complexity and inflectional possibilities holds for nouns as well. Objects (e.g., people, books, automobiles, etc.) can be individuated and specified in a way that abstract nouns such as *liberty* and dummy nouns like *there* cannot. So it follows that the semantic structure of concrete nouns will have the general potential to map onto more layers of nominal functional structure than that of abstract nouns.

There are two problems, however, that are faced by an exclusively semantic account of restrictions on inflection. The first is that some languages have inflections that are restricted to some forms but not others, even though there appears to be no semantic explanation for the restriction. For example, Croft (1990: 82) notes that process verbs in Quiché take tense-aspect inflectional prefixes, while stative verbs do not and writes:

There is no apparent reason for this, since there is no semantic incompatibility between the inflectional prefixes...and in fact in a language like English stative predicates do inflect for tense. It is simply a grammatical fact regarding the expression of stative predicates in Quiché. As such, it provides very strong evidence for the markedness of stative predicates compared to process predicates.

Although I do not pretend to have a full explanation for cases such as these, I would venture to guess that what we have here are pragmatic factors overriding semantic ones. Both process verbs and stative verbs can logically manifest tense, aspect, and modality, though in many discourse contexts such distinctions are irrelevant for the latter. Thus pragmatic factors have kept the grammars of Quiché and languages manifesting similar phenomena from grammaticalizing tense, aspect, and modality for stative verbs. No appeal to prototypicality is necessary.

A second problem with a semantic approach to inflection is that inflections that appear to be semantically *empty* also manifest prototype effects. Take agreement inflections, for example.

---

[11] Grimshaw (1997) derives Minimal Projection from the principles of Economy of Movement and Oblig Heads.

As is noted in Croft (1988), where languages have a "choice" as to object agreement, it is always the more definite and/or animate (i.e., more prototypical) direct object that has the agreement marker. Does this fact support prototype theory? Not necessarily: In the same paper Croft argues that agreement has a *pragmatic function*, namely to index important or salient arguments. So, if agreement markers are not "pragmatically empty," then their presence can be related to their discourse function and need not be attributed to the inherently prototypical properties of the arguments to which they are affixed.

4. THE NONEXISTENCE OF FUZZY CATEGORIES

We turn now to the question of whether categories have distinct *boundaries*, or, alternatively, whether they grade one into the other in fuzzy squish-like fashion. I examine two phenomena that have been appealed to in support of fuzzy categories—English *near* (section 4.1) and the Nouniness Squish (section 4.2)—and conclude that no argument for fuzzy categories can be derived from them.

4.1. English *Near*

Ross (1972) analyzes the English word *near* as something between an adjective and a preposition. Like an adjective, it takes a preposition before its object (44a) and like a preposition, it takes a bare object (44b):

(44) a. The shed is near to the barn.
     b. The shed is near the barn.

So it would appear, as Ross concluded, that there is a continuum between the categories Adjective and Preposition, and *near* is to be analyzed as occupying a position at the center of the continuum. A prototype theorist would undoubtedly conclude that the intermediate position of *near* is a consequence of its having neither prototypical adjectival nor prototypical prepositional properties.

In fact, *near* can be used either as an adjective or a preposition. Maling (1983) provides evidence for the former categorization. Like any transitive adjective, it takes a following preposition (45a); when that preposition is present (i.e., when *near* is adjectival), the degree modifier must follow it (45b); it takes a comparative suffix (45c); and we find it (somewhat archaically) in prenominal position (45d):

(45) a. The gas station is near to the supermarket.
     b. Near enough to the supermarket.
     c. Nearer to the supermarket.
     d. The near shore.

Near passes tests for Preposition as well. It takes a bare object (46a); when it has a bare object it may not be followed by *enough* (46b), but may take the prepositional modifier *right* (46c):

(46) a. The gas station is near the supermarket.
     b. *The gas station is near enough the supermarket.[12]
     c. The gas station is right near (*to) the supermarket.

---

[12] Maling (1983) judges sentences of this type acceptable, and on that basis rejects the idea that *near* is a P. I must say that I find (46b) impossible.

It is true that, as a Preposition, it uncharacteristically takes an inflected comparative:

(47) The gas station is nearer the supermarket than the bank.

But, as (48) shows, other prepositions occur in the comparative construction; it is only in its being inflected, then, that *near* distinguishes itself:[13]

(48) The seaplane right now is more over the lake than over the mountain.

Thus I conclude that *near* provides no evidence for categorial continua.

4.2. The Nouniness Squish

Recall Ross's Nouniness Squish (5), repeated below:

(5) The "Nouniness Squish":
   that clauses > *for to* clauses > embedded questions > Acc-*ing* complements > Poss-*ing* complements > action nominals > derived nominals > underived nominals

This squish grades nouns (or, more properly, the phrases that contain them) along a single dimension—their degree of nominality. Subordinate and relative clauses introduced by the complementizer *that* are held to be the least nominal; underived nominals (i.e., simple nouns) are held to be the most nominal. But, according to Ross, there is no fixed point at which the dominating phrase node ceases to be S and starts to be NP; each successive element on the squish is held to be somewhat more nominal than the element to its left.

As Ross is aware, demonstrating a fuzzy boundary between S and NP entails (minimally) showing that syntactic behavior gradually changes as one progresses along the squish; that is, that there is no place where S "stops" and NP "starts." We will now examine two purported instances of this graduality. As we will see, the facts are perfectly handlable in an approach that assumes membership in either S or NP.

First, Ross claims that "the nounier a complement is, the less accessible are the nodes it dominates to the nodes which command the complement" (Ross, 1973b: 174). That is, it should be harder to extract from a phrase headed by an underived N than from a *that* clause. He illustrates the workings of this principle with the data in (49) and concludes that "the dwindling Englishness of [these] sentences supports [this principle]" (p. 175):

(49) a. I wonder who he resented (it) that I went steady with.
   b. I wonder who he would resent (it) for me to go steady with.
   c. *I wonder who he resented how long I went steady with.
   d. ?I wonder who he resented me going out with.
   e. ??I wonder who he resented my going out with.
   f. ?*I wonder who he resented my careless examining of.
   g. ?*I wonder who he resented my careless examination of.
   h. ?*I wonder who he resented the daughter of.

But one notes immediately that, even on Ross' terms, we do not find consistently 'dwindling Englishness': (49c) is crashingly bad. Furthermore, he admits (in a footnote) that many speakers find (49h) fine. In fact, the data seem quite clear to me: (49a–b, d–e, h) are acceptable,

---

[13] Presumably the inflectional possibilities of *near* are properties of its neutralized lexical entry; not of the ADJ or P branch of the entry.

and (49c, f–g) are not. The latter three sentences are straightforward barriers violations, given the approach of Chomsky (1986), while the others violate no principles of Universal Grammar. The degree of 'nouniness' plays no role in the explanation of these sentences.

Second, Ross suggests that the phenomenon of pied piping—that is, wh-movement carrying along material dominating the fronted wh-phrase, is sensitive to degree of nouniness. He cites (50a–f) in support of this idea. It would appear, he claims, that the more nouny the dominating phrase, the more pied piping is possible:

(50) a. *Eloise, [for us to love [whom]] they liked, is an accomplished washboardiste.
　　 b. *Eloise, [us loving [whom]] they liked, is an accomplished washboardiste.
　　 c. *Eloise, [our loving [whom]] they liked, is an accomplished washboardiste.
　　 d. ?*Eloise, [our loving of [whom]] they liked, is an accomplished washboardiste.
　　 e. ?Eloise, [our love for [whom]] they liked, is an accomplished washboardiste.
　　 f. Eloise, [a part of [whom]] they liked, is an accomplished washboardiste.

Again, there is no support for a categorial continuum in these data. *For to* clauses, Acc-*ing* complements, and Poss-*ing* complements are all dominated by the node S, which can *never* pied pipe. Hence (50a–c) are ungrammatical. (50d–e), on the other hand, are all fully grammatical, though this is masked by the stylistic awkwardness of the *loving . . . liked* sequence. By substituting *was a joy to our parents* for *they liked* some of the awkwardness is eliminated and both sentences increase in acceptability.

5. CONCLUSION

The classical view of syntactic categories assumed in most models of generative grammar has seen two major challenges. In one, categories have a prototype structure, in which they have "best case" members and members that systematically depart from the "best case." In this approach, the optimal grammatical description of morphosyntactic processes is held to involve reference to degree of categorial deviation from the "best case." The second challenge hypothesizes that the boundaries between categories are nondistinct, in the sense that one grades gradually into another.

This paper has defended the classical view, arguing that categories have discrete boundaries and are not organized around central "best cases." It has argued that many of the phenomena that seem to suggest the inadequacy of the classical view are best analyzed in terms of the interaction of independently needed principles from syntax, semantics, and pragmatics.

REFERENCES

Adger, D. (1992). 'The licensing of quasi-arguments'. In P. Ackema and M. Schoorlermer (eds.), *Proceedings of ConSole* i. Utrecht: Utrecht University, 1–18.

——(1994). 'Functional heads and interpretation'. Ph.D. thesis, University of Edinburgh.

Armstrong, S. L., L. Gleitman, and H. Gleitman (1983). 'What some concepts might not be'. *Cognition* 13: 263–308.

Bach, E. (1980). 'In defense of passive'. *Linguistische Berichte* 70: 38–46.

Bates, E., and B. MacWhinney (1982). 'Functionalist approaches to grammar'. In E. Wanner and L. Gleitman (eds.), *Language Acquisition: The State of the Art*. Cambridge: Cambridge University Press, 173–218.

Bolinger, D. (1977). *Meaning and Form*. London: Longman.

Bresnan, J. W. (1978). 'A realistic transformational grammar'. In M. Halle, J. Bresnan, and G. Miller (eds.), *Linguistic Theory and Psychological Reality*. Cambridge, Mass.: MIT Press, 1–59.

Chomsky, N. (1986). *Barriers*. Cambridge, Mass.: MIT Press.

Churchward, C. M. (1940). *Rotuman Grammar and Dictionary*. Sydney: Australasian Medical Publishing.

Coleman, L., and P. Kay (1981). 'Prototype semantics'. *Language* 57: 26–44.

Comrie, B. (1989). *Language Universals and Linguistic Typology*, 2nd edn. Chicago: University of Chicago Press.

Crazzolara, J. P. (1955). *A Study of the Acooli Language*. London: Oxford University Press.

Croft, W. (1988). 'Agreement vs. case marking and direct objects'. In M. Barlow and C. A. Ferguson (eds.), *Agreement in Natural Language: Approaches, Theories, Descriptions*. Stanford, Calif.: Center for the Study of Language and Information, 159–79.

——(1990). *Typology and Universals*. Cambridge: Cambridge University Press.

——(1991). *Syntactic Categories and Grammatical Relations*. Chicago: University of Chicago Press.

Cruse, D. A. (1992). 'Cognitive linguistics and word meaning: Taylor on linguistic categorization'. *Journal of Linguistics* 28: 165–84.

Dixon, R. M. W. (1977). 'Where have all the adjectives gone?' *Studies in Language* 1: 1–80.

Dowty, D. R. (1979). *Word Meaning and Montague Grammar*. Dordrecht: Reidel.

Dryer, M. S. (1997). 'Are grammatical relations universal?' In J. Bybee, J. Haiman, and S. A. Thompson (eds.), *Essays on Language Function and Language Type*. Amsterdam: Benjamins, 115–43.

Fodor, J. A., and E. Lepore (1996). 'The red herring and the pet fish: why concepts still can't be prototypes'. *Cognition* 58: 253–70.

Gazdar, G., and E. Klein (1978). Review of E. L. Keenan (ed.), *Formal Semantics of Natural Language*. *Language* 54: 661–7.

Geeraerts, D. (1993). 'Vagueness's puzzles, polysemy's vagaries'. *Cognitive Linguistics* 4: 223–72.

Givón, T. (1984). *Syntax: A Functional-Typological Introduction*, vol. i. Amsterdam: Benjamins.

Goldsmith, J., and E. Woisetschlaeger (1982). 'The logic of the English progressive'. *Linguistic Inquiry* 13: 79–89.

Grimshaw, J. (1990). *Argument structure*. Cambridge, Mass.: MIT Press.

——(1993). *Minimal Projection, Heads, and Optimality*. Piscataway, NJ: Rutgers Center for Cognitive Science.

——(1997). 'Projection, heads, and optimality'. *Linguistic Inquiry* 28: 373–422.

Heine, B. (1993). *Auxiliaries: Cognitive Forces and Grammaticalization*. New York: Oxford University Press.

Hopper, P. J., and S. A. Thompson (1984). 'The discourse basis for lexical categories in universal grammar'. *Language* 60: 703–52.

——(1985). 'The iconicity of the universal categories "noun" and "verb" '. In J. Haiman (ed.), *Iconicity in Syntax*. Amsterdam: Benjamins, 151–86.

Jackendoff, R. (1972). *Semantic Interpretation in Generative Grammar*. Cambridge, Mass.: MIT Press.

——(1983). *Semantics and Cognition*. Cambridge, Mass.: MIT Press.

——and F. Lerdahl (1981). 'Generative music theory and its relation to psychology'. *Journal of Music Theory* 25: 45–90.

Kamp, H., and B. H. Partee (1995). 'Prototype theory and compositionality'. *Cognition* 57: 129–91.

Kearns, K. S. (1991). 'The semantics of the English progressive'. Ph.D. dissertation, Massachusetts Institute of Technology.

Keil, F. C. (1989). *Concepts, Kinds, and Cognitive Development*. Cambridge, Mass.: Bradford Books.

Lakoff, G. (1970). *Irregularity in Syntax*. New York: Holt, Rinehart, & Winston.

——(1972). 'Hedges: A study in meaning criteria and the logic of fuzzy concepts'. In *Papers from the Eighth Regional Meeting of the Chicago Linguistic Society*, 183–228.

——(1973). 'Fuzzy grammar and the performance/competence terminology game'. In *Papers from the Ninth Regional Meeting of the Chicago Linguistic Society*, 271–91.

Lakoff, G. (1987). *Women, Fire, and Dangerous Things: What Categories Reveal about the Mind*. Chicago: University of Chicago Press.

Langacker, R. W. (1987). 'Nouns and verbs'. *Language* 63: 53–94.

——(1991). *Foundations of Cognitive Grammar*, vol. ii: *Descriptive Application*. Stanford, Calif.: Stanford University Press.

Langendonck, W. van (1986). 'Markedness, prototypes, and language acquisition'. *Cahiers de l'Institut de Linguistique de Louvain* 12: 39–76.

Levin, B. (1993). *English Verb Classes and Alternations: A Preliminary Investigation*. Chicago: University of Chicago Press.

Lewis, G. L. (1967). *Turkish Grammar*. Oxford: Oxford University Press.

Maling, J. (1983). 'Transitive adjectives: a case of categorial reanalysis'. In F. Heny and B. Richards (eds.), *Linguistic Categories: Auxiliaries and Related Puzzles*, vol. i: *Categories*. Dordrecht: Reidel, 253–89.

Mervis, C. B., and E. Rosch (1981). 'Categorization of natural objects'. *Annual Review of Psychology* 32: 89–115.

Moravcsik, E. A. (1983). 'On grammatical classes: the case of "definite" objects in Hungarian'. *Working Papers in Linguistics* 15: 75–107.

Newmeyer, F. J. (1998). *Language Form and Language Function*. Cambridge, Mass.: MIT Press.

Pustejovsky, J. (1991). 'The syntax of event structure'. *Cognition* 41: 47–81.

——(1995). *The Generative Lexicon*. Cambridge, Mass.: MIT Press.

Rosch, E. (1971/1973). 'On the internal structure of perceptual and semantic categories'. In T. E. Moore (ed.), *Cognitive Development and the Acquisition of Language*. New York: Academic Press.

——and B. B. Lloyd (eds.) (1978). *Cognition and Categorization*. Hillsdale, NJ: Erlbaum.

Ross, J. R. (1972). 'Endstation Hauptwort: the category squish'. In *Papers from the Eighth Regional Meeting of the Chicago Linguistic Society*, 316–28.

——(1973a). 'A fake NP squish'. In C.-J. N. Bailey and R. Shuy (eds.), *New Ways of Analyzing Variation in English*. Washington, DC: Georgetown University Press, 96–140.

——(1973b). 'Nouniness'. In O. Fujimura (ed.), *Three Dimensions of Linguistic Theory*. Tokyo: TEC, 137–258.

——(1975). 'Clausematiness'. In E. L. Keenan (ed.), *Formal Semantics of Natural Language*. London: Cambridge University Press, 422–75.

——(1981). 'Nominal decay'. MS, Dept. of Linguistics, Massachusetts Institute of Technology.

——(1987). 'Islands and syntactic prototypes'. In *Papers from the Twenty-Third Regional Meeting of the Chicago Linguistic Society*, 309–20.

——(1995). 'Defective noun phrases'. In *Papers from the Thirty-First Regional Meeting of the Chicago Linguistic Society*, 398–440.

Rudzka-Ostyn, B. (ed.) (1988). *Topics in Cognitive Linguistics*. Amsterdam: Benjamins.

Silverstein, M. (1976). 'Hierarchy of features and ergativity'. In R. M. W. Dixon (ed.), *Grammatical Categories in Australian Languages*. Canberra: Australian Institute of Aboriginal Studies, 112–71.

Smith, C. (1991). *The Parameter of Aspect*. Dordrecht: Kluwer.

Smith, E. E., and D. N. Osherson (1988). 'Conceptual combination with prototype concepts'. In A. Collins and E. E. Smith (eds.), *Readings in Cognitive Science: a Perspective from Psychology and Artificial Intelligence*. San Mateo, Calif.: M. Kaufman, 323–35.

Swart, H. de (1998). 'Aspect shift and coercion'. *Natural Language and Linguistic Theory* 16: 347–85.

Taylor, J. R. (1989). *Linguistic Categorization: Prototypes in Linguistic Theory*. Oxford: Clarendon Press.

Thompson, S. A. (1988). 'A discourse approach to the cross-linguistic category "adjective"'. In J. Hawkins (ed.), *Explaining Language Universals*. Oxford: Blackwell, 167–85.

Tsohatzidis, S. L. (ed.) (1990). *Meanings and Prototypes: Studies in Linguistic Categorization*. London: Routledge.

Van Oosten, J. (1986). *The Nature of Subjects, Topics, and Agents: A Cognitive Explanation*. Bloomington: Indiana University Linguistics Club.

Vendler, Z. (1967). *Linguistics in Philosophy*. Ithaca, NY: Cornell University Press.

Warner, A. R. (1993a). *English Auxiliaries: Structure and History*. Cambridge: Cambridge University Press.

——(1993b). 'The grammar of English auxiliaries: an account in HPSG'. *York Research Papers in Linguistics Research Paper* (YLLS /RP 1993–4), 1–42.

Wierzbicka, A. (1986). 'What's in a noun? (Or: How do nouns differ in meaning from adjectives?)' *Studies in Language* 10: 353–89.

——(1990). ' "Prototypes save": on the uses and abuses of the notion of "prototype" in linguistics and related fields'. In S. L. Tsohatzidis (ed.), *Meanings and Prototypes: Studies in Linguistic Categorization*. London: Routledge, 347–67.

Winters, M. E. (1990). 'Toward a theory of syntactic prototypes'. In S. L. Tsohatzidis (ed.), *Meanings and Prototypes: Studies in Linguistic Categorization*. London: Routledge, 285–306.

Žegarac, V. (1993). 'Some observations on the pragmatics of the progressive'. *Lingua* 90: 201–20.

Subject Index

Author Index

Language Index

DATE DUE

MAY 1 7 2007